HUMAN
RIGHTS
WATCH

Kosovo

Hungary
Slovenia
Romania
Croatia
Serbia
Bosnia and Hecegovina
Federal Republic of Yugoslavia
Montenegro
Kosovo
Bulgaria
Albania
Macedonia
Italy
Greece
NORTH
SERBIA
Novi Pazar
LEPOSAVIC
FEDERAL REPUBLIC OF YUGOSLAVIA
MONTENEGRO
ZVECAN
KOSOVSKA MITROVICA
ZUBIN POTOK
Mitrovica
Vucitrn
PODUJEVO
ISTOK
Srbica
VUCITRN
SRBICA
PRISTINA
Pec
OBILIC
Pristina
KOSOVSKA KAMENICA
PEC
KLINA
Glogovac
KOSOVO POLJE
NOVO BRDO
Decani
GLOGOVAC
Lipljan
GNJILANE
DECANI
LIPLJAN
Gnjilane
ORAHOVAC
STIMLJE
DJAKOVICA
Orahovac
Urosevac
Djakovica
SUVA REKA
UROSEVAC
VITINA
Prizren
STRPCE
KACANIK
ALBANIA
PRIZREN
Kumanovo
Kukes
GORA
Tetovo
Skopje
0 km 20
0 miles 20
MACEDONIA
Michael S. Miller for Human Rights Watch, 2001

UNDER ORDERS

War Crimes in Kosovo

HUMAN RIGHTS WATCH

NEW YORK · WASHINGTON · LONDON · BRUSSELS

Printed in the United States of America

ISBN: 1-56432-264-5
Library of Congress Control Number: 2001096623

Cover photo: Refugees from Kosovo. Albania, 1999.

Cover design by Rafael Jiménez
Text design by Jenny Dossin

Addresses for Human Rights Watch
350 Fifth Avenue, 34th Floor, New York, NY 10118-3299
Tel: (212) 290-4700, Fax: (212) 736-1300, E-mail: hrwnyc@hrw.org

1630 Connecticut Avenue, N.W., Suite 500, Washington, DC 20009
Tel: (202) 612-4321, Fax: (202) 612-4333, E-mail: hrwdc@hrw.org

33 Islington High Street, N1 9LH London, UK
Tel: (171) 713-1995, Fax: (171) 713-1800, E-mail: hrwatchuk@gn.apc.org

15 Rue Van Campenhout, 1000 Brussels, Belgium
Tel: (2) 732-2009, Fax: (2) 732-0471, E-mail:hrwatcheu@skynet.be

Web Site Address: http://www.hrw.org

Listserv address: To subscribe to the Human Rights Watch news e-mail
list, send a blank e-mail message to subscribe@igc.topica.com.

Human Rights Watch is dedicated to protecting the human rights of people around the world.

We stand with victims and activists to prevent discrimination, to uphold political freedom, to protect people from inhumane conduct in wartime, and to bring offenders to justice.

We investigate and expose human rights violations and hold abusers accountable.

We challenge governments and those who hold power to end abusive practices and respect international human rights law.

We enlist the public and the international community to support the cause of human rights for all.

Human Rights Watch

Human Rights Watch conducts regular, systematic investigations of human rights abuses in some seventy countries around the world. Our reputation for timely, reliable disclosures has made us an essential source of information for those concerned with human rights. We address the human rights practices of governments of all political stripes, of all geopolitical alignments, and of all ethnic and religious persuasions. Human Rights Watch defends freedom of thought and expression, due process and equal protection of the law, and a vigorous civil society; we document and denounce murders, disappearances, torture, arbitrary imprisonment, discrimination, and other abuses of internationally recognized human rights. Our goal is to hold governments accountable if they transgress the rights of their people.

Human Rights Watch began in 1978 with the founding of its Europe and Central Asia division (then known as Helsinki Watch). Today, it also includes divisions covering Africa, the Americas, Asia, and the Middle East. In addition, it includes three thematic divisions on arms, children's rights, and women's rights. It maintains offices in New York, Washington, Los Angeles, London, Brussels, Moscow, Dushanbe, and Bangkok. Human Rights Watch is an independent, nongovernmental organization, supported by contributions from private individuals and foundations world wide. It accepts no government funds, directly or indirectly.

The staff includes Kenneth Roth, executive director; Michele Alexander, development director; Reed Brody, advocacy director; Carroll Bogert, communications director; Barbara Guglielmo, finance director; Jeri Laber special advisor; Lotte Leicht, Brussels office director; Michael McClintock, deputy program director; Patrick Minges, publications director; Maria Pignataro Nielsen, human resources director; Jemera Rone, counsel; Malcolm Smart, program director; Wilder Tayler, general counsel; and Joanna Weschler, United Nations representative.

The regional directors of Human Rights Watch are Peter Takirambudde, Africa; José Miguel Vivanco, Americas; Sidney Jones, Asia; Holly Cartner, Europe and Central Asia; and Hanny Megally, Middle East and North Africa. The thematic division directors are Joost R. Hiltermann, arms; Lois Whitman, children's; and Regan Ralph, women's.

Contents

ACKNOWLEDGEMENTS

A report of this magnitude would not have been possible without the active participation of many individuals. This book has been a collaboration of Human Rights Watch staff, consultants, volunteers, and numerous people working on human rights issues in Kosovo.

The project was coordinated by Fred Abrahams, senior researcher at Human Rights Watch. Primary field research was conducted by the following Human Rights Watch researchers, in alphabetical order: Fred Abrahams, Bogdan Ivanisevic, Andre Lommen, Joanne Mariner, Martina Vandenberg, and Benjamin Ward, as well as Human Rights Watch consultant James Ron. Secondary research was conducted by Human Rights Watch associates Sahr MuhammedAlly, Alexandra Perina, Kerry McArthur and Laura Rusu, and two research interns, Kristie Evenson and John Walkup.

The report was written primarily by Fred Abrahams and Benjamin Ward, although many of the above researchers provided important editorial input. Joanne Mariner wrote the sections on Prizren and Pusto Selo, Martina Vandenberg wrote the sections on rape, William M. Arkin, Human Rights Watch military consultant, wrote most of the chapter on NATO, and Kristie Evenson helped write the section on landmines. Betsy Andersen, advocacy directory for the Europe and Central Asia division of Human Rights Watch contributed greatly to the background chapter dealing with the international community.

The entire report was edited by Susan Osnos, consultant to Human Rights Watch, and Michael McClintock, deputy program director of Human Rights Watch. Dinah Pokempner, general counsel of Human Rights Watch provided a legal review. Pro bono legal advice was generously provided by Craig Bloom and Jeremy Feigelson of the law firm Debevoise & Plimpton.

Background sections of the report relied on research and writing conducted by many present and former Human Rights Watch staff who began work on Kosovo in 1990. These people include: Ken Anderson, Jeri Laber, Ivana Nizich, Vlatka Mihalovic, Julie Mertes, Gordana Igric, and Peter Bouckaert. This report, and the Kosovo work as a whole, greatly benefited from the dedication and professionalism of numerous other individuals at Human Rights Watch, including: Ken Roth, executive director of Human Rights Watch, Lotte Leicht, director of the Brussels office, Jean-Paul Mathoz, Brussels communications director, Bessie Skoures, Brussels office administrator, Carroll Bogert, communications director, Minky Worden, electronic communications director, Wilder Taylor, general counsel, and Rachael Reilly, who conducted research in Macedonia during the war on the treatment of refugees. Most importantly, Holly Cartner, director of the Europe and Central Asia Division, provided insight, poise, and guidance throughout the Kosovo war and this project.

The maps in this report were designed by Michael Miller. Photographs were taken by Human Rights Watch staff Fred Abrahams, Peter Bouckaert, Joanne Mariner, and Benjamin Ward, as well as professional photographers Alban Bujari and Wade Goddard. Assistance with photographs and design was provided by Veronica Matushaj, photo editor and creative services manager at Human Rights Watch.

Various associates at Human Rights Watch also provided invaluable assistance, specifically Alexandra Perina, Alex Frangos, Rachel Bien, Laura Rusu, Kerry McArther, Skye Donald, and Adam Bassine. Alex Frangos designed and maintained the "Crisis in Kosovo" page on the Human Rights Watch website (www.hrw.org/campaigns/kosovo98/index.shtml), which received 1.2 million visitors in 1999. A number of interns and volunteers also provided valuable help. These include Darja Radulovic-Watkins, Cveta Popovic, and Erkan Ates.

The statistical analysis in this report was conducted by an array of experts and interns, many of whom graciously volunteered their time. Dr. Patrick Ball, deputy director of the Science and Human Rights Project at the American Association for the Advancement of Science (AAAS), designed the statistical analysis. The coding process was coordinated by Rebecca Morgan, a consultant to Human Rights Watch. Dr. Herbert F. Spirer, adjunct professor at Columbia University, professor emeritus at the University of Connecticut, and consultant to AAAS, conducted the analysis, generated the initial graphs, and provided crucial advice and guidance on deadline. Matt Zimmerman at AAAS produced the final graphs and diagrams. Outside reviews were conducted by Dr. Fritz Sheuren and Tom Jabine. Dr. Wray Smith provided his professional expertise. Many hours of data entry were logged by a long list of volunteers: Benedicte Benoit, Sabrina Ait-Aoudia, Mirela Gegprifti, Artan Kafexhiu, Haim Samuels, Miguel Morales, Yulia Dultsina, Sarah Millar, Aida Repak, Susana Kevorkova, Adam Greenfield, and Jasmina Repak. Human Rights Watch sincerely thanks them for their time.

None of the Kosovo research would have been possible without the cooperation and assistance of human rights groups and activists in Kosovo and the region, who work at far greater risk than any foreign-based organization or individual. Particular thanks go to the Council for the Defense of Human Rights and Freedoms in Pristina and its many sections throughout Kosovo, the Humanitarian Law Center, the Center for the Protection of Women and Children, the Mother Theresa Society, the Kosova Helsinki Committee, the Helsinki Committee for Human Rights in Serbia, the Kosovo Association of Political Prisoners, the Albanian Counseling Center for Women and Girls in Albania, and El Hilal in Skopje and Tetovo, Macedonia.

Many professionals—diplomats, journalists, lawyers, humanitarian and human rights activists—provided invaluable help throughout the process. They cannot all be named here. In particular, Human Rights Watch would like to thank the following people: Nora Ahmetaj, Sevdie Ahmeti, Dejan and Duska Anastasijevic, Ardian Arifaj, Judith Armata, Tina Babarovic, Agron Bajrami, Adem Bajri, Ilir Bajri, Fazli Balaj, Sonja Biserko, Zoran Cirjakovic, Vjosa Dobruna, Robin Ellis, Agim Fetahu, Sheri Fink, Josh Friedman, Carlotta Gall, Benedicte Giaever, Bukerija Gjonbalaj, Wade Goddard, Dukagjin Gorani, Baton Haxhiu, Mayke Huijbregts, Ylber Hysa, Natasa Kandic, Flamur Kelmendi, Kosovare Kelmendi, Nekibe Kelmendi, Asif Khan, Bajram Krasniqi, Andrea Lako, Ibrahim Makolli, Paul Miller, Fron Nazi, Lirije Osmani, Marta Palokaj, Jane Perlez, Paul Risley, David Rohde, Destan Rukiqi, Bexhet Shala, Milbert Shin, Eric Stover, Veton Surroi, Gjeraqina Tuhina, Volker Turk, Mark Vuksani, Mary Wyckoff, and Ariana Zherka for their trusted guidance.

Human Rights Watch is also thankful to the following organizations for their assistance: OSCE KVM in Kosovo and Macedonia, OSCE Mission to Kosovo, UNHCR Skopje and Pristina, Amnesty International, ICTY, Office of the UN High Commissioner for Human Rights in Skopje and Pristina, UNMIK, KFOR PIC (Skopje and Pristina), and ABC News.

Lastly, but perhaps most importantly, Human Rights Watch worked with a large number of highly professional translators and interpreters before, during, and after the war, who did much more than just translate words, and thereby contributed immensely to this report. In particular, Human Rights Watch acknowledges the work of Fisnik Abrashi, Ylber Bajraktari, Ilda Daci, Virtyt Gaceferi, Ilir Gocaj, Albana Kasapi, Adriatik Kelmendi, Garentina Kraja, Yllze Mustafa, Beni Qena, Bujar Saiti, Birol Urcan, and Mimoza Zabergja. Agron Musa and Malsor Krasniqi drove Human Rights Watch staff safely through the precarious roads of northern Albania and Kosovo. Many of these people also undertook personal risks to assist in the gathering of reliable human rights information.

Introduction

This report's main aim is to document the war crimes committed by Serbian and Yugoslav government forces in Kosovo between March 24 and June 12, 1999—the period of the NATO bombing of Yugoslavia. Through well-researched case studies, as well as scientifically rigorous statistical analysis, the goal is to provide a credible account of the terrible events that have taken place in the hope that the perpetrators will be brought to justice.

At the same time, the report acknowledges that Serbian and Yugoslav government forces did not have a monopoly on abusive behavior. The report therefore provides documentation of international humanitarian law violations committed by the Kosovo Liberation Army (KLA) as well as by the North Atlantic Treaty Organization (NATO).

Given the intense focus on Kosovo in 1999, it is not surprising that similar studies documenting violations of international humanitarian law in the province have already appeared, including a two-volume work by the Organization for Security and Cooperation in Europe (OSCE), as well as numerous reports by nongovernmental organizations. We hope that this report breaks new ground by providing both a broad and detailed account of war crimes in Kosovo, along with the political background and context of the conflict. By including first-hand accounts and testimony, the report also gives voice to the innocent victims of war.

Given the poisonous atmosphere in post-conflict Kosovo, with regular attacks on Serbs and Roma, one must ask whether this report will remind people of past crimes and perhaps provoke further revenge. Is it worth dredging up these terrible stories?

First, it is crucial to provide a historical record. Along with the other reports produced thus far, *Under Orders: War Crimes in Kosovo* will hopefully help future generations to understand better both the conflict and the region. Second, the evidence presented here will be of assistance to war crimes investigators in putting together cases against the Serbian and Yugoslav leadership, as well as against members of the KLA. Assigning individual accountability can help dispel the notion of collective guilt. Lastly, some sectors of Serbian society have expressed interest in evaluating the past. This report might assist that process by providing facts and analysis.

The report presents an overview of the Serbian and Yugoslav government campaign between March and June 1999, with an analysis of the governments' aims and strategies and a breakdown of the kinds of abuses documented, both by region and type of abuse. Another chapter provides a detailed description of the forces in the conflict, including the chain of command of the Serbian police, Yugoslav Army, and the KLA. The crux of the report follows: chapters that document the abuses committed in particular geographic areas, usually defined by municipality.

The report includes a chapter of statistical analysis, prepared in conjunction with the Science and Human Rights Program of the American Association for the Advancement of Science (AAAS), which uses data gleaned from more than 600 Human Rights Watch interviews to examine the trends and patterns of the crimes committed that may not be evident from narrative information. The numbers and graphs help deal in a systematic way with the reports of violations, as well as lend credence to the argument that the Serbian and Yugoslav government campaign of murder, destruction, and "ethnic cleansing" was systematic and well organized.

In a chapter on the background to the conflict, the report provides an analysis of the history and human rights abuses that precipitated the armed conflict. A constant theme is the international community's willingness to turn a blind eye to these abuses in the interest of short-term political stability, and the West's lack of a strategic approach to the region.

Three other chapters are of great importance, although they fall outside the main focus of the report. One deals with violations after NATO's entry into Kosovo on June 12, 1999, primarily abuses by ethnic Albanians against non-Albanians—Serbs, Roma, Gorani, and others—and the international community's inability and apparent unwillingness to protect these populations. The Background chapter also presents important material about war crimes committed by the Kosovo Liberation Army in 1998, including hostage-taking and summary executions. Another chapter addresses NATO's violations of international humanitarian law, specifically the alliance's failure to minimize civilian deaths during the bombing campaign and its use of cluster bombs. A more comprehensive report on the NATO bombing, *Civilian Deaths in the NATO Air Campaign,* was published by Human Rights Watch in February 2000.

Lastly, the report contains a detailed chapter on the international and domestic legal standards that apply to the Kosovo conflict and a chapter describing the work of the International Criminal Tribunal for the Former Yugoslavia (ICTY).

Without question, the serious violations being committed by some Albanians in Kosovo today require urgent attention. In addition to the documentation provided in this report, Human Rights Watch has repeatedly condemned these abuses, most comprehensively in a report issued in August 1999, *Abuses Against Serbs and Roma in the New Kosovo.* This report, however, focuses primarily on the crimes committed against ethnic Albanians during the NATO bombing—crimes that were both wide-ranging and carefully planned by a government. As this report shows, Kosovo from March to June 1999 experienced a coordinated, state-sponsored campaign of killings and expulsions.

METHODOLOGY

Human Rights Watch began documenting human rights violations in Kosovo in 1990. A series of reports then and in subsequent years was based primarily on field missions to the province.

The nature of the research changed in 1998 with the beginning of the armed conflict. Four missions in that year and early 1999, including one to northern Albania, focused on documenting violations of international humanitarian law by all sides in the conflict.

On March 28, 1999, four days after the commencement of NATO bombing, Human Rights Watch dispatched its first researcher to Macedonia, followed the next day by a researcher sent to Kosovo's border with northern Albania. For the duration of the war, researchers were based in both places. Brief fact-finding trips to Montenegro and Bosnia to interview the refugees being expelled from the province were added to ensure more complete coverage. Visa restrictions and security concerns did not allow travel within Kosovo.

In general, the research had two aims: to identify and draw public attention to the crimes being committed and to assist the investigations of the ICTY. The former was done by methodically documenting the most serious abuses through the testimony of refugees, as well as trying to discern the patterns of abuse. "Kosovo Flashes" were produced with updates from the field on a near-daily basis and released to the public. Several lengthier, more in-depth reports were also released during this period. Human Rights Watch assisted ICTY investigators by alerting them to alleged crimes and, at times, introducing them to potential witnesses.

All information was based on refugee accounts, because foreign press and human rights monitors had been expelled from Yugoslavia. Still, the consistency of the refugee statements and their high degree of corroboration allowed a fairly accurate picture to be formed.

On June 13, 1999, a Human Rights Watch researcher entered Kosovo just after NATO troops. At least one researcher remained in the province for the next six months to investigate first-hand the extent of the crimes. The strategy was to look into those incidents that Human Rights Watch had reported on in its initial reports, such as those occurring in Meja, Djakovica (Gjakove), and Velika Krusa (Krusha e Madhe). In addition, many new sites were chosen in order to get a full geographic representation of the abuses.

The accuracy of the refugee accounts was astounding. In virtually all of the sites visited by Human Rights Watch after the war, researchers found the facts to be as the refugees in Albania and Macedonia had claimed, down to the names and ages of victims. In one village in the Suva Reka municipality, for example, the bodies of twelve elderly men were found, eleven of them in the village well. Six weeks before, women refugees from the village had told Human Rights Watch that eleven elderly men had been taken away by the Serbian police (the twelfth man was detained after they had left). All of the names matched.

With time, many previously unreported incidents surfaced. The executions in Shraravina went unreported because witnesses had remained trapped in Drenica. The killings at Dubrava prison were not known because the survivors had been transferred to prisons inside Serbia. Human Rights Watch pursued these and other cases, although many incidents had to remain uninvestigated due to the sheer number of sites across the province at which atrocities had occurred. Most of the sites of major killings, however, are covered in this report, with a few notable exceptions, such as Kotlina (Kotline), Kacanik, Lukare (Llukare) Duz (Dys), Goden, and Beleg. In general, incidents in the municipalities of Podujevo (Podujeve) and Kosovo Polje (Fushe Kosove) are also under-reported.

As with all research of this kind, there are limitations. Witnesses and victims sometimes had trouble remembering the details of events due to the extreme trauma they had experienced. In some cases, they had been instructed by the KLA not to speak of certain events. All of these complications have been taken into account. Multiple sources were always interviewed for each and every incident in this report. All facts have been corroborated by at least a second source. Whenever necessary, sources are cited in an endnote. In addition, Human Rights Watch researchers visited all of the large-scale killing sites mentioned in this report, inspecting the physical evidence that remained.

The naming of alleged perpetrators was undertaken with particular care. Although Kosovar Albanians often did not know their tormenters, a few names are mentioned in this report. For each, at least three independent sources confirmed their participation in a crime.

ON NAMES AND TERMINOLOGY

Much confusion stems from the existence of both Albanian and Serbian names for villages and towns in Kosovo, as well as for the province itself ("Kosova" in Albanian and "Kosovo and Metohija" in Serbian). For the sake of clarity and consistency, Human Rights Watch provides both the Serbian and the Albanian name at first mention of any location. Subsequent references are in the Serbian language only, since this is the English language practice (for example, Pristina and not Prishtina). Names of individuals are always in the spelling of that person's mother-language and ethnicity, i.e. all Albanian names are spelled in Albanian. Again for the sake of simplicity, accents and diacritics are not used.

The Federal Republic of Yugoslavia—comprised of Serbia and Montenegro—is referred to as "Yugoslavia." The Former Yugoslav Republic of Macedonia is called "Macedonia." Bosnia and Hercegovina is called "Bosnia."

Much care has been taken to avoid possible recriminations against the witnesses and victims who provide testimony in this report. Although some names are provided when there is no perceived danger, Human Rights Watch has withheld the identity of many sources, even if permission was granted to use a name in full. As such, many witness and victim names are presented either as initials or, when stated, changed entirely. Two villages where rapes are known to have taken place are not mentioned by name.

Glossary

AK47/Kalashnikov	Russian or Chinese-made semi-automatic rifle
APC	Armored Personnel Carrier
Arkan	Real name, Zeljko Raznjatovic, paramilitary leader during the wars in Croatia and Bosnia-Herzegovina. Indicted by the International Criminal Tribunal for the former Yugslavia (on September 30, 1997, and publicly on March 31, 1999); wanted by Interpol. Shot dead in Belgrade by unknown assailants, February 2000
Arkan's Tigers	Serbian paramilitary formation run by "Arkan"
Black Hand	Serbian paramilitary group
CDHRF	Council for the Defense of Human Rights and Freedoms, Kosovo-based human rights organization
Chetnik	Term with connotations to First World War Serbian combat forces under Kosta Pecenac, and to Second World War combat forces under Draza Mihailovic. The term, now derogatory, is used to indicate a hard-line nationalistic Serb
DM	Deutschmark/German mark, widely used as hard currency in Kosovo

DU	Depleted Uranium
EU	European Union
FRY	Federal Republic of Yugoslavia
ICRC	International Committee of the Red Cross
ICTY	(United Nations) International Criminal Tribunal for the former Yugoslavia
IDP	Internally displaced person
IOM	International Organization for Migration
KDOM	Kosovo Diplomatic Observer Mission
KFOR	(NATO) Kosovo Force
KLA	Kosovo Liberation Army (*Ushtria Clirimtare e Kosoves* (UCK) in Albanian)
KPC	Kosovo Protection Corps (*Trupat e Mbrojtjes se Kosoves* (TMK) in Albanian)
KPS	Kosovo Police Service
KVM	Kosovo Verification Mission of the Organization for Security and Cooperation in Europe
LDK	Democratic League of Kosovo (Lidhja Demokratike te Kosove in Albanian)
LPK	People's Movement of Kosovo (Levizija Popullare e Kosoves in Albanian)
MTA	Military Technical Agreement

MUP	Serbian Ministry of Internal Affairs (Ministarstvo Unutrasnjih Poslova in Serbian)
NATO	North Atlantic Treaty Organization
NGO	Non-governmental organization
OSCE	Organization for Security and Cooperation in Europe
OUP	Unit of Internal Affairs in the Serbian Ministry of Internal Affairs (Odeljenje Unutrasnjih Poslova in Serbian)
PJP	Serbian Special Police Units (Posebne Jedinice Policije in Serbian)
SAJ	Serbian Special Anti-terrorist Units (Specijalne Antiteroristicke Jedinice in Serbian)
SDB	State Security Service (Sluzba Drzavne Bezbednosti in Serbian)
Serbian cross	Serbian nationalist symbol, comprising a cross and four Cyrillic "S"s derived from the slogan "Only Unity Saves the Serbs" (Samo Sloga Srbina Spasava in Serbian)
SFRY	Socialist Federal Republic of Yugoslavia
SPS	Socialist Party of Serbia (Socijalisticka Partija Srbije in Serbian)
SRS	Serbian Radical Party (Srpska Radikalna Stranka in Serbian)
SUP	Secretariat for Internal Affairs in the Serbian Min-

	istry of Internal Affairs (Sekretarijat Unutrasnjih Poslova in Serbian)
UCK	Ushtria Clirimtare e Kosoves (Kosovo Liberation Army in English)
UNHCHR	United Nations High Commissioner for Human Rights
UNHCR	United Nations High Commissioner for Refugees
UNICEF	United Nations Children's Fund
UNMIK	United Nations Interim Administration Mission in Kosovo
VJ	Yugoslav Army (Vojska Jugslavije in Serbian)
WFP	World Food Programme
White Eagles	Serbian paramilitary formation
WHO	World Health Organization

UNDER ORDERS

"Unidentified."

1

EXECUTIVE SUMMARY

This report documents torture, killings, rapes, forced expulsions, and other war crimes committed by Serbian and Yugoslav government forces against Kosovar Albanians between March 24 and June 12, 1999, the period of NATO's air campaign against Yugoslavia. The report reveals a coordinated and systematic campaign to terrorize, kill, and expel the ethnic Albanians of Kosovo that was organized by the highest levels of the Serbian and Yugoslav governments in power at that time.

Naturally, these crimes did not occur in isolation. This report outlines the historical and political context of the war, with a critique of the international community's response to the developing crisis over the past decade. Three chapters also document abuses committed by the ethnic Albanian insurgency known as the Kosovo Liberation Army (KLA), which abducted and murdered civilians during and after the war, as well as abuses by NATO, which failed adequately to minimize civilian casualties during its bombing of Yugoslavia. Nevertheless, the primary focus of this report is the state-sponsored violence inflicted by the Serbian and Yugoslav governments in 1999 against ethnic Albanian citizens of Yugoslavia.

THE 1999 OFFENSIVE

The Serbian and Yugoslav government offensive in Kosovo that began on March 20, 1999, four days before NATO bombing commenced, was a methodically planned and well-implemented campaign. Key changes in Yugoslavia's security apparatus in late 1998, including a new head of Serbian state security and a new chief of the Yugoslav Army General Staff, suggest that preparations for the offensive were being made at that time. In early 1999, a distinct military build-up in Kosovo and the arming of ethnic Serb civilians was observed. Police and army actions in late February and early March around Vucitrn (Vushtrri) and Podujevo (Podujeve), called "winter exercises" by the government, secured rail and road links north into Serbia.

More than 80 percent of the entire population of Kosovo, and 90 percent of Kosovar Albanians, were displaced from their homes.

Serious violations of international humanitarian law had accompanied all previous government offensives, but the period of the NATO bombing saw unprecedented attacks on civilians and the forced expulsion of more than 850,000 ethnic Albanians from Kosovo. For the first time in the conflict, fighting moved from the rural areas to the cities.

While the government campaign seems to have been an attempt to crush the KLA, it clearly developed into something more once the NATO bombing began. With a major offensive underway, then-Yugoslav President Slobodan Milosevic took advantage of the NATO bombing to implement a plan to crush the rebels and their base of support among the population, as well as forcibly to expel a large portion of Kosovo's Albanian population.

No one predicted the speed and scale of the expulsions. Within three weeks of the start of NATO bombing, 525,787 refugees from Kosovo had flooded the neighboring countries, according to the United Nation High Commissioner for Refugees (UNHCR). All told, government forces expelled 862,979 ethnic Albanians from Kosovo, and several hundred thousand more were internally displaced, in addition to those displaced prior to March 1999. More than 80 percent of the entire population of Kosovo—90 percent of Kosovar Albanians—were displaced from their homes.

Areas with historic ties to the KLA were hardest hit. The municipalities of Glogovac (Gllogofc) and Srbica (Skenderaj) in the Drenica region, the cradle of the KLA, were the scene of multiple massacres of civilians, as well as arbitrary detentions, torture, and the systematic destruction of homes and other civilian property. Mass killings, forced expulsions, and the destruction of civilian property were also common in the southwestern municipalities of Djakovica (Gjakove), Orahovac (Rrahovec), and Suva Reka (Suhareke), where many villages had long supported the insurgency. Sixty-five percent of the violations documented by Human Rights Watch took place in the above-mentioned five municipalities (see Figure 2 in the chapter Statistical Analysis of Violations).

Explanations for the abuses in other municipalities are more complex and less conclusive. The municipalities of Pec (Peja) and Lipljan (Lipjan), both of which had significant Serbian populations, were targeted for mass expulsion of ethnic Albanians, but killings were more localized, such as in the villages of Slovinje (Sllovi), Ribare (Ribar), Ljubenic (Lubeniq), Cuska (Qyshk), and the town of Pec. Although the KLA was active in the Pec municipality and present in the western-most part of Lipljan municipality during 1998 and early 1999, there is little or no evidence to tie the KLA to some of the villages in which massacres occurred. The killings were consistent with a broader pattern of operations to terrorize the population into fleeing Kosovo employing military, police, and paramilitary forces.

There was little KLA presence or violence during 1998 and early 1999 in the ethnically-mixed northwestern municipality of Istok, for example. Nevertheless the municipality suffered mass expulsions of its Albanian residents into Montenegro spurred by the burning and looting of their homes. Istok was also the scene of one of the bloodiest incidents of the war, when Serbian forces killed more than ninety ethnic Albanian inmates in the Dubrava prison in May 1999, after two days of NATO air strikes had killed an estimated nineteen inmates.

The forced expulsion was well organized, which suggests that it had been planned in advance. Villages in strategic areas were cleared to secure lines of communication and control of border zones. Areas of KLA support, as well as areas without a KLA presence, were attacked in joint actions by the police, army, and paramilitaries. Large cities were cleared using buses or trains and long convoys of tractors were carefully herded toward the borders. Refugees were driven into flight or transported in state organized transportation to the borders in a concerted program of forced expulsion and deportation characterized by a very high degree of coordination and control.

There is little or no evidence to tie the KLA to some of the villages in which massacres occurred.

Human Rights Watch also documented the common practice of "identity cleansing": refugees expelled toward Albania were frequently stripped of their identity documents and forced to remove the license plates from their cars and tractors before being permitted to cross the border. Before reaching the border, many Albanians had their personal documents destroyed, suggesting the government was trying to block their return.

The mass expulsion of Kosovar Albanians may have served a number of purposes. First, it might have been intended to alter Kosovo's demographic composition—a policy often mentioned by Serbia's extreme nationalist politicians throughout history. Demographic shifts might also have led to an eventual partition of the province into two parts, one for Serbs and one for Albanians. Second, the expulsions might have been intended to destabilize the neighboring countries of Albania and Macedonia. Lastly, the goal might have been to tie down NATO forces in the neighboring countries, thereby hindering a ground invasion, or at least to weaken the resolve of the NATO alliance. If undercutting the international community's determination was the aim, it clearly failed, as the images of beleaguered refugees only provoked public outrage and increased calls for action.

Deliberate and unlawful killings of civilians—extrajudicial executions—were a key part of the "cleansing" campaign. Throughout the province, civilians who were clearly noncombatants, including women and some children, were murdered by Serbian police, Yugoslav army soldiers, and associated paramilitary forces in execution-style killings.

In general, the killings had three apparent motives. The first was to expedite the "cleansing" process through intimidation and fear. The second was the targeting of individuals suspected of fighting with or assisting the KLA—a distinction that was often difficult to make. Targeted individuals included some prominent political leaders, human rights activists, and wealthy businessmen. The third was killing for revenge: some massacres were committed after Serbian or Yugoslav forces suffered casualties at the hands of the KLA.

Deliberate and unlawful killings of civilians–extrajudicial executions–were a key part of the "cleansing" campaign.

Although reliable figures are beginning to emerge, the final death toll from the Kosovo war remains unknown, and has become the focus of considerable debate. Through its own research, Human Rights Watch documented 3,453 killings by Serbian or Yugoslav government forces, but that number is definitely lower than the total, because it is based on only 577 interviews (and these interviews were not randomly sampled to allow for extrapolation of the data to all of Kosovo). At the same time, the number is certainly not as large as some Western government and NATO officials suggested during the war, when figures went as high as 100,000.

There is incontrovertible evidence of grave tampering and the removal of bodies by Serbian and Yugoslav troops.

As of July 2001, the International Criminal Tribunal for the former Yugoslavia (ICTY) had exhumed approximately 4,300 bodies believed to have been victims of unlawful killings by Serbian and Yugoslav forces in Kosovo. This is certainly less than the total number of those killed by government troops. Most importantly, there is incontrovertible evidence of grave tampering and the removal of bodies by Serbian and Yugoslav troops, as the post-Milosevic Serbian government was beginning to confirm in summer 2001. Human Rights Watch documented attempts to hide or dispose of bodies in Trnje (Terrnje), Djakovica, Izbica (Izbice), Rezala (Rezalle), Velika Krusa and Mala Krusa (Krushe e Madhe and Krushe e Vogel), Suva Reka, Slovinje, Poklek, Kotlina (Kotline), and Pusto Selo (Pastasel). In addition, 3,525 persons, including ethnic Serbs, remain missing from the conflict, according to the International Committee of the Red Cross (ICRC).

The statistical analysis conducted by Human Rights Watch and the American Association for the Advancement of Science (AAAS) revealed killing patterns that further expose the systematic nature of the government's campaign. When recorded extrajudicial executions are plotted over time, for example, three distinct waves emerge, as seen in Graph 5 in the chapter on Statistical Analysis of Violations. The graph is not a perfect reflection of killings since Human Rights Watch did not randomly sample the interviewees. However, the extreme nature of the waves, with three distinct surges over short periods of time, strongly suggests that the killings were not the result of random violence by government forces. Rather, they were carefully planned and implemented operations that fit into the government's strategic aims.

Likewise, the extrajudicial executions by municipality over time (Graphs 6 through 10, 14, and 15) show similar spikes in violence over short periods.

Killing "sprees" tended to occur in municipalities over distinct periods, suggesting a strategic order to commit these killings in certain areas.

Rape and sexual violence were also components of the campaign. Rapes of ethnic Albanians were not rare and isolated acts committed by individual Serbian or Yugoslav forces, but rather were instruments to terrorize the civilian population, extort money from families, and push people to flee their homes. In total, Human Rights Watch found credible accounts of ninety-six cases of sexual assault by Yugoslav soldiers, Serbian police, or paramilitaries during the period of NATO bombing, and the actual number is certainly much higher.

Rape and sexual violence were also components of the campaign.

In general, rapes in Kosovo can be grouped into three categories: rapes in women's homes, rapes during flight, and rapes in detention. In the first category, security forces entered private homes and raped women in front of family members, in the yard, or in an adjoining room. In the second category, internally displaced people wandering on foot or riding on tractors were stopped, robbed, and threatened by the Yugoslav Army, Serbian police, or paramilitaries. If families could not produce cash, security forces told them their daughters would be taken away and raped; in some cases, even when families did provide money, their daughters were taken away. The third category of rapes took place in temporary detention centers, such as abandoned homes or barns.

The destruction of civilian property by government troops in 1999 was widespread. According to a November 1999 UNHCR survey, almost 40 percent of all residential houses in Kosovo were heavily damaged or completely destroyed. Municipalities with strong ties to the KLA were disproportionately affected, in part because attacks against them began in 1998. But other areas without a history of KLA activity were also affected, such as the city of Pec, where more than 80 percent of the city's houses were heavily damaged or destroyed.

Schools and mosques were similarly affected. According to a United Nations damage assessment of 649 schools in Kosovo, more than one-fifth of the schools surveyed were heavily damaged and more than 60 percent were completely destroyed. Throughout Kosovo, Serbian and Yugoslav forces also deliberately rendered water wells unusable by dumping chemicals, dead animals, or human remains into the water. Human Rights Watch documented cases in four villages in which murder victims had been dumped into the water supply.

Endless witnesses and victims told Human Rights Watch how government forces robbed them of valuables, including wedding rings and automobiles, either at their homes or along the road during their expulsion. Police, soldiers, and especially members of paramilitary units threatened individuals with death if they did not hand over sums of money, usually demanding German marks. Such theft was mentioned repeatedly, even by members of the security forces who spoke with the international media after the war. For some of the men, it was the reason they went to Kosovo. Some volunteers said they were released from prison in Serbia if they agreed to serve with the army or police.

Endless witnesses and victims told Human Rights Watch how government forces robbed them of valuables, including wedding rings and automobiles.

This report also documents the practice of forcing detainees to dig trenches or clear bunkers, as well as the use of civilians as human shields to protect troops from NATO or KLA attacks. The Yugoslav government also placed both antipersonnel and antitank landmines, especially along the borders with Albania and Macedonia, most probably in preparation for a ground invasion.

THE CHAIN OF COMMAND

The government forces involved in the conflict were a complex combination of the Serbian Ministry of Internal Affairs police and special police, Yugoslav Army soldiers and special units, paramilitary forces, local militias, and an assortment of gunmen from abroad, all operating under orders from the government in Belgrade.

The Yugoslav Army had overall command during the period of NATO bombing, with the police and paramilitary forces subservient to its orders according to law, although top officials in the Serbian Ministry of Internal Affairs clearly exercised significant influence over the campaign. The army controlled the main roads and the borders, coordinating and facilitating the "ethnic cleansing." The police and paramilitary forces were more involved directly in the expulsion of civilians and destruction of villages, with artillery support from the army. It is during these operations that men sometimes were separated from women and children, interrogated about the KLA, and summarily executed.

According to Yugoslav law, the Yugoslav Army (Vojska Jugoslavije, or VJ) is under the command of the Yugoslav president in both wartime and peace. Until October 2000, this was Slobodan Milosevic. The controlling body of the VJ is the Supreme Defense Council, comprised of the presidents of Serbia, Montenegro, and Yugoslavia and chaired by the Yugoslav president. The chief of the army's General Staff during the war was Gen. Dragoljub Ojdanic, who was appointed after the war to serve as Yugoslav minister of defense—the position he held until October 2000.

The VJ is divided into three armies. The Third Army, commanded during the war by Col. Gen. Nebojsa Pavkovic, was responsible for Kosovo and southern Serbia. As of August 2001, Pavkovic was Chief of the Yugoslav Army's General Staff. Under Pavkovic, during the war, was Maj. Gen. Vladimir Lazarevic, who commanded the Pristina Corps of the Third Army that was based in Kosovo. Under Lazarevic were five brigades, one military police unit, and one aviation regiment. All of their commanders are named in the chapter Forces of the Conflict.

The structure of the Serbian Ministry of Internal Affairs (Ministarstvo Unutrasnjih Poslova, or MUP), run during the war by Minister Vlajko Stojiljkovic, is more complicated than that of the VJ, which has a transparent chain of command. Within the MUP were the regular police in Kosovo commanded by Sreten Lukic, the special police (Posebne Jedinice Policije, or PJP) commanded by Lt. Gen. Obrad Stevanovic, and the Anti-Terrorist Forces (Specijalna Antiteroristicka Jedinica, or SAJ) commanded by Col. Zivko Trajkovic. Col. Gen. Vlastimir Djordjevic was head of the public security sector of MUP, as well as assistant to the minister of internal affairs. The new Serbian government replaced Djordjevic and Stevanovic in January 2001, but promoted Lukic to chief of public security as well as deputy minister of internal affairs.

The Yugoslav Army (Vojska Jugoslavije, or VJ) is under the command of the Yugoslav president in both wartime and peace.

The Serbian Ministry of Internal Affairs also contains the state security service, or secret police, which played a major role in Kosovo. In addition to covert activities monitoring and harassing ethnic Albanian political activists and the KLA, state security also deployed its special operations unit, the JSO (Jedinica za Specijalne Operacije), and assisted various paramilitary organizations. Also known as the "Red Berets" or "Frenki's Boys" (after Frenki Simatovic, a key personality in the Ministry of Internal Affairs who allegedly founded the group), the JSO was commanded during the war by Milorad Lukovic, a man better known as "Legija." Until January 2001, the head of the Serbian state security was Col. Gen. Radomir Markovic. He was dismissed in late January and arrested one month later by Serbian police for his alleged involvement in a 1999 attack against a Serbian politician, Vuk Draskovic. David Gajic was the head of state security in Kosovo during the war.

Lastly, various paramilitary forces as well as foreign gunmen were active in Kosovo, largely under the control of the central government. Aside from being among the most violent forces in Kosovo, one of the paramilitaries' primary activities was looting and theft.

Although the precise lines of command and control of these paramilitary forces remain unclear, they clearly cooperated closely with the Yugoslav Army and Serbian police. Paramilitary members who spoke with the international press after the war said that local officials had sometimes given them lists of ethnic Albanians to target for murder. Some men were released from Serbian prisons if they agreed to fight in Kosovo. At times, individual members of the police or army tried to warn or protect ethnic Albanian civilians from paramilitary forces, although this was rare; more commonly, regular militias and police personnel worked closely with paramilitary units, often maintaining a cordon around targeted communities while paramilitary troops moved in.

The various units and groups within the MUP make the chain of command less discernible than with the VJ, although it is clear that ultimate authority for the MUP rested with Yugoslav President Slobodan Milosevic. According to Yugoslav law, in a declared state of war, the Yugoslav Army has jurisdiction over the Serbian police, thereby making Slobodan Milosevic the de facto and de jure commander of the police during the period of NATO bombing. Then-Yugoslav Deputy Prime Minister Nikola Sainovic also played an important role.

International law is clear on individual criminal responsibility for the leaders who organize or tolerate the commission of war crimes. Both the direct perpetrator of a crime as well as the military or political leaders who ordered that crime, or who fail to take steps to prevent a crime or to punish the perpetrator, can be held accountable.

As this report proves, the extent and systematic nature of the abuses in Kosovo make it impossible that the Serbian and Yugoslav leaderships were unaware of those violations, despite their public denials. In only a few cases were members of the security forces punished for having committed serious crimes, such as murder. On the contrary, the postwar period saw hundreds of promotions and awards for police and army personnel, including some of the top leadership, such as Dragoljub Ojdanic, Nebojsa Pavkovic, Vladimir Lazarevic, Obrad Stevanovic, Sreten Lukic, Vlastimir Djordjevic, and Zivko Trajkovic, as well as many of the brigade commanders in Pristina Corps. A complete list of those promoted and awarded is included as an appendix to the chapter Forces of the Conflict.

The extent and systematic nature of the abuses in Kosovo make it impossible that the Serbian and Yugoslav leaderships were unaware of those violations.

THE WAR CRIMES TRIBUNAL

After a slow start in 1998, the International Criminal Tribunal for the Former Yugoslavia (ICTY) began a full investigation into the war crimes committed in Kosovo. On May 27, 1999, the tribunal announced its most significant indictment to date: that of Yugoslav President Slobodan Milosevic and four other top officials for "murder, persecution, and deportation in Kosovo" between January 1 and late May 1999. The other indictees are: Milan Milutinovic, president of Serbia and member of the Supreme Defense Council, Dragoljub Ojdanic, Chief of General Staff of the Yugoslav Army, Nikola Sainovic, deputy prime minister of the FRY, and Vlajko Stojiljkovic, Serbian minister of internal affairs. ICTY investigations of war crimes are ongoing, including a review of KLA crimes. On April 1, 2001, the Serbian police arrested Milosevic on charges of corruption. On June 28, he was transferred to the war crimes tribunal in The Hague. As of August 2001, the other indictees remained at large.

The tribunal also conducted an internal assessment of NATO actions during the war, concluding that there were no grounds for a further investigation. The Human Rights Watch assessment of NATO's air campaign differs slightly. Although Human Rights Watch found no evidence that NATO committed war crimes, it did violate international humanitarian law by taking insufficient precautions to identify the presence of civilians when attacking convoys and mobile targets. As previously reported in a February 2000 Human Rights Watch report, *Civilian Deaths in the NATO Air Campaign,* the NATO bombing caused the deaths of approximately 500 civilians throughout Yugoslavia. Between 56 and 60 percent of these deaths were in Kosovo. NATO's use of cluster bombs, although halted in the course of the conflict, is also criticized in this report. As inherently indiscriminate weapons when used in urban areas and because of their high failure rate, cluster bombs pose a serious and disproportionate danger to the civilian population. Between March 24 and May 7, 1999, more than 1,500 cluster bombs were dropped over Kosovo and the rest of Yugoslavia.

ABUSES BY THE KLA

As presented in the Background chapter, the KLA was responsible for serious abuses in 1998, including abductions and murders of Serbs and ethnic Albanians considered collaborators with the state. In some villages under KLA control in 1998, the rebels drove ethnic Serbs from their homes. Some of those who remained are unaccounted for and are presumed to have been abducted by the KLA and killed. According to the International Committee of the Red Cross, ninety-seven Kosovo Serbs who went missing in 1998 were still missing as of May 15, 2000.

The KLA was responsible for serious abuses in 1998, including abductions and murders of Serbs and ethnic Albanians considered collaborators with the state.

The KLA detained an estimated eighty-five Serbs during its July 19, 1998, attack on Orahovac. Thirty-five of these people were subsequently released but the others remain missing as of August 2001. On July 22, 1998, the KLA briefly took control of the Belacevac mine near Obilic. Nine Serbs were captured that day, and they remain on the ICRC's list of the missing.

In September 1998, the Serbian police collected thirty-four bodies of people believed to have been seized and murdered by the KLA, among them some ethnic Albanians, at Lake Radonjic near Glodjane (Gllogjan). Prior to that, the most serious KLA abuse was the reported killing in August of twenty-two Serbian civilians in the village of Klecka, where the police claimed to have discovered human remains and a kiln used to cremate the bodies. The manner in which the allegations were made, however, raised questions about their validity.

The KLA, which evolved between 1996 and 1999 from a scattered guerrilla group to an armed movement and ultimately to a more formidable armed force, engaged in military tactics in 1998 and 1999 that put civilians at risk. KLA units sometimes staged an ambush or attacked police or army outposts from a village and then retreated, exposing villagers to revenge attacks. Large massacres sometimes ensued, helping publicize the KLA's cause and internationalize the conflict.

Elements of the KLA are also responsible for post-conflict attacks on Serbs, Roma, and other non-Albanians, as well as ethnic Albanian political rivals. Immediately following NATO's arrival in Kosovo, there was widespread and systematic burning and looting of homes belonging to Serbs, Roma, and other minorities and the destruction of Orthodox churches and monasteries. This destruction was combined with harassment and intimidation designed to force people from their homes and communities. By late-2000 more than 210,000 Serbs had fled the province; most of them left in the first six weeks of the NATO deployment. Those who remained were increasingly concentrated in mono-ethnic enclaves, such as northern Mitrovica, Kosovo Polje, or Gracanica.

Immediately following KFOR's arrival in Kosovo, there was widespread and systematic burning and looting of homes belonging to Serbs, Roma, and other minorities and the destruction of Orthodox churches and monasteries.

Most seriously, as many as one thousand Serbs and Roma have been murdered or have gone missing since June 12, 1999. Criminal gangs or vengeful individuals may have been involved in some incidents since the war. But elements of the KLA are clearly responsible for many of these crimes. The desire for revenge provides a partial explanation, but there is also a clear political goal in many of these attacks: the removal from Kosovo of non-ethnic Albanians in order to better justify an independent state.

Ethnic Albanians are not exempt from the violence. Albanians accused of "collaboration" with Serbian authorities have been beaten, abducted, or killed, notably in the municipalities of Prizren, Djakovica, and Klina. Attacks against political party activists, especially against the Democratic League of Kosovo (LDK), continued after municipal elections on October 28, 2000.

ROLE OF THE INTERNATIONAL COMMUNITY

The slow response by the international community is partially to blame for the post-war violence; the U.N. and NATO failed to take decisive action from the outset to curb the forced displacement and killings of Kosovo's non-ethnic Albanian population, which set a precedent for the post-war period. In mid-1999, there were no more than a handful of U.N. police, leaving NATO's KFOR troops to perform civilian policing functions for which they were ill-prepared. NATO was largely preoccupied with protecting its own troops, rather than defending civilians. Two years after the war, a functioning judiciary system had not been established, which contributed to an atmosphere of impunity.

The familiar refrain from the United Nations is that poor security results from a lack of resources. It is true that there are insufficient funds to pay police, judges and prosecutors. But the more fundamental shortcoming is the lack of political will. Senior NATO and U. N. officials know that persons linked to the former KLA, including some of Kosovo's key political figures, are implicated in violence against minorities and in criminal activities, but they have chosen not to confront them.

The international community's errors in this regard are hardly their first in Kosovo. In the Background chapter, this report tracks the international community's response to the conflict since 1990. The West failed to support the Kosovar Albanians' peaceful movement from 1990 to 1998, concerned during the wars in Bosnia and Croatia with keeping Kosovo out of the headlines. The West essentially watched as the KLA emerged, the Yugoslav state responded forcefully, and the province slid toward armed conflict.

The West essentially watched as the KLA emerged, the Yugoslav state responded forcefully, and the province slid toward armed conflict.

Throughout the conflict, the international community failed to develop a unified position to resolve the crisis. Slobodan Milosevic used this disharmony to his advantage, appearing to deal with one state, and then another, all the while buying time to advance his campaign. Members of the international community took advantage of the disunity as well, pointing to each other as the excuse for inaction. In the instances in which the international community strongly condemned the violence, words and symbolic action proved meaningless, with deadlines postponed, conditions abandoned, and sanctions poorly enforced or even withdrawn.

Primary blame for the Kosovo tragedy must be placed on former Yugoslav President Slobodan Milosevic and the then-Serbian and Yugoslav leadership.

The report concludes that the international community's interest in preserving its political settlement in Bosnia and an allergy to altering international borders blinded it to the imperative of halting abuses before they escalated into open warfare. If the international community wanted to promote territorial integrity in the Balkans, it should have pressed for the national unity that comes from respect for the rights of all citizens—a respect that had been sorely lacking in Kosovo as well as in other parts of the Balkans. Permitting serious abuses to go unchallenged led to the regional instability that the international community had sought to avoid.

In the end, primary blame for the Kosovo tragedy must be placed on former Yugoslav President Slobodan Milosevic and the then-Serbian and Yugoslav leadership, who not only failed to seek any peaceful compromises with the Albanians in Kosovo, but also devised and implemented a violent campaign against armed insurgents and civilians alike. As this report shows, all evidence points to their direct involvement in war crimes of the most serious nature.

The autumn 2000 electoral victory of the Democratic Opposition of Serbia (DOS) opened the door for change in Serbian and Yugoslav society and a peaceful resolution to long-standing conflicts in the region. But lasting stability in Kosovo, Serbia, and the region will not be achieved without accountability for past crimes committed by all sides.

2

BACKGROUND

INTRODUCTION

In 1989, when the Serbian government revoked Kosovo's status as an autonomous province within the Socialist Federal Republic of Yugoslavia, political analysts and activists in that country and abroad anticipated deterioration. "A lit fuse," "a powder keg," and other clichés were used to describe the prospect of armed conflict in the province and the country.

The danger became more apparent with each passing year, even though the wars that engulfed the other parts of the former Yugoslavia did not spill over into Kosovo. Serbian government oppression against Kosovar Albanians intensified and, seeing no potential for improvement, the ethnic Albanians gradually lost faith in the nonviolent politics that they had pursued since 1990. By late 1996, a previously unknown guerrilla group called the Kosovo Liberation Army (KLA) began coordinating attacks against the Serbian police. The government responded with indiscriminate force and the downward cycle of violence had begun.

Despite the repeated warning signs during the decade, the international community failed to stop a predictable conflict. Short-term and piecemeal political tactics took precedence over long-term strategic policy. Divisions and competition between governments and international bodies made unified action weak and directionless—characteristics that the Milosevic government craftily exploited.

Serious and unified international engagement came only after the conflict had deteriorated into full-scale war. Faced with limited options at that point, the West chose military action by NATO—the so-called "humanitarian intervention" in 1999.

Ethnic Albanian man in Plocica village, September 1998. PHOTO BY WADE GODDARD

Taking advantage of the NATO bombing, Serbian and Yugoslav forces "ethnically cleansed" more than 850,000 Kosovar Albanians, and killed thousands more. The NATO bombing eventually forced government troops out of the province, but not before serious war crimes had been committed—atrocities which continue to poison Kosovo's post-war environment.

The pages of graphic human rights testimony in this report are one result of the West's failures in dealing with this foreseeable crisis. The large-scale expulsions and killings of Serbs and Albanians, even after the entry of NATO into Kosovo, provide a crucial lesson: left unattended, government oppression and human rights abuses, especially against minority populations, can easily produce violent confrontations that result in more serious abuse. Put another way, genuine and lasting stability in the Balkans is impossible without democratic governments respectful of human rights.

There have been many debates over what the international community could have done to stop Kosovo's violence. One fact is clear: the international community could have implemented creative economic and political measures designed to halt the Yugoslav government's abusive behavior against civilians. The cost of such measures would surely have been less than that of NATO's intervention and the subsequent U.N. mission in Kosovo.

What follows is a chronology of Kosovo's downward spiral and the international community's missed opportunities.

BRIEF HISTORY OF THE KOSOVO CONFLICT

One must go back centuries to address fully the relationship between Albanians and Serbs and their struggles in Kosovo. Both consider the province central to their cultures and political well-being, and have proven willing to fight for control of the region. Keeping Kosovo and its historic sites a part of Serbia has become a centerpiece of Serbian nationalist policy. Violent confrontations have marked the area's history, although Albanians and Serbs have also fought as allies on occasion. Mutual accusations of atrocities in the Balkan Wars, World War I, and World War II, as well as battles long before, cloud the region's history.

While this background is central to understanding the conflict, and the region's history plays an important role in contemporary affairs, historical debates are secondary to the more recent developments that influenced the Kosovo war. Selective versions of history and past grievances provided fertile ground for opportunistic politicians in the 1980s and 1990s to exploit the fears and frustrations of Albanians and Serbs. History was abused by aggressive nationalist politicians who benefited by promoting hatred, xenophobia, militarization and, ultimately, war.

Kosovo in the Socialist Federal Republic of Yugoslavia

After World War II, the federal constitution defined ethnic Albanians in Yugoslavia as a "nationality" rather than a constituent "nation," despite being the third largest ethnic group in the country. This was a status distinct from that of the other major ethnic groups in the country—Serbs, Croats, Bosnians, Slovenes, and Macedonians. Still, Yugoslavia provided a semblance of minority rights to all ethnic groups in the name of socialist "brotherhood and unity."

Kosovo was the poorest region in Yugoslavia. With the exception of the bountiful Trepca mines, most of the province is agricultural. Poverty and underdevelopment among all ethnic groups in Kosovo exacerbated tensions. Some improvements came after student demonstrations in the late sixties, such as increased public investment, the opening of a university in Pristina, and the recruitment of Kosovar Albanians into the local administration.

Endeavoring to strike a better balance among the country's competing ethnic groups—and to check the power of Serbia within the federation—Yugoslav leader Josip Broz Tito orchestrated a new constitution in 1974 to provide two regions in Serbia with more autonomy: Kosovo and Vojvodina (with a large ethnic Hungarian population). Although they did not achieve the status of federal republics like Bosnia, Croatia, Macedonia, Montenegro, Serbia, and Slovenia, the two provinces were declared "autonomous regions," which gave them representation in the federal presidency alongside Yugoslavia's republics, as well as their own central banks, separate police, regional parliaments and governments. Ethnic Albanians were brought into some of the ruling elite's inner circles.

History was abused by aggressive nationalist politicians who benefited by promoting hatred, xenophobia, militarization and, ultimately, war.

Ethnic Albanians, who made up approximately 74 percent of the Kosovo population in 1971, took most key positions of power in Kosovo and controlled the education system, judiciary, and police, albeit under control of Tito and the Communist Party, which was the dominant political force in the country. The Albanian-language university in Pristina, opened in 1970, was promoted by the authorities.

Kosovo's autonomy was never embraced by a wide sector of the Serbian ruling elite, which viewed it as a threat to Serbia's interests and sovereignty. Autonomy for Kosovo and Vojvodina, some argued, had diluted Serbia's power in Yugoslavia. Criticism was muted during the seventies, but began to mount after Tito's death in 1980. The following year, ethnic Albanians, led by university students initially discontented with bad food and poor dormitory conditions, took to the streets to demand higher wages, greater freedom of expression, the release of political prisoners, and republic status for Kosovo within Yugoslavia. Their demonstrations were dispersed forcibly by the Yugoslav Army and federal police, resulting in a number of ethnic Albanian deaths and numerous arrests over the ensuing months. Some political prisoners from that time, together with young men who fled Kosovo to avoid arrest, later formed the radical emigre groups in Western Europe that evolved fifteen years later into the KLA.[1] A new ethnic Albanian communist leadership was installed by Belgrade. From 1981 on, pressure grew in Serbian political circles to rein in what was viewed as a growing "Albanian secessionism."

Ethnic Serbs and other minorities, such as Turks and Roma, were subjected to harassment, intimidation, and sometimes violence by extremist members of the ethnic Albanian majority.

Treatment of Non-ethnic Albanians

Throughout the late 1970s and 1980s, Kosovo's Serbs complained of harassment and discrimination by the ethnic Albanian population and leadership, with the intention, Serbs claimed, of driving them from the province. According to a report submitted to the influential Serbian Academy of Sciences and Arts in 1988, more than 20,000 ethnic Serbs moved out of Kosovo in the years 1981–1987.[2] Albanians claim that Serbs left for economic reasons because Kosovo remained Yugoslavia's poorest province.

Ethnic Serbs and other minorities, such as Turks and Roma, were subjected to harassment, intimidation, and sometimes violence by extremist members of the ethnic Albanian majority. The government in Kosovo, run by ethnic Albanians, did not take adequate steps to investigate these abuses or to protect Kosovo's minorities against them.[3]

At the same time, the ethnic Albanian population was consistently growing with Kosovar Albanians having the highest birthrate in Europe, resulting in what the Serbian Academy of Sciences and Arts called, "heavy pressure not only on available resources, but also on other ethnic groups."[4]

The Rise of Serbian Nationalism

The mid- and late-eighties were marked by a distinct rise in Serbian nationalism, especially among Serbs living outside of Serbia proper, who felt increasingly isolated and threatened by the nationalism that was rising around them in Croatia, Bosnia, and Kosovo. The most vocal were Serbs in Kosovo who complained about their mistreatment at the hands of ethnic Albanians.

In September 1986, a document from the Serbian Academy of Sciences and Arts was published that addressed "the Serbian question" in Yugoslavia. Known as the *Memorandum,* the document attacked Serbian politicians for doing nothing in the face of threats, attacks, and even "genocide" against the Serbs of Kosovo. Among other inflammatory claims, the *Memorandum* stated:

> The physical, political, legal, and cultural genocide of the Serbian population of Kosovo and Metohija is a worse historical defeat than any experienced in the liberation wars waged by Serbia from the First Serbian Uprising in 1804 to the uprising of 1941.[5]

Criticized by then-Serbian President Ivan Stambolic, the *Memorandum* reflected a common, albeit unspoken, sentiment among the Serb populace. With communism failing as an ideology, Serb politicians began to harness this discontent for their own political means.

No politician understood this better than Slobodan Milosevic, by that time communist party chief of Serbia. A communist apparachik and Stambolic protegé, Milosevic grasped the potency of fear and nationalism to fuel his own rise to power.

On April 24, 1987, Milosevic was sent to address a crowd of Kosovo Serbs in Kosovo Polje who were protesting maltreatment by Albanians. He rallied the demonstrators with the exhortation that: "No one should dare to beat you!" The phrase was repeated frequently on the Serbian state television that was under Milosevic's control and became a rallying cry for Serbian nationalists. Making the conversion from communist to nationalist, Milosevic continued:

Milosevic grasped the potency of fear and nationalism to fuel his own rise to power.

> You should stay here. This is your land. These are your houses. Your meadows and gardens. Your memories. You shouldn't abandon your land just because it's difficult to live, because you are pressured by injustice and degradation. It was never part of the Serbian and Montenegrin character to give up in the face of obstacles, to demobilize when it's time to fight... You should stay here for the sake of your ancestors and descendants. Otherwise your ancestors would be defiled and descendants disappointed. But I don't suggest that you stay, endure, and tolerate a situation you're not satisfied with. On the contrary, you should change it with the rest of the progressive people here, in Serbia and in Yugoslavia.[6]

With determined precision, Milosevic used his new found nationalist populism to eliminate political opponents, including Stambolic.[7] The state media, especially the Serbian Radio and Television (RTS), purposefully spread misinformation on abuses against Serbs in Kosovo, including the rape of Serbian women, and campaigned to promote negative images of Albanians. Over the next two years, massive gatherings were held in Yugoslavia called the "Rallies of Truth" in which Milosevic invoked Serb glory and demanded constitutional changes to revoke Kosovo's autonomy. In one such rally, Milosevic said:

> We shall win the battle for Kosovo regardless of the obstacles facing us inside and outside the country. We shall win despite the fact that Serbia's enemies outside the country are plotting against it, along with those in the country. We tell them that we enter every battle . . . with the aim of winning it.[8]

Ethnic Albanians organized their own strikes and public protests against the growing restrictions and repression in the province. Unlike the rallies in Serbia proper, the Albanian demonstrations were often broken up by force, and many ethnic Albanians were arrested. On November 17, 1988, the

Excerpts of speech by Slobodan Milosevic at Gazimestan, Kosovo, on 28 June, 1989 (600th anniversary of the Battle of the Blackbirds between Serbian and Ottoman forces)

At the time when this famous historical battle was fought in Kosovo, the people were looking at the stars, expecting aid from them. Now, six centuries later, they are looking at the stars again, waiting to conquer them. On the first occasion, they could allow themselves to be disunited and to have hatred and treason because they lived in smaller, weakly interlinked worlds. Now, as people on this planet, they cannot conquer even their own planet if they are not united, let alone other planets, unless they live in mutual harmony and solidarity.

Therefore, words devoted to unity, solidarity, and cooperation among people have no greater significance anywhere on the soil of our motherland than they have here in the field of Kosovo, which is a symbol of disunity and treason.

In the memory of the Serbian people, this disunity was decisive in causing the loss of the battle and in bringing about the fate which Serbia suffered for a full six centuries.

Even if it were not so, from a historical point of view, it remains certain that the people regarded disunity as its greatest disaster. Therefore it is the obligation of the people to remove disunity, so that they may protect themselves from defeats, failures, and stagnation in the future.

This year, the Serbian people became aware of the necessity of their mutual harmony as the indispensable condition for their present life and further development.

I am convinced that this awareness of harmony and unity will make it possible for Serbia not only to function as a state but to function as a successful state. Therefore I think that it makes sense to say this here in Kosovo, where that disunity once upon a time tragically pushed back Serbia for centuries and endangered it, and where renewed unity may advance it and may return dignity to it. Such an awareness about mutual relations constitutes

Kosovo communist party leadership was dismissed. A few days later, Kosovar Albanian miners went on strike at the Trepca mines near the town of Kosovska Mitrovica. On November 25, the Federal Parliament passed constitutional amendments that paved the way for changes to the Serbian

an elementary necessity for Yugoslavia, too, for its fate is in the joined hands of all its peoples. The Kosovo heroism has been inspiring our creativity for six centuries, and has been feeding our pride and does not allow us to forget that at one time we were an army great, brave, and proud, one of the few that remained undefeated when losing.

Six centuries later, now, we are being again engaged in battles and are facing battles. They are not armed battles, although such things cannot be excluded yet. However, regardless of what kind of battles they are, they cannot be won without resolve, bravery, and sacrifice, without the noble qualities that were present here in the field of Kosovo in the days past. Our chief battle now concerns implementing the economic, political, cultural, and general social prosperity, finding a quicker and more successful approach to a civilization in which people will live in the 21st century. For this battle, we certainly need heroism, of course of a somewhat different kind, but that courage without which nothing serious and great can be achieved remains unchanged and remains urgently necessary.

Six centuries ago, Serbia heroically defended itself in the field of Kosovo, but it also defended Europe. Serbia was at that time the bastion that defended the European culture, religion, and European society in general. Therefore today it appears not only unjust but even unhistorical and completely absurd to talk about Serbia's belonging to Europe. Serbia has been a part of Europe incessantly, now just as much as it was in the past, of course, in its own way, but in a way that in the historical sense never deprived it of dignity. In this spirit we now endeavor to build a society, rich and democratic, and thus to contribute to the prosperity of this beautiful country, this unjustly suffering country, but also to contribute to the efforts of all the progressive people of our age that they make for a better and happier world.

Let the memory of Kosovo heroism live forever!

Long live Serbia!

Long live Yugoslavia!

Long live peace and brotherhood among peoples!

constitution. Azem Vllasi, the communist party chief of Kosovo and then the leading ethnic Albanian politician at the Yugoslav federal level, was dismissed.

On February 20, 1989, the Trepca miners struck again, demanding the reinstatement of the Kosovo party leaders. The government deployed the army and imposed "special measures" on the region, which amounted to a form of martial law. An atmosphere of fear prevailed in the province, especially among ethnic Albanian political leaders and intellectuals. The other Yugoslav republics, especially Slovenia, began to protest Serbia's aggressive nationalism.

After a massive pro-Milosevic rally in Belgrade, Vllasi was arrested on March 2.[9] Three weeks later, a new Serbian constitution was announced. The Kosovo assembly—mostly ethnic Albanians but under direct pressure from Belgrade—accepted the proposed changes to the Serbian constitution which returned authority to Belgrade.

While Belgrade celebrated, Kosovar Albanians vehemently protested the changes. On March 28, 1989, riot police opened fire on a protesting crowd, killing at least twenty-four persons. Although government forces may have come under attack, the state's response was indiscriminate and excessive. A joint report by Helsinki Watch and the International Helsinki Federation for Human Rights at the time found that there was "no justification for firing with automatic weapons on the assembled crowds."[10]

Riding an ever stronger wave of nationalism, Slobodan Milosevic was elected president of Serbia on May 8, 1989, a post he held for the next eight years, until he was elected president of Yugoslavia on July 23, 1997—the position he held until October 2000.

In July 1989, the Serbian parliament passed the Law on the Restriction of Property Transactions, the first in a series of laws that severely discriminated against ethnic Albanians in Kosovo. The law forbade Albanians to sell real estate without the approval of a special state commission run by the Serbian Ministry of Finance. On March 30, 1990, the Serbian government adopted a new program that laid the ideological foundation for the government's policy in Kosovo. Ironically called, "The Program for the Realization of Peace, Freedom, Equality, Democracy, and Prosperity of the Socialist Autonomous Province of Kosovo," the program stated:

> The autonomy of Kosovo may not serve as an excuse or reason for the malfunctioning of the legal state and possible repetition of nationalistic and sep-

aratist unrest and persistent inter-ethnic tension. It may not be misused in pursuit of unacceptable and unfeasible goals: prevention of the return of Serbs and Montenegrins, displaced under pressure, and all the others who wish to come and live in Kosovo, and especially for any further emigration of Serbs and Montenegrins and secession of a part of the territory of the Republic—the state of Serbia so as to constitute a new state within or without Yugoslavia.[11]

Kosovo in the 1990s

The Revocation of Kosovo's Autonomy

On July 2, 1990, ethnic Albanian members of Kosovo's politically gutted assembly declared Kosovo's independence. Two months later, on September 7, members of the parliament, which had been dissolved on July 5, met secretly and adopted a new constitution of the Republic of Kosova. A clandestine government and legislature were elected. Three weeks later, on September 28, the Serb Assembly promulgated the new Serbian constitution that formally revoked the autonomous status of both Kosovo and Vojvodina.

The new Serbian constitution was important because, by formally revoking the autonomy of Kosovo and Vojvodina, Serbia assumed two additional seats in the eight-member Yugoslav presidency. In coalition with its partner Montenegro, the "Serbian Block" controlled half of the federal body.

In September 1991, Kosovar Albanians held an unofficial referendum on independence. Ethnic Albanians voted overwhelmingly for independence from Yugoslavia. The Yugoslav government refused to recognize the results. Only the government in Albania, at that time still ruled by the communist party, recognized Kosovo's independence.[12]

Human Rights Abuses in the 1990s

Kosovo became a police state run by Belgrade. A strong Serb military presence, justified by the need to fight "Albanian secessionists," committed ongoing human rights abuses. Police violence, arbitrary detentions, and torture were common. Ethnic Albanians were arrested, detained, prosecuted, and imprisoned solely on the basis of their ethnicity, political beliefs, or membership in organizations or institutions that were banned or looked upon with disfavor by the Serbian government.[13]

A strong Serb military presence, justified by the need to fight "Albanian secessionists," committed ongoing human rights abuses.

Hundreds of thousands of ethnic Albanians were fired from government institutions and state-run enterprises under a series of discriminatory laws. Already in August 1990, the Serbian parliament had abolished the independence of the Kosovo educational system and instituted a new curriculum to be administered centrally from Belgrade. Albanian teachers were forced to sign a loyalty oath; those who refused were dismissed. Throughout 1990, the government closed most of the Albanian-language schools and, in January 1991, it stopped paying most Albanian high school teachers. By October 1991, all Albanian teachers had been fired; only fifteen Albanian professors remained at the university in Pristina, and they all taught in Serbian.

The deliberate economic and social marginalization of ethnic Albanians forced the emigration of an estimated 350,000 Albanians from the province over the next seven years. While Albanians were being forced to leave, Milosevic's government provided incentives and encouraged the settlement of Serbs in the region. In 1996, 16,000 Serb refugees from Bosnia and Croatia were settled in Kosovo, sometimes against their will.[14]

The Yugoslav government maintained that the military presence and legal measures were necessary for two reasons: to protect Kosovo's minority populations—principally Serbs and Montenegrins—and to contain the Albanian successionist movement. Such a movement, the government argued, would seek Kosovo's independence from Yugoslavia, and possible unification with neighboring Albania. The government's actions with regard to both concerns were extreme and produced violations of human rights.

Albanian Non-Violence and the Parallel State

Kosovar Albanians responded to the revocation of autonomy by creating their own parallel state which was, based on the September 1991 referendum, declared independent from Yugoslavia. Albanian deputies of the dissolved parliament established "underground" institutions of government, and Kosovar Albanians refused to recognize the Serbian state.

A parallel system of private schools was set up with donated funds and taxes. For eight years, Albanian school children and university students attended classes in private homes, empty businesses, and abandoned school buildings. Teachers, students, and administrators in the private schools were routinely harassed, detained, and beaten by the police and security forces. Funds collected for educational purposes were sometimes confiscated by the police.

Underground parliamentary elections on May 24, 1992, established the three-year-old Democratic League of Kosova (Lidhja Demokratike te Kosoves, or LDK) as the strongest ethnic Albanian party and a previously little-known literary figure, Ibrahim Rugova, was named president. The LDK expanded the parallel system and established structures to collect taxes from Albanians in Kosovo and from the ever-growing diaspora community.[15] Rugova and a prime minister, Bujar Bukoshi, represented the "Kosova Republic" abroad.

The revocation of Kosovo's autonomy and the subsequent abuses garnered little response from the international community, which was increasingly preoccupied with the growing conflict in Slovenia, Croatia, and then Bosnia. In the summer of 1992, the Conference for Security and Cooperation in Europe (now the Organization for Security and Cooperation in Europe (OSCE)) sent missions to Kosovo, Vojvodina, and Sandzak, but the missions were forced to leave in July 1993 when the Yugoslav government refused to renew the mandate.

In December 1992, after Serbian special police forces had enforced rule in Kosovo, U.S. President George Bush issued what became known as the "Christmas Warning." Bush reportedly wrote, in a letter to President Milosevic, that the U.S. would be "prepared to employ military force" in the event of conflict in Kosovo caused by Serbian action—a warning that was repeated by President Clinton when he came to office a few months later.[16] Kosovar Albanians interpreted the warnings as a message that the U.S. would come to their defense.

Largely out of a realistic assessment of ethnic Albanians' military capabilities, the LDK declined offers from the Croatian and Bosnian leadership to open another military front against Serbia.[17] While calling for Kosovo's independence, the LDK preached nonconfrontation and urged Albanians to support the parallel structures.

The exception was an attempt in 1992 and 1993 to set up a Kosovar Ministry of Defense, with its own forces made up mostly of former policemen. The Serbian police crushed the nascent group through large-scale arrests in 1993, and no armed movement was discernible again until the emergence of the KLA in 1996.

The United States and West European governments strongly encouraged ethnic Albanians to pursue a moderate approach, fearing that a conflict in Kosovo would spin out of control and engulf the region. The primary goal was to avoid a conflagration in Kosovo, and non-confrontation, the West believed, was the best way to achieve this.

Rugova was identified as the prime advocate of this moderate line and received the unconditional support of Western governments, especially the United States. He was frequently invited for high level meetings in Washington and West European capitals which greatly boosted his popularity among the strongly pro-Western Kosovar Albanian public. At the same time, however, Western governments never expressed support for Kosovo's independence, although most Kosovar Albanians believed the West did so.[18]

In some respects, Rugova and Milosevic derived benefits from each other. Milosevic tolerated Rugova because Rugova allowed the Kosovar Albanians an outlet for their frustrations and a public expression of their political will, while his nonconfrontational policies excluded a challenge to Serbian rule over the province. Albanians also continued paying taxes to the Serbian government. At the same time, Milosevic's repressive policies helped justify the Albanians' drive for independence.[19] The West was comfortable with this arrangement because it helped guarantee the status-quo. Human rights abuses continued, but Kosovo stayed off the front pages while the West was dealing with the fighting in Croatia and Bosnia.

At the same time, West European governments and the U.S. were providing strong financial and political support to the government of Sali Berisha in Albania, partly because Berisha supported Rugova and promised not to meddle in the affairs of Kosovo or Macedonia. Unqualified support for Berisha, despite his clear pattern of human rights violations against Albanian citizens, greatly contributed to the eventual destabilization of Albania which, in turn, negatively affected Kosovo.[20]

Meanwhile, thousands of Kosovar Albanian men were leaving Kosovo for the United States and Western Europe due to ongoing persecution or fear of being drafted into the Yugoslav Army. Many of these disenfranchised young men abroad and in Kosovo, without education or steady employment, later joined the insurgency.

The Downward Cycle of Violence

A crucial shift came after the Dayton conference in December 1995 that stopped the fighting in Bosnia. Kosovar Albanians were not invited to the conference, and Kosovo was kept off of the agenda. This left many Kosovar Albanians with the impression that the West had forgotten the Kosovo issue and that their peaceful approach was not working. Furthermore, with international recognition for the new borders of the Republika Srpska, Albanians understood that the international community responded to the facts on the ground rather than high-minded principles of nonviolence—not the force of argument but the argument of force.[21]

In early 1996, the first organized violence took place against Serbian civilians and police. Although individual attacks had occurred before then, the first coordinated attack occurred on February 11, when grenades were thrown at the gates of Serbian refugee camps in Pristina, Mitrovica, Pec, Suva Reka, and Vucitrn. No one was injured.

Albanians understood that the international community responded to the facts on the ground rather than high-minded principles of nonviolence—not the force of argument but the argument of force.

On April 21, 1996, an ethnic Albanian student, Armend Daci, was shot and killed in Pristina by a local Serb who reportedly thought Daci was breaking into his car. The next day, four assassinations of Serbs took place within one hour.[22] That same night, in the village of Stimlje (Shtimje), policeman Miljenko Bucic was killed, and a police car was attacked by machine gun on the road between Mitrovica and Pec, killing a Serbian woman who was in custody. Revenge for the Daci killing was generally considered the motive for these attacks, but post-war interviews with KLA leaders revealed that the April 22 actions had been planned in advance.[23]

In this climate of increasing violence, Milosevic allowed the U.S. government to open a U.S. Information Agency office in Pristina, which was welcomed warmly by Kosovar Albanians as a sign of increased American involvement. The office, considered wrongly by some Albanians as an embassy, was announced in early February and opened in July 1996.

Violent attacks on Serbian police continued throughout the summer and fall of 1996, resulting in four deaths and two injuries.[24] Kosovar Albanian leaders and Serbian officials both denied any involvement in the violence and accused the other side of provoking conflict. Rugova, unconvincingly, claimed that the attacks were committed by the Serbian secret police in order to provoke retaliation against Albanians.

Meanwhile, a previously unknown organization called the Kosovo Liberation Army claimed responsibility for the attacks. In letters faxed to the media, the group criticized the "passive" approach of the ethnic Albanian leadership and promised to continue their attacks until Kosovo was free from Serbian rule.

By mid-1996, there was a clear pattern of arbitrary and indiscriminate retaliation by the Serbian police and special security forces against ethnic Albanians who lived in the areas where KLA attacks were taking place. Police broke into private homes without warrants and detained ethnic Albanians, often abusing them physically. Many individuals traveling through the areas of suspected KLA activity were stopped, interrogated and beaten. In October, the police arrested forty-five ethnic Albanians who, they claimed, were involved in the attacks.[25]

By mid-1996, there was a clear pattern of arbitrary and indiscriminate retaliation by the Serbian police and special security forces.

In the West, Milosevic continued to be viewed as a necessary partner for regional stability because of the Dayton Accords. The concern in Washington and West European capitals was that Milosevic should not be challenged on Kosovo because he was needed to implement the accords. Fear of attacks on Western soldiers deployed in Bosnia to monitor and enforce the agreement reinforced the West's reluctance to alter the status-quo in Kosovo. Human rights abuses were deemed acceptable in the name of regional stability.

At the same time, the Western military presence in Bosnia was unwilling to arrest the leading individuals indicted for war crimes by the U.N.'s war crimes tribunal, notably Bosnian Serb leader Radovan Karadzic and General Ratko Mladic. Their arrest might have sent a message that the West would not tolerate further violent and abusive behavior in the Balkans, deterring Serbian forces from atrocities in Kosovo.

The next important political development came on September 1, 1996,

Albanian children in Kosovo had restricted access to Albanian-language education despite a 1996 agreement between Slobodan Milosevic and Ibrahim Rugova. 3+3 refers to the six-person commission (three Serbs and three Albanians) that was supposed to implement the agreement. DRAWING BY JETON MIKULLOVCI-*KOHA DITORE*

when Rugova and Milosevic signed a much-heralded education agreement that envisaged unconditional return to Albanian-language schools for ethnic Albanian pupils, students, and teachers.[26] The details were to be worked out by a joint commission of three Serbs and three Albanians. Despite the international fanfare, the agreement was never implemented, and ethnic Albanian pupils remained locked out of most school buildings. The harassment, beatings, and arrests of ethnic Albanian teachers and school administrators continued.

The failure of the education agreement to bring any concrete improvements in the daily lives of Kosovar Albanians was a serious blow to Rugova's peaceful politics. Ethnic Albanians were losing faith in his increasingly empty promises that the West would help. The inability or unwillingness of the West to reward Albanians' patience and nonviolence with concrete improvements, such as in education, helped push the community closer to the military option.

On September 31, 1996, the U.N. lifted sanctions on Yugoslavia that had been in place since May 1992, and many European states upgraded diplomatic relations with Yugoslavia. European Union countries began to reestablish diplomatic relations with Belgrade—broken during the war in Bosnia. France, Italy, and Greece restored a high level of economic relations.

The main exception was the U.S. insistence on maintaining the so-called "outer wall" of sanctions, which, most importantly, kept Yugoslavia out of international financial institutions such as the International Monetary Fund and the World Bank. The sanctions were to stay in place, the U.S. government said, until, among other things, the Kosovo issue was resolved.[27]

Human rights abuses in the province intensified toward the end of 1996 as the government attempted to weed out the growing insurgency. Police acted with near total impunity as they maltreated, and occasionally killed, ethnic Albanians. Police abuse generally took three basic forms: random beatings on the streets and other public places, targeted attacks against politically active ethnic Albanians, or arbitrary retaliation for KLA attacks on Serbian policemen.[28]

Publicly, the Serbian government continued to deny that human rights violations existed and officials defended the need to protect the sovereignty of the state. In July 1996, Serbian Deputy Minister of Information Rade Drobac told Human Rights Watch: "The situation of human rights is excellent in Kosovo. Albanians have more rights than anywhere in the world."[29]

At the same time, ethnic Albanians did not drop their demand for full independence, and the KLA continued its attacks.

The international community was trapped on the one hand by its general desire to stop the Serbian government's violations and a distaste for Kosovo's potential independence on the other. An independent Kosovo, it was argued, would join Albania and, eventually, the Western part of Macedonia, which is predominantly inhabited by ethnic Albanians. In the very least, an independent Kosovo would disrupt the delicate balance between ethnic Macedonians and ethnic Albanians in Macedonia, considered a young and fragile state.[30] Most Western governments also feared the precedent that Kosovo's independence would set for ethnic separatist movements in other countries, such as those of the Basques and Corsicans.

To tread the middle line, the international community called for increased minority rights in Kosovo and encouraged dialogue between Serbs and Albanians through a variety of channels. A political settlement on autonomy within Yugoslavia, the West hoped, was still attainable, despite the escalating violence and abuse.

At the end of 1996, the political scene inside Serbia changed. In municipal elections on November 17, opposition parties won in fourteen of Serbia's nineteen largest cities. The government declared "unspecified irregularities" in those areas where the ruling party had lost, sparking eighty-eight days of peaceful demonstrations by opposition party supporters and students, some of which were broken up forcibly by the police.[31] The government recognized the election results on February 22, 1997, but it did so without losing power on the national scene. Internal bickering and power struggles quickly weakened the opposition's power and support.

Although most western governments criticized the 1996 electoral violations and the ensuing police abuse, many states continued welcoming Yugoslavia back into the international community. In April 1997, the European Union offered Yugoslavia preferential trade status—which grants a country beneficial conditions when trading with E.U. states—despite the ongoing abuses in Kosovo. On May 15, the European Commission approved an aid package to Yugoslavia worth U.S. $112 million. Such concessions squandered a prime source of leverage that the international community had to press for improvements in Milosevic's human rights record, repression in Kosovo, and the government's compliance with the Dayton Accords.

Growth of the Kosovo Liberation Army

The KLA continued its attacks against Serbian policemen and civilians in early 1997, especially in the more rural areas, although the group's size, structure, and leadership remained a mystery. The insurgency's impact was limited by restricted access to arms.

This changed with the dramatic 1997 events in Albania. By March, the so-called "pyramid schemes" (linked with money laundering and other illegal activities) that the Albanian government had allowed to flourish collapsed, creating mayhem throughout the country. In the ensuing lawlessness, weapons depots were looted and, in some cases, opened by the government. More than 100,000 small arms, mostly Kalashnikov automatic rifles, as well as some heavier weapons, were readily available for prices as low as fifty German Marks. Many of these arms found their way across the northern border into Kosovo.

By late 1997, the central region of Drenica was known among ethnic Albanians as "liberated territory" because of the strong KLA presence. Serbian police only ventured into the area during the day.

The still-loosely organized guerrillas made their first public appearance on November 28, 1997, at the funeral of a Kosovar Albanian teacher, Halit

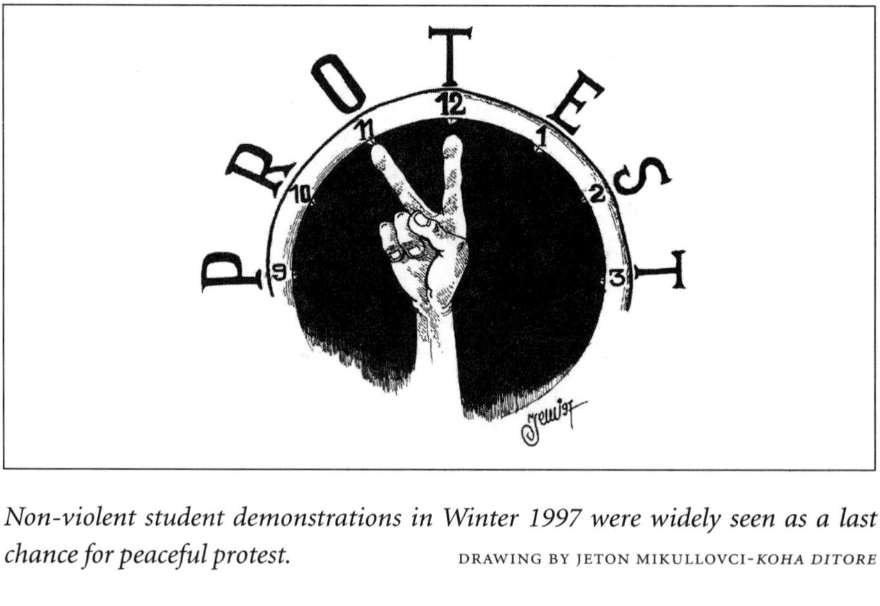

Non-violent student demonstrations in Winter 1997 were widely seen as a last chance for peaceful protest. DRAWING BY JETON MIKULLOVCI-*KOHA DITORE*

Gecaj, who was killed by a stray bullet during fighting with Serb police in the village of Lausa (Llaushe). In front of an estimated 20,000 mourners, three masked and uniformed KLA fighters, two of whom reportedly took off their masks, addressed the crowd.[32]

Around this time, Kosovar Albanian students began organizing peaceful demonstrations in Kosovo's cities to demand the implementation of the 1996 education agreement and the reopening of the Albanian-language university. Some of the nonviolent protests were broken up forcibly by the police. For many people, Albanians and Serbs, the peaceful student movement was the last chance to avoid an outright armed conflict in the province.

The international community condemned the rising state violence in Kosovo while stressing its respect for the territorial integrity of Yugoslavia. At the same time, most West European governments, as well as the U.S., condemned as "terrorist actions" the KLA attacks. A February 1998 statement of the Contact Group on former Yugoslavia—comprised of the U.S., Germany, France, Russia, Italy, and the U.K.—stated:

> The Contact Group reaffirmed its commitment to uphold human rights values, and their condemnation of both violent repression of non-violent expressions of political views, including peaceful demonstrations, as well as terrorist actions, including those of the so-called Kosovo Liberation Army.[33]

In late February, President Clinton's special representative, Robert Gelbard, visited Yugoslavia to address, among other issues, the brewing Kosovo crisis. During a press conference in Pristina on February 22, he declared that "the UCK [KLA] is a terrorist group by its actions. I used to be responsible for counter-terrorist policy in the American government. I know them when I see them."[34]

Gelbard reiterated his condemnation of the KLA in a Belgrade press conference the next day, and also announced some concessions to the Yugoslav government due to cooperation in Bosnia. Consistent with the view that Milosevic was a necessary ally for the implementation of the Dayton Accords, Gelbard said that the U.S. had been "particularly encouraged by the support that we received from President Milosevic," although, Gelbard added, "we still have a large number of areas where there are differences in views." In order to encourage "further positive movement," Gelbard announced that the U.S. was upgrading diplomatic relations with Yugoslavia, that Yugoslavia could open a consulate in the U.S., that Yugoslavia had been invited to join the Southeast European Cooperative Initiative, and that Yugoslav airlines (JAT) had regained landing rights in the U.S. Regarding Kosovo, Gelbard said:

> The great majority of this violence we attribute to the police, but we are tremendously disturbed and also condemn very strongly the unacceptable violence done by terrorist groups in Kosovo and particularly the UCK—the Kosovo Liberation Army. This is without any question a terrorist group. I refuse to accept any kind of excuses. Having worked for years on counterterrorist activity, I know very well that to look at a terrorist group, to define it, you strip away the rhetoric and just look at actions. And the actions of this group speak for themselves.[35]

Gelbard later retracted the allegation about the KLA, and the group was never placed on the U.S. government's list of terrorist organizations.[36] At the time, however, some analysts interpreted the U.S. statement as a green light for Milosevic to begin a counter-insurgency campaign.

The 1998 Armed Conflict

The Drenica Massacres

Five days after Gelbard's comments, the Serbian government launched a major assault on the central Drenica valley, a stronghold of the KLA. On February 28 and March 1, responding to KLA ambushes of the police, special forces attacked two adjacent villages, Cirez (Qirez) and Likosane (Likoshane). On March 5, special police attacked the nearby village of Prekaz—home of Adem Jashari, a known KLA member. Jashari was killed along with his entire family, save an eleven year-old-girl.[37] In total, eighty-three people lost their lives in the three attacks, including at least twenty-four women and children.[38]

Although the KLA engaged in combat during these attacks, Serbian special forces fired indiscriminately at women, children, and other non-combatants. Helicopters and military vehicles sprayed village rooftops with gunfire before police forces entered the village on foot, firing into private homes. A pregnant woman, Rukia Nebihi, was shot in the face, and four brothers from one family were killed, apparently while in police custody. Ten members of the Ahmeti family were summarily executed by the police.

The Serbian police denied any wrongdoing in the attacks and claimed they were pursuing "terrorists" who had attacked the police. A police spokesman denied the "lies and inventions" about indiscriminate attacks and excessive force carried by some local and foreign media and said "the police has never resorted to such methods and never will."[39]

In total, eighty-three people lost their lives in the three attacks, including at least twenty-four women and children.

These events in Drenica were a watershed in the Kosovo crisis. If the government's aim was to crush the nascent insurgency, it had the opposite effect: the brutal and indiscriminate attacks radicalized the ethnic Albanian population and swelled the ranks of the KLA. Many ethnic Albanians who had been committed to the nonviolent politics of Rugova or the peaceful student movement decided to join the KLA, in part because they viewed the armed insurgency as the only means of protection. The various armed families and regional KLA groups active in Kosovo up to that point began to merge as a more organized popular resistance took shape.

The Drenica massacres also marked the beginning of the Kosovo conflict in the terms of the laws of war. It was only after February 28, 1999, that the fighting clearly went beyond mere internal disturbances to become an internal armed conflict, a threshold which once passed obliges both government forces and armed insurgencies to respect basic protections of international humanitarian law—the rules of war. In particular, Article 3 common to the four Geneva Conventions of 1949, Protocol II to those conventions, and the customary rules of war would henceforth apply to the conduct of hostilities in Kosovo.

The significance of the Kosovo conflict being classified an "armed conflict" went beyond a mere invocation of standards. Once open conflict broke out, the jurisdiction of the International Criminal Tribunal for the Former Yugoslavia over Kosovo began. Mandated to prosecute crimes against humanity and violations of the laws or customs of war in the territory of the former Yugoslavia, the tribunal, on March 10, stated that its jurisdiction "covers the recent violence in Kosovo," although tribunal investigators did not visit the province until four months later.[40]

As the conflict grew, so too did the insurgency. Money from the diaspora community that was previously given to the LDK was increasingly diverted to the fund of the KLA, known as Homeland Calling. Increasingly, Albanian men from Western Europe and later the U.S. joined the insurgency.

Role of the International Community

The killings in Drenica drew the attention of the international community, despite Yugoslav government pleadings that the conflict was an internal affair. The international community criticized the state's excessive violence in Drenica but took minimal steps beyond verbal condemnations. On March 2, State Department spokesman James Rubin said that the U.S. was "appalled by the recent violent incidents" and threatened that "the outer wall" of sanctions would stay in place until there was improvement in Kosovo. He also called on Kosovar Albanian leaders to "condemn terrorist action by the so-called Kosovo Liberation Army."[41]

Over the next seven months, notwithstanding continued state violence, threats of sanctions and other punitive measures were weakly, if ever, enforced. Concessions were granted after the slightest progress, after which Serbian commanders, under the command of Milosevic, would often order renewed violence.

On March 9, the Contact Group met in London and gave the FRY government ten days to meet a series of requirements, including: to withdraw the special police from Kosovo and cease actions against the civilian population by the security forces; to allow access for the ICRC and other humanitarian organizations as well as by representatives of the Contact Group and other diplomatic representatives; and to begin a process of dialogue with the Kosovar Albanian leadership.[42] The Contact Group proclaimed that, if President Milosevic took those steps, it would reconsider the four punitive measures that it had adopted.[43] If he failed to comply, the group would move to further international measures, including an asset freeze on FRY and Serbian government funds abroad.

Threats of sanctions and other punitive measures were weakly, if ever, enforced.

In a parallel move, the U.S. State Department announced on March 13 that it was providing $1.075 million to support the investigations of the war crimes tribunal in Kosovo.[44]

Allowing ten days to slip to sixteen, the Contact Group met again on March 25. In the days prior to the March 25 meeting, the Milosevic government briefly reduced the police attacks in Kosovo and agreed to implement the education agreement, a long-standing demand of the international community and one of many needed confidence-building measures cited in the March 9 Contact Group statement. Though not enough to bring the Contact Group to lift its previously adopted measures, the FRY gestures kept the group from imposing new measures and bought Milosevic some time. The Contact Group agreed to meet again in four weeks to reassess the situation.[45]

As Milosevic raised the level of violence, the international community lowered the bar he needed to clear to regain international acceptance.

On March 31, the Security Council passed resolution 1160 which condemned violence on all sides, called for a negotiated settlement, and imposed an arms embargo on Yugoslavia. In April 1998, Milosevic organized a popular referendum on whether there should be international mediation in the Kosovo conflict. The vote for no international involvement was overwhelming.

The Contact Group meeting of April 29 set in motion a new round of maneuvering between the international community and the FRY government. Finding that the conditions set on March 9 remained unfulfilled, the Contact Group decided to take steps to impose the asset freeze. The freeze, first threatened if Belgrade did not meet Contact Group conditions by March 19, was finally endorsed by the Contact Group a month and a half later. It was not implemented by the European Union until late June—plenty of time for the Yugoslav authorities to shelter any funds that might otherwise have been affected. The Contact Group also promised to pursue an investment ban if Milosevic did not meet new conditions by May 9.[46] These new conditions were watered down from the March 9 ultimata, substituting a general call for "cessation of repression" for the earlier "withdraw the special police units," and dropping the demand for access for the ICRC and humanitarian organizations altogether. As Milosevic raised the level of violence, the international community lowered the bar he needed to clear to regain international acceptance.

During the second quarter of 1998, the KLA, called a "liberation movement" by most ethnic Albanians and a "terrorist organization" by the Yugoslav government, took loose control of an estimated 40 percent of Kosovo's territory, including the Drenica region and the area around Malisevo. KLA spokesmen, increasingly in the public eye, spoke of "liberating Pristina" and eventually Kosovo. Serb civilians in areas under KLA control were harassed or terrorized into leaving, by assaults, kidnaping, and sporadic killing.

In late April and early May, the KLA took control of the villages northeast of the main road running between Decani (Decane) and Djakovica, with a headquarters in Glodjane. Serbs were forced out of these villages and fled to Decani town, where inter-ethnic tensions increased sharply. The KLA appeared to be attempting to establish a corridor between Albania and Drenica.

In retrospect, some analysts believe that the Serbian police and Yugoslav army purposefully allowed the KLA to expand. Aware that the lightly armed and poorly organized insurgency could not hold territory, the security forces allowed the rebels to spread themselves too thin across a large swath of territory. Government forces did not attack, but positioned themselves, such as on the Suka Crmljanska hill near Lake Radonjic. Other analysts, however, believe that the rapid growth of the KLA caught the Serbian government by surprise.

After five days of intense shuttle diplomacy by U.S. Special Envoy Richard Holbrooke, Milosevic and Rugova agreed to meet on May 15 in Belgrade, together with four other Kosovar Albanian representatives.[47] In a major concession to Milosevic, the meeting took place without the presence of foreign mediators, a long-time condition set by both the international community and the Kosovar Albanians. Milosevic agreed to continue negotiations and named a team to be headed by Ratko Markovic, Deputy Prime Minister of Serbia. After the meeting, Milosevic's office issued the following statement:

> President Milosevic pointed out that it is only by political means—through a direct dialogue on the basis of principle—that peaceful, human, just and lasting solutions to the problems in Kosovo and Metohija can be found. These solutions should be based on the equality of all citizens and ethnic communities in Kosovo and Metohija.[48]

Considering this a "framework for dialogue and stabilization package," as stipulated in the April 29 Contact Group statement, the Milosevic-Rugova meeting caused the international community to ease the pressure. At the May 25 meeting of the European Union General Affairs Council, the foreign ministers of E.U. member states concluded that, in light of the Milosevic-Rugova meeting in Belgrade, "the proposed measure to stop new investment in Serbia would not be taken forward."[49]

That week Belgrade launched a major offensive along its border with Albania that involved serious breaches of international humanitarian law. Kosovo Albanians called off all negotiations in light of the offensive.

In the first known joint action between the Serbian special police and the Yugoslav Army, government forces attacked a string of towns and villages along the border with the specific intent of depopulating the region and ousting the KLA. Until then, the KLA had been receiving arms and fresh recruits from Albania. The Serbian offensive so soon after the meeting hurt

Main street of Decani, destroyed by Serbian and Yugoslav forces in the May-June 1998 offensive along Kosovo's border with Albania

© PETER BOUCKAERT / HUMAN RIGHTS WATCH

Rugova's popularity among Albanians, but he was quickly brought to Washington, along with Bujar Bukoshi and independent publisher Veton Surroi, for a meeting with President Clinton to bolster his public image.[50] The offensive was also another reminder of Milosevic's now-familiar tactics: talk peace and conduct war.[51]

Although there was clearly fighting between the government and the KLA, many villages from Pec in the north to Djakovica in the south were shelled indiscriminately without consideration for civilian lives. Noncombatants who fled the attacks were sometimes fired on by snipers, and a still undetermined number of people were taken into detention. In three cases, helicopters marked with the Red Cross emblem reportedly fired on civilians. Anti-personnel landmines were placed in strategic points along the border, as well as along the southern border with Macedonia. Most villages in the region were looted and systematically destroyed, and farmers' livestock was shot, to ensure that no one could return in the short run. Fifteen thousand people fled to Albania and an estimated 30,000 went north to Montenegro.[52]

Around the same time, Milosevic also took steps to consolidate his power in Serbia proper. In May 1998, the Serbian parliament passed a highly restrictive university law that marginalized independent or opposition-oriented academics. The government also continued its assault on the independent media by refusing broadcast licenses to some independent radio and television stations.[53] Milosevic's political ally from Montenegro, Momir Bulatovic, was appointed Yugoslav prime minister.

By the June 9 meeting of E.U. foreign ministers, the pattern of deception could no longer be ignored. The ministers adopted the investment ban on Serbia, together with a declaration that stated:

> President Milosevic bears a special responsibility as head of the FRY government for promoting a peaceful settlement to the problems of Kosovo. He should not believe that the international community will be taken in by talk of peace when the reality on the ground is ever greater repression. . . . The European Union remains ready to press ahead with other measures against Belgrade if the authorities there fail to halt their excessive use of force and to take the steps needed for genuine political progress. Furthermore, the E.U. encourages international security organizations to pursue their efforts in this respect and to consider all options, including those which would require

> an authorization by the [United Nations Security Council] under Chapter VII.[54]

On June 11, NATO defense ministers directed NATO military authorities to develop a range of options for "halting or disrupting a systematic campaign of violent repression and expulsion in Kosovo."[55] As a demonstration of military might, NATO agreed to conduct air exercises over neighboring Albania and Macedonia. Exercise "Determined Falcon," carried out on June 15, was presented as a demonstration of NATO's "capability to project power rapidly into the region."[56] Planes flew over Tirana, the Albanian capital, but not over North Albania where they would have been seen by Serbian forces and the KLA alike.

The June 12 Contact Group meeting reaffirmed the asset freeze and investment ban, with Russia in dissent and promised additional measures unless certain steps were taken immediately. These steps were essentially the same as those that were supposed to have been implemented within ten days of March 9, except that what had once been internationally mediated dialogue and then a "framework for dialogue and a stabilization package" had become "rapid progress in the dialogue with the Kosovar Albanian leadership."[57]

Taking advantage of the division between Russia and the other Contact Group members, Milosevic agreed to meet Russian president Boris Yeltsin on June 16. The Milosevic-Yeltsin meeting yielded Yugoslav commitments to continue talks with Kosovar Albanians, to commit no repressive actions against the peaceful population, to guarantee full freedom of movement on the whole territory of Kosovo, and to provide unimpeded access for humanitarian organizations. The joint statement between Milosevic and Yeltsin was honored in the breach, but it bought Milosevic time at a critical juncture, when NATO threats were stronger than they had been at any time up to that point.

One concrete result of the Yeltsin meeting was the creation of the Kosovo Diplomatic Observer Mission (KDOM), established on July 6, 1998, which was mandated to observe and report on freedom of movement and security conditions in Kosovo. Coordinated by the Contact Group ambassadors in Belgrade, the European Union Presidency (Austria), and the Chairman-in-Office of the OSCE (Poland), the mission consisted of three groups: U.S.-KDOM, Russian-KDOM, and EU-KDOM, each of which had teams traveling and monitoring throughout the province. By December 1998, KDOM had 400 personnel in Kosovo, many of them defense and intelligence experts.

An estimated forty Serbs also vanished during the brief time that the city was under KLA control.

KDOM members in the field began to establish contact with the KLA, such as a U.S.-KDOM outpost in the village of Dragobilje (Dragobil), where the KLA had a base of operations. The U.S. government also maintained public contact with the KLA in July as negotiators tried to sell a political settlement for "enhanced autonomy" within Yugoslavia.

While the first FRY government offensive partially dislodged the KLA along the border with Albania, the insurgents gained territory in other parts of Kosovo, especially around Malisevo. The rebels' growth throughout the spring dispelled thoughts of international military action as too likely to tip the balance in favor of Kosovo independence. Forceful KLA statements about "liberating Pristina" and even eventual unification with Albania made the international community even more reluctant to take any action that might be construed as supporting the insurgency.

Emboldened, the KLA's first major offensive began on July 19 when it attempted to capture the town of Orahovac. The offensive failed badly, as the police recaptured the town two days later, as well as the KLA stronghold of Malisevo. In the Orahovac fighting, at least forty-two ethnic Albanians were killed. Witnesses reported summary executions and the use of human shields by the police. An estimated forty Serbs also vanished during the brief time that the city was under KLA control, most of whom were still missing and are presumed to have been murdered as of August 2001 (see section below on KLA Abuses in 1998).

The government forces intensified their offensive throughout July, August, and September despite repeated promises from Milosevic that it had stopped. By mid-August, the government had retaken much of the territory previously held by the KLA. Unable to protect the civilian population, the KLA retreated into the hills of Drenica and some pockets in the west and south of Kosovo.

Government Abuses in 1998

The government offensive, which continued unabated despite the deployment of KDOM, was an apparent attempt to crush civilian support for the rebels. Government forces attacked civilians, systematically destroyed towns, and forced thousands of people to flee their homes. The police were repeatedly seen looting homes, destroying already abandoned villages, burning crops, and killing farm animals, as well as committing summary executions, all violations of the rules of war. The majority of those killed and injured were civilians. At least 250,000 people were displaced between May and September 1998, according to UNHCR, many of them women and children. The border region with Albania was particularly hard hit, but so were other areas of KLA activity, such as Drenica and the area around Orahovac.

An ethnic Albanian woman in front of her home in Plocica, destroyed by government forces in September 1998. © PETER BOUCKAERT / HUMAN RIGHTS WATCH

The government restricted the ability of humanitarian aid agencies to assist the internally displaced. On various occasions, the police hindered access to needy populations, confiscated supplies, harassed, and even attacked humanitarian aid workers. The government justified the restricted access by arguing that some humanitarian organizations had distributed supplies, including arms, to the KLA.

The Yugoslav government also restricted the work of domestic and foreign journalists who sought to report the atrocities. Some ethnic Albanian journalists were threatened, detained, or beaten by the police. Independent radio and television stations in the Albanian language were denied licenses or, in one case, closed down.

The independent Serbian-language media was not exempt from state pressure. News wires, newspapers, and radio stations that attempted to report objectively on Kosovo were labeled “traitors” and threatened with legal action. A complex and contradictory legal framework in Serbia made it virtually impossible for independent radio or television stations to obtain a broadcast frequency.[58] As was the case during the wars in Bosnia and Croatia, the state-run radio and television purposefully spread disinformation and promoted images of "the enemy" intended to inflame passions in the conflict.

The international media covering Kosovo also faced a number of restrictions on its work, starting with the denial of visas to critical journalists whom the state considered "anti-Serb." One journalist was declared persona non grata, and a few foreign journalists were beaten or fired upon by the police.

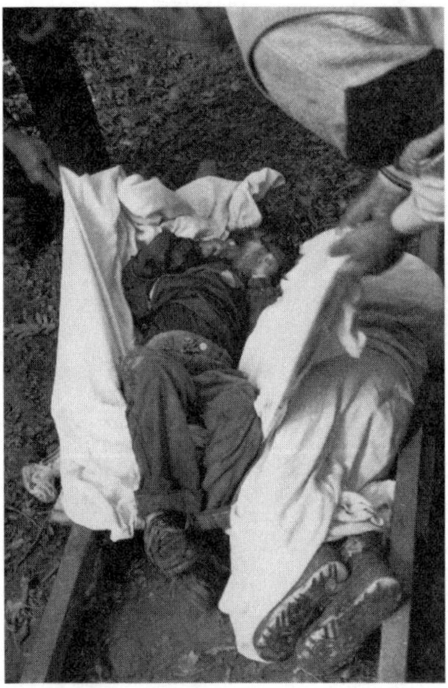

The bodies of Gentiona and Donietta Delijaj, seven and five years old, being removed from the forest spot in Gornje Obrinje where they were killed on September 26, 1998. Eighteen members of the family were killed in the attack. © PETER BOUCKAERT/HUMAN RIGHTS WATCH

At least one hundred ethnic Albanians "disappeared" in Kosovo between February and October 1998, about half of whom were last seen in the custody of the police. The precise number was impossible to determine since the Yugoslav authorities refused to make public the number of people they had in detention, a problem that continued after the NATO bombing commenced in March 1999. In addition, some Albanians, considered "collaborators with the Serbs" were abducted by the KLA.

More than 500 ethnic Albanians were arrested and charged with committing "terrorist acts." In July and August, detained individuals increasingly included human rights activists, humanitarian aid workers, political party members, doctors, and lawyers, many of whom were physically abused. The use of torture against detainees was widespread, and at least six people died from abuse in prison.[59]

The Serbian and Yugoslav government offensive closed in late September with serious combat around Suva Reka and in the Drenica region. On September 27, KDOM observers discovered the bodies of twenty-one ethnic Albanian civilians executed in the forest near the village of Gornje Obrinje (Abri i Eperme). The next day, researchers from Human Rights Watch and journalists visited the site and documented the killings, as well as the execution of thirteen ethnic Alban-

From Human Rights Watch report, *A Week of Terror in Drenica,* February 1999

The worst incident documented in this report took place in late September 1998 at the Delijaj family compound in Gornje Obrinje, a village where there had been intense fighting between government forces and the KLA that left at least fourteen policemen dead. Special police forces retaliated by killing twenty-one members of the Delijaj family, all of them civilians, on the afternoon of Saturday, September 26. Fourteen people were killed in a nearby forest where they were hiding from government shelling, six of them women between the ages of twenty-five and sixty-two. Five of the victims were children between eighteen months and nine years of age. Of the three men killed in the forest, two were over sixty years old.

Human Rights Watch visited the scene on September 29 while the bodies were being carried out of the forest for burial. All fourteen victims were wearing civilian clothing; most appeared to have been shot in the head at close range, and several of the bodies had been mutilated. In one case, the leg of sixty-two-year-old Hava Delijaj was cut off below the knee save for some skin.

In addition to the fourteen persons killed in the forest, seven other members of the Delijaj family were killed by government forces in and around the family compound. The ninety-four-year-old family patriarch Fazli Delijaj, an invalid, was found burned to death in his burned-out home. Habib and Hysen Delijaj were summarily executed by Serbian police in front of Hysen's wife and children. Adem Delijaj was found near the forest hide-out with his throat cut. Over the next few weeks, the decomposed bodies of two girls, Antigona and Mihane Delijaj, and of Hajriz Delijaj, were found in the general area of the massacre. One man, Sherif Delijaj, remains missing to this day.

ian men in nearby Golubovac.[60] The massacre galvanized world opinion and helped spark a new round of diplomatic negotiations led by the U.S.

KLA Abuses in 1998

The KLA also committed serious violations of international humanitarian law during this time, as well as in early 1999, including the taking of hostages and extrajudicial executions.[61] On June 21, 2000, in Pristina, ICTY chief prosecutor Carla Del Ponte announced that "five episodes" of alleged KLA crimes were under investigation by the tribunal.

In some villages in areas of KLA control, the rebels drove ethnic Serbs from their homes. In some cases, elderly Serbs stayed behind, either too old to flee or unwilling to abandon their homes. Some of these people went missing and are presumed dead. The KLA also attacked and killed or seized

An ethnic Serbian man surveys his destroyed home in Jelovac, near Klina. There were twelve Serbian and twenty Albanian homes in the village until June 1998, when the KLA kidnaped one Serbian man and expelled the Serbs of the village.

© FRED ABRAHAMS/HUMAN RIGHTS WATCH

some ethnic Albanians and Roma whom it considered "collaborators" with the Yugoslav government.

According to the ICRC, ninety-seven Kosovo Serbs abducted in 1998 were still missing as of May 15, 2000.[62] According to the Humanitarian Law Center, a highly respected Yugoslav human rights group, 103 Serbs went missing between January and August 1998, thirty-nine of whom were last seen in KLA custody. The center also documented the abductions of three Kosovar Albanians by the KLA.[63]

The KLA detained an estimated eighty-five Serbs during the offensive in Orahovac on July 19, 1998. Thirty-five of these people were subsequently released but the others remain unaccounted for at the time of this writing. According to the ICRC, thirty-nine Serbs went missing from the Orahovac municipality on July 17 and 18.[64] On July 22, the KLA briefly took control of the Belacevac mine near Obilic. Nine Serbs were captured that day, and they remain on the ICRC's list of missing.

On September 9, the Serbian police announced that they had found a number of bodies of people reportedly killed by the KLA near Glodjane. By September 16, the authorities recovered thirty-four bodies, eleven of whom were identified, some of them as ethnic Albanians. Prior to that, the most serious reported KLA abuse involved the reported execution of twenty-two Serbian civilians in the village of Klecka, where in August the police claimed to have discovered human remains and a kiln used to cremate the bodies. The manner in which the allegations were made, however, raised serious questions about their validity.[65]

The KLA, slowly transforming from a disorganized guerrilla group into a more serious armed force, did not abide with their stated commitments to respect international law and the laws of war, and in public statements appeared not to recognize some of the basic principles of these norms. Indeed, executions were acknowledged and justified in the early months of the war. In an interview given to a Kosovo newspaper, KLA spokesman Jakup Krasniqi said:

> [T]he KLA has never dealt with civilians, or only if they have been in the service of the army and the police and have done serious harm to the people and the Albanian national cause. There have been cases in which they have been kidnaped, but in this event they have been handed over to international organizations, of course when they have been innocent.

> First of all, all Serbian forces, whether the police, the military, or armed civilians, are our enemy. From the start, we had our own internal rules for our operations. These clearly lay down that the KLA recognizes the Geneva Conventions and the conventions governing the conduct of war, even though it has not been offered the chance of signing them, as it would have done. We do not go in for kidnaping. Even if some people have suffered, these have been more Albanian collaborators than Serbian civilians. We do not deal with civilians, and we return those whom we take as prisoners of war. A few days ago we handed over two Serbs originating from Croatia to the International Red Cross. Those we have kidnaped are either announced in a list or reported to be executed, but we do not behave in a base fashion like Serbia.[66]

The KLA's disregard for ethnic Albanian civilians is also striking. Villages declared "liberated" by the KLA were often smashed shortly thereafter by the Serbian security forces, who vented their anger on the civilians who did

A skull with an apparent bullet wound in Klina, Kosovo, where Serbian authorities exhumed the remains of four people they claimed were killed by the Kosovo Liberation Army.

© PETER BOUCKAERT / HUMAN RIGHTS WATCH

not retreat into the hills with the KLA. Ambushes of police or army checkpoints often provoked a response against the nearest village, if the KLA was based there or not. The pattern of KLA behavior suggests that the rebels, relying on the predictable aggressiveness and brutality of the Serbian forces, may have deliberately provoked attacks against ethnic Albanian civilians, since innocent victims would promote their cause and help bring the West, especially the United States, into the conflict. In the very least, the KLA understood the political benefit of civilian casualties.

Response of the International Community

The international response to the summer offensive was considerably weakened by persistent disunity within the international community. In the Security Council, China and Russia, both permanent members with veto power, maintained that the conflict was an internal matter for resolution by the Yugoslav authorities. This position effectively blocked a forceful Security Council response to the conflict.

A similar degree of disunity emerged in the Contact Group, where Russia in particular played the role of spoiler, although Russia's resistance was at times used by Western states as an excuse for their own inaction.

Throughout the Serbian and Yugoslav offensive, the international community condemned the government's abuses but took no steps to halt the ongoing offensive. Inaction by the West left the impression that it was tolerating the attacks against civilians, and may have been interpreted by Milosevic as a green light to continue. Advocates of inaction in the West presumed the offensive would drive the Kosovar Albanians to the negotiating table. As one Western official was quoted in the press, "There is a general recognition that the KLA was getting too big for its boots and needed to be taken down a peg or two before there can be negotiations."[67]

Inaction by the West left the impression that it was tolerating the attacks against civilians, and may have been interpreted by Milosevic as a green light to continue.

The U.S. position was aptly presented by Secretary of Defense William Cohen who said that NATO did "not want to see" Serbian or Yugoslav government troops attacking civilians or using disproportionate force, but that NATO did not want to take action that "could be construed as lending support, either moral or military, to those seeking independence," meaning the KLA.

Prior to September, the only measure adopted by the Security Council having any bite had been resolution 1160, passed on March 31, 1998, imposing an arms embargo on FRY, a position reached with China abstaining and only after repeated warnings by the Contact Group had been ignored. U.N. Security Council Resolution 1199, passed on September 23, 1998, (again with China abstaining), went further by condemning acts of violence committed in Kosovo, reaffirming the arms embargo and, under authority of Chapter VII of the U.N. Charter, demanding an immediate cessation of hostilities.[68]

Resolution 1199 also called upon the FRY and Kosovar Albanian leadership to enter into immediate and meaningful dialogue and demanded that FRY implement immediately the measures set out in the June 12 statement of the Contact Group. The resolution called on the president of FRY to implement his own commitments from the June 16 joint statement with Yeltsin, among other things, not to carry out any repressive actions against the peaceful population, to facilitate refugee return, and to ensure full access for the ICRC and UNHCR. The resolution also called on the government of FRY, the Kosovar Albanian leadership, and all others to cooperate fully with the prosecutor of the ICTY, and it underlined the need for FRY authorities to bring to justice members of security forces involved in mistreatment of civilians and the deliberate destruction of property. It stated that the Security Council would consider "further action and additional measures" if the measures demanded in its two resolutions were not taken. Porous borders, a well established Balkan arms market, and weak enforcement had kept the embargo from having any substantial impact on the ground.

On September 24, NATO took the first formal steps toward military intervention in Kosovo, issuing an "ACTWARN" for both a limited air option and a phased air campaign in Kosovo.[69]

The Deployment of the Kosovo Verification Mission

The September 26 massacre in Gornje Obrinje, in which twenty-one members of one ethnic Albanian family were killed, garnered major media coverage in the West and catalyzed a more unified international response to the crisis. With winter approaching, international concern was also focused on the estimated 250,000 internally displaced ethnic Albanians.

U.S. envoy Richard Holbrooke flew to Belgrade for talks with Milosevic. At the same time, after the Gornje Obrinje killings, the Serbian police and Yugoslav army wrapped up the summer offensive in the end of September and began a partial withdrawal from Kosovo. As one Serbian journalist wrote of the Gornje Obrinje massacre, government forces "slammed the door on the way out."[70]

With the offensive over, Milosevic had largely achieved his goals, and then granted Holbrooke some concessions: a cease-fire, NATO air surveillance to verify compliance with UN Security Council Resolution 1199, and the deployment of an observer mission from the Organization for Security and Cooperation in Europe (OSCE) called the Kosovo Verification Mission (KVM). By January 1999, the KVM had 2,000 observers in the field, many of them westerners with military experience. Human rights officers were also deployed throughout the province to monitor, document, and publicly report on violations.[71] A subsequent agreement brokered by NATO set the limit of Yugoslav Army and Serbian Ministry of Internal Affairs troops allowed in Kosovo. Hours before the deadline for meeting these limits, the Yugoslav government complied.

Key late-1998 Promotions in the Serbian and Yugoslav Security Structure

- Radomir Markovic replaced Jovica Stanisic as chief of Serbia's state security service (secret police)
- Dragoljub Ojdanic replaced Momcilo Perisic as Yugoslav Army Chief of the General Staff
- Nebojsa Pavkovic promoted from commander of the Pristina Corps to commander of the Third Army (with responsibility for Kosovo)
- Vladimir Lazarevic appointed commander of the Pristina Corps
- Ljubisa Stojimirovic appointed Chief of Staff of the Third Army

Around this time, other developments in Serbia had an impact on Kosovo. On November 3, Milosevic fired the Chief of the General Staff of the Yugoslav Army, Momcilo Perisic, and replaced him with a known loyalist, Gen. Dragoljub Ojdanic. Col. Gen. Nebojsa Pavkovic, commander of Pristina Corp, was promoted to commander of the Third Army, which had responsibility for southern Serbia and Kosovo. In late October, Milosevic dismissed the Yugoslav Air Force commander Col. Gen. Ljubisa Velickovic, and the chief of Serbia's security service, Jovica Stanisic, who had been a close confidant of Milosevic for the past seven years.[72] Velickovic was replaced by Lt. Col. Gen. Spasoje Smiljanic. Stanisic was replaced by Radomir Markovic.

Late-October 1998 to March 1999 saw continued provocations by both government forces and the KLA.

The precise reason for these dismissals remains unclear. Some analysts speculate that the individuals removed disagreed with government policy on Kosovo, fearing that Milosevic was heading into a direct conflict with the West. In particular, it was believed the Perisic had warned Milosevic against a direct confrontation with NATO (as well as having argued against a military deployment against Belgrade demonstrators in late 1996 and early 1997).[73] The replacements were generally viewed as personally loyal to Milosevic and hardline, perhaps necessary for another offensive against the KLA.

Notwithstanding the KVM presence in Kosovo, late-October 1998 to March 1999 saw continued provocations by both government forces and the KLA. The KLA captured two Serbian journalists and nine Yugoslav Army soldiers during this time, all of whom were later released, and conducted periodic strikes on police and army posts—an apparent attempt to provoke the government into a response in front of international monitors. As KLA commanders later admitted, they used the calm from the monitors' presence to continue mobilization, training, and arms procurement.[74]

Serbian and Yugoslav forces also repositioned during this time. Gradually throughout January and February reinforcements and heavy armor made their way back into Kosovo, as detailed in the OSCE report on Kosovo, *As Seen, As Told—Part I.*[75]

On December 13, the army killed more than thirty ethnic Albanians along the border with Albania, ostensibly while they were smuggling in arms. On December 14, unidentified armed men attacked the Panda Cafe in the western city of Pec, killing six Serbian youths. On December 23, the army and police undertook military action against the KLA near Podujevo, in northern Kosovo, along the main road linking Pristina with Belgrade.

On February 25, the Yugoslav Army announced the beginning of "winter exercises" in the Vucitrn municipality, where the KLA had positions in the Cicavica mountains along the Mitrovica-Pristina road (based in the village of Pantina (Pantine)). Skirmishes were ongoing throughout February, as were KLA abductions of local Serbs. According to the OSCE report on Kosovo:

> As armed engagements between Yugoslav/Serbian forces and the UCK continued in the areas of the "exercises," it became clear that these "exercises" had a strategic aim: for the VJ [the Yugoslav Army] to secure the main road and rail routes between Kosovska Mitrovca and Pristina by pushing the UCK back into their strongholds in the Cicavica mountains.[76]

In some cases, the "exercises" included the army's shelling of villages and the forced expulsion of noncombatants. Fighting between the army and KLA was ongoing as the OSCE left the Vucitrn area on March 19. According to U.S. General Wesley Clark, NATO thought Milosevic was "preparing for a spring offensive that would target KLA strongholds." No one expected the "wholesale deportation of the ethnic Albanian population."[77]

During the military buildup by all sides, the U.S. government was engaged in shuttle diplomacy to reach a political solution. U.S. Ambassador to Macedonia Chris Hill, working closely with Richard Holbrooke, continued work on draft plans that would provide Kosovo with substantial autonomy within Yugoslavia. Previous drafts were scuttled after they were leaked and published in a Kosovo-based newspaper, *Koha Ditore.*

A major turning point took place on January 15, 1999, when forty-five ethnic Albanians were killed in the village of Racak. Although the attack was possibly provoked by a KLA ambush that killed three Serbian policeman a few days before, government forces responded by shooting at civilians, torturing detainees, and committing summary executions.[78]

The massacre in Racak was well documented by the OSCE mission, and immediately condemned by the mission's head, U.S. diplomat William Walker. The Yugoslav government said that the Albanians were KLA fighters killed in combat, and threatened to expel Walker—labeled "a representative and a patron of separatism and terrorism"—from the country.[79] On

January 18, Chief Prosecutor Louise Arbour of the war crimes tribunal was denied entry into Kosovo, where she planned to investigate the Racak incident.

The Racak massacre provoked an outcry among the Western public and Western governments began consulting on ways to back up diplomacy with force. NATO increased its threats of military action if attacks on civilians did not stop.

The Rambouillet Conference

Kosovar Albanians and Serbs were hastily summoned to a government chateau in Rambouillet, France, for negotiations between February 6 and 22, 1999. The British and French foreign ministers co-sponsored the talks, with negotiators from the U.S., Austria (as president of the E.U.) and Russia. A diverse delegation of Kosovar Albanians representing the various political forces elected Hashim Thaci, political leader of the KLA, as their spokesman. Milosevic refused to attend and sent Serbian president Milan Milutinovic to head a motley delegation of ethnically diverse but unimportant representatives from Kosovo—an attempt to demonstrate his multiethnic and tolerant approach to the province.

After two weeks, the negotiators presented both sides with an interim agreement that would have provided for substantial autonomy and self-government for Kosovo inside Yugoslavia, protected by a strong NATO presence on the ground. The final status of Kosovo was to be worked out in three year's time by an international conference.

The Serbian delegation refused to sign, stating that Kosovo was an integral part of Yugoslavia. Some parts of the accords were clearly of particular concern to the delegation, such as NATO's unrestricted access throughout Yugoslavia and NATO's authority to detain individuals.[80] The Kosovar Albanian delegation, while more inclined to give support, said it needed approval from the regional commanders of the KLA—a reflection of the group's decentralized character. The conference was halted while Thaci returned to Kosovo to get the commanders' agreement. The conference reconvened in Paris on March 15. Three days later, under great pressure from the West, the Kosovar Albanian delegation signed.

Throughout the conference, Serbian and Yugoslav forces were observed positioning themselves around the Kosovo border with Serbia proper, a clear indication—coupled with the Serbian delegation's intransigence—that a military offensive was in preparation. According to the OSCE, "a significant build up of VJ forces" was taking place throughout Kosovo.[81] Many observers believe that Milosevic never had any intention of signing an agreement; he simply used the time to further reinforce his troops, and he gained three weeks because of Thaci's need to consult commanders inside Kosovo.

Media reports later claimed that the Austrian government had warned NATO before the bombing that a large-scale Serbian offensive was in preparation. The allegation was repeated two weeks into the bombing by the German government, which said that Operation Horseshoe—a plan to expel Albanians from Kosovo—had been drafted six months prior to the air war.[82] A retired brigadier general in the German Army, however, later stated that the claims of a plan were faked from a vague intelligence report in order to deflect growing criticism in Germany of the bombing.[83]

In anticipation of the NATO bombing and the deteriorating security situation, the OSCE's KVM mission withdrew from Kosovo on March 20. Although there had been fear the observers would be seized as hostages, government forces welcomed rather than hindered their withdrawal. That day, attacks against Kosovar Albanians began in parts of Kosovo, notably Drenica and the Llap region near Podujevo. Yugoslav soldiers, Serbian special police, paramilitaries, and armed irregulars poured into the province. With no local information, ethnic Albanian civilians sat waiting for the worst.

In a final effort to avoid bombing, U.S. special envoy Richard Holbrooke flew to Belgrade to meet Milosevic and threaten air strikes unless he signed the agreement. He left empty-handed on March 23 and, the next day, NATO air strikes commenced without awaiting approval from the United Nations Security Council.

CONCLUSION

Kosovo dominated the headlines in 1999, but the conflict was predictable as long ago as 1989. The international community failed to implement effective preventive measures, acting only after the crisis had evolved into an armed conflict.

Even after open conflict began, the international community failed to take meaningful steps to stop the serious abuses committed against civilians in Kosovo. Throughout 1998, the international community repeatedly failed to develop a unified position to resolve the conflict. Slobodan Milosevic used this lack of consensus to his advantage in a series of bilateral negotiations buying time to advance the campaign in Kosovo. Members of the international community took advantage of the disunity as well: pointing to each other as the excuse for inaction. When the international community sent a strong message of condemnation to the parties to the conflict, words and symbolic action proved meaningless, with deadlines postponed, conditions abandoned, and sanctions poorly enforced or withdrawn as abusive violence persisted.

In addition to concerns over the stability of Bosnia and supporting the Dayton Accords, the international community's approach to Kosovo was strongly influenced by its desire to avoid independence for the province. The redrawing of Yugoslav borders, it was (and still is) feared, might destabilize Montenegro, Bosnia and Macedonia, as well as encourage secessionist movements in other parts of Europe and around the world.

This is not a trivial concern. But the international community's interest in preserving international borders should not have been elevated above the imperative of halting abuses before they escalated into open warfare, leading to thousands of dead and many more displaced. If the international community wanted to promote territorial integrity in the Balkans, it should have pressed for the national unity that comes from respect for the rights of all citizens—a respect that had been sorely lacking in Kosovo as well as in other parts of the region. But seeking to preserve borders by tolerating serious abuses led to the regional instability that the international community was trying to avoid.

3

FORCES OF THE CONFLICT

The Serbian and Yugoslav government security forces are a complex combination of republican and federal institutions, along with more clandestine groups of irregulars and paramilitaries. The Yugoslav Army's military police and army special forces, antiterrorist units of the Serbian police and special police, special forces of the secret police, paramilitary groups, international mercenaries, and armed local Serbs were all active in Kosovo in 1998 and 1999 in operations coordinated by Belgrade.[1]

The various forces often engaged in joint operations, in close coordination, and at times used interchangeable uniforms. Insignias were not always displayed, and name tags or identification numbers were rarely visible.[2] Many of the government's forces came from outside Kosovo, making it difficult for Kosovar Albanians to identify either a particular force or individuals, compounded by the difficulties of observation in a violent and shocking environment.

There were some exceptions, particularly in the areas where Albanians and Serbs lived in closer proximity, such as in and around Pec, Orahovac, and Lipljan. Forces of the Yugoslav Army were more easily identified due to their more standarized procedures, equipment, and uniforms. But the army's soldiers usually came from outside of Kosovo, and were therefore unknown to the local population.

The Yugoslav Army, Serbian police, and paramilitaries were all responsible for war crimes in Kosovo. In general, however, paramilitaries appear to have been more extensively involved in the most violent abuses, specifically the executions and rapes. While police and army units are by no means

Chief of the Yugoslav Army General Staff during the Kosovo war Gen. Dragoljub Ojdanic (left), Yugoslav President Slobodan Milosevic (center), and head of the Third Army Col. Gen. Nebojsa Pavkovic attend a ceremony in Belgrade on March 17, 2000. After the war, Milosevic promoted Ojdanic to Yugoslav Minister of Defense and Pavkovic to Chief of the General Staff. Milosevic and Ojdanic have been indicted by the war crimes tribunal. AFP PHOTO exempt from responsibility in this regard, the paramilitaries were more commonly engaged in arbitrary killings and sexual violence.

But paramilitary forces were not operating on their own. On the contrary, paramilitary units were operating in close concert with the police, army, and secret police (known as the state security sevice). There may have been specific incidents when paramilitary units or individuals got out of control, but the general deployment of paramilitary units and their coordination with other sectors of the security apparatus were planned components of the Kosovo campaign.

Paramilitary units were operating in close concert with the police, army, and secret police.

In general, it appears that the Yugoslav Army was in command during the war, with the police and paramilitaries subordinate to its orders, although top officials of the Serbian Ministry of Internal Affairs exercised significant influence over the campaign. The army controlled the main roads and the borders, coordinating and facilitating the "ethnic cleansing." The police and paramilitaries were more directly involved in expulsions and the destruction of villages, with artillery support from the army. It is during these operations that men were separated from women and children, interrogated about the KLA, and sometimes executed.

Typically, as told by witnesses from all over Kosovo, the army and special police forces surrounded a village and shelled it from a distance. Regular and special police forces then moved in, swept the village, and gathered the villagers in a centralized location. Men were separated from women and children for interrogation about the KLA. Regular police and paramilitaries then looted the village, as well as stealing whatever the villagers carried with them and destroying their identity documents. The village was then left to the police, paramilitaries, and local Serbian militias, who looted and burned the remains. The women, children, and elderly were often expelled, and men with suspected ties to the KLA were sometimes executed.

There are a few examples of police officers and soldiers having tried to treat civilians fairly, and even going out of their way to protect them. In a few cases documented by Human Rights Watch, Kosovar Albanians reported that police or soldiers gave them food or medical assistance, or warned them to hide from oncoming paramilitaries. In one example, army officers tried to investigate women's allegations of sexual abuse.[3] In another case, a witness to the April 30 killings in Vrbovac (see Drenica Region) said that he had heard VJ soldiers pleading with paramilitaries not to fire on civilians.[4] But these examples are the exceptions. Too often, the police and army either tolerated paramilitary behavior, facilitated it, or engaged in criminal acts themselves.[5]

The Serbian and Yugoslav security structure, especially Serbian state security, was also strongly linked to criminal activity in Kosovo and the rest of the country, such as illicit trade in cigarettes, arms, and drugs. "Volunteers" to fight in Kosovo were sometimes recruited directly from Serbian prisons. Funding for the police and army also came from unorthodox sources within Serbia, such as the Federal Customs Agency, run by long-time Milosevic ally Mihalj Kertes, who was arrested for embezzlement in December 2000.[6]

The sections below describe in more detail the various forces that operated in Kosovo, including the responsible officers, when known. All information is from open sources and is cited. Two official sources are used heavily: *Vojska* magazine, the official publication of the Yugoslav Army, and *Policajac* magazine, the official publication of the Serbian Ministry of Internal Affairs.

In addition to the forces of the conflict, this section identifies the key political and military leaders in Serbia and Yugoslavia, some of them no longer in their positions, who have the highest level of responsibility for the war crimes committed in Kosovo. These people either directed the campaign against ethnic Albanians or in full awareness of the events did nothing to stop it. They can be held legally accountable for both.

FORCES OF THE FEDERAL REPUBLIC OF YUGOSLAVIA

The two principal military forces in Yugoslavia in 1998 and 1999 were the Yugoslav Army (Vojska Jugoslavija, or VJ) and the Republic of Serbia's Ministry of Internal Affairs (Ministarstvo Unutrasnjih Poslova, or MUP). The Republic of Montenegro's Ministry of Internal Affairs remained loyal to the Montenegrin government and were not active in Kosovo.

From the time he became president of Serbia in 1989, Slobodan Milosevic gradually strengthened and expanded the MUP over the VJ and the Yugoslav federal police, both of which he viewed as less loyal forces. Friction between the MUP and VJ occasionally emerged over the increased resources and prestige provided to the former. One noted incident regarding Kosovo occurred after the first police attacks on Drenica in late February and early March 1999, in which more than eighty people were killed, including twenty-four women and children (see Background). An unnamed high official of the Yugoslav Army cited in the Serbian press criticized the police for their "completely amateurish manner," saying that the operation had acquired "the dimensions of a massacre" because the police "succumbed to emotions."[7]

Only the Serbian regular police, special police, and possibly state security special forces were active in Kosovo in the first half of 1998. The army, although present in the province, was restricted to maintaining security along the borders with Macedonia and Albania. This changed in April 1998, when the army participated in military actions in southwestern Kosovo along the border with Albania. The army and the police cooperated from that point on, but for the most part, actions against the KLA remained the responsibility of the Serbian Ministry of Internal Affairs throughout 1998.

The primacy of the MUP began to change in late 1998 and early 1999 when President Milosevic reshuffled some key members of the police and army, placing known loyalists in top positions. Among other changes, Dragoljub Ojdanic replaced Momcilo Perisic[8] as Chief of General Staff of the Yugoslav Army and Nebojsa Pavkovic was promoted to commander of the VJ's Third Army, which had responsibility for southern Serbia and Kosovo. Radomir Markovic replaced Jovica Stanisic as head of Serbia's security service (for more details, see Background). In late March 1999, when faced with attacks by NATO, the police, army, paramilitaries, and other irregulars units coordinated their attacks on the KLA and their defense against air strikes.[9]

It should also be noted that Serbian state security played a major role in Kosovo throughout the 1990s, monitoring Kosovar Albanian political circles, especially the KLA. State security also had a special operations unit called the JSO (Jedinice za Specijalne Operacije—Special Operations Unit), which was active in Kosovo in 1998 and 1999.

Yugoslav Army (Vojska Jugoslavije)

According to the OSCE report *Kosovo/Kosova: As Seen, As Told—Part I*, the VJ had from 85,000 to 114,000 total personnel with a reserve force of as much as 200,000. In Kosovo, there were an estimated 15,000 troops in early 1999, increased to 20,000 by the end of April. This does not include the additional 30,000 police, paramilitaries, and other irregulars also in the province.[10]

The emblem of the Yugoslav Army.

According to the Yugoslav Constitution, the VJ is under the command of the Yugoslav president in both wartime and peace. The president is also empowered to appoint, promote, and dismiss officers as stipulated by law.[11]

The controlling body of the army is the Supreme Defense Council (SDC), of which the Yugoslav president is chairman. The other members of the SDC are the presidents of Serbia and Montenegro. Secretary of the council was Slavoljub Susic.[12] According to the Serbian media, the SDC rarely if ever met to consult on Kosovo, presumedly because Montenegrin President Milo Djukanovic would not have agreed to Milosevic's plans.[13]

Although the Yugoslav president is entitled to command the VJ only "pursuant to decisions of the Supreme Defense Council," in reality Milosevic took personal command of the army, as he did with all of Yugoslavia's governing structure. At times, the VJ undertook actions without the approval of the SDC, provoking criticism from Montenegrin President Djukanovic. In March 1999, for instance, when the VJ increased its presence in Kosovo, Djukanovic denounced the action and proclaimed: "Any decision made by the [Supreme] Defense Council without me would be illegal."[14]

The VJ is under the command of the Yugoslav president in both wartime and peace.

The main organ of the VJ is the General Staff, headed during the 1999 war by Gen. Dragoljub Ojdanic, who was chief of the VJ General Staff.[15] The deputy chief of the General Staff was Gen. Svetozar M. Marjanovic.[16]

The VJ is divided into three armies, as well as the Navy, Air/Air Defense

Forces, and the Counter Intelligence Service (known as KOS—Kontraobavestajna Sluzba).[17] The First Army covers northern Serbia, the Second Army covers central Serbia and Montenegro, and the Third Army covers southern Serbia and Kosovo.[18] In addition, the VJ has a Special Forces Corps, known as the Red Berets, specially trained for anti-terrorist actions.[19]

The Third Army, headquartered in Nis, was further broken down into the Timok Tactical Group, the Nis Corps, the Leskovac Corps, and the Pristina Corps (also known as the 52 Corps).[20] The Pristina Corps, which covered Kosovo, is comprised of the following:[21]

- 15th Armored Brigade (Pristina), commanded by Col. Mladen Cirkovic.[22]
- 125th Motorized Brigade (Kosovo Mitrovica and Pec), commanded by Col. Dragan Zivanovic.[23]
- 549th Motorized Brigade (Prizren and Djakovica), commanded by Col. Bozidar Delic.[24]
- 243rd Mechanized Brigade (Urosevac and Gnjilane), commanded by Col. Krsman Jelic.[25]
- 52nd Mixed Artillery Brigade (Gnjilane) commanded by Col. Radojko Stefanovic.[26]
- 52nd Military Police Unit, (Pristina) commanded by Maj. Zeljko Pekovic.[27]
- 83rd Aviation Regiment[28]
- 52nd Engineers Regiment (Krusevac)
- 311th Air-Defense Regiment (Djakovica)
- 53rd Border Guard Battalion (Djakovica)
- 55th Border Guard Battalion (Prizren)
- 57th Border Guard Battalion (Urosevac)

During the war, the Third Army was commanded by Col. Gen. Nebojsa Pavkovic, who was promoted to the position in November 1998—at the same time Ojdanic became Chief of the VJ General Staff.[29] Until then, Pavkovic had commanded the Pristina Corps of the Third Army. The commander of the Third Army before Pavkovic had been Col. Gen. Dusan Samardzic, with Col. Mirko Starcevic in a subordinate position to him.[30]

The Pristina Corps was commanded during the war by Maj. Gen. Vladimir Lazarevic, who was assigned to the post at the end of 1998 by

Yugoslav Army (VJ) — Basic Structure Related to Kosovo, March-June1999

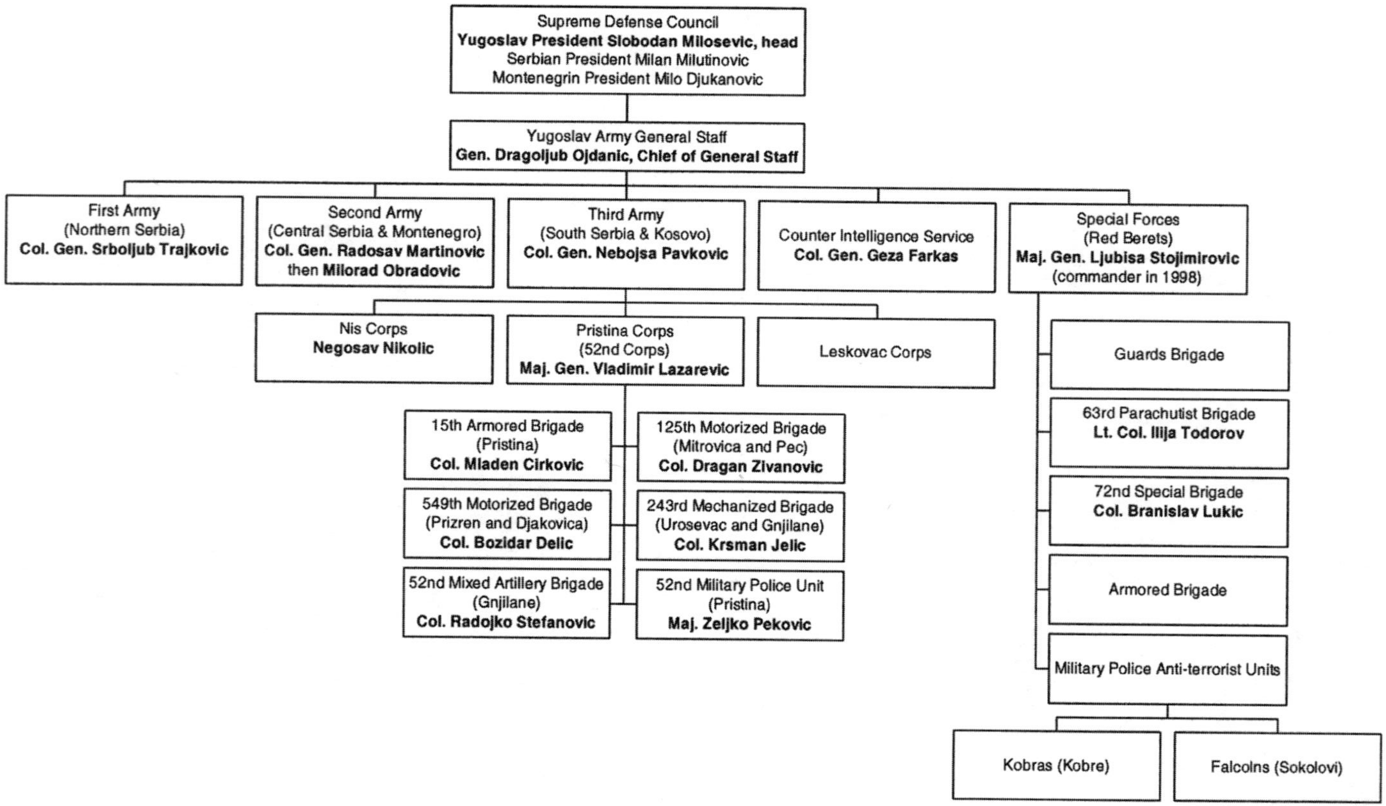

President Milosevic.[31] Other generals in the Third Army included Ljubisa Stojimirovic, chief of staff of the Third Army,[32] Negoslav Nikolic, commander of the Nis Corps,[33] Tomislav Mladenovic, and Milan Djakovic.[34]

The Pristina Corps was deployed in the following cities: Pristina, Pec, Prizren, Kosovska Mitrovica, Urosevac, Djakovica, and Gnjilane. The total strength of the corps was approximately 15,000.[35]

The evidence suggests that the VJ's Special Forces Corps was also active in the province during the Kosovo conflict. According to Western defense and intelligence officials cited in the *Washington Post,* the 72nd Special Operations Unit was conducting operations in the Rogovo mountains in June 1999.[36] The longtime commander of the Special Forces Corps, Maj. Gen. Ljubisa Stojimirovic,[37] was appointed Chief of Staff of the Third Army by President Milosevic in the end of 1998.[38] His replacement as commander of the Special Forces Corps is unknown.

Maj. Gen. Vladimir Lazarevic (left), commander of the Pristina Corps during the Kosovo war, and Col. Gen. Nebojsa Pavkovic (right), commander of the Third Army during the war, salute Yugoslav Army soldiers in Pirot, Serbia, on September 1, 2000. After the Kosovo war, President Milosevic promoted Lazarevic to commander of the Third Army and Pavkovic to Chief of the Yugoslav Army General Staff. AFP PHOTO

According to *Vojska* magazine, the Special Forces Corps in April 1998 included:[39]

- Guards Brigade;
- 63rd Parachutist Brigade, commanded by Lt. Col. Ilija Todorov;[40]
- 72nd Special Brigade commanded by Col. Branislav Lukic;[41]
- Anti-terrorist units of the Military Police - Cobras and Falcons;
- Armored Brigade.

Soldier Interview

Journalists Stephen Smith and Michael Montgomery from American RadioWorks interviewed Serb fighters who were active in Pec and surrounding villages up to June, 1999. Their documentaries on Kosovo and specifically the village of Cuska (see Pec Municipality) are available at www.americanradioworks.org. This interview with Vaso (a pseudonym) was conducted in Montenegro in September 1999. Vaso, in his early thirties, served in a special tactical unit in the Third Army.

ARW: Was it unusual for the men to be executed in Cuska?

Vaso: It was more than unusual and yet it was so common. It was unusual in the sense that this isn't what people are supposed to do, I mean killing unarmed men . . . But we went there with one aim, to defeat the terrorists. It was out of patriotic reasons I went to fight. And now I ask myself: Should I have been there? Was I delirious? Had I known what I know today, maybe I wouldn't have gone. Again, when you live through difficult trauma, it's hard to figure things out. I walk the streets, alone. I walk all day just thinking. Sometimes I find that I was right to go to fight, other times I feel I was wrong. The pictures from all that are still with me. I still see those innocent people dying. I see a fighter killing a woman in front of her husband and her child. It's something I can never forget.

ARW: What did your officers tell you about the war, about the Albanians?

Vaso: They always held these classes during training and at other times. They would tell us what the Albanians were doing to us, how many people the Albanians had killed. I don't know if it was true but they talked in great detail. They would show us pictures of mutilated bodies and talk about this

According to the Federation of American Scientists (a non-profit, non-governmental organization based in the United States), which has monitored the Yugoslav security structure, the Falcons (Sokolovi) and the Cobras (Kobre) were special units of the Special Forces Corps' Military Police. These highly trained units were reportedly used for anti-terrorist operations; the Cobras consist of two platoons with a total of sixty members.[42] According to *Vojska,* their use was regulated by the Chief of the VJ General Staff.[43]

Regular VJ soldiers were usually identifiable by their green camouflage

village or that village where the Serbs were killed or driven out by Albanian terrorists. I don't know if these were true stories but we were blinded by them, by the whole campaign across Serbia. The media was saying the same thing, just one thing. All day, you have one station, one channel, one newscast, one source of information and you have your general, and all of them are talking against the Albanians. You had no chance to like the Albanians, to see them as human beings.

ARW: What would you think if the Hague Tribunal ruled that what happened in Cuska was a war crime and tried to punish the people responsible?

Vaso: Those people should be punished. I agree. I think this was a mistaken policy. And Milosevic, as the person who created this policy, should go to the Hague. I didn't know what was going to happen when I went (to Kosovo). But they (Milosevic's regime) calculated everything that happened. He should be the first to go to the Hague and they'll probably find others.

ARW: How do you feel when you go to your hometown in Serbia and talk to people who support Milosevic, who believe nothing bad happened in Kosovo?

Vaso: It's terrible. I think it's a catastrophe for anyone who thinks that way. I tried to explain to people what I saw, what he (Milosevic) has done. I explained the failed policies but I don't have the nerves or the patience to convince people. I've tried to tell people what I saw. But what am I to say to the person who doesn't believe me . . . that he's crazy. Then, either he'll kill me or I'll kill him.

ARW: What does your family (in Serbia) think?

Vaso: My family thinks the same way I do. It was my influence. They used to think like Milosevic's people. Now they think the complete opposite . . . Unfortunately, there are still a lot of people who think the old way.

uniforms and the red and white, double-headed eagle insignia on the shoulder. The soldiers tended to be younger—often conscripts.

Some volunteers also fought with the VJ. In an interview with the Serbian newspaper *Vecernje Novosti,* Col. Gen. Nebojsa Pavkovic confirmed that "there were about 1,000 volunteers, but they were under the strict command and control of our officers."[44] The presence of volunteers was confirmed by a document obtained by Human Rights Watch in Pec, which lists by name twelve volunteers coming from Vojvodina. The one-page document from the Department of General Management and Public Service in Debeljaca, Vojvodina, is to allow public transportation free of charge from Debeljaca to Bubanj Potok and back for the "below cited volunteers."[45] The document does not, however, specify whether the listed individuals were volunteers for the army or a paramilitary unit.

In an interview with the *Guardian* newspaper (London), a VJ volunteer named Milan Petrovic said he had gone to Kosovo to "cleanse" Albanians, along with 2,000 other volunteers. "We gave most of them [the Albanians] twenty-four hours to get out," he told the paper. "The rich ones, and they're all criminals you know, with satellite TVs and big houses were tougher to move. But if you push hard enough, they all go in the end. They're cowards, those Albanians, they run like rabbits."[46] According to Petrovic, normally a truck driver, "one in a hundred" of the volunteers committed some rapes or killing. He said:

> About six guys in my unit got out of hand one night and started killing Albanians. But they only killed three or four of them before they started taking stuff out of their houses. The next day our army came and took the six of them away.[47]

Another volunteer, identified as "K," was interviewed by the United States documentary program Frontline. In a filmed interview, he said that the volunteers were strictly following VJ orders:

> Every action that was about to be done, there was an order . . . in writing. I had principles. I saw every order before going into action. We had orders for V., M., and G [referring to Kosovo villages]. . . . those were the actions of "cleaning" that I participated in. . . . We had an order to get them from the hills, and that's what we did.[48]

At the same time, "K." admitted that some volunteers went out of control, although he claimed they were stopped by the VJ commander. He told Frontline:

> [T]here were groups of people that wanted to go into cleaning actions of their own accord. That's not cleaning. That's theft, robbery. . . . A few villages

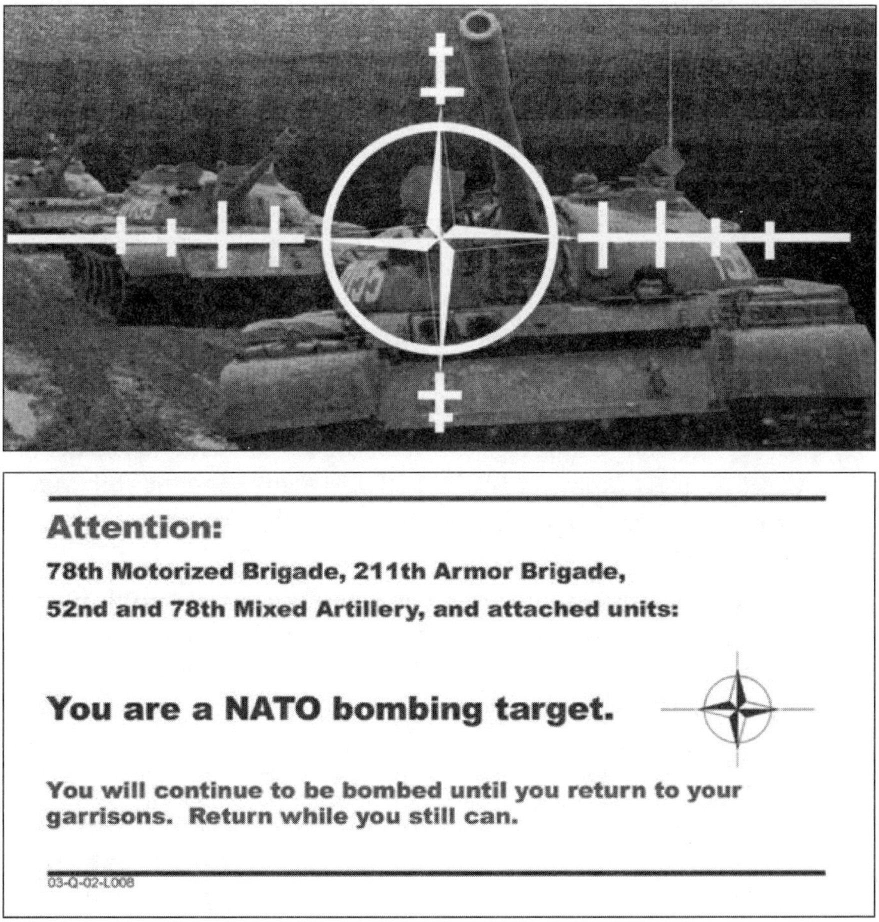

NATO dropped leaflets like this over Kosovo as part of a psyops (psychological operations) campaign. This leaflet indicates the precise brigades that NATO believed were active in Kosovo. The 52nd Mixed Artillery Brigade is known to be in the Third Army, which has jurisdiction over Kosovo. NATO MEDIA ARCHIVE

> were done without orders until [a] general saw one of the unauthorized actions. He ordered the soldiers to stop, he told [those] that have already formed a column to go because there was fear already and he couldn't have guaranteed them safety. When volunteers are being accepted, sometimes even thieves turn up. You can't control everything. We were careful that the group of volunteers that joined for patriotic reasons, the good people, were following orders to defend themselves and act against the terrorists.[49]

According to NATO and the U.S. State Department, some other army forces outside of the Third Army's Pristina Corps were also active in Kosovo between March and June 1999. On April 7, the State Department issued a statement that named nine commanders in the Yugoslav Army, placing them on notice, with the International Criminal Tribunal for the former Yugoslavia (ICTY) in mind, that "VJ and MUP forces are committing war crimes and crimes against humanity in Kosovo."[50] Among those named as commanders of such forces was Col. Milos Mandic, commander of the 252nd Armored Brigade, with a home garrison in Kraljevo, Serbia.

At some time during the air war, NATO dropped leaflets on Kosovo as part of its psychological operations (Psyops) campaign. One leaflet was addressed to the 78th Motorized Brigade, the 211th Armor Brigade, the 52nd Mixed Artillery (known to be in the Third Army), and the 78th Mixed Artillery Brigade, suggesting NATO's belief that these brigades were also active in Kosovo.

According to *Jane's Defense Weekly,* a reinforced brigade from the Nis Corps and a brigade from the Leskovac Corps were believed to have moved into Kosovo on the weekend of March 20–21, just before the NATO bombing. In addition, two reinforced brigades, one from the First Army and one from the Second Army were believed to have moved into Kosovo around that time.[51]

The precise number of VJ casualties remains unknown. According to former commander of the Third Army Pavkovic, 161 soldiers died and 299 were wounded during the NATO bombing. Nine others went missing. Regarding equipment, Pavkovic said in a June 1999 statement published in *Vojska,* that NATO had destroyed thirteen VJ tanks, six armored personnel carriers, eight artillery pieces, nineteen anti-aircraft guns, and one radar.[52]

Serbian Ministry of Internal Affairs (MUP)

The structure of the Serbian Ministry of Internal Affairs (MUP) is far more complicated than that of the VJ, which has a transparent chain of command. The profusion of units and groups within the MUP make such a hierarchy less discernible, although it is clear that, according to law, ultimate authority for the MUP during the war rested with then-Yugoslav President Slobodan Milosevic. Although he was not at the top of the MUP's de jure chain of command during times of peace, a position nominally held by the Serbian Minister of Internal Affairs, he was the indisputable de facto commander of its forces. According to Yugoslavia's Law on Defence, during a state of war, the republican police come under the jurisdiction of the Yugoslav Army. A state of war existed in Yugoslavia between March 24 and June 10, 1996.

The emblem of the Serbian Ministry of Internal Affairs.

The security apparatus of the Serbian MUP is divided into three branches: the public security service, the state security service (known as the SDB—Sluzba Drzavne Bezbednosti), and educational institutions, such as the police academy.[53] The public security service has eleven departments, including the police department. The state security service, or SDB, is also known as the secret police. There is also a

An undated photo of Vlajko Stojiljkovic, Serbian Minister of Internal Affairs during the Kosovo War. The war crimes tribunal indicted Stojiljkovic, Yugoslav President Slobodan Milosevic, Serbian President Milan Milutinovic, Yugoslav Deputy Prime Minister Nikola Sainovic, and chief of the Yugoslav Army General Staff Dragoljub Ojdanic for war crimes in Kosovo on May 27, 1999. AFP PHOTO

Yugoslav Ministry of Internal Affairs, run by Zoran Sokolovic, but all evidence suggests that he and the federal ministry had a limited role.[54]

From April 1997 to October 2000, the minister of the MUP was Vlajko Stojiljkovic, known informally as "Deda" ("Grandpa"). On May 27, 1999, he was indicted by the ICTY along with four other top Serbian and Yugoslav officials for crimes against humanity committed in Kosovo.[55] Legally, Stojiljkovic reported to the Serbian government and the National Assembly. It is not clear how much de facto power he wielded within the ministry.

Until January 2001, the head of the public security service was Col. Gen. Vlastimir Djordjevic, known informally as "Rodja" ("Cousin"), who was also an assistant to the minister. Djordjevic was replaced by Sreten Lukic, who commanded the uniformed police in Kosovo during the war (see below). Head of the state security service during the war was Col. Gen. Radomir Markovic. Markovic was fired by the new Serbian government on January 25, 2001. On February 23, he was arrested along with three other officials in the state security service for their alleged involvement in the 1999 car crash that injured opposition politician Vuk Draskovic and killed four of his associates.[56] According to the MUP's own website, www.mup.sr.gov.yu/domino/mup.nsf/pages/index-e (April 22, 2001), the other assistants to Minister Stojiljkovic were: Maj. Gen. Nikola Curcic, deputy of the state security service and director of the Security Institute, Lt. Gen. Obrad Stevanovic, Maj. Gen. Stojan Misic, and Maj. Gen. Petar Zekovic.

Until January 2001, Col. Gen. Obrad Stevanovic commanded the police department of the public security service.[57] The department was broken down into various groups: the regular police, the special police, and the antiterrorist special forces.

The special police units were most frequently known as the PJP (Posebne Jedinice Policije). They surpassed the regular police in the specialization and intensity of their training and the sophistication of their equipment, which included mor-

Undated photo of Col. Gen. Vlastimir Djordjevic, head of the Public Security Service at the Serbian Ministry of Internal Affairs during the Kosovo war. PHOTO COURTESY OF VREME

Serbian Ministry of Internal Affairs (MUP) — Basic Structure Related to Kosovo, March-June 1999

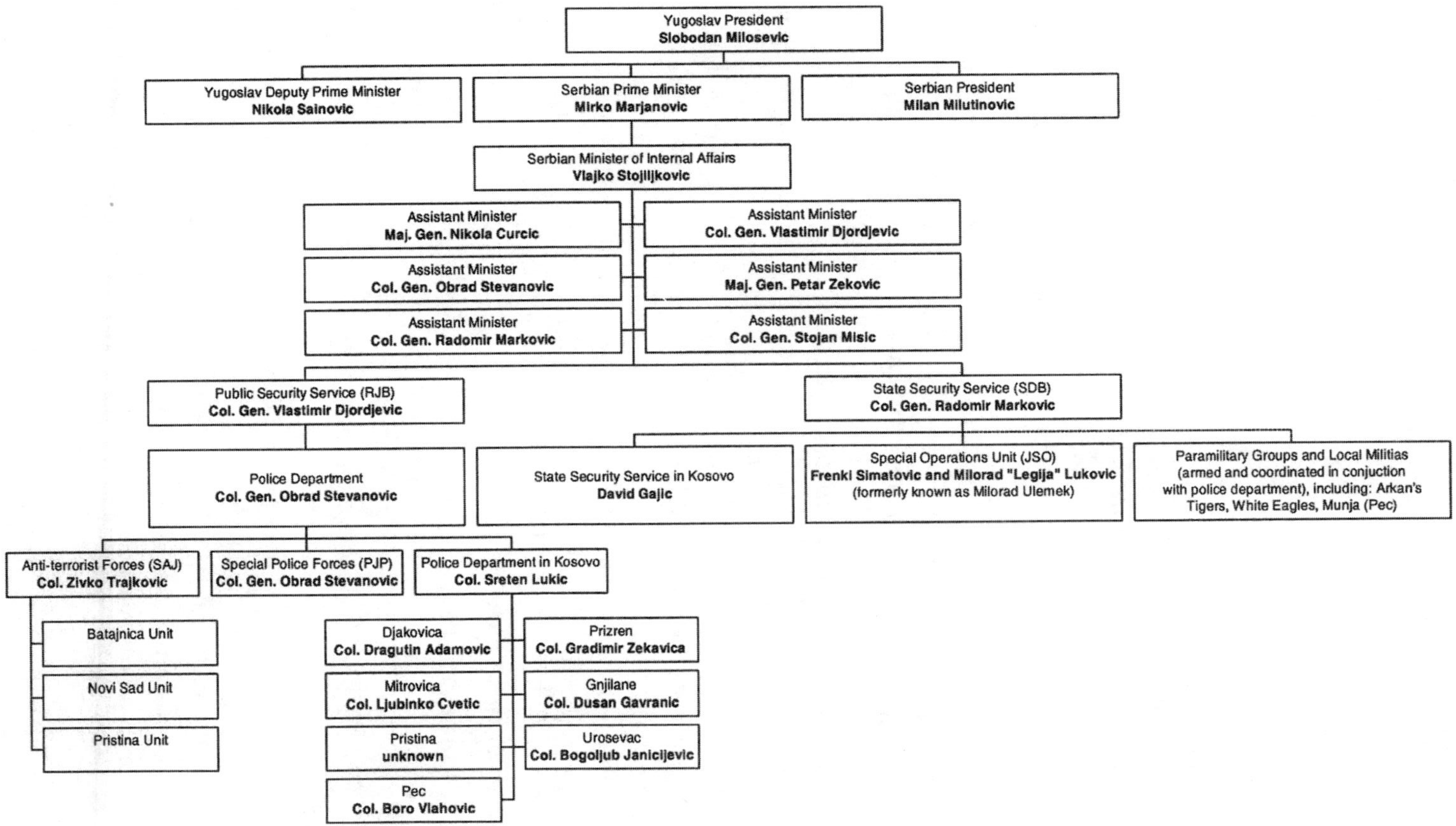

tars and heavy machine guns. According to the Federation of American Scientists and a leading Belgrade police analyst, the PJP had an estimated 7,000 men, although their numbers could be quickly expanded by recruiting from the regular police.[58] The U.K. Ministry of Defense, however, claimed that the PJP had 5,000 members in 1999 divided into six detachments in Serbia, as well as 8,000 reservists.[59] It is believed that Obrad Stevanovic, head of the police department, also commanded the PJP.

The police department also had special antiterrorist units, known as the SAJ (Specijalna Antiteroristicka Jedinica), and commanded by Col. Zivko Trajkovic.[60] The unit used to be commanded by Radovan Stojicic, a.k.a. Badza, who was killed by unknown assailants in downtown Belgrade in 1996.

The SAJ had three units: in Batajnica (near Belgrade), Pristina, and Novi Sad.[61] The units are reportedly well equipped and enjoy support from helicopter units. Their uniforms are often black and the emblem, according to the Serbian newspaper *Blic,* was a double-headed white eagle with a red shield and the Serbian symbol of four Cs.[62]

Serbia also had the regular police stationed throughout the republic, all under the command of Col. Gen. Obrad Stevanovic. In Kosovo, there were seven regional police centers, known as SUPs (Sekretarijat Unutrasnjih Poslova, or Secretariat for Internal Affairs) in Pristina, Kosovska Mitrovica, Pec, Prizren, Urosevac, Gnjilane, and Djakovica. Each of these SUPs were broken up into smaller OUPs (Odeljenje Unutrasnjih Poslova, or Unit of Internal Affairs), within which were the local police stations in towns and villages. Spokesman for the MUP in Kosovo was Col. Ljubinko Cvetic.

A central figure in the regular police was Sreten Lukic, who commanded the force in Kosovo.

A central figure in the regular police was Sreten Lukic, who commanded the force in Kosovo.[63] His precise position in the MUP chain of command during the war remains somewhat unclear, although his importance in the province is undisputed. In various MUP documents, he is referred to as the Chief of the Headquarters of the Ministry of Interior in Pristina.[64] He is also related to Milan Lukic and Sredoje Lukic, both under indictment by the war crimes tribunal for abuses in Bosnia,[65] as well as Mikailo Lukic, the former secret police chief in Bajina Basta.[66]

On numerous occasions, Lukic was presented by the MUP in Kosovo as its main interlocutor with foreigners. On June 7, 1998, Lukic met a large delegation of foreign diplomats and defense attaches who were on a Yugoslav government-organized tour of western Kosovo after the government's first large offensive against the KLA. In response to a question from a Dutch diplomat about the whereabouts of the villagers, Lukic replied, "The terrorists evacuated their nearest and dearest, their wives, children and old people . . ."[67] Lukic denied the rumors that thousands of ethnic Albanian civilians had been forced to flee.

Some journalists also covered the tour. According to one account, Lukic claimed that the KLA had deliberately blown up their own houses. He attributed the damage to some mosques in the area to the Albanians' "misuse of religious facilities during shooting."[68] According to the MUP website, Lukic said:

> [S]ome 5,000 people left the areas around the road. But instead of going to Albania, as reported in some media, they fled for Djakovica, Prizren, and a smaller number of them went to their relatives working in Western Europe and a significant number of those along the border went to their cousins and to their mountain sheds on the slopes where they graze their cattle in summer. Following the unblocking of the road, all the conditions have been created for people to return to their homes.[69]

Human Rights Watch visited northern Albania in July 1999 to interview the refugees who had fled the offensive. They reported indiscriminate shelling of villages, widespread looting, and burning of private property by Serbian forces. Fifteen thousand people fled to Albania and an estimated 30,000 fled north to Monte-negro.[70]

Lukic was also the main contact person with the police for the KDOM observer mission. In one incident, on August 21,

Undated photo of Col. Gen. Obrad Stevanovic, head of Serbia's Police Department during the Kosovo war.

PHOTO COURTESY OF VREME

1998, a joint U.S. and Canadian KDOM team was stopped and detained by three drunken police officers near Pec, according to the internal KDOM daily report from that day, which was viewed by Human Rights Watch. After thirty minutes of verbal abuse and harassment, the KDOM team was released. U.S. KDOM immediately contacted Kosovo administrator Veljko Odalovic and "provincial MUP commander General Lukic." Lukic was reportedly in Belgrade but Odalovic apologized and guaranteed that the individuals responsible would be punished. Three hours later, according to the KDOM report, Odalovic called back to say that the MUP official responsible had been fired and that the two other officers would be dealt with. He also advised that, "General Lukic would ensure that MUP units in the field would be advised and instructed to maintain discipline."[71] This statement supports a conclusion that the MUP rank and file was under the control of its superiors.

Lukic's name appeared again in January 1999, after the killing of forty-five ethnic Albanians in Racak. According to the *Washington Post,* Western governments had intercepted conversations between "Serbian Interior Minister General Sreten Lukic" and Yugoslav Deputy Prime Minister Nikola Sainovic (who was indicted by ICTY on May 24, 1999). Western sources familiar with the intercepts claimed that the two officials ordered their forces to "go in heavy." In a series of conversations after the attack, Lukic and Sainovic allegedly discussed ways to cover up the massacre.[72]

After Milosevic's fall in October 2000, Lukic reportedly became head of the Ministry of Internal Affair's Department for Border Affairs, which deals with passports and visas.[73] But on January 30, 2001, the new Serbian government appointed him the ministry's new chief of public security, replacing Vlastimir Djordjevic, as well as Deputy Minister of Internal Affairs.[74]

The commanders of the regional Kosovo SUPs were under Lukic. The commander of the Djakovica SUP, established in early 1996, was Dragutin Adamovic.[75] The commander of the Pec SUP, which covers the municipalities of Pec, Klina, and Istok, was Col. Boro Vlahovic.[76] The commander of the Klina OUP, within the Pec SUP, was Sgt. Maj. Jovica Mikic.[77] Lt. Vukmir Mircic was the commander of the Decani OUP. [78]

SUP Prizren covers the municipalities of Prizren, Orahovac, Suva Reka, and Gora, each of which has its own OUP. Based on a February 1998 *Policajac* article, as well as awards issued to MUP officers after the war, the commander of Prizren SUP was Col. Gradimir Zekavica (and Lt. Milan Djuricic was section head of Prizren SUP's police department).[79] But there is conflicting information because, according to *Policajac*, in January 1999 a new Prizren SUP head was appointed: Col. Milos Vojnovic, who was also assistant chief of the police department in the Ministry of Internal Affairs.[80] As of February 1998, the chief of police in OUP Suva Reka was Lt. Dobrivoje Vitosevic and Sub-Lt. Radojko Repanovic was his deputy.[81]

Kosovska Mitrovica SUP covers Kosovska Mitrovica, Leposavic, Zvecane, Zubin Potok, Vucitrn, and Srbica, with OUPs in Srbica, Leposavic, and Vucitrn. The head of the SUP in 1998 (since 1996) was Col. Ljubinko Cvetic, formerly the police chief in Kragujevac and later also a spokeman of the Ministry of Internal Affairs in Kosovo. Section head of the Kosovo Mitrovica police department was Lt. Milorad Radevic.[82] In OUP Srbica, Major Branko Jaredic was the head and Capt. Milenko Bozovic was commander of the police.[83]

SUP Gnjilane covers the municipalities of Gnjilane, Kosovska Kamenica, Vitina, and Novo Brdo. Up to January 1999, the head of the Gnjilane SUP was Col. Vlada Milicevic. He was then replaced by Col. Dusan Gavranic, former head of the SUP in Zrenjanin (in Vojvodina, Serbia).[84]

The Pristina SUP covered Pristina, Glogovac, Kosovo Polje, Lipljan, Obilic, and Podujevo. The Glogovac OUP head was Petar Damjanac, and his deputy was Nebojsa Trajkovic ("Lutka"). The Urosevac SUP covered Urosevac, Stimlje, Strpce, and Kacanik, and was run by Bogoljub Janicijevic, according to residents of Urosevac.

In addition to these seven SUPs, individual policemen and probably police units from outside the province were also active in Kosovo, as shown by the list of policemen killed in Kosovo during 1998 and 1999 that is provided on the MUP website. In September 1998, for instance, five policemen were killed in a landmine incident near Likovac. All of them were from the Novi Sad SUP, although it is not clear whether they were regular or special police (either the PJP or SAJ).[85] Police units from Pozarevac were apparently also engaged in Kosovo, as evidenced by the killing of a policeman from Pozarevac, Milan Tenic, in Kosovo on April 24, 1998.[86] Policemen from Pancevo, Serbia were also killed in Kosovo in 1998.[87]

Within the MUP were also many local militia and reservist groups, such as Munja ("Lightning") in Pec, which was responsible for the massacre in Cuska village on May 14, 1999 (see Pec Municipality). The group had a reputation for violence and criminality. According to Munja members who spoke with journalists from the United States radio documentary company American RadioWorks, the Yugoslav Army supplied them with food and ammunition, as well as travel documents to allow them to pass checkpoints. One Munja member called "Branko" said:

> We would get a list of names of people to arrest. If they resisted, we killed them. Some Albanians paid money, protection money. We knew who we should move out and those we shouldn't.[88]

The Serbian Ministry of Internal Affairs also contains the state security service (SDB), otherwise known as the secret police, which was organized into directorates and sectors. The state security's role in the wars of the former Yugoslavia generally and Kosovo in particular should not be underestimated. The SDB maintained a large network of operatives and informants in Kosovo, among them many ethnic Albanians. KLA commanders claimed

Vidomir Salipur, a Pec policeman who was killed by the KLA on April 8, 1999, is standing in the center of the back row wearing a cap. Allegedly the head of a local Pec militia called "Munja", or Lightning, Salipur had a reputation for brutality against ethnic Albanians. To his right is a man witnesses identified as Nebojsa Minic, who is implicated in the extortion and killing of six family members in Pec on June 12 (see Pec Municipality). The date and location of the photograph are unknown, as are the identities of the other men. © HUMAN RIGHTS WATCH the SDB had in some cases successfully infiltrated the KLA (and sometimes used these claims to justify the torture and summary executions of suspected ethnic Albanian spies).

During late 1998 and 1999, the director of state security was Col. Gen. Radomir Markovic, formerly head of the Belgrade SUP. (As mentioned above, Markovic was arrested in February 2001.) Markovic's deputy was Maj. Gen. Nikola Curcic, who was also the director of the Institute for Security, according to the MUP website at the time. In Kosovo, the head of the SDB was David Gajic.[89] According to the U.K. Ministry of Defense, there were three main SDB centers in Kosovo: Pristina, Prizren, and Gnjilane.[90] According to Suva Reka residents, the head of the local SDB in Suva Reka was "Misko" Nisevic (see Suva Reka Municipality). According to Djakovica residents, the local head of state security was Sreten Camovic (See Djakovica Municipality).

"Frenki's Boys kill everything. Believe me, you do not want to see them."

—Serbian policeman

Radomir Markovic was appointed SDB head on October 27, 1998, replacing Jovica Stanisic, a long-time confidante of President Milosevic. There is speculation that Stanisic's dismissal was related to his disapproval of policy in Kosovo. Some analysts also believe that Stanisic was at odds with Milosevic's powerful wife, head of the Yugoslav United Left Party (JUL) Mira Markovic.

The precise role and organization of the SDB remains murky, although its surveillance and military activities in Kosovo are indisputable, both before and during the war. Most notorious was the SDB's special operations force, the JSO (Jedinice za Specijalne Operacije—Special Operations Unit), which was very active in Kosovo. The commander of the unit during the war was Milorad Lukovic, a man better known as "Legija."[91] According to Serbian press reports, Ulemek changed his last name in 1997 from Ulemek to Lukovic.[92] A central figure in the JSO organization, if not its

An undated photo of Col. Gen. Radomir Markovic, head of Serbia's State Security Service from late 1998 to early 2001.

PHOTO COURTESY OF VREME

founder, was Franko "Frenki" Simatovic: a common nickname for JSO fighters was "Frenki's Boys." The JSO was also sometimes called the "Red Berets" which has caused some confusion, because the VJ's Special Forces Corps has gone by the same name.

The JSO often appeared in the uniforms of other military or police units, and were known for carrying large knives, as well as their distinctive Australian-style cowboy hats, something many witnesses reported seeing. The JSO also had a reputation for ruthlessness. In the words of a Serbian policeman who spent six months in Kosovo in 1998, interviewed by Human Rights Watch in Belgrade, "Frenki's Boys kill everything. Believe me, you do not want to see them."[93] According to a VJ soldier who spoke with Human Rights Watch in September 1998, the JSO was operating on the border with Albania around Decani.[94]

American RadioWorks interview with "Milos," who claimed he belonged to Frenki's Boys.

MILOS: We were a special unit of the secret police. I got to Kosovo a few weeks before the NATO bombing. We expelled Albanians from areas that had been the strongest bases for the fighters. Not to exterminate them, but to drive them out for good. The least harmful thing that happened in the war was when the army arrived and said you have two hours to get out. Those were the lucky Albanians.

There were many Albanian terrorists. We were outnumbered. And the most powerful armies of the world start bombing you—it's a totally exceptional situation. Anything goes.

We were a special unit. But the paramilitary groups—I call them gangs. Everything below us, the army and the police, they were gangs. Nevertheless, there was some control. These groups were all given their zones of operation. They were allowed to do what they wanted. They were put into places intentionally and told to do what they wanted to get the job done. It was their job to kill and rape and do what they liked.

I think a man who is prepared to rape and mutilate civilians, someone who would attack a village just to massacre civilians, whatever nation that man is from that person brings no honor to his nation. I would liquidate them immediately. No courts, just executions.

According to the U.K. Ministry of Defense, the JSO had between 400 and 500 men, mostly recruited from the VJ's special forces.[95] The Serbian media has written that the JSO was a unit assembled in special circumstances whose members wear "a variety of uniforms with emblems that are officially not in use by any police or army units in the province."[96] *Vreme* magazine claimed that the JSO, formed in 1991, did not have more than 300 members. Armed with the most up-to-date weapons, the group reportedly trained at Kula (near Vrbas), which was bombed by NATO during the war, as well as at other camps near the Tara river.[97] Unconfirmed reports claim that during the NATO bombing the JSO was based at the Dubrava prison near Istok, which NATO bombed on May 19 and 21 (see Istok Municipality).

The background of Frenki Simatovic is enigmatic. Various reports on Kosovo have cast him as a commander of the state security's special operations or an assistant head of the state security service.[98] An article on the JSO by Belgrade-based journalist Dejan Anastasijevic and Andrew Purvis for Time.com claims that Simatovic, then a young Yugoslav intelligence officer, was tasked in 1991 with setting up a paramilitary force closely connected to the state security apparatus for Belgrade to use in Croatia. The article concludes: "Simatovic's solution was to set up a small unit of ex-policemen, exconvicts and other self-proclaimed volunteers who would answer only to Serbian secret police."[99]

Milorad Lukovic (or Ulemek) remained in charge of the JSO after the fall of the Milosevic government in October 2001, raising suspicions about the organization's role in the country's political changes. Serbian newspapers suggested that Lukovic (or Ulemek) had pledged his support to the new Serbian Prime Minister Zoran Djindic. On May 6, 2001, however, the Serbian Ministry of Internal Affairs announced that JSO commander "Milorad Lukovic" had been suspended from duty due to a violent incident at a disco club in the town of Kula. Disciplinary proceedings and a criminal suit are to follow, the ministry announced.[100] According to the newspaper *Danas,* a group of JSO members had gathered in the club to celebrate the JSO's tenth anniversay.[101]

The Serbian SDB is also believed to have assisted and armed paramilitary forces in Kosovo, as they did in Bosnia and Croatia, although the nature of this work remains unclear. The U.K. Ministry of Defense has maintained that Simatovic has a "long history of organizing, arming, and directing Serbian paramilitaries in the Bosnian war and now in Kosovo."[102]

In an interview, a former member of the Serbian state security told

American RadioWorks that the SDB had helped strengthen command and control over paramilitary forces in Kosovo through the provision of communications equipment:

> Initially, we received orders from the high command to provide some things for leaders of the paramilitary groups. Mobile phones, radio links, satellite communications. They already had weapons and ammo from the army. The communications were so they could be in direct contact with the command in Pristina.[103]

[Paramilitaries] operated in Kosovo with the approval and ongoing political and logistical support of the government.

According to KLA commanders who spoke with Human Rights Watch, the SDB had a good knowledge of KLA personalities and activities, largely from informants and infiltrators. Evidence suggests that the Serbian government was well aware of the militant movement among Kosovar Albanians throughout the 1980s and 1990s, including the first organized KLA actions in 1996.

Paramilitaries

In an interview with the Serbian newspaper *Vecernje Novosti,* former head of the Third Army Col. Gen. Nebojsa Pavkovic denied that there were any paramilitaries in Kosovo.[104] Witness statements collected by Human Rights Watch, OSCE reports, and numerous articles in the international media convincingly counter this claim. The composition and command structure of the various paramilitary forces and the precise connections they each had to the Serbian and Yugoslav governments remains unclear. But the evidence reveals that they operated in Kosovo with the approval and ongoing political and logistical support of the government, and often in close coordination with regular forces. There is little, if any, evidence to suggest attempts by the government to hinder paramilitary operations, despite repeated and credible reports that they had committed atrocities.

The paramilitary forces believed active in Kosovo include, but are not limited to, Arkan's Tigers,[105] Seselj's White Eagles,[106] and the Republika Srpska Delta Force, a group of police from Republika Srpska.[107] It is believed that many of these groups were armed and organized with assistance from the SDB. Unlike in Croatia and Bosnia, however, in Kosovo these paramilitary groups were mostly integrated into VJ or MUP units, rather than allowed to operate on their own.

According to the OSCE report on Kosovo, Arkan's Tigers are believed to have had a training camp between Leposavic and Kosovska Mitrovica, and the forces supposedly operated around Kosovska Mitrovica, Pec, Djakovica, and Prizren. The Republika Srpska Delta Force reportedly operated to the south of Gnjilane in early April.[108] The SDB unit known as Frenki's Boys are also sometimes referred to as paramilitaries.

According to witnesses, paramilitaries wore an array of uniforms—they were sometimes recognizable due to the lack of uniformity. Some had shaved heads while others had long hair with beards. They often wore black or red head scarves or bandannas, and carried hand axes or long knives on their belts.

Aside from being among the most violent forces in Kosovo, one of their primary activities was looting and theft. According to the OSCE report, some paramilitaries may have arrived in Kosovo in mid-February to prepare for the transportation of looted goods back to Serbia.[109]

At times, the police or army tried to warn or protect ethnic Albanian civilians from paramilitaries, although this was rare. One ethnic Albanian man who was forced to walk with a group of prisoners from Lipljan prison back to Pristina in May said that a policeman saved him from threatening paramilitaries. He told Human Rights Watch: "When we were coming back, we were stopped by paramilitaries and they wanted to kill us. A police officer hit one of the paramilitaries over the head with a gun. The police officer spoke Albanian to us, gave us water, and told us to hide in Pristina."[110]

After the war, some paramilitaries spoke with foreign journalists about their time in Kosovo. One man named "Dragan" said he fought with the Pitbull Terrier paramilitary unit, which was comprised of boxers from his home town in Niksic, Montenegro, who had also fought in Bosnia. Dragan said that his group killed fifty Albanians in retaliation for losing seven of their men.[111]

A *Wall Street Journal* reporter interviewed eight paramilitaries, ranging from a thug who was released from prison to fight to a Serbian nationalist who believed he was defending the homeland. One man, "Tony," said he fought with Arkan's Tigers. Local Kosovo officials, he said, gave his unit computer printouts with the names and assets of wealthy Albanians. Other units got lists of those to be executed. Another man identified as "Il Mon-

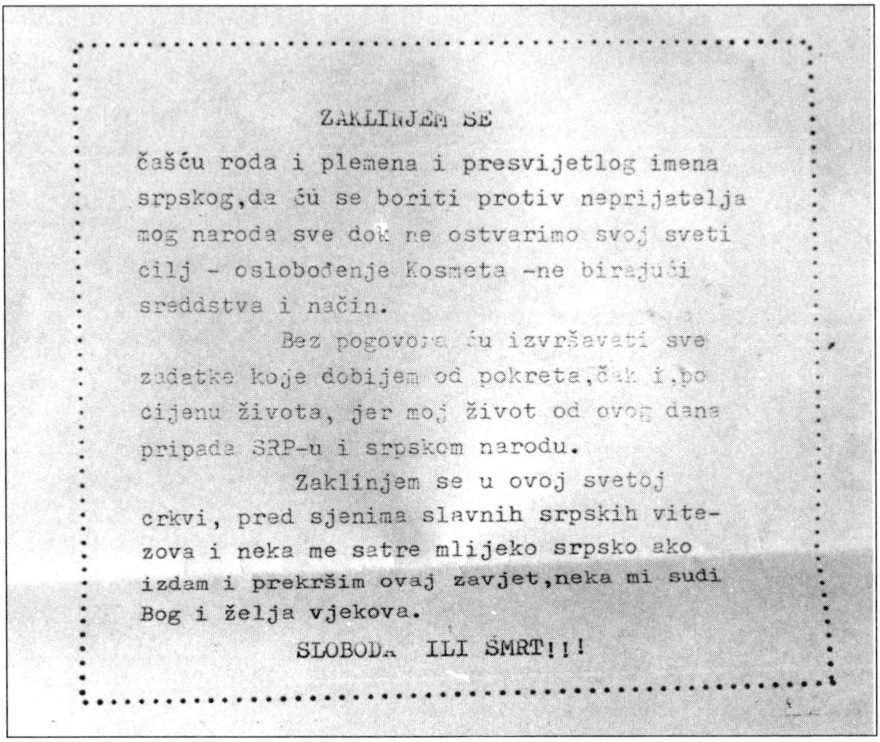

ZAKLINJEM SE

čašću roda i plemena i presvijetlog imena srpskog,da ću se boriti protiv neprijatelja mog naroda sve dok ne ostvarimo svoj sveti cilj - oslobođenje Kosmeta -ne birajući sreddstva i način.

Bez pogovora ću izvršavati sve zadatke koje dobijem od pokreta,čak i,po cijenu života, jer moj život od ovog dana pripada SRP-u i srpskom narodu.

Zaklinjem se u ovoj svetoj crkvi, pred sjenima slavnih srpskih vitezova i neka me satre mlijeko srpsko ako izdam i prekršim ovaj zavjet,neka mi sudi Bog i želja vjekova.

SLOBODA ILI SMRT!!!

© HUMAN RIGHTS WATCH

This oath was found in Pec after the war. It is not known whether "SRP" refers to a political group, paramilitary unit, local militia, or some other type of organization.

I SWEAR

On the honor of my family and clan and the most holy name of the Serbs that I will fight against the enemy of my people until we achieve our holy aim—liberation of Kosmet [Kosovo]—regardless of ways or means.

I will execute without question all tasks that the movement assigns to me, even at the expense of my own life, because my life from this day belongs to SRP and the Serbian people.

I take the oath in this holy church, before the shadows of famed Serbian knights, and let Serbian milk crush me if I betray or violate this oath, let God and the wish of the centuries judge me.

FREEDOM OR DEATH!!!

tenegrino" was offered early release from prison if he went to fight in Kosovo. He accepted along with sixteen of his twenty-five cell mates. A third paramilitary called "Jacques" said his unit acted on information from the army, the police, local Serbs, and Albanian collaborators.[112]

Another article in the U.S. press, based on more than a dozen interviews with paramilitary members, said that the units were acting on orders from state security, the MUP, and the VJ. In return for their services, paramilitaries were reportedly allowed to keep 10 percent of the goods they stole. Some of the fighters showed the journalist official MUP documents that allowed them to transport stolen goods back into Serbia. Some of the men denied that they had orders to rape women, but claimed that their commanders had done nothing to stop it.[113]

American RadioWorks produced a series of radio programs on war crimes in the Pec area, especially the massacre at Cuska village. Its reporters spoke with Serbian militia members, some of whom admitted taking part in the Cuska killing. One man, identified as "Marko," said that he had been released from a Serbian prison to fight in Kosovo with Arkan's Tigers. He said:

> Formally, Arkan didn't come to the prison. It was one of his men. He had a list of prisoners and their dossiers. They had to be the right profile. All he asked was if you were ready to go, to Kosovo . . . this wasn't a judge's, or a prison warden's decision. It was Arkan's. He is the law in Serbia.
>
> We would receive a list of names. Bring this person in alive or dead. I was assigned to arrest people, and had permission to kill them if necessary. You look at the guy, his attitude. If there's attitude, you might just kill him. I mean, there's no point in taking someone in who's just going to cause trouble . . .
>
> We interacted a lot with certain people at the MUP. There was a kind of crisis council, and some of the information came from there. The lists came from all over, police, city authority, because they had been collecting this kind of information for years. Who were the rich ones, where they lived, who were the important ones, where they lived. And we had local spies to help us on operations. We would use locals from a particular village to guide us, tell us where so-and-so lived, and they might get some money, if they were Serbs. We also had Albanian spies and Gypsies, too.[114]

In some places, local Serbs also participated in the "cleansing" campaign, although in no way can this be said for the Serbian population in Kosovo as a whole. Some local Serbs were reservists in the police, but village defense groups were also formed. Some Serbian villages in Kosovo had complained to the Serbian government in 1998 about the lack of protection from armed Albanians. The government responded by arming these individuals and groups. Armed local Serbs were apparently coordinated through the police, although some also joined paramilitary forces.

Although some of the most violent behavior was by local Serbs, there were also examples of local Serbs providing assistance to Albanians. Around Pec and Orahovac, for example, especially near the all-Serbian village of Velika Hoca, armed Serbs participated in the looting and burning of private property, as well as executions.

The most common criminal activity by local Serbs, however, was probably looting Albanian homes after security forces had swept through an area and the population had either fled or been expelled. Perhaps the most telling proof of looting comes from the diary of a Serbian woman from Pec, who recorded her observations during the war. The diary, found after the war by international journalists, says:

> They say these [the looters] are patriots who are breaking into the houses of Shiptars [derogatory word for Albanians], and a traitor is he who does not do that. Let them call me a traitor, but I will not stain my hands. I fear for the future of children whose parents teach them how to steal, how to loot, and to set houses on fire. What will come out of those kind of persons in the future? What recollections will they have of their childhood? They do not play soccer or roller-skate. Their play consists of breaking into homes and taking all they can carry, and then, with a liter of gasoline, destroying everything.[115]

According to many ethnic Albanians, members of Kosovo's Roma population also participated in crimes, and this is the justification most often given for their expulsion from post-war Kosovo (see Abuses After June 12, 1999). Indeed, the evidence collected in this report includes descriptions of a number of cases where local Roma collaborated with the police, army, or paramilitaries, either by guiding them through Albanian villages or by actively participating in crimes. But many Roma were also victims in the offensive, and it is patently wrong to blame the group as a whole for crimes during the war. A substantial number of Roma were expelled to Albania and

Macedonia. Others were killed by the government's security forces. Some Roma were forced by the government's security forces to work, such as the group in Djakovica that was ordered to pick up and bury bodies in the city. According to a report by the Humanitarian Law Center: "The Serbian police and local authorities forced Roma civilians, including minors, to bury the bodies of Albanian civilians and Kosovo Liberation Army members, to dig trenches for the military, and to pillage and destroy ethnic Albanian property."[116]

The local Serbs and Roma who committed crimes or collaborated with the security forces during the war are generally believed to have left Kosovo with the departing forces in early June 1999. Those who remained did so either because they believed in their innocence or because they were too old or poor to flee. They face exceedingly difficult conditions in post-war Kosovo, including harassment, abductions and murder (see Abuses After June 12, 1999).

Lastly, there are many reports of foreigners fighting with the Serbian and Yugoslav forces, as well as a few with the KLA. It is not known whether any of these individuals was paid for their services. Human Rights Watch interviewed more than a dozen witnesses who claimed to have seen Russian fighters among the Serbian forces, although no evidence has emerged to suggest official involvement by the Russian government. Some reports in the international media also described the presence of foreign fighters from Russia as well as from other countries.[117] An article in an Israeli newspaper, *Tel Aviv Yedi'ot Aharonot,* claimed that some forty Israeli citizens joined the "Serb foreign volunteers unit," most of them originally from the former Soviet Union and veterans of the wars in Afghanistan or Chechnya.[118] A male Danish citizen who claimed that he had fought with Serbian forces in Kosovo was arrested in Denmark after telling a Danish newspaper, *Extra Bladet,* that he had taken part in "ethnic cleansing." He was later released for lack of evidence.[119]

Chain of Command and Superior Responsibility

The chain of command for the Yugoslav Army is public. As set out in this chapter, local commanders in Kosovo reported to the commanders of the Pristina Corps, led by Maj. Gen. Vladimir Lazarevic. The Pristina Corps reported to the Third Army, commanded by Col. Gen. Nebojsa Pavkovic, who reported to the General Staff, commanded by Gen. Dragoljub Ojdanic. The overall commander of the VJ was Yugoslav President Slobodan Milosevic, who chaired the Supreme Defense Council.

The chain of command for the MUP is considerably less clear. While much of the de jure hierarchy has been presented in this chapter, there are still gaps, such as the relationship between the state security and paramilitary forces and the roles of the various MUP formations. Additional structures of command and control with the MUP and VJ probably existed.

In addition, the MUP's de jure structure does not necessarily reflect the de facto reality. The role of Serbia's Minister of Internal Affairs Vlajko Stojiljkovic, for instance, is considered by Serbian and foreign observers of the Serbian security structures to have been subordinate to that of President Milosevic and perhaps also to Yugoslav Deputy Prime Minister Nikola Sainovic, widely considered Milosevic's point-man on Kosovo.[120] Various lines of command and control within and between state security, public security, the paramilitary forces, and the president are still unknown. Lastly, the methods and structure of cooperation between the MUP and VJ also remain unclear, including a possible coordination center in Pristina.

Despite this, the case against the Serbian and Yugoslav leadership is convincing. The ICTY statute is clear on individual criminal responsibility for the leaders who organize or allow the commission of serious crimes. Article 7 of the statute says:

1. A person who planned, instigated, ordered, committed or otherwise aided and abetted in the planning, preparation or execution of a crime referred to in articles 2 to 5 of the present Statute, shall be individually responsible for the crime.

Nikola Sainovic, Yugoslav Deputy Prime Minister and high official of the Socialist Party of Serbia (SPS) during the Kosovo war at a press conference in Belgrade, October 13, 2000. Sainovic, widely considered Milosevic's representative on Kosovo, was indicted by the war crimes tribunal on May 27, 1999. AFP PHOTO

2. The official position of any accused person, whether as Head of State or Government or as a responsible Government official, shall not relieve such person of criminal responsibility nor mitigate punishment.

3. The fact that any of the acts referred to in articles 2 to 5 of the present Statute was committed by a subordinate does not relieve his superior of criminal responsibility if he knew or had reason to know that the subordinate was about to commit such acts or had done so and the superior failed to take the necessary and reasonable measures to prevent such acts or to punish the perpetrators thereof.

4. The fact that an accused person acted pursuant to an order of a Government or of a superior shall not relieve him of criminal responsibility, but may be considered in mitigation of punishment if the International Tribunal determines that justice so requires.[121]

In other words, both the direct perpetrator of a crime as well as the military or political leaders who ordered that crime can be prosecuted. Paragraph three adds that a superior is accountable for crimes committed if he or she failed to take steps to prevent such acts or to punish the perpetrators.

The extent and systematic nature of the crimes in Kosovo make it highly implausible that the Serbian and Yugoslav leadership did not know that crimes were being committed, despite their public denials.[122] Numerous statements by the Serbian and Yugoslav government or military demonstrate that the top leadership was regularly apprised of the security situation in Kosovo. Well distributed reports by the media and nongovernmental organizations, including Human Rights Watch, were repeatedly documenting abuses by Serbian and Yugoslav forces.

Serbian President Milan Milutinovic during a press conference in Paris on March 18, 1999. Milutinovic was indicted by the war crimes tribunal for crimes in Kosovo on May 27, 1999.

AFP PHOTO

At the beginning of the war, on March 26, 1999, for example, President Milosevic received top officials from the army and police, including Zoran Sokolovic, Yugoslav minister of internal Affairs, Vlajko Stojiljkovic, Serbian minister of internal affairs, Col. Gen. Vlastimir Djordjevic and Radomir Markovic, chiefs of public security and state security, respectively, as well as Col. Gen. Geza Farkas, chief of Yugoslav Army counterintelligence. In a statement issued after the meeting, the government said:

"Everything was well orchestrated over there."

—General Nebojsa Pavkovic

> The officials of internal affairs and security notified President Milosevic that all service organs as well as security services are functioning very well, and that their members perform the necessary tasks efficiently, responsibly and highly professionally. . . . It is estimated that the moral, patriotic consciousness and readiness of all the members of the internal affairs organs are on the highest level.[123]

On May 4, 1999, President Milosevic met with Gen. Ojdanic, Gen. Pavkovic, Maj. Gen. Sreten Lukic, and Serbian President Milutinovic, among others. The Ministry of Internal Affair's statement after the meeting said: "[I]t was concluded that all tasks directed towards the defense of the country, anti-terrorist combat and the establishment of the general security in Kosovo and Metohija are being successfully realized."[124]

In an interview with the U.S. television news show Frontline conducted after the war, General Pavkovic was asked if, during the NATO war, he had met with his political counterparts, like President Milosevic. The following exchange ensued:

> PAVKOVIC: Of course, I was present as a member of the top brass on many occasions, and I can tell you that there was a feeling of unity in the headquarters and amongst the people.
>
> FRONTLINE: What impression did Milosevic give you?
>
> PAVKOVIC: He is the top command, and as such, he knows the political and the military climate very well. He gave optimism to us soldiers as well as the people.
>
> FRONTLINE: Did you partake in the military planning of the pullout?
>
> PAVKOVIC: No, but I was in constant touch with the team that did. No decision could have been put through without our participation.[125]

In addition, all evidence suggests that, with a few localized exceptions, the police, army, and paramilitary units were under strict control, only operating with written orders from their commanders. The fact that all security forces withdrew from Kosovo in an orderly manner after the Military Technical Agreement with NATO was signed on June 10 further suggests that the forces were under the strict and effective command of their superiors. Indeed, in an interview given on January 16, 2001, to Belgrade's Radio B92, General Pavkovic said, referring to military operations in Kosovo, "everything was well orchestrated over there."[126]

There is also evidence to prove that local police stations were functioning during the war, dispelling claims that the governing structures had broken down. In Pec, for instance, the police kept careful records of deaths in the city, attributing most of them to "NATO bombs" or "terrorist acts", referring to the KLA.[127] Witnesses in various parts of Kosovo told Human Rights Watch that they saw police investigators inspecting crime scenes, such as in the village of Sudimlja after the killing of the Gerxhaliu family on May 31 (see Vucitrn Municipality).

The Serbian and Yugoslav leadership also had to have known about the actions of paramilitary forces operating in Kosovo. At the very least, the leadership knew of these forces' reputations for brutality in Croatia and Bosnia. Despite this, the authorities either deployed paramilitaries or allowed them to operate in Kosovo without taking any precautions to prevent their committing war crimes. With their reputations for brutality, dispatching a paramilitary force under certain leaders was tantamount to ordering excessive violence without having to issue an explicit command to do so.

This was reflected in the interview given on page 84 by a self-proclaimed member of "Frenki's Boys" to American RadioWorks. In the interview, the man identified as "Milos" says:

> We [Frenki's Boys] were a special unit. But the paramilitary groups—I call them gangs. Everything below us, the army and the police, they were gangs. Nevertheless, there was some control. These groups were all given their zones of operation. They were allowed to do what they wanted. They were put into places intentionally and told to do what they wanted to get the job done. It was their job to kill and rape and do what they liked.[128]

With a handful of exceptions at the lower levels, there were few cases in which the Milosevic government punished security forces for serious crimes or even placed anyone under investigation.[129] On the contrary, the postwar period saw hundreds of promotions and awards for police and army personnel who had served in Kosovo, including some of the top leadership. A more complete list of promotions and awards is provided as an appendix to this chapter. But some of the more prominent individuals commended or promoted for their work in Kosovo include:

- Dragoljub Ojdanic, Chief of the Army's General Staff, promoted to General of the Army (four stars) and, subsequently, Yugoslav Minister of Defense (a position he held until October 2000).
- Nebojsa Pavkovic, commander of the Third Army, promoted to Chief of the Army's General Staff.
- Maj. Gen. Vladimir Lazarevic (one star), commander of the Pristina Corps, promoted to Major General (two star).
- Col. Bozidar Delic, commander of the 549th Motorized Brigade, promoted to One Star General.
- Col. Radojko Stefanovic, commander of the 52nd Mixed Artillery Brigade, promoted to Brigadier General.
- The Order of the War Flag was given to the 243rd Mechanized Brigade, the 211th Armored Brigade, and the 15th Armored Brigade.
- President Milosevic presented the Order of Freedom to Army General Dragoljub Ojdanic and Col. General Nebojsa Pavkovic, Commander of the Third Army.
- President Milosevic presented the Order of the National Hero to the following VJ brigades: the 125th Motorized Brigade (accepted by Commander of the Brigade, Col. Dragan Zivanovic), the 549th Motorized Brigade (accepted by commander of the Brigade, Col. Bozidar Delic), and the 37th Motorized Brigade (accepted by commander of the Brigade, Col. Ljubisa Dikovic).
- The Order of the Yugoslav Flag of the First Degree was given to Col. General Vlastimir S. Djordjevic, head of MUP Public Security, Obrad M. Stevanovic, head of police special forces, and Sreten Lukic, head of MUP forces in Kosovo.
- Obrad Stevanovic and Sreten Lukic were promoted to Major Generals in the police.
- Assistant Ministers of Internal Affairs Nikola Curcic, Stojan Misic, and Petar Zekovic, were all promoted.

- The Order of the Yugoslav Flag of the Third Degree was given to Col. Zivko Trajkovic, commander of the SAJ.
- The Order of Merit in Matters of Defense and Security of the First Degree was given to Col. Dragutin Adamovic, Djakovica SUP; Col. Dusan B. Gavranic, Gnjilane SUP; Col.Gradimir R. Zekavica, Prizren SUP; Lieutenant Col. Milan S. Djuricic, Prizren SUP; and Maj. Milenko M. Bozovic, Srbica police commander.
- President Milosevic awarded the Order of the Yugoslav Flag to Zoran Andjelkovic, president of the Temporary Executive Council of Kosovo and Metohija, Nikola Sainovic, Deputy Prime Minister of the Yugoslav Government, Col. Gen. Vlastimir Djordjevic, Maj. Gen. Obrad Stevanovic, and Maj. Gen. Sreten Lukic.
- Decoration of the Yugoslav Flag First Class was given to Vlajko Stojiljkovic, Serbian minister of internal affairs, and Col. Gen. Radomir Markovic, assistant to the minister and chief of state security.

In addition to these promotions, public statements by Milosevic, both while he was president and afterwards, repeatedly praised the security forces for their actions in Kosovo without any mention of crimes that were committed. On November 25, 2000, at a special congress of the Serbian Socialist Party, Milosevic declared that the four other Serbian and Yugoslav leaders indicted by the war crimes tribunal were "national heroes."[130] On May 13, 1999, known as "Security Day" in Serbia, then-President Milosevic extended congratulations to the country's security forces.

> You have achieved great success in crushing the separatist movement and its terrorist gangs in Kosovo and Metohija, which had the support of the foreign powers which have also committed criminal aggression on our country. Many members of the security authorities and services have bravely died in that battle and they are a shining example of courage and loyalty to their people and their country.
>
> With your high sense of patriotism, loyalty and professionalism, you have thwarted the activities of the enemy forces and prevented them from undermining the strength of our defense.
>
> Congratulating you on your holiday, I wish to express my conviction that you will continue, just as so far, honorably, professionally and in the spirit of the freedom-loving traditions of our people to carry out your duties in the

defense of the sovereignty, territorial integrity, independence and the constitutional order of the Federal Republic of Yugoslavia.[131]

After the war, there was very limited discussion within Serbia of crimes committed by government forces, although this is changing with the fall of the Milosevic government in October 2000. Two individuals who attempted to present the issue in public while Milosevic was still in power both faced retaliation by the government. On July 26, 2000, a journalist with Agence France Presse, *Danas* newspaper, and the Institute for War and Peace Reporting, Miroslav Filipovic, was sentenced to seven years in prison by a military court for espionage and spreading false information. He was released on October 10. Filipovic had written about the role of government forces in abuses against Albanians in Kosovo. In July 2000, an outspoken and well-respected human rights activist, Natasa Kandic, was threatened with legal action by the Yugoslav Army after she condemned the Filipovic verdict and spoke out about "the horrors [VJ] generals sent young recruits to witness in Kosovo."[132]

Although the process of dealing with the past will take time, there have been some promising steps inside Serbia since Milosevic's fall. The local media is beginning to report more openly—and without fear of retribution—on atrocities by Serbian forces, a truth commission sponsored by new Yugoslav President Vojislav Kostunica has been initiated, and the VJ has begun legal proceedings against more than 150 VJ soldiers for their actions in Kosovo. Most notably, in April 2001, Serbian police arrested Slobodan Milosevic on charges of corruption. On June 28 he was transferred to the war crimes tribunal in The Hague.

STRUCTURE AND STRATEGY OF THE KLA

Since World War II, small groups of militant Albanians had sought Kosovo's independence from Yugoslavia, although their activity and impact were minimal. Some of these organizations, such as the Levizja Popullore per Republiken e Kosoves (People's Movement for the Republic of Kosovo) and later the Levizja Kombetare per Clirimin e Kosoves (National Movement for the Liberation of Kosovo) gained strength in the 1980s, especially after the government's crackdown in 1981. Support was provided by Kosovar Albanians living abroad, as well as through illegal activities by Kosovar Albanians in the Balkans and Western Europe.

Throughout the 1990s, the majority of the population pursued the peaceful politics of Ibrahim Rugova, but a fringe element of militants was active in some areas, especially Drenica. As repression in Kosovo continued, the movement gradually gained members and, as noted above, the initial fragments of the Kosovo Liberation Army were, by 1996, attacking police outposts in Kosovo. The flow of weapons from Albania in 1997, after the government there fell, greatly assisted the nascent insurgency.

A crucial turning point came with the police crackdown in Drenica in February and March 1998, in which more than eighty civilians were killed. The brutality of the Serbian government radicalized the Albanian community. Many villagers turned to the KLA either out of frustration with Rugova's ineffective nonviolent approach or because they saw the KLA as

KLA press conference in Kosovo on March 13, 1999. Seated are Fatmir Limaj (left), member of the General Staff, Hashim Thaci (center), member of the General Staff and political representative of the KLA, and Sylejman Selimi (right), member of the General Staff and chief military commander. One month later, Selimi was replaced by Agim Ceku, a former brigadier general in the Croatian Army. AFP PHOTO their only means of protection. At the same time, some villages clearly did not encourage the presence of the armed group, since they feared it would provoke a government response, which it often did.

Throughout early 1998, the KLA was primarily a disorganized collection of armed villagers, often built around family structures, without a clear chain of command. Strong regionalism dominated the organization, as evidenced by the post-war splintering of the insurgency. Operational areas raised their own funds and purchased their own weapons.

This changed gradually throughout the year as the KLA secured a steadier arms supply and organized itself into a more centralized structure.[133] Ethnic Albanians with experience in the Yugoslav Army or its predecessor in the former Yugoslavia, the Yugoslav National Army (Jugoslovenska Narodna Armija, or JNA), gradually joined the insurgency. Contacts with Western governments, mostly through KDOM or the KVM, were strengthened. The ceasefire period from December 1998 to March 1999 was used to strengthen the central command and to reorganize operations. By March 1999, the KLA was a better organized rebel force, albeit with strong personalities in the various regions who did not always agree with one another. A military police force and military courts were more firmly established with detention facilities, along with civilian political structures that issued decrees in areas under KLA control.

By 1999, the main political representative of the KLA was Hashim Thaci (a.k.a. Snake), who represented the insurgency at political negotiations such as the Rambouillet conference in February 1999. In April 1999, Agim Ceku, an ethnic Albanian former brigadier general in the Croatian Army with close ties to the United States government and military, was appointed head of the KLA's General Staff, making him the chief military commander.[134] He replaced Syleman Selimi (a.k.a. Sultan). Both Ceku and Thaci sat on the KLA's General Staff (Stafi i Pergjithshem), the main decision-making body of eighteen people, along with many of the other key members of the insurgency.[135]

The KLA was organized into seven operational zones, each with a regional commander and chief of staff: Drenica (Glogovac, Srbica, Malisevo, and Klina municipalities), Shala (Kosovska Mitrovica), Dukagjin (Pec, Prizren, Decani, and Djakovica municipalities), Llap (Podujevo), Nerodine (Urosevac), Kacanik, and Pastrik. Prominent among the regional commanders were Ramush Haradinaj in the Dukagjin zone, Ekrem Rexha (a.k.a. Commander Drini) in the Pastrik zone,[136] Rrustem Mustafa (a.k.a.

Remi) in the Llap zone, and Sami Lushtaku in Drenica. Each region had brigades and companies, usually based around a village or series of villages.[137] Rexhep Selimi was head of the military police and Kadri Veseli (a.k.a. Luli) was head of the KLA's secret service, that later became known as the Sherbimi Informativ i Kosoves (SHIK).

There are no known cases of KLA soldiers having been punished for committing abuses against civilians.

Given the regional divisions within the KLA, a central chain of command was sometimes difficult to discern. Even within the operational zones, it was not always clear how much control the various commanders had over their troops.

On the other hand, as 1998 progressed, regionally-based and central command structures were increasingly discernible. Local commanders initiated military actions and issued decrees within their areas of responsibility. The military police and courts were functioning, albeit haphazardly, in areas of KLA control. The General Staff coordinated military actions and political activities to an extent throughout Kosovo, a structure which allowed decisions to be transmitted down to the fighters. It also coordinated logistical and financial support from Albania and the Albanian diaspora in Western Europe and the United States.

Although there were often examples to the contrary, KLA fighters in late 1998 and early 1999 displayed discipline, manning checkpoints, checking identification papers, and adhering to orders from their commanders. A KLA office in Pristina (allowed to function by the authorities) distributed passes to allow foreign journalists and human rights researchers access to areas under KLA control.

Despite these structures, there are no known cases of KLA soldiers having been punished for committing abuses against civilians or government forces no longer taking active part in hostilities. It is clear that in certain cases, such as the September 1998 murder by KLA forces of thirty-four people near Glodjane, that the local commanders must have known, if not directly ordered, the killings. There were, however, reported but unconfirmed cases of KLA soldiers being disciplined by their own commanders for having harassed or shot at foreign journalists.

In interviews and public statements, KLA spokesmen repeatedly expressed the organization's willingness to respect the rules of war. In an interview given to the Albanian-language newspaper *Koha Ditore* in July 1998, KLA spokesman Jakup Krasniqi said:

> From the start, we had our own internal rules for our operations. These clearly lay down that the KLA recognizes the Geneva Conventions and the conventions governing the conduct of war.[138]

KLA Communique number 51, issued by the KLA General Headquarters on August 26, 1998, stated that, "The KLA as an institutionalized and organized army, is getting increasingly professional and ready to fight to victory."[139]

In November 1998, Human Rights Watch representatives had a meeting in Banja village near Malisevo with Hashim Thaci and Fatmir Limaj to discuss the KLA's commitment to the laws of war generally and, specifically, the treatment of Serbian civilians in KLA custody. The KLA representatives informed Human Rights Watch that the KLA had a soldiers' code of conduct but that it could not be made public. Disciplinary measures for abusive soldiers were in place, they said, but no details were provided.

The precise size of the KLA was difficult to calculate given its loose organization, the participation of village defense forces, and the continual ebb and flow of Albanians from abroad. Perhaps the best indication comes from the International Organization for Migration (IOM), which was mandated after the war with registering and assisting former combatants. According to the IOM, as of March 2000, it had registered 25,723 ex-combatants, although it's certainly possible that this number was inflated by noncombatants looking for assistance.[140] Some international volunteers are known to have fought with the KLA.[141]

After the Drenica killings in March 1998, major fundraising for the KLA was conducted among the Albanian diaspora communities in Europe and the United States, with money flowing through the Homeland Calling Fund. Various reports in the media have also linked the KLA's fundraising to drug trafficking, money laundering, and migrant smuggling.[142]

Ramush Haradinaj, former KLA commander of the Dukagjin Operational Zone, became chairman of a political party, Alliance for the Future of Kosovo (AAK), after the war. Here he speaks at an election rally in Pristina on September 22, 2000. AFP PHOTO

Lightly armed in comparison to Serbian and Yugoslav forces, the KLA remained a mobile guerrilla force throughout 1998 and 1999, choosing mostly to attack police or army checkpoints or lay ambushes, and then retreat. The only large scale offensive, an attack on Orahovac in July 1998, failed miserably, as the government retook the town after two days.

Throughout the conflict, the KLA engaged in military tactics that put ethnic Albanian civilians at risk; specifically, attacking Serbian checkpoints or patrols near ethnic Albanian villages, exposing civilians to revenge attacks. It is a troubling fact that the 1998 and 1999 Kosovo war was marked by well-publicized massacres of civilians, such as in Prekaz, Gornje Obrinje, and Racak, which were all turning points in the war. All of the evidence shows that these crimes were committed by habitually brutal Serbian and Yugoslav forces, but it is clear that the KLA understood the political benefit of publicizing civilian deaths.

A number of top KLA officials and officers hold important positions in post-war Kosovo. Hashim Thaci became head of the Democratic Party of Kosovo. Agim Ceku was named head of the Kosovo Protection Corps (Trupat e Mbrojtjes se Kosoves (TMK) in Albanian), the successor to the KLA, where some other former KLA commanders also hold important positions, such as Sylejman Selimi. Ramush Haridinaj left the Kosovo Protection Corps in 2000 to form a political party, Alliance for the Future of Kosova. Some KLA commanders and fighters have continued their military activities in Macedonia with the National Liberation Army (Ushtria Clirimtare Kombetare).

APPENDIX: Post-War Promotions of Serbian Police and Yugoslav Army Members

On May 13, 1999, then-Serbian President Milan Milutinovic promoted Sreten Lukic (identified as "Leader of the Headquarters of the Ministry of Internal Affairs in Pristina") to Police General (two star). On the same occasion, then-Minister of Internal Affairs Vlajko Stojiljkovic promoted seventy-two officers and 307 sub-officers of the police.[143]

On June 7, 1999, Yugoslav President Milosevic commended 911 members of the MUP for "the suppression of terrorism in Kosovo and defense of the country from aggression." Among those who received awards were three generals, seventeen colonels, seventeen lieutenant colonels, twenty majors, thirty captains, forty-five lieutenants, thirty-seven sub-lieutenants, fifty sergeant majors, 652 noncommissioned officers and forty members of other parts of MUP.[144]

Some of the leadership was honored in particular. The Order of the Yugoslav Flag of the First Degree was awarded to Col. Gen. Vlastimir S. Djordjevic, Col. Gen. Obrad M. Stevanovic, and Col. Gen. Sreten D. Lukic.

The Order of the Yugoslav Flag of the Third Degree was awarded to Col. Zivko Trajkovic, commander of the SAJ. The Order of Merit in Matters of Defense and Security of the First Degree was awarded to Col. Dragutin Adamovic, head of Djakovica SUP (also listed as Novi Sad SUP) and Jr. Sgt. of the First Order Vidomir N. Salipur, who was notorious in and around Pec for his brutality against ethnic Albanians (see Pec Municipality).

Also in June 1999, former president and "supreme commander" Slobodan Milosevic issued a decree on promotions, decorations, and appointments for three thousand officers, noncommissioned officers, soldiers, and civilians serving the Yugoslav Army.[145] This included giving the Order of the National Hero to the following VJ brigades: the 125th Motorized Brigade, the 549th Motorized Brigade, and the 37th Motorized Brigade.

Among the notable promotions, Dragoljub Ojdanic was promoted to General of the Army. Vladimir Lazarevic, commander of the Pristina Corps, and Ljubisa Stojimirovic, Chief of Staff of the Third Army, were both promoted to the rank of Major General.

"For the phenomenal successes and exceptional results in directing and commanding over the VJ in combat for defense of the freedom and sovereignty of the homeland against aggressors," the Order of Freedom was awarded to General of the Army Dragoljub Ojdanic and Col. Gen. Nebojsa Pavkovic.[146]

"For manifestations of bravery, determination, self-sacrifice, discipline and responsible execution of martial tasks, in which they served as an example to other members of their units," the Order of Bravery was awarded to Maj. Gen. Vladimir Lazarevic, commander of the Pristina Corps. Lazarevic also received the Order of the War Flag of the First Degree two months prior to receiving this reward. The Order of Bravery was also given to the following members of the Third Army:

- Bgd. Gen. Milan N. Djakovic, Member of the Third Army
- Col. Milivoje P. Branic, Member of the Third Army

- Col. Zoran M. Jablanovic, Member of the Third Army
- Col. Miloje R. Miletic, Member of the Third Army
- Col. Dragan S. Petrovic, Member of the Third Army
- Col. Radojko M. Stefanovic, Member of the Third Army
- Col. Veroljub J. Zivkovic, Member of the Third Army
- Lt. Col. Simo R. Ivosevic, Member of the Third Army
- Lt. Col. Stojan O. Konjikovac, Member of the Third Army
- Lt. Col. Pera V. Petrovic, Member of the Third Army
- Maj. Zoran M. Bojkovic, Member of the Third Army
- Maj. Uros V. Nikolic, Member of the Third Army
- Maj. Radivoje Dj. Paravinja, Member of the Third Army
- Maj. Ljubisav D. Stojanovic, Member of the Third Army
- Cpt. of the First Order Ljubisa S. Vucetic, Member of the Third Army
- Cpt. of the First Order Zoran R. Raseta, Member of the Third Army
- Cpt. of the First Order Boban R. Rajkovic, Member of the Third Army
- Cpt. Dragan L. Lukic, Member of the Third Army
- Cpt. Jovica L. Milak, Member of the Third Army
- Cpt. Perica B. Nastasijevic, Member of the Third Army
- Cpt. Milos R. Ralevic, Member of the Third Army
- Cpt. Cedo S. Trpkovski, Member of the Third Army
- Cpt. Sladjan D. Hristov, Member of the Third Army
- Lt. Boban S. Kuzmanovic, Member of the Third Army
- Lt. Nikola M. Mijatovic, Member of the Third Army
- Sub. Lt. Nenad M. Popovic, Member of the Third Army
- Snr. Sgt. of the First Order Radisa V. Ilic, Member of the Third Army
- Snr. Sgt. Zeljko J. Alar, Member of the Third Army
- Snr. Sgt. Branko N. Vukovic, Member of the Third Army
- Sgt. Aleksandar R. Rakovic, Member of the Third Army
- Jr. Sgt. Ivan S. Niciforovic, Member of the Third Army
- Cor. Branislav M. Fungerhut, Member of the Third Army
- Soldier Dragan R. Belosevic, Member of the Third Army
- Soldier Milan M. Bogdanovic, Member of the Third Army
- Soldier Veroljub M. Mijatovic, Member of the Third Army
- Soldier Sasa T. Pejic, Member of the Third Army
- Soldier Milinko M. Pendic, Member of the Third Army
- Soldier Nikola R. Popovic, Member of the Third Army

On July 7, 1999, another batch of MUP employees was decorated, according to *Politika,* for "outstanding results accomplished in direction of units of the police, manifestations of bravery, determination and discipline in carrying out security tasks by stopping terrorism in Kosovo and Metohija and in defense of the country from aggression, in which they acted as an example to other individuals and members of the police."[147] In particular, the Order of the National Hero was awarded to the 124th Intervention Brigade of the Special Police Units. The Order of the Yugoslav Flag of the Third Degree was awarded to Col. Zoran B. Simovic, former commander of the SAJ, and Col. Zivko T. Trajkovic, commander of the SAJ. The Order of Merit in Matters of Defense and Security of the First Degree was awarded to the following MUP official in Kosovo:

- Col. Dragutin R. Adamovic—Djakovica SUP
- Col. Dusan B. Gavranic—Gnjilane SUP
- Col. Gradimir R. Zekavica—Prizren SUP
- Lt. Col. Milan S. Djuricic—Prizren SUP (head of police department)
- Maj. Milenko M. Bozovic—Srbica police commander

Former Yugoslav President Slobodan Milosevic, by decree, appointed Bgd. Gen. Radojko Stefanovic to the post of commander of the Pristina Corps of the Third Army of the Yugoslav Military. The man who had been occupying this post, Maj. Gen. Vladimir Lazarevic was promoted to the Chief of Command Headquarters of the Third Army.[148]

Many other members of the VJ were promoted and appointed to new posts by decrees of President Milosevic. They included Negosav Nikolic, commander of the Nis Corp from the Third Army, promoted to Maj. Gen., Col. Bozidar Delic, commander of the 549th Motorized Brigade, promoted to Brigadier General, and Col. Radojko Stefanovic, commander of the 52 Mixed Artillery Brigade, promoted to Brigadier General.

Maj. General Ljubisa Stojimirovic was appointed as the Chief of Staff of the First Army. The Order of the War Flag was awarded to the following brigades:

- The 243rd Mechanized Brigade
- The 211th Armored Brigade
- The 15th Armored Brigade

President Milosevic also presented the highest possible decorations of the

Federal Republic of Yugoslavia—The Order of Freedom, The Order of the National Hero, The Order of the Yugoslav Flag, and The Order of the War Flag of the First Degree to top commanders in Kosovo.[149]

The Order of Freedom was awarded to:

- General of the Army Dragoljub Ojdanic.
- Col. Gen. Nebojsa Pavkovic, Commander of the Third Army.

The Order of the National Hero was awarded to:

- The 125th Motorized Brigade of the VJ; accepted by commander of the Brigade, Col. Dragan Zivanovic.
- The 549th Motorized Brigade of the VJ; accepted by commander of the Brigade, Col. Bozidar Delic.
- The 37th Motorized Brigade of the VJ; accepted by commander of the Brigade, Col. Ljubisa Dikovic.
- The 63rd Parachuting Brigade of the VJ; accepted by commander of the Brigade, Lt. Col. Ilija Todorov.
- The 124th Intervention Brigade of the Police; accepted by commander of the Brigade, Col. Zarko Brankovic.

The Order of the Yugoslav Flag was awarded to:

- Zoran Andjelkovic, President of the Temporary Executive Council of Kosovo and Metohija
- Nikola Sainovic Deputy Prime Minister of the Yugoslav Government
- Col. Gen. of the Police Vlastimir Djordjevic.
- Maj. Gen. of the Police Obrad Stevanovic.
- Maj. Gen. of the Police Sreten Lukic.

On May 13, 2000, Security Day, President Milosevic decorated 135 members of the MUP. Decoration of the Yugoslav Flag First Class was given to Vlajko Stojiljkovic, Serbian minister of internal affairs, and Col. Gen. Radomir Markovic, assistant to the minister and chief of state security.[150]

On July 5, 2000, Serbian President Milan Milutinovic promoted some of the Ministry of Internal Affair's top officials. Assistants to the minister, Nikola Curcic, Stojan Misic, and Petar Zekovic were all promoted to the rank of major general.[151]

An ethnic Albanian man surveys the destruction in Kosare (Koshare) village.

PHOTO BY ALBAN BUJARI

4

MARCH–JUNE 1999: AN OVERVIEW

On March 24, 1999, the eyes of the world turned to Kosovo as aircraft from the North Atlantic Treaty Organization began to bomb targets in the Federal Republic of Yugoslavia. The start of NATO's air war against Yugoslavia was also the beginning of the bloodiest period in Kosovo since the end of the Second World War. In the twelve weeks that followed, Serbian and Yugoslav military, police, and paramilitaries expelled more than 850,000 ethnic Albanians from Kosovo, internally displacing several hundred thousand more.[1] Many were robbed and beaten as they were forced from their homes, which were frequently looted and burned. Scores of women were raped. Thousands of adult males were detained, and many of them were executed, in some cases together with women, children, and the elderly, although the total number of civilians executed is still unclear (see section on Death Toll below). In more than a dozen mass killing sites, government forces tried to hide the evidence by destroying or removing bodies. The brutal campaign against ethnic Albanian civilians came to a halt only after the withdrawal of Yugoslav soldiers and Serbian police and paramilitaries and the entry of NATO forces on June 12, 1999.

Many observers mark the date of the NATO air war as the beginning of the Serbian and Yugoslav campaign. While March 24 saw a marked intensification of the campaign, the start of the operation actually came four days earlier, on March 20, when the monitors of the OSCE Kosovo Verification Mission (KVM) withdrew en masse from Kosovo. Most of the remaining international nongovernmental organizations evacuated their personnel at the same time. The departure of the KVM, together with international aid workers, deprived Kosovo not only of some of its most important witnesses, but also ended any deterrence that the presence of the OSCE verifiers might have provided.[2] According to the OSCE report on its work in Kosovo from October 1998 to June 1999, based in part on interviews with refugees during the NATO bombing, "the level of incidents of summary and arbitrary killing escalated dramatically immediately after the OSCE-KVM withdrew on March 20."[3]

As the Background chapter of this book demonstrates, the abuses after March 20, 1999, were a continuation and intensification of the attacks on civilians, displacement, and destruction of civilian property carried out by Serbian and Yugoslav security forces during 1998 and the first months of 1999. By March 1999, the combination of fighting and the targeting of civilians had left an estimated 1,500–2,000 civilians and combatants dead.[4] More than 200,000 Albanian civilians were internally displaced, almost 70,000 Albanians had fled the province to neighboring countries and Montenegro, and a further 100,000 Yugoslav nationals, mostly Kosovar Albanians, had sought asylum in Western Europe.[5] Thousands of ethnic Albanian villages in Kosovo had been partially or completely destroyed by burning or shelling.[6]

The state-organized campaign that began in late March 1999 was nevertheless different in scale and scope than the violence that had occurred in 1998 and early 1999. Earlier operations by Serbian and Yugoslav security forces were directed at areas and families in Kosovo with ties to the KLA. Although the actions undertaken by Serbian police and Yugoslav soldiers in the Drenica region and southwestern Kosovo were egregious (in that they targeted civilians, illegal under international humanitarian law), they could be understood as brutal counterinsurgency against the KLA rebels.

The operations that began in late March 1999 went far beyond counterinsurgency: Serbian and Yugoslav forces carried out a systematic campaign of violence and forcible depopulation that left an estimated 80 percent of the civilians displaced from their homes.[7] Areas with no history of support for the KLA and which had previously escaped the violence in Drenica and southwestern Kosovo, such as Pristina and eastern Kosovo, were targeted for mass expulsion. The killing and terror against civilians began to encompass any area with a current or historic link to the KLA, as well as some areas without any such link. In short, localized counterinsurgency was joined by systematic "ethnic cleansing."

Despite the scale of the displacement during 1998 and early 1999, many observers believed Kosovo, with its 90 percent ethnic Albanian population, would be exempt from large-scale ethnic cleansing, if only for the practical obstacles to the expulsion of an entire people. In ethnically-mixed Bosnia and Herzegovina, and contested areas of Croatia where no one ethnic group had an absolute majority, the expulsion of one ethnic group was a means of consolidating control over that territory by a rival group. By contrast, Kosovo with its overwhelming ethnic Albanian majority had experienced a steady outflow of its Serb population over preceding decades, with Belgrade resorting to forced resettlement of Croatian Serbs in an attempt to reverse the migration of Serbs out of the province. The slow initial response of UNHCR and NATO to the human tide of refugees into Macedonia and Albania in late March and early April is evidence that few in the international community believed the government of Slobodan Milosevic would attempt the "ethnic cleansing" of Kosovo.[8] Many observers also believed that Milosevic would quickly capitulate once NATO airstrikes began.

The operations that began in late March 1999 went far beyond counterinsurgency.

If the conventional wisdom among Western observers held that "ethnic cleansing" was unlikely in Kosovo, what is the explanation for the systematic mass expulsion of the province's Albanian population by Serbian and Yugoslav forces between March and June 1999? Was it a coordinated plan or a spontaneous reaction to the NATO bombing? Although only Slobodan Milosevic and his top aides know the real explanation for the "ethnic cleansing" of Kosovo, several strong theories have emerged.

First, evidence suggests that the Milosevic government began preparing a large-scale anti-insurgency campaign to crush the KLA back in September 1998, long before anyone suspected NATO airstrikes, when the summer offensive was coming to a close (see Background). After routing the KLA from some of its strongholds—and influenced by growing international criticism and the onset of winter—the government halted the offensive and accepted the KVM monitors.

Between October and December 1998, a number of key individuals in the security apparatus were either removed or promoted, including the dismissal of Jovica Stanisic, head of Serbian state security, and Momcilo Perisic, chief of the army's general staff. A loyalist, Gen. Dragoljub Ojdanic, replaced Perisic, and Col. Gen. Nebojsa Pavkovic was promoted to commander of the Third Army, which had responsibility for southern Serbia and Kosovo. These changes, along with others in the Yugoslav Army and Serbian Ministry of Internal Affairs, suggest that a new strategy on Kosovo was being devised.

December 1998 and January 1999 saw a gradual increase of security forces in Kosovo, in violation of the KVM agreement, but without serious criticism from the international community. The killing of forty-five ethnic Albanians in Racak provoked an international outcry, but the Serbian and Yugoslav buildup inside Kosovo continued unabated. According to the OSCE, paramilitary groups were set up in Kosovo in February to organize transportation routes for looted goods.[9] The buildup continued during the negotiations in Rambouillet, France, including the arming of local Serbs. According to the OSCE, which still had its monitors in Kosovo, February 6–23 saw "a significant build up of VJ forces throughout Kosovo leading to the arming of civilians and the training of reservists, the arrival of anti-aircraft weapons, the digging of tank pits and the preparation of demolition explosives along key routes in from the south and an increase in military air activity."[10]

The first attacks on KLA strongholds in the rural areas began immediately after the KVM departed on March 20, and these involved indiscriminate attacks on villages. According to the OSCE, emphasis was also placed on the strategically important route to the west of Vucitrn that links Kosovo to Serbia proper.

The character and intensity of the campaign appeared to change, however, after the commencement of NATO bombing. On March 24 began the full-scale cleansing of cities, such as Pec in Kosovo's southwest, and later Pristina, as well as the burning of Djakovica's old town. March 24–26 saw an aggressive operation to secure the southwest border with Albania, which involved large-scale displacement accompanied by killings of civilians.

While this evidence suggests that a powerful anti-insurgency campaign had long been in preparation before the NATO bombing, it seems that the Milosevic government took advantage of NATO air strikes to further impose terror on Kosovo's Albanian population and to expel large numbers of ethnic Albanians from the province. Using the pretext of the NATO bombing, the government was free to unleash a full-scale offensive on the KLA as well as to order the expulsion of more than 850,000 Kosovar Albanians.

One explanation is simply revenge. As hundreds of refugees testified, government forces repeatedly told them to "Go to NATO!" Unable to strike back at NATO air power, government forces took their vengeance on the civilian population. But the systematic nature of the expulsions contradicts this theory; clearly, there was a well-conceived plan to "ethnically cleanse" large portions of the Albanian population. Revenge was nothing more than an added factor to motivate the troops.

One credible theory is that Belgrade intended permanently to alter the demographic composition of Kosovo by expelling a large proportion of Kosovar Albanians—a strategy that had occasionally been proposed by Serbia's far-right, including former Serbian Deputy Prime Minister and head of the Serbian Radical Party Vojislav Seselj.[11] This explanation is supported by the multiple accounts from refugees arriving in Albania of document confiscation and destruction and the removal of car license plates at the border. This so-called "identity cleansing" documented by Human Rights Watch and other organizations gathering testimony in Albania strongly suggests an attempt by Belgrade to strip Kosovo Albanians of their citizenship and to frustrate future efforts to return home.[12]

A second explanation for the "ethnic cleansing" is that it was designed to destabilize the neighboring countries of Albania and Macedonia. In March 1999, the young state of Macedonia, with two million inhabitants, at least 25 percent of whom are ethnic Albanian, was widely perceived as unstable and, at the same time, as a pivotal country for regional stability. The mass influx of refugees from Kosovo could easily have disrupted the fragile ethnic balance, if not destablized the entire country.[13]

Although Albania did not have these ethnic tensions to contend with, its stability had been repeatedly threatened in the 1990s by political and economic upheaval. The influx of more than 400,000 refugees could have pushed the impoverished country into turmoil.

There was a well-conceived plan to "ethnically cleanse" large portions of the Albanian population.

With luck, none of these scenarios played out. There can be little doubt that the arrival of some 260,000 refugees from Kosovo placed an enormous strain on relations between ethnic Macedonians and ethnic Albanians in Macedonia. The government's go-slow policy in admitting refugees during the spring of 1999, the occasional police violence against the refugees, and the government's periodic refusal to admit additional refugees[14] created enormous resentment and anger among Macedonia's Albanians. Equally, the common cause shown by Macedonian Albanians for their Albanian neighbors from Kosovo fueled fears about succession among ethnic Macedonians. The restraint shown by the leadership of the Albanian party in the ruling coalition, the Albanian Democratic Party, as well as the NATO presence, certainly helped prevent open conflict in Macedonia in the spring of 1999.

In Albania, the refugees were accepted with open arms. Despite difficult economic conditions, especially in northern Albania, refugees were successfully accommodated in refugee camps and private homes. The country even experienced an economic boom due to the influx of foreign humanitarian aid organizations, NATO, and the media.

Destabilizing Macedonia and Albania may also provide a third explanation for the "ethnic cleansing"—to weaken the resolve of the NATO alliance to continue the air war. It was clear from the outset that some members of the alliance, such as Italy, France, and Greece, were apprehensive about the airstrikes. Belgrade may have hoped that the flood of refugees would convince governments and the public that the bombing had made the situation worse, if not directly caused the refugee flow. (The Yugoslav government repeatedly claimed that the refugees were fleeing NATO bombs.) If this was Belgrade's intention, it badly failed: the "ethnic cleansing" and the need to reverse it became the strongest justifications for NATO's actions and helped to galvanize support among the alliance and the public to continue the bombing. Extensive media coverage of the expulsions, invoking images of Nazi deportations, helped solidify NATO support, notably during periods of intense criticism over civilian casualties by NATO and the bombing of the Chinese embassy in Belgrade.[15] The refugee crisis handed NATO its greatest evidence that this was a war in defense of human rights.

Some commentators have suggested that the forced expulsion of Kosovo's Albanian population was an attempt by Belgrade to create conditions for the partition of Kosovo, presumably areas bordering Serbia in the northern and eastern parts of the province to be retained by Belgrade. The existence of such a plan, however, remains unclear since the expulsions were generally heaviest in those areas with high KLA activity rather than along any of the lines proposed as possible partition borders.

Finally, the "ethnic cleansing" apparently served some militarily strategic objectives. Villages in areas where the KLA was active, such as around Podujevo, Malisevo, and Djakovica, were cleared because of the logistical support they were providing to the KLA. Since it was difficult to discern between combatants and civilians, government forces drove the entire populations from many of these areas, essentially "draining the sea," to better engage the rebels. The one exception is the Drenica region, where many civilians were prevented from leaving the area and used as human shields.

Expelling refugees to Macedonia and Albania might also have been intended to tie down NATO forces in those countries and to hamper a possible ground invasion. Likewise, the crisis in Albania might have been an attempt to disrupt supply lines and hinder incursions by the KLA, who were based in the northern part of the country.

THE GEOGRAPHY OF ABUSES

Beyond the systematic "ethnic cleansing" of Kosovo, some parts of the province were disproportionately affected—suffering the mass execution of civilians, rape, torture, and the destruction of civilian property through arson and looting. Many of these areas had already witnessed violence during 1998 and early 1999. The documentation and analysis of the abuses in these towns and villages form the main body of this report. (See Statistical Analysis of Violations for a study of Kosovo's most impacted municipalities.)

Areas with historic ties to the KLA were hardest hit. The municipalities of Glogovac and Srbica in the Drenica region, the cradle of the KLA, were the scene of multiple massacres of civilians, as well as arbitrary detentions, use of human shields, and the destruction of civilian property (see Drenica Region). With the exception of a mass expulsion from Glogovac town, most Drenica residents were prevented from fleeing, or unwilling to leave the area. Mass killings, expulsions, and the destruction of civilian property were also common in the municipalities of Djakovica, Orahovac, Prizren, and Suva Reka in the southern border area, where many of the villages had historically supported the KLA. (There are no reports of mass expulsion or killings among the almost exclusively Muslim Slav population of the southern-most municipality of Gora (Dragash).) With close ties to neighboring northern Albania, the southwestern region was the principal conduit for KLA weapons, supplies, and

Areas with historic ties to the KLA were hardest hit.

trained recruits, and it was across the Albanian border that hundreds of thousands of civilians were expelled over the course of a few weeks during the spring of 1999. The slaughter and terrorizing of civilians and the destruction of their homes in these municipalities between March and June 1999 can be understood, at least in part, as a continuation of the effort to eliminate the KLA's base of support in the civilian population that began in early 1998.

Explanations for the concentration of abuses in other municipalities investigated in detail by Human Rights Watch are more complex and less conclusive. The municipalities of Pec and Lipljan, both of which had significant Serb populations, were targeted for mass expulsion, but killings were more localized. Although the KLA was active in the Pec municipality and present in the western-most part of Lipljan municipality during 1998, there is little or no evidence to tie the KLA to some of the villages in which massacres occurred. The killings may simply have been designed to terrorize the remaining population into fleeing Kosovo, with the majority from Pec crossing into Montenegro and most of those from Lipljan being sent to Macedonia. Whatever the case, the frequent acquaintance between perpetrators and victims in these ethnically-mixed municipalities sets them apart from Drenica and southwestern Kosovo, where Albanians had scant familiarity with their tormenters. There was little KLA presence or violence during 1998 in the ethnically-mixed western municipality of Istok, for example. Nevertheless the municipality suffered mass expulsions of its Albanian residents into Montenegro and the burning and looting of their homes. Istok was also the scene of one of the bloodiest incidents of a bloody spring, when more than ninety Albanian inmates in the Dubrava prison were killed by unknown perpetrators in May 1999 after two days of NATO airstrikes that had already killed an estimated nineteen inmates (see Istok Municipality). By contrast, a massacre of more than one hundred civilians in the municipality of Vucitrn, as the villages around Sudimlja (Studime) were being forcibly expelled from Kosovo into Albania, appears almost certainly tied to the presence of KLA fighters in the area. Many of Vucitrin's residents were also expelled, some toward Albania and others toward Macedonia.[16]

In other municipalities in Kosovo during the spring of 1999 (not covered in detail by this report), the picture is generally one of mass expulsion combined with more limited numbers of killings and other abuses. In northern

Kosovo, the municipalities of Leposavic (Leposaviq), Zvecan, and Zubin Potok were relatively untouched, as reflected in the chapter on statistics, a fact mostly attributable to the majority Serb population in each.[17] The Albanian-majority municipality of Kosovska Mitrovica (Mitrovice) was less fortunate. The ethnically-mixed and eponymous capital of the municipality, which has since become the most potent symbol of post-war ethnic division in Kosovo, was the scene of conflict between the KLA and Serbian security forces beginning in 1998.[18] As elsewhere, the departure of the OSCE was followed by an increase in killings of Albanians and the forced expulsion to Albania of much of the town's Albanian population.[19]

Fighting between the KLA and Serbian security forces also occurred in the municipality of Podujevo (Podujeve) to the east of Mitrovica, although this region is less covered in this report. The violence and the accompanying crackdowns that began in September 1998 led some of its residents to flee to Pristina in December of that year.[20] Tensions rose further in March 1999, notably in Podujevo town, with much of the remaining population expelled towards Macedonia or fleeing into the nearby hills, where a large number of displaced persons had taken shelter.[21] The ethnically-mixed municipalities of Obilic (Obiliq) and Kosovo Polje (Fushe Kosove) had also witnessed some sporadic fighting during 1998, much of it linked to the seizure of a mine in the village of Grabovac (Graboc) in Kosovo Polje municipality.[22]

Following the departure of the KVM, events in both Kosovo Polje[23] and Obilic[24] followed a similar pattern, with much of the Albanian population forcibly expelled to Macedonia. The railway station in Kosovo Polje was also used as a transit point for the expulsion of tens of thousands of Albanians to Macedonia by train. The village of Ade (Hade) appears to have been singled out for punishment, perhaps because of an association with the KLA: five men from a single family in the village were executed and four of the corpses set on fire.[25] A week later the entire population was forced to board buses and was expelled to Macedonia and Albania.[26]

The eastern municipalities of Klina (Kline) and Decani also suffered the forced expulsion of much of their Albanian populations during late March and early April. Ethnically-mixed Klina to the immediate west of the Drenica region had witnessed fighting between the KLA and Yugoslav and Serbian security forces during 1998. Much of the municipalities Albanian majority was expelled to Albania on March 31 and April 1, 1999.[27] The predominantly Albanian population of Decani had also experienced KLA activity as well as substantial internal displacement prior to March 1999. Many of its inhabitants were expelled to Albania over the month of April 1999.[28]

March 1999 saw a broadening and deepening of the conflict in Kosovo to encompass areas that had previously experienced little violence and which had few links to the KLA.

March 1999 saw a broadening and deepening of the conflict in Kosovo to encompass areas that had previously experienced little violence and which had few links to the KLA. Kosovo's capital Pristina is a case in point. Although Pristina was spared the large-scale killing that occurred to the west in Drenica during the spring of 1999, a large proportion of the city's population was expelled towards Macedonia in the first wave of "ethnic cleansing" in late March and early April 1999. Robbery and looting were also widely reported, although far fewer properties were burned than in Pec or Djakovica. The eastern municipalities of Gnjilane (Gjilan) and Kosovska Kamenica (Kamenice) suffered a similar fate: although they largely escaped the killing and burning, thousands of their Albanian residents were expelled from their homes during April and May, with many robbed and detained on their way to the Macedonian border. (Little is known about the experience of the tiny Serb-majority municipality of Novo Brdo, which lies to Gnjilane's west.)

Municipalities close to the Macedonian border were not known for their links to the KLA, although the border was used by the group for smuggling weapons and supplies and was a focus of Yugoslav counterinsurgency efforts. Once the conflict broadened, however, Yugoslav and Serbian security forces moved quickly to expel or otherwise displace the population away from the border, with frequent reports that villages were being shelled and burned. Preparation for a NATO ground invasion may be one explanation.

The municipality of Kacanik, on the Macedonia border, had been mostly quiet during 1998. According to the OSCE KVM, the KLA moved into the area in February 1999, and armed clashes were reported between Yugoslav and Serbian security forces and the KLA in a number of villages during February and March.[29] Efforts by the Yugoslav army and Serbian police to expel villagers to Macedonia began almost immediately following the departure of the OSCE, but many residents were reluctant to leave, leading to substantial and rapidly shifting internal displacement in the municipality before residents were forced into Macedonia in April 1999.[30] There were also a number of killings in the municipality, notably in the village of Kotlina (Kotlino) where twenty-five men were executed (some of them members of the KLA) before the residents were expelled.[31]

The municipality of Urosevac (Ferizaj) to the north also experienced mass expulsion within weeks of the KVM departure. By mid-April, thousands of Urosevac residents were sheltering in camps in Macedonia, although a few were also forced to go to Albania.[32] The railway line in Urosevac town made the municipality a convenient staging point for deportations from southern Kosovo into Macedonia. The ethnically-mixed border municipality of Strpce (Shterpce) experienced similar patterns of displacement to Kacanik, at least in its eastern half and other areas with Albanian populations. While initially resisting expulsion by moving from village to village, most of the municipality's Albanian inhabitants were in refugee camps in Macedonia by mid-April 1999.[33] Many of the Albanian residents of Vitina (Viti) municipality, on the border to the east of Kacanik, were also expelled to Macedonia in early April 1999.

THE KILLINGS

Executions of ethnic Albanians took place throughout Kosovo. As the chapter on statistics makes clear, the vast majority of the victims were males, although females and children were not exempt. In numerous cases, such as the Vejsa household in Djakovica on April 1, the Gerxhaliu family in Donja Sudimlja (Studime e Poshtme) on May 31, or the Berisha household in Suva Reka on March 26, young children were killed along with adults. The statistics chapter also reveals how the killings generally occured in three distinct waves (see Graph 5).

Witness testimonies suggest three general motives for killings. The first was to expedite the "cleansing" process. Typically, security forces would shell and then enter a village, ordering the Albanian population to leave. A few individuals might be killed to spread panic and accelerate the deportation.

The second motive was to target individuals suspected of participating in or assisting the KLA. In village after village, security forces separated the men from the women and children, and interrogated the men about the insurgency, sometimes detaining them for days. As interviews with witnesses and survivors confirm, as well as statements in the international media given by Serbian and Yugoslav forces after the war, men suspected of KLA involvement were often shot on the spot. Such suspicion could be based solely on the fact that the man was of fighting age. Men were sometimes forced to strip, such as in Bela Crkva, to look for military uniforms under their civilian clothes, injuries from combat, or even dirt on their hands to suggest fighting. Since it was often difficult to distinguish civilians from KLA, not to mention village guards, government forces often took no chances, and killed those they thought might be a threat.

Witness testimonies suggest three general motives for killings. The first was to expedite the "cleansing" process. . . . The second motive was to target individuals suspected of participating in or assisting the KLA. . . . A third factor was revenge.

In other cases, prominent political leaders, community activists, or wealthy individuals were specifically targeted. As the chapter Forces of the Conflict makes clear, paramilitary units sometimes had lists of those to be killed, provided by local officials or the police.

A third factor was revenge. In certain cases, such as Meja near Djakovica or the Tusus neighborhood of Prizren, large-scale killings took place after the KLA had killed Serbian or Yugoslav forces. In Drenica, the killings in Vrbovac and Stutica occurred in late April immediately after NATO bombed the Feronikel plant, where security forces had been based.

Lastly, while most of the expulsions and killings were carefully planned, there are also cases where forces went out of control, especially volunteers or paramilitaries. The general lawlessness in Kosovo during the NATO bombing allowed for criminals and thugs to extort, rob, and kill with impunity. With very few exceptions, the government did nothing to stop these people. On the contrary, paramilitaries were dispatched to Kosovo despite their reputation for brutality, and some criminals were even released from prison if they agreed to go to Kosovo to fight.

DEATH TOLL, THE MISSING AND BODY REMOVAL

More than two years after the end of the war, the total number of victims killed between March and June 1999 remains unclear. Although the explanations for the lack of clarity in the death toll are straightforward and common to many post-conflict situations, the total number of dead remains one of the most controversial aspects of the war. Ultimately, however, what matters is not whether the dead number 5,000 or 15,000, but that large numbers of civilians were targeted for execution by Serbian and Yugoslav security forces.

One reason for the number controversy is the exaggerated claims made by NATO and NATO governments during the war. Some U.S. officials, including Secretary of Defense William Cohen and State Department Special Envoy on War Crimes David Scheffer suggested that up to 100,000 Albanian men were missing and feared dead.[34] Such figures contrast with the more measured U.S. government and NATO estimates from the same period of between 3,000 and 4,000, based on refugee accounts.[35] After the war, head of the U. N. administration in Kosovo, Bernard Kouchner, said that "around 11,000 people" had died, although his press office later backpedaled from that estimation.[36] Still, the unproven claims by top government officials at the height of the war led to charges of propaganda to justify NATO intervention both by journalists and by NATO's political opponents in the West.[37] These allegations also fueled predominantly left-wing critics of Western policy towards the former Yugoslavia, some of whom dispute that the mass exodus of Albanians was caused by Serbian government forces and even that mass killings of Albanian civilians occurred.

The more direct reason for the uncertainty, however, is a deliberate attempt on the part of the Serbian and Yugoslav government to destroy evidence and remove bodies. Both the ICTY and Human Rights Watch have documented cases where bodies were disinterred and removed from the crime scene, in an apparent attempt to conceal the killing. A radio documentary broadcast on National Public Radio in the United States on January 25, 2001, called *Burning the Evidence,* claims that Serbian and Yugoslav forces systematically transported the bodies of Kosovar Albanians to the mining complex at Trepca near Kosovska Mitrovica, where they were incinerated. Citing Serbian fighters and "a well-placed Serbian intelligence officer," between 1,200 and 1,500 bodies were destroyed at Trepca, according to the report.[38]

The credible allegations of body removal and destruction were apparently confirmed in May 2001, when the Serbian government announced that a truck filled with eighty-six bodies had been dumped in the Danube River in Serbia during the Kosovo war—allegedly the bodies of ethnic Albanian civilians taken from Kosovo. A top Serbian Ministry of Internal Affairs official announced on May 25 that Milosevic had ordered then-Interior Minister Vlajko Stojiljkovic to eliminate "all traces which could lead to any evidence of crimes" in Kosovo.[39] As of July 2001, the Serbian authorities had announced the discovery of four additional graves in Serbia with as many as 1,000 Kosovar Albanian bodies.

[There was] a deliberate attempt on the part of the Serbian and Yugoslav government to destroy evidence and remove bodies.

As of July 2001, the ICTY had exhumed approximately 4,300 bodies, far less than the 11,334 bodies initially reported to the ICTY by Kosovar Albanians.[40] According to the International Committee of the Red Cross, as of April 2001, 3,525 people remain missing from the conflict — the vast majority of them Kosovar Albanians.[41]

Between June and November 1999, ICTY teams exhumed 2,108 bodies from 195 grave sites. During the second phase of exhumations, between April and November 2000, forensic experts examined another 325 sites and found an additional 1,577 bodies and 258 incomplete remains. In her November 2000 address to the U. N. Security Council, ICTY Chief Prosecutor Carla Del Ponte stated that the provisional total of exhumed bodies was "almost 4,000 bodies or parts of bodies." It should be noted, however, that the ICTY apparently made no distinction between combatants and non-combatants, and that in some areas the KLA was present among the civilian population (eg: in the Vrbovac-Stutica area of Drenica during the April 30 offensive that left dozens of ethnic Albanians dead).

Of crucial importance, however, are the statements about grave tampering made by Del Ponte in both her 1999 and 2000 address to the Security Council. In 1999, after exhuming 2,108 bodies, she said:

> This figure [2,108 bodies] does not necessarily reflect the total number of actual victims, because we discovered evidence of tampering with graves.

There are a significant number of sites where the precise number of bodies cannot be counted. In these places, steps were taken to hide the evidence. Many bodies have been burned, but at those sites the forensic evidence is nevertheless consistent with the accounts given by witnesses of the crimes.[42]

Testimony on the removal of bodies

"Early in the morning I heard a truck come from Leshan. I heard them stop, and they opened the metal doors, and I knew they came to take the bodies. I heard when they put them in the truck, and I heard the Serbs complain about the smell. They put them all in, and went back to Leshan . . . In the evening, I went out into the yard of Musli, and saw they had taken all the bodies, there was just one children's jacket left in the yard."

Human Rights Watch interview with N.B., Trnje, Kosovo, August 29, 1999

"On April 24 I saw the Serbs come and take the bodies away. Two civilian trucks came. Besides trucks, they used a small bulldozer. There were men wearing medical outfits and masks. They took the bodies away toward Rahovec [Orahovac] in the two trucks. Not to know where the bodies are hidden is, for us, as if they've been killed again."

Human Rights Watch interview with T. K., Pusto Selo, Kosovo, June 26, 1999

"Four days after the killings [in Velika Krusa], the Serbian police arrived with bulldozers, a truck, and some army vehicles. They collected corpses and took them away. We weren't able to film this. We don't know what they did with the bodies."

Human Rights Watch interview with R.E., Kukes, Albania, June 8, 1999

"Evidence of tampering, should such evidence become available, is, in fact, excellent circumstantial evidence of guilt. . . . If one can trace where the order to tamper came from, it permits a pretty strong inference that it was done for the purpose of hiding the truth, which demonstrates consciences of guilt."

Former ICTY Chief Prosecutor Louise Arbour quoted in Agence France Press, "Don't Tamper with Evidence, UN Prosecutor Tells Belgrade," January 21, 1999

In the next year's address, Del Ponte stressed that "it will never be possible to provide an accurate figure for the number of people killed, because of deliberate attempts to burn the bodies or to conceal them in other ways."[43]

Sites at which the ICTY has reported clear evidence of grave tampering include Izbica, Trepca, Mala Krusha and Crkolez (Cerkolez). Human Rights Watch, the OSCE, and other organizations documenting violations of humanitarian law and human rights have also collected evidence of grave tampering and other efforts to conceal evidence of killings by Yugoslav and Serbian forces prior to June 12, 1999. These include the removal of bodies, the reinterring of bodies from mass graves into individual graves, the burning of corpses, and the removal or exchange of clothing and personal effects in order to complicate the process of identification.

Human Rights Watch gathered credible testimony relating to grave tampering in Mala and Velika Krusa, Pusto Selo, Slovinje, Poklek, Kotlina, Rezala (Rezalle), Izbica, Trnje (Trrnje), and Djakovica, where at least seventy-seven bodies were removed from the town cemetery. In Trnje near Suva Reka, between twenty-four and thirty-six village men were killed by Serbian forces on March 25. Four days later, a witness saw unidentified men taking the bodies away on a truck. He said:

> Early in the morning I heard a truck come from Leshane [Lesane in Serbian]. I heard them stop, and they opened the metal doors, and I knew they came to take the bodies. I heard when they put them in the truck, and I heard the Serbs complain about the smell. They put them all in, and went back to Leshane.[44]

In Slovinje, Human Rights Watch visited a temporary grave site outside the village in which the sixteen victims of an April 16 killing had been buried by their relatives the following day (see Lipljan Municipality). The bodies were later removed by Serbian security forces with excavation equipment, and the relatives have no information about the remains. In Poklek, the estimated forty-seven victims of an April 17 killing were first machine-gunned before hand-grenades were thrown into the room where they lay (see Drenica Region). Several other corpses were pulled from the garden well. Finally the house was set on fire. Relatives showed a Human Rights Watch researcher a box of human bones reportedly collected from the room during a July 1999 visit to the site. In the village of Kotlina, Human Rights

Watch saw a wooded site where Serbian security forces had attempted to conceal evidence of the killing of twenty-two men by putting their bodies into two deep natural wells and dropping explosives into the holes.

There have been two scientific studies to address the question of how many Albanians were killed. The first study, released in June 2000 by the U.S. Centers for Disease Control,[45] is an epidemiological analysis of all deaths in Kosovo during 1998 and 1999. It concludes based on its household surveys and pre-war mortality rates that an estimated 12,000 persons died as a result of "war-related trauma." It is important to emphasize, however, that the study includes 1998 (when approximately 1,500 Albanians were killed as a result of the conflict) and does not undertake the difficult distinction between civilians and combatants.

The second study, *Political Killings in Kosova/Kosovo,* published in October 2000 by the Central and East European Law Initiative (CEELI) of the American Bar Association and the American Association for the Advancement of Science (AAAS), concluded that approximately 10,500 Kosovar Albanians were killed between March 20 and June 12, 1999, with a 95 percent confidence interval from 7,449 to 13,627.[46] The report further analyzes the timing and location of the killings, showing that the killings correlated closely with the flow of refugees out of Kosovo (see Statistical Analysis of Violations).

TARGETED KILLINGS

In addition to the general killings that took place throughout Kosovo, some prominent Kosovar Albanians were specifically targeted for execution. A number of politicians, doctors, human rights activists, and other public figures were killed in this way, as well as individuals who had worked with the OSCE or rented their homes to the organization.

The first reported case was the murder of a well-known human rights lawyer, Bajram Kelmendi, and his two sons, Kushtrim and Kastriot, aged eighteen and thirty-one. Bajram was active with the Council for the Defense of Human Rights and Freedoms and had been providing information during 1998 to the war crimes tribunal. He was highly respected for his skills as a defense attorney in numerous politically-motivated trials over the previous decade.[47] Most recently, he had defended the Albanian-language newspaper *Koha Ditore,* which was on trial for publishing a statement by the KLA's political representative, Hashim Thaci.

On the night of March 24, the beginning of the NATO bombing, five uniformed policemen forced their way into the Kelmendi house on Vellusha Street in Pristina.[48] According to Kelmendi's wife, Nekibe Kelmendi, herself a prominent lawyer, Kastriot called the police to tell them that someone had broken into their home, but the police hung up the receiver. Nekibe tried to call and they hung up on her as well. The family was forced to lie down, and Bajram was hit in the stomach. The police searched the house but didn't steal anything. Around 1:30 a.m., Bajram, Kushtrim, and Kastriot were taken away in Kastriot's car. Kushtrim was told that he should "kiss his children for the last time."

Nekibe tried without success to get information about her husband in the police stations and hospitals of Pristina. She also contacted Natasa Kandic, executive director of the Humanitarian Law Center, one of Yugoslavia's most respected human rights groups, who publicized the abduc-

Përkujtime 31

Dje, u bënë katër muaj nga dita kur gjakatarët shuan me dhunë jetën e më të dashurve tanë

BAJRAM (SOKOL) KELMENDI (1937 - 1999)

KASTRIOT (BAJRAM) KELMENDI (1968 - 1999)

KUSHTRIM (BAJRAM) KELMENDI (1982 - 1999)

Ditët po kalojnë me peshë plumbi, dhimbja për Ju vetëm sa po rëndohet. Ishit të mençur e të vendosur, ishit njerëz të vërtetë. E deshët atdheun Tuaj, pa u frikësuar nga vdekja. Armiku shfryu urrejtjen më të egër ndaj jush, por mbetët të papërkulur. Përjetë të jetëve do të mbeteni të dashur e të gjallë në zemrat tona.

Ju kujtojmë me mall, me dashuri e me respekt të përjetshëm: Nekibja, Kosovarja, Vjollca, Elena, Sokoli, Anyla dhe Fadili.

Prominent human rights lawyer Bajram Kelmendi and his two sons, Kastriot and Kushtrim, were murdered by Serbian security forces on the night of March 24, 1999.

COURTESY OF KOHA DITORE

tion. On the morning of March 26, Nekibe received word that the bodies of Bajram and her two sons had been found at a gas station on the Pristina road leading to Kosovo Polje. All three had been shot.

The murder of Bajram Kelmendi and his sons terrorized Pristina and Kosovar Albanian professionals—anyone with a public profile as a politician, human rights activist, journalist, artist, or academic. Panic spread in Pristina out of fear that unaccountable forces would liquidate prominent members of Kosovar Albanian society. Upon receiving news of Kelmendi's death, many Albanians decided to leave Kosovo.

Other prominent Albanians were killed in different parts of Kosovo around the same time. On March 25, Serbian security forces broke into the home of a respected physician in Djakovica, Dr. Izet Hima, and shot him in front of his wife. A well-known lawyer, Urim Rexha, and an LDK leader, Mark Malota, were also killed in Djakovica that day (see Djakovica Municipality). Two high level LDK activists in Mitrovica were also killed in unclear circumstances: Agim Hajrizi and Latif Berisha.

On March 27, unknown security forces reportedly took into detention the LDK secretary in Kosovo Polje, along with his wife and another Albanian family which lived nearby. According to the OSCE's report on Kosovo, the males were beaten badly in detention. They were released on March 28 and eventually made their way to Macedonia. On April 4, the LDK secretary, who is not named in the OSCE report, died from his wounds in a hospital in Tetovo, Macedonia.[49]

Perhaps the most prominent killing was the murder of Fehmi Agani, a professor and leading member of the LDK. Agani was a politician respected by most people involved in Kosovo politics: his own party, the KLA, international negotiators, and even his Serbian interlocutors. For many years, he was viewed as the key player

Fehmi Agani, a professor and leading member of the Democratic League of Kosovo, was killed in unclear circumstances on May 6, 1999, after being taken off a train by Serbian police.

PHOTO COURTESY OF ZERI

The Humanitarian Law Center is one of Yugoslavia's most professional and respected human rights organizations. The organization's director, Natasa Kandic, wrote this on the occasion of Bajram Kelmendi's murder:

HUMANITARIAN LAW CENTER
Natasa Kandic

ON THE MURDER OF BAJRAM KELMENDI
27 March 1999

It was confirmed yesterday morning, 26 March, that Bajram and his sons were murdered. A relative of the Kelmendi family found their bodies at the first gasoline station on the road from Pristina to Pec. I learned of their disappearance two hours after they were taken from their home. At about 3.30 a.m., Bajram's wife Nekibe phoned me and her first words were: "Natasa, they have taken Bajram and the children." "Who, Nekibe?" I asked. Her reply was very specific. "Five men in dark uniforms with police insignia and long-barrel rifles." She had heard the front door being broken down and voices shouting, "You have five seconds to come out of your rooms!" As the attackers climbed the stairs to the upper floor, Nekibe seized the opportunity to call the local police station. They heard her out and did not come. She called again after Bajram and their sons were taken away. This time the police hung up on her . . .

Bajram Kelmendi. A man of stature in court and among people. His defense of accused Albanians from Urosevac before the Pristina District Court will be remembered as the best legal and political analysis of the events in Kosovo. I had never seen him so vulnerable as during a trial in Pec on 11 February. With misty eyes he listened to Marija and her son Miomir Pejuskovic, Serbs, giving testimony at the trial of their Albanian neighbors in Grabovac village, alleged "terrorists." Marija and her son spoke movingly of Avdi, Sadri and Syl Krasniqi, of the help they gave them in all circumstances, especially when the situation in Kosovo worsened. Their Albanian neighbors protected them, encouraged them, told them things would go back to normal, like they were over the past forty years they lived together.

My respects to Bajram Kelmendi. Justice for Bajram and his sons! Justice for Kosovo!

behind LDK politics, and a person in genuine search of a peaceful solution to the crisis. His intelligence and popularity are a possible motive for his murder.

The circumstances behind Agani's death remain unclear. On May 6, Agani attempted to leave Kosovo by train with his family. On the border with Macedonia, the train was sent back. Somewhere near Kosovo Polje, police stopped the train and ordered everyone off. Various accounts in the press have Agani being taken away either in a bus with other Albanian men or separately with police in a private car. His body was found the following day next to a dirt road near Lipljan. The Serbian government claimed that the KLA had killed Agani to prevent him from negotiating between Rugova and the Serbian government. A statement from the police issued on May 7, 1999, said:

> It is assumed that the terrorists of the so-called KLA kept Agani isolated in order to prevent his engagement in negotiations between Ibrahim Rugova and the Government of Serbia. When Rugova left for Rome they had no further interest to keep him, so they killed him. This most recent terrorist act can be, without any doubt, interpreted as a confirmation of an already announced decision of the KLA to do the same thing to Mr. Ibrahim Rugova.[50]

Other well-known individuals, such as Latif Berisha, the LDK president in Kosovska Mitrovica,[51] Din Mehmeti, a poet, and Teki Dervishi, a writer, were also reportedly killed.[52] On March 24, the guard at the newspaper *Koha Ditore* was shot and killed by police who were raiding the offices.

Another targeted group were Albanians who worked with the OSCE's KVM mission. Once the KVM withdrew from Kosovo on March 19, many of their offices were looted and burned, and some of the Albanian staff was sought by police or paramilitaries for beatings or execution. The worst case of revenge took place in Suva Reka against the Berisha family, which had rented two houses to the OSCE. Serbian forces killed at least twenty-four members of the family on March 25 and 26, including eleven children aged sixteen or younger (see Suva Reka Municipality).

RAPE AND SEXUAL ASSAULT

Rape and other forms of sexual violence were used in Kosovo in 1999 as weapons of war and instruments of systematic "ethnic cleansing."[53] Rapes were not rare and isolated acts committed by individual Serbian or Yugoslav forces, but rather were used deliberately as an instrument to terrorize the civilian population, extort money from families, and push people to flee their homes. Rape also furthered the goal of forcing ethnic Albanians from Kosovo.

In total, Human Rights Watch found credible accounts of ninety-six cases of sexual assault by Yugoslav soldiers, Serbian police, or paramilitaries during the period of NATO bombing, and the actual number is probably much higher. In six of these cases, Human Rights Watch was able to interview the victims in depth. Human Rights Watch met two other women who acknowledged that they had been raped but refused to give testimony. Finally, Human Rights Watch documented six cases of women who were raped and subsequently killed.

The ninety-six cases also include rape reports deemed reliable by Human Rights Watch that were compiled by other nongovernmental organizations.[54] To the extent possible, Human Rights Watch corroborated these accounts through interviews with dozens of nurses, doctors, eyewitnesses, and local human rights and women's rights activists. It is important to note that some of these cases may have been double-counted by local and international organizations. Despite this, Human Rights Watch believes that the actual number of women raped in Kosovo between March and June 1999 was much higher than ninety-six, since Kosovar Albanian victims of rape are generally reluctant to speak about their experiences. At the same time, it should be noted that Human Rights Watch was not able to confirm the allegations of rape camps in Kosovo that were presented during the war by the U.S. and British governments, as well as by NATO.

In general, rapes in Kosovo can be grouped into three categories: rapes in women's homes, rapes during flight, and rapes in detention. In the first category, security forces entered private homes and raped women in front of family members, in the yard or in an adjoining room. In the second category, internally displaced people wandering on foot and riding on tractors were repeatedly stopped, robbed, and threatened by the Yugoslav Army, Serbian police, or paramilitaries. If families could not produce cash, security

The sites shown on this map are based on accounts reported by Human Rights Watch, the Counseling Center for Women and Girls (Tirana), the Center for the Protection of Women and Children (Pristina), the Organization for Security and Cooperation in Europe, Médecins Sans Frontières, the Council for the Defense of Human Rights and Freedoms (Pristina), the Humanitarian Law Center (Belgrade and Pristina), as well as credible first-hand victim and witness accounts carried in the international news media. Human Rights Watch could not confirm the validity of each of these accounts. All of the information used to develop this map stems only from direct witness or victim interviews conducted by representatives of these organizations or by journalists.
KOSOVO
Reported Incidents of Rape
February - June 1999
Each symbol represents one reported incident of rape in Kosovo.
Notes:
1. Many reported and mapped incidents involved multiple rapes at one location.
2. In addition to the mapped incidents, there have been 16 reported incidents of rape with unknown location within Kosovo.
3. Locations of incidents shown on this map have been modified to protect the confidentiality of individuals while preserving the regional distribution of incidents.
Kosovo Municipality (Optsina)
Border
PRIZREN
Name
SERBIA
Novi Pazar
LEPOSAVIC
Kosovo
FEDERAL REPUBLIC OF YUGOSLAVIA
MONTENEGRO
ZVECAN
KOSOVSKA MITROVICA
ZUBIN POTOK
Mitrovica
PODUJEVO
Vučitrn
ISTOK
VUCITRN
Srbica
SRBICA
PRISTINA
Glogovac
OBILIC
Priština
KOSOVSKA KAMENICA
Peč
PEC
KLINA
KOSOVO POLJE
NOVO BRDO
GLOGOVAC
Decan
Lipljan
LIPLJAN
GNJILANE
DECANI
Gnjilane
ORAHOVAC
Orahovac
STIMLJE
Uroševac
Djakovica
UROSEVAC
DJAKOVICA
SUVA REKA
VITINA
STRPCE
KACANIK
Prizren
Kumanovo
ALBANIA
PRIZREN
Tetovo
Skopje
GORA
0 km 20
0 miles 20
MACEDONIA
Michael S. Miller for Human Rights Watch, 2000

forces sometimes threatened that their daughters would be taken away and raped; in some cases, even when families did provide money, their daughters were taken away. The third category of rapes took place in temporary detention centers, such as abandoned homes or barns.

As an example of the second category, one rape victim recounted to Human Rights Watch how she was dragged off a tractor by a Serb paramilitary near the border village of Zur (Zhur) and sexually assaulted in front of dozens of other refugees. The victim, a thirty-year-old mother traveling with her mother, mother-in-law, and two children, told Human Rights Watch:

> Two uniformed Serbian men stopped us. A big guy with red hair called me from the tractor. The red-haired one came around the tractor and said, "You," pointing at me. When he told me to get off the tractor, I didn't. Then he yelled, "You! Get off!" My three-year-old son was asleep on my lap. He kept yelling, "Get off! Get off!" He pulled me off the tractor and ripped my clothes. His pants were already open and his penis was out. He tore off my bra. I started screaming and crying. The other Serb came close and pointed his automatic weapon at my chest. I was wearing dimije [baggy pants] so they'd think I was old. The red-haired one took my pants off, tearing the drawstring. He told me to sit down. He took the 10 DM that I had with me. He took off his pants and pulled me close to him. We were right next to the tractor, next to the driver's cabin. I had my period. When he took off my pants, he saw the pads with blood on them, so he didn't have sex with me. Instead he turned me around and grabbed my breasts, trying me on the other side [anal rape]. I contracted myself very tightly and he didn't succeed. He may have ejaculated. I don't know. It took three or four minutes, then he told me that I could get back on the tractor.[55]

Witnesses to this attack, which occurred on June 2, 1999, corroborated the account and provided additional, credible details of the incident. A tractor driver who passed that same point later in the day, as well as his other passengers on the tractor, corroborated the description of the two uniformed men. One eyewitness to the sexual assault, an eighteen-year-old man from Djinovce (Gjinoc) in the Suva Reka municipality, told Human Rights Watch:

> He took her onto the asphalt road and raped her right there in front of everyone. Only one Serb raped her. The other Serb hit people with the butt of his

> automatic weapon and said, "Silence, silence!" We all averted our eyes. It took three or four minutes. He did it right next to the tractor.[56]

With few exceptions, the rapes documented by Human Rights Watch were gang rapes involving at least two perpetrators. In several cases, victims and witnesses identified the perpetrators as Serbian special police, in blue or blue-camouflage uniforms, or Yugoslav Army soldiers, in green military uniforms. The majority of rape cases, however, were evidently committed by Serbian paramilitaries, who wore various uniforms and often had bandanas, long knives, long hair, and beards. These paramilitary formations worked closely with official government forces, either the Serbian Ministry of Internal Affairs or the Yugoslav Army, throughout Kosovo (see Forces of the Conflict).

The Serbian and Yugoslav authorities knew that their paramilitaries had used rape and other forms of sexual violence in Bosnia and Herzegovina. Yet, the paramilitaries were deployed to or allowed to operate in Kosovo by the Serbian and Yugoslav authorities apparently without any precautions being taken to prevent their committing further such war crimes.

The participation of Serbian and Yugoslav forces in gang rapes renders it unlikely that senior officers were unaware of the assaults. Rapes occurred frequently in the presence, and with the acquiescence, of military officers. Several rape victims actually reported the crimes to Yugoslav military officers. Yet there is no evidence that the Yugoslav Army or the Serbian Ministry of Internal Affairs made any attempt to apprehend or punish those responsible for the attacks. Despite this seeming dereliction of duty, many leading police and military officers from the Kosovo campaign have been honored or promoted within the Serbian and Yugoslav forces since the end of the conflict.

There is also no evidence that the Yugoslav Army or Serbian Ministry of Internal Affairs took any measures to prevent rape and other forms of sexual violence, such as issuing orders or warning troops that they would be punished for these crimes, although there were some cases where soldiers or police tried to protect women from paramilitaries. Moreover, soldiers, police, and paramilitaries often raped their victims in front of many witnesses. In addition to actual rapes that took place in front of others, the process of pulling women out of refugee convoys often occurred in full view of other internally displaced persons.

FORCED EXPULSIONS

During 1998 and the first months of 1999, there was substantial displacement in Kosovo: more than 200,000 Kosovar Albanians were internally displaced, almost 70,000 fled the province to neighboring countries and Montenegro, and a further 100,000 Yugoslav nationals, mostly Kosovo Albanians, sought asylum in Western Europe.[57] But as the discussion above makes clear, few Western observers believed that Belgrade would attempt to expel the entire Albanian population of Kosovo. None could have predicted the speed and scale of the expulsion: within three weeks of the start of NATO airstrikes, there were 525,787 refugees from Kosovo in neighboring countries.[58] A month later, on May 12, the total had risen to 781,618.[59] All told, the Yugoslav military and Serbian police and paramilitaries expelled 862,979 Albanians from Kosovo,[60] and several hundred thousand more were internally displaced, in addition to those displaced prior to March.[61] These figures indicate that by early June 1999, more than 80 percent of the entire population of Kosovo and 90 percent of Kosovar Albanians were displaced from their homes. Approximately 440,000 refugees crossed the border to Albania and 320,000 to Macedonia (of whom almost 80,000 were transferred to third countries outside the region). Montenegro hosted around 70,000 refugees, while Bosnia and Herzegovina received more than 30,0000.

Yugoslav military and Serbian police and paramilitaries expelled 862,979 Albanians from Kosovo, and several hundred thousand more were internally displaced.

Refugee flows from Kosovo between March and June generally followed the principle of proximity to borders. Residents from the western half of Kosovo generally crossed the southwestern border into Albania and residents from the eastern half generally crossed the southeastern border into Macedonia. Conversely, residents of Kosovska Mitrovica, Vucitrn, and other ethnic Albanian areas in northern Kosovo were generally sent to the Albanian border. Many residents from Pec and the western-most part of Kosovo crossed into Montenegro, while some residents in the eastern-most municipalities entered first into southern Serbia before crossing the border into Macedonia. Some areas saw relatively few departures: A military cordon and an unwillingness to leave meant that few residents from the

Drenica region in central Kosovo fled the province, other than those expelled from Glogovac town in early May (see Drenica Region). While the fact of proximity in most cases may suggest voluntariness, the statements of hundreds of refugees interviewed by Human Rights Watch and other organizations in Albania, Macedonia, and Bosnia indicate otherwise.

The flight of the ethnic Albanian population from Kosovo was executed with a degree of coordination and control that render it impossible to reach any conclusion other than systematic forced expulsion. At least four factors are key in determining that a policy of "ethnic cleansing" was carried out in Kosovo: First is the timing of the refugees' arrival—refugees arrived in Macedonia and Albania from the same areas on the same dates, and at various times (notably during negotiations) the flow of refugees stopped or was switched from one border to another. Second is the means of departure: refugees were expelled into Macedonia by train, which allowed the efficient removal of thousands of persons a day. Others, including many of those sent to Albania who did not have their own transportation, were taken by trucks and buses organized by the Serbian police. Collection points were used to facilitate expulsion. Third is the use of threats and violence to terrorize the population into departing, a central element of "ethnic cleansing," observed frequently during the wars in Bosnia and Croatia. Fourth is the practice of "identity cleansing": refugees expelled toward Albania were frequently stripped of their identity documents and forced to remove the license plates from their cars and tractors before being permitted to cross the border.

Since almost 90 percent of the refugees who left Kosovo crossed the Albanian or Macedonian border, the analysis of the timing and pattern of expulsion must necessarily focus on arrivals in those two countries. Human Rights Watch had researchers present in both countries from the last week of March until the end of the war in mid-June 1999. Researchers were therefore able to observe both the timing and pattern of refugee arrivals. If refugees were fleeing the NATO bombing or the fighting between Yugoslav and Serbian forces and the KLA, one would expect that refugees would arrive in a somewhat random fashion, based on an individual family's decisions about when the risks became too great to remain. In fact, almost all refugees arrived village-by-village and municipality-by-municipality in Albania or in Macedonia. The exceptions were cases where some residents from the same place were directed to Albania and some to Macedonia.

Although they were necessarily selective, the chronologies of Human Rights Watch interviews provide some insight into that process. In Macedonia, Human Rights Watch interviewed mostly newly arrived refugees from Pristina in the first week (beginning March 24). In the second and third weeks most of the new arrivals were from Kacanik and Strpce municipalities. In the fourth week, large numbers of refugees arrived from Gnjilane. In week five, many of the new arrivals were from Lipljan municipality. Similarly in northern Albania, Human Rights Watch interviewed large numbers of new arrivals from Prizren municipality during the first week; in the second week, many of the refugees came from Suva Reka and Djakovica, and in the third week, there was a large influx of refugees from Mitrovica and more from Djakovica. Refugee flows to Macedonia were abruptly stopped on several occasions, notably in early June, when the details of a settlement between the Yugoslav government and NATO were being negotiated. And as the OSCE noted, "the flow of refugees was also regulated, with the result that many thousands would arrive at the border crossing points with Albania, the former Yugoslav Republic of Macedonia and Montenegro (FRY) on some days, but then only a handful of refugees would arrive at particular crossing points on succeeding days."[62]

A more systematic effort to analyze the pattern of refugee flows into Albania, conducted by the American Association for the Advancement of Science (together with the East-West Management Institute and the Institute for Legal and Policy Studies in Albania), confirms this analysis. The statistical study primarily utilized data collected during the crisis by Albanian guards at the Morina border crossing in northern Albania. The study concludes that "the mass exodus of refugees from Kosovo [into Albania] occurred in patterns so regular that they must have been coordinated." The report further compared the expulsion times and patterns to the NATO bombing and found that "only a small fraction of Kosovo Albanians fled Kosovo as a direct result of NATO bombing raids."[63] (See Statistical Analysis of Violations for a further discussion.)

The pattern of departure of many of the refugees also strongly points to organized expulsion rather than spontaneous departure. The depopulation of Kosovo's capital, Pristina, is a case in point. Within days of the start of the NATO airstrikes, Serbian police and paramilitaries began systematically to clear the city of large sections of its Albanian population. Witnesses from the neighborhoods of Vranjevac (Kodra e Trimave), Tashlixhe, Dragodan, and Dardanija (Dardania) told Human Rights Watch that police and masked paramilitaries went door to door at the end of March, telling residents that they had to leave at once. M.B., a mother of two from Tashlixhe said that she had been told: "Come on, get out! You must go to the railway station."[64] In some cases witnesses were told they would be killed if they failed to comply. A medical doctor and his family were told by masked men "if you don't leave in one minute we will kill you all!"[65]

Upon leaving their homes, residents were directed by police towards the central railway station in Pristina, while others left by car. The side roads were blocked by armed police and paramilitaries: a Vranjevac resident said that "people who tried to walk in another direction were forced back by police."[66] Thousands of Pristina residents were gathered at the railway station, with armed police posted around the area, where they were herded onto a passenger train headed for the Macedonian border. The trains were extremely overcrowded: one refugee said he was one of twenty-eight people forced into a compartment meant for eight passengers.[67] Several refugees also described people being loaded onto buses and trucks at the railway station, which suggests that it served as a general collection point for the organized expulsion of ethnic Albanians from Pristina. Refugees interviewed by Human Rights Watch saw police drag people from cars and beat them. Most indicated that police and especially paramilitaries demanded hard currency for safe passage, and reported witnessing the theft of jewelry and vehicles. The use of collection points was also reported by refugees in the towns of Glogovac and at the central railway stations in Urosevac and Kosovo Polje, and in the village of Belanica (Bellanice) in Suva Reka municipality.

As the case of Pristina suggests, violence and threats were frequently used to terrorize the population into departing. Residents from Lipljan municipality told Human Rights Watch that the first massacre in the municipality (in the village of Slovinje) made them nervous. A climate of fear was created by subsequent killings in Malo Ribar (Ribar i Vogel) and Mali Alas (Hallac i Vogel), which left them with no choice but to leave (see Lipljan Municipality). Random gunshots, police checks, and house burnings also contributed to their decision to flee.

In areas with a history of support for the KLA, killings and other violence served the dual purpose of terrorizing the population and eliminating persons associated with the rebels. The experience of the town of Djakovica is indicative: a wave of organized terror early in the war left dozens dead and thousands as refugees in northern Albania (see Djakovica Municipality). This first wave of violence in Djakovica began on March 24, when NATO initiated its attack on Yugoslavia, and continued until April 2.

Violence and threats were frequently used to terrorize the population into departing.

Following the principles of "ethnic cleansing" in Bosnia and Herzegovina, prominent residents, including doctors, lawyers, and politicians, were targeted for death—a strategy designed to terrorize the remainder of the population into believing that no one was safe and to eliminate important sources of leadership in the community. Approximately 200 Djakovica residents are believed to have been killed between March 24 and April 2, 1999, many of them in a series of house-to-house operations by Yugoslav soldiers, Serbian police, and paramilitaries.

Much of the population was expelled during this period. Witnesses interviewed by Human Rights Watch in northern Albania—most of them women— described their forced expulsion at the hands of police, paramilitaries, and the army. Many reported seeing clusters of dead bodies as they left the city.[68] According to one Djakovica resident:

> It was all very organized. They went from one neighborhood to another. Some soldiers are in charge of destroying things, while others are in charge of accompanying people to the border.[69]

The widespread confiscation of identity documents and car license plates by Serbian police and border guards from departing Kosovar Albanian refugees also points to the systematic nature of the expulsions. Hundreds of refugees arriving in Albania spoke of being forced to hand over ID cards, passports, and birth certificates, which were often torn up in front of them, before they were permitted to cross the border. Those who crossed the border by car were given screwdrivers and ordered to remove the license plates from their vehicles. By contrast, refugees who were expelled to Macedonia generally were permitted to retain their documents, even after having them inspected by Serbian police officers. (As noted in the section discussing explanations for the "ethnic cleansing," the difference in approach may reflect an expectation that those sent to Albania could be more easily characterized as Albanians from Albania and blocked from returning, whereas

Macedonia was unlikely to tolerate the permanent residence of large numbers of Albanians from Kosovo.)

Whatever the explanation, the practice of "identity cleansing" was clearly not a random initiative by Serbian officials on the border. After the war, piles of license plates and burned documents were discovered by the border crossings into Albania and elsewhere in Kosovo.

Each one of these four factors (the timing of arrivals, the means of departure, the use of terror and the practice of "identity cleansing") strongly suggest that the flight of some 860,000 Albanians from Kosovo in twelve weeks adds up to systematic forced expulsion. Taken together, the evidence is overwhelming. The prosecutor of the ICTY was in no doubt when her office prepared the indictment for Slobodan Milosevic, Milan Milutinovic, Nikola Sainovic, Dragoljub Ojdanic, and Vlajko Stojiljkovic (see Forces of the Conflict). The first of the charges reads:

> The forces of the FRY and Serbia have, in a systematic manner, forcibly expelled and internally displaced hundreds of thousands of Kosovo Albanians from their homes across the entire province of Kosovo. To facilitate these

Hundreds of license plates lying by the side of the road in Kosovo just across the border from Albania. Serb border police had stripped them from the vehicles of fleeing refugees as part of a systematic effort to destroy proof of Yugoslav citizenship.

© JOANNE MARINER/HUMAN RIGHTS WATCH

expulsions and displacements, the forces of the FRY and Serbia have intentionally created an atmosphere of fear and oppression through the use of force, threats of force, and acts of violence.[70]

ARBITRARY ARRESTS AND DETENTIONS

Throughout the armed conflict in 1998 and early 1999, arbitrary arrests and detentions of Kosovar Albanians were commonplace. Physical abuse and torture of detainees was widespread.[71] The practice intensified during the period March-June 1999. Thousands of Kosovar Albanians were detained during the NATO bombing. Very often, men were separated from women and held in makeshift detention centers, such as schools or factories, for a period of days, during which time they were beaten and interrogated about the KLA. Some men were held for longer periods in the prisons at Smrekovnica, Lipljan, Istok (Dubrava), or Pristina.

Ethnic Albanian men, interviewed in May 1999 as refugees in Albania, who were separated from their families and detained in Smrekovnica prison (see Vucitrn Municipality). © JOANNE MARINER/HUMAN RIGHTS WATCH

Most of the men in detention at the end of the war—between 1,000 and 2,000—were transferred out of Kosovo to prisons in Serbia proper; as of March 2001, more than 400 Kosovar Albanians were still being held.

As an example, more than 300 men and women were taken into detention from the streets and private homes in Djakovica between May 7 and May 11 after fighting in the Cabrat neighborhood between government forces and the KLA (see Djakovica Municipality). Women were held temporarily in the Gorenje Elektromotor factory and then released. The men were held in an unknown location on the edge of the city along the Djakovica-Pec road.

Approximately half of the men were released after six days but the rest—an estimated 150 people—were transferred to the jails in Pec, Lipljan, and then Dubrava (prior to the NATO bombing of that prison). Most, if not all, of the detainees were transferred to prisons inside Serbia just before NATO troops entered Kosovo on June 12. On May 22, 2000, a court in Nis sentenced 143 men from Djakovica to a total of 1,632 years in prison for acts of terrorism. The Serbian Supreme Court released them on April 23, 2001.

More than 300 ethnic Albanians were held in Prizren's prison beginning in April. One man, who spent two months in detention, spoke about the treatment he and others received:

> I went straight to the prison; they never brought me to the police station. There they tortured me for breakfast, lunch, and dinner. The first thing they did to me when I arrived was beat me using rubber police batons. They hit me on the palms of my hands and in my groin. There were more than 300 Albanians there. Every time they served us food, they beat us. During my first four days, they beat me every day in the hall. Other inmates got the same treatment.[72]

In the town of Glogovac, police raided neighborhoods and detained large groups of adult men in the local police station for one week beginning April 22 (see Glogovac Municipality). Almost all of the men were beaten in front of their homes or on the way to the station, and some were forced to sing Serbian nationalist songs. Most of the detainees were questioned about the KLA and then released after no more than one day in custody. One month later, hundreds of Glogovac men were detained and held in the basements of local shops. The majority of the men were released after three days, but only after interrogations and beatings with sticks, shovel handles, and metal bars. Approximately ninety men were transferred to Lipljan.

In some villages, women were held in makeshift detention facilities, such as barns or abandoned homes, where they were sexually abused or raped (see section on rape).[73] A few women were reported to have been held in Kosovo's prisons, such as the doctor Flora Brovina, who was transferred to Serbia proper after the war, sentenced to twelve years in prison, but released in November 2000 (see Abuses After June 12, 1999).

Signs of physical abuse, such as black eyes, severe bruises, and skin abrasions were visible on their bodies.

More than 2,000 Kosovar Albanian men were detained in Smrekovnica prison near Mitrovica in May (see section on Smrekovnica prison in Vucitrn Municipality). Human Rights Watch interviewed more than thirty of these men; all of them reported regular beatings by police during their detention, especially during interrogations about the KLA. Signs of physical abuse, such as black eyes, severe bruises, and skin abrasions were visible on their bodies when they were interviewed as refugees in Albania. Most of the men were forced to sign confessions that they were engaged in terrorist activities before being released.

Human Rights Watch also spoke with former detainees from Lipljan prison, who testified to the beatings and indecent conditions at the prison, including a cordon of policemen and prison guards who beat new arrivals. One former prison from Glogovac, who was in Lipljan for fifteen days before being transferred to Sremska Mitrovica prison on June 10, said:

> At first when we got out of the bus [at Lipljan prison] we had to walk thirty meters through two columns of police, and they beat us with bars and sticks. Inside they told us to disrobe. And they beat us again. They took us to another room with about 500 prisoners—in a sports hall. We all stayed together.[74]

Another detention facility was Dubrava penitentiary near Istok—Kosovo's largest prison. Between 900 and 1,100 prisoners were being held there when the NATO bombing began, including approximately thirty ethnic Serbs, but additional prisoners were transferred to Dubrava after the bombing had begun (including the 150 men from Djakovica), some of them from prisons in Serbia proper.

NATO bombed the prison on May 19 and May 21, killing at least nineteen ethnic Albanian prisoners (see section on Dubrava prison in Istok Municipality). On May 22, Serbian security forces lined up the approximately 1,000 prisoners in the courtyard and fired on them with snipers, machine guns, and grenades from the prison walls and guard towers, killing at least seventy people. At least another twelve prisoners were killed over the next twenty-four hours as prison guards, special police, and possibly paramilitaries attacked prisoners who were hiding in the prison's undestroyed buildings, basements, and sewers. The injured were taken away in trucks, while the remaining prisoners were transported to Lipljan prison, where they were beaten. On June 10, they were transferred to prisons in Serbia proper.

On June 10, two days before NATO's entry into Kosovo, an estimated 2,000 ethnic Albanian prisoners were transferred from Kosovo to prisons inside Serbia proper. More than 1,400 of these people were released at different times in 1999, 2000, and 2001, some of them under a Yugoslav amnesty law passed in February 2001. As of March 2001, approximately 400 Kosovo Albanians were known to be in Serbian prisons. (See Abuses After June 12, 1999.)

DESTRUCTION OF CIVILIAN PROPERTY AND MOSQUES

Between March and June 1999, Yugoslav soldiers and Serbian police and paramilitaries destroyed thousands of Albanian homes throughout Kosovo with the use of artillery, bulldozers, explosives, and arson. There was also widespread looting. In some areas, especially those with close ties to the KLA, entire villages were destroyed. A number of towns, including Pec and Glogovac were also badly damaged. Albanian-owned shops and businesses, schools, and mosques were also targeted for destruction and were frequently looted. In addition, there was widespread contamination of water wells in the province (see following section).

These actions were the continuation of policies carried out by security forces in Kosovo during 1998 and early 1999, notably in the Drenica region and Orahovac municipality (particularly in the town of Malisevo) and Decani municipality.[75] A UNHCR shelter survey released in November 1998 demonstrates the widespread nature of the destruction during 1998.[76]

The survey assessed 285 villages, of which 210 had been affected by the conflict. In the 210 affected villages with an estimated pre-conflict population of 350,000 persons, 28 percent of the homes—9,809 out of a total of 35,185 homes—had been completely destroyed. Another 15 percent of the homes (5,112 homes) had severe damage, while an additional 6,017 homes sustained moderate to minor damage, leaving only 40 percent of the homes in the affected regions undamaged.

Much of the remaining housing stock in Kosovo was destroyed in 1999. According to a November 1999 UNHCR survey, almost 40 percent of all residential houses in Kosovo were heavily damaged (categories III and IV) or completely destroyed (category V).[77] Out of a total of 237,842 houses, 45,768 are heavily damaged and 46,414 are destroyed. Municipalities with strong ties to the KLA were disproportionately affected (probably in part because they began to be attacked in 1998): almost half the 12,887 houses in Orahovac municipality were heavily damaged (4,334 houses) or completely destroyed (1,943 houses); in Suva Reka, 4,552 homes were heavily damaged and 2,018 destroyed, or more than 55 percent of the total number (11,622). In the Drenica region, out of a total housing stock of 17,340 units, 7,155

A damaged mosque on the road between Djakovica and Prizren, July 1999.

were heavily damaged and 6,209 completely destroyed, or 77 percent of the total. The city of Pec was also hit especially hard, with more than 80 percent of the city's 5,280 houses heavily damaged (1,590) or destroyed (2,774).

Schools and mosques were similarly affected. According to a United Nations damage assessment of 649 schools in Kosovo, more than a fifth of the schools surveyed were heavily damaged and more than 60 percent were completely destroyed.[78] After June 1999, Human Rights Watch observed damaged and destroyed mosques in Djakovica, Pec, Istok, and Cirez (Srbica municipality). Field visits by Human Rights Watch over the summer of 1999 also revealed extensive damage to shops and businesses in Suva Reka, Urosevac, Pristina, Pec, Glogovac, and Djakovica. An August 1999 report by Physicians for Human Rights documented 155 destroyed mosques throughout Kosovo, based on refugee accounts.[79]

CONTAMINATION OF WATER WELLS

One of the more blatant forms of civilian property destruction in Kosovo during 1998 and 1999 was the widespread practice of water well contamination, which is forbidden by the laws of war.[80] Throughout Kosovo, Serbian and Yugoslav forces deliberately rendered water wells unusable by disposing of chemicals, dead animals, and even human corpses into the water. According to the International Committee of the Red Cross (ICRC), which ran a water-sanitizing operation in Kosovo, "Of the 20,000 wells in Kosovo, over half are believed to have been contaminated with animal or human remains or with rubbish, or have simply grown stagnant through lack of use." Between January and September 1999, the ICRC cleaned over 1,700 wells.[81]

Serbian and Yugoslav forces deliberately rendered water wells unusable by disposing of chemicals, dead animals, and even human corpses into the water.

Human Rights Watch documented a number of villages in Kosovo where murder victims were dumped into a local well. In one village in Suva Reka—which is not named because of the rape that occurred there—eleven men were killed in April 1999 and thrown into the well (see Suva Reka Municipality). As noted in the above discussion of the death toll, at least four of the estimated forty-seven members of the Muqolli family, executed in the village of Poklek in April 1999, were thrown into a well in the yard of the family compound. In another village in Drenica region (that will also remain nameless to protect the identity of the victims), eight women were raped, shot, and then thrown into a well.[82] Human Rights Watch has also received reports that human remains were found in water wells in the villages of Donji Streoc (Strellc i Poshtem) and Dubovik in Decani municipality, the village of Damjane (Dehje) in Djakovica municipality, and Studenica (Studenice) in Istok municipality. The two wells outside the village of Kotlina, into which twenty-three men were thrown together with hand-grenades in April 1999, were not used by the villagers for water and the decision to put the men into the wells appears to have been an attempt to conceal their murders rather than to contaminate the water.

Secondary sources also reported that wells had been contaminated, both prior to and during the NATO bombing. According to an article in *The Washington Post* on December 10, 1998, at least fifty-eight villages had informed foreign aid organizations that their wells contained "dead dogs, chickens, horses, garbage, fuel oil, flour, detergent, paint and other contaminants." In one village, Ovcarevo, 70 percent of the wells "might be contam-

A village man looks into a water well where Serbian forces threw the bodies of eleven murdered men. © FRED ABRAHAMS/HUMAN RIGHTS WATCH inated."[83] After the NATO bombing, *The Los Angeles Times* cited UNHCR statistics on the Djakovica area indicating that the wells in thirty-nine of forty-four villages were contaminated with "either human or animal bodies."[84] According to the Council for the Defense of Human Rights and Freedoms in Pec, human remains were found in wells in the villages of Donja Luka (Lluke e Eperme), Banja (Banje), and Kosuric (Kosuriq).[85] The Italian newspaper *Corriere Della Sera* also reported on the contamination of the Donja Luka well, in which a villager found thirteen relatives and neighbors, aged twelve to seventy.[86]

ROBBERY AND EXTORTION

The killing and mass expulsion in Kosovo in the spring of 1999 was often accompanied by robbery and extortion. Typically, Albanians were robbed immediately prior to or during their expulsion from Kosovo. Those who refused were threatened with death, or their children were snatched and threatened until they complied. Serbian paramilitaries or persons in unknown uniform were most often implicated in the crimes, although there are also reports of the involvement of Serbian police. Incidents of robbery were not confined to any particular area: there are notable examples in regions with significant KLA activity and widespread killings, such as Glogovac, Suva Reka, and Pec, and in regions that experienced fewer killings and relatively light destruction, such as Lipljan, Pristina, and Gnjilan. As in Bosnia and Herzegovina, robbery and extortion may simply have been motivation and reward for Serbian paramilitaries, although the widespread nature of the abuses and the involvement of the police in at least some cases suggests complicity by, and possibly profit to, the state.

One of the most egregious cases of mass robbery occurred in the village of Belanica in Suva Reka municipality (see Suva Reka Municipality). On March 31, Serbian police and paramilitaries entered the village and rounded up residents and the large number of internally displaced persons from the surrounding area. Serbian paramilitaries and police then repeatedly demanded money, threatening those who refused or their children with death. They made good on their threats: at least a dozen Albanians were killed. A woman who was in the village at the time told Human Rights Watch:

> At one point, the police came up to a man on the tractor in front of me. They said, "Give us money!" He didn't have anything for them. He was from Ostrozuk village. So they pulled him off the tractor and killed him. When he didn't give them anything they [four policemen] pulled him off the tractor by his arms and legs. They brought him around to the back of a house, then I couldn't see him anymore. I heard shooting and I could see one of the policemen aiming his gun and firing. The man didn't come back to his tractor.[87]

In the weeks leading up to the mass expulsion from Glogovac at the start of May 1999, the town's residents and displaced persons suffered persistent visits to their homes by Serbian paramilitaries and police demanding money and valuables (see Drenica Region). In some areas, demands for money by paramilitaries were so frequent that residents took the unusual step of going to the police on April 23 to request protection. Protection was provided only intermittently and did little to curtail criminal activity, suggesting a degree of official complicity.

The robberies followed a similar pattern: one or two paramilitaries or police officers would break in the door of a private apartment, sometimes wearing masks, but always carrying automatic rifles. The families were physically threatened until they handed over everything of value. A fifty-nine-year-old man from Glogovac, A.H., described what happened when men with "green uniforms and red bandanas on their arms" came to the four-house compound he shared with his three brothers in early May:

> Two days before we left, at around 9:00 or 10:00 a.m., they [the police] came into the house and searched us . . . They pointed their guns at us . . . They asked me for money . . . [then] they forced me to strip to my underwear — looking for money. One of them said, "If I find any money on your body, I'm going to shoot you . . ." They took rings and gold from the women . . . The next day . . . they took two radios from my brother and a small TV.[88]

During some of the robberies, paramilitaries and police reportedly threatened children with knives and automatic guns in order to extort money from their parents. According to H.M., a forty-six-year-old man, from Glogovac: "A week before we left [paramilitaries] started to take very strong action to take money. They would take your daughter and say, 'Give me money or I won't let her go.'"[89] Another man from Glogovac in his late fifties said that "paramilitaries came, they took children, held a knife against their throats [and threatened to kill them] unless they were given money."[90]

Areas that escaped multiple killings and widespread destruction were nonetheless targeted for robbery and extortion. Residents of Pristina reported frequent robberies as they were forced from the city at the end of March. The municipality of Gnjilane, which was among the least affected by the war, also experienced robbery and extortion as its population was forced to flee toward Macedonia. The experiences of the residents of Malesevo village are typical of the pattern in Gnjilane. After green-uniformed paramilitaries with "a white eagle with four C's"[91] insignia entered their village on the morning of April 16, Malesevo residents were given two hours to leave. Two villagers were shot in a field as the rest of the village stood by. The villagers were beaten, robbed of cars, money, and jewelry, and threatened with death before they were forced to walk to nearby Gnjilane. Later, on the road between Gnjilane and Urosevac, the villagers were repeatedly robbed by bands of paramilitaries. One villager said that the column had been stopped nine times between Gnjilane and the town of Klokot (Kllokot), approximately ten kilometers by road. Each time the villagers were stopped they were slapped, beaten, and threatened with death if they did not hand over all their foreign currency, jewelry, and other valuables. Several witnesses indicated that paramilitaries had threatened to detonate hand grenades if their demands were not met. According to one witness: "They took hand grenades and were threatening that they would throw them in the midst of the children if they didn't get anything."[92]

Areas that escaped multiple killings and widespread destruction were nonetheless targeted for robbery and extortion.

DETENTIONS AND COMPULSORY LABOR

There is clear evidence that between March and June 1999, Yugoslav and Serbian security forces detained adult males and compelled them to dig trenches, clear bunkers, and perform other manual work. The majority of the work appears related to the Yugoslav Army's strategic objectives. The most notable incidents occurred in Glogovac municipality during May and June 1999. Human Rights Watch also documented the compulsory labor of detainees in Prizren municipality during April 1999, where on at least two occasions, Serbian police and Yugoslav soldiers rounded up men in Prizren town and transported them to the Albanian border where they were forced to serve on trench-digging brigades (see Prizren Municipality). There are also reports of work brigades in Orahovac, Suva Reka, and Djakovica, where Roma were allegedly compelled to dig trenches on the border with Albania during the month of April 1999.[93]

Human Rights Watch received detailed accounts of compulsory labor from the group of prisoners who were detained at the mosque in Cirez in Drenica on April 31, 1999. While many of the detainees were executed at the Shavarina mine near Cikatovo on May 1, 1999, the remainder were transferred to Glogovac (see Drenica Region). Around seventy-six of the survivors were taken by Serbian police from Glogovac to the villages of Krajkovo (Krajkove), Vukovce (Vukofci), and Poturk on May 5 and 6 and handed over to Serbian soldiers. According to seven witnesses interviewed by Human Rights Watch, the men were then forced to work for approximately six weeks until the withdrawal of Serbian security forces from Kosovo in mid-June. Tasks included digging trenches and bunkers. Witnesses reported incidents of beating and torture of prisoners at the hands of the soldiers, although some noted that they were fed and received better treatment than they had at the hands of Serbian police and paramilitaries in Cirez and Glogovac.

HUMAN SHIELDS

Between March and June 1999, Yugoslav and Serbian security forces compelled some Albanian civilians to remain close to them or situated them between Serbian positions and those of the KLA. Both strategies were designed to create a human shield to protect Yugoslav and Serbian forces from attack from NATO aircraft or the KLA. The use of such "human shields" is prohibited by Article 28 of the Fourth Geneva Convention, which states that "The presence of a protected person may not be used to render certain points or areas immune from military operations."

In some cases, the use of human shields was direct, with Albanian civilians compelled to march alongside Yugoslav soldiers and Serbian police in order to protect them from attack by NATO aircraft or the KLA. Human Rights Watch interviewed witnesses from Suva Reka, Klina, and Lipljan who described being held as human shields. Witnesses reported to the OSCE that they were detained as human shields in Djeneral Jankovic (on the Macedonian border), in Djakovica municipality, in Pristina, and on the road between Cirez and Stutica.[94] There are also allegations that the displaced Albanian civilians killed in the Korisa woods by NATO bombs had been compelled by Serbian forces to remain there as "human shields" but the evidence is inconclusive (see The NATO Air Campaign).[95]

Serbian and Yugoslav forces placed an estimated 50,000 anti-personnel and anti-tank mines in Kosovo.

There is also evidence of the indirect use of human shields, through efforts to create barriers of civilians between Serbian security forces and the KLA, thereby limiting the ability of the KLA to attack, or defend from attacks by, Serbian positions. Most of the reports are from the Drenica region. The case of Staro Cikatovo village is a notable example (see Drenica Region). One witness from the village told Human Rights Watch, "We were between the KLA and Feronikel. [Serbian forces] started grenading from Feronikel to attack [KLA] soldiers."[96] The OSCE reports a similar incident in the village of Trnavce (Trnoc) in Srbica municipality, as well as in Belanica village in Suva Reka municipality.[97] A witness from Malisevo (Orahovac municipality) interviewed by Physicians for Human Rights reported being in a group of 500 civilians who were detained close to the Albanian border and used as human shields by Yugoslav soldiers as they attacked a nearby KLA position.[98]

LANDMINES

Throughout 1998 and the first six months of 1999, Serbian and Yugoslav forces placed an estimated 50,000 anti-personnel and anti-tank mines in Kosovo, especially along the borders with Macedonia and Albania.[99] The KLA also placed mines in areas under its control during this period. In addition, NATO's use of cluster bombs during at least six weeks of the air war resulted in some civilian deaths and unexploded ordinances (UXO) scattered in Kosovo and elsewhere in the Federal Republic of Yugoslavia after the war.

Mines and UXO represent the deadliest legacy of the conflict in Kosovo. According to the U.S.-based Vietnam Veterans' Foundation, from the end of the war to mid-November 2000, 103 people were killed and 394 wounded in accidents with mines and unexploded ordinance.[100] This differs only slightly from a July 2000 report of the U.N. secretary general, which said that 101 people had been killed and 395 injured in mine or unexploded ordnance incidents between June 12, 1999, and July 2000.[101] The U.N. Mine Action Coordination Center (MACC) established in Kosovo after the war, reported that by mid-July 2000, 1.1 million square meters of land had been demined or cleared of unexploded ordnance.[102] The secretary general's report also noted that teams coordinated by MACC had cleared 3,405 anti-personnel mines, 3,768 anti-tank mines, 3,066 cluster bombs, and 9,327 items of unexploded ordnance. In addition, KFOR had cleared over 16,000

A sign warning of mines on the road near Mitrovica, July 1999.

© FRED ABRAHAMS/HUMAN RIGHTS WATCH

homes, 1,165 schools, and almost 2,000 kilometers of roads during the same period.[103]

The Yugoslav government, one of the world's largest producers of anti-personnel mines, is not a signatory to the 1997 treaty banning the use of landmines, but Yugoslav officials have stated that landmines are used only for the purposes of training.[104] In fact, landmines were used extensively by Yugoslav forces during the 1998–99 conflict as a tactical measure against the KLA and NATO. According to the International Campaign to Ban Landmines 2000 report, the Yugoslav Army primarily placed barrier minefields along the southern border with Macedonia. Serbian Ministry of Internal Affairs forces and paramilitaries laid anti-personnel mines in and around civilian population centers.[105] According to a report by the HALO Trust, a non-profit demining group, "[M]any villages are afflicted with random mines laid with the sole aim of causing civilian casualties and thereby discouraging the return of refugees."[106] According to a U.S. Agency for Inter-

In late September 1998, this ICRC vehicle struck an anti-tank mine placed by the KLA on a road leading to Likovac, a regional KLA headquarters in Drenica. A Kosovar Albanian doctor was killed and three others were injured.

© FRED ABRAHAMS/HUMAN RIGHTS WATCH

national Development report, more than 900 schools needed mine clearance.[107]

In the Military Technical Agreement signed between NATO and the Yugoslav government on June 9, 1999, the Yugoslav authorities agreed to "mark and clear minefields, booby traps and obstacles."[108] The Yugoslav Army informed NATO of 616 mined areas. Mines placed by Serbian paramilitaries, however, were generally unrecorded and are therefore difficult to locate.[109]

The same is true for many of the mines planted by the KLA. The KLA is known to have placed mostly anti-tank mines but also some anti-personnel mines around regional bases, headquarters, and safe houses. In late September 1998, a Canadian armored car from KDOM and a vehicle from the ICRC both hit anti-tank mines laid by the KLA in central Drenica. A Kosovo Albanian doctor, Dr. Shpetim Robaj, was killed and three ICRC medical workers were injured.

Cluster bombs dropped by NATO forces during the air war also pose a continued risk to civilians in post-war Kosovo. Both U.S. and British forces have acknowledged the use of cluster bombs in the bombing campaign.[110] The White House issued a directive to the Pentagon in May 1999 to restrict cluster bomb use (at least by U.S. forces) after fourteen civilians were killed and twenty-eight were injured in a May 7 cluster bomb attack on an airfield in Nis (see The NATO Air Campaign).[111]

According to the International Campaign to Ban Landmines, "[T]he U.S dropped 1,100 cluster bombs of the type CBU-87/B, each containing 202 BLU-97/B bomblets and the UK dropped 500 RBL/755 cluster bombs, each containing 147 Bl-755 bomblets."[112] Because of the high failure rate of the submunitions inside cluster bombs—estimated conservatively at 5 percent[113]— these "bomblets" in effect become anti-personnel landmines.

As of July 2000, NATO had provided the United Nations MACC with information regarding 333 cluster bomb drop-sites where 1,392 bomblet-dispensing canisters (cluster bomb units) had been dropped.[114] According to NATO, "[N]early 30,000 individual bomblets may have failed to function and will require clearance." NATO estimated that as of July 4, 2000, approximately 30 percent of the cluster bomb units had been cleared. NATO has faced criticism for the pace of its clean-up of cluster bomb areas. According to the BBC, as of May 2000, 40 percent of the known risk areas had not been cordoned off.[115]

5

DRENICA REGION

Glogovac (Gllogofc) and Srbica (Skenderaj) Municipalities

Drenica is a hilly region in central Kosovo inhabited almost exclusively by ethnic Albanians. The inhabitants of the region have a tradition of strong resistance to outside powers, dating back to Turkish rule in the Balkans. By 1997, Albanians had begun to refer to Drenica as "liberated territory" because of the local KLA presence. The government considered Drenica a hotbed of "Albanian terrorism."

The region, flanked by the Drenica mountains on the west, consists of the municipalities of Glogovac (Gllogofc) and Srbica (Skenderaj). The towns of Glogovac and Srbica are the respective municipal capitals and major population centers of each municipality. Prior to 1998, both municipalities had an almost entirely Albanian population. The villages that surround the two towns are the birthplace of the Kosovo Liberation Army, which began armed operations in Drenica in 1996. They are also the scene of some of the worst abuses against civilians in Kosovo.[1]

In operations that began in January 1998, Serbian special police raided villages in Drenica linked to the KLA. Between January and March, police launched multiple military-style attacks on the villages of Donje Prekaz, Likosane, and Cirez using armored personnel carriers and a helicopter.[2] The attacks, and the fighting that ensued, left eighty-three villagers dead, including at least twenty-four women and children, and helped to crystallize armed opposition to Belgrade's rule. In May, an estimated 300 special police forces attacked the village of Novi Poklek (Poklek i Ri), a suburb of the town of Glogovac. Ten Albanians were detained during the attack; one of them was later found dead, while the nine others remain missing.[3]

Low intensity conflict between government forces—the Serbian police—and the KLA continued until September 1998, when the deaths of

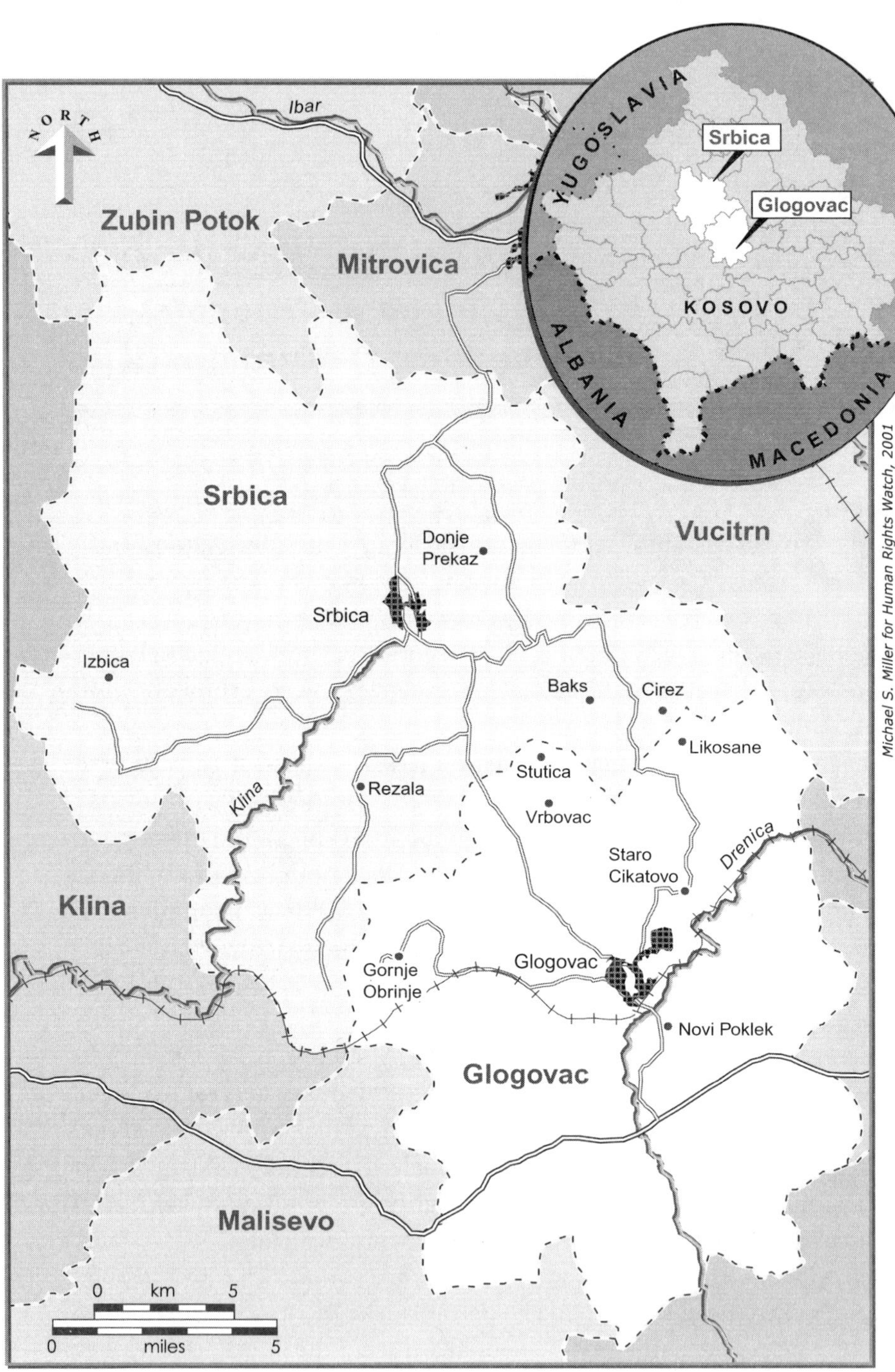
NORTH
Ibar
Zubin Potok
Mitrovica
YUGOSLAVIA
Srbica
Glogovac
KOSOVO
ALBANIA
MACEDONIA
Srbica
Vucitrn
Donje Prekaz
Srbica
Izbica
Baks
Cirez
Likosane
Stutica
Vrbovac
Rezala
Klina
Klina
Staro Cikatovo
Drenica
Gornje Obrinje
Glogovac
Novi Poklek
Glogovac
Malisevo
0 km 5
0 miles 5
Michael S. Miller for Human Rights Watch, 2001

fourteen policemen in a gun battle provoked multiple reprisal killings of civilians from the villages of Gornje Obrinje and Golubovac and the detention and abuse of hundreds of Albanian men in Glogovac police station.[4] The deployment of the OSCE Kosovo Verification Mission reduced but did not eliminate abuses against civilians in police raids on villages in the region or the resulting displacement of civilians, which continued throughout the winter.

Serbian police and paramilitaries backed by the army attacked and cleared of its civilian population village after village.

The withdrawal of the KVM in March 1999 signaled an intensification of Serbian police and military activities in Drenica. Any restraint imposed by the presence of international monitors was now removed. Three months of terror followed, as Serbian police and paramilitaries backed by the army attacked and cleared of its civilian population village after village in its efforts to destroy both the KLA and its base of support. Adult males were detained en masse and hundreds were executed. Killings were not confined to persons regarded as potential combatants. As with earlier massacres in Gornje Obrinje and Racak (Stimlje municipality), women and children from the families of persons linked to the KLA were also killed. Many of the killings occurred in the days following the NATO bombing of the Feronikel mineral plant near Glogovac on April 29, as thousands of civilians were forced onto buses and expelled from the town to the border with Macedonia.

Abuses in the Drenica region were so widespread that a comprehensive description is beyond the scope of this report. Few villages were left intact, and few families without victims.[5] Instead, this chapter will concentrate on the key atrocities from the period of March to June 1999 in the villages of Izbica, Rezala, Poklek, and Staro Cikatovo; the major offensive in the area of Vrbovac, Stutica, and Baks that followed the NATO bombing of the Feronikel mineral plant on April 29 and its bloody aftermath; and the forcible expulsion of thousands of people from Glogovac, the region's largest town during the first week of May.

IZBICA (IZBICE)

Human Rights Watch interviewed almost a dozen witnesses to the events in Izbica on March 28, 1999. Their testimonies, coupled with NATO satellite imagery and video footage produced by Kosovar Albanians, document one of the largest massacres of the Kosovo conflict. The exact number of ethnic Albanian victims remains unknown, although villagers who buried the dead reported counting between 146 and 166 bodies. The killings were cited in the war crimes tribunal's indictment of Slobodan Milosevic, and others, made public on May 27, 1999.[6]

Set beneath the mountains and a half hour from the nearest Serb village, Izbica was considered a safe place for Albanians from neighboring areas to take refuge, in part because of the KLA presence in and around the village. By March 27, thousands of ethnic Albanians from the area had gathered in Izbica. Most had come after NATO started bombing, when government forces began to shell the surrounding area.[7]

By all accounts, the shelling of Izbica began during the night of March 27, and a group of at least fifty soldiers, police, and paramilitaries entered the village that evening. Nearly all of the adult men fled to the mountains, leaving mostly women, children, and old men in the village on March 28. H.D., a forty-year-old man from Brocna (Buroje), near Izbica, recounted:

> At least 30,000 people were crowded in Izbica that day. Unfortunately, we believed that the women and old men would not be harmed, which turned out to be wrong. There was shelling from all directions. Younger men, including me, fled into the mountains in the morning. I left with my thirteen-year-old son at about 10 am. We had brought our family to Izbica the morning of the previous day. We had stayed overnight in a field in the open air there. I was so tired that the shelling didn't even wake me up, but my wife woke me up because of it at around 9 am. So we fled into the mountains. The shelling came closer, and so did the Serbs. I was about 200 meters away, in the mountains, trying to watch. The Serbs came close to our families. Our families were huddled in the midst of their tractors and cars; the Serbs burnt all this. I couldn't see it, but I could hear the women and children crying. We didn't dare move to see what was happening; we knew we could be killed by snipers.[8]

Villagers left their houses to congregate in the field in the early morning hours of March 28, as the shelling continued. S.E., a twenty-year-old woman from Izbica whose father, uncle, and cousin were killed, told Human Rights Watch:

When we saw the Serbs coming we didn't dare stay in our houses. We went by tractor to a nearby field (about 500 meters from the village)—me, my mother and father, my brother, my sister, her family, and her mother-in-law—a total of ten people. We joined the rest of the inhabitants of the village in the field, all of the other families. Families had started leaving their houses at about 4 a.m. By 10 a.m. everyone was in the field. There were thousands of people, almost all women, children, and old people. Only about 150 men were among us.

At the field, everyone got off their tractors and huddled together. We had chosen the field because we wanted to be together. We were too scared to stay alone in our houses; it would be too easy for the Serbs to kill us there. From the field, we could see the Serbs setting our houses on fire. They were shooting in the air and yelling loudly: insulting us and scaring the children. [9]

Two women who encountered the Serb forces that day said that the men wore both camouflage and dark blue or black uniforms, and carried long knives. Both women recalled that some men wore dark ski masks and others had their faces blackened with greasepaint.[10] Another woman reported that several of the paramilitary men had been recognized as local police officers.[11]

At around 10 a.m., the group of Serbs reportedly swept through the village, forcing the few remaining inhabitants to flee. Those who were unable to leave were killed. S.E.'s sister, who returned to Izbica three days after the massacre, reported:

On March 28, the day of the massacre, the Serbs set Shaban Rexhepi, age ninety, on fire. He had been sitting on a straw mat near his house; the Serbs set the mat on fire. I saw his bones; there was no flesh left on them.

The family of a paralyzed woman put her in the trailer of a tractor, which was full of mattresses. The Serbs found her and lit the trailer on fire with the woman inside. Her name was Zyka Bajrami, age about seventy. This also happened on March 28.[12]

When the Serb security forces arrived at the field, at about 10 a.m., they threatened to kill the villagers and burn their tractors, and demanded money. S.E., whose father was later killed, told Human Rights Watch:

They told us, "give us money if you want to survive." They said it cost 1,000

> DM to save your family and 100 DM to save your tractor. Everyone paid, each man paying for his own family. My father paid 1,100 DM.
>
> After the Serbs got the money, they shot out the tires of everyone's tractors, and then burned all our belongings, which were bundled up on the tractors.[13]

All witnesses reported that the Serb security forces then separated the men from the women and children, expelled the women from the village, and executed the men with automatic weapons. It was around noon. S.E., her mother, and her paralyzed brother were part of the convoy that was forced out of the village. She described how the Serb security forces harassed them and forced young boys to return to the field:

> At about 11 a.m., they separated the women from the men. We asked them why they were doing this and they told us, in a very scary voice: "shut up, don't ask, otherwise we'll kill you." The children were terrified. The Serbs yelled, "we'll kill you and where is the United States to save you?" All the women had covered their heads with handkerchiefs out of fear of the Serbs, hiding their hair and foreheads. The Serbs called us obscene things, saying "fuck all Albanian mothers," and "all Albanian women are bitches."
>
> They took the men away and lined them up about twenty meters away from us. Then they ordered us to go to Albania. They said, "you've been looking for a greater Albania, now you can go there." They were shooting in the air above our heads. We followed their orders and moved in the direction we were told, walking away from the men.
>
> About 100 meters from the place we started walking, the Serbs decided to separate out younger boys from our group. Boys of fourteen and up had already been placed with the men; now they separated out boys of about ten and up. Only very small boys were left with us, one old man who had lost his legs, and my handicapped brother, who can't walk because of spinal meningitis.
>
> So they took the ten to fourteen- years-olds to join the men. The boys' mothers were crying; some even tried to speak to the Serbs, but the Serbs pushed them. We were walking away very slowly because we were so worried about what would happen to our men.
>
> We stopped moving when we heard automatic weapon fire. We turned our heads to see what was happening but it was impossible to see the men.

> We saw the ten to fourteen-years-olds running in our direction; when they got to us we asked them what was happening. They were very upset; no one could talk. One of them finally told us, "they released us but the others are finished."
>
> We stayed in the same place for some twenty minutes. Everyone was crying. The automatic weapon fire went on non-stop for a few minutes; after that we heard short, irregular bursts of fire for some ten minutes or so.
>
> Then ten Serbs caught up with us. They said lots of obscenities and again told us, "now you must leave for Albania—don't stop, just go." We had to leave.[14]

Her account was corroborated by a thirty-year-old woman, interviewed separately, whose husband and son survived by hiding in the mountains.

> In the field we crowded together in a tight circle. The men were separated from the women, and were led away. Then they told us to go to the asphalt road. We heard the sound of shooting, but I myself couldn't see anything. It happened at about when the convoy reached the main road, about twenty minutes after we left the men. We understood that our men had been killed from those women at the back of the convoy: word spread through the convoy.[15]

During the following several days, men began to come down from the mountains and several of the women who had been forced out of the village returned in search of relatives. In the field where the massacre took place, they found, by all accounts, four groups of men who had been shot. Three groups were in the field, and one smaller group was beyond the field, near the foot of the mountain. Men who buried the victims reported that most of the bodies had a bullet through the side of the head. Some bodies were badly mutilated.

H.D., who hid in the mountains with his son during the massacre, was among the first to discover the bodies.

> On the fourth day, unfortunately, I returned to Izbica. I say unfortunately because I would rather not have seen what I saw. It was a terrible massacre. I saw my uncle, who had been executed by the Serbs. I saw one of my aunts; she had been burned in her garden. I saw many more dead. The total num-

> ber of people killed was 150. Most of the men were elderly. A cousin of mine was over ninety.
>
> I was among the first to find the bodies. When we came down from the mountain, we found the first group of dead bodies in a pasture at the foot of the mountain. There were three separate groups of dead bodies in the field, the men who had been separated from the women, and a few bodies in the mountain. The second group was just beyond a stream of water. I myself had heard the sound of automatic weapon fire when they were killed. When I heard the burst of fire, I said, "Oh my God, they've killed them all." It was at midday.[16]

Another man from Izbica, fifty-two years old, also hid in the mountains and returned to look for his brother. His description matches those of the other witnesses to the site.

> The first group was about 200 meters from the tractors, above the houses at the foot of the mountain. We saw a group near a small stream, about twenty to twenty-five meters from the previous group; this group included my brother. There were about twenty-three people in this group.
>
> The group with my brother included many bodies in bad condition. You couldn't recognize some of them. You could only recognize the ears of one man: the upper part of his head had disappeared. Most of them had been shot in the head. Most had small holes on one side of their heads, while the other side was completely destroyed.[17]

The testimony of a survivor of the massacre, published by Amnesty International, corroborated the descriptions of the site gathered by Human Rights Watch. The survivor recounted that the men were divided into groups, led to different areas, and lined up facing away from the soldiers. Serb forces shot them from behind with automatic weapons, and the man was able to survive by feigning death.[18] Witnesses interviewed by Human Rights Watch claimed to know of between six and sixteen men who had survived the execution.

"When I heard the burst of fire, I said, 'Oh my God, they've killed them all.'"

Villagers who returned to Izbica set about the task of burying the victims. According to the participants interviewed by Human Rights Watch, between sixty and eighty people buried the bodies in the field in three rows.

The graves were shallow, approximately sixty to ninety centimeters deep, because the villagers were tired and working quickly. The name of each victim, when identifiable, was recorded on stones near the graves and on a master list.

One man buried his brother, a victim of the massacre, and his brother's wife and daughter, who were killed in a tractor accident as the families were driving to the field on March 28.

> . . . [W]e organized a council of men to decide how and when to bury the bodies. We started digging graves the next day, sixty to eighty of us. All of us had been hiding in various local mountains. It took us all day to dig the graves. Four or five bodies were left unburied that day because there wasn't time. All day we tried to find flat pieces of stone to write the names of the dead on. We buried them about ninety centimeters deep.
>
> I saw all the bodies when they were brought together. There were 156 or

NATO released these satellite images of a field near Izbica on April 17, 1999, as part of its publicity campaign. The photo on the left was reportedly taken on March 9. The photo on the right, with what NATO claimed was "up to 150 graves," was reportedly taken on April 15. NATO MEDIA ARCHIVE

> 157 of them. The council made a list of the dead. Each dead person has a number that corresponds to the number on the grave.[19]

A woman from Izbica who returned to the village on March 31 and assisted in the burials told Human Rights Watch:

> I saw my father dead. The families had brought the bodies to the village from the mountain where they were killed, less than a kilometer away. My husband and nephew carried my father.
>
> I saw all the bodies. We counted them. It was horrible. They had been brought to a field and placed in three rows. They were buried in three rows. Relatives of the dead were there, mostly men. Each family buried their dead. Each family opened up the graves. There were many people there. The graves were very shallow. We had to bury them fast.[20]

In May 1999, CNN aired video footage that a Kosovar Albanian, Dr. Liri Loshi, claimed was taken at the scene of the Izbica massacre. The footage shows a large number of bloody corpses in civilian clothing—ethnic Albanians who the doctor claimed were killed in the massacre. Two witnesses who helped bury the dead reported independently to Human Rights Watch that two local villagers had filmed the site, and both identified the man who then gave the video footage to Dr. Loshi.[21]

NATO satellite images taken on April 15, 1999, and released two days later appeared to confirm the three rows of graves in the Izbica field, holding what NATO believed was "up to 150 graves."[22] NATO compared the photograph to a March 9, 1999, satellite image of the same field that showed no signs of disturbed earth.

The witness cited above, H.D., interviewed by Human Rights Watch on June 9, 1999, claimed that Serbian forces returned to Izbica in the first days of June to dig up the bodies and bulldoze the field, although he did not observe this himself.[23] The ICTY investigated the site in July 1999, with 142 graves reported, but was unable to find any of the bodies.[24]

REZALA (REZALLE)

The village of Rezala is located in the southern part of Srbica municipality, close to the Drenica mountains. It is not clear whether the village had strong links with the KLA. The village was reportedly the scene of clashes between Serbian security forces and the KLA on May 15.[25] Whatever the motive, Serbian forces entered the village on April 5 early in the morning, entered and burned houses, ordering the population outside. Most of the men from the village were in the hills at the time, but according to witnesses, the eighty-three men who were present were detained together with women and children. Some of the men were from the nearby village of Morina. One of two remaining survivors, X.X. (initials changed), a sixteen-year-old boy, explained how the villagers were detained:

> Early in the morning they [Serbian police] surrounded the village—they were shooting from all sides. Then they came inside the village—into every house. They took us outside the house. After they took us outside they set fire to the houses. They told us to walk towards a hill, saying to us, "you can go to [Hashim]Thaci or Clinton." [Then] they took us into the yard of [H.D.'s] house. They kept us there from 11 to 5 p.m. They separated the men from age fourteen to fifty and beat us—they tied our hands behind our backs. [26]

The testimony of sixty-year-old M.D., the other remaining survivor, suggests that although men were questioned during the course of the day, the decision to kill them had been made in advance:

> When they took us in the yard they started to check us. They told us to take everything we had out of our pockets. We were all kinds of people—old men, blind men, young men. There was a thirteen-year-old boy and they shot him [with everyone else]. When we were surrounded they were asking us [questions]. We heard when they said 'is it enough so we can kill them now?'[27]

Serbian police appear to have gone to considerable lengths to create a pretext for the killings. X.X. said that one group of Serbian forces fired toward the village while others told their Albanian captives that the shots were coming from the KLA. Since the killings were intended to leave no survivors, it is possible that the Serbian police hoped to be able to characterize the deaths as being the result of crossfire or accidental fire from the KLA rather than deliberate murder. According to M.D., "sometimes when we were standing in the yard they were shooting. They were saying that our army was shooting at us."[28] Whatever Serbian forces hoped to achieve, the survival of X.X. and M.D. leaves no doubt as to the actual cause of death for the villagers of Rezala. At around 5 p.m., the men were ordered to line up in pairs. X.X. continued his testimony:

> At 5 p.m. another group of police came from Marina [village]. Those that were with us there went to another side [of the village] toward Likovac [village]. The [police] who went [toward] . . . Likovac started shooting and the others were telling us that the KLA were shooting at us. Then they took the women and children in the direction of Likovac and sent them to Srbica. One man there who was blind was trying to take his thirteen-year-old son away, but they brought him back and were beating him. They told us to get in line two by two. They took us down to the road to Likovac [Likofc]. Then they brought some others—three or four of them—from some houses. . . . After [the police] brought these men they started to prepare their guns. One of them went to the roof of the house of [H.D.]. There were about thirty police there with us. The one who was on the roof was the first one to shoot. Then the others started to shoot. I was wounded with three bullets. They were shooting for half an hour. Then after that another one came closer and started to shoot with an automatic. When he came close to me he didn't have any bullets. When he came back from reloading he went somewhere else and fortunately didn't shoot me. Then they took the trucks and tractors and started to drive away. I stayed there for two hours because I was afraid to move.[29]

Like X.X., M.D. survived by playing dead. He explained, "They told us to walk to the left. We walked about 100 meters. The police were hiding behind the tractors. I didn't see anything after that—I just found myself wounded."[30] Initially, there were four survivors. In addition to M.D. and X.X., fifty-year-old Sadri Gashi, and sixty-eight-year-old Pajazit Khelmendi were both alive after the killings. Neither man survived for long. According to M.D., Sadri Gashi was captured ten days later together with his brother and killed. Pajazit Khelmendi died of his wounds four days after the massacre. M.D. and X.X. are the sole remaining survivors. For M.D., whose brother was killed in the massacre, relief at survival is shaded with loss:

"When I woke up from that place and the other people were dead, I thought, 'these people are lucky, because I don't know anything about my family.' I don't know how I survived—I was with them—together with them."[31]

The horror of Rezala did not end with the killings. Information from KLA fighters suggests that in late May, the bodies were dug up with bulldozers from the shallow graves in the field.[32] It appears that the human remains in the graves were replaced with the carcasses of dead cows. Journalists visiting the site in June confirmed that the top layer of the graves contained animal remains. M.D. believed that the bodies of the villagers lie below those of the animals, although none were found by ICTY investigators. His frustration is evident: "People are saying that they took the bodies away but I am not satisfied that that's what happened. . . . Everyone wants to find the body of their father, the body of their son. We know that they are not going to live again but we just want to know where they are."[33] The present location of the bodies is unknown.

POKLEK

Poklek is a relatively wealthy village with two parts—old and new—located on the outskirts of Glogovac. The KLA had been active in and around the area since at least March 1998. The village also suffered a fair amount of damage, as well as human rights violations, throughout that year. A damage assessment conducted for the European Union by the International Management Group in January 1999 determined that 40 percent of New Poklek's (Novi Poklek, or Poklek i Ri) seventy houses had been damaged, while 47.6 percent of the 164 homes in Old Poklek (Stari Poklek, or Poklek e Vjeter) had been damaged.[34]

The most serious human rights violation during 1998 took place on May 31 when an estimated 300 special police forces attacked Novi Poklek. Ten local ethnic Albanians were seized that day during the attack; one of them (Ardian Deliu) was later found dead, while the nine others have never been found.[35] Poklek remained a dangerous place up until March 1999 because of the presence of Serbian forces in the nearby Feronikel plant. Many villagers had moved to Glogovac or to the neighboring village of Vasiljevo a few kilometers away. A Human Rights Watch researcher visited Vasiljevo in June 1998 and observed a KLA checkpoint and other forces.

None of the abuses that took place in and around Poklek throughout

1998 compare to what happened on Saturday, April 17, 1999, in the old part of the village. According to numerous testimonies, including one survivor, at least forty-seven people were forced into one room and systematically gunned down. The precise number of dead is unknown, although it is certain that twenty-three children under the age of fifteen died in the attack.[36]

At least forty-seven people were forced into one room and systematically gunned down.

A Human Rights Watch researcher visited the site of the killings—the house of Sinan Muqolli—on June 25, 1999. The house had been largely burned, which was consistent with witness testimony. The room where the killings took place had bullet marks in the walls and bullet casings from a large-caliber weapon on the floor. The basement below the room had dried blood stains dripping from the ceiling and walls, and a large pool of dried blood on the floor. Surviving family members displayed a cardboard box containing some of the bones they said were collected from the room and showed the nearby well where they claimed some of the bodies had been dumped.

Human Rights Watch first heard about the Poklek killing on May 8 from a member of the Muqolli family, F.M., who was in the Cegrane refugee camp in Macedonia. The thirty-nine-year-old woman told Human Rights Watch that the police had attacked Poklek on April 17, a rainy day, around 6:00 a.m. She said:

> The police were first based in the Gorani family compound. The massacre took place about 150 meters from there. At 8:30 a.m. the shooting began. We were running away in a field toward Glogovac. Sometimes we stopped for the group to gather. The police were in a Zastava 101, white jeeps, and a grey Niva. We made it finally to Glogovac, but a second group behind us was blocked by the police and sent back.[37]

F.M. stayed in Glogovac for eight days before going back to Poklek. When she returned to her village with a cousin, four members of the group that had been turned back eight days before told her what had happened on April 17:

> They said that they went into the house of Sinan Muqolli. "You will change your clothes here," Sinan told them. "You will be safe here." The police

> entered and the children screamed. Sinan said, "Don't scream because they won't hurt you." The police counted sixty-four people and said, "Don't leave the house because we have counted you. If you want to save these people, then bring us four people from the UCK." Sinan said he has two sons in Germany and their wives are here. The police asked why all of these women were there. "Where are the men?" they asked.

F.M's story is supported by a fifty-five-year-old member of the Muqolli family, R.M., who was in Sinan's house and survived the attack. His detailed and damning testimony, as told to Human Rights Watch, is presented here in its entirety:

> Something happened that you can see nowhere. I think it was April 17. It was Saturday. They [the police] came from the hill. They had tanks and a car. They just started to shoot. We didn't know where to go, but we tried to go to

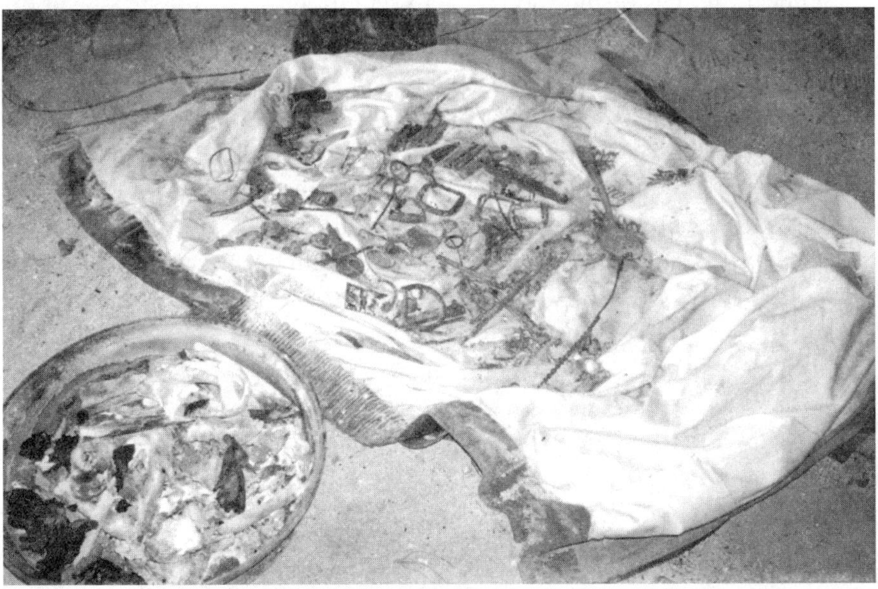

Personal effects from those killed on April 17, 1999, in the Muqoli family home. At least forty-seven people were murdered in the house, including twenty-three children under the age of fifteen.

© BENJAMIN WARD / HUMAN RIGHTS WATCH

Glogovac. They saw us and came with three cars to the house there [indicates a house close to the town], and they told us, "Just go back, because nothing is going to happen in Poklek." When we came back, they started shooting in the air.

We came back and gathered together, four brothers. There were seven of us. We wanted to stay together. We stayed there all day. At about 5:00 in the evening they came. Sinan opened the door for them. They told us to get out, all of us. We went outside. They asked us, "Do you have guns?" We said no. Then they told us to go inside. We went inside. Then he [sic] called Sinan and Ymer, and he took them out and killed them. The women started to scream. I was trying to tell the women, "No, no, they are just shooting in the air." After five minutes they came. There were a lot of us. First they just dropped a bomb, and the children and women started screaming. Then he [sic] started shooting with an automatic rifle. The rifle was firing for a long time. Then I heard someone from outside say, "Come on, leave them, they are all dead," but he saw someone alive and started to shoot again.

I heard him leave and was trying to get out. I got up and saw one of my neighbors, [H.M.], who was wounded and another woman and a daughter of [S.M.], who was wounded too. After that I was trying to help those who were wounded, because there was only me and a five-year-old child who were not wounded.

Fifteen or twenty minutes later I saw the police forces coming into this house. It's the house of my cousins. So the girls were trying to go to the village, but me and H.M. couldn't go to the village because they were watching us from Feronikel. After that, the police forces came and started to burn.

"I heard someone from outside say, 'Come on, leave them, they are all dead," but he saw someone alive and started to shoot again.'"

That night, when it got dark, we went out and saw that they had burned the houses, not once, but twice. We were trying to go to the village Vasiljevo. We stayed that night in Vasiljevo, and after four days we came back and found Sinan and Ymer who had been burned and thrown in the well. There are others who were killed and put in the well. They found the mother of Ymer, killed her and put her in the well. Halim was killed, and they put him in the well too. We were trying not to disturb the remains and to hide them from the police.

... Twenty-three or more [of those killed] were children between six and

> thirteen. Some old women around sixty years old [were also killed]. I lost a daughter, a three-year-old, two nephews—a three-year-old and ten-month-old—and a big daughter, twenty-one. There are thirty-four victims from the families of two of my brothers. There was a daughter of my cousin and three children and a sister-in-law.[38]

In response to a question about the identity of the single gunman who carried out the killings inside the house, referred to in his testimony only as "he," R.M. responded:

> I didn't recognize him, but he was uniformed, like a policeman. It was the same man who told us to go outside and go back home. The same man who dropped the bodies in the well. It was one man who threw the bombs and shot. It was the same person who did all of this.

STARO CIKATOVO (CIKATOVE E VJETER)

The village of Staro Cikatovo (Cikatove e Vjeter), which lies a few kilometers north-east of Glogovac, had a 1991 population of 1,300, all of them ethnic Albanians. The village is located close to the Feronikel plant, which at times since early 1998 had served as a base of operations for Serbian security forces against KLA insurgents active in the area.

The KLA was in and around the village throughout 1998 and 1999, and Serbian forces had inflicted a fair amount of damage on Staro Cikatovo long before the March 1999 offensive. A U.N. damage assessment conducted on November 2, 1998, determined that 60 percent of the village had been damaged, 20 percent of it severely.[39] At the time, only ninety Albanians were living in the village, mostly due to the proximity of the dangerous garrison at the Feronikel plant and the ongoing clashes in the area between Serbian forces and the KLA.

Human Rights Watch visited Staro Cikatovo on June 25, 1999. Residents said that there are 114 houses in the village. Between forty and fifty percent of the village was badly destroyed. Most houses had been burned from the inside, which indicates that they were purposefully burned rather than damaged in combat. Several structures had also been demolished by bulldozers.

According to witnesses from the village and Glogovac, government attacks on Staro Cikatovo began on Saturday, March 20, five days before the start of NATO bombing, when military operations were launched from the Feronikel plant against KLA positions around the village. A witness from the village, A.A.,[40] told Human Rights Watch: "We were between the KLA and Feronikel. [Serbian forces] started grenading from Feronikel to attack [KLA] soldiers."[41] Another villager described incessant gunfire that day.

Villagers told Human Rights Watch that they had been advised by OSCE personnel prior to the OSCE's departure that "if anything happened" the villagers should relocate to Glogovac. As the attacks continued on March 20, most villagers followed this advice. Most were able to reach Glogovac safely, but one group, consisting of members of the extended Morina family, were detained by police near the school as they tried to exit the village. One of the women from the family, B.B., told Human Rights Watch:

> In front of the school, we were stopped by the police in tanks. They took our men and put them to one side, asking them if they were soldiers. They put us in the school—women and children in one classroom and men in the other. They kept us from 7 a.m. to 3 p.m. They told us, "If a bullet is fired by the KLA, we're going to kill all of you." [Then the] police and military left us in the classroom and went towards the mountains, where the KLA was. They were shooting from Feronikel with cannons and rockets.[42]

By mid-afternoon, all of them were released and told to return to their homes. The following day, March 21, the Serbian Red Cross arrived around 1 p.m. and evacuated some of the remaining women and children from the village. Many refused to leave because, they said, the Serbian Red Cross would only take women and children, and they did not want to leave their menfolk behind. Those who were evacuated to Glogovac stayed there for periods ranging between ten and twenty days before returning to Staro Cikatovo. In the words of one of the women evacuated by the Red Cross, B.B., who later returned to Staro Cikatovo, "We came back ten days later because half of our family had stayed."[43]

Over the ensuing three weeks, the remaining inhabitants of Staro Cikatovo watched as unoccupied houses were looted by the police and paramilitaries. According to several witnesses, Serbian security forces also commandeered civilian cars and tractors, which they used to move around the village. For the most part, however, the remaining residents were left undisturbed during this period, although they were frightened by the threats made during their detention in the school.

A.A., a twenty-nine-year-old woman from Staro Cikatovo, described to Human Rights Watch how on or around April 14, three police officers entered the house of her uncle during the afternoon for what appeared to be a routine check. At 8 p.m. that same evening, the three men returned wearing masks made from sheets they had taken from the clothesline outside. Women and children were inside the house as well as an eighty-two-year-old man. According to A.A., who was present, "They harassed the old man, saying, 'Give us money or gold or we will kill you all.'" The three men demanded 500 Deutsche Marks. B.B., who was also present, tried to collect the money: "We said, 'Can we go and ask others, because we don't have any money?' So my sister went to look for money and gave them 300 Deutsche Marks. They also took our gold." Before leaving, one of the police pointed at a one-year-old child and, according to B.B., said, "It is thanks to this small baby that you are still alive, otherwise we were going to kill all of you."

The April 14 robbery was a precursor of the horror that was to follow. In the early hours of Saturday, April 17, the village was again raided by Serbian forces. By the end of the day, twenty-four men from the Morina family had been kiiled. A seventeen-year-old boy and an elderly man were forced to endure life-or-death negotiations with paramilitaries and police about whether they should be put with the men, i.e. killed, or allowed to leave with the women and children. They were eventually allowed to go. The survivors from Staro Cikatovo insist that none of the dead men were involved in the KLA, although several members of the family are admittedly KLA soldiers, including two who were wounded in the assault.

Prior to the April 17 attack, the Morina family had gathered in a few houses in one part of the village for safety. According to statements from six witnesses, the houses were attacked in the early morning from four sides: "from the direction of Feronikel, the school, the KLA-held area and the electricity generating stations." A.A. described what she saw:

> At 6:00 a.m. a lot of shooting started.... We didn't go outside. We were afraid because of the shooting, and we had no idea what was happening to the neighbors.... At around 7 or 7:30 a.m. they came to my uncle's house.... When they told us to get out we saw that the yard was full of heavily armed police. We came out—men, women and children; we women came out behind the men.[44]

Witness D.D., a mother of five children, was in another house nearby. She said:

> They took a very strong action against the village at 5:30 a.m. Our children were still sleeping. There was a lot of shooting from automatic rifles and grenades. Glass from the windows and tiles from the roof were falling on us. We lay down on the floor inside our house with our children. . . . They entered the house, breaking the door and came into the rooms. They took us by our arms and forced us outside. They didn't even let us get dressed. . . .[45]

Villagers describe a mixture of police, paramilitary and military forces in either dark blue or green camouflage uniforms and iron helmets. Some had either a red, blue, black, or yellow bandana tied onto their arms, which may have been used to cover the insignia on their uniforms or to identify troops. D.D. claimed that she saw a tiger emblem sewn onto some uniforms and that the troops were wearing black fingerless gloves. If true, the tiger emblem might indicate the presence of Arkan's Tigers, the notorious paramilitary group. Witnesses also emphasized that the forces were heavily armed, with flak jackets, automatic rifles (in some cases with bayonets), and grenades.

C.C. described how the occupants of the houses were taken outside. The men were separated from the women, he said, and lined up against the walls of the nearby houses. Since the houses were close to one another but not adjacent, the families were gathered in several groups in the village, and the evidence points to a time lapse between the operations against each of the groups. C.C. told Human Rights Watch:

Villagers describe a mixture of police, paramilitary and military forces in either dark blue or green camouflage uniforms and iron helmets.

> They came to our house and shouted, "Come out one by one." We came out and walked into the street. There was already another group there. The forces were all drunk and wearing iron helmets. They were all red in the face and had bandanas on their arms: red, blue, and black. We were afraid. Then that group separated us—men from women. They didn't let us talk or do anything. They were angry, out of their minds. Our mothers were grabbing us, but they were hitting them. Fathers who had children in their arms

had the children taken away. My sister held my father's hand. One of them said to her, "Let go of his hand, and go to your mother." She wouldn't, so they hit her in the head with a rifle butt. My father's eyes were full of tears.[46]

It was during this operation to empty the houses and separate men from their families that the first killing occurred. According to several relatives, the security forces caught Avdil Morina as he was trying to sneak his family away to safety. Avdil was stabbed in the throat and then shot dead in front of his family. B.B., who witnessed the killing, told Human Rights Watch, "He had a big wound in his throat—they stabbed him in the neck, pushed his wife and child away, and shot him."

Meanwhile, the women were being ordered to leave the village. Another witness, E.E., explained:

> They brought us to the house of a neighbor. From that house they took four men. From our house they took three men—my father-in-law, his uncle, and my husband. All the men were separated on one side. My mother-in-law tried to intervene . . . but they forced us out and told us to go to Glogovac. Then they took the men to a lower place. When we left on the road, they just started shooting. I didn't see whether they shot in the air or on the ground, but I heard a lot of shooting. We knew at that point that they had killed them. My mother-in-law fainted.[47]

Despite the efforts to kill the men out of sight, one woman, Witness A.A., saw eleven of the men being shot around 8 a.m. She told Human Rights Watch:

> They lined up all the men against a wall, and they directed all of us away, but I didn't go with the rest [because] my husband has only one son. Women were screaming and children were crying, but it was useless. They put the men in the yard of a neighbor, [shots were fired], and I saw them fall down. The children didn't want to go away—they were crying. After I saw them fall down I started to scream [to the others]: "Hey, they killed them all!" There was a lot of shooting. . . .[48]

Several of the male Morina family members, including an elderly invalid and a young boy, did manage to escape with their lives, but only after negotiating police checkpoints and the threat of execution. The younger of the two survivors, C.C, explained what happened:

> They took me too. My grandmother wouldn't let me go, but they kept screaming, "Go away from here, because we are not releasing them." One police officer told me, "Go" and the other put his rifle against my chest and said, "Where are you going?" It happened three times. Then they talked among themselves and decided to let me go. They released my grandfather too. After this they didn't release anyone else. . . . Then they screamed at us, "Go to Glogovac." But we didn't want to leave, so they started acting crazy. Then we went a little further away. They told the men to line up behind a wall. After they had lined them there—they had rifles. I didn't see them directly, but I was five meters away. I think I saw their blood splash.[49]

After being sent down side streets and walking through ploughed fields, the group with C.C. and his grandfather were stopped by police outside the school, where many of them had been detained almost one month earlier. Again the fate of the two male family members was the subject of discussion. According to C.C.:

> They called my grandfather, and they asked him about me. They separated me from the line so I had to go to them. They asked me, "Why did they let you go? They shouldn't have let you go." My grandfather said, "The others down there released him." They searched him and said over and over again, "Why did they release you?" Women were crying for me, my mother, grandmother, and others. They said, "Let him go, he's the only one left, and he's young." Fifteen minutes later, one of them told me to go. So then we started towards Glogovac.

The group was stopped again on the road to Glogovac by military personnel at the Feronikel plant, and faced similar questions but was eventually allowed to proceed to the town.

Despite at least three subsequent attempts by some of the older women to return to Staro Cikatovo, in order to locate and bury the bodies of their dead men, they were not permitted to return to the village. According to A.A., the women "never made it further than the school. . . . The third time they went, they were told, 'We can let you in but there are police in the houses, and they might kill you.'"

THE APRIL 30 OFFENSIVE

As the testimony from Rezala, Cikatovo, and Poklek suggests, actions by Serbian security forces in Drenica were designed in part to control the flow of the civilian population. Just as certain villages were attacked early on and their populations forced to flee, other villages were left comparatively untouched to serve as so-called "free zones" where displaced civilians could take shelter. The strategy of forcibly concentrating the civilian population into a few villages was complicated by efforts to create barriers of civilians between Serbian security forces and the KLA, thereby limiting the ability of the KLA to attack Serbian positions, or defend from attack. As noted above, the villagers of Staro Cikatovo found themselves hostage to that strategy, as they were forced to remain in their village caught between Serbian forces based in the Feronikel plant and the KLA positions these forces were attacking.

As mentioned above, the Feronikel plant was frequently used as a base by Serbian and Yugoslav forces throughout 1998 and 1999. There are unconfirmed reports that the large mine and industrial complex was also used as a detention facility for Albanians beginning in March 1998. OSCE personnel who visited the site in June 1999 were shown what is characterized in their report as "possible evidence of torture" of civilians by Serbian security forces, such as a pole with nails hammered into either end.[50] The testimony of Glogovac area residents certainly confirms a consistent presence by Serbian security forces during March and April 1999.

On the night of April 29, NATO aircraft bombed the Feronikel facility, causing extensive damage to the buildings and plant. The extent of the casualties among Serbian forces and damage to military capability is unknown. However, the response of Serbian soldiers, police, and paramilitaries was swift, clear, and brutal. Early on April 30, Serbian forces attacked the villages of Stutica, Vrbovac, and Baks and surrounding areas. As many as one hundred Albanian men were killed and more than two hundred taken prisoner during the operation.[51] The prisoners were taken to a destroyed mosque in nearby Cirez and held overnight. The next day, they were loaded onto trucks for jails in Glogovac and Lipljan. Some of the trucks stopped at the Shavarina mine near Staro Cikatovo. At least one hundred men were taken off trucks at Shavarina and executed. The survivors were taken to Glogovac, where they were interrogated and beaten for five days before being transported to three villages where they were forced to work until June. The final death toll is believed to be in excess of two hundred.

Vrbovac (Vrbofc)

On April 30, the village of Vrbovac and the surrounding area were under KLA control. Although the area had been attacked by government forces before, witnesses present in the area described the village and its environs as a "free zone," meaning that it was an area where Albanian civilians were safe from attacks by Serbian security forces. As a result there were a large number of displaced persons from other villages sheltering in the Vrbovac area, including Gladno Selo, Trstenik, Poljance, Globare

The Feronikel plant near Glogovac was used as a base by Serbian and Yugoslav forces throughout 1998 and 1999. NATO bombed the facility on April 29, 1999.

© BENJAMIN WARD/HUMAN RIGHTS WATCH

and Poklek. An attack on the village in early April had already forced the inhabitants to flee to the woods for one night. According to R.K., a Vrbovac resident:

> April was the worst month because it was the month when most of the people were killed. I'm going to tell you when my father was killed. He was eighty-four-years old. When the Serbs attacked us we all ran away from the house but he stayed here. They killed him at night in the yard. We couldn't come back that evening. We had to sleep in the woods. When I came back I found him in the yard. He was shot in the head.... My father was killed April 7 but most of the people were killed April 30....[52]

The April 30 attack on Vrbovac began at dawn. Six witnesses interviewed independently by Human Rights Watch state that the village was attacked between 5 a.m. and 7 a.m. All the witnesses describe how the village was surrounded. Given the presence of the KLA in the Vrbovac area, the surrounding of the village by Serbian security forces made tactical sense. According to F.P., a twenty-two-year-old Vrbovac resident who described himself as a member of the KLA:

> The village was surrounded on all sides. The forces came from the direction of Gladno Selo, Poljance and Cirez.... The offensive began at about 6 a.m. and lasted until about 4 p.m. They were shooting with tanks and mortars.... There were only [KLA] ten soldiers [in the village] ... the rest were civilians. Most of the soldiers were in the woods.[53]

F.P. who was "in the woods, watching with binoculars," also said that at around 3 p.m. his unit had encountered a Serbian police position in the woods and had fought with them for an hour. According to R.N., a seventy-eight-year-old Gladno Selo resident who was present in the woods near Vrbovac on April 30, " a few" of the people killed in the woods were KLA."[54] R.N. also said that members of the group he was hiding with in the woods had rifles and a pair of binoculars, although he did not specify if they were KLA members.

Although large numbers of civilians were present and some of the dead, who included elderly men and boys, were clearly civilians, the presence of the KLA and the admission from a KLA soldier that the KLA was engaged in combat with Serbian security forces on the day of the killings complicates the analysis of the killings. The largest number of killings appears to have taken place in what witnesses refer to as a "dell." The testimony of M.H., a twenty-six-year-old man from Poklek who was sheltering in Vrbovac at the time, suggests that the attacking Serbian forces left an escape route, which led into the "dell" area. He explained:

> We were surrounded. The offensive started at around 5 a.m. My aunt told us to go away because the police had arrived. We were still sleeping. When we left [Vrbovac] we saw there were forces all over the area. We saw there was only one way out. So we went to that field and to the mountains. It was like a dell. . . . We could hear the voices of the Serbs talking. They surrounded us. They were about two kilometers away. They started shooting, but not at us. When they came close they shot at us. Some of us were killed—I was only wounded. My brother was shot in the chest with three bullets. The police heard him talking, came back and shot him again with nineteen bullets. I saw him [being shot]. . . . A policeman was looking at me. I was covered in blood so he thought I was dead. I stayed in that place for twelve hours. There were twenty-nine people killed at that time.[55]

S.G. a sixty-two-year-old man from Vrbovac, became separated from some of his family members who had decided to take shelter in the dell:

> It was April 30, about 6 a.m. . . . We were all sleeping when we heard shots from all sides. . . . After about half an hour all the people from the houses higher up in the village were coming this way. The women, children, and elderly went in the direction of the field and the youngest—the men—we went in the direction of the woods. . . . When I was up in the woods I could see forces coming from all sides, from Globar, Trstenik, Cirez, Stutica and Gladno Selo. We were surrounded. I met some of the refugees [displaced people] from my house and my son-in-law. None of us knew what to do. As a parent I felt responsible for my children. I told them to run away from the hill. We thought that it [the place where our children took shelter] was some kind of dell so they [Serbian forces] wouldn't find them there. But they [Serbian forces] killed them all there . . . Among the people they caught in the dell—some were brought to a neighborhood of the village—including my brother—and they killed them there.[56]

Whether they were ordered to limit killings or were simply permitted to kill whomever they wished, Serbian forces did not kill all the Albanian men they encountered in the Vrbovac area. S.G. was captured by Serbian soldiers the following morning, after having the spent the night at home, and was taken to Glogovac unharmed, where he was detained (see section on detentions below). Capture did not necessarily end the risk of being killed, however. B.R., a forty-five-year-old Vrbovac resident narrowly escaped death after intervening to save his son:

> It was April 30, about 7 a.m. The forces were inside the village. They were coming from all sides with all kinds of vehicles. We men decided to run away. . . . We went to the woods. I was with my son. My oldest son didn't stay with us. [Serbian forces] saw this son [who was with me] in a bush. They surrounded my son and shot around him. They told him to call for his friends but he didn't understand Serbian so one of them said 'he's pretending he doesn't understand Serbian, let me shoot him.' When I saw that they were going to shoot my son I went to them and said 'he doesn't understand.' They took us close to the water and told us to take off our jackets. Then they beat us very badly. Then one of them, a commander, saw some more of us [Albanians] so they took my son, [R.], as a hostage to go and find the others. One of the Albanians had a gun and shot once at the paramilitaries. Three police put their guns on my shoulders and began shooting. They killed two and caught another one, I.F. I saw when they cut him with a knife [indicates across throat]. When I saw my son was in danger I said to the police let him go and take me.
>
> They didn't listen to me. They beat me with a stone and the butt of a gun. They cut my hand with a knife. I don't know how many of them there were—ten or fifteen. They took us and made us stand in a line. They brought another person [V.B.], and told him to go and find the gun that the Albanian had had. But he found only one gun. They said there were two guns so they shot him. I was ten meters away. They told us to go in the direction of Cirez. Along the road, there was another group of police—special police—and a tank. The special police beat us at that location. One of us, Ismet Prokshi, they tied behind a tank. Then he was executed. I saw it. . . .
>
> My son was helping me to walk because I was covered in blood. I had a head wound and I couldn't see where I was going. About one kilometer before we reached the school in Cirez I collapsed. My son wanted to stay

> with me but they didn't let him. One of them was saying, 'why don't you kill him.' Another said, 'no, he is already dead.' They thought I was going to die so they left me. . . . It was the last time I saw my son. He was executed at Shavarina.[57]

B.R.'s beating and the execution of Ismet Prokshi by paramilitaries was confirmed by Z.Z. (initials altered), a forty-four-year-old man from Poljance, who was also captured outside Vrbovac on April 30.[58] According to the man, Prokshi, who was already wounded, was beaten to death after two NATO aircraft flew overhead in the afternoon. A.D. a twenty-four-year-old man from Trstenik was captured together with B.R. He confirmed the overflight by the NATO aircraft, and B.R.'s beating:

> They [Serbian forces] caught me with [B.R.] and his son at 11 a.m. First they started to beat us with everything they had in their hands. There is not much to say but they were trying to cut me. One of them had a red bandana on his arm. They took us to a stream and told us to lie down. . . . they beat [B.R.] and his son too. They took us to Stutica. On the road we met a group of thirty civilians. They told us to put our hands up. They took my ID card and passport. When I came back from England, I found my passport in that place. There were about sixty of us in Stutica. We saw dead bodies. I saw the body of one of my cousins. They told us to lie down and to take off all the clothing we were wearing. They left us with just t-shirts. . . . then they ordered us to go to the mosque in Cirez. It was 4 p.m. . . . On the road to Cirez we left [B.R.] because we thought he was dead. . . . One paramilitary wanted to shoot him but another said, 'leave him, he's already dead.'[59]

Y.Y. (initials altered) a middle-aged man from Globar was also caught near Vrbovac.

> It was April 30. [Serbian forces] attacked us from Globar, Staro Cikatovo, Cirez and from the side of Poljance, Stutica, and Vrbovac at about 6 a.m. There were more than 5,000 people staying in the woods. We call it "Fusha E Molles" (Field of Apples). We didn't have guns, but there was a small number of KLA inside [Vrbovac]. It was a terrible day, that day. They killed so many people. . . . Vrbovac was a free-zone. . . . It was 5p.m. There were about twenty or thirty of us. [Serbian forces] came close to us. The woods were on fire. There were army, police, and paramilitaries with masks. They came

> close to us, and surrounded us. We decided to give up. They beat us up and sent us to a house in Vrbovac close to the mountains. They told us to take off our jackets. Some of us were even without trousers. . . . [then] they sent us to the mosque in Cirez.[60]

Forty-five-year-old Baks resident A.S. was captured in "Fushe e Molles" earlier in the day at around 2 p.m. According to A.S., he and eighty-five others were told to lie down and were beaten in the field before being taken to the mosque in Cirez.[61]

Thirty-seven-year-old Z.K., from Gladno Selo, was also captured by Serbian soldiers on April 30 in what he referred to as "a dell," together with six others, and added to another group of thirty or forty Albanian prisoners. The men, one of whom had a weapon and may have been a KLA fighter, were detained, questioned about KLA involvement and beaten. At least two men were killed and another disappeared before the group was taken to Cirez:

> It was morning but I can't remember exactly what time, on April 30. We were running. They were shooting from all sides, coming closer and closer. . . . We were trapped so we surrendered. We were in a dell. I was with six others, four uncles and two men from Cikatovo. We gave up. . . . Other soldiers came. One of them said to us "give us everything you have"—we gave them everything—money, watches, jackets. . . . They took us with our hands up onto the road. There were more people there—thirty or forty of them—with a guard. Then they took us about 200 meters away. . . . We were lined up one by one. . . . They were beating [H.B.] because he had a gun and they took another man, [B.B.], into a stream and killed him. We don't know . . . [what happened to] [H.B.] . . . One of their soldiers came back covered in blood. He asked the others to choose one of us because "one of them is mine." At that time they killed [S.], my uncle's son. I heard them talk about how they had killed him. Then they came to us and said "we're going to kill you all." They beat the young people with a stick. Then they took us to a house. . . . [There was] an officer there with four soldiers. They said "we'll call you by name." They had a list of people in the KLA but no one among us was on the list. From that place they took us to "Fusha E Molles". . . . There was a tank. They asked us to take off our clothes so they could cover the tank, because they were afraid of NATO. They told us lie down and asked us 'are you in the KLA." [H.B.] was very bad[ly wounded]. He couldn't speak. I was hit with the butt of a rifle

and questioned and hit with a fist. . . . They questioned everyone there. After they brought another group there—there were about thirteen of them—and did the same things to them, asking questions and beating them. Then they took us in the direction of Cirez.[62]

Stutica (Shtutice)

The nearby village of Stutica was also attacked early on April 30. Stutica had been attacked on March 20, forcing residents to flee to Cirez for a week, and villagers had also evacuated the village during a two-day offensive by police in early April. The village then remained quiet for three weeks. Several witnesses noted that Stutica and Vrbovac were the only villages in the area without a permanent Serbian security presence during the month of April. As in Vrbovac, displaced persons from Dosevac, Cirez, and other surrounding villages had taken refuge in Stutica as a result. When the village was attacked on April 30, male residents and displaced persons fled to the surrounding woods. Many of the men were caught later the same day, and were taken to Baks and then ultimately to Cirez. Forty-four-year-old Stutica resident R.B. narrowly escaped death when the group of twenty-five men he was part of was attacked in the woods:

It was April 30 in the morning. I had just woken up. We saw that we were surrounded. The grenades started, so we had to leave the house and find a safer place. . . . There were about twenty-five persons in one place outside. . . . The women and children of the village were in the school. The men ranged [in age] between fifteen and seventy. During the day Serb forces were coming closer and closer to us. At about 5 p.m. they came very close to us. [It was] Serbian paramilitaries and army. They shot at us. I was the first one to be wounded [in the fingers]. . . . We heard somebody say "don't shoot, we are civilians." We put our hands on our heads. . . . I saw that more than eighteen [people] had been killed. Seven of us got out from there—four of us were wounded. I was wounded in the fingers, chest, and side [indicates bullet holes in jacket]. They checked our clothing for gold, watches and money. . . . Then we went to Baks. . . . When we got to Baks they ordered us to go to one house and lie down on the floor . . . they beat us with a big stick. When we went out on the road we saw some civilians who had been arrested—a lot of people

> including three of my brothers and some children. They took seven from that group and killed them. We know where they are buried. They were beating us and insulting us. . . . Near the mosque in Cirez they stopped us. One soldier came (who was very tall with dark skin) and a lot of other soldiers were beating us. One of them killed a man in front of us.[63]

A.A., a nineteen-year-old man from the village, was in the same group. His account corroborates R.B.'s statement:

> Early in the morning, Stutica and Vrbovac were attacked. There were so many refugees and a large number of people [from the village] there. The men decided to go into the woods. A large number of forces came here on foot and with tanks. They were shooting in the woods with mortars and tanks. It was about 3 p.m. when we got to the side of Baks. . . . At about 5 p.m. we were surrounded by military forces. At that moment there were about thirty of us. They shot at us for about five minutes. They were fifteen to twenty meters away from us. There were so many dead in that place—I was wounded in my left arm at that time. We screamed "we are civilians, don't shoot at us." They stopped shooting. They captured us and moved us away from the dead. My uncle was wounded but alive. He was trying to walk but he couldn't so they executed him. I was wounded in my left arm. They were telling us to keep our hands behind our heads but I couldn't. . . .
>
> They asked us for money and told us to take off our jackets. . . . They took us to Baks into the yard of a house. We were lying down with our hands behind our heads for one hour. After they took us out of there I saw some other [Albanian] civilians there. [Then] they took us on the road toward Cirez. I was at the start of the line with my father. As I told you, I couldn't put my hands up. One soldier came close to me and started to [verbally] abuse me. I didn't understand Serbian. Then my father began translating for me. Then he started to abuse him too saying, "why do you understand Serbian but your son doesn't." [The soldier] took a hand- grenade and wanted to put it into my mouth but another soldier told him to leave me alone. They put me back in the line. We heard some shots at the end of the line but I didn't see what happened. . . . Then they told us to go to Cirez.[64]

Twenty-two-year-old Stutica resident, A.S., was in another group hiding in the woods that was captured at around the same time. Although the group was not fired upon immediately, the circumstances of their capture were similar. A.S. explained what he saw:

> It was April 30, a Friday. The day after they bombed Feronikel. We woke up before 5 a.m. and we were surrounded. Vrbovac and Dosevac [were] also surrounded. The youngest men ran away from the houses to the woods, leaving the rest of [our] families here. We were hiding in the woods. There were shots all day long. It was between 4 and 5 p.m. when [Serbian forces] caught us. They came in a tank. . . . There were forty or fifty of us staying there. After they took us from that place they told us to lie down with our hands behind our heads. They began to beat some of us immediately. They killed a boy there [who was] thirteen years old. After that they took money and some clothing, put us in a line and took us to Cirez. [65]

It is notable that many of the men captured near Stutica and Vrbovac were told to remove their jackets and other clothing. Survivor Z.K.'s explanation is that "they asked us to take off our clothes so they could cover the tank because they were afraid of NATO."[66] It is certainly possible that just as farm buildings and houses were used to shelter tanks and other military equipment, clothing may have also been used to make identification by NATO aircraft more difficult. Another possibility is that the security forces were searching the men for signs of fighting, such as a uniform under their clothes or bruising on the shoulder from firing a gun.

Baks

As witnesses from Stutica and Vrbovac have testified, many of those captured were taken to the village of Baks before being sent to Cirez. Baks appears to have served as a collection point for the prisoners prior to their detention in Cirez (described in detail below). Both R.B. and A.A. from Stutica describe their detention in a house in Baks before being moved to Cirez with another group of Albanian civilians. In addition, Stutica resident A.S., as well as F.R., a thirty-nine-year-old man from Cirez who had been staying in Stutica, describe the detention of fifteen or sixteen men in the yard of a house in Baks. According to both A.S. and F.R., the men lying on the ground were ordered to join the new arrivals and directed toward Cirez.

F.R. identified the owner of the house:

> When we came into Baks, near the house of [name withheld], fifteen or sixteen civilians were lying on the ground with their hands behind their heads. We thought they were all dead. We stayed there about fifteen minutes. They were ordered to get up. We saw that they were alive. Then they went in front of us [in the line of prisoners]. . . . .We started to walk towards Cirez with a tank behind us. When we got to [name withheld]'s house [Serbian forces] ordered us to stop. They shot at houses near to us. We didn't know what they were shooting at. When they came back they began beating us with guns. My father and uncles were part of a group of five who were ordered to stay there. The rest of us were ordered to go to Cirez. Four of them [the five] came later and one man from Dosevac was killed.[67]

R.B.'s testimony describes the execution of seven of the Albanian men being held prisoner in Baks. The seven were part of a group of eight men who were detained outside Baks by paramilitaries after a Serbian policeman had been killed. The eight men were beaten and forced to carry the police officer's body to Baks, where they were lined up and shot. The sole survivor, twenty-two-year-old M.F., recounted his ordeal:

> It was April 30, a Friday. . . . I was with two brothers, a nephew, an uncle and three cousins. We went towards Baks through the hills. It was about four o'clock in the afternoon. Paramilitaries came. They surrounded us and took the eight of us. They brought us to a field and started to beat us. There was [the body of] some police guy who had been killed. After they beat us they took us towards Baks. On the road to Baks they stopped us and began beating us, saying "are you in the KLA? Do you have guns?" We weren't in the KLA and didn't have guns. We were carrying that dead [police] man. When we got to Baks they asked us to tell them which one of us killed him. . . . They beat us again, asking us the same question. There were about thirty or thirty-five police officers there. They told us to go two or three meters away. One person began shooting. We ran. Some others came out of a tank and fired as well. One of my brothers and a cousin were the first to be killed. I fell down. I was wounded in my leg. They thought we had all been killed so they took the tanks and went away. After they had gone about 250 meters away, two of them came back and walked around for about five minutes then walked off. After that I got up, looked around and saw that everyone had been killed.[68]

M.F. described the paramilitaries as wearing "uniforms, but not like a soldier. They had green and brown bandanas on their heads and a red scarf tied around their arms. The uniforms were green and yellow camouflage." M.F. showed a Human Rights Watch researcher entry and exit wounds on his leg consistent with his statement. M.F. eventually made his way to Stutica where he was helped by a relative.

"They thought we had all been killed so they took the tanks and went away. "

According to Q.Q. (initials altered), a forty-six-year-old Dosevac resident, twenty-five-year-old Bexhet Shabani was executed by paramilitaries in a separate incident in Baks.[69] A.S., the twenty- two-year-old from Stutica, claims that he saw the body of "a young man lying dead in the road" upon entering Baks.[70] Q.Q. and many of the others witnesses interviewed claim that there were more executions in the Baks area, but Human Rights Watch was not able to confirm these reports.

The Mosque in Cirez (Qirez)

Many of the men captured in the Baks, Stutica, and Vrbovac areas on April 30 were taken to the mosque in Cirez and detained there overnight. The mosque, which is located in the center of the village, had been ransacked and burned prior to March 1999. Human Rights Watch interviewed twelve witnesses who were detained in the damaged mosque on April 30. The witnesses are from the villages of Baks, Cirez, Dosevac, Gladno Selo, Globare, Poljance, Stutica, Trstenik, and Vrbovac, all of which lie within a five kilometer radius of Cirez. Most stated that an Albanian man, S.K., had been ordered to count the prisoners, and that he had counted 176 men in the mosque. S.K. was subsequently executed. Several witnesses indicated to Human Rights Watch that the count did not include a smaller group of men who were being held on the upper floor of the mosque. Whatever the total, the purpose of the count would become clear the following morning, May 1. After spending the night in the mosque, the men were taken outside in two groups, the first at around 8 a.m. and the second at around noon. Some were beaten. On both occasions, the prisoners were then organized into smaller groups and ordered to get on to trucks. The size of the groups and the number of trucks had clearly been calculated from the count conducted the night before. On each occasion there were three trucks, and the prisoners were split into groups of between twenty and thirty.

Underlying all the statements from witnesses who were detained at the mosque in Cirez was that they had feared execution at any moment. Cirez resident, F.R., who was detained in Baks after having fled his village, was part of the first group to be taken out of the mosque. He was badly beaten before being put on the first group of trucks:

> We arrived at the mosque in Cirez. We were lined up two by two. They called an Albanian guy and he started to count us. At that time they brought a man on a tank. They put him about one hundred meters away from us. They took a belt and put it around his head and ordered him to put his hands up. He walked for ten meters and they shot him twice. They ordered us to go into the mosque. We were about 175. Most of us were from Cirez, Baks, Stutica, and Vrbovac. . . . [We spent the night there]. . . . The next day at around 8 a.m.

More than 170 ethnic Albanian men were held in this mosque in Cirez on April 30, 1999, where they were interrogated and beaten. The next day two groups were taken to the nearby Shavarina mine, where an estimated 121 of the men were executed. © BENJAMIN WARD/HUMAN RIGHTS WATCH

> . . . we were told to line up two-by-two and face the wall. . . . An hour later paramilitaries came . . . They said whoever speaks Serbian come here. About twenty people went and were sent outside [the mosque]. Then they beat them. You could hear the screams. It was like [listening to] wild animals. They ordered us to go out of the door two by two. When I went out one Serb soldier (or whatever he was) said to another that I was a Turk. He cut my head with a knife. Another one said "give him to me." They took me to the side of the mosque. [The second one] had a big knife and started to cut my clothing. . . . He was cutting my jacket. Then he put the knife on my stomach. But another one said, "don't kill him," so he put the knife down. As I was standing there someone broke a pane of glass over my head. They told me, "you are the second one we are going to kill." I was standing like this [indicates position] with my hands behind my head. [One of them] broke one of my fingers. . . . My father saw me covered in blood. . . . [Then] me and another guy were ordered to get on a yellow truck. There were three trucks at first that were going to Glogovac. . . . We were in the last truck.[71]

Nineteen-year-old Stutica resident A.A. was also in the first group to be taken out of the mosque early on May 1. After being beaten, he witnessed one man's execution with gunfire and another who was burned alive:

> They put us in the yard of the mosque in Cirez. Some officer started beating me. Then he took another man from Vrbovac and executed him in front of our eyes. There were more people in the mosque when we entered. They told S.K. from Gladno Selo to count how many we were. I can remember that there were 176 of us in the mosque. We spent one night there. The morning after, at 7 or 8 a.m., they took us outside the mosque again. Then they put us into groups—one group in the graveyard of the mosque and another at the back of the mosque. There were about twenty soldiers. They were saying "we are going to take you to the new graves of Mohammed." Behind us I can remember there was one person (alive) lying down and they set fire to him. . . . They told us to stay on our knees with our hands behind our heads, looking down. They asked for money again. . . . .I was trying to take money out of my pocket but I couldn't do it with one hand. Then a soldier came with a knife and cut my pocket. I had two pairs of trousers on. When I tried to take one pair off a soldier took me out of the line and asked me why I was wearing two pairs. I told them it was because it was cold and I had been sleeping

> in the woods. Then they said "you are KLA." . . . I tried to tell them I wasn't a KLA soldier. They sent me back to the line. Then they put us in a truck. As we came close to the truck a soldier hit me on the head with a bottle because I couldn't get on the truck . . . because I was wounded. I don't know how but I managed to get on the truck. There were twenty of us on the truck.[72]

Another witness from the first group, twenty-four-year-old A.D. from Trstenik, also described the burning of prisoners with gasoline.[73]

It is unclear whether the intention of the operation in Cirez was to distinguish KLA members among the prisoners or simply to round up presumed sympathizers. Some of the lines of interrogation and threats against the prisoners were on their face designed to identify which among them were affiliated with the insurgency. The experience of Z.K., the witness from Gladno Selo who was captured in "the dell," shows that whatever the motivations, the theme of KLA membership was constant during the prisoners' detention in the Cirez mosque (and later). According to Z.K:

> A major came and asked for one of us who could speak Serbian. One of our cousins, [S.K.], acted a translator (he was killed later). . . . It was Friday. They took us into the mosque. He said "on Monday you will all be released, except members of the KLA.". . . We spent the night there. The next day paramilitaries came. They screamed and threatened us with knives. They came inside and started beating us but they saw there were so many of us so they took us outside, lined us up against the wall and beat us until we collapsed. After twenty or thirty minutes of beating us, one of them (who was in charge) ordered us to strip. They hit me with an automatic rifle. After that [the one in charge] told them to stop beating us. There was a wounded Albanian man. Two paramilitaries took him and said "you are free but must tell us who among them is in the KLA." . . . That Albanian was scared. He didn't care who was and who wasn't in the KLA and he chose some men there. . . . He told them that I am in the KLA. I said "I'm not." They said, "please don't lie to us because we'll kill you if you do it again." Then they brought some trucks and sent some to Shavarina and some to prison in Lipljan. They told us to go back inside the mosque and after three or four hours they came back and took us. . . .[74]

As his testimony suggests, Z.K. was part of the second group of prisoners who were detained in the mosque until the early afternoon. Despite this difference, the subsequent fate of both groups was the same. Each group was loaded onto three flatbed trucks (some witnesses from both groups said the trucks were painted yellow but it is not clear if the same trucks were used).The men were ordered to lie on the floors of the trucks and armed paramilitaries rode in the back of each truck. Some witnesses said the paramilitaries forced them to sing Serbian songs and beat them en route. The trucks were driven towards Glogovac town, and on both occasions at least two of the trucks stopped at the Shavarina mine near the village of Staro Cikatovo. The open-cast mine is part of the Feronikel complex. On May 1, more than one hundred prisoners were taken off trucks at Shavarina, lined up, and executed in the course of the day.

The Shavarina Mine

Despite being taken out of the mosque in the early morning, the first group was not loaded onto the trucks for several hours. A survivor from the second group said the first group of prisoners was ordered onto the trucks at around 11 a.m., which is roughly consistent with a statement from a witness from the first group who said that his truck had reached Shavarina at around noon. The separation of the prisoners into smaller groups and their assignment to individual trucks appears to have been made at random. While the selection of the groups was left to chance, the horrific consequences for those selected to board the second truck were no accident. The first of the three trucks was allowed to proceed directly to Glogovac and on to Lipljan. Trucks two and three were stopped at Shavarina. The men from truck two were ordered off the truck and lined up along a drainage trench at the side of the road and shot. The prisoners from truck three were there to witness the killings.

As noted above, F.R., in the first group of prisoners taken from the mosque, was on the last truck. He witnessed some of the executions in Shavarina:

> We went to a place called Shavarina. The first truck didn't stop. The second did. The third truck stopped and they told us to get up [and] told us to look at the other truck. They said "This is going to happen to you." They killed five

> or six people in front of us. It's near Feronikel—it's a place called Shavarina. Then with my own eyes, I saw my uncle get off the truck with another seventy-year-old. They were standing by one another facing the soldiers. The soldiers were about ten or twelve meters away, just watching. There were groups of people [of various sizes]. First they killed the groups of five—one by one. When they finished them they started on the group of fifteen or sixteen. After that another person came and shot the people who had fallen down at close range. I couldn't watch anymore. There was a small explosion and the Serbs started to laugh at us. We were just waiting for our turn to be killed. We were lucky not to have to get out of the truck.. [then] they took us to the police station in Glogovac . . .[75]

"First they killed the groups of five—one by one. When they finished them they started on the group of fifteen or sixteen."

A.S., the Baks resident who was captured in "Fushe e Molles," was on the same truck as F.R. His testimony underscores the terror of the prisoners in truck three as they witnessed fellow villagers being executed:

> They brought three trucks and put us in the trucks lying on top of one another. Then they drove towards Glogovac. When we arrived in Cikatovo, at Shavarina, they stopped two trucks there. People from one truck were all killed. They put them in three groups. Some of [the Serb forces] had bandoliers of bullets. Then they shot at them and they fell down there in that hole. Then another car came from Glogovac. We were thinking they would kill us but they took us to Glogovac.[76]

The second group was out of the mosque at around noon, although witness statements suggest that they were not ordered to board the trucks until several hours later. The pattern of their transportation and murder was broadly similar to that of the first group. The prisoners were ordered to form smaller groups before getting on to the three trucks. The first truck went to Glogovac, although it first stopped at Shavarina for between thirty minutes and an hour, allowing enough time for several witnesses to hear gunshots, even though they were unable to see what was happening. The second and third trucks stopped at Shavarina as before. This time, however, the occupants of both trucks were taken off, lined up and shot. Almost all were killed, but several were able to escape. Their testimony is the only eyewitness record of the events that afternoon.

Forty-four-year-old Z.Z. (initials altered), the Poljance resident who witnessed the beating death of Ismet Prokshi near Vrbovac, was one of the survivors. He described his escape:

> They took us out of the mosque. It was 4 p.m. when they put us on the trucks. It was May 1. (We had stayed one night in the mosque.) The first truck in front of us went on the road to Glogovac. I was in the second truck with four paramilitaries with automatic weapons trained on us. They asked us to sing "Serbia, Serbia." We were going to Shavarina. They stopped at the crossroads to Dobrasevac and Feronikel. I don't know about the truck in front of us, but in my truck they put us in tens and took us out of the truck ten by ten. . . . I was in the third group and there were twelve of us, so I knew we were thirty-two in total. Close to me was a guy called ["Q.Q"] so I just touched him a little on the hand so he understood I was trying to tell him to run away. He was the first to try to run away from here. I was behind him. There were three paramilitaries with rifles and seven with machine guns. They were twenty meters away from us. . . . When we started to run they began shooting at us. I was wounded in the shoulder by a bullet. Then I said: 'why don't you shoot me?—I'm a robot—you can't kill me.' . . . They chased us for two kilometers—shooting at us . . . After two or three kilometers they stopped shooting at us. I saw a stream [and went to it]. I was wounded. . . . the other man who was with me was trying to take care of the wounds. He said to me "we must leave here and find you a doctor.". . . we stayed there until it was dark. . . . In the evening I went to Dosevac. There was a doctor there who gave me first aid.[77]

Q.Q. (initials altered), a Dosevac man who had been captured in Stutica (see above), stood next to Z.Z. (initials altered) as they waited to be shot. Although less detailed, his account corroborates the other survivor's testimony:

> They put us on the trucks. I'm not sure what time it was—around 2 or 3 p.m. . . . They took us towards Glog, beating us on the way. They told us to sing "Serbia is big." They were beating us in the truck until we reached Shavarina.

> I was in the second truck. The first truck went to Glogovac. Everyone on the second and third trucks was shot. It was only me and another man from Poljance who survived. They took us out of the truck in groups. I was in the second group but I escaped with ["Z.Z"]. I don't know how many they killed because I didn't see. I think there's another one from Gladno Selo who survived. We were lucky [to have escaped] because they were shooting all around us. . . .[78]

Human Rights Watch was unable to locate any survivors from truck three. Testimony from Q.Q. and others indicate that truck three never arrived in Glogovac, nor were its occupants heard from again.

The total death toll from the Shavarina killings is believed to be 121. This figure is the total number of bodies discovered at two sites. Forty-nine bodies were found in the drainage canal at Shavarina, and another seventy-two corpses of those killed at Shavarina were exhumed from a site opposite the school in Staro Cikatovo. As of October 1999, thirty-seven of the forty-nine bodies from the Shavarina site had been identified, together with fifty-seven of the seventy-two corpses from the school site.[79] The total of 121 probably includes some or all of the twenty-four persons reported killed in Staro Cikatovo on April 16, as there were thought to be around ninety men on the three trucks whose occupants were killed. As noted above, however, the figure of 176 taken from the mosque on May 1 may be an undercount, since several witnesses suggested that a smaller group of prisoners on the upper floor of the mosque were omitted. Whatever the total, the executions at Shavarina provide some of the best evidence of the systematic nature of the killings by Serbian security forces during the spring of 1999.

Forty-nine bodies were found in the drainage canal at Shavarina, and another seventy-two corpses of those killed at Shavarina were exhumed from a site opposite the school in Staro Cikatovo.

Detention and Interrogation in Glogovac

Those who had climbed aboard the "safe" trucks in Cirez were taken to Glogovac and detained, questioned, and beaten by police for up to five days before being transferred to other detention facilities or taken to villages around Glogovac where they were forced to work. At least one man was killed while in detention in Glogovac. A.S. from Baks saw the man being chosen for death. According to A.S.: "There was a man sitting beside me from Gladno Selo. A soldier came said, 'I want to kill one of them,' so they took him [the man next to me] ten or fifteen meters away and we heard four shots."[80] R.B. from Stutica was also present. He explained what he saw: "a policeman came with a bottle of alcohol and said 'I'm going to kill Albanians.' The police who were there said you can have anyone you want. He took a man called Topila from Gladno Selo. He took him to a burned house and we heard four shots and the man didn't come back."[81]

Not all those detained in Glogovac were brought from the mosque. S.G., a sixty-two-year-old man from Vrbovac who was captured outside his house, was taken straight to Glogovac together with eighteen other prisoners from surrounding areas. The men were unharmed until they reached the police station. There they were beaten severely in police custody and detained for five days before being transferred to villages, where they were forced to work for security forces. S.G. explained what happened upon his arrival in Glogovac:

> They took us from Trstenik to Glogovac. There were one hundred police in the yard of the police station in Glogovac. At that moment there were nineteen of us [prisoners]. Some of the police had sticks and some had iron bars. Then they started to beat us. [By the end] most of us were beaten unconscious and covered in blood. After an hour they took us into another room. There were some other prisoners there. After another hour they told us to come out. They told us to face the wall. There were three lines of us. They beat us non-stop from 12 o'clock until 5 p.m. Nobody knew what was going to happen to us. We stayed there for five days without food—we got water only once a day. After five days they took us out of the police station. We were about two hundred then. They called us one by one and questioned us, beating us all the time, although they didn't beat me that day. They took our ID cards but returned them to us. We thought they were going to release us, but they only released a thirteen-year-old boy and a seventy-five-year-old man. . . . Unfortunately, [Serbian forces] killed both of them in Globar. . . . Then they brought two trucks and told us to get in—beating us all the time. They put us in the trucks, closed the doors and took us to Lapusnik. . . .[82]

Some prisoners were taken from Glogovac almost immediately. Y.Y. (initials altered) the fifty-three-year-old Globar resident who was captured in Vrbovac (see above), was detained in the Cirez mosque and taken on a "safe" truck through Shavarina to Glogovac. Y.Y. was beaten and detained overnight in Glogovac. He confirmed the release of the elderly man and boy, who were subsequently killed in Globar. Y.Y. was taken to Pristina before being transferred to the prison in Lipljan. He described what happened after he arrived in Glogovac:

> There were about thirty people on my truck. They didn't kill anyone from the truck. [Instead] they took us to the police station in Glogovac. It's near the municipal offices. There were more people [detainees] there. We were about fifty altogether. They [the police] beat us with iron bars, sticks and the back of shovels. They were beating us. After we collapsed they put water on our faces, even benzine [gasoline]. They told us to stand up and then started to beat us again. In the evening they put us in the nearby cinema. We stayed there until the following day. There were around sixty of us. The following day they [police] took us out and some civilians came and took our names, dates of birth, and took us one by one for questioning. They put thirteen of us in police cars and took us to prison in Pristina. We spent one night there. This happened on May 2. On May 3, we were taken to Lipljan on a large truck. We were not only from Glogovac, but also from Podujevo and Pristina. At the prison in Lipljan we were beaten very badly. I was there for twenty-six days. . . . Sometime they gave us one loaf between five but not every day. We were twenty-four in one room. They didn't beat us every day, but they did most days. I was injured in the chest because of the beatings. . . . [83]

On May 26, Y.Y. and sixty other prisoners were taken to the Macedonian border on buses and expelled. A.D., the twenty-four-year-old man from Trstenik, provided a similar account, adding that he was questioned in Pristina at police headquarters and at the prison in Lipljan about KLA involvement.[84] He was part of the same group of sixty-one expelled on May 26. The questioning and different treatment of this group suggests that Serbian authorities either suspected them of KLA involvement or believed that they were more of a threat than those prisoners who were made to work in the villages around Glogovac.

Detention and Compulsory Labor

Most of the surviving prisoners from the Cirez mosque were transferred from Glogovac to three nearby villages on May 5 and 6. Seven of the Cirez prisoners interviewed by Human Rights Watch stated that they had been taken in trucks to the villages of Krajkovo, Vukovce, and Poturk and handed over to Serbian security forces. The men were forced to work for approximately six weeks until the withdrawal of Serbian and Yugoslav security forces from Kosovo in mid-June. Tasks included digging trenches and bunkers. Witnesses reported incidents of beating and torture of prisoners at the hands of the government forces, although some noted that they were fed and received better treatment than they had at the hands of Serbian police and paramilitaries in Cirez and Glogovac.

R.B., the Stutica resident who received multiple gunshot wounds during the April 30 offensive, was among those detained by the police in Glogovac during the first week of May. On May 6, he was taken with seventy-five others to Krajkovo and later to Vukovce, where he was forced to work until June 15. He described his ordeal:

> In the afternoon the military police came in two trucks. They put us in the trucks—lying on top of one another. They were beating us and asking us to sing the song "Kosovo is Serbia." We had no idea where we were going until the truck stopped in the village of Krajkovo. They brought us a little bread and water and put us in three groups—two groups of twenty-five and one of twenty-six. I was with the twenty-six. They put us back on the truck and took us to the village of Vukovce. [There] they put us in five groups—four groups of five and one group of six. That day they asked us to dig bunkers. The young guy who was with me was saying to me "we are digging our graves" but I told him don't be afraid, we are opening a bunker. In the evening they put us all in the same room. . . . In that time they were beating and insulting us every time they lost someone to the KLA or NATO. They gave us food—we were working—but they didn't care if we were wounded; [there was] no medical treatment. I had my fingers wounded but I couldn't tell them I was wounded by soldiers. I told them I was wounded by police.
>
> The worst thing was done to Z.M., a seventy-year-old man who ate a piece of cheese [without permission]. One soldier made him stand for two days with his legs on two blocks. They didn't give him any food. After that they

> forced him to take off his clothes and get into a rain barrel and stay there all day. Another day he tied him in three places and left him like that—giving him very little bread. In the evening some soldiers came. One had three red lines on his jacket. . . . He untied [Z.M.] and started to beat him. Then they let him sleep for three days on the floor. Whenever they thought there was a risk—of mines for example—they made us go first. . . . I was in detention for forty-seven days.[85]

The men were forced to work for approximately six weeks until the withdrawal of Serbian and Yugoslav security forces.

Gladno Selo resident Z.K., who was also part of the group detained in Vukovce, confirmed the torture of Z.M., and that the group was forced to walk ahead of the soldiers in case of mines. Z.K. also said that towards the end of their detention Serbian soldiers had severely beaten S.G., a former director of the PTT (Yugoslav Post, Telegraph and Telephone) over the course of three days.[86]

There is some evidence to suggest that not all soldiers were willing to dehumanize their prisoners entirely. Several witnesses told Human Rights Watch that they were treated better by soldiers than by police or paramilitaries, noting the food that was provided and the more limited use of violence. The experience of nineteen-year-old A.A. from Stutica illustrates the differences in approach. After surviving a mass killing in the woods near Vrbovac that left him wounded in the arm and multiple beatings by paramilitaries in the mosque in Cirez and by police in Glogovac, A.A. was transferred to military custody, and provided medical treatment. He explained what happened after he was taken to Krajkovo on Wednesday May 5: "When we arrived in Krajkovo, they hit me in the same arm [that was wounded]. They took us to some houses there and told us to clean a garage there. It was the place we were supposed to stay. The following day I told them I was wounded. They didn't treat us very badly there—it was not the same as in the police station. In the evening, one of them who was in charge brought a doctor for me. I had been wounded for seven days. The day after (Friday) they took me to the hospital in Pristina. . . . I stayed there for six weeks."[87]

Several witnesses told Human Rights Watch that they were treated better by soldiers than by police or paramilitaries.

GLOGOVAC (GLLOGOFC) TOWN

The largest town in the Drenica region, Glogovac lies approximately twenty-five kilometers southwest of Pristina. Prior to the outbreak of Kosovo fighting in March 1998, it had a population of approximately 12,000, almost exclusively ethnic Albanians. Although Drenica, as a stronghold of the KLA, was a focal point of conflict throughout 1998 and the beginning of 1999, Glogovac itself, like most towns and cities in Kosovo, was spared any fighting or destruction. The Serbian police always held the town, and the police station was frequently used as a detention center for ethnic Albanians arrested from the surrounding villages, especially during the major government offensive in September 1998.[88] Police harassment, arrests, and beatings were commonplace in the period before NATO began bombing on March 25, 1999.

Serbian police and Yugoslav military operations in the villages around Glogovac began almost immediately after the OSCE's Kosovo Verification Mission (KVM) left Kosovo on March 19, 1999. Right away, many ethnic Albanians from the rural areas fled or were expelled from their villages and went to Glogovac.[89] By the end of April, the influx of displaced persons had swelled the town's population to more than 30,000, and residents were sheltering large numbers of displaced persons in their houses.

While the level of violence against civilians in Glogovac during the NATO airstrikes was lower than that inflicted on villages in the same municipality, eyewitness accounts describe multiple violations of human rights and humanitarian law in the town after the end of March 1999. At least five—and as many as nineteen civilians—were reportedly executed by Serbian police and paramilitary forces in the town. Glogovac's residents were repeatedly harassed by Serbian security forces and suffered detentions, beatings, house-to-house searches, robbery, and extortion. Some private homes, shops and businesses were ransacked, looted, and deliberately burned.[90] As with the April 30 offensive in the area of Vrbovac, Baks, and Stutica, the bombing of the Feronikel plant on April 29 seems to have spurred retaliation against the civilian population by Serbian security forces in Glogovac. Over a five-day period beginning on May 1, the majority of the population was expelled from the town and sent toward the Macedonian border.

Accounts from residents indicate a large presence of both Serbian police and paramilitaries. Witness testimony repeatedly referred to armed Serbian men having long hair and long beards, as well as bandanas on their heads and arms. One person said that a few paramilitaries even had UCK patches (Albanian for KLA) on their sleeves as a joke.[91] Some Glogovac residents claimed to have seen members of Arkan's Tigers—the notorious paramilitary group run by the late indicted war crimes suspect Zeljko Raznjatovic (Arkan)—but their claims could not be confirmed.

The only person identifiable by witnesses was a deputy police chief from Glogovac known as Lutka, which means "doll" in Serbian. Lutka's real name is Nebojsa Trajkovic. A known policeman in the town, residents said that he did not behave brutally, unlike many of the paramilitaries, although he was clearly involved in many thefts, and he was a principal organizer of the forced depopulation in early May, telling Albanians that they should "get on the buses or go to Albania by foot."[92]

Human Rights Watch visited Glogovac on June 25, 1999, nine days after NATO forces had arrived in the town. Many windows had been broken, cars burned, and there had clearly been a great deal of looting. There were approximately fifty burned houses in the town, most of them private homes.

Killing of Civilians

Some civilians were killed in Glogovac itself during the month of April, although the killings were on a much smaller scale than those in the villages. Human Rights Watch interviewed more than fifteen residents of the town, as well as a number of displaced persons from surrounding villages who were sheltering in the town. The majority of the interviewees had knowledge of between four and twelve killings in Glogovac, although one person claimed that nineteen people had been killed. Human Rights Watch has only been able to confirm the killings of Haxhi Selimi, Sokol Saiti, and two men from Banjica village with eyewitness testimony. Most of the killings, witnesses said, were carried out by paramilitaries and police during house-to-house searches and robberies.

Shortly after the March 19 departure of the OSCE from Glogovac (the witness did not know the precise date), the Serbian police killed sixty-year-old Haxhi Selimi and two men displaced from the village of Banjica, according to B.K., a fifty-two-year-old Glogovac resident.[93] He explained that Selimi, a displaced person from the village of Negrovce, was among forty people sheltering in his house at the time. Three armed police officers wearing green uniforms with white eagle insignia on their jackets, came to his house at around 10 a.m. One of the officers, who had a moustache and a dark complexion, demanded 2000DM (approximately U.S. $1042), he said, while the men in the house were forced to go outside. Haxhi Selimi was shot seven times by the officer with the moustache at point blank range, according to B.K.. Two of the shots were fired after Selimi had already died, he said. The witness also heard additional shots and later saw the bodies of the two men from Banjica, who were reportedly shot by the same police officer in the yard of a nearby house.

Most of the killings, witnesses said, were carried out by paramilitaries and police during house-to-house searches and robberies.

Late in the afternoon of March 28, paramilitaries entered the home of Sokol Saiti in Glogovac, demanding money and valuables. A fifty-three-year-old displaced man from Domanek village, A.H., who was staying near Saiti's house, told Human Rights Watch that the paramilitaries had informed local residents, including him, that they were "Arkan's men."[94] They were wearing black uniforms, with black camouflage makeup on their faces, and had bandanas around their heads. According to the man, the paramilitaries then shot Saiti. He told Human Rights Watch, "They shot him in the leg around 6 p.m. They didn't touch him or let anyone give him first aid until he had bled to death. The paramilitaries stayed in his house until he died at 1 a.m." Although he did not witness the shooting, Saiti's neighbor helped bury the man's body later the same day. This man claimed knowledge of an additional twelve killings, although he had not personally witnessed the deaths or seen the bodies.

A forty-four-year-old man from Glogovac, A.G., told Human Rights Watch that two ethnic Albanians were killed in his apartment building. He did not witness the killings, but as paramilitaries were robbing his apartment, he heard the shooting on the floors above. He told Human Rights Watch:

> They [paramilitaries] broke into my apartment about 4 p.m. on Friday, April 20. Two of them broke in. We were eighteen people. They were wearing green

> uniforms. They broke in and shot into the ceiling. Then they said, "All of your money, Deutsche Marks, gold, watches—give it all!" They even took our wedding rings.
>
> We were on the fourth floor. In the other apartment they killed Brahim Shala. Two others went there, and we heard one shot. They said they killed him because he was wearing a *plis* [the traditional Albanian white cap worn by older men]. On the fifth floor they killed another—Hysen Morina—because he looked at the policeman. We heard the shooting.[95]

Eight other residents from the town interviewed by Human Rights Watch, three women and five men, claimed knowledge of as many as nineteen civilian killings in Glogovac during late March and April, although they did not witness the deaths or see the bodies. The reported dead included thirty-four-year-old Hysen Morina, reportedly killed by paramilitaries during a robbery; Qazim Kluna (from Poklek); Sokol Hajrizi; and Rahim Krasniqi. At the very least, the residents' claims strongly suggest that further killings did take place during this period, mostly in the context of robberies, extortion and looting. Five of the witnesses said paramilitaries were responsible for the killings.

Detention and Abuse

Throughout the period between the departure of the OSCE and the expulsion of the population in early May, paramilitaries and police made frequent visits to the homes of Glogovac's inhabitants and displaced persons. Until the third week of April, most of these visits were connected with extortion and robbery, although threats of violence helped to intimidate the population, keeping most inside their homes unless it absolutely necessary to leave.

On April 22, the nature of these visits began to change. Over the course of a week, the regular police carried out early morning raids against various neighborhoods in the town, conducting house-to-house searches in which large groups of adult men were separated from their families and taken to the local police station. Almost all of the men were beaten in front of their homes or on the way to the station, and some were forced to sing Serbian nationalist songs.

Although some beatings took place in the police station and in the nearby garage, where many men were held, some detainees also reported that the police in the station generally behaved correctly, and even offered them cigarettes. Most of the detainees were questioned about the KLA and then released after no more than one day in custody. Their treatment is in marked contrast to the treatment of the "Cirez" prisoner group who were detained by the police in Glogovac during the first week of May (see above).

A thirty-five-year-old man from Glogovac was among the first group to be detained. He told Human Rights Watch:

> The police came in the morning at 8 a.m. on April 22. . . . They brought everyone out of their houses. . . . They separated men aged between fourteen and sixty from the women, children, and elderly. They put us against a wall and threatened to shoot us, saying, "Shall we shoot them or not shoot them?" Ninety percent of the men were beaten up as they were searched by the police. Then they said to us, "Go to the police station." They put us in a garage at the station . . . [and] said to us, "You are not safe here anymore. From now on the military will take responsibility. . . ." Around 3 p.m. the last person was released. . . . We were asked, "Have you been in the KLA?"[96]

The searches, beatings, and detentions on April 22 established a pattern that would be repeated throughout the week. On April 24, I.X., a fifty-nine-year-old male resident from the center of Glogovac close to the police station, received a visit. He told Human Rights Watch:

> In my house, around ten soldiers and paramilitaries came at 8 a.m. They knocked on the door. [When I opened it] they pointed their automatic rifles at me and told me to put my hands up. They took me outside with my family and checked all of us. . . . They beat up the men and ransacked the house. They hit me twice inside the house, while they were searching the house. My sons were beaten up on the street and taken to the police station.[97]

Although he was not detained due to his age, and his sons were later released, the message of the visit was clear: "They never let us relax and sleep," I.X. said. "We were always in anticipation of when they were going to come inside."

Some Glogovac residents received visits from the military as well as the police. On April 25, police came to the house of a fifty-six-year-old man,

B.B., in Glogovac around 9 a.m. After a weapons sweep, the men were lined up against the wall. The younger men were taken to the police station and beaten. The man subsequently received a second visit from the military. He told Human Rights Watch:

> Three or four days after the police came, the military came around at 1 p.m. and harassed us. They took our identification cards and told us to gave 100 Deutsche Marks if we wanted them back. After we paid the money they returned them. Then they checked our pockets.[98]

The raids and detentions continued on April 28 and 29, the day NATO first bombed the Feronikel plant. A displaced man in his forties from Gornje Obrinje who was staying in the center of Glogovac described what happened to him during an early morning operation:

> The police came on the 28th of April around 8 a.m. They searched us and . . . asked, "Do you have weapons?" They searched our house but they didn't take anything. . . . We [eighty-three men] were taken to the police station at 9 a.m. It was a garage. They put us with our faces against the wall and said, "If you turn around we will shoot you." . . . We were detained until 2 p.m. Other people were held there for three days . . . An inspector from the Ministry of the Interior wearing civilian clothes was asking me questions in Albanian. . . . The deputy chief of police, "Lutka," [Nebojsa Trajkovic] was also present while I was being questioned. He said, "We are leaving and the military are taking our place. If they find you they will execute you immediately."[99]

Another detainee, R.M., told Human Rights Watch what happened in the police station when the Feronikel plant was bombed. He said:

> Around 2 p.m. NATO began bombing Feronikel. We were in a part of the station with cars, and one high official with stars on his shoulders said, "You asked for NATO, and look what they are doing to us." He beat some of us with a shovel handle.[100]

Another man who was detained on April 30, N.B., explained how he was arrested and how the police responded to his group when the Feronikel plant was struck.

> They took me on April 30 at around 8 a.m. I was in my house, and around nine police surrounded the homes in the center. They took men up to sixty years old, altogether about 150 men. They took us to the police station. They beat us on the way with batons and shovels. It was the normal police. We went with our hands on our heads, and we were made to sing Serbian songs. We were put in the car garage. Most of us were released after about one and one-half hours, but about forty people stayed [including myself].
>
> We stayed until the next day around 5 p.m. In the moment when NATO attacked Feronikel, the police got so nervous. They beat some of us. They took me by the hair and slammed my head against the wall. Some people were made to work and clean the station. They were also beaten.
>
> They put us in a room in the cultural center that is near the station. There were forty others there, those who had been taken the day before. They said, "You asked for NATO, and now you've got it." Nine people were taken away for questioning, but they were later released.[101]

Subsequent events now make it clear that these operations were the prelude to the mass expulsion of the population: by instilling fear among the population, the security forces expedited their forced removal from the town.

Forced Expulsion

To some of Glogovac's residents, the objective of the detentions was made immediately clear. A small group of residents in the center of the town was informed on April 24 that buses would be arriving to take them to Macedonia if they wished to go. They were to be the first group to leave the town, whose residents had been effectively under siege since March 19. One of the residents, a twenty-three-year-old man, had the stark choice made explicitly clear:

> On Saturday (April 24) the police came into our house and told everyone to get out. They took me while they searched the rooms, forcing me to kick the doors open. The police hit me and my aunt.... They took us into the street. The police [in the street] were even worse. They threatened to kill us.... They gathered men from the houses and took us to the police station. There they told us, "There is no more safety in the town. We heard on the news that we

are keeping you as hostages. We are going to bring buses and take you to Macedonia if you want to go."[102]

Around 11:30 a.m. on April 26, the police went door to door in central Glogovac, telling residents that there were two buses going to Macedonia and that they were free to stay or go. The police, who reportedly included Petar Damjanac, the commander of Glogovac police and Nebojsa Trajkovic, the deputy commander known as "Lutka", also told people of their limited options. According to M.S., a twenty-year-old woman resident, "The police chief came with another police officer and said, 'We are not forcing you' but, he said, 'From now on the military will be in charge of this place.'"[103] Approximately two hundred residents were told that their safety could not be guaranteed if they remained, and they were given fifteen minutes to decide whether they wanted to leave. Most decided to go and boarded one of the two waiting buses, paying 50 Deutsche Marks per adult. They were then transported to the Macedonian border without incident, arriving around 4 p.m. the same day. The buses were clearly organized by the Serbian authorities: Several refugees said the way was clear to the border because the buses had a special pass from the Interior Ministry authorizing their safe passage through the multiple roadblocks and checkpoints.

The mass expulsion of Glogovac's residents and displaced persons did not begin until five days later, on May 1. The timing appears to be linked to the NATO attack on the Feronikel plant, and the April 30 offensive against the villages of Vrbovac, Stutica, and Baks (see section on April 30 offensive, above). The pattern established with the early expulsions continued, with organized buses being used to transport thousands of people out of the municipality over a five-day period. Buses went either directly to the Macedonian border or, in some cases, to a railway station near Kosovo Polje for transit to Macedonia. All adults were required to pay 50 Deutsche Marks if they were being taken directly to the border, or 25 Deutsche Marks for transfer to the train. Diesel fuel was also accepted as payment for travel. Again, it was the Glogovac police that were responsible for informing people about the buses and ensuring that they boarded them. Many witnesses identified the deputy police chief known as "Lutka" as the person responsible for organizing the expulsions and informing residents that the police "could no longer guarantee their

"They beat us on the way with batons and shovels."

security," while attempting to emphasize that their decision to leave was "voluntary."

On Saturday, May 1 at 10 a.m., a group of displaced persons from Staro Cikatovo and Poklek paid 50 Deutsche Marks each and boarded buses for Macedonia. According to a fifty-three-year-old displaced man from Domanek, A.H., that same day, white armored Land Rovers with loudspeakers were announcing further departures on the following day, with the message: "We cannot defend you, but your way to the border will be open, and no one will touch you." The next morning the man made his way to the center of the town and boarded one of an estimated twenty-five buses that left at around 10 a.m. [104] A seventy-three-year-old displaced man from Gladno Selo told Human Rights Watch that he left on the same day under similar circumstances.

Many witnesses identified the deputy police chief known as "Lutka" as the person responsible for organizing the expulsions and informing residents that the police "could no longer guarantee their security."

The following morning, Monday, May 3, police visited apartment buildings in the town. According to a seventeen-year-old boy: "Those of us who had apartments in Glogovac didn't want to leave. . . . [but] they entered by force and told us to get out because the military needed the apartments."[105] When the boy came out of the building with his family, buses were waiting. Two other witnesses interviewed by Human Rights Watch left the same day.

The clearance of apartment buildings continued on May 4, according to H.M., a forty-six-year-old man from Glogovac. He told Human Rights Watch, "The police came into the building at 9 a.m. They were going building by building. They indicated with their hands that we had to leave. There was a deputy commander with the name "Lutka," who was responsible for the evacuation."[106]

A fifty-six-year-old Glogovac resident who was transferred to the train near Kosovo Polje on the same day had a similar account.

> They [the police] were going through the streets and shouting at around 9 or 10 a.m. "Go out as soon as possible, go to the bus station to take the bus," they said. So we took some food for the children and some clothes and left the house. At the bus station they were putting us in the buses in lines by neighborhood. The buses were shuttling to Milosevo (near Kosovo Polje),

> and from there people went by train. We had to pay 25 Deutsche Marks per person for a ticket for adults. We arrived in Milosevo around 5 p.m. We were told to get off the bus, and the police put us on the train immediately. They didn't let us go left or right—we had to go straight to the train. We waited for two hours there. We had no problems after that except that they put twenty people in one compartment—it was very crowded. . . . There were police escorts on the train . . .[107]

Statements from other witnesses who left on May 4 corroborate these accounts. A.H., a fifty-nine-year-old man from Glogovac (originally from Domanek) who left the same day, was told by the police: "'Whoever has diesel can go.' I had fifteen liters in my tractor, so they let me go on the bus. Otherwise they wanted 50 Deutsche Marks."[108] Another man who was displaced from Gornje Obrinje described seeing "fifteen buses in an open area [in Glogovac]. There were more than a thousand people there."[109]

The expulsions continued on May 5, according to those who were forced from the town on that date, although in smaller numbers. By that time, much of the displaced and resident population of the town had been forced out. The police action in the first days of May was dedicated to the systematic expulsion of the civilian population from Glogovac. Following weeks of harassment, intimidation, robbery by paramilitaries and police, as well sporadic killings, a dwindling food supply, a heavy military and police presence, and the temporary detention of hundreds of men, the population was in no position to decline an offer of transport to Macedonia, especially when they were repeatedly told that their security could no longer be guaranteed. A small number of people remained; most became refugees.

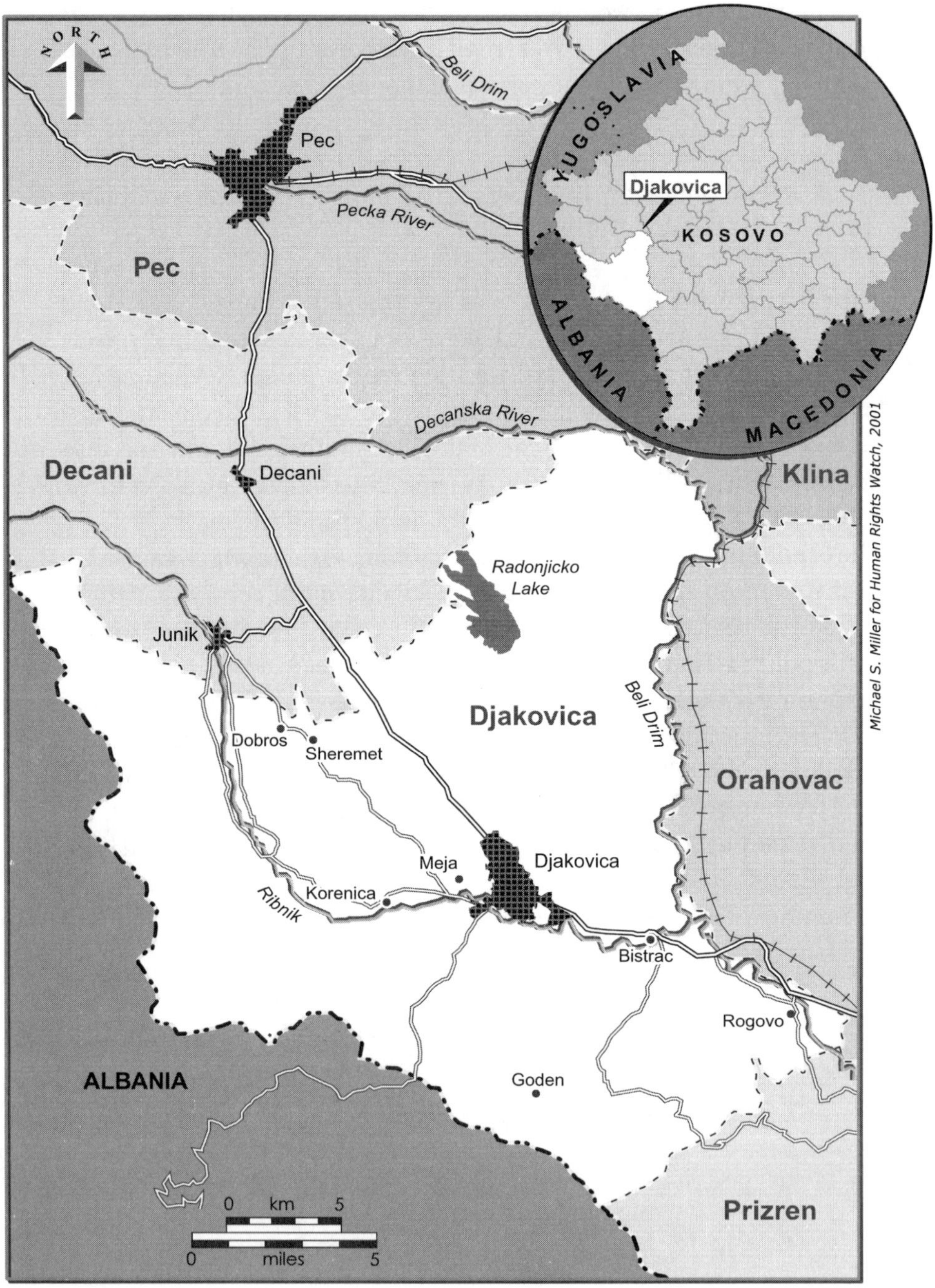

NORTH
YUGOSLAVIA
Djakovica
KOSOVO
ALBANIA
MACEDONIA
Beli Drim
Pec
Pecka River
Pec
Decanska River
Decani
Decani
Klina
Radonjicko Lake
Junik
Djakovica
Beli Drim
Dobros
Sheremet
Orahovac
Meja
Djakovica
Korenica
Ribnik
Bistrac
Rogovo
ALBANIA
Goden
0 km 5
0 miles 5
Prizren
Michael S. Miller for Human Rights Watch, 2001

6

DJAKOVICA (GJAKOVE) MUNICIPALITY

Djakovica municipality had a pre-war population of approximately 131,700, ninety-three percent of whom were ethnic Albanian, according to the United Nations High Commissioner for Refugees (UNHCR).[1] The area was severely affected by the war in 1998 and 1999 due to its strategic location along the border with Albania. The KLA was active in the villages of the municipality and used the border region for the smuggling of arms and supplies.

Government abuses increased with the withdrawal of the OSCE/KVM on March 20, but intensified dramatically with the NATO bombing on March 24. Villages along the border to the northwest of Djakovica city, in the direction of Junik, were depopulated. Prominent Albanians, including those who had worked for the OSCE, were targeted for murder in Djakovica city, and the old city center was burned. Reprisals for fighting in the Cabrat neighborhood between the KLA and government forces is one explanation for the severity of government crimes against civilians in the city proper (see below).

Some villages in the municipality were also hard hit.[2] As explained below, more than one hundred men are missing from an April 27 attack on Korenica. That same day, thousands of Albanians from the villages northwest of Djakovica were forcibly expelled to Albania and fled in a giant convoy. In the village of Meja, men were separated from the cordon, and approximately 300 of them remain missing as of April 2001. Twenty men were executed in Goden on March 25.

Meja was also the site of a NATO attack on a convoy of internally displaced Albanians on April 14. Later that same day, NATO bombed another

IDP convoy near the village of Bistrazin (Bistrazhin).[3] (For details see The NATO Air Campaign.)

DJAKOVICA (GJAKOVE) CITY

Djakovica suffered the most intense violence against civilians of Kosovo's larger cities. While not all of the city's estimated 100,000 residents (including 20,000 internally displaced) were expelled, threats and killing drove a majority of the population from the city. Serbian police and paramilitaries, as well as Yugoslav soldiers, killed approximately 200 people between March 24 and June 12 alone in the city, and many more were killed in nearby villages such as Meja and Korenica. Approximately 1,200 other people from the Djakovica municipality remained missing as of February 2000. At least 150 others were arrested during the war and taken to Serbia proper where they were convicted by Serbian courts for "terrorist acts," although most were later released.

The violence in Djakovica was well organized. Although some killings took place almost every day, the large-scale violence and destruction occurred in distinct phases and appeared well coordinated by the security forces. A few large-scale killings also took place, such as the murders of twenty people in one house, aged two to seventy-three, on the evening of April 1. Prominent residents of the city, such as lawyers, doctors, and political activists, appeared to have been expressly targeted for murder.

Those active in the repression in Djakovica included local police, police from other parts of Serbia, the army, and paramilitaries, all working in close concert with one another. Witnesses identified certain local policemen, as well as some other local Serbs. Some local Albanians were also said to have helped the police identify individuals, especially political activists, wealthy businessmen, or families with members in the KLA.

Djakovica suffered the most intense violence against civilians of Kosovo's larger cities.

Djakovica's proximity to the Albanian border was one factor in the intensity of violence. The nearby mountains were a common route for arms and personnel infiltration by the KLA which made the city strategically significant. From May 7 to May 11, intense house-to-house fighting between government forces and the KLA took place in the Cabrat neighborhood of the city—followed by a wave of state violence against civilians, as well as many detentions.

But Djakovica also has a tradition of resistance and Albanian national pride that may have contributed to the government's violent determination. The city's population—over ninety percent ethnic Albanian—strongly supported the Democratic League of Kosovo (LDK), the main Kosovar Albanian political party in the 1990s, and many young men from Djakovica joined the KLA in 1998 and 1999. Albanians from Djakovica also believe that the city was targeted because of its reputation as a cultural and intellectual center in Kosovo.

Because an estimated 25 percent of the population remained in the city throughout the war, there are a number of credible witnesses who observed the looting, burning, and killing that enveloped the city. Among these are the municipal workers who were ordered by the police to remove and bury the dead. Faton Polloshka, head of the Djakovica Public Works Department, and his team of eight workers, all of them ethnic Roma,[4] remember many of the names of victims and the dates and places of their deaths, as well as general observations about the events in Djakovica. They were some of the few non-military personnel allowed to travel freely throughout the city. Polloshka told Human Rights Watch:

> Every day there were two, three, four, or five [killings]... If it was one body, we went with a car. If it was two bodies, we went with two cars. If it was more than that we took a tractor.[5]

Polloshka and his crew claim that the Serbian police systematically catalogued the deaths that took place, which was also the case in Pec. Many of the victims were identified and photographed, they said. And they said an investigative judge named Marinkovic was often present at the site of the killings.

The total number of deaths in Djakovica is unclear, since so many men remain missing. The Council for the Defense of Human Rights and Freedoms estimated the missing at 1,200 and compiled a list with names, dates of birth, places of abduction, and the names of the persons who reported the missing. As of July 11, 1999, the list had 948 names, but approximately 250 more names were being added to the database. The council also had a list of 200 persons killed from Djakovica municipality which included fourteen KLA fighters.[6]

The *Washington Post* conducted in-depth research into the killing in Djakovica. Based on information from Faton Polloshka, the Council for the Defense of Human Rights and Freedoms and its own independent investigation, the paper came up with an "incomplete" list of 199 people killed between March 24 and June 12 in Djakovica, 186 of whom are listed by name.[7]

One hindrance to counting the dead was the authorities' apparent attempt to remove or destroy evidence. According to Faton Polloshka, as well as one of his street cleaners, interviewed separately, seventy-seven bodies that had been buried in the Djakovica cemetery in early May were removed sometime after May 7. Polloshka told the *New York Times* that approximately one hundred bodies were removed from the cemetery on May 22.[8] Another city employee, who worked in the cemetery for six years, told Human Rights Watch: "Bodies were taken from the cemetery. They came with bulldozers. I didn't see this but we saw the next day that they had come. It was after the Cabrat offensive."[9]

On July 24, Human Rights Watch observed large tire tracks and disturbed earth at the spot in the cemetery where the bodies were allegedly removed. A number of other graves were marked "Paidentifikuar"—"Unidentified." One grave said: "Wool socks, black jacket and pants with white stripes." According to Polloshka, during the war, his team also buried eighteen bodies in private gardens throughout the city.

All evidence suggests close cooperation between the various security forces present in and around the city: police, army and paramilitaries. Djakovica residents named Sreten Camovic, who was the local head of state security, as the officer responsible for the city, although nobody witnessed him committing any crimes. Milan Stanojevic was the local head of the police—a cousin of Djakovica's mayor, Momcilo Stanojevic. According to Polloshka, he had a brief conversation with Mayor Stanojevic during the war: "I was close with the mayor and I asked him 'What are you doing? Don't you want to live here after this?' He answered that his 'orders are coming from above.'"[10]

Seventy-seven bodies that had been buried in the Djakovica cemetery in early May were removed sometime after May 7.

In an article from April 30, 1999, the *Washington Post* reported on some of the Yugoslav forces active in the Djakovica region. Citing "U.S. intelligence reports," the article mentioned the Yugoslav Army's 125 Motorized Brigade, commanded by Col. Srba Zdravkovic;[11] the 252nd Armored Brigade, commanded by Col. Milos Mandic; and the 52nd Mixed Artillery Brigade, commanded by Col. Radojko Stefanovic.[12] Colonels Mandic and Stefanovic were both named by the State Department in early April as commanders known to be operating in Kosovo.[13]

Many Albanians from Djakovica also spoke about a local Albanian family, the Jakupis, that had long-term ties with the police. In its report on Kosovo, the OSCE also mentions the Jakupi family as having been mandated by the police to contribute to "local security" in 1998 and 1999.[14] Many people in Djakovica said the family assisted the police, at least by guiding them around the area, during the NATO bombing.

One further clue regarding government forces active in the Djakovica area emerged from the trial of 143 Kosovar Albanians, who were convicted by a Serbian court on charges of terrorism on May 22, 2000 (see the section on Kosovar Albanian Prisoners in Serbia Since War's End in the chapter

Graves in the Djakovica cemetery. According to witnesses, Serbian forces exhumed and moved at least seventy bodies in May 1999.

© FRED ABRAHAMS/HUMAN RIGHTS WATCH

Abuses After June 12, 1999). According to Judge Goran Petronijevic, the verdict was based in part on the testimony of Yugoslav Army Capt. Radovan Bogavac, who participated in a May 7, 1999, action in Djakovica to help a group of police under attack by the KLA, as well as a Yugoslav Army report on activities in the Djakovica area. While this does not suggest Captain Bogavac's participation in war crimes, it clearly shows that the Yugoslav Army was active inside Djakovica city.

Phase One—March 24 to April 2

The first wave of violence began on March 24, when NATO initiated its attack on Yugoslavia, and continued until April 2. Djakovica's historic old town, including the Hamudi Mosque, was set on fire and sporadic killings took place throughout the city. On March 25, unknown security forces broke into the home of a respected physician, Dr. Izet Hima, and shot him in front of his wife.[15] According to the *Washington Post,* Faton Polloshka picked up Dr. Hima's body at 5:00 p.m. and then collected the bodies of three other ethnic Albanians killed that day: Kujtim Dula, forty-four, Qamil Zherka, seventy, and his son, Nexhdet, forty-one.[16] Prominent Djakovica residents Urim Rexha, a lawyer, and Mark Malota, an LDK leader who had rented his house to the Mother Theresa Society, were also killed.[17] On March 26, armed Serbs shot and killed six men in one house on Ymer Grezda Street, including a Muslim cleric, Zenel Dana, and his sons Emin and Fahri. The killing is cited in the war crimes tribunal's indictment of Milosevic, Milutinovic, Sainovic, Ojdanic and Stojiljkovic.[18]

By the end of March, thirty-two people had been killed in the city, according to the *Washington Post.*[19] Thirty-one were killed in March, according to the Council for the Defense of Human Rights.[20]

Many people were expelled from Djakovica during this time. Interviewed in northern Albania, refugees—most of them women—spoke of the old town's burning and their forced expulsion at the hands of police, paramilitaries, and the army. Many refugees reported seeing clusters of dead bodies lying around Djakovica as they left the city.[21] One refugee from Djakovica interviewed in northern Albania said:

> There was heavy shooting in Djakovica; people were killed by Serbs, and people are terrified. They don't even bury the bodies. . . . The soldiers were

> telling us: "Go to Albania, this is our land, not yours." The violence began on March 24 in Djakovica. There was no KLA there. The Serbs began setting homes on fire. Many of them are Serbian civilians. . . . I saw seven bodies in the Qyli neighborhood of Djakovica, located in the northwest part of the city, on the outskirts. Two or three from several different families. The entire neighborhood had been destroyed by tanks that entered into the neighborhood on March 25.[22]

Refugees in Albania and Djakovica residents interviewed after their return spoke of an order to the chaos, as armed forces moved systematically neighborhood by neighborhood. As one refugee in Albania said, "It was all very organized. They went from one neighborhood to another. Some soldiers are in charge of destroying things, while others are in charge of accompanying people to the border."[23]

Some of the most intense violence took place on April 1 and 2, when fifty-six people are believed to have been killed. A coordinated police action on two adjacent streets in the Qerim neighborhood—Milos Gilic and Sadik Stavileci—resulted in numerous executions.

According to witnesses, who said the neighborhood had organized men to keep watch in the area, Serbian police forces attacked the streets in a systematic sweep beginning around midnight on April 1. One woman, N.C., told Human Rights Watch:

> I saw fire from the end of the street near the Sofes Mosque. They came nearer. Others were waiting on the other end of the street. The first massacre was near the mosque against the Leshi family, a man and his wife. Then Hysen Deda with his wife, daughter and her five-year-old child. Then they came to the Vejsa family and twenty of them with some others were killed. They then came to the Cana family, where four people were killed.[24]

The witness mentioned a policeman—she believed a deputy commander—who lived in the neighborhood: Novak Pitolic. Although she didn't see Pitolic on the night of the attacks, a neighbor and witness to the attack, A.N., interviewed separately, claimed that he saw Pitolic that night.[25] Another man, a former policeman in Djakovica, confirmed that Pitolic was an active policeman in town, although he didn't see him committing any crimes.[26]

The neighbor, A.N., said the attack began between 11:00 p.m. and 12:00

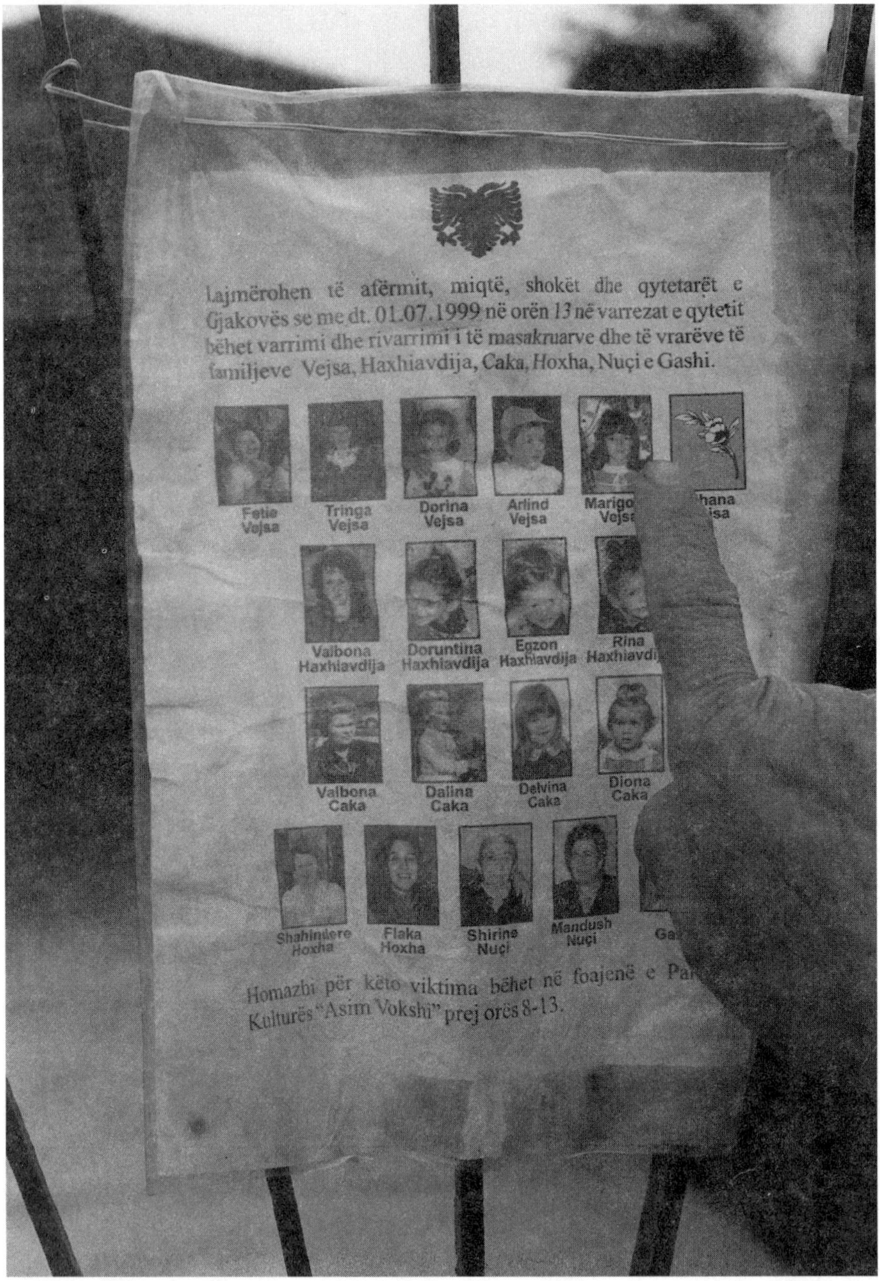

These twenty people were killed and their bodies burned in the Vejsa house at 163 Milos Gilic Street in Djakovica. © FRED ABRAHAMS/HUMAN RIGHTS WATCH a.m. He watched from a hole in his attic that gave him a view of the street,[27] and told Human Rights Watch:

> I saw Novak Pitolic and he made a signal with a lighter two times. At that moment, an armored vehicle turned on its lights. One vehicle with two policemen without lights went on the road. It left two policemen behind. I saw them with a small machine gun near Fehmi Leshi's house and I heard sounds and screams and then shots.[28]

Based on refugee testimony in Albania during the war, the *Washington Post* reconstructed a lot of what happened in the Qerim neighborhood that night. It said the police moved down Sadik Stavileci Street, killing fifty-four people and burning most of the houses apart from those homes belonging to local Serbs.[29] Witnesses believed that the police were looking for Besim Bokshi, the local leader of the LDK, but he managed to escape along with approximately 300 other residents of the neighborhood.

The most brutal killings occurred in the Vejsa family house at 163 Milos Gilic Street, where twenty people from five different families were killed and then burned, including twelve children under the age of sixteen. ICTY forensic experts found evidence of twenty bodies at the site, and the killing is included in the indictment of Milosevic.[30]

According to N.C., approximately ten policemen arrived at the Vejsa house around 12 a.m. All of the men had already fled the area, except Hysen Gashi, who was mentally disturbed. Those who remained were shot in the kitchen, and then the house was set on fire. One ten-year-old boy, whose name is withheld, survived. A.N., a neighbor, told Human Rights Watch:[31]

> When they came near the Vejsa house, I heard the voice of my good Serbian friend Nenad Rajcevic and his five brothers. I saw all of them. There were thirty or forty police in total. All of them in police uniforms. I saw [Serbian] civilians too. They went to the Vejsa house. I then heard screaming in that house. I also saw them go in with Milos Sepanovic. . . . They stayed only five minutes. I heard screams and shooting. Then they went to Jonus Cana and they killed the whole family, four people, within two minutes.[32]

A.N. described Rajcevic as thirty-six years old and originally from Montenegro. He worked in the main post office. His five brothers were: Tihomir, aged approximately forty-two, Nenad, thirty-six, Sasa, thirty-three, Lubisa approximately thirty-nine, and Micko, approximately thirty-four. Milos Sepanovic, approximately forty-three years old, was described as a former mechanic who worked in the police.

The Rajcevic brothers and Sepanovic were also named by N.C. She told Human Rights Watch she saw the Rajcevic brothers in blue police uniforms as she and her family were walking in a column of internally displaced persons out of Djakovica. Human Rights Watch interviewed another ethnic Albanian man, a former policeman in Djakovica, who said that Sepanovic was an active policeman during the war, and that he was a local leader in Qerim neighborhood, although he was not a witness to his actions. The man also confirmed that Novak Pitolic was a Djakovica policeman, but said he didn't see him during the war.[33]

Faton Polloshka from the Djakovica Public Works said he helped take the twenty bodies away, as well as thirty other people killed on April 1 and 2. He told Human Rights Watch: "The bodies in the Vejsa house were completely carbonized. I went for blankets in the hospital but they had only one. Nineteen of them were in one blanket. They were buried in three graves.[34]

The victims were:

Hysen Gashi, 50	Fetihe Vejsa, 60	Mandushe Nuci, 52
Valbona Haxhiavdija, 38	Tringa Vejsa, 31	Shirine Nuci, 73
Rina Haxhiavdija, 7	Dorina Vejsa, 11	Valbona Caka, 34
Doruntina Haxhiavdija, 3	Marigona Vejsa, 9	Delvina Caka, 7
Egzon Haxhiavdija, 5	Sihana Vejsa, 7	Diona Caka, 2
Shaindere Hoxha, 55	Arlind Vejsa, 5	Dalina Caka, 14
Flaka Hoxha, 15	Rita Vejsa, 2	

Smaller scale killings took place in other parts of the city on April 1 and 2. One witness, who gave her story to Human Rights Watch while she was a refugee in Albania, said that the police forced her and her family out of their house in the first days of April. Her husband, Hajdar, fifty-two, was killed on the street, and she saw many other corpses on her way out of the city. She said:

> They sent me and my children out of the house, but they kept my husband. They finally let him go, but while he was walking out, he came across three

> policemen in the street. They were special police with masks over their faces and mouths. They also stopped my brother-in-law and told him to stop and fight. When I was running away, they killed them in our yard. Maybe ten minutes later, when it all became a little bit more quiet, I went back and found my husband dead with a gun shot wound in his temple. In the streets, I saw about ten dead people and one of them had his throat cut.[35]

Sporadic killing took place throughout April, although with less frequency than on the first two days of the month. According to the figures provided by the *Washington Post,* thirty-five people were killed between April 3 and May 6. One woman told Human Rights Watch how three of her neighbors who lived at 86 Commune Parisit Street in the Blloku i Ri (New Block) neighborhood, two brothers and a sister, were killed on April 23. She said:

> The three of them [Teki, Agim, and Femije Deda] were having lunch on April 23. Around 1:30 p.m., a bunch of us in the neighborhood saw the police

The blood-stained living room of a home in Djakovica, in which Serbian police executed a woman and her two brothers on April 23, 1999. A neighbor found the victims kneeling down into the cushions. © JOANNE MARINER/HUMAN RIGHTS WATCH

> enter their house. There were no more than fifteen police; they rushed into the house, smashing their way in. I know one of them: Nebojsa Obradovic, aged thirty-eight or forty. He's a local policeman from Djakovica. We heard lot and lots of shooting—maybe one hundred shots—it was automatic weapons fire. They killed the three first, then they ransacked the house. They tried to burn the living room where the bodies were.
>
> I waited several hours before I came into the house. It was about 5:30 p.m. I came with two friends, a neighbor and a brother of the victims' uncle. The gate to the garden had been blasted open and the doors to the house were broken—they were wide open. The three bodies were riddled with bullets. Each one had a puddle of blood below it. The brothers were killed as they were kneeling face down, one on the sofa and one on a chair. The sister was lying back on the other chair, face up. They had bullet holes in their bodies and even in their hands.[36]

Human Rights Watch visited the house where the killings took place in June 1999. Parts of it had been burnt but three large bloodstains were still visible on the sofas where the three victims had allegedly been shot. Bullet casings were littered all over the living room.

Phase Two—May 7 to May 13

The second killing wave began on May 7, the day intense fighting between government forces and the KLA began in the Cabrat neighborhood. According to Hekuran Hoda, commander of KLA Battalion II, Brigade 137, the fighting lasted until May 11 and many KLA and Serbian police died.[37] According to the *Washington Post,* fifty-seven civilians not involved in combat were killed during this period.

Witnesses told Human Rights Watch that the fighting in Cabrat began on May 7 around 9 a.m. Around 6 p.m., a crowd of civilians was fleeing the area toward the city center, when they were stopped by security forces on the Tal-icit Bridge. The men were separated from the women and children, and then brought to the Mulla Jusuf neighborhood, where they were divided into two groups and executed. One resident of the neighborhood who lived on Zejnel Luzha Street told Human Rights Watch:

> I didn't see it [the killing] with my own eyes. But I was inside my house. I

> heard steps first as the group came and some words in Serbian from the police: "Stand in a line," they said. He repeated this many times. I heard nothing from the group. Then there was shooting. It was automatic fire, very short. Then they went one by one with a bullet to each person. I don't know how many. From what I heard, there were only two soldiers. I saw the bodies the next day from my window. I couldn't recognize any of them. There were eleven bodies and one was alive for twenty hours and then died. All of them were men. The bodies stayed there for forty hours before the police took them away with workers from Cabrat on tractors. I heard that another group was killed on a nearby street at the same time—nine people and two escaped.[38]

Another man, B.E., was among the other group of men who were taken into custody from the Talicit Bridge. He told Human Rights Watch that the security forces separated out twenty-six men and held them for approximately twenty minutes. Three armed men watched over them, all of them in camouflage and two of them wearing masks. Twelve of the men, B.E. among them, were then taken into a nearby street, where they were shot two by two. He said:

> They sent us to a street, twelve of us. One of them was in a green uniform with a blue mark on his shoulder. The other one was in a blue uniform, I think they were brothers because they looked alike. Their accent was not like Serbs from Djakovica. Only these two took us.
>
> They demanded our documents and money. Most of us gave our documents and money. One of them, the one in blue, said, "Let's finish this because the group is waiting." The other wanted to take us further along the street and he ordered us to break open the front door on one house. We did and two of our group went in. At that moment, one guy from our group [Agim Efendia] said "Don't do this Dragan," because he had heard someone say his name. They said, "Go on!" and they killed him. Then one of our group managed to escape.
>
> Agim was still alive and Dragan said, "Let's stop his suffering." The other guy in the garden came and they told him and two others to bring Agim into the garden. The other one went in and we heard shots inside the garden and no one came out. Then we were ordered to go into the garden two by two, and they were killed. Me and another guy were the last. When I got to the garden I saw them all dead. They shot at us. They said "Turn your back." The

> bullets first hit me in the legs, then the chest, fingers, and two more on the leg. I was hit twelve times.
>
> They checked all of us to see who was alive. They stepped on my back—I was the last one they checked. At that moment I didn't breathe or move. Then I heard them say they were going to execute some others, and they left.[39]

B.E. showed Human Rights Watch his scars. He had what appeared to be bullet wounds on the right side of his chest, his right knee, his left ankle, and the middle finger of his right hand.

Testimony from Faton Polloshka corroborates the two stories provided above about the May 7 killings. Without being told about the two witnesses, Polloshka told Human Rights Watch that his team of street cleaners picked up two groups of bodies from Zejnel Luzha Street of men who "had been executed" on May 7. According to Polloshka, one group had twelve bodies, the other had nine bodies.[40] These numbers differ slightly from those provided by L.V. and B.E., but Polloshka's account otherwise matches the details provided by the witnesses.

Individual killings also took place in other parts of the city on May 7. One woman, S.G. who lived on Maslan Shazivari Street, told Human Rights Watch that, around 10 a.m. on May 7, four paramilitaries burst into her home and murdered her husband, Ibrahim. She said:

> The doors opened and four paramilitaries entered. They had come from our neighbor's house. They shot two bullets into the house: one went upstairs and one went into the kitchen. . . . They demanded money. My husband said we didn't have any money. They laid him on the floor and told me to go outside. They killed him with three bullets on the fifth stair of the stairway. One of the bullets hit him in the face. There was lots of blood. When the shots were fired, I was on the fourth stair of the stoop in front of the house, just a few steps from the front door. I knew my husband was dead but they didn't allow me to go back inside.[41]

Human Rights Watch visited the home on June 15, 1999, and saw blood stains on the stairs where S.G. said her husband had been killed. According to S.G., the Djakovica street cleaners buried her husband seven days later in the city cemetery—grave number 28.

Many men and women were also taken into detention after the fighting in Cabrat. According to Polloshka and the local Council for the Defense of Human Rights and Freedoms,[42] the women were held temporarily in the Gorenje Elektromotor factory in Djakovica and then released. The men were held somewhere on the edge of the city along the Djakovica-Pec road. Some thirty men were released after six days, but the rest—an unknown number—were transferred to the jail in Pec.[43] Many are believed to have been subsequently transferred to other jails inside Serbia just before NATO troops entered Kosovo on June 12. While some of these men have appeared on official lists of prisoners provided by the Serbian government, others remain missing. Approximately 1,200 Djakovica men were unaccounted for more than one year after the conflict.

Paramilitaries entered her apartment building where approximately 250 people were staying, and sexually abused six young girls.

In May 2000, 143 Djakovica Albanians were convicted as a group in Serbian courts for terrorist acts. Lawyers and human rights groups like the Humanitarian Law Center protested the fairness of the trials and the exceedingly high sentences. On April 23, 2001, the Serbian Supreme Court, citing "fundamental violations of criminal proceedings" and "erroneous and incomplete collecting of evidence," released all of the defendants pending a review of the case by the district court.[44]

The Withdrawal

A final wave of looting and burning took place around June 10–12 as Serbian and Yugoslav forces were withdrawing from the city. Human Rights Watch confirmed some attempted rapes during this time. A witness told Human Rights Watch how, on June 12, paramilitaries entered her apartment building where approximately 250 people were staying, and sexually abused six young girls. Among the victims was the witness's sister, who was spared being raped because she was menstruating at the time:

> At 11:00 or 11:30 six paramilitaries with the insignia "ARKO" or "ARKAN" [on their uniforms] came. They entered the building. First they took the cars we had, then they went into every building. There were 250 people in my building. In every family they took young and beautiful girls. I was with my

> father's family. After they burned his house he took shelter in my building. They told my father to give them all our jewelry or, "I'll take your daughter." He [the paramilitary] had long hair with a pony tail and a big machine gun and ammo belt. They took my sister into another room because my father said he had no money. My father showed them a document that he was not allowed to work and they hit him. They took her in another room in the flat, locked the door, and told her to take off her clothes, "Because you look like a face that has money." She is seventeen. When my father got up to go after my sister they hit him and he fell and hit his head on the table. They hit my father in the chest [before this]. The second time they hit him was when he went to help his daughter. One of them took my sister and two went out with her. Another two were in the room with us. My father got up and they hit him with a fist—they were wearing brass knuckles. He fell and hit his head on the small coffee table made of thick glass.
>
> I heard from my sister what happened and I heard everything through the wall. She looked pale and then she fainted. She looked like she had come back from the dead. She was gone for ten minutes. It felt like days. I heard this through the wall. The walls are thin. I got close to the door and I heard him say, "You have your period and you are worth nothing." I also heard my sister begging them, "Please in the name of God, if you have a sister or a wife, don't touch me."
>
> My sister took off her T-shirt but they told her, "No, not that part, take off the lower part." She took off her pants and panties. She was having her period. My mother was hitting the door and yelling, "Release my daughter!" She offered them 100 DM—the last money she had. When my mother was banging on the door, she was yelling, "I have 100 DM." They said to my sister, "you have your period . . . You are worth nothing anyway. Get out!" My sister fainted and for a few hours she could not talk from the trauma and the stress.[45]

Rape in Djakovica was reported by reliable secondary sources as well. Dr. Sejoullah Hoxha, chief of the gynecology department at Pristina hopital, told Human Rights Watch that his department had treated two cases of rape from the war, one of which took place in Djakovica (the other was near Klina). Both women were raped by more than one man. The Djakovica rape took place, Dr. Hoxha said, on the street sometime between April 5 and April 15.[46]

Sexual abuse was also documented by a reliable NGO based in Albania, the Counseling Center for Women and Girls, which collected refugee testimony during the war and compiled twenty-eight cases of rape in Kosovo, as well as some unconfirmed reports of sexual abuse around Djakovica.[47]

On April 20, NATO claimed that, according to Kosovar refugee accounts, Serbian forces had established rape camps in the Hotel Karagac in Pec and at an army base near Djakovica.[48] Neither Human Rights Watch nor foreign journalists were able to confirm the allegations in either city. (See March - June 1999: An Overview, section on Rape and Sexual Assault.)

MEJA

One of the more notorious mass killings in Kosovo took place on April 27 in the small Catholic village of Meja, a few miles northwest of Djakovica.[49] The precise number of ethnic Albanian victims remains

Personal items—lighters, cigarette boxes, pens, a key—in a field in Meja, where up to 300 men are believed to have been murdered by police and paramilitaries.

© JOANNE MARINER/HUMAN RIGHTS WATCH

unknown, although an estimated 300 men, ranging in age between fourteen and sixty, are believed to have been killed. Very few bodies have been recovered but, according to the ICRC, 282 men taken from Meja were missing as of May 15, 2000.[50] The massacre was apparently revenge for the KLA killing of five Serbian policemen in Meja on April 21.

Human Rights Watch first learned of the massacre on the early morning of April 28, as traumatized refugees were entering Albania from the Morina border crossing near Kukes, Albania.[51] Tractors were pulling wagons carrying only women, children, and elderly men who reported how Serbian and Yugoslav forces had expelled them from their villages around Djakovica on April 27 and forced them into a convoy that went through Meja and then towards the Morina border crossing. In Meja, they said, the police and paramilitary forces robbed most of the Albanians, took many of the men off the tractors and wagons, and forced the convoy to continue. Later in the day, refugees entering Albania reported seeing men lined up along the road in Meja. By evening, and over the next days, refugees claimed that they had seen large numbers of dead bodies along the road in the village.

Human Rights Watch visited Meja on June 15, after NATO entered Kosovo, and saw the decomposing remains of several men, burned documents, and personal possessions that apparently belonged to the men who had been killed there, as well as spent bullet casings. A second visit was conducted on July 25, bringing the total number of interviewees regarding the Meja killings above twenty. The information provided during these two visits corroborated what refugees had originally reported two months before.

According to all of the witnesses, in the early morning of April 27 Serbian special police and paramilitary units, together with soldiers of the Yugoslav Army, systematically evicted all ethnic Albanians from the villages between Djakovica and Junik—the region near the Albanian border known in Albanian as Reka e Keq. Beginning around 6 a.m., the security forces forcibly expelled residents from the following villages: Pacaj (Pecaj), Nivokaz, Dobras (Dobrash), Seremet (Sheremet), Jahoc, Ponasevac (Ponashec), Racaj (Rracaj), Ramoc, Madanaj, and Orize. All of the witnesses interviewed from these villages, including people from other areas who had sought refuge there over the previous month, told Human Rights Watch that soldiers and special police forces surrounded their villages, rounded up the inhabitants, and forced them to flee along the road towards Djakovica, some in wagons drawn by tractors and some on foot. Many of the villages were then systematically burned. One eighteen-year-old woman from Dobras told Human Rights Watch:

> The police and military came and forced us out. They burned the houses. They had a spray and a kind of pistol with fire. Everyone left Dobras and the surrounding villages. They took two men in Dobras, Iber Hasani and Avdyl Avdyli [both aged approximately forty-five]. The police told us to walk on and then we heard the shooting of automatic guns.[52]

This testimony about Dobras, including the killing of Iber Hasani and Avdyl Avdyli, was corroborated in a separate interview with a man from Sisman who had sought shelter in Dobras. He said:

> On April 27, around 6:30 a.m., the army entered Dobras with police and paramilitaries. Iber, me, and another guy went to the upper part of the village to flee. Iber said, "I can't go with you because I'm afraid they'll rape my twenty-year-old daughter if I'm not there to protect her." So he returned to the village. My friend and I stayed in the mountain separated from our families. The family later told me that they heard lots of shooting when the army entered the village. My family and Iber's family took to the road, along with Avdyl Avdyli. Avdyl and Iber were separated from their families on the road in the village of Dobras, not far from their houses. They killed Avdyl with a knife, mutilating his body, and killed Iber with a bullet to his heart. I saw the bodies later. The families didn't see their men killed; the Serbs had told them to leave before they killed them.[53]

A nineteen-year-old woman originally from Orize, whose father was taken away in Meja later that day, told Human Rights Watch:

> We were in Ramoc that morning, as we weren't able to stay around Djakovica because of the danger. An order to leave came at 5:00 a.m. The police came to the door. They knocked and said, "get out of your house because we're going to burn it." I had to leave immediately with my mother, father, and fifteen-year-old brother.[54]

The villagers from the region were all forced to follow the road to Meja. Their accounts reveal how, during the course of the day, the many police and military present at a checkpoint in the village center systematically robbed the displaced villagers of their possessions. One woman, thirty-six years old, told Human Rights Watch:

> When we arrived in Meja, the Serbs stopped us; they wanted money and jewelry. They threatened my children, even my baby. They had beards, and wore masks. They took our necklaces, rings, earrings, identity papers, even our bags with clothing. They took everything. They threw our clothes in the bushes. They spoke to us harshly, and slapped one woman.[55]

More ominously, the security forces pulled hundreds of ethnic Albanian men out of the convoy and away from their families. As noted, ICRC records show 282 men who were reported abducted in Meja as still missing as of May 15, 2000.[56] A nineteen-year-old man who arrived in Meja between 10:00 and 11:00 a.m. described the scene to Human Rights Watch.

> Many people were in the convoy with tractors. The ones who were walking were mostly let through, but some were taken. They [the police and military] stopped the tractors and began to hit people with pieces of wood and they broke the tractor windows. The men were stopped and taken away, about one hundred men, to a field near the road. The police screamed for us to keep moving so we left the hundred men and we don't know what happened to them.[57]

One witness originally from Nivokaz who did not give her name said she was forced out of Seremet village around 8 a.m. on April 27 and arrived in Meja with her family on a tractor around 10 a.m. "They took the men from the tractors," she said. "There were about forty people on our tractor, and they took twelve men. They took all of the men."[58] Another witness said her husband was taken off their cart to join a group of Albanian men at the side of the road and forced to shout: "Long live Serbia! Long live Milosevic!"[59]

Other refugees who traveled through Meja that day confirmed that security forces took men as young as fourteen and as old as sixty out of the convoy. Ray Wilkenson, a spokesman for the United Nations High Commissioner for Refugees in Kukes who was on the border as the refugees arrived in Albania, told Human Rights Watch that, in his estimation, sixty tractors crossed into Albania on April 28, and people on "six out of seven" of them reported that some men had been taken from their vehicles.[60] Journalists who were on the border at the same time told Human Rights Watch that the refugees repeatedly said that at least one hundred men had been killed.

"There were about forty people on our tractor, and they took twelve men. They took all of the men."

Refugees who passed through Meja between 12:00 and 3:00 p.m. reported seeing large numbers of ethnic Albanian men in the custody of security forces, even as many as "hundreds." One witness, a thirty-eight-year-old teacher who passed through Meja around 1:00 p.m., told Human Rights Watch:

> I saw a big crowd of people separated from their families: old and young men. I think it was more than 250. They were kneeling on the ground . . . along the road at a small forest on the side of a hill about twenty or thirty meters from the road. They were in the village center.[61]

Another witness who was in Meja at the same time, interviewed separately, provided a corroborating account, adding that the group of men was kneeling with their hands behind their backs, surrounded by soldiers.[62]

Other witnesses who were in Meja in the early afternoon provided largely consistent variations of this scenario with varying numbers. A forty-year-old woman who was in Meja around 12 p.m. said she saw "seventy men or more" squatting with their hands behind their heads in a small canal that ran parallel to the road.[63] All of the witnesses said that Meja was full of police and special forces dressed in blue and green camouflage uniforms, respectively. Many members of the forces wore black ski masks, and some wore red bandanas on their heads, they said. Some reported seeing red patches with a double-headed eagle, a symbol of Yugoslavia, on the soldiers' sleeves.

Some refugees who passed through Meja in the afternoon reported seeing dead men near the road. One eighteen-year-old woman who passed through Meja around 12:00 p.m. claimed to have seen fifteen dead men on the right side of the road. She told Human Rights Watch, "The road was full of blood. On the right side of the road there were fifteen men. I counted them. They were lying face down with blood all around, and they were not moving."[64]

Another woman in Meja around 1:00 p.m. said:

> [W]e saw dead young men, men with their hands tied behind their head. The Serbs said, "Look what we did to them. Do you want us to do that to you?" We saw a lot of blood. We were in shock, traumatized. There were about twenty young men lined up neatly in a row, face down, with their hands tied behind their heads. The Serbs said, "Look what we've done to these men; now give us your money." It was in the center of Meja. The bodies were about four meters away from the road, behind some thorn bushes. I saw some men who had died crouched; other people told us that blood had been taken from them.[65]

The refugees who passed through Meja later in the afternoon told of seeing many dead bodies in the village. An eighteen-year-old man and a nineteen-year-old woman, interviewed together, who arrived in Meja on foot around 5:30 p.m., said they saw a large pile of bodies about three meters from the right side of the road in the center of the village. The bodies, tumbled together, covered an area of ground about twelve by twenty feet, and were

The remains of an ethnic Albanian man killed by Serbian security forces on April 27, 1999, in Meja. © JOANNE MARINER/HUMAN RIGHTS WATCH

stacked about four feet high, they said. The witnesses admitted to being very scared and to being rushed along by the police, factors which prevented them from making any more than a rough estimate of the body count. Admittedly basing their estimate on the number of men that they believed were missing, they thought the number of dead totaled 300. Fifteen other men, they said, were sitting on the ground with their backs to the pile of dead bodies facing a group of security forces.[66] The female witness said:

> As we were walking through Meja we saw about 300 dead bodies piled up on top of each other in a pasture. It was a big pile of bodies heaped together in a mess, not laid out in any orderly way. The Serbs didn't let us look at them; they said "fast fast fast."...
>
> The bodies in Meja were in a pasture on our left. The pile of bodies was about the size of a tent. Up to four feet high, piled on top of each other. I recognized a couple of men who were alive. There were about fifteen men with their backs to the bodies, facing the Serbs. I recognized Rame Mehmeti and his son Mehmet Mehmeti. [67] They're from Brovina but we stayed together with them in a house in Ramoc. We saw them taken off their tractor.[68]

On June 15, a Human Rights Watch researcher inspected Meja and found the decomposed remains of several men. The bodies were on the edge of a field next to the road that runs through Meja. One intact body and the top half of another were located on the side of a ravine adjacent to the field, roughly thirty meters up from the road. Another two bodies were a few meters further up the ravine, and the bottom half of another body was located in the field near the ravine. All of the bodies were in an advanced state of decay. The bones of some of the bodies were broken, and they all appeared to be headless. Pieces of a skull were found next to one of the bodies.

Closer to the road, the Human Rights Watch researcher saw three large piles of straw and cow manure, which a villager claimed covered many more bodies. The villager also stated that the bodies of most of the men killed in the massacre had been collected by Roma street cleaners, which was also the case in Djakovica (see section on Djakovica).[69]

In the field were clusters of burned documents and personal possessions—items such as cigarette cases, keys, and family photos—that apparently belonged to the dead men. Spent bullet casings were also littered about. There were four recently dug graves located in a small Catholic cemetery further up the hill which, according to one villager, held the remains of four local men who had been killed in the massacre.

One possible motive for the killings was the KLA's ambush of a Serbian police car one week before the massacre.

Human Rights Watch collected the names of twelve men whom witnesses claimed had been taken from Meja by the Serbian security forces on April 27. Eight of the twelve are included in the ICRC's list of persons missing since their detention in Meja on April 27. Villagers in Meja also reported to Human Rights Watch that eight men had been killed in the village on that day. All eight men are on the ICRC's missing list, which suggests that bodies were removed from the site.

Motives: Five Policemen Killed

One possible motive for the killings was the KLA's ambush of a Serbian police car one week before the massacre, in which five policemen were killed. Numerous witnesses from the area told Human Rights Watch that the KLA had killed the five policemen in their car near the center of Meja. One policeman, Milutin Prasevic, was known by many villagers in the area.[70] One villager from Meja told Human Rights Watch:

> The five [policemen] were killed in one car, a brown Opel Ascona. They came to us a few minutes before they were killed, asking, "where is the KLA?" An Albanian policeman was driving. They left and then we heard the bazooka. We heard that the Albanian in uniform was from Ratis.[71]

Human Rights Watch saw the badly damaged car lying on one side of the road in the village on June 15, 1999.

Other sources also mentioned the killing of the Serbian policemen. Marie Colvin, a reporter for London's *Sunday Times,* and Ian Fisher from the *New York Times,* separately told Human Rights Watch that the KLA had boasted to them about killing a Serbian commander and his bodyguards in Meja during the third week of April.[72] Villagers also told Jonathan Landay from the *Christian Science Monitor* that the attack on Meja was "in revenge for the KLA killing a senior Serbian policeman, Milutin Prasevic, and four other policemen."[73]

Indeed, on its website, the Serbian Ministry of Internal Affairs lists three policemen who were killed in "a terrorist attack" in Meja on April 21, including Prasevic, for whom there is a photo. Born on August 6, 1968, in Vranic, Kosovo, Prasevic is said to have worked in the police since 1990. The two other policemen killed in Meja who were identified are named as Ljubodrag Lazarevic, born November 1, 1973, and Boban Lazovic, born February 25, 1976. They were policemen for one and two years, respectively.[74]

Perpetrators

Witnesses interviewed by Human Rights Watch identified some of the Serbian policemen who were present in Meja on April 27, although none of these policemen were seen killing or committing other abuses. Three people claimed to have seen a Serbian policeman they knew as "Stari" ("Old Man") at the checkpoint on the day of the killing; and one of these witnesses believed his real first name was Milutin.[75] Another man, a villager from nearby Koronica who was not in Meja, told Human Rights Watch that Stari was a policeman active in the area whose name was Milutin Novakovic.[76] The three witnesses independently said that Stari, who used to work in Ponasevac, was tall with a thin face, dark skin, and black hair. He is approximately forty years old and has two brothers. One witness claimed that Stari's father was Vucko, and his brother was Miladin, but this could not be confirmed.

One witness identified another policeman who he claimed was in Meja on April 27: a man known as "Guta," who was the police commander of Ponacevac village.[77] The villager from Koronica mentioned above independently claimed that Guta was the police commander in Ponacevac. His real name is not known.

In general, witnesses described the Serbian forces at the checkpoint in Meja as wearing dark blue or green camouflage uniforms. Some of the men had black masks covering their faces, and some had red bandanas. One woman described the two Serbian men who took away her father at gunpoint:

> The two Serbs were wearing black masks that covered their head and hair; you could only see their eyes and mouth. It was ninja style. They had dark

> blue police uniforms with loose red stripes on the arm just below the shoulder, I believe on the right arm.[78]

Another woman, forty years old, provided this description:

> The Serbs were wearing camouflage uniforms, black masks, black gloves, and carrying automatic weapons. You could only see their mouth and two eyes. They had stripes with the colors of the Serbian flag falling loose. Some had their heads covered; some uncovered. Some had bandanas; I don't remember the color. Some had short hair; some had long hair. They carried knives in their hands: straight knives that were bent at the end, about as wide as one's arm, and two feet long. . . . To look at them was scary. The Serbs weren't driving military vehicles; they were driving cars stolen from Kosovars.[79]

KORENICA (KORENICE)

On the same day as the killing in Meja, April 27, Serbian police forces violently expelled the inhabitants of the nearby village of Korenica, another predominantly Catholic village near Djakovica. At least thirteen men were killed at this time, according to villagers, and 120 people from the area were abducted and remained missing as of August 1999.

Upon their return to Korenica in June, villagers found the remains of the thirteen men, twelve of them largely burned. But another sixty-seven people from Korenica remain missing, as well as fifty-three other villagers from the surrounding area who were seeking refuge in Korenica (twenty-six of them from Guska and twenty-seven from the following villages: Duznje, Babaj Boks (Babaj i Bokes), Brekovac (Brekoc) and Djakovica.[80]

Villagers found the remains of the thirteen men, twelve of them largely burned.

It remains unclear precisely what happened to the missing villagers, or how the thirteen Korenica men were killed, since no direct eyewitnesses are known to have survived. But, based on interviews with villagers after their return in June and a Human Rights Watch inspection of Korenica, a relatively clear picture emerges of forced expulsions and summary executions by the Serbian police.

According to villagers, Serbian security forces first entered the village on April 4. Five or six policemen, led by Alexander Micunovic and Milutin Prasevic (who was later killed in Meja by the KLA—see above), ordered all of the villagers to leave Korenica, but then allowed them to return. The village was then quiet until April 27, when the police returned. One villager, M.M., explained:

> [On April 27] at 6:00 a.m. we heard shooting at the beginning of the village and we saw some houses on fire. In the two first houses a ninety-six-year-old man was shot who was later found burned—Kole Palokaj. They [the police] continued to burn and kill until they got near the center. I was in my house with my family and some twenty-five refugees from other places, about fifty-three people in total.[81]

The witness and his family fled through the nearby fields to the road, which they took in the direction of Meja. In Meja around 11:00 a.m., they encountered the police checkpoint where they claimed to have recognized some policemen from Djakovica, even though they were wearing masks. The police separated out two brothers from the family, aged thirty-five and thirty-six, as well as four men from Guska, five men from Duznje (Duxhnje), one man from Brekovac (Brekoc), and ten other men from Korenica. As of July, all of these men were still missing. The witness said:

> They took the twenty-two men and made them lie down and shout "Serbia! Serbia! Slobodan is master!" Then they shot above their heads. I didn't see them killing anyone because they made us move on for Djakovica . . . Of the twenty-two men taken in Meja we have no news.[82]

Another villager, Anton Dedaj, also escaped Korenica on April 27. He described the scene:

> Huge numbers of Serbs—army, police and paramilitaries—arrived in the village on April 26 in several buses. Some wore red bandanas on their heads or tied on their arms. The following day, in the early morning, the Serb forces surrounded the area and began burning homes. A local policeman came inside the house [where I was staying]; the owner knew him and invited him for coffee. The policeman said, "It's too late for you now." They took 9,000 DM from my brother before they killed him.[83]

Yet another villager, Tom Dedaj, was in his house as the Serbian forces arrived. He said:

> The Serbs arrived in the early morning, all kinds of Serbs, army, paramilitaries, police, local police. The local police gave information to the outside security forces. Five bus loads of Serbs arrived in the upper part of the village, and two more were near this house. Police were everywhere, every twenty meters on the road. About ten villages were surrounded. They lied to us; they told us that they were going to Ponosevac [a nearby village]. The local police wore masks. Some paramilitaries wore green camouflage trousers and T-shirts, with red bandanas tied on their arms.[84]

Tom Dedaj fled into the forest with his family. That evening, he told Human Rights Watch, he met Daniel Berisha, aged forty, another man from Korenica who had been shot that morning in the ankle and knee and had burns on his arms. Berisha told Dedaj that the police had captured him and four other male members of his family, all of whom were shot in Berisha's house. Berisha miraculously survived and escaped to the forest.

According to Dedaj, Berisha told him that the Serbian forces arrived at his home around 7:30 a.m., made everyone leave the house, and then separated the women and children from the men. The Serbian forces initially agreed to allow Berisha's sixty-eight-year-old uncle, Mark Berisha, to leave with the women and children, and told him to drive away on a tractor. When he responded that he didn't know how to drive a tractor, they made him return to the house and go to the third floor, where the other detained men were being held.

When the men reached the third floor, Berisha told Dedaj, they began to plead for their lives. A local policeman whom Berisha said was called "Bajo," ordered the men to turn their backs, and then shot them at close range with an automatic weapon. According to Dedaj, who was relaying Berisha's story:

> The Serbs lined them up on the third floor. Daniel's uncle pleaded with them. He asked the Serbs, "Aren't you people just as we are? Aren't you human? Why would you kill us?" He said a prayer and made the sign of the cross. Bajo said, "It's too late for you now." He ordered the men to turn their backs to him and shot them at close range with an automatic weapon. They said, "Fuck your mothers; it's too late for you."[85]

Berisha told Dedaj that he fell first, after being hit twice in his leg, and was covered by other bodies. He then pretended to be dead while the police brought blankets upstairs, lit them, and threw them on the bodies. Berisha escaped from the blaze as the police left, and made his way to the forest, where he met Dedaj.

"He ordered the men to turn their backs to him and shot them at close range with an automatic weapon."

The next day, April 28, Berisha attempted to escape this hiding place in the forest along with some other villagers, but was captured by the Serbian forces together with a man named Kolë Merturi, another woman, and some children. All of these people were released except Berisha, Merturi later told Dedaj. Berisha's body was found the following day by another villager. Dedaj helped bury Berisha and told Human Rights Watch that, in addition to the wounds Berisha had the night before in the forest, he had five more bullet wounds—two in the forehead and three in the chest. They buried him in the forest near where his body had been found.

On June 16, a Human Rights Watch researcher inspected Daniel Berisha's house, which had been looted and burned. On the third floor were the gruesomely burned and broken remains of what appeared to be five men. Anton Dedaj, a relative of Tom Dedaj, told Human Rights Watch that the bodies in the house were those of his brother Gjoke Dedaj, age forty; Musa Dedaj, age sixty-one, Gjoke and Anton's uncle; Nikolle Dedaj, age eighteen, Gjoke's son; Kole Berisha, age forty-three, the brother of the house's owner; and Mark Berisha, age sixty-eight, the uncle of the house's owner.

After inspecting the five bodies, the Human Rights Watch researcher visited three badly burnt houses nearby in which bodies, or in one instance, small pieces of charred bones, were found. The bodies were burned beyond recognition, but were identifiable by relatives or neighbors familiar with the deceased persons' personal belongs, such as jewelry and eyeglasses. According to Tom Dedaj, the houses contained:

- House one—Gjergj Mala, age fifty-nine and Pal Kabashi, age forty-one;
- House two—Mire Palokaj, approximately forty-five (whose husband, Muse Palokaj, is missing);
- House three—Kole Palokaj, age eighty, and Brahim Kamberi, approximately sixty-seven.

In the nearby forest, Dedaj also claimed to have found the body of Ded Sadriaj, a mentally disturbed man from Nec village who was approximately twenty-three years old.

Human Rights Watch visited Korenica a second time on July 26, the day the villagers were exhuming some graves in the village cemetery with the help of Italian KFOR. After a landmine team declared the area safe, the villagers found one body that had been wrapped in a blanket and buried. According to the villagers, Roma from the area told them that they had buried thirty-four people in Korenica around May 7, but that they police had taken the bodies away.

Human Rights Watch spoke with one ethnic Rom, who said that he worked for the state mortuary as a driver. He said:

> I was present when bodies were picked up and buried. Every day we picked up a few bodies, five, six, or ten. The Serb police would come and tell me where there were bodies. There were proper procedures: the police would take photos of the body; they'd write down the name of the dead; they'd attach a number to the corpse and put it in a grave with that number. They were very organized. They'd take photos before the burial; sometimes they'd even film the bodies. My sector worked in street cleaning and road maintenance; we were forced into this job. The week after NATO started bombing they made us start doing this.
>
> Bodies that we could identify we buried in their village cemetery. Other bodies, those without identity cards, went into the cemetery of this village [Korenica]. I saw lots of dead bodies in Korenica: one day we found eight [bodies] underneath a bridge, near a stream. There are thirty-five or forty bodies buried in the Korenica burial site. We didn't bury any women, except one old woman. The bodies that I've seen were

Picture found on the floor of an Albanian Catholic home in Koronica, in which five men were killed on April 27, 1999.

© JOANNE MARINER/HUMAN RIGHTS WATCH

> killed with automatic weapons. It was disgusting to look at them. I've only found burned bodies once.[86]

Witnesses from other villagers also saw dead bodies in Korenica. One married couple, R.R. and S.R. from Sisman (Shishman), near Djakovica, told Human Rights Watch that they went through Korenica on April 27. S.R. said: "We saw twelve dead men in Korenica. They were laying in the street with their hands over their head. It was about 1 or 2 p.m. [on April 27]."[87]

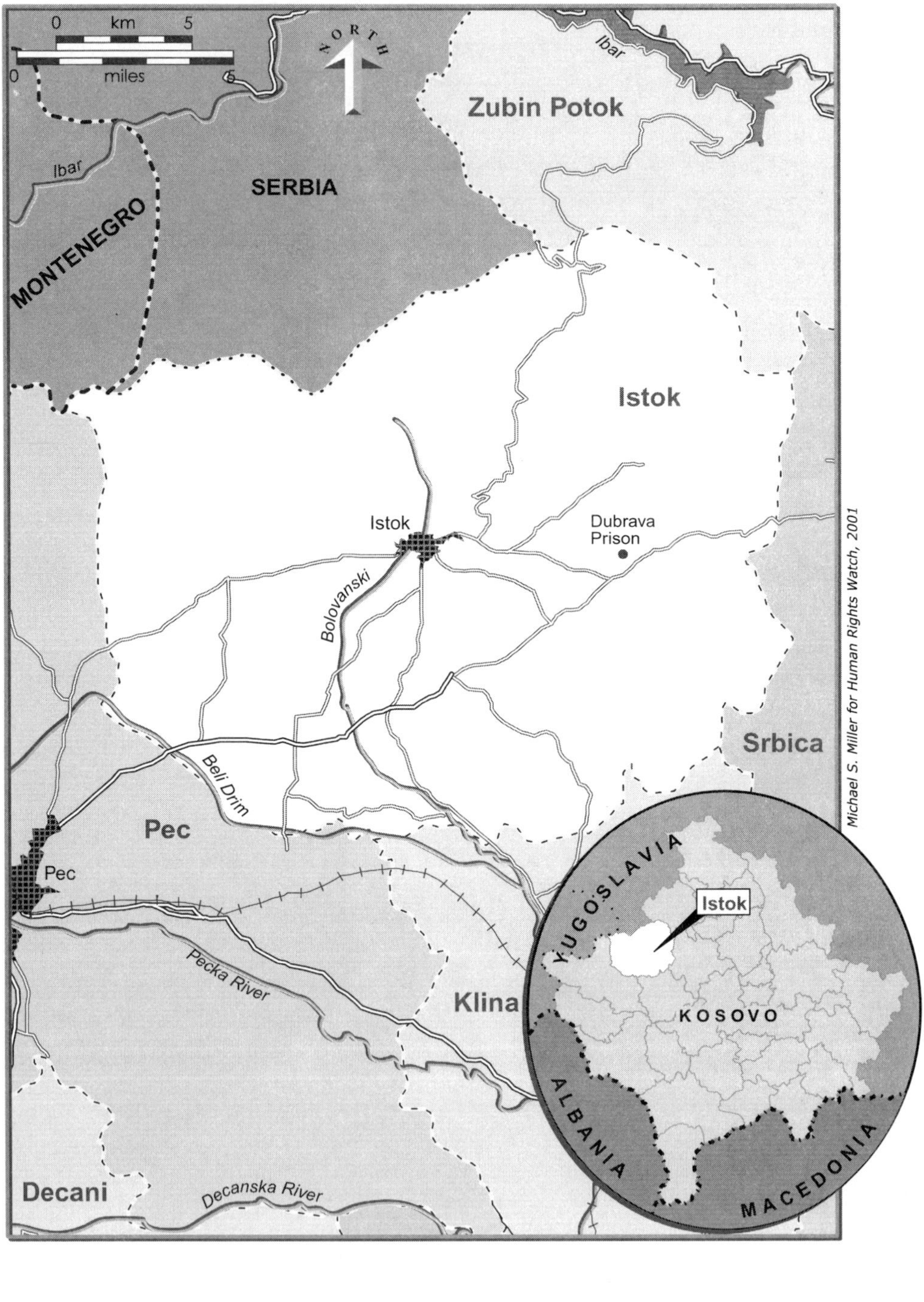
0 km 5
0 miles 5
NORTH
Ibar
Zubin Potok
Ibar
SERBIA
MONTENEGRO
Istok
Istok
Dubrava Prison
Bolovanski
Srbica
Beli Drim
Pec
Pec
Pecka River
Klina
Decani
Decanska River
YUGOSLAVIA
Istok
KOSOVO
ALBANIA
MACEDONIA
Michael S. Miller for Human Rights Watch, 2001

7

ISTOK (ISTOG) MUNICIPALITY

Istok was relatively quiet in 1998, compared to the other municipalities of Kosovo. Serbs made up between 15 and 20 percent of the area's 50,000 inhabitants.

Tension increased in early 1999, as the KLA increased its activities in Istok and the Serbian police responded with violence. During the NATO bombing, there was direct fighting between the KLA and the Yugoslav Army and Serbian police. Paramilitary forces were also present in the area. According to a UNHCR shelter survey, 5,049 of the 7,081 houses in Istok municipality were either heavily damaged or completely destroyed, although it is not clear how much of this damage was due to NATO bombing.[1]

According to the OSCE, thousands of ethnic Albanians in Istok were forcibly expelled from their homes and fled to Starodvorane (Staradran) and Zablace (Zablaq) villages, which was under KLA control. When the KLA retreated from the area in April, government forces robbed and beat many of the ethnic Albanians who had fled there as well as committed some extrajudicial exeuctions.[2]

The single largest killing in Istok municipality took place in the Dubrava prison, to the east of Istok town. Citing Serbian and military activity in the direct vicinity, NATO bombed the prison on May 19 and May 21, killing an estimated nineteen inmates. Over the following days, as many as ninety-six inmates were killed by government forces.

The Serbian police in Istok were under the jurisdiction of the Secretariat of Internal Affairs (SUP) in Pec, which covered the municipalities of Pec, Klina, and Istok. The commander of the Pec SUP during the war was Col. Boro Vlahovic.[3]

DUBRAVA PRISON

One of the worst incidents of the war took place in the Dubrava prison, Kosovo's largest detention facility, when prisoners were massacred by security forces after a NATO bombing attack there. Since all of the survivors of the massacre were transferred to prisons in Serbia after the attack, reliable accounts of the killings did not emerge until after the war, when some of the prisoners were released.[4] Human Rights Watch spoke separately with two survivors who had witnessed the killing. Their stories closely match the testimonies of four other survivors that have appeared in the Serbian, Albanian, or international press.[5]

Citing Serbian and Yugoslav military activity in the area, NATO bombed the prison on May 19 and again on May 21, 1999, killing at least nineteen ethnic Albanian prisoners and causing chaos in the facility. According to the Yugoslav government, some prisoners took advantage of the bombing and tried to escape the prison; the guards were struggling to maintain order. On May 22, prison officials ordered the approximately 1,000 prisoners to line up in the prison yard. After a few minutes, they were fired upon from the prison walls and guard towers with machine guns and grenades, killing at least seventy people. Over the next twenty-four hours, prison guards, special police, and possibly paramilitaries attacked prisoners who were hiding in the prison's buildings, basements, and sewers, killing at least another twelve inmates.

It is not clear precisely how many prisoners were killed by NATO bombs and how many were killed subsequently by prison guards and other government forces. Nor is it known to what extent the Albanian prisoners tried to escape or offered resistance. But the consistency of witness testimony, with specific details about times and locations, leaves no doubt that Serbian and possibly Yugoslav government forces deliberately and without need killed a substantial number of ethnic Albanians in the prison, probably more than seventy, and wounded many others. The Yugoslav government claimed that NATO bombs killed ninety-five inmates and injured 196.[6] NATO admitted to bombing the prison, but never acknowledged any related civilian deaths.

The Prison

Located a few miles east of Istok, near the border with Montenegro, Dubrava prison had three pavilions with a capacity of more than 1,000 prisoners. The walled facility contained a cultural center, sports hall, health center, and a hotel for prisoners' visitors.

As with all of Kosovo's detention facilities, credible reports of torture and abuse emanated from Dubrava prison throughout 1998 and early 1999. According to the OSCE, at least four male prisoners died as a result of beatings sustained in Dubrava between October 1998 and March 1999. Defense lawyers reported restricted access to their clients in Dubrava, and the Kosovo Verification Mission itself was never allowed access to the prison.[7]

Former prisoners who were in Dubrava during the war told Human Rights Watch that there were between 900 and 1,100 prisoners in the prison when the NATO bombing of Yugoslavia began on March 24, 1999, including approximately thirty ethnic Serbs. Some prisoners were transferred to Dubrava after the NATO bombing had begun. One former prisoner, R. T., transferred to Dubrava on April 30, said that approximately 165 ethnic Albanians from Djakovica came to Dubrava a short time after he had arrived.[8] This was confirmed during the April-May 2000 trial in Nis, Serbia, of 143 Albanians arrested in Djakovica in May 1999, who testified that they had been transfered from Djakovica to prisons in Pec, Lipljan, and Dubrava.[9] Another former prisoner, Bajrush Xhemaili, was transferred to Dubrava from Nis prison on April 29.[10]

Among the ethnic Albanians in Dubrava was one of Kosovo's most prominent political prisoners, Ukshin Hoti, who was finishing the last year of a five-year sentence.[11] Three witnesses said that Hoti was released from Dubrava on May 16 because his sentence had expired. His current whereabouts, however, are unknown, and many former prisoners and human rights activists fear that he is dead.

Fellow inmates said that Ukshin Hoti, one of Kosovo's most prominent political prisoners, was released from Dubrava prison on May 16, 1999. No one has seen him since. PHOTO COURTESY OF SHUKRIE REXHA

The prison authorities claimed that many of the ethnic Albanian prisoners in Dubrava were KLA members, including at least eleven commanders.[12] In November 1999, Human Rights Watch interviewed two ethnic Albanian men who had been in Dubrava during the NATO bombing, and both of them admitted to having been in the KLA, but it is not known whether the government's claim holds true for other prisoners.

One of the former prisoners who spoke with Human Rights Watch, A. K. (initials changed),[13] said there were approximately 1,100 prisoners in Dubrava by March 1999. While the treatment in Dubrava was generally acceptable before then, he said, the prison guards beat the prisoners every day once the NATO bombing began.[14]

A.K.'s testimony about events in the prison is highly consistent with Human Rights Watch's other interviewee from Dubrava, B.K. (initials changed), who, like A.K., was serving a one-year sentence for "terrorist activities against the state."[15] As stated above, these two testimonies match interviews with four other former prisoners that were published in the Serbian, Albanian, or English-language press to paint a consistent picture of the events in the prison between May 19 and May 25.

The NATO Bombing

According to all of the witnesses, as well as Yugoslav government and NATO sources, NATO aircraft first bombed Dubrava prison without warning on the morning of May 19. B.K., who was being held in Pavilion C, told Human Rights Watch that four bombs hit the prison, two striking Pavilion C, one an adjacent pavilion, and antoher the prison director's building. He said:

> When the rockets fell, we called on the guards to open the doors but they left. When we saw that they had run, we started to break down the doors. It took us about one and a half hours to break them down. In my pavilion, three people died and fifteen others were wounded. The Serbs sent three of the wounded to Pec. We went outside into a courtyard within the prison. They came and took the bodies two hours later.[16]

A.K. claimed that four or five prisoners were killed in Pavilions B and C, and some others were hit by shrapnel when running into the prison field. Both former prisoners, interviewed separately, said that, once gathered in the courtyard, the prisoners tried to contact the NATO jets flying overhead by spelling out the word "HELP" with long florescent light bulbs.

In Brussels, NATO spokesmen acknowledged the bombing and said Dubrava was an "army facility." At a press conference on May 20, Major General Walter Jertz explained:

NATO spokesmen acknowledged the bombing and said Dubrava was an "army facility."

> It [Dubrava] is a militarily significant target, we know it is a military security complex and this target has been attacked because it was a legitimate military target and we have no evidence that any weapons did go someplace else or the crew was wrong. I can add that we used precision-guided munition and, to sum it up, it was a military security complex, a military legitimate target.[17]

According to the Yugoslav Ministry of Foreign Affairs, NATO bombed Yugoslav Army and Serbian police forces near the prison at 1:15 p.m. on May 19, killing three civilians. Three weapons also reportedly hit the penitentiary, killing two prisoners and a guard.[18]

A.K. and B.K., as well as the four other former prisoners whose interviews were published in the press, all said that the prisoners spent the next two nights sleeping outside, but within the walls of the prison. Then, on May 21, prison guards ordered the prisoners to line up in the courtyard. As they were gathering, however, a second wave of NATO bombing began. B.K. told Human Rights Watch:

> On May 21, they lined us up again in the courtyard. We were surrounded by the structures of the prison. The guards did not shoot at us. We were sitting in the grass, all of us—about 900 people. They said, "don't be afraid, NATO won't fire." Around 10 or 11 a.m. the planes started flying. The first rocket fell on the kitchen. Others fell nearby. One of them fell inside the walls near us. Sixteen people were killed when a chunk of land five meters wide blew apart near us. They included: Fadil Bezeraj from Rasic, Naim Kurmehaj from Srellc e Eperme, Ali Kelmendi from Kosoriq, Qaush Ahmeti from Sheremetaj, and Mete Osmajaj from Isniq.

> Three times they [NATO] bombed. When it began, we just lay there all day. When the guards heard the planes, they left the prison. We stayed in the courtyard until about 12:00 p.m., then we retreated to places in the yard about 300 meters away where there were fewer buildings. . . . Around 2:00 p.m., some four armed guards came near. We thought they came to shoot us, but the planes roared overhead and they ran away. We slept in the field that night. . .[19]

The May 21 bombing of Dubrava was confirmed by western journalists who had been escorted to the prison by Serbian authorities on the same day, ostensibly to see the damage from NATO's May 19 bombing. Jacky Rowland, a correspondent for the BBC, saw some of the corpses from the May 19 bombing before having to flee the prison as NATO continued its raid. She wrote in *Scotland on Sunday*:

> We walked across the grass, stepping between the bodies covered by blankets. One man was still alive, his blood-spattered body shaking convulsively. Then we heard the drone of planes overhead: the bombers were returning. It was time to leave. As we sped down the dirt track away from the prison, the bombs fell. Three of them in close succession.[20]

Paul Watson from the *Los Angeles Times*, who spent most of the war inside Kosovo, was also in Dubrava that day. "At least nine bodies lay scattered on the grass and in shrubs," he wrote. "All had shaved heads, indicating they were inmates." He wrote further:

> During two previous hours of morning attacks [on May 21] ending at 10:20 a.m., two blasts breached the high outer wall and left large craters on either side. Angry Yugoslav guards, who were trying to keep inmates locked in the yard while coming under attack, said they thought the North Atlantic Treaty Organization warplanes were attempting to spring scores of KLA fighters from jail.[21]

Watson quoted a man he identified as the prison warden, Aleksander Rakocevic, as saying: "The prisoners are still inside the walls but we cannot put them back into the cellblocks where they're supposed to be because NATO is hitting the buildings as well. . . . Maybe some have already escaped because there are several holes in the walls."[22]

An Associated Press article did not provide a first-hand account of the May 21 bombing, but asserted that reporters "saw seven bloodied corpses covered by blankets in the jail's grassy courtyard, as well as shrapnel-pocked buildings, and nervous-looking guards with automatic weapons keeping prisoners at bay."[23]

As with the previous attack on Dubrava, NATO acknowledged bombing the prison, and claimed that it was a legitimate military target. In a morning briefing on May 22, NATO spokesman Jamie Shea said:

> As you know already, in Istok, Kosovo, NATO forces attacked a barracks and an assembly area that has been in use for a long time by both the Yugoslav Army and the MUP special police forces as part of their operations against the KLA and also against Kosovar civilians, and this military facility abuts a prison, but I want to stress, as I did yesterday, that it is a military facility, the prison is part of this but it is only a small part of what is quite a major military facility.[24]

The international journalists who visited Dubrava on May 21 did not see any military activity in the area, although this does not prove that military troops and equipment were not near the prison when the bombing occurred. Paul Watson wrote that the press, "found no evidence of military vehicles or equipment amid the rubble, although it was difficult to confirm what might have been at the site during the earlier attacks."[25]

Some of the former prisoners claim that they saw anti-aircraft fire coming from near the prison during the NATO bombing. According to an article in the Serbian-language *Beta News Agency,* former prisoner Bajrush Xhemaili claimed to have seen "constant provocation from a strong anti-aircraft base set up near the prison."[26] Ahmet Ahmeti, who gave an interview to the Serbian- language daily newspaper *Danas,* said that an air defense system was near the prison.[27]

The Yugoslav government claimed that the second round of NATO bombing had caused further civilian casualties. On May 21, the state news agency *Tanjug* reported that at least nineteen prisoners had been killed and ten wounded in the May 21 attack, including the deputy warden, Nedzmedin Kalicanaj, aged forty-one. This was in addition, the report said, to the two prisoners who had been killed in the May 19 bombing.[28] The next day, Tanjug reported that nineteen prisoners and guards had been killed and more than ten were wounded.[29] Another Tanjug report that same day claimed that, "dozens of inmates and guards" had been killed.[30]

The Massacre

The day after the second round of bombing, May 22, according to all of the witness testimony available, the prison guards ordered all of the inmates to assemble in the prison's main courtyard. B.K. explains what happened next:

> In the morning, 5:40 a.m., May 22, we heard a megaphone from the guard tower. Some commander said, "Get in a line because we want to move you to Ni_ for your own security." They put us in a line. Around 6:10 a.m., they said we have ten minutes to get in a line. The line was not clean, but had four to six people in a line, about 200 meters long. After a few seconds, we were twenty to twenty-five meters from the walls, they threw some three or four hand grenades. At the same time, they began shooting with RPGs [rocket propelled grenades], and snipers [sniper rifles]. Whoever could manage just fell to the ground.[31]

A.K. told a similar story:

> We were made to stand in a line on a cement football field surrounded by guard towers. About 100 people were in one line. We stood there about ten minutes until we were all in a line. Then a guy named "Ace" climbed up one of the towers and gave the order to shoot. We saw that. It was something like twenty minutes of constant shooting from the five meter-high walls—it was all prepared. They had hand-held RPGs, sniper rifles, machine guns, AK47s, hand grenades, and mortars. They were shooting from the walls. The bombs fell on everyone and people were flying.[32]

In the *Beta News Agency* interview, Bajrush Xhemaili[33] explained his version of the May 22 attack: "The Serbian forces opened fire from the watchtowers on the northern and western parts of the prison walls. They used sniper rifles, automatic weapons, and portable grenade launchers. The shooting lasted about thirty minutes."[34]

Chaos ensued as prisoners ran for cover in the various buildings of the prison, their basements, or the prison's sewer system. B.K. said:

> Me and a group who was closer to the wall, heard them reloading. I screamed "Get up and run!" Whoever wanted to, or could, started to run. We went into the basements, into manholes, into the pavilions, and behind mounds. They continued shooting. From all the towers there was sniper and automatic rifle fire. It lasted ten to fifteen minutes.
>
> We went back to the field in the middle of the buildings to try and get the wounded. After one hour, we went to check who had died. They were still there but they didn't shoot. We counted approximately ninety-seven dead. Among them were: Sahit Ibrahimi from Kotradic, Agim Elshani from Klina, Zahir Agushi, Iber Gergoci, and Zeke Hasan Metaj from Strellc. We collected the dead and covered them with blankets. Those we knew, we wrote their names on paper which we stuck somewhere in their clothes. Then we organized some food for ourselves. We broke into the medical clinic for supplies.[35]

"They had hand-held RPGs, sniper rifles, machine guns, AK47s, hand grenades, and mortars. They were shooting from the walls. The bombs fell on everyone and people were flying."

A.K. explained:

> People were running. Since the prison is so big, there are many sewers. We opened a grate and five to ten of us jumped in. . . . We went into the destroyed buildings and took things to defend ourselves. Since NATO hit the kitchen, there was food, so we cooked for ourselves.[36]

That evening, all of the witnesses say, a group of special police or paramilitaries entered the prison and tried to reassert control. The assault lasted approximately twenty minutes, during which time hand grenades were thrown into the school building, allegedly killing at least two people. The prisoners remained hidden during the night, some of them preparing to defend themselves with makeshift weapons made from broken furniture or garden tools.[37] B.K. said:

Around 5:00 or 6:00 p.m., some paramilitaries entered the prison. They demolished the prison school. That night they killed everyone who was hiding in the sewers. Three or six, up to twelve people were in there. They opened up the manholes and shot them.

I was in Pavilion C. Others were in the kitchen basement. We organized ourselves for the night so they could not come and kill us. We took shovels, sticks, whatever we could, even furniture legs. We prepared some traps and I filled two big canisters with water. We had the wounded in the Pavilion C basement. There were about 120 or 150 of them.

That night, one person, twenty-five-years-old, hung himself with a rope. Another was found hanging in the school. On May 23, around 5:00 a.m., they began shooting and bombing. From the twenty-two people hiding in the cultural center, they killed nine people, one by one. Zef Keqiraj from Zhub—his brother saw this. Kabeshi from Zahaq was killed too.

Bloody mattresses lay in a pavilion of the Dubrava prison after the war. NATO bombed the facility on May 19 and 21, 1999, citing military activity in the area, killing an estimated nineteen inmates. Serbian forces killed as many as ninety-six inmates over the following days. PHOTO BY ALBAN BUJARI

A.K. explained what happened the next morning, around 6:00 a.m., when another group of special forces entered the prison. He told Human Rights Watch:

> We were hiding in the basements and small rooms, and we didn't know if they wanted to kill us or take us away. I saw "Grga," "Mladja," and some others from Pec. When they caught us, they grabbed us by the hair and hit people in the head.
>
> I was behind a heating pipe in the basement with eighteen others. We were hiding. The fiberglass around the pipes was scratching us. Some twenty-eight others came but they couldn't get in because there was no room. Then the forces saw us and surrounded us. I saw them come with machine guns and big knives and they hit the twenty-eight guys in the basement. People's organs were spilling out everywhere. They stabbed people. At that spot, all of the twenty-eight people were killed, including: Zef Kqira, Lush Prelazi, Nikolle Bibaj, Jonus Krasniqi, and Arsim Krasniqi.

"From the twenty-two people hiding in the cultural center, they killed nine people, one by one."

Naser Husaj, a prisoner in Dubrava who relayed his story to the *New York Times,* said that he spent the night hiding with a group of other prisoners in a laundry room beneath the cafeteria. The police attacked the building in the morning, he said, "with rocket-propelled grenades and shot through the windows straight into the basement."[38] Visiting the spot with Husaj on December 7, the *Times* journalist, Carlotta Gall, noticed the "overpowering" stench of death. She wrote:

> The green linoleum floor is still sticky with blood, which has been smeared around in an attempt to clean it. Mr. Husaj moved quickly in the dark, showing a familiarity with the underground rooms. But even he gagged as he showed where he saw six people gunned down in one corridor.[39]

Another prisoner, Remzi Tetrica, told his story to the Kosova daily newspaper *Kosova Sot.* About the morning attack on May 23, he said:

> On May 23, in the early hours, a massacre was carried out by the paramilitaries. We were again attacked by the same arsenal of weapons, just like the

> day before. They killed many prisoners in cellars, shafts, and in rooms, where they would be caught. They also wounded many other prisoners. I was wounded by the bombs as well. That same day, Xhemail Alimani was killed. . . . I personally know about 108 killed and ninety-eight wounded prisoners.[40]

Later in the morning, the security forces had reasserted some control over the prison, and they issued an ultimatum for the prisoners to emerge from their hiding places within fifteen minutes. With no other options, the prisoners revealed themselves, and were then gathered in the prison's sports hall, which was still undamaged. According to the witnesses, VJ soldiers were present this time, and they were more friendly to the surviving prisoners, even giving them cigarettes in the name of "Miki"—a man two of the interviewees identified as the prison warden, although they didn't know his full name. According to A.K., he recognized a policeman from Pec nicknamed "Bata."

The injured were taken away in trucks, while the remaining prisoners were transported in approximately ten buses to Lipljan prison in south-central Kosovo. All of the former prisoners claimed to have been beaten in Lipljan. A.K. and Bajrush Xhemaili, claimed that the new arrivals had to walk through two cordons of police wielding batons and metal sticks, who beat the prisoners as they passed.[41]

On the morning of June 10, just after NATO and the Yugoslav Army signed the Military Technical Agreement that ended the war, all of the ethnic Albanian prisoners in Lipljan were transferred to other prisons inside Serbia proper, such as Sremska Mitrovica, Nis, Prokuplje, or Pozarevac. According to the Belgrade-based Humanitarian Law Center, in October 1999, wounded prisoners from Dubrava were being held in the prisons at Sremska Mitrovica, Zabela and Nis.[42]

Human Rights Watch interviewed three other prisoners who had been in Lipljan prison at this time, in addition to the two men who were in Dubrava, about the transfer. All of the men said that the inmates had their hands tied and were then transferred in buses out of Kosovo. B.K. said:

> On June 9, at 10:00 p.m., they woke us up. They tied us with ropes and put us in groups of fifty. We could not sit. They started withdrawing and shooting in the air. We were afraid they would kill us there. At 6:00 a.m., June 10,

> they held us until 12:00 p.m. without food or water. Then they put us onto buses with our heads down. Half of us were on the floor. It was cold. They beat those who moved. There were two policemen and a driver in each bus. We realized that the army and police were withdrawing from Kosovo. We got to Nis, where we stayed one hour in the bus. They untied us and put us in the prison.[43]

Other prisoners stopped at Nis prison, but were then moved on. B. Z., an eighteen year-old who was not a prisoner from Dubrava, told Human Rights Watch:

> On June 10 we were transferred out. First they said we would go to Nis. But they said there was no room there, so we changed buses and went on. From Lipljan, I was in the first bus with my hands tied behind my back. The bus was full. They took us to Sremska Mitrovica. We were about 300 people.[44]

All of the former prisoners interviewed by Human Rights Watch had been released between September and December 1999, usually because their prison terms had expired. But, as of April 2001, at least 70 ethnic Albanians from Kosovo remained in Serbian prisons, among them some survivors of the Dubrava massacre (see section on Kosovar Albanian Prisoners in Serbia Since War's End in Abuses After June 12, 1999).

The precise number of Dubrava inmates killed by the two NATO bombing raids and by prison guards and special police remains unclear. After initially reporting on May 21 that at least nineteen inmates had been killed, the Yugoslav government's figures rose sharply four days later, without, however, attributing killings to measures to control rioting or escaping priosiners. Serbian authorities, in contrast, attributed the new deaths to the bombings in stark contradiction to survivor testimonies. A May 25, 1999, Tanjug report said that "in days-long bombardment of the Penitentiary Institute Istok, some 100 prisoners died, and some 200 were wounded."[45] On May 27, Tanjug quoted Vladan Bojic, investigative judge in the Pec district court, as saying that ninety-six corpses had been pulled from the ruins and that forty wounded

As of April 2001, at least 70 ethnic Albanians from Kosovo remained in Serbian prisons, among them some survivors of the Dubrava massacre.

were in critical condition.[46] On May 29, the Yugoslav government stated that "the number of casualties in the Correctional Institution in Istok is increasing. Out of 196 people wounded in the vandal bombing of this institution another three persons died, and seven more were taken out from under the rubble, while the search for the dead continues."[47] On May 30, Tanjug reported that seven more bodies had been found, bringing the death total to ninety-three.[48] The final Yugoslav government figures were published in a July report by the Ministry of Foreign Affairs called "NATO Crimes in Yugoslavia: Documentary Evidence, 25 April–10 June 1999." NATO bombs had killed ninety-five inmates and injured 196, the report said.[49]

Ostensibly to help make its case that all of the prisoners had been killed by NATO bombs, the Serbian authorities again escorted a group of foreign journalists to Dubrava prison on May 24. Reporting for the BBC, Jacky Rowland said that the prison had clearly been struck again since the journalists' first visit on May 21. "One building was smouldering while the dining hall and several cell blocks were badly damaged," she reported.[50] However, it was less clear to Rowland how the victims in the prison had died:

> Walking around the prison we counted forty-four bodies, about half of these appeared to be the victims of the first bombing raid on Friday [May 19], still lying under blankets on the grass. Then we were taken to a room in a damaged cell block where there were twenty-five corpses. The men appeared to be ethnic Albanians, some of them had shaved heads, others had longer hair. A couple of the corpses had their trousers pulled down around their knees. We were told they had died between Friday and Sunday although it was not clear how all of them had met their deaths, nor why they were all in one relatively undamaged room.

Another reporter who visited the prison on May 24, Daniel Williams with the *Washington Post*, also questioned the government's version of the deaths:

> This time, the official version—that bombs again were to blame—did not match what reporters saw at the scene, where twenty-five more ethnic Albanian corpses were on display. The corpses were piled in the foyer of a

> clinic. Except for a ruined dining hall, however, no new bomb damage was visible inside the prison, and none of the newly dead had been crushed, or touched by the concrete dust that covered the dining hall floor.[51]

Williams visited Dubrava again on June 12, after NATO troops had entered Kosovo. He wrote:

> Once inside, it didn't take long to see that ugly things had happened—things that had nothing to do with bombing. At the clinic where the twenty-five bodies had lain, mattresses and pillows lined a hallway I had not been able to see before. Some had bullet holes and dried blood where heads might have rested. Bullet holes and splattered blood marked walls. A copy of the Hippocratic oath hung at an angle in one office.
>
> In a cellblock, bullet holes marred inner walls and more mattresses bore dried bloodstains. At the rear of the compound, piles of clothing filled a cowshed. Again, walls bore bullet pockmarks. Mattresses and clothing were stuffed into open manholes.[52]

Visiting the prison in early November with former prisoner Naser Husaj, Carlotta Gall from the *New York Times* saw evidence that suggested many people were killed inside the prison's buildings and basements. She wrote:

> And in the basements of the buildings, the blood lies still sticky on the floor, bullet holes scar the walls, and impact marks of grenade explosions crater the floors . . . In the basement of the cultural center, under insulated heating pipes and industrial washing machines, the weapons still lay around: a spade, metal spikes, wooden bars and stretches of metal piping, wrapped with rags for a better grip. Pools of dried blood still stained the floor, and discarded clothes. Two small round craters from a hand grenade pockmarked the concrete floor.[53]

The Exhumations

On August 13, a Spanish forensic team began exhuming ninety-seven graves that were found outside the village of Rakos/Rakosh near Dubrava prison.[54] A legal advisor to the International Criminal Tribunal for the Former Yugoslavia, Karl Koenig, claimed that the bodies appeared to have "been here since the 26th or 27th of May." All of the graves were marked "KPD," which stands, in Serbian, for Kazneno Popravni Dom, or Penal Correctional Facility. In her November 10, 1999, report to the U.N. Security Council, ICTY chief prosecutor Carla Del Ponte said that ninety-seven bodies had been found at the Rakos site, although no details on the cause of death were provided.[55]

Perpetrators

Precisely who was in charge during the killings in Dubrava prison remains unclear. Still, from witness testimonies and press accounts, a few leads have emerged.

Ninety-seven graves outside the village of Rakos near Dubrava prison are believed to hold the bodies of inmates killed first by NATO bombs and then by Serbian forces, who went on a rampage through the facility. "NN" means name unknown and "KND" stands for Kazneno Popravni Dom (Penal Correctional Facility).

© BENJAMIN WARD/HUMAN RIGHTS WATCH

According to an article in the *Washington Post,* then-Serbian Justice Minister Dragoljub Jankovic, claimed that "his people" were not in charge in Dubrava between May 19 and 25, meaning, ostensibly, the Serbian Ministry of Justice. The article said that, "He [Jankovic] does not know what happened during the bombardment, and seemed to suggest that if any atrocities occurred, it was others—special police, paramilitaries—who were responsible."[56]

Journalist Paul Watson, who visited Dubrava on May 19 and May 21, quoted one official from the prison—Aleksander Rakocevic—whom he identified as a warden.[57] Former prisoners told Human Rights Watch that they recognized a few of the Serbian security personnel in the prison, although they did not know their full names. Both of the former prisoners who spoke with Human Rights Watch said that the director of the prison was known as "Miki"—a dark-skinned man who spoke perfect Albanian. According to A.K., the deputy director was known as "Ace," and he was the one who allegedly gave the order to fire on the assembled prisoners on May 22. A.K. and B.K. both also claimed that the prison guards had released and armed some of the ethnic Serbian prisoners after the first NATO raid on May 19. Both witnesses said they saw some of these people back in the prison attacking the Albanians with whom they had, until recently, been incarcerated.

Lastly, the Kosovo Liberation Army has claimed to possess further information about the Dubrava killings. In an interview with Human Rights Watch, KLA spokeswoman Faton Mexhmeti Ramusij said that the KLA possesses Serbian police documents that portray all the deaths in Dubrava as having been the result of NATO bombing. The names of four policemen who allegedly compiled the report were provided to Human Rights Watch, although the original document was not seen.[58]

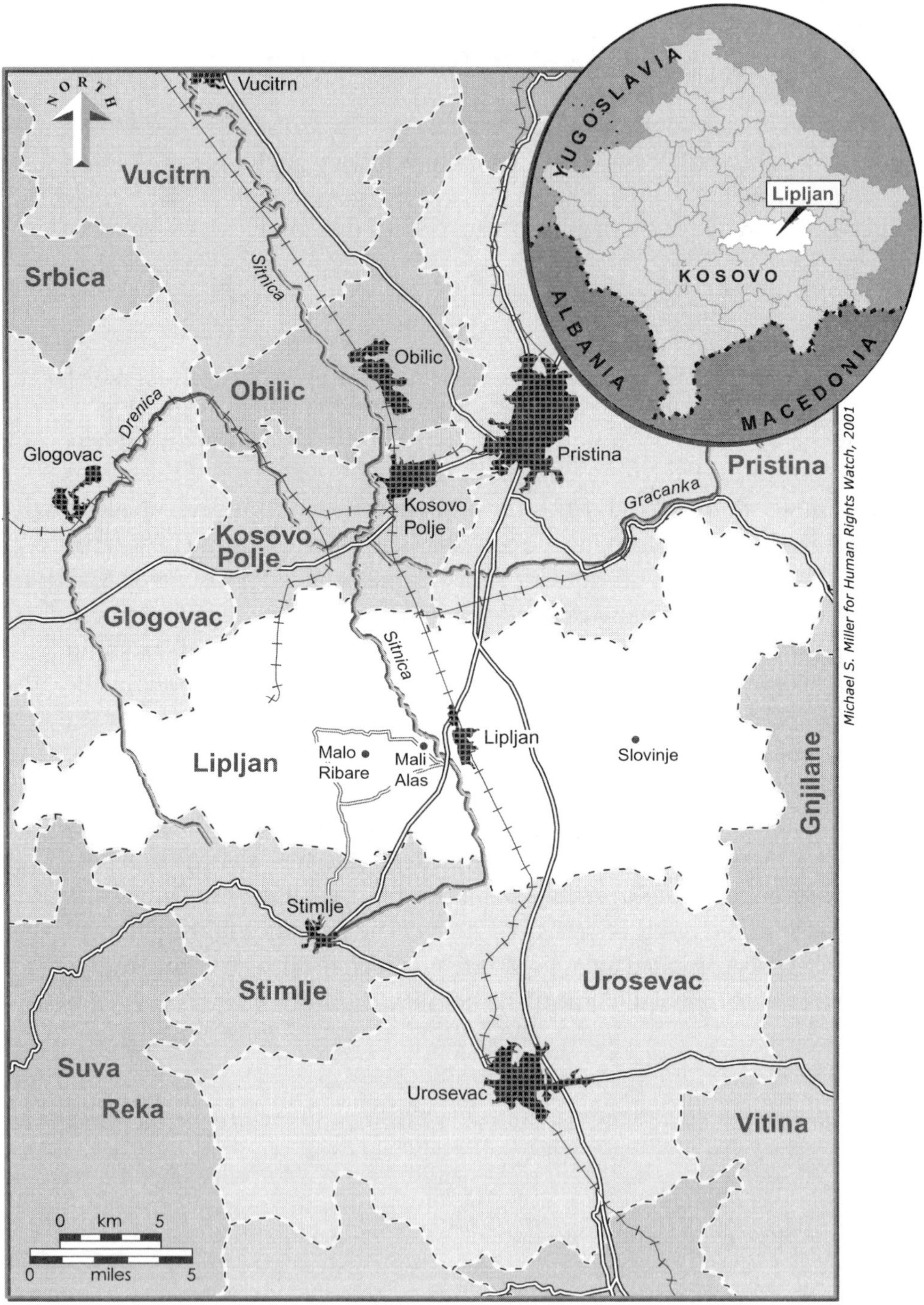
NORTH
Vucitrn
Vucitrn
Srbica
Sitnica
Obilic
Obilic
Drenica
Glogovac
Pristina
Pristina
Kosovo
Polje
Kosovo
Polje
Gracanka
Glogovac
Sitnica
Lipljan
Lipljan
Malo
Ribare
Mali
Alas
Slovinje
Gnjilane
Stimlje
Stimlje
Urosevac
Suva
Reka
Urosevac
Vitina
0 km 5
0 miles 5
YUGOSLAVIA
Lipljan
KOSOVO
ALBANIA
MACEDONIA
Michael S. Miller for Human Rights Watch, 2001

8

LIPLJAN (LIPJAN) MUNICIPALITY

The municipality of Lipljan (Lipjan) is situated in central Kosovo, with the main Pristina-Skopje highway passing close to its municipal capital, Lipljan town. Unlike the neighboring municipalities of Glogovac and Stimlje, Lipljan was not a focus of KLA activity or counter-insurgency by Serbian security forces during 1998, perhaps as a result of its ethnically-mixed population. This included large numbers of Serbs and a significant Roma and ethnic Croat population. Almost immediately after NATO airstrikes began, however, Serbian military and police began to enter and attack ethnic Albanian villages, forcing their inhabitants to flee to neighboring areas. In addition to large-scale displacement, there was arson and looting of Albanian homes and businesses in the municipality. Although Lipljan did not experience the level of killings suffered in Glogovac or Suva Reka, there were large-scale killings in three villages—Slovinje, Malo Ribare and Mali Alas—in mid-April. In Slovinje, for example, at least thirty-five people were killed on April 15 and 16. Finally, over the last week of April and first week of May 1999, thousands of Lipljan-area residents were forced to board trains and were expelled into Macedonia while others were sent towards Albania.

Although Lipljan municipality was not a center of KLA activity, it was the focus on considerable attention from Serbian security forces between March and June 1999. The testimony of the more than thirty witnesses from the area interviewed by Human Rights Watch indicates a pattern of attacks against many villages even while certain villages were spared direct assault. The objective of the attacks seems to have been to concentrate the population within a small area, prior to their subsequent expulsion from Kosovo.

There were several waves of offensives, first immediately following NATO airstrikes at the end of March. Subsequent offensives in April aimed at driving away villagers who tried to return home, while massacres in several villages served to terrorize many of the municipality's inhabitants into fleeing to Macedonia.

Albanian residents in the town of Lipljan were forced out of their homes within days of the start of NATO airstrikes through the burning of Albanian homes and house to house searches by Serbian police, and indirectly, out of fear at the large concentration of Serbian security forces in the town following the departure of the OSCE Kosovo Verification Mission. A.I., a thirty-three-year-old Lipljan resident, described the climate of fear that forced him and his family to leave:

> I was living in the center [of the town] in a building. On March 23, more than one hundred police were stationed at the administrative office for agriculture, four meters away from our [apartment] building. On Wednesday March 24 we felt fear when we saw a lot of movement of police and military in front of the building. At around 3:00 p.m. we were forced [by fear] to take our children and go to my nephew's house in the suburbs about 300 meters away from the town. We stayed two days in that house. On March 28 at around 9 p.m. the shooting and burning of Albanian homes in the town began. The burning houses were getting closer and closer to us. At around 10:30 p.m. we saw seven police officers from the window [of the house] about five meters away. Fortunately . . . they went to a neighbor's house which was empty. In the space of three minutes, all seventeen of us in the house left. We crossed through muddy fields to a village two kilometers away with our children in our arms. We arrived in Bandulic village at around 1:00 a.m.[1]

A.I. and his family left Bandulic (Banulle) around April 8 for Lugadzija (Llugagji), a village several kilometers farther south which served as a wartime refuge for many displaced families from the municipality. They spent several weeks there before returning to Lipljan on April 24. On their return to Lipljan, the family spent another week in A.I.'s nephew's house in the suburbs before fleeing to Macedonia. Most Bandulic residents fled to Macedonia in the last week of April, following an ultimatum from the police for the villagers "to hand over all their weapons" and several bouts of arson and robbery by police and paramilitaries.[2] Lipljan residents interviewed by the OSCE describe a similar pattern of police activity and arson in the town in late March, as well as direct expulsions of Albanian residents.[3]

Villages east of Lipljan were targeted in operations staged from Babus, a Serb village in the northernmost part of Urosevac municipality. Neighboring Muhadzer Babus (Babush i Muhaxhere), a predominantly ethnic Albanian village in southern Lipljan, was attacked with gunfire and grenades by Serbian forces the same evening that NATO airstrikes began, causing the villagers to flee. Several weeks later, after some inhabitants had returned, the village was attacked again with gunfire. Although residents initially fled to nearby Gornje Gadimlje (Gadime e Eperme) which had itself been attacked within days of the start of airstrikes, the inhabitants of Muhadzer Babus eventually took refuge in the village of Lugadzija, which in contrast with most of the surrounding villages was largely left undisturbed.[4] S.S., a thirty-six-year-old man from the village, explained to Human Rights Watch what he had experienced:

"They were shooting with automatic rifles and anti-aircraft weapons. We had five minutes to leave the village."

> On the first day of airstrikes we were very pleased, but the airstrikes began at 8:00 p.m. in our village and at midnight the first grenades fell on our village from Srpksi Babus. It's two kilometers away. The inhabitants are all Serbs—they were our neighbors. . . . It wasn't until the morning when we saw the craters [blast damage] that we realized that the grenades had come from Babus. Those of us who had small children took them to other villages. I took mine to Gadimlje. It was the second day of airstrikes [March 25]. . . . About ten days or two weeks after the NATO bombing [commenced] when we went back to our houses suddenly a column of between ten and thirteen tanks entered [Muhadzer Babus] without warning. They were shooting with automatic rifles and anti-aircraft weapons. We had five minutes to leave the village. We couldn't take any clothes. I couldn't take my passport. Then we went to Lugadzija.[5]

On April 26, after learning of mass killings in the villages of Slovinje, Malo Ribare, and Mali Alas (see below), S.S. decided to take his family to Macedonia. He explained his decision: "We were not frightened by the massacre in Slovinje. . . . but when it happened in [Malo] Ribare and [Mali] Alas we were afraid. We were unarmed and the children were very afraid so we had no choice but to leave."[6]

The village of Donje Gadimlje (Gadime e Ulet) was shelled from Babus within days of the start of NATO strikes. A witness from Donje Gadimlje interviewed by Human Rights Watch described the arrival of residents from Crnilo (Cernille), a village in northern Urosevac close to Muhadzer Babus, "five or six days after NATO started bombing."[7] He explained that "we couldn't sleep at all at night, because once NATO bombardments stopped, they [Serbian forces] would shell our village." Several days later (around April 1), Serbian forces entered Donje Gadimlje with tanks at around noon, causing the villagers to flee to a nearby river. After reassurances that the forces were just there to find shelter from NATO bombing, some residents returned the same day, only to flee again at around 5:00 p.m. after the arrival of the Serbian army with five tanks, which according to two witnesses, were shooting in the air.[8] Some villagers fled to Gornje Gadimlje to the east, some to Smolusa in the north and others to Glogovce, a village close to Lipljan. Although nearby Gornje Gadimlje was also attacked in late March, causing some of its residents to flee to Smolusa, many of the villagers either remained or returned, since residents from Muhadzer Babus and Donje Gadimlje both report taking shelter there in mid-April, together with large numbers of displaced persons from other villages.[9] On April 16 or 17, however, Serbian police and paramilitaries entered Gornje Gadimlje at around 1:30 p.m. and ordered everyone in the village to leave for Albania within two hours.[10]

Some villagers were on the move for most of April. M.L., a thirty-six-year-old man from Donje Gadimlje described his ordeal:

> It was nine days after the bombing started that we had to leave the first time [approximately April 2]. The military came at around 2:00 p.m. and did a patrol with tanks and then left. Two hours they returned and forced us out. Nobody was allowed to take cars or tractors. . . . We were obliged to go to Smolusa. After one week they came to Smolusa at 6:00 a.m.—we heard the shooting. It was the [same] military who were in Gadimlje. First they said no one is going to touch you. Then they came back after two or three hours and said "it's not safe for you here anymore. You have to leave Smolusa." So we went back to Gadimlje at 3:00 p.m., but not back to our houses. They had

> burned about half of the village. We stayed for twenty-four hours then the military came again and said "between 1:00 p.m. and 3:00 p.m. everyone has to leave, including Gornje Gadimlje." So we left and went to Lugadzija. We stayed only two days there because it was overcrowded. Then we went back to Smolusa. We stayed in Smolusa one week and then went back to Gadimlje after a villager was told by a police commander that it was safe to go back. But when we went back the shooting continued all night long and three houses were burned so we left for Macedonia after two nights. [11]

The villages of Marevce and Glavica were targeted several weeks later. According to S.S., the tanks located in Muhadzer Babus relocated to the villages of Glavica and Marevce at around 4:30 a.m. a week after they had entered. S.S. explained that he knew this because the road from Muhadzer Babus to Glavica passes through Lugadzija and he had heard the tanks.[12] This account is consistent with the testimony of Q.F., a woman from Marevce, who told Human Rights Watch that the village was attacked early on the morning of April 15, exactly three weeks after the inhabitants of Muhadzer Babus had initially fled their village. Q.F. described the attack:

> The Serb offensive came early in the morning before sunrise. We heard the noise of tanks from Babus village. When they entered the side of our village we could hear the shooting. The noise and fear woke us up and we went into the yard. When they were shooting we lay down on the ground. No one was hit. There were about ten of us. Bullets were going over our heads. [There were] a lot of tanks, armored personnel carriers, and civilian cars. Afterwards, ground troops came down from the upper part of the village. They went to Upper Glavica and our neighborhood and gave an order to leave the houses. After that the situation became calmer. [The villagers from] Glavica and Marevce ran away but our part of the village stayed until the afternoon at around 3:00 p.m. After that a tank and armored car came and started to burn houses in Glavica village. After they burned the houses in Glavica, they burned houses in the upper part of Marevce. After that we left and went to Lugadzija.[13]

Q.F., who was pregnant, decided to travel to Macedonia soon after because of "fear that something might happen again."[14]

On the same day that Marevce and Glavica were attacked, Serbian police and paramilitaries entered the village of Slovinje, executed eighteen of its Albanian inhabitants, and ordered the remainder to go to nearby Smolusa (see below). The following day, April 16, paramilitaries surrounded a large number of residents taking shelter in the hills close to the village and separated the men from the women. Fifteen men were then shot dead and a woman was burned to death on a tractor by the paramilitaries, according to witnesses. Some residents fled to Macedonia at the beginning of May, although many took shelter in neighboring villages or hid in the hills. Together with the villages of Malo Ribare and Mali Alas (see below), Slovinje endured the worst wartime abuses in the entire municipality.

Fifteen men were then shot dead and a woman was burned to death on a tractor by the paramilitaries,

The villages of Toplicane (Toplican) and Glogovce south of Lipljan were not attacked directly, but were frequently visited by Serbian security forces in March and April, creating a climate of fear and uncertainty that led many residents to flee to Macedonia. Both villages suffered widespread arson as well as robbery and extortion by police and paramilitaries. According to F.P., the intimidation in Toplicane began soon after the start of NATO airstrikes: "First they burned three houses where the OSCE had been staying. This was about four days after the NATO airstrikes started. Around one week after the strikes, they started to rob houses."[15] Finally, F.P. took his family to Macedonia by train on April 22, "because of fear and because of our children."

In Glogovce (Gllogoc), the house burning and looting were accompanied by threats and extortion. In early April, Glogovce residents were forced to leave their houses for an hour and half, while police looted and burned them. According to M.L., a twenty-five-year old man from the village: "The police entered Bandulic. After that they came to our village. It was around three weeks ago [approximately April 6]. We had to leave our houses and go one hundred meters away just for somebody not to be killed."[16] When M.L. and the other villagers returned home they found that the police "had burned twenty-five houses and stolen money and anything else they could find." The family of forty-year-old A.A, suffered escalating violence that culminated in his daughter's kidnap for ransom:

> The day that they burned our houses was Saturday. Six days later they came and took my car. They caught my daughter three days before we left—Friday

> or Saturday. We were inside around 9:00 a.m. They caught my child outside playing. . . . They had a white van. They were Serb civilians, always armed. . . . They said "give us money or we'll kill the child." I gave them a thousand Deutsche Marks and a gold necklace. They released her half an hour later and left. One hour later regular police came. I told them what happened. They knew who they were but pretended to ask for a description of the car etc.[17]

A.A. and his family left Glogovce for Macedonia on Monday, April 26. When asked why he left, he explained: "It was a very big panic. If you stayed any longer it might be too late."[18] According to witness statements obtained by the OSCE in Macedonia, many Glogovce residents had reached the same conclusion by the end of April.[19]

Serbian security forces launched a series of offensives against the villages west of Lipljan on April 18. Bujance, a village southwest of Lipljan close to the Lipljan-Stimlje road, was attacked with mortars or grenades early on the morning of April 18 according to B.B, a thirty-three-year-old resident of the village interviewed by Human Rights Watch.[20] A witness from the nearby village of Toplicane said that he saw grenades being fired on Bujance at around 6 a.m. from neighboring Staro Gracko, a predominantly Serbian village to the north of Bujance.[21] As a result of the attack, the younger inhabitants of Bujance fled to the hills near to the village of Varigovce (Varigove), although some elderly residents remained in the center of the village. Bujance also suffered looting and arson during the offensive, according to B.B. and witnesses interviewed by the OSCE.[22] The nearby village of Krajiste (Krajishte) was also targeted on April 18, according to a thirty-five-year-old woman from the village: "on Sunday, our village was attacked at 6:00 a.m. by three tanks. All the village left immediately."[23] According to the witness, three villagers were killed on the day of the attack, including a middle-aged woman, a teenage boy, and twenty-year-old woman.[24] After spending five days in the hills close to the village of Varigovce, the villager returned to Krajishte after Serbs from the village told them it was safe to return. The decision of most of the villagers to flee to Macedonia several days later seems to have been prompted more by fear that Serbian forces would return than by any specific incident.

The villages of Malo Ribare and Mali Alas were attacked on April 18 and 19. The villages, which lie approximately three kilometers apart, are close to the village of Novo Rujce (Rufc i Ri), which although its residents remained, was spared the same violence as its close neighbors. Nevertheless, the proximity of Novo Rujce to the two villages left its inhabitants in no doubt as to what was happening nearby. Y.S., a twenty-eight-year-old man from Novo Rujce described his experiences on April 18:

> I was at home in Novo Rujce with my family when the incidents happened in [Malo] Ribare and [Mali] Alas. It was Sunday when the massacre happened in [Malo] Ribare. We heard the first shots at 6:15 am. At 7:00 a.m., smoke was rising from the first houses. . . . then the women began screaming. We were forced to leave our house . . . Then us men went there [Malo Ribare] to try and help them at around 8:00 or 9:00 a.m. We went around the village. . . . We found some wounded people. There were four of them—an old man, an old woman, and two young men (around twenty-five-years-old). So we tried to help them. After an hour the lady died. . . . We couldn't see anyone else.[25]

Despite assurances from his Serb neighbors that the attack on Malo Ribare would not be repeated in Novo Rujce, house-to-house visits from paramilitaries demanding money and the burning of a house in nearby Mali Alas convinced Y.S. to leave. He took his family to Velika Dobranja (Dobraje e Madhe) for one week. Y.S. tried to return to Novo Rujce but was ordered out by paramilitaries after two nights, forcing him to flee to Lugadzija before eventually being forced to board a train to Macedonia on May 4.

The fears generated by the attack on Malo Ribare for Y.S. and his family proved to be well-founded. Early on April 18, Serbian forces, including tanks, police, and paramilitaries entered the village. According to multiple eyewitnesses, the paramilitaries then went on a rampage of murder that left between twenty-four and twenty-seven dead, including women, children and the elderly.[26] J.K., a forty-year-old resident of Malo Ribare described what he witnessed:

> The massacre happened on Sunday April 18 at 6:00 a.m. Four different kinds of paramilitaries arrived with tanks. They executed whoever they saw in the streets from seven [years old] to eighty-seven [years old]. . . . They didn't choose by sex or age. Most of the people they killed were killed by a gun shot in the neck, heart, or forehead. They burned nineteen houses and stayed two days. . . . They came without warning. . . . A force of about seventy entered the village with a few tanks and APCs. There was a tank at the start [of the

> convoy] with a heavy gun, after that two APCs and after them a truck loaded with paramilitaries who got off the truck and spread around the village. . . . As soon as the forces entered and the shooting started, people began running away. I was going around knocking on doors telling people to get out. In half an hour the whole village was empty. . . . I saw everything. I saw one person shot in the neck. I saw another person shot in the heart. A woman with me was shot from behind. I saw almost all the people being shot apart from four. . . .[27]

J.K. named eighteen persons from the village who were executed, including a seven-year-old girl and fourteen-year-old boy, as well as six displaced persons from the village of Vrsevce (Vershec) in the western part of Lipljan municipality. J.K. described paramilitaries wearing "various hats and uniforms," including Chetnik hats, bobble hats, red bandanas, as well as green camouflage uniforms without insignia."[28] J.K. returned to the village one week later, but found the "village was burned and demolished." He fled to Macedonia soon after.

The neighboring village of Mali Alas was attacked the following day. On the morning of April 19, Serbian paramilitaries entered the village and separated men from women. The paramilitaries demanded money from and then executed at least twenty men. One witness interviewed by Deutsche Presse Agenteur said he was among thirteen men lined up against the wall of a house and shot.[29] While he and another man escaped by feigning death, eleven men were killed. Another nine men from the village were also shot the same day, according to this witness. Witnesses interviewed by the OSCE (who may include the same man) describe the same event, including the shooting of the eleven in identical terms; they also provide additional information about the other killings.[30] Although most of the details are common to all accounts, some witnesses claimed twenty were executed and others twenty-one.[31] An explanation for the disparity may lie in the statement of an elderly woman from Suvi Do (Suhodoll) village who was interviewed by the *Boston Globe* in June 1999.[32] The woman, who was present in the village at the time of the killings, said that Serbian forces had demanded that a Roma man from the village help to bury the bodies of the dead, a detail echoed in other witness statements, and stated

J.K. named eighteen persons from the village who were executed, including a seven-year-old girl and fourteen-year-old boy.

that after the Roma man had refused to do so, he was shot dead. Most accounts suggest that the bodies of the victims were initially buried in a single grave, but were reinterred sometime in early May into the individual graves that postwar visitors to the village observed, presumably in an attempt to conceal the nature of the deaths.

SLOVINJE (SLLOVI)

Some of the worst atrocities in Lipljan municipality occurred in the village of Slovinje. Slovinje, which lies approximately eight kilometers east of Lipljan was a mixed village prior to the war, comprising around 500 Albanian and sixty Serb homes. Relations between the Albanian and Serb villagers were reportedly good prior to March 1999. The villagers do not appear to have been involved in the KLA and, unusually for Kosovo, many of the Serb villagers spoke Albanian in addition to Serbian. The violence that occurred on several days in April shattered that community: at least thirty-five Albanian villagers were executed on April 15 and 16. The survivors fled to neighboring villages, and many continued on to Macedonia. As the war neared its end in early June, two elderly brothers who had returned early were detained and beaten. One died from his injuries. Today Slovinje is a community in tatters: almost every Albanian family has had one or more relatives killed, all of the Serb and most of the Roma population have fled the village, dozens of Albanian and Serb homes have been burned to ground and the Orthodox church lies in ruins.

Tensions in Slovinje were raised following the departure of the OSCE KVM on March 20 and the start of NATO airstrikes four days later, with Albanians from the village particularly concerned about deteriorating security elsewhere in Kosovo. Those concerns were brought home on April 14, 1999. According to F.B, a thirty-eight-year-old Albanian man from the village, an armored personnel carrier entered the village at around 4:30 p.m. and left without incident.[33] Another villager, F.G., told Human Rights Watch that he observed a Serb villager from Slovinje in a military vehicle the same evening.[34] Both men stated that Serb villagers had advised their Albanian neighbors and the local Democratic League of Kosovo (LDK) office on the evening of April 14 that tanks were going to be brought into the village the following day, but that

The villagers do not appear to have been involved in the KLA

"there would be no consequences," since the tanks were simply being moved to evade NATO bombers.[35]

At around 4:00 or 5:00 a.m. on April 15, six tanks entered Slovinje. According to witnesses, the forces with them were a combination of police, military, and paramilitaries, some of them wearing masks. Villagers allege that some of the paramilitaries were residents of Slovinje.[36] Aside from reports that soldiers or paramilitaries painted the four C's (a Serbian symbol of four Cyrillic letter S's in the shape of a cross) on doors and windows during the morning, the village was quiet until around 1:30 p.m., when multiple witnesses report hearing gunshots and seeing smoke and flames from burning houses in the north side of the village (closer to the road from Lipljan). Soon after, the village suffered its first victims: Fatushe Dubova, a nineteen-year-old woman, was shot in the yard of her house, possibly by a sniper. According to several witnesses, Hedije Krasniqi, a fifty-two-year-old woman, was shot at close range in the street outside her house around 2:00 p.m. Next to die were the men of the Gashi family, whose family compound was close to the entrance of the village, across from the school. Z.G., a female relative who was present in the Gashi compound at the time, described seeing "forces from Gusterica and Dobratin villages in military uniform" as well as persons wearing "masks and police uniforms." She explained to Human Rights Watch how she witnessed the execution of her male relatives:

"Only one person fired. He was given a hand signal."

> We were all inside when the Serbs came. They were wearing masks and police uniforms. They knocked on the door and came inside the house. It was around 2:00 p.m. They told us to get out of the house because they were going to burn it. When we left the house, they took the men among us, and told us [women and children] to go to Smolusa. My husband didn't want to leave . . . but they even took him. . . . Then a man said "should I burn the house or should I kill them?" Another replied "better kill them and then take care of the house.". . . . All of the us started to scream "don't do that," but they didn't listen. Only one person fired. He was given a hand signal. I didn't recognize him. He was thin, had red hair and red beard. He was wearing a police uniform, and was in his late twenties or early thirties.[37]

According to Z.G., five male members of the Gashi family were executed in the yard: sixty-three-year-old Murat; forty-year-old Enver, and thirty-four-year-old Omer, his two sons; twenty-year-old Bekim Haziri, his grandson, and sixteen-year-old-old Arben, Enver's son. Z.G. alleges that several Serb residents of Slovinje were involved in the murder of her relatives (see below). On or around the same time, Rifat Gashi and his cousin Milaim were shot dead by a sniper. Three witnesses told Human Rights Watch that forty-six-year-old Rifat Gashi and twenty-two-year-old Milaim were killed by a sniper in the yard of their house on the afternoon of April 15.[38] Three girls from the family were also wounded in attack. Two of the witnesses interviewed by Human Rights Watch had helped bury the two cousins in temporary graves.

In the meantime, the Albanian residents were being ordered to leave the village and go to nearby Smolusa by Serbian police and paramilitaries. According to I.N., a sixty-year-old man, "We heard rifle shots outside on the other side of the village. We went outside the house and a Serbian officer gave a 'thumbs up' indicating that we had to leave. I asked him which way to go and he told us to go to Smolusa. He was wearing a green uniform, not camouflage, like a soldier."[39] Several elderly men refused to leave their homes. Fifty-nine-year-old Adem Bytyqi, remained in his home on April 15 and was found dead in a field by his brother five days later. Avjaz Gashi, a sixty-two-year-old man also refused to leave and was subsequently found shot in the yard of his house.

A memorial for the victims in Slovinje, where Serbian forces killed at least thirty-five ethnic Albanian villagers on April 15 and 16, 1999.

Some residents had already decided to leave once the shooting began. Most were able to flee, but some were executed as they tried to leave. One witness, M.B., saw Gafur Hyseni pulled off his tractor by police and shot.[40] Another witness from Gadimlje told Human Rights Watch how paramilitaries took his nephew Faik Krasniqi off his tractor and shot him, in front of his children.[41] A third witness, F.G., saw both bodies. Ramadan Kryeziu, a twenty-nine-year-old man, was stopped by the police as he drove out of the village and then allowed to proceed. Kryeziu was later found dead, according to several witnesses, including his father.[42] Three elderly villagers were also found dead near to their home. The bodies of seventy-three-year-old Mehmet Sopa, eighty-seven-year-old Shehide Sopa, and sixty-four-year-old Qamille Sopa were found with knife wounds in a horse stable. Relatives found blood in the yard of their house. In all, eighteen residents of Slovinje were killed on April 15. Latife Kryeziu, a forty-seven-year-old woman who was wounded on April 15, died several days later in Smolusa.

While part of the village went southwest to Smolusa, others, including many of the men, fled east toward the village of Zhegovac (Zhegofc) to a place in the hills called "the Dell of Deme" (Lugu i Demas). The dell consists of a large field surrounded by woods connected to a smaller field on higher ground. The villagers spent the night in the dell, sleeping on open ground in the rain. According to one villager, "that night we began to talk about who was dead and who was missing."[43] People from other villages were also sheltering nearby. One witness estimates that there were around 800 people in the dell on the morning of April 16. The villagers spent the morning building temporary shelters and organizing food supplies and vehicles. At around 2:00 p.m., Serbian paramilitaries appeared at the top of the dell. S.B., a sixty-two-year-old man from the village told Human Rights Watch:

> At 2:00 p.m. they came from the higher part of the hill and started to force us [down the hill]. The woods were full of soldiers and paramilitaries. Ten of them came closer to us and began to shoot.... They told us all to move down [the hill]. One of them with a gun told us to take out all the money, identification papers and gold that we had. Another one started to search us to see if we kept anything.... They separated thirteen people, made them put their hands up.... One kicked me in the shoulder and I fell down. They beat the younger [men] one by one with fists and the butts of their guns.... Then they ordered us to separate from the women and children. The women and chil-

> dren were ordered down to the field [below]. They ordered us men to go to another side. They told us to go up into the woods, all the time saying "you were asking for NATO, now let NATO come and help you."[44]

F.B, a twenty-nine-year-old male relative of S.B., was also present. He told Human Rights Watch:

> The shooting was very intense and very close to us. At around 2:00 p.m. Serbian forces entered the field from two sides—above and below. That's when we saw them for the first time. . . . .In a panic, we put up our hands to surrender. They began to tell us to get together. . . . They moved us to the lower part of the field. As they were moving us, one person was killed—a man who didn't want to leave his sick wife. My nineteen-year-old nephew was wounded because the young people were moving around a lot, trying to hide. We were all in the lower part of the field. Five armed Serbs were standing in front of us with dark military uniforms. They were all between thirty and forty years old. One who spoke to us in Albanian had a black mask on his face. Most of the Serbian forces were 300 meters lower down in another field.[45]

F.G. confirmed the killing of Jonuz Pacolli, the man with the sick wife.[46] According to F.G., "the biggest abuses began" after Jonuz Pacolli was executed [47] Each of the witnesses described the confiscation of documents and money by Serbian security forces, and that foodstuffs, tractors and other vehicles were set alight at that time. According to F.G., "one started to pour petrol over everything. H. [a villager] had to set fire to these things." Having earlier put six men in a line, the same man who forced H. to set fire to foodstuffs and vehicles then began to call people from the line. F.G. told Human Rights Watch that the man "called the first [person] from the line and beat him, although not badly. The second one—Gazmend [Zeqir Hetemi] was ordered to untie his shoes—they were kicking him. They beat him very badly. The third one was asked to take off his clothes and they kicked him. All of this in front of the women and children."[48]

Each of the witnesses described the confiscation of documents and money by Serbian security forces

A.B who was also present when the beatings occurred, provided a similar account:

> Then they separated six men and started to beat them up, one by one in a way that I have never seen before. I remember a young man—who is dead now—one Serb told him to untie his sneakers—he kicked him in the face and another one kicked him above his head. . . . I remember another case. They called him too—three police or paramilitaries tied a machine gun belt around his head in front of his eyes and around his forehead and started to pull the belt. When they told him to go back to the line with his hands up, the blood started to flow from his forehead down his face because his skin was very badly damaged.

Isak Bytqyi was the next person to be shot. The forty-five-year-old Bytyqi had worked as a policeman in the Socialist Federal Republic of Yugoslavia, which likely placed him under greater suspicion of involvement in the KLA. According to his cousin, A.B., "three or four Serbs in uniform came. One of them seemed like he was in charge—he was around forty-five and had a moustache. He called for Isak Bytyqi. . . . I heard when [Isak] was told "you are commanding these people." I couldn't hear the rest of the conversation (which went on for about three minutes). They took him in front of a vehicle and I heard gunshots—I couldn't see because I was in the upper part of the field.[49] Isak's brother S.B. found his body later the same day. According to S.B., Isak Bytyqi "had been shot in the back of the head, behind the left ear."[50]

Following Isak Bytyqi's death, Serbian police and paramilitaries took the remaining women, children and elderly down the hill to the lower field, leaving only younger men in the upper field. According to witnesses, H., who had been ordered earlier to burn the vehicles, was again called from the line. He was badly beaten and told that he was going to get "a bullet in the forehead." When he was ordered back to the line, H. escaped into the bushes, despite being pursued by two paramilitaries who fired after him. After questioning the men as to H.'s identity, shots were fired at the other men in the line from lower down the hill, killing Fatmir Bytyqi, Gazmend (Zeqir) Hatemi, and Heset Lekiqi and wounding a fourth man. The other men from the village were then told to run into the woods. According to S.B.: "They told the men who remained there to go deep into the woods. When we started to run, they began to shoot.[51] As shots rang out, the men scattered into the woods. A.B. described hearing "firing and branches falling" as he fled, which may have been the result of stray bullets hitting trees. Those who escaped hid in the woods.

At around 6:00 or 7:00 p.m. the same day, the survivors returned to the field site, drawn by the cries of women and children and anxious to know what had become of their families. The villagers began to search the woods to retrieve the bodies of those who had been killed. The wounded were carried back and given first aid. In the morning, after a night sheltering under plastic sheeting and in those vehicles that had not been burned, the villagers finished collecting the corpses. In addition to the bodies of fifteen men who had been shot in the field and the woods, the body of seventy-four-year-old Halime Gerbeshi was also discovered. Gerbeshi appears to have been burned to death while she was sheltering under a plastic sheet on a tractor which had been set alight. In order to bury the bodies quickly, it was decided to prepare a large single temporary grave. Some from the villagers, including a local politician, attempted to persuade the villagers otherwise, arguing that it would hamper subsequent investigations of the deaths. The villagers nevertheless dug a single grave and prepared a list of the names and ages of the dead (prepared in triplicate in case one of the persons carrying the list was killed or captured). At around 1:00 p.m. on April 17, the bodies were buried in a simple funeral service.

The Slovinje residents hid in the hills for three more days, before attempting to return to their village. On April 20 or 21, some residents returned to the village. Villagers sheltering in Smolusa were reportedly invited back to the village around the same time by their Serb neighbors. Within days of returning, gunshots and the burning of an Albanian house prompted the Albanian residents of the village to leave for Smolusa, which throughout this period appears to have been safe, if overcrowded. It was not without its victims, however: Latife Kryeziu, a forty-seven-year-old woman who had been wounded in the village on April 15, died of her wounds in Smolusa. The remaining villagers who were sheltering in the hills also made their way to Smolusa, so that by the end of April, most of the surviving Albanian inhabitants of Slovinje (and several other villages) had taken refuge there.

Towards the end of April, some of the villagers were invited by police to return to Slovinje. The primary motivation for this invitation was apparently to arrange the reburial of the eighteen villagers who had been killed by Serbian police and paramilitaries in Slovinje on April 15. According to H.K., the eighteen corpses initially placed in a mass grave were dug up by Serbian soldiers and taken to the school in Slovinje.[52] The Albanian villagers were instructed by police to visit the school to identify and arrange for reburial of their relatives. The official logic of such an action was presumably to mask the circumstances of the deaths, albeit one complicated by the involvement of the dead villagers' relatives. According to Z.G., the bodies were dug up following the visit of "a doctor from Belgrade."[53] Several witnesses interviewed by Human Rights Watch participated in the reburials, which took place at the end of April.

The bodies of seventeen residents of Slovinje once buried in the Dell of Deme are missing.

Almost as soon as the burials had taken place, the villagers were given an order to leave the village. According to S.B., Serbian forces gave the following ultimatum: "Everyone must leave. If we find anyone here after 6:00 p.m. we're going to kill them."[54] Those villagers who had returned left again for Smolusa, Gadimlje, and Glogovac (Lipljan). Several of the persons interviewed by Human Rights Watch boarded overcrowded trains to the Macedonian border outside Lipljan, eventually ending up in refugee camps in Macedonia. Most of the village did not return until the withdrawal of Serbian forces and the entry of KFOR in June.

In late May, the seventeen bodies temporarily buried in a single grave in the Dell of Deme were removed.[55] According to unconfirmed reports, the bodies were removed with a bulldozer by Serbian security forces and loaded onto a truck on May 25. None of the villagers interviewed by Human Rights Watch had seen the bodies being bulldozed or loaded onto a truck, although one villager did reportedly witness the exhumation. During a visit to the gravesite on July 23, Human Rights Watch observed that the earth had been disturbed and found clothing fragments that supported the villagers' accounts. Reports of exhumations by Serbian forces to conceal the evidence of murders elsewhere in Kosovo also lend support to the account. What is certain is that the bodies of seventeen residents of Slovinje once buried in the Dell of Deme are missing, and that the anguish it has caused their relatives is real.

Most of Slovinje's Albanian inhabitants did not return until Serbian security forces withdraw in mid-June following KFOR's entry into Kosovo on June 12. Some elderly residents sheltering in nearby villages did attempt to return earlier however, with tragic consequences. On June 3, S.S. and his forty-five-year-old brother Shefki returned to Slovinje. Early in the morning the two men were stopped by unknown paramilitaries in the village and taken to the local school, where they were detained for several hours. While under detention they were questioned and beaten repeatedly by the paramilitaries and several soldiers. The two brothers were accused of being NATO informants and asked about the location of a satellite telephone they allegedly possessed. Their denials were met by beatings. Shefki, who suffered from a kidney ailment, was beaten so badly that he died an hour after his release.

S.S. described their detention to Human Rights Watch:

> They [paramilitaries] stopped us, checked our pockets and checked us for weapons. They tied our hands and forced us to get in the car and took us to the school. We were teachers and the Serbs [from the village] told them we were spies. Then they began asking us about the telephone, saying "call NATO to help you." Then they started to torture us. There were five people—three paramilitaries and two soldiers . . . My brother and I were in the same place and got beaten at the same time. Two officers—paramilitaries—were asking the questions. After they left, the three others came and we were beaten by them. . . . They questioned us six times and beat us on six occasions. The questioning was longer [than the beating. We were questioned for] about twenty minutes each time. . . . The three of them all beat us at the same time.[56]

The two men were detained until around 11:45 a.m., when it apparently became clear that Shefki was close to death as a result of his beatings. According to S.S. "When they saw my brother was dying, they said 'Leave now! Go! Go away!'"[57] The brothers then left the school on foot and headed towards their home in the village. S.S. continued, "we were walking on the road when my brother died. I went to the neighbor's and told them what happened. We took his body into a neighbors garden. He died an hour after [we were released]—we were walking very slowly toward my house. It was 12:30 p.m. when he died—it took us an hour to walk [from the school]."[58] When asked the cause of Shefki's death, S.S. replied, " My brother died because they beat him so much in the kidneys."[59]

Shefki collapsed and died outside the home of P.F. As a result, P.F. was the first person other than S.S. to see Shefki's body. He told Human Rights Watch that on June 3 at around 1:00 or 2:00 p.m., "I was in this [location of interview] house with my daughter and I saw S. in my garden, yelling 'Oh my God they killed my brother.' I took some wood and a small wagon and went to the place [where the body lay]. I took the body and went to the village cemetery where my brother was and buried the body there. . . . S. stayed here because he was wounded."[60] When asked to describe the condition of the body P.F. stated "when I saw the body it had some wounds. [There were] bruises on the side of the cheek and on the side of the his body. I could see bruises all over his body—on his legs. There was no blood."[61]

Several days later P.F. himself was detained in the school, following the killing of a policeman. During his detention, he was pressured into making a false confession that he had killed the man he helped to bury. According to P.F.:

> The military came and took me to the school at around 11:00 a.m. They were wearing long boots, uniforms and bullet proof vests. They asked me who killed Shefki. I answered "the police and the military." In the end, I had to admit that I killed him, even though I didn't [kill him]. They wanted to scare me. They took their knives [out] . . . [One of them] threatened me, saying "I will kill your brother and your daughter if you don't show where in the mountains the people are [hiding]." I said "I don't know anything."[62]

P.F. was also questioned about the KLA. He alleges that two Serb civilians from the village were present at the school during his detention, and that his head was pushed against a wall although he was not beaten. Human Rights Watch observed a cut on P.F.'s head that was consistent with the latter allegation. Although the soldiers who questioned him managed to force P.F. to admit that he had killed Shefki, they were unable to get him to sign a confession before police arrived at the school and ordered P.F. released.

S.S. was taken to the hills by a KLA doctor for treatment, returning the following day. Almost three weeks after his beating, Human Rights Watch saw faded bruising and skin damage all over S.S.'s body consistent with his account of the beating. The remainder of his family returned to the village unharmed on June 9.[63]

Perpetrators

Witnesses from Slovinje describe three kinds of forces active in the village and surrounding areas between April and June—police, military, and paramilitary.[64] The military appear to have played a much less active role in the expulsion and murder of civilians than police and paramilitaries. By contrast the police and paramilitaries are frequently implicated by witnesses. There is some confusion among witnesses between police and paramilitaries, possibly related to the allegation that local Serbs from Slovinje put on police uniforms to participate in the violence.

As always, identification of perpetrators proved difficult for witnesses. Nine Serbs from Slovinje were named by various witnesses as participants in killings, forcible expulsion and arson in the village, but Human Rights Watch was unable to confirm their participation. Several police officers were named by multiple witnesses from Slovinje, however. Mr. Tosic (first name unknown), a police commander from Lipljan, was identified by four witnesses as present in Slovinje during the atrocities on April 16 and 17. Although individual witnesses from Slovinje and the village of Toplicane allege that Tosic was variously involved in acts of arson and ordering civilians to leave Slovinje, another witness, D.N. who described Tosic as "a person in charge," told Human Rights Watch that he had intervened to save her husband from execution by paramilitaries on April 16.[65] Milivoje Pejic, the deputy police chief in Janjevo, was named by four witnesses as a commander in Slovinje at the time of the April 16 killings. A third police officer from Slovinje, identified as "Tomce, the son of Milic," was named by two witnesses interviewed by Human Rights Watch as present in the village in April and May.

Several police officers were named by multiple witnesses from Slovinje.

9

ORAHOVAC (RRAHOVEC) MUNICIPALITY

With regular KLA activity in the area throughout 1998 and early 1999, Orahovac municipality was tense and violent both before and during the NATO air campaign. Approximately 90 percent of the municipality is ethnic Albanian and there is one predominantly Serbian village: Velika Hoca (Hoce e Madhe).

On July 19, 1998, the KLA tried to capture Orahovac town. The police regained control two days later and began a summer-long offensive that retook the nearby KLA base at Malisevo and much of the territory throughout Kosovo that the KLA had declared "liberated." Serbian and Albanian civilians died in the Orahovac battle, and dozens of people are still missing.[1]

War crimes such as killings and abductions of civilians on both sides continued throughout 1998 and early 1999, with a primary target of the KLA being Serb civilians in Velika Hoca.[2] During the NATO bombing, ethnic Albanians from the municipality recognized Serbian villagers from Velika Hoca among the troops that committed large-scale executions of Albanian civilians in the area.

During the air war, Orahovac town experienced forced expulsions and sporadic killings. The most serious crimes were committed between March 24 and March 26 in the southwestern part of the municipality, between Bela Crkva and Pirana, along the border with Prizren municipality. Because these villages were attacked in a single offensive, they are dealt with as a unit in the chapter on the Prizren-Djakovica Road. The major atrocity in Orahovac municipality away from the road was the killing of more than one hundred men in Pusto Selo, as documented below.

The Serbian police in Orahovac fell under the jurisdiction of the Prizren

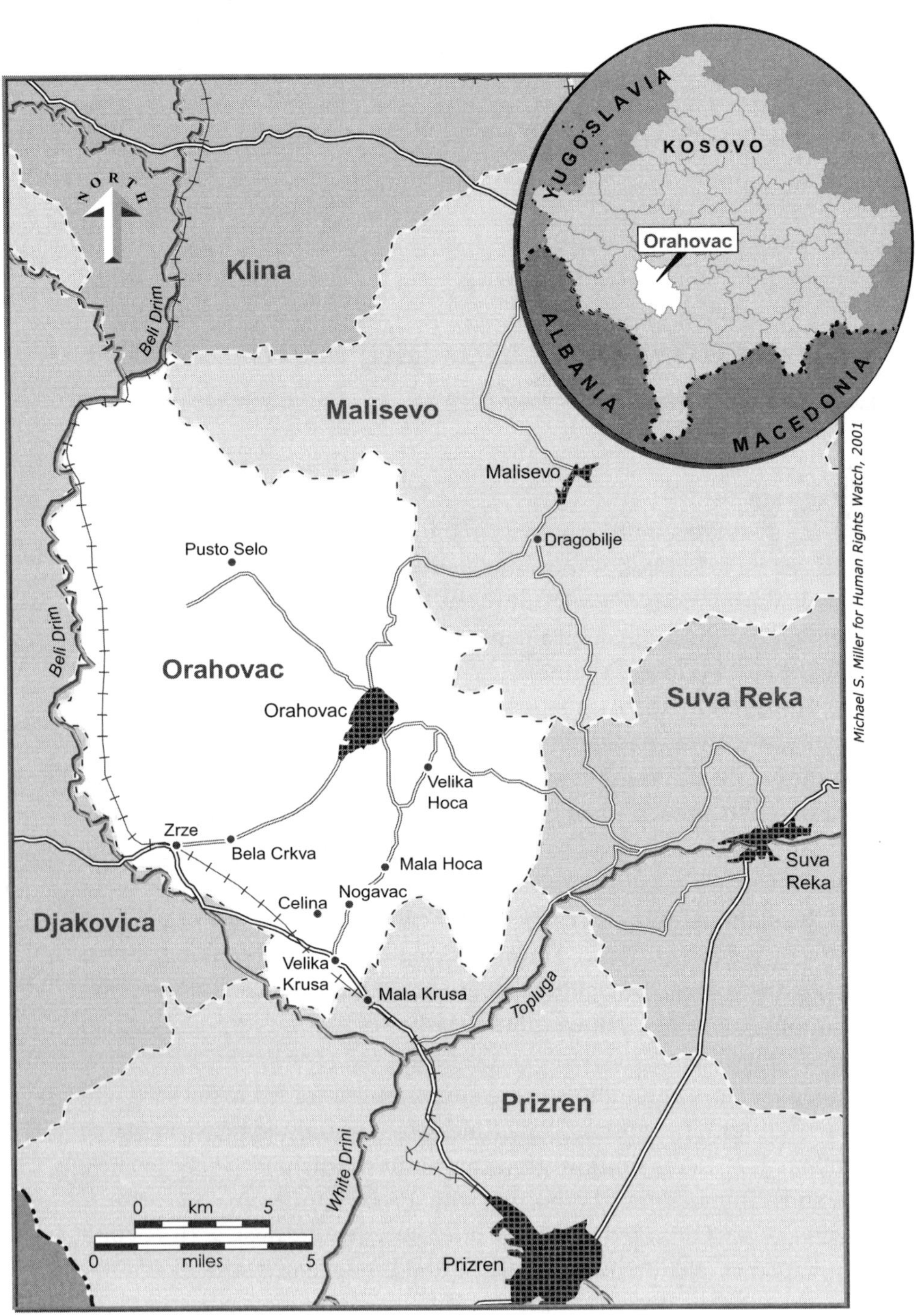

NORTH
YUGOSLAVIA
KOSOVO
Orahovac
ALBANIA
MACEDONIA
Klina
Beli Drim
Malisevo
Malisevo
Dragobilje
Pusto Selo
Beli Drim
Orahovac
Orahovac
Suva Reka
Velika Hoca
Zrze
Bela Crkva
Mala Hoca
Suva Reka
Nogavac
Celina
Djakovica
Velika Krusa
Mala Krusa
Topluga
Prizren
White Drini
0 km 5
0 miles 5
Prizren
Michael S. Miller for Human Rights Watch, 2001

Secretariat for Internal Affairs, or SUP (which covered Prizren, Orahovac, Suva Reka, and Gora municipalities). Col. Gradimir Zekavica was the commander of Prizren SUP until at least January 1999, with Lt. Milan Djuricic the section head of Prizren SUP's police department.[3] According to Policajac Magazine, in January 1999, Col. Milos Vojnovic became the new Prizren SUP commander, while also serving as assistant chief of the police department in the Ministry of Internal Affairs.[4] But, according to awards given to MUP officers after the war, Zekavica was the Prizren SUP commander in 1999 (See Forces of the Conflict).

In August 1999, KFOR forces arrested the former mayor of Orahovac, Andjelko Kolasinac, along with more than a dozen other Orahovac Serbs. On June 14, 2001, the Prizren district court found Kolasinac and another Orahovac Serb, Cedomir Jovanovic, guilty of war crimes against the civilian population of Orahovac, and sentenced them to five and twenty years imprisonment respectively. According to the Humanitarian Law Center, which monitored the trial, the defendants were denied a fair trial.

PUSTO SELO (PASTASEL)

One hundred and six ethnic Albanian men were summarily executed on March 31, 1999, in Pusto Selo, a small village near the town of Orahovac. Human Rights Watch visited the village on June 26, 1999, interviewing three of the massacre's thirteen survivors, as well as another man who helped bury the bodies. The men spoke of a well-coordinated military attack on the village followed by the expulsion of the village women and the killing of its men. Previous clashes between the KLA and government forces, possibly in the nearby village of Drenoc, may have precipitated the slaughter.[5]

One hundred and six ethnic Albanian men were summarily executed.

B.K., age fifty-seven, is one of the survivors who described the events in detail. He explained how large numbers of Serbian security forces, including paramilitaries wearing red bandanas, attacked Pusto Selo on March 31 using tanks, artillery, and mortars. "Two tanks were up on the hill; four tanks came into the village, and one tank went down to where the people were," said B.K.[6] The villagers of Pusto Selo, joined by residents of other villages from the area—well over 2,000 people in all—took refuge in a nearby field just downhill from Pusto Selo. Around 3:00 p.m. they surrendered by waving white bandages at paramilitaries who had surrounded them.

The Serbian forces separated the men from the women and children, searched the women, and confiscated their money and jewelry. The men were mostly older than fifty-five, as almost all of the younger men had fled into the hills. Around 4:30 p.m., the women were sent away from the village under orders to "Go to Albania!"

After the women left, the Serbian forces ordered the men to empty their pockets, stealing the several thousand German marks that they found. "We begged them to spare our lives," said T.K., age fifty-four, another survivor. "We gave them all of our money so that they wouldn't kill us."[7] The Serbs also confiscated the villagers' identity documents. B.K. said that when they took his papers they told him: "You won't need any ID where you're going."

The Serbian forces separated a group of seven or eight younger men for interrogation and severe beatings, demanding to know whether the men belonged to the KLA. The group was then lined up nearby and shot with automatic rifles by seven or eight members of the Serbian security forces, believed by witnesses to be paramilitaries. "The Serbs were in green camouflage police uniforms. They had shiny metal insignias on their caps, the Arkan or Seselj sign; we're not sure," said T.K. Another group of about twenty-five men was then taken to the edge of a nearby gully and killed in the same manner.

"They came back to us and asked if we had seen what happened, telling us, 'you're going to go there too,'" B.K. said. In all, four groups, each consisting of between twenty-five and thirty men, were taken to the edge of the gully and executed using automatic weapons.

Shreds of clothes and some shoes were scattered around in the gully amidst shrubs where the men had been killed.

A Human Rights Watch researcher spoke separately to survivors from the second, third, and fourth groups, who on June 26, 1999, brought the researcher to the field where the villagers had gathered and the nearby gully where the men had been killed. The three men each gave consistent accounts of the day's events. There was no visible blood at the scene but shreds of clothes and some shoes were scattered around in the gully amidst shrubs where the men had been killed. "I fell before they started to shoot," explained B.K., who was in the fourth group of men. He continued: "Two dead men fell on top of me. I didn't move. After a couple of minutes, someone said shoot again and I was hit. I stayed hidden under the bodies for another twenty minutes until I was sure that they were gone; then I escaped down the hill."[8] A Human Rights Watch researcher saw the bullet scar on B.K.'s left buttock, as well as the bloody undergarments he was wearing at the time.

Serbian forces returned to Pusto Selo to remove the physical evidence of the crime.

Another man with the initials B.K., age sixty—a cousin of the other B.K—also escaped death. "They [the Serbian forces] were from somewhere else and they didn't know the terrain," he explained. "I was too quick for them; I slipped behind some rocks."[9] In all, thirteen men survived the massacre, including one of the younger B.K's brothers, although a third brother, M.K., age fifty-five, was killed.

The following day, the Serbian forces removed between twenty and twenty-five bodies from the ravine and burned them in a house in the village, the three survivors said. Village men who later buried the remains of these men stated that they were burnt beyond recognition, with little more than bones remaining.

Serbian forces abandoned the village that same day, leaving the remaining bodies, approximately seventy-five or eighty of them, in the gully. Returning villagers spent two days transporting the bodies up the hill to a site by the village mosque where they were buried. Serbian paramilitaries returned to the village once before the burial was complete, forcing the villagers to flee into the mountains. The burial resumed that same day after the Serbs had left; it was finished on April 3. "We were very afraid; we rushed to bury them," said R.K., a villager who assisted in digging the graves.[10]

Four days after the burial, another Serb attack on the village forced villagers to flee again, with Serb forces temporarily occupying the village.[11] "Every day we watched the village to see if the Serbs would leave," said T.K., who explained that they used binoculars to monitor the Serbs' actions.

On April 11, 1999, NATO released imagery taken by an aerial reconnaissance flight on April 9 that appeared to reveal a large burial site in Pusto Selo. The photograph showed two long parallel lines, each made up of several dozen mounds of dirt; it was paired with what NATO spokesmen said was an earlier photograph, one in which the freshly turned earth does not appear.[12] The evidence of mass graves was widely noted in the Western media.[13]

Roughly two weeks after the photographs were released, Serbian forces returned to Pusto Selo to remove the physical evidence of the crime. T.K. told Human Rights Watch that on approximately April 24 he saw unidentified individuals exhume the bodies, using a small tractor to dig up the burial site. "There were men wearing medical outfits and masks," he said. "They took the bodies away toward Orahovac in two civilian trucks."[14] Panorama, a BBC news program whose reporters visited Pusto Selo after NATO's entry into Kosovo, obtained video footage that was said to have been taken by Kosovar Albanian villagers monitoring the exhumation from a hill above the burial site. The footage shows a large truck, with police and workers in protective clothing at work near the mosque. The BBC claimed that its

NATO released satellite images of an alleged mass grave in Pusto Selo on April 11, 1999. Two weeks later, Serbian forces removed the bodies, witnesses said.

SOURCE: U.S. STATE DEPARTMENT

investigations established that some of the exhumed bodies were brought to the village of Zrze, southwest of Orahovac, where they were reburied in the village cemetery.[15]

Also on April 24, according to Agence France Presse, the Dutch daily newspaper *Algemen Dagblad* ran a story casting doubt on the veracity of NATO claims of a grave site in Pusto Selo.[16] A Dutch map expert quoted in the newspaper claimed that the aerial photographs of Pusto Selo displayed suspicious inconsistencies. Indeed, stories disputing accounts of the killings in Pusto Selo continued to circulate well after survivors' first-hand descriptions of the massacre became known.[17] Human Rights Watch's own interviews and inspection of the scene confirmed that the massacre had, in fact, occurred such as initially reported, and that the government had acted first to bury and then to remove the bodies.

When Human Rights Watch visited Pusto Selo in June 1999, villagers pointed out the burial site next to the village mosque. Part of the fence surrounding the site was broken down; within it was a long stretch of rough and uneven ground. Villagers, who spoke of close relatives whose bodies were missing, looked at the spot with anguish. "Not to know where the bodies are hidden is, for us, as if they've been killed again," T.K. stated, voicing a sentiment shared by others.[18]

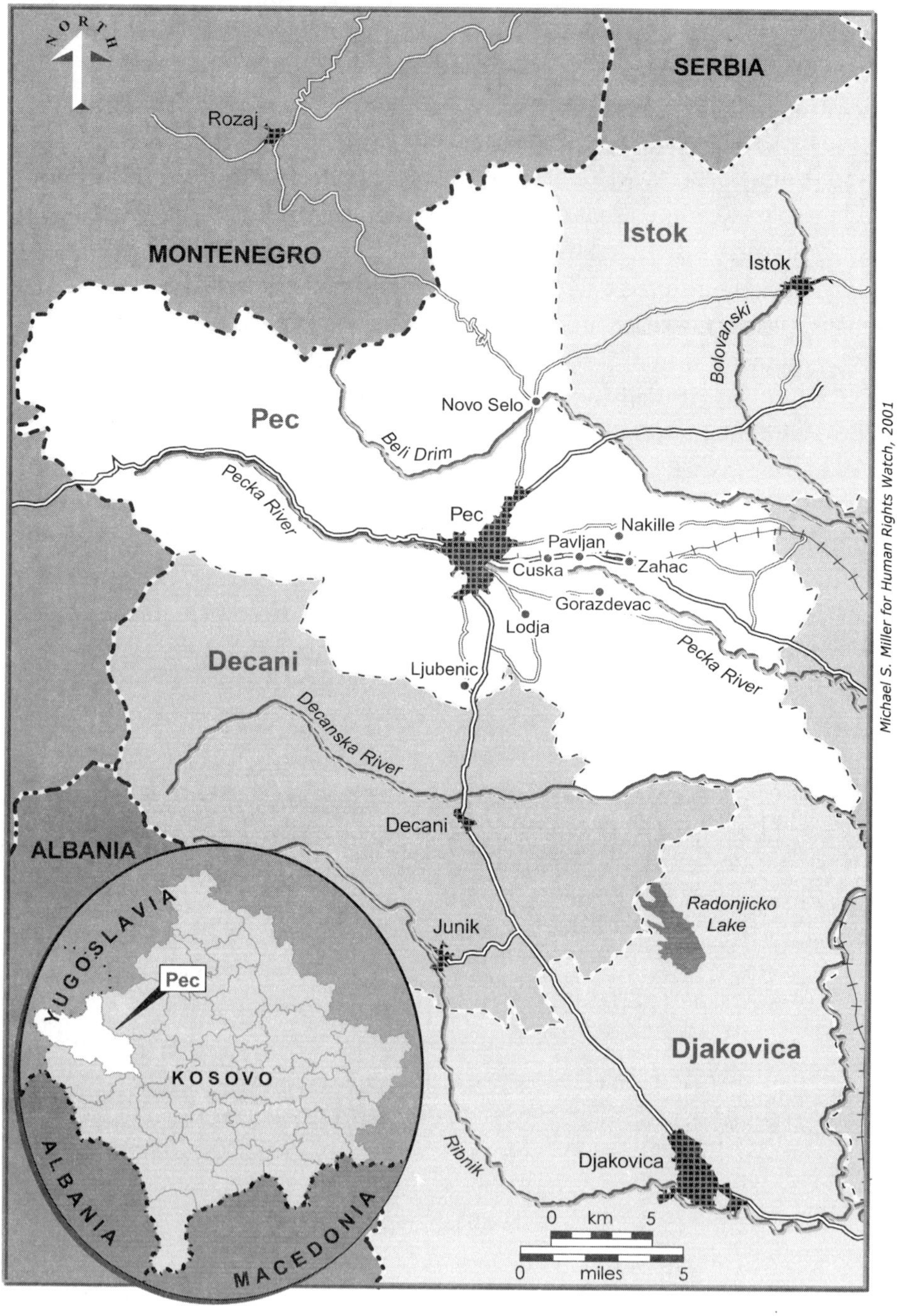
NORTH
SERBIA
Rozaj
MONTENEGRO
Istok
Istok
Bolovanski
Novo Selo
Pec
Beli Drim
Pecka River
Pec
Nakille
Pavljan
Cuska
Zahac
Gorazdevac
Lodja
Decani
Ljubenic
Pecka River
Decanska River
Decani
ALBANIA
YUGOSLAVIA
Pec
KOSOVO
ALBANIA
MACEDONIA
Radonjicko Lake
Junik
Djakovica
Ribnik
Djakovica
0 km 5
0 miles 5
Michael S. Miller for Human Rights Watch, 2001

10

PEC (PEJA) MUNICIPALITY

More than other areas in Kosovo, Pec municipality holds special significance for Serbs. The area is home to several important Serbian Orthodox sites, including the sixteenth century Pec Patriarchy just outside of Pec city. Prior to 1999, Serbs made up approximately 15 percent of the municipality's 150,000 people.

With its mixed population, Pec city was very tense from the beginning of the internal armed conflict in March 1998. The KLA was in the hills to the west and the highlands to the southeast, and numerous ambushes occured against the police, especially along the road south of Pec towards Decani and Djakovica. In the summer of 1998, there was intense fighting between the KLA and Serbian forces in the village of Lodja (Loxha), just a few kilometers from the city center. For the first time in the war, government forces used airplanes to attack the KLA.[1]

The city became palpably more tense after December 14, 1998, when unknown perpetrators opened fire and killed six Serbian youths in the Panda Cafe.[2] The police responded by searching the Zatra and Kapeshnica neighborhoods around the cafe, and abusing many of the ethnic Albanian residents. The winter, up until the NATO bombing, saw many beatings of ethnic Albanians and a series of enigmatic murders. The government said the KLA was killing Albanians because they were loyal to the government.

During the NATO bombing, Pec city did not suffer such intense violence as in other cities. While there were large-scale killings in the surrounding villages, such as Ljubenic (Lubeniq), Cuska (Qyshk), Pavljan (Pavlan), and Zahac (Zahaq)—more than 500 killings, according to a local human rights group[3]—and some serious incidents in the city itself,

Pec was generally spared the large-scale killings that took place, for example, in Djakovica.

The effectiveness of the police's "ethnic cleansing" campaign in the city is one explanation. Within the first week of the war, an estimated 90 percent of Pec's ethnic Albanian population had been forcibly expelled. The "ethnic cleansing" operation was among the best organized in Kosovo, with buses waiting in the city's center to take people south towards Albania.

Ethnic Albanians in the area are able to provide valuable information about the specific individuals that committed crimes.

Another difference with other municipalities is that, due to Pec's mixed population, ethnic Albanians in the area are able to provide valuable information about the specific individuals that committed crimes, as well as insights into the various police and military structures that were in operation during the war. In some cases, Albanians recognized Serbian neighbors participating in looting as civilians or with military units that committed executions. Based on their testimonies, Human Rights Watch has positively identified some of the individuals involved in the looting, beatings, and killings that took place in parts of the city, as well as in the surrounding villages. A section in this chapter on Cuska village is particularly long and detailed because some of the perpetrators have been identified by name and photograph.

From sources in Pec who wished to remain anonymous, Human Rights Watch also obtained a copy of an official Yugoslav Army document, marked "Military Secret, Highly Confidential" and signed by Lt. Col. Dusko D. Antic. Although the authenticity of the document cannot be verified with certainty, the headings, numbering, and stamps are all consistent with official documents of the army. The document, dated March 30, 1999, places all republic and municipal organs of Pec under the control of the army, and refers to a "moving of the part of the population from the Pec Military Department." Legally speaking, all actions in Pec were under the authority of the Yugoslav Army.

Lt. Col. Antic was also the author of a journal found in the Pec area and viewed by Yugoslav human rights activists and foreign journalists, who believed that it was authentic. According to Natasa Kandic from the Humanitarian Law Center, one of Yugoslavia's most reliable human rights groups, the book, which she saw, was signed by Antic and registered the military activities in the Pec area after March 24, 1999.[4] As described in Forces of the Conflict, the commander of the Pec Secretariat for Internal Affairs, which covers the municipalities of Pec, Klina, and Istok, was Col. Boro Vlahovic.[5]

There is overwhelming evidence that the police, special police, and paramilitaries were acting in close cooperation with the army in the Pec area. In interviews given to foreign journalists, various police and army officials, as well as paramilitary members spoke about their coordinated activities. One unnamed Yugoslav Army official told a reporter, "The Yugoslav Army consciously and deliberately protected [the paramilitaries]."[6]

More directly, witnesses in Pec and the surrounding area repeatedly spoke about the violent actions of paramilitaries allowed to operate by the army. Like in Cuska, the army secured the perimeter of villages under attack or controlled the major roads while small militia groups attacked the villages themselves, committing serious abuses in the course of their actions. In Pec, the army or police never interfered with the paramilitaries' violent actions.

Various paramilitary groups were operating in the Pec area, some of them with links to the Serbian Ministry of Internal Affairs. One such group was called Munja ("Lightning"), and was run by a policeman named Vidomir Salipur. Salipur, as he was known in Pec, was killed by the KLA on April 8 (see death certificate). His public death announcement states that he was a member of the PJP (Posebna Jedinica Policije, or Police Special Unit) and a group called OKB (believed to be Operativni Grupa, or Operative Group). Other groups that were repeatedly mentioned by Pec residents include the Black Hand, Arkan's Tigers, and Serbian Deputy Prime Minister Vojislav Seselj's White Eagles, although we possess only anecdotal evidence of these groups' direct participation in abuses.

Serbian civilians also took part in some of the abuses, especially the looting and burning of Albanian property. Numerous witnesses in Pec city reported seeing their neighbors carting away private possessions, or even participating in some of the militia groups. The diary of a Serbian woman from Pec, who wrote about the activities of local Serbs, is cited above in the chapter Forces of the Conflict.

The following document, dated March 30, 1999, places all governmental authorities in the municipalities of Pec, Istok, Klina and Decani under the command of the Yugoslav Army. The introduction also refers to an order from the "Supreme Commander" for "moving a part of the population."

Састанак ... 99 у 9 часова

1КОМАНДА ВОЈНОГ ОДСЕКА ПЕЋ
Стр.пов.бр. 612-1
Дана,30.03.1999.године

ВОЈНА ТАЈНА
СТРОГО ПОВЕРЉИВО

Функцијонисање живота
и рада у Зони одговорности
ВОд-а Пећ,НАРЕЂЕЊЕ.-

Бранислав Вуковић

На основу Наредбе Врховног Команданта о проглашењу ратног стања, те пресељења дела становништва из зоне одговорности ВОд-а Пећ, а у циљу правилног функцијонисања укупног живота у зони одговорности ВОд-а Пећ,

НАРЕЂУЈЕМ:

1.- Сви Републички и општински органи власти стављају се под команду ВОд-а Пећ, и то на територијама општина: Пећ, Исток, Клина и Дечане.
На територији општине Ђаковица одговорна команда гарнизона Ђаковица.

2.- За општину Пећ формирати штаб састава (овај штаб је претпостављени и штабовима општина Исток, Клина и Дечане)
- Командант штаба: командант ВОд-а Пећ
- заменици команданта: Јово Поповић, начелник Пећког округа и Симеон Радовић председник извршног одбора општине Пећ.
- Чланови штаба по виталним областима функцијонисања живота и рада:
а)- За снадбевање становништва животним намирницама: Бијелић Томо, директор ДД "17 Новембар", а његов заменик Томовић Небојша, начелник одељења тржишне инспекције.

б)- За здравство становништва
- примаријус ДР Вујошевић Драгутин директор здравства Пећ а његов заменик примаријус Др. Војислав Поповић.

в)- За комуналне послове и асанацију територије у случају дејства штг
Влаховић Слободан, директор јавног комуналног предузећа, а његов заменик Здравковић Миливоје директор дирекције за грађу.

г)- За привредне делатности:
професор доктор Слободан Јокић. директор"Застава"а његов заменик Меденица Данило, директор "Пећке Пиваре"

д)- За снадбевање и расподелу нафтних деривата, Кнежевић, директор "Југопетрола", а његов заменик Лазовић Бранко, управник бензинске пумпе "Југопетрола" Рајковић

е)- За информисање јавности,
Зечевић Драгана, главни и одговорни уредник радио " Метохије", а њен заменик Дашић Весна, дописник РТС.

ж)- За правосуђе:
Гојковић Радомир, председник Окружног суда Пећ,
а његов заменик, Миладин Поповић окружни тужилац.

з)- За прикупљање материјалних добара расутих деловањем
штг
Бранислав Вуковић, координатор финансијске полиције, а
његов заменик Небојша Девић шеф одељења тржишне инспекције
Пећког округа.

и)- За јавни превоз и транспорт:
Радош Радуловић, директор ДД "Аутопревоз", а његов заменик
Новица Антић, Републички инспектор друмског саобраћаја.

ј)- За збрињавање расељених лица дејством штг:
Томислав Лакићевић, секретар општинске организације СПС
Пећ, а његов заменик, Олга Обрадовић, директор центра за
социјални рад.

љ)- За јавни ред, мир, сузбијање криминала, гашење пожара
и друге задатке из надлежности МУП-а:
начелник МУП-а Пећ а заменик начелник полиције МУП-а Пећ.

3.- У општинама Исток , Клина и Дечане формирати исте овакве
штабове под командом команданата ВТОд-а а у општини Дечане
под командом председника општинског већа Ђурковић Миливоја.
Исти су у обавези да донесу Наређење о формирању штабова
у својим зонама одговорности које ми у писаној форми доставити
дана 31.03.1999.године до 16,00 часова.

4.- Начелник МУП-а Пећ, својом наредбом регулисаће јавни
ред, мир, спречавање крађа разбијање објеката, злостављање
грађана, гашење евентуалних пожара и сузбијању свих криминалних
радњи коју ми у писаној форми доставити дана 31.03.1999.године
до 16,00 часова.

5.- Начелник одељења НО својом наредбом регулисаће питање
заштите цивила од ваздушних удара (узбуњивање, обавештавање,
склањање људства у склоништа) и друга питања за заштиту
цивила а исту ми доставити на увид дана 31.03.1999.године
до 16,00 часова .

6.- Чланови штаба општине Пећ реферишу ми свакодневно у
09,00 часова о проблемима, предлозима за решавање истих
и појавама чије деловање може имати негативног утицаја
на одбрамбену способност становништва.

7.- Команданти штабова општина Исток, Клина и Дечани свакодневно
у 11,00 часова извештавају ме по питањима из тачке 6, овог
наређења.

8.- У командовању са свим штабовима у општинама Пећ, Клина,
Исток и Дечане из ВОд-а Пећ ангажовати:
мајора Гојковић Ранка, рез. мајора Дашић Илија, кIк Булатовић
Дејана, кIк Ивичић Милана и кIк Радослава Арсенијевића.

9.- Ова Наредба ступа на снагу дана 31.03.1999.године у 8,00 часова и ће се строго придржавати до укидања исте. У случају не извршења или пропуста у извршавању задатака из ове Наредбе важе ратни закони СРЈ.

ДА/АЕ

К О М А Н Д А Н Т
потпуковник
Душко Д. Антић

ВОЈНИ ОДСЕК
П е П

Headquarters of the Pec Military Department — MILITARY SECRET
Str. Pov. No. 612-1 — HIGHLY CONFIDENTIAL
March 30, 1999.

Daily functioning of life in the Pec Military Department Branislav Vukovic area of responsibility, ORDER. [*handwritten*]

As per the Order of the Supreme Commander, concerning the declaration of martial law and moving a part of the population from Pec Military Department area of responsibility for the purpose of correct functioning of total life in the Pec Military Department area of responsibility,

I ISSUE THIS ORDER:

1. —All republic and municipal organs of authority are to be placed under the command of the Pec MD [*military department*] in the following municipalities: Pec, Istok, Klina and Decani. The Djakovica garrison Headquarters is responsible for the territory of the Djakovica municipality.
2. —Headquarters are to be formed for the Pec municipality, and are to comprise the following (these headquarters are to be considered superior to the headquarters of the Istok, Klina and Decani municipalities):
   —The headquarters commanding officer: commander of the Pec MD.
   —The deputy commanding officer: Jovo Popovic, chief of Pec district, and Simeon Radovic, chief of Pec municipality executive council.
   —Staff members in the area of vital concern to the daily functioning:
   a) —Responsible for supplying food to the general population: Bijelic Tomo, CEO of DD "17. November", and as his deputy Tomovic Nebojsa, chief of the section for market inspection.
   b) —For population health
   Hospital chief of staff Vujosevic Dragutin, MD, the director of Pec health department, and as his deputy hospital chief of staff Vojislav Popovic, MD.
   c) —Responsible for public utilities and cleaning in the case of stg

action Vlahovic Slobodan, CEO of the public communal enterprise, and as his deputy Zdravkovic Milivoje, chief of building department.

d) —For economic/business/market matters:
Prof. Dr. Slobodan Jokic, CEO of "Zastava" and as his deputy Medenica Danilo, CEO of "Pecka Pivara"

e) —For the supply and distribution of oil derivatives, Knezevic, CEO of "Jugopetrol", and as his deputy Lazovic Branko, "Jugopetrol" gas station manager.

f) —For distribution of public information,
Zecevic Dragana, editor in chief of radio station "Metohija", and as her deputy Davic Vesna, RTS correspondent.

g) —For justice administration:
Gojkovic Radomir, chief of Pec Municipal Court, and as his deputy, Miladin Popovic, District Attorney.

h) —For gathering of material goods dispersed as a result of stg actions Branislav Vukovic, coordinator of the financial police, and as his deputy Nebojsa Davic, chief of the department of market inspection of the Pec municipality.

i) —For public transportation:
Rados Radulovic, CEO of DD "Autoprevoz", and as his deputy Novica Antic, traffic inspector.

j) —For the care of persons misplaced by the action of stg:
Tomislav Lakicevic, secretary of the municipal SPS organization, and as his deputy Olga Obradovic, director of the social services center.

k) —For public order, peace and suspension of criminal activities, handling of fire emergencies and other MUP [*Ministry of Internal Affairs*] responsibilities:
The chief of Pec MUP and deputy chief of Pec police department.

3. —In Istok, Klina and Decani municipalities the same headquarters are to be set up under the command of commanders of VTOand in the municipality of Decani under the command of the president of the municipal council Djurkovic Milivoje. The aforementioned are

responsible for issuing a written order concerning the set up of the headquarters in their respective areas of responsibility, which are to be submitted to me on March 31, 1999, no later than 16:00 hours.

4. —The chief of Pec MUP will with this order regulate public security, order, prevention of theft, breaking of building structures, mistreatment of citizens, prevention of possible arson, and eradication of all criminal activities, and will present [the order] it to me in the written form on March 31, 1999, no later than 16:00 hours.
5. —Head of the NO section will with this order regulate the question of the protection of civilians from the air attacks (air raids, informing, placing people in shelters) and other questions for protection of civilians, and will present it [the written order] to me for inspection on March 31st 1999, no later than 16:00 hours.
6. —Headquarters members of the Pec municipality are to report to me daily at 09:00 about problems and suggestions for their solution, as well as occurrences that may have a negative influence on the population's defending capability.
7. —Headquarters commanders of Istok, Klina and Decani municipalities will report to me daily at 11:00 o'clock regarding the question from the item 8 of this Order.
8. —In commanding the headquarters in Pec, Klina, Istok and Decani municipalities, the following persons are to be engaged:
Mayor Gojkovic Ranko, Reserve Mayor Dasic Ilija, Capt. First Class Bulatovic Dejan, Capt. First Class Ivicic Milan, and Capt. First Class Radoslav Arsenijevic.
9. —This order goes into effect on March 31, 1999, at 08:00 o'clock and it is to be strictly observed until it is repealed. In the case of non-observance or neglect in the execution of the assignments from this order, martial laws of FRY are to be applied.

COMMANDER
Lieutenant Colonel
Dusko D. Antic
[*signed*]
[*stamp*] Pec Military Department

PEC (PEJA) CITY

The "Cleansing"

The violence against the city's ethnic Albanian population began immediately with the first NATO bombs on March 24. The next day, the Zatra neighborhood was "cleansed," followed by the Kapeshnice neighborhood, and then Dardania. According to the OSCE's report on Kosovo, the police targeted in particular former OSCE-KVM staff and Serb civilians looted the OSCE office in Pec.[7]

Whole neighborhoods were cleared, with residents ordered to gather at collection points in the center. The police organized buses to take people south to Prizren and then on to Albania. Others were forced to walk on foot north to Montenegro. By March 29, the vast majority of the ethnic Albanian population had been forced to leave the city.

Some killing also took place, apparently to incite fear and expedite the depopulation of the city. The most vicious incidents took place in the Dardania neighborhood where, according to the local Council for the Defense of Human Rights and Freedoms, forty-one people were killed on March 27.[8] Human Rights Watch did not verify every one of these alleged killings, but the general research in Pec and the Dardania neighborhood confirmed the approximate number of forty-one.

One man told Human Rights Watch how his wealthy neighbor, Namik Bilalli, was killed. He said:

> My neighbor, Namik Bilalli, was shot on the night of March 26–27. He was a wealthy man in Pec and he lived next door to me. Serbs wanted to rob everything he had. They knocked on his door, rang the bell, and asked for money. Namik said he had no money, so they shot him with a gun fitted with a silencer.[9]

Another man who declined to give his name told Human Rights Watch:

> On Saturday, March 27, Serb neighbors came and said "you must leave." All of them were armed. They went into Albanian homes demanding money and telling us to leave. They said that a human life was worth 1,000 Deutsch marks. If we could pay that, we would live. My cousins and their children were killed. One of them was Mustafa Lajci, aged fifty-five, and his two sons,

> Halil, aged twenty, and Florim, aged seventeen. The other was Adem Lajci, aged sixty-five, and his two sons, Gani, aged twenty-five, and Myftar, aged eighteen. Mustafa and Adem were brothers, and they lived next door to each other.[10]

Other ethnic Albanians interviewed in refugee camps in Albania explained how they were forced out of Pec. One man told Human Rights Watch:

> The Serbs came into our basement on Sunday, March 28. They pointed guns at us and said: "Where is everyone?" We had been hiding in the basement for five days. We hadn't moved. We had heard shooting, and we had been afraid they would come down into the basement and kill us. . . .
>
> They gathered us in the center of town, searched us, and took our passports and money if they found them, as well as jewelry, necklaces. They threatened us and cursed us. We waited for two hours, and then they put us on buses. When the buses were full, they made people walk. When night fell, we were still in Pec. Some of the people were put in schools. While people were leaving, the Serbs would shoot to create panic. Some people tried to escape from the crowd, hiding in the schools. It was terrible; there was fear and panic everywhere, it was incredible. There was no sleeping, no rest. Vehicles were stolen from people.[11]

Another man, Bujar Tabaku, said:

> They put people on buses. These were private bus companies from Kosovo that had been taken over by the army. There were police drivers on the buses. They were wearing green uniforms and black masks. There were some civilians with guns. I think that these civilians were men from Pec, and it was them who helped organize the buses.[12]

After "cleansing" the city, the government turned its attention to the villages around Pec. The first villages to be "cleansed" were in the Barane valley that lies to the southeast of Pec. A series of villages, such as Rasic (Rasiq), Brolic (Broliq) and Vranovac (Vranoc) were forcibly depopulated in the first week of April. Villages along the Pec-Pristina road to the east of Pec were also "cleansed" at this time. Three villages along the road—Cuska, Zahac, and Pavljan—were an important exception. They were not touched until May 14, when a series of mass killings took place there (see below). It remains unclear why these three villages were left unaffected in the beginning of April, and then were hit so hard in mid-May.

Looting and Burning

Looting and burning took place throughout the city, often at the hands of local Serbian civilians. The Serbian government, on the state-controlled radio and television, claimed that the city had been damaged by NATO bombs. A member of the Serbian Orthodox Church, Father Jovan, who was working in the Pec Patriarchy after the war, reiterated this claim and told Human Rights Watch that Pec had been bombed by NATO.[13] Another member of the church, however, Father Sava, gave an interview to the Serbian-language magazine "Nin" that painted a different picture. In the interview, he said:

> We believe the truth will be fully unveiled. How many people died exactly, how many mass graves exist, where they are located. . . . We'll learn about it in these days. That is not a matter of propaganda now, but of material proof which is being found on a daily basis—reports, photos, films are being shot on these sites, and many corpses—unfortunately, mainly of women and children. The Serbian people have to know this tragic truth.
>
> The worst is precisely in areas like Pec, which is a completely ruined town, not because of the NATO bombardments, but because of a systematic burning and destruction of property. All people who lived there, or came and saw what happened, knew what it was about. That is the sad truth about Kosovo and Metohija, the one that not many are ready to talk about, but the one which the Serbian people has to face and do what is necessary.[14]

Much of Pec's central shopping district was systematically looted and burned.

Much of Pec's central shopping district was systematically looted and burned in the beginning of April. Many of the municipality's mosques were also destroyed. According to the municipal Islamic office, of thirty-one mosques in the municipality, thirteen were completely destroyed, although three of these were destroyed in 1998 (in Lodja, Rausic (Rausiq), and Vranovac). All of the other mosques were defaced in some way, with graffiti or partial destruction.[15] On July 19,

1999, Human Rights Watch visited the ruins of the 300-year-old Islamic archive, which had been destroyed by fire.

A Final Killing

One of the worst incidents in Pec took place on June 12 as Serbian and Yugoslav troops, as well as most of Pec's Serbian population, were preparing to leave Kosovo. In one house, armed forces believed to be members of the Munja militia group killed six members of one family, including children aged five, six, seven, twelve, and thirteen. Four people survived, one of them an eight-year-old boy who pretended he was dead. One man from the family was taken and later found dead.

The incident involved two households, whose family names are withheld to protect them from possible reprisal. The head of one of the households, called here Agim, told Human Rights Watch that, on June 12, around 8:30 p.m., he heard three knocks on the front gate of his garden.[16] Before he could open the door, three armed men in uniform jumped over the wall. The door was opened and between fifteen and twenty armed men came into the garden. Agim's three daughters were interrogated for fifteen minutes in a separate room, and then Agim was taken outside, where he saw five or six vehicles waiting. He was driven to the house of his close friend, Ibrahim.

According to Agim, army troops were staying in a house across from Ibrahim's home. Ibrahim was taken from his house and put in a jeep with Agim, who had been hit on the head and body while waiting outside. The two men were then taken back to Agim's house.

In a separate interview, Ibrahim told Human Rights Watch the same story from his perspective.[17] On June 12 around 9 p.m., he said, some armed uniformed men jumped over his gate. He was at home with his wife, brother, sister-in-law, three of his brother's children, and four children of his own, as well as his elderly mother, who was an invalid.

The armed men demanded money, and Ibrahim gave them 3,000 DM, as well as some jewelry. Ibrahim and his brother, Musa, were then ordered to go outside. There they saw Agim, who had been beaten, waiting in a jeep. They were all driven back to Agim's house.

Five or six armed men came into Agim's house with the three men, Ibrahim said. They were wearing green army uniforms, black bandanas around their necks, and were armed with automatic guns, grenades and bottles of gasoline. Among them was Nebojsa Minic, a known criminal and paramilitary leader in Pec, who was known by his nickname Mrtvi ("Death"). Both Agim and Ibrahim recognized him at the time, and from the photographs shown in this report. They described him as dark skinned with tattoos all over his upper body, including a dead man on his chest.

Minic asked Ibrahim how much money he had brought. Ibrahim said 3,000DM and Minic replied that he would count the money and kill him if it was not all there. Ibrahim then said he could go home and get some more, so he went back to his house and handed over another 4,900DM that he had hidden.

After Ibrahim gave the additional money, the armed men ordered the family to sit on one couch. They told the sister-in-law to come with them into the next room, Ibrahim recalled. They took her into the bathroom where she was raped by a man with a small beard. Ibrahim's invalid mother

Witnesses identified the man on the right as Nebojsa Minic, known as "Mrtvi" ("Death"). He is implicated in the extortion and killing of six family members in Pec on June 12. On the left is Vidomir Salipur, a Pec policeman and alleged head of the Munja gang, who was killed by the KLA on April 8, 1999. The date and location of the photograph are unknown. © HUMAN RIGHTS WATCH was in the next room and heard them screaming at her daughter-in-law: "Brzo! Brzo!" ("Faster! Faster!"). "They dehumanized her," Ibrahim's mother later told Ibrahim.

The armed men brought the sister-in-law back, sat her on the couch with the rest of the family, and then opened fire. Ibrahim explained:

> He started shooting. I jumped with my young son out and then off the balcony. My wife who was bleeding went to the balcony and said "please help me." I ran with my son and went to the neighbor's, and left him there. I came to Slavka [a Serbian neighbor] but she didn't come out. I waited to see what would happen and I saw them leaving. But they dropped two grenades. I hid in the grass and when they went out they shot all over the house.
>
> I went in and asked my mother what had happened. She said I don't know but something is moving. I saw the son of my brother, four years old, who survived. My wife was badly wounded. She crawled to the neighbor's house bleeding. The daughter of my brother was wounded too, but I didn't realize that until the next morning. We took her to the hospital but the doctor said she had lost a lot of blood. They operated on her but she died.

The dead are Vjollca, 28 (raped and killed); Rena, 7; Nita, 5; Hajri, 13; Dardane, 12; Agon, 6; and Musa, 31 (taken away and found dead five days later)

While this was taking place, Agim was sitting with the other armed men, including Minic. There were ten members of his family present, he told Human Rights Watch, as well as Ibrahim's brother, Musa, who had been taken from Ibrahim's house. Musa was then taken away. His body was found five days later in the Kalaja neighborhood with a slit throat.

Minic, appearing reflective, said to Agim, "Old man, these are hard times. And this is the cleansing of the inner city." He drank coffee offered by the family and then, according to Agim, told him about his orders. Agim recalled:

> When they took Musa away, Minic said, "You see, old man, your family and Musa's family must be executed." He said, "Every half hour the orders are changing." He said, "I feel sorry I must tell you, but Ibrahim's family has been executed, liquidated." He said, "You were first on the list but unfortunately we had to kill Ibrahim's family first." I said, "please save the lives of my children." He said he would spare them until morning.

> Minic had a radio. That night he wore only a green T-shirt. We saw his arms had tattoos. On one forearm was a knife, an axe and a grenade. There was a dead man on his chest. We heard people speaking to him on the radio. We heard only "the city is safe. No entrance or exit to the city. You are secure. Do what you want." We heard this when they were in our house.

The armed men left Agim's house, except for Minic and another man. Minic and the other man then stated that they had to take Agim's two daughters "to the Major." According to Ibrahim, Minic swore by the cross around his neck that nothing would happen to the girls. They were gone for approximately one hour and returned unharmed, according to Ibrahim and the two girls who were interviewed by Human Rights Watch in their father's presence. The men tried to convince them to have sex with them, they said, but they refused and were brought back home.

The next morning, Ibrahim showed up outside Agim's house with a friendly Serbian policeman, whom the Albanians affectionately called "Kaplan."[18] According to Agim, Kaplan told him about the plans to execute his family, and advised him to flee, which they did.

That day, Ibrahim buried the five killed members of his family who were killed with the help of four policemen whose names are withheld to protect them from possible reprisals.

The motivation for the killing is unclear, although robbery is one explanation. But both Ibrahim and Agim claim that the armed forces knew them by name and they therefore believed that they had been targeted for some reason. One explanation, posited by Ibrahim, was that his brother Musa had recently been caught trying to escape to Montenegro. According to Ibrahim, in late May, Musa paid a Serbian policeman named Zharko Backovic 3,000 DM to smuggle him and his family out of Kosovo. They were caught on their way, and Musa spent one week in prison. Backovic allegedly got in trouble for helping an Albanian family. Ibrahim and Agim believed that the killing might have been his attempt to redeem himself in front of his colleagues, but this is their speculation. The knowledge that the family had wealth is another possibility.

Rape

The rape in the incident mentioned above was the only case of sexual assault in Pec directly confirmed by Human Rights Watch, although circumstantial evidence suggests that many more women were raped in and around the city. A gynecologist in Pec told Human Rights Watch that, after the war, he had given abortions to three Pec women whom he believed had been subjected to rape.[19] Womens' reluctance to speak about rape and sexual assault makes it very difficult to confirm these allegations. (See March–June 1999: An Overview.)

On April 20, NATO alleged that, according to Kosovar Albanian refugees, Serbian and Yugoslav forces had set up rape camps in Djakovica and Pec. In Pec, refugees claimed, "Serb forces have rounded up young Albanian women and taken them to the Hotel Karagac where the local commander apparently has organized a roster of his soldiers to allow them all an evening at the hotel."[20]

In its report on war crimes in Kosovo, the U.S. State Department also made allegations about rape camps in Djakovica and Pec.[21] The report's section on Pec cites as its sole source a June 22 *New York Times* article about rape in Pec. The cited article, however, mentions "Department of State officials" as the original source of the allegations.[22]

Neither Human Rights Watch nor any foreign journalists were able to confirm the presence of a rape camp in the Hotel Karagac.[23] According to the OSCE, the KLA inspected the Hotel Karagac once they entered Pec around June 12. A local deputy brigade commander of the KLA told the OSCE that they had found used condoms and women's clothes in the hotel.[24]

CUSKA (QYSHK)

In the early morning of May 14, 1999, Serbian security forces descended on the small village of Cuska a few miles east of Pec. Fearing reprisals, many men fled into the nearby hills while the rest of the population was forcibly assembled in the village center. An estimated twelve men were killed during the roundup in various parts of the village.

At approximately 8:30 a.m., security forces in green military uniforms with painted faces and masks separated the gathered women, children, and elderly from the remaining men who had not managed to flee. The more than 200 villagers were threatened and systematically robbed of their money, jewelry, and other valuables. Their identification papers were destroyed.

Thirty-two men between the ages of nineteen and sixty-nine were divided into three groups and taken into three separate houses, where they were forced to stand in a line. In each house, uniformed men sprayed them repeatedly with automatic weapons. In one of the houses, a gunman finished off several of the fallen men with pistol shots. Each house was set on fire and left to burn.

The Cuska case has two special characteristics that make it worth a detailed investigation. First, in each of the three groups of men, there was one survivor. Through pure chance, three people managed to crawl from the burning homes, none of them seriously injured. They, and many others present that day, have told Human Rights Watch their stories.

Second, while ethnic Albanian villagers in Kosovo are usually unable to differentiate between soldiers, special police, and paramilitaries, let alone identify individuals, in this case there is powerful evidence to point the finger at some of the specific people involved in these war crimes. Local villagers are adamant that ethnic Serbs from the immediate area were involved in the action. Some of the forces addressed the Albanians by name and asked for specific valuables.

Villagers positively identified in photographs two of the individuals that they claim were present in Cuska on May 14

Villagers positively identified in photographs two of the individuals that they claim were present in Cuska on May 14—Srecko Popovic and Zvonimir Cvetkovic—and a third man—Slavisa Kastratovic—who was present in the nearby village of Zahac on the same day, when nineteen other men were killed. While none of the individuals identified are known to have opened fire on the ethnic Albanian men, their presence in Cuska and Zahac on May 14 means that they should be able to identify the perpetrators, as well as the commanders of the unit. That information should be invaluable to the International Criminal Tribunal for the former Yugoslavia, as well as to Serbian courts, which may begin some prosecutions after the October 2000 fall of Slobodan Milosevic. The photographic evidence is discussed further below in the section on perpetrators.

The motivation for the killing in Cuska, as well as the attacks that same day on Pavljan and Zahac, remains unclear. There is no evidence to suggest an active KLA presence in the villages in 1998 or 1999, and no policemen or soldiers are known to have died in the immediate vicinity during the NATO bombing, which might have made revenge a possible motive. One explanation offered by local villagers is that Cuska was the home of Hasan Ceku, the father of Agim Ceku, the military head of the KLA.[25] Hasan and his brother, Kadri, were both among the murdered in Cuska on May 14. One villager in Cuska told Human Rights Watch that the police showed her a picture of Agim Ceku and said: "We are doing this because of him."[26] This is supported by testimony given to the Lawyers Committee for Human Rights, a U.S.-based human rights group. In video footage taken by the committee's Witness Project, members of the Ceku family testify that the security forces specifically asked for Agim Ceku's father before killing him.[27]

Motivation aside, the killings in Cuska, Pavljan, and Zahac were closely coordinated. This was not random violence by a rogue element in the Serbian security forces. As in other villages throughout Kosovo during the war, the Yugoslav Army maintained security on the periphery of the fighting, installing checkpoints on roads leading out, while special police forces and paramilitaries went into the villages to kill and "cleanse." Whether the principal perpetrators in Cuska were a local militia, a special police unit, or perhaps both, there is no question that they were working in concert with the local police and military authorities.

There is also evidence of direct Yugoslav Army involvement in the attack. A number of sources reported seeing documents from the army regarding a military buildup around Cuska shortly before May 14. One Western journalist claimed to have seen Yugoslav Army documents that ordered the village to be "cleansed".

To protect the identities of survivors and witnesses, altered initials are used.

Background

Cuska is a small village about five miles east of Pec near the main Pec-Pristina road that had approximately two hundred houses and 2,000 residents. Three ethnic Serbian families lived in the village, each named Jasovic, as well as one Montenegrin family named Bojovic. Relations between Serbs and Albanians were good, the ethnic Albanian villagers said. All of the non-ethnic Albanian families left Kosovo when the Serbian and Yugoslav forces withdrew from the province on June 12.

According to villagers, there was never any KLA activity in Cuska, Zahac, or Pavljan, although some of the military-age men in the area were admittedly members of the KLA who fought in the Pec municipality, including in the village of Lodja. The immediate Cuska area was not the scene of fighting between government forces and the KLA in 1998 or 1999. The only known incident occurred in Zahac on December 22, 1998, when the police killed one ethnic Albanian man, Sali Kabashi, and arrested five others in disputed circumstances. The Serbian government said the police came under fire during the arrest,[28] but ethnic Albanian sources claimed that Kabashi was summarily executed.[29]

During the NATO bombing of Yugoslavia in 1999, Cuska, Zahac, and Pavljan were initially left relatively untouched even though most of the surrounding villages and the city of Pec were systematically "cleansed" beginning on March 25. By March 29, as noted, more than 90 percent of Pec's population had been sent to Montenegro in the north by foot or to Albania in the southwest by bus. Other villages along the Pec-Pristina road were also vacated of ethnic Albanians in March and April, except for Cuska, Zahac, and Pavljan. Why they were not "cleansed" at this time is unknown. One unproven theory is that the villages were paying protection money to the local security forces.

Special police forces came to Cuska three times before the May 14 attack to demand weapons and money, and they burned a few houses, but nobody was injured or killed, and everyone was allowed to stay. The first visit was April 17 around 4:00 p.m., and the forces only entered the Kristal neighborhood of the village. Between four and seven houses were burned, villagers told Human Rights Watch.

Four days later, at around 12:00 p.m., security forces entered Cuska, Zahac, and Pavljan. Witnesses told Human Rights Watch that the men were in green camouflage uniforms, and some of them had green cowboy hats. Villagers also said that the forces told them not to worry. "All of you can go home. No one will touch you. You're safe," they allegedly said. The forces came again the following day and searched Cuska for weapons. A number of witnesses said that some villagers had handed over guns they had in their possession at this time. Syl Gashi reportedly handed over a hunting rifle and his brother gave a pistol, as did Brahim Lushi, even though he possessed a gun license. The police also reportedly took Syl Gashi's BMW car and 1,200 DM.

The police action on May 14 was clearly "more aggressive" than on previous visits, many villagers said. From the beginning, it was clear that the forces' objectives and orders went beyond a routine search for weapons.

The Killings

The May 14 offensive began without warning around 7:30 a.m. when a large force believed to be special police and paramilitaries entered Cuska from the direction of Pec. Villagers told Human Rights Watch that they heard automatic gunfire at about that time and saw some houses on the edge of the village being burned. Many of the young and middle-aged men fled in fear into the nearby hills, as they had during the previous police visits to Cuska, although some decided to stay with their families.

The police swept from west to east, forcing people towards the center of the village. Some villagers went willingly to the center since, as one woman said, they thought they were being expelled to Albania and "it would be safer to assemble in one place."[30] An estimated twelve men were killed at this time in various parts of the village, including Hasan Ceku.

The Witness Project of the Lawyers Committee for Human Rights interviewed two witnesses to Hasan Ceku's killing. Both of them testified about the incident on video, the transcript of which was made available to Human Rights Watch. One witness said:

> They [the security forces] then asked who was the father of Agim Ceku, that he was big now, that we brought NATO to them, now they will eliminate us. . . . They took Hasan, let him go two times, and released the cattle. When he came back the last time, they had even stabbed one of the cows. They shot Hasan right there, and set him on fire. I snuck close by and saw Hasan dead, with his legs on fire.[31]

Another witness testified to the Witness Project:

> We knew that they were killing the families of Albanian officers. I believed it was just a matter of time before they killed us all. They separated us, not knowing who Agim's father was, and asking about it. [Hasan] came forward.

> They told him to take his family and separated us. They took [Hasan] to find a picture of Agim, while they questioned me and my sister-in-law. They asked us when was the last time we saw him [Agim]. Where? But we had already decided that no matter what, we would never admit that we have any contact with him. I was telling him never. At that moment [Hasan] brought the picture, in which I was with Agim. He recognized me, but I denied it. He told me I was lucky because I was carrying a little child with me. They asked me to follow them and tell them whose house was the one across the street. Then I heard the shots. I ran but my uncle did not let me see [Hasan] dead.[32]

An estimated twelve men were killed at this time in various parts of the village, including Hasan Ceku.

Despite these initial killings, some men decided to stay with their families. One thirty-eight-year-old man, B.B., remained with approximately forty people from his family, including his mother and children. He explained for Human Rights Watch:

> When I saw them [the Serbian forces] near my house they looked very aggressive, so I decided to run. Down the road I saw some young men who told me they [the Serbian forces] had killed three men. I decided to come to the neighborhood of the Gashi family. When I got there I spoke with some old men who had decided to wait for the military to come. Right after that, the Lushi and Kelmendi families came—women, men, and children.[33]

B.B. and other villagers interviewed separately told Human Rights Watch that a group of approximately 200 ethnic Albanians from the village was soon surrounded by an estimated one hundred security forces. All of the witnesses said that the forces were wearing green military-style uniforms. All of them had their faces covered in some way, either with black grease paint or a mask, and some of them had black scarves and green cowboy-style hats.

All of the villagers believed that some of the security forces were from the Pec area, such as the ethnic Serbian village of Gorazdevac (Gorazhdec), which is across the Bistrica River from Cuska. Some of the forces seemed to know a few of the local Albanians personally, villagers told Human Rights Watch, since they asked for specific valuables, such as the "car keys to your Mercedes." One woman who was in close contact with the forces told Human Rights Watch:

> They wore green camouflage uniforms. Most of them had handkerchiefs around their heads, and two of them had hats, but some of them had their heads uncovered. All of them had their faces painted. We could only see their eyes, so we could not recognize them. But it was obvious that some of them knew us. There is a very short man from Cuska, a drunkard, whom people make fun of. Some soldiers started making fun of him, and from the way they did it, it was clear they knew him. . . . Also, some of the soldiers would say to a person: "Get the keys of your Mercedes!" or "Give us the keys to your van!" That is, they knew who was who and who owned what.[34]

B.B. told Human Rights Watch: "I think they were from around here because they knew the men by name and they told them to get their cars. I recognized some of their faces."[35] For more details on the identities of the security forces, see below.

After the crowd of villagers was concentrated in the village center, twenty-nine men were separated from the women and children. The entire group was then systematically robbed of their valuables. B.B. explained:

> They ordered us to empty our pockets of all valuables—money, jewelry, gold. After they finished that, they ordered two kids, aged thirteen and fourteen. One was to take our IDs and the other to collect the valuables. The man who [later] executed us put a knife to the childrens' throats and said "give us everything you have." They shot near the kids' legs and above their heads.[36]

C.C., aged fifty-seven, was also captured as he tried to leave his house and forced to gather in the village center. He told Human Rights Watch:

> The wife of my brother was twenty meters away. They told her to stop and they put a machine gun to her neck. They took about 850 DM from her. One of them cursed me and hit me in the face with his hand. "What do you think, you will never have a democracy," they said. "This is Serbia. America or NATO have no business here."
>
> They took us to the cemetery. The Gashi, Lushi, and Kelmendi families were there, along with some guests from Lodza, Graboc, Rausic, and Gorazdevac. . . . They started to separate the women, children, and old men

"I think they were from around here because they knew the men by name and they told them to get their cars. I recognized some of their faces."

> from the younger men. I didn't recognize them because at that moment most of them were masked or with black color on their faces. They stole from us; from me they took about 200 DM. They took our watches, documents, some of which they burned, our gold, and jewelry.[37]

Another woman who was present, D.D., told Human Rights Watch that the women and children stayed in the village center for approximately one hour. She said:

> The soldiers were taking things from us: money, cigarettes, watches, jewelry. . . . One soldier took a knife and started licking it. He put it under the throat of a child. One of my children, my three-year-old son, broke free from my hands and started running to the direction of the group of men, where my husband was. The soldiers shot into the ground close to my son's legs to stop him.[38]

Another woman, A.A., corroborated this account. She added:

> We [the women] stayed at the square. A soldier told us that they had an order to kill all of the villagers, but that they would spare women and children. He asked: "Do you want us to take you to Albania or to Montenegro?" We did not answer.[39]

After stripping everyone of their documents and valuables, the security forces separated twelve men from the group of thirty-two and brought them into a yard between the houses of Ajet and Haki Gashi. The twelve men were led into the nearby house of Syle Gashi. What happened next is best described by the testimony of C.C., who was in the group:

> Four of them came with us, three soldiers and one policeman. One had an automatic machine gun with two legs and the other three had normal machine guns. They put us near the wall. One of them was at the door with the machine gun—a young soldier. He said, "We will execute all of your families at the cemetery. You'll give us all your money if you want to be saved." We said we didn't have any more money and you can do anything you want with us.
>
> Then he said he would talk with his colleagues to see what he'd do with

> us. They spoke by walkie-talkie with their commander but I didn't hear what they said. At once he stepped into the door with the machine gun. We were against the wall with our hands up. He said, "In the name of Serbia you will all be shot."
>
> Ibro [Iber] Kelmendi was on the left side. He has a weak heart and when he heard what he said, he died and fell on top of me. I pretended like I was dead too. Then he opened fire and everyone was killed except one guy. He shot once more at that person—I don't know who it was. I was wounded too, in the upper leg. Another guy came and shot again, then a third guy emptied his machine gun, then the fourth. I was alive under Ibro Kelmendi and my brother.
>
> They cursed Albanians and then they set the house on fire. They broke a window and lit the stuffing from a mattress and put it over the bodies. I pushed the bodies aside and got out. I decided it was better to kill me than to be burned alive, so I jumped out the window. I went 100 meters and hid. I hid from 10:00 a.m. to 5:00 p.m.[40]

"In the name of Serbia you will all be shot."

Human Rights Watch inspected Syle Gashi's house on July 16. Only the walls were standing, and the interior had been completely burned. Small fragments of bone were scattered among the charred roof tiles and wooden beams that lay on the ground.

B.B. was among the men waiting outside the garden gate. He told Human Rights Watch that he heard shooting two or three minutes after the first group had been taken away, and he knew they had been killed. He told Human Rights Watch:

> The police returned, talked among themselves and asked some young boys around fifteen and sixteen to go with the women and children. Then they separated us into two groups. When they took us [eleven men], one guy didn't know which way to go and they hit him with a gun and said "Go this way!" They told us to go with our hands on our head and walk quickly. When we came here [house of Sahit Gashi], one said, "put them here." Another said, "It's not good to put them here because it will smell." So we went to Sahit Gashi's house.
>
> First they said stand near the bathroom. I first thought they would execute us there, but one guy with many bullets on his chest—12.7 mm bul-

> lets—said, "No, go in this room." They were very calm. They cursed us but they were not shouting. I wonder how they can kill us when they are so calm. We went into the kitchen. I saw the fire from the machine gun and I fell to my left. I think everyone was killed but I wasn't even wounded. He sprayed three times. The same man went to the other side of the room and shot again at those who had fallen. Three times again. One bullet hit me in the leg. I was hit on my left leg below the knee. Then I was hit on the right leg above the knee. The third bullet hit me in the right shin and broke the bone.[41]
>
> Then he took out his pistol and shot six or seven people but I wasn't watching because my eyes were closed. Then everything stopped. There was silence. I waited for two or three minutes and slowly opened my eyes. When I saw no one was around I looked to my right and saw Isuf Shala was dead. Arian Lushi was dead on my right. The others were dead too.
>
> I saw five police from the window and I heard one of them coming. I stayed lying down with my eyes half closed watching what he was doing. He just put his head in the room and threw something and very quickly some black smoke started going from that. After a few seconds, I couldn't breathe. When I thought I was going to scream because I was choking, I was thinking "please God, help" and I got up and went to the door. I thought I'd be killed but it is very hard to be burned alive.
>
> I went to the other room and jumped from the window. I jumped out and saw their cars. One had a big Gulinov. They had civilian vehicles, trucks, and tractors and military vehicles too.[42]

Like Syle Gashi's house, Sahit Gashi's home was also burned, with only the walls remaining, when visited by Human Rights Watch on July 15.

E.E. was in the last group of nine men waiting outside the garden gate on the day of the killing. In a brief interview with Human Rights Watch he confirmed that his group had been taken into Deme Gashi's house and was shot there. He survived uninjured. During the discussion, however, the photographs of his deceased family members and neighbors arrived for use in the ceremonial service that was planned to take place in Cuska the next day, July 18, rendering the moment inappropriate for an in depth interview.

Some foreign journalists, however, did speak in detail with E.E. about his experience. In an article published in the June 28 edition of *Time,* the survivor is quoted about what happened after the security forces took him into the two-story house:

> I was together with eight others. When we entered the hallway of the house, one of the VJ [Yugoslav Army] soldiers gave us a lighter and told us to burn down the house. When I bent down to take the lighter, the shooting started. I started crawling, not lifting my head.[43]

Human Rights Watch also spoke with E.E.'s niece, A.A., in Montenegro where she was a refugee. She told Human Rights Watch that she met her uncle near Cuska the night of May 14 and relayed what he had said to her at that time:

> At twilight, our uncle E.E. came and told us that the men had been separated into three groups and led into three houses. He was the first to enter one of the houses. He was given a lighter by a soldier and ordered to light a curtain in the room. When he kneeled down to set the curtain on fire, he heard a machine gun burst. He jumped out of the window and ran away.[44]

The events described by the three survivors were corroborated by other individuals in Cuska on May 14, including the group of women who were in close proximity to the security forces before being sent out of the village around the time the first group of men was being led into Syle Gashi's house. As they were leaving, they heard shots, some of them said, but they were not able to determine where they came from. A.A. told Human Rights Watch:

"I wonder how they can kill us when they are so calm."

> While we were leaving Cuska, the soldiers started shooting in our direction, but they were only shooting into the ground. Because of the noise and the fear we felt, we were unable to discern precisely what was shot at, and all the places the shooting was coming from. Maybe there was some other shooting as well at the same time, but we were not able to discern it.[45]

The women and children in the village were loaded onto tractors and escorted by the Serbian forces to the nearby Trepca battery factory on the Pec-Pristina road. One women in the group told Human Rights Watch that they met the commander of the Pec-Klicina police station at a checkpoint near the factory. He was apparently surprised to see the women and children, asked who had sent them there, and returned them in the direction of

Cuska, accompanied by men in three civilian cars, a grey Audi and two Zastavas. D.D. said:

> The soldiers set Sali's house on fire. The roof began to fall. Then they put us on tractors and horses. Around 10:00 a.m. they took us—women, children, and several old men—in front of the Trepca factory, which is between Cuska and the center of Pec. While we were leaving, we heard gunfire. The soldiers didn't say much on the way to the factory.
>
> We stayed for four hours in front of Trepca. The police there told us to go back to Cuska. When we got close to the village, we saw the burnt houses. I entered the house of Ram Binaku. I saw burnt bodies in one of the rooms. Most of the bodies were impossible to recognize. The woman recognized pieces of things belonging to their husbands, such as lighters, watches, keys. . . . I think Skender Dervishi was burned alive, because next to his body I saw traces in the ground, as if somebody was scratching his hand in the surface. I fainted.[46]

Another man, F.F., aged thirty-five, fled into the hills when the security forces arrived but returned later that day to discover many of the bodies, ultimately burying thirty-five of the forty-two victims. He told Human Rights Watch:

> We went about 300 meters from the village where there is a wooded hill. We saw the burning houses and heard shooting and screaming. Then the forces went away. About thirty or forty-five minutes later, [E.E.] came. We saw he was not okay. I asked him what happened. He couldn't speak a word but just replied, "What happened to us. What happened to us" while putting his hands on his head. He looked inhuman.[47]

E.E. told the men in the hills that people had been killed in the village but he was too traumatized to explain, F.F. said. About an hour later, F.F. and another man named Ajet went into Cuska to see what happened. On the way, they saw Zoran Jasovic, an ethnic Serb civilian who lived in Cuska, waving a Yugoslav flag in front of a burning house, apparently to let the security forces know that he was Serbian. He didn't see the ethnic Albanian men and then he left the area. F.F. explained what happened next:

> He [Jasovic] left and we went to that house. I went inside and saw the bod-

> ies burning. It was the house of Deme Gashi. I didn't identify them or count them. We went back to the woods and invited Sadik Gashi to come with us. We went back and tried to put the fire out. The forces had left at that time. None of our family members were around. . . .
>
> I saw the burning house of Syle Gashi and we saw a large number of burning victims. I cannot tell how many people were there, it's better to speak with an eyewitness. I decided to inspect each house. In the house of Ahmet Gashi we found burning bodies but we couldn't put out the flames. In Ajet's house we saw two other burning bodies: Syle Gashi and Skender Gashi . . . Then we went to Sali Gashi's house. We saw the body of Ibish Gashi with many bullet holes. We saw an outhouse near the road riddled with bullets. I opened the door slowly, very slowly, and I saw Qaush Lushi dead. He was killed with a 7.9 mm machine gun.

Human Rights Watch inspected the outhouse where Qaush Lushi was reportedly killed. It was a small wooden structure on the side of the road with ten bullet holes in the front door, and nine bullet holes on the far wall inside (see photograph at left). Danish forensic experts who were coincidentally examining the site for the International War Crimes Tribunal for the Former Yugoslavia at the time told Human Rights Watch that they had gathered positive evidence of human blood inside. Two bullets were found, they said, one inside the outhouse and one wedged into the wood. They appeared to be 7.6 mm caliber.[48]

Villagers in Cuska told Human Rights Watch that Qaush Lushi was the richest man in the village, and that he had been forced to give the police 10,000 DM before he and his son, Osman, were killed. An article in *Time* covering the killings in Cuska also said that Lushi returned from his house with money

Villagers in Cuska, one of whom saw the body, said the Serbian security forces killed Qaush Lushi in this outhouse in Cuska on May 14, 1999. A Danish criminal investigator examining the site in July found ten bullet holes and positive traces of human blood. © FRED ABRAHAMS/HUMAN RIGHTS WATCH

for the police to find his son already dead. He was then forced into the outhouse where he was killed.[49]

B.B. confirmed that the police had targeted Qaush Lushi. He told Human Rights Watch:

> They [the security forces] said "Do you want a state? We are 11 million Serbs so if you want a state ask for help from Clinton and Blair. Ask for NATO's help now." Qaush said "We have a state." And one of them said, "While I was defending you, you got rich." Two times they took Qaush to his home and when he went to this garden [near Azem Gashi's house], they shot above his head. Qaush came back with his car.[50]

F.F. told Human Rights Watch what happened the next day, May 15, after he and other villagers had spent the night in the forest:

A memorial service held in Cuska on July 18, 1999, for the forty-one ethnic Albanian men killed in the village on May 14 by Serbian security forces. Villagers are carrying photographs of the deceased.

© FRED ABRAHAMS/HUMAN RIGHTS WATCH

List of those killed in Cuska on May 14, 1999

1. Muse Gashi, age 64
2. Emin Gashi, age 60
3. Brahim Gashi, age 60
4. Ibish Gashi, age 56
5. Halil Gashi, age 55
6. Syle Gashi, age 49
7. Jashar Gashi, age 47
8. Ahmet Gashi, age 35
9. Skender Gashi, age 37
10. Rame Gashi, age 60
11. Xhafer Gashi, age 42
12. Brahim Gashi, age 56
13. Selim Gashi, age 42
14. Haki Gashi, age 38
15. Iber Kelmendi, age 52
16. Skender Kelmendi, age 46
17. Besim Kelmendi, age 36
18. Erdogan Kelmendi, age 19
19. Brahim Kelmendi, age 40
20. Deme Kelmendi, age 41
21. Mentor Kelmendi, age 23
22. Avdi Berisha, age 64
23. Rasim Rama, age 40
24. Muhamet Shala, age 50
25. Hasan Ceku, age 69
26. Kadri Ceku, age 68
27. Sefedin Lushi, age 41
28. Osman Lushi, age 47
29. Xhafer Lushi, age 46
30. Skender Lushi, age 44
31. Avdulla Lushi, age 60
32. Uke Lushi, age 57
33. Ramiz Lushi, age 41
34. Qaush Lushi, age 51
35. Arian Lushi, age 20
36. Gani Avdylaj, age 42
37. Hasan Avdylaj, age 40
38. Isuf Shala, age 50
39. Emrush Krasniqi, age 49
40. Ismet Dinaj, age 32
41. Zeqir Aliaj, age unknown

The next day, the families who had slept in the Kelmendi house, Ajet, Milaim, and me, decided to bury the bodies because we didn't want the families to see them in that condition. I proposed and we decided to dig one mass grave because it was too dangerous to take the time digging many graves. Some women and children came and realized that their men had been killed and burned. They asked me "where is so and so." I said, "everyone who is not here is dead."

We found thirty-one burned bodies and buried them with two unburned bodies, that of Ibish Gashi and Qaush Lushi . . . [The next day] it rained very hard. We decided that we, Skender, Ajet, Milaim, and me would go and take two other bodies, one near my house, with a stretcher and we saw one old man who was watching the body of my uncle Brahim, who was killed by a bullet to the heart. We took him to the grave site. We went to look for our neighbor Rasim. . . . We found Rasim in his garden. He had been killed by many bullets. In his garden another executed person, Mete Shala, had been, but he had already been taken by his brother.[51]

We found thirty-one burned bodies and buried them with two unburned bodies.

By mid-afternoon, the group of women, children, and elderly had been sent back to Cuska. Uniformed men put people from three families—Lushi, Gashi, and Kelmendi—into the house of Shaban Binaku. They, and those who had managed to escape the attack, stayed in the village or the nearby forest until the end of the war.

The Attacks in Zahac (Zahaq) and Pavljan (Pavlan)

The killing in Cuska is the focus of this section. But it appears that the May 14 offensive also included attacks on the neighboring villages of Zahac and Pavljan as a coordinated action. The evidence suggests that some of the same forces were involved in the attacks in at least two of the villages. Many witnesses, for example, told Human Rights Watch that the security forces moved on in the direction of Zahac and Pavljan after the killings in Cuska.

Zahac

Villagers told Human Rights Watch that the police had come to Zahac, a village with approximately 140 houses, a few times prior to May 14, mostly to demand money. After the NATO bombing began, the police and paramilitaries were based in private properties near the village, including shops on the Pec-Pristina road and the house of Xhemail Rama.

The police arrived on May 14 at around 8 a.m. Many people fled into the hills, but a number of villagers were captured in the village. Sadri Gashi, Fatos Gashi, and Valdet Gashi were reportedly killed at this time. Forces described as police and paramilitaries ordered most of the villagers to flee toward Pec on tractors and on foot, with orders to "go to Albania."[52]

Another group of paramilitaries stopped the convoy on the road and sep-

List of those killed in Zahac on May 14, 1999

1. Ismet Hyseni, age 41
2. Sabit Hyseni, age 31
3. Naim Hyseni, age 38
4. Agim Hyseni, age 28
5. Bajrush Hyseni, age 24
6. Shpend Hyseni, age 31
7. Shaban Rama, age 45
8. Sadri Rama, age 50
9. Faton Rama, age 24
10. Valdet Rama, age 36
11. Deme Hatashi, age 28
12. Shaban Neziri, age 41
13. Zenel Neziri, age 67
14. Fehmi Gjukiqi, age 23
15. Hysen Gjukiqi, age 21
16. Bekim Delia, age 21
17. Zymber Smajlaj, age 26
18. Shaban Smajlaj, age 23
19. Gezim Cukaj, age 19

arated out fourteen men. The rest of the group continued on to the Trepca battery factory near Pec, but they were stopped there by police around 1:00 p.m., held for a while, and turned back toward Zahac. Around 5:00 p.m. the convoy passed the spot where the fourteen men had been detained, villagers said. They didn't see any bodies, but they later heard from other villagers that the fourteen men were dead in a ditch there parallel to the road.

Back in Zahac, security forces robbed the villagers who had returned on the convoy and then separated the men from the women and children. The men were ordered to hand over all of their money if they didn't want to be executed. After all of the valuables had been handed over, the forces left. The villagers stayed in the hills for more than one month, coming back to the village only for food, until NATO forces arrived in Kosovo on June 12. In total, nineteen people were killed In Zahac on May 14. Nine others were killed at other times during the war, but Human Rights Watch did not investigate these killings.[53]

Pavljan

The security forces arrived in Pavljan around 10:30 a.m. on May 14, according to villagers.[54] Many of the men fled the village since they had heard that people were being executed in the area. Forty-six people from the village were captured, however, including six men. After the police took

List of those killed in Pavljan on May 14, 1999

: 1. Zymber Gashi, age 70
2. Niman Gashi, age 56
3. Shaban Kelmendi, age 52
4. Haxhi Dreshaj, age 41
5. Brahim Nikqi, age 55
6. Hatixhe Nikqi, age 55
7. Alush Selmanaj, age 46
8. Zenun Shala, age unknown
9. Muqe Lulaj, age unknown
10. Xhejrone Nikqi, age unknown

their identity documents, they detained the six men but let the others go. As they were leaving, the villagers said they heard three rounds of shooting. When they returned to Pavljan that evening, they found the six men dead in the burned house of Zymer Gashi.

Human Rights Watch visited Zymer Gashi's two-story house on July 17, 1999. It was completely burned with only the walls standing. On the wall at the height of the second floor, opposite the door, there were fourteen bullet holes. The villagers had collected the fragments of some bones, which were placed in a plastic bag hanging on the wall by a nail.

The villagers told Human Rights Watch that Ajshe Gashi, aged forty-three, had had the most direct contact with the security force since she spoke good Serbian. According to them, when the police returned to Pavljan later in May after the massacre, Ajshe told them that she knew they were from the area. She was killed in unknown circumstances on June 8.

All together, thirteen people were seized and shot by Serbian forces in Pavljan during the NATO bombing, ten of them on May 14. The others were killed on June 5, 8, and 10.

The Perpetrators

As noted, ethnic Albanians had difficulty indentifying the perpetrators of abuses against them. On occasion, a specific individual or police chief was recognized, but witnesses and victims generally refer to abusers in generic terms like "the paramilitaries" or "soldiers."

Abuses in the Pec area, however, offer new possibilities for perpetrator identification, since, unlike in other parts of Kosovo, the local Albanians had regular contact on a variety of levels with the many ethnic Serbs who lived in the area. Pec itself, seat of the Serbian Orthodox Church, had a sizable Serbian population, as did some of the area's villages, such as Gorazdevac and Nakle (Nakille).

In Cuska, many of the local Albanians believed that the security forces who were in the village on May 14 included ethnic Serbs from the area. As described above, the security forces seemed to know some of the individual Albanians. Other villagers told Human Rights Watch that the forces spoke Serbian with a clear Kosovo accent, as opposed to Serbs from southern Serbia or Belgrade. One villager in Pavljan said she recognized some of the forces in her village as Serbs from the area, although she knew no names. "One of them worked as a doorman where they sell cheese and milk in Lloma e Bilmetit," she said.[55]

In numerous interviews with villagers, a number of physical descriptions emerged. One woman, H.H., described the man she thought was a commander in Cuska (because he spoke on a walkie-talkie) as approximately six feet tall, slightly fat and aged forty. He had short black hair, shaved on the sides, with a bit of white on the top, she said. He had a beard that was speckled with gray and he wore an army uniform with no hat.[56] Other villagers also described the commander as having a light beard. B.B. told Human Rights Watch: "One guy with a short beard with grey speckles looked like a commander because he gave the orders."[57]

The most damning evidence, however, is from witness identifications using a series of twenty-one photographs obtained by Human Rights Watch that depict armed and uniformed men who were apparently in some form of military unit or units, either police reservists, special forces, a local militia, or paramilitaries. Two individuals in the photographs were positively identified by multiple witnesses as having been present in Cuska on May 14, and a third person was seen in Zahac on the same day. A number of other individuals were identified, although not alleged to be in Cuska on May 14, and some were not identified at all.

Human Rights Watch obtained the photographs on July 16 from the municipal administration in Pec, which was run at that time by former members of the KLA. The photographs depict various individuals and groups in an assortment of military poses. Some show men in military uniforms posing in a field or village. Others have men in full military outfits with automatic weapons in front of burning houses or displaying the three-fingered Serbian nationalist salute. The KLA officials told Human Rights Watch that the photographs had been found in the homes of ethnic Serbian citizens in the Pec area after Serbian and Yugoslav forces withdrew from Kosovo on June 12. Human Rights Watch also obtained two other group photographs dated May 6, 1999, of what, from the shoulder insignia, appears to be special police forces, from villagers in Zahac. The villagers told Human Rights Watch that they had found the photographs in the home of an ethnic Serb in Nakle.

Human Rights Watch scanned all of the photographs into a laptop computer and then showed them to villagers in Cuska, Zahac, and Pavljan, as well as to people in Pec, to see if anyone recognized or could identify any of the individuals. Human Rights Watch cannot confirm the authenticity of the photographs, since their origin, method of procurement, and ownership record are unknown. The fact that they were provided by the KLA, in whose interest it is to identify possible Serbian war criminals, should heighten suspicion about their accuracy. But, even if the photographs were doctored, there is no question that the villagers interviewed by Human Rights Watch positively identified some of the people in the photographs—and it is highly unlikely that this was coordinated between them and the KLA. Human Rights Watch asked the KLA for the photographs, rather than receiving them on the KLA's initiative, and did not mention that they would be shown to villagers in the area.

The results of Human Rights Watch's investigation are as follows. One man was recognized by six different people, interviewed separately, who said they had seen him in Cuska on May 14. Five of these people identified him from photograph no. 1 (second from left), and only one of these people qualified this, saying "I am 90 percent sure he was here." The others were emphatic in their answers. Two of the interviewees said the man in the photographs was a commander in Cuska on May 14, and one other who had also placed him there said he "might be the commander," i.e. a person who was directing the others in the group and talking on a walkie-talkie.[58]

Photographs no. 2 (man on right) and no. 3 appear to show the same person, although he is cleanly shaven. One of the five witnesses who recognized the man from photograph no. 1 said the same man was on the right in photograph no. 2 and photograph no. 3, and that the other security forces had called him "Popa." One further witness, who did not react to photograph no. 1, said that the man on the right in photograph no. 2 was in Cuska on May 14, and that he had gone to Deme Gashi's house where eight people were killed. "He had no beard," she said. When viewing photograph no. 3, the witness claimed that the man had visited Cuska with the Serbian forces in April, and that he had worn a beard at that time. By her account, he "waved his assault rifle and said 'you can't run from this.'"

Aside from having heard the nickname "Popa," none of these witnesses knew the man's name when they identified him in the photographs: they only claimed that he had been in Cuska. His name, Srecko Popovic, had been provided previously to Human Rights Watch by the local KLA, but it was later confirmed by two American journalists who were also investigating war crimes in the Pec area, and using the same set of photographs to identify perpetrators. According to Stephen Smith and Michael Montgomery from American RadioWorks, whose radio series on Cuska and war crimes in Kosovo generally, "The Promise of Justice", has aired on National

PHOTOGRAPH NO. 1: *Second from left is a man identified as Srecko Popovic, who multiple witnesses said was a member of the Serbian security forces in Cuska, Kosovo, on May 14, the day forty-one people were executed. Third from left is a man identified as Slavisa Kastratovic, who was seen in Zahac, Kosovo, with Serbian security forces on May 14, when nineteen other men were killed. Their knowledge of the events and other members of their units would make them invaluable witnesses to the International Criminal Tribunal for the former Yugoslavia. The identities and activities of the other men in the photograph are unknown, as is the date and place of the photograph.* © HUMAN RIGHTS WATCH

Public Radio in the United States in 2000 and 2001, the three men they interviewed—one ethnic Albanian and two ethnic Serbs—identified Popovic by name when they saw photograph no. 3.[59] In addition, Smith and Montgomery found another five people who didn't know Popovic's name but placed him in Cuska on May 14. Two of these people considered Popovic a commander.[60]

Another man identified as being in Cuska on May 14 is Zvonimir (Zvonko) Cvetkovic. One witness claimed to have seen Cvetkovic in Cuska on that day, and even to have spoken with him. The witness identified him immediately from the group photograph of the men in front of the truck, photograph no. 4 (Cvetkovic on far right), saying, "Of course I know Zvonko. We lived on the same street." Human Rights Watch later obtained a copy of Cvetkovic's passport that was found in the Petrans trucking company in Pec where he worked. The passport photo (photograph no. 5) appears to match the man in the group picture on the right. Another man, F.F., separately told Human Rights Watch that he had seen Zvonko Cvetkovic in Cuska on May 14, but he admitted to only learning his name later, and he did not see the photographs in Human Rights Watch's posses-

PHOTOGRAPH NO. 2: *The man on the right has been identified as Srecko Popovic (see* PHOTOGRAPH NO. 1*). The date and location of this picture is unknown, as are the identities of the other men.* © HUMAN RIGHTS WATCH sion. Smith and Montgomery, however, had two other people separately identify Cvetkovic by name from the Petrans photograph. Both people claimed to have seen him in Cuska on May 14.[61]

Based on these identifications, Human Rights Watch believes there is strong evidence to place both Srecko Popovic and Zvonko Cvetkovic in Cuska on May 14. We do not have evidence, however, that either of these men participated directly in the execution of the forty-one men. It can only be said that they were present with the security forces when these executions, as well as the burning of homes and the theft of private property, took place. At the very least, they possess valuable information about the war crimes that were committed, including the names of commanders, and they should, therefore, be the subject of an investigation by the International Criminal Tribunal for the Former Yugoslavia (ICTY).

"Of course I know Zvonko. We lived on the same street."

Two other ethnic Albanian men from Zahac, interviewed separately, said they recognized Slavisa Kastratovic in photograph no. 1 (third from left, next to Srecko Popovic) as a member of the security forces present in Zahac on May 14. One of the men who claimed to have had regular contact with local Serbs through his job, said that Kastratovic was from Gorazdevac and that he had worked in the Pik Trading Company. The other man claimed to have known Kastratovic personally. He told Human Rights Watch: "On May 14, I saw Slavisa Kastratovic. He spoke with me. He asked how I am. "I'm glad your sons are alive," he said. I only have young kids."[62]

Another person from Cuska, H.H., recognized Kastratovic from photograph no. 1, although she did not know his name. She told Human Rights Watch that he had been in

PHOTOGRAPH NO. 3: *The man at left has been identified as Srecko Popovic (see* PHOTOGRAPHS NO. 1 AND NO. 2 *). Date and location unknown.* © HUMAN RIGHTS WATCH

Cuska on May 14, as well as on previous occasions in April when the security forces had checked the village.[63] The testimony of the three witnesses from Cuska and Zahac provides some evidence that the same forces were involved in the actions in both places on May 14.

The other name that came up repeatedly in interviews was Vidomir Salipur, known by almost everyone in Pec and the surrounding villages simply as Salipur. Interviews and conversations with dozens of Pec residents relayed Salipur's reputation for brutality. A member of the Pec police department, he was known for eagerly beating and torturing ethnic Albanians on the street or in detention. Local human rights activists, journalists, and the KLA, as well as a number of ordinary Pec citizens told Human Rights Watch that Salipur was also the head of a local militia group or paramilitary called Munja, or "Lightning" in English, which was also Salipur's nickname.[64] The group was apparently made up of local Serbs, some of whom were in the police and others who were civilians. According to

PHOTOGRAPH NO. 4: *This photograph shows a man identified as Zvonimir Cvetkovic (far right) with a group of unidentified men at the Petrans trucking company in Pec, Kosovo, where Cvetkovic worked. Cvetkovic was seen in uniform with Serbian security forces on May 14 in Cuska, when forty-one ethnic Albanian men were executed. The identities of the other men are not known, and there is no evidence about their involvement in military activities. The date of the photograph is also unknown.*

Salipur's death announcement (see photograph no. 6), obtained by Human Rights Watch, he was killed by the KLA on April 8, 1999:

> With great sadness we announce to family and friends that our dear
>
> Salipur Vidomir—"The Lightning"
> (1970–1999)
>
> Died a heroic death defending the Holy Serbian land on April 8th 1999 in the 29th year of his life, at the hand of Albanian terrorists.
>
> The funeral will take place tomorrow, April 11th (Easter), at the Dobrilovici cemetery at 1:00 p.m.
> The procession leaves in front of the family house. . . .
>
> LAST SALUTE FROM COLLEAGUES AND OFFICERS FROM "OPG" AND "PJP" UNITS—PEC POLICE DEPARTMENT

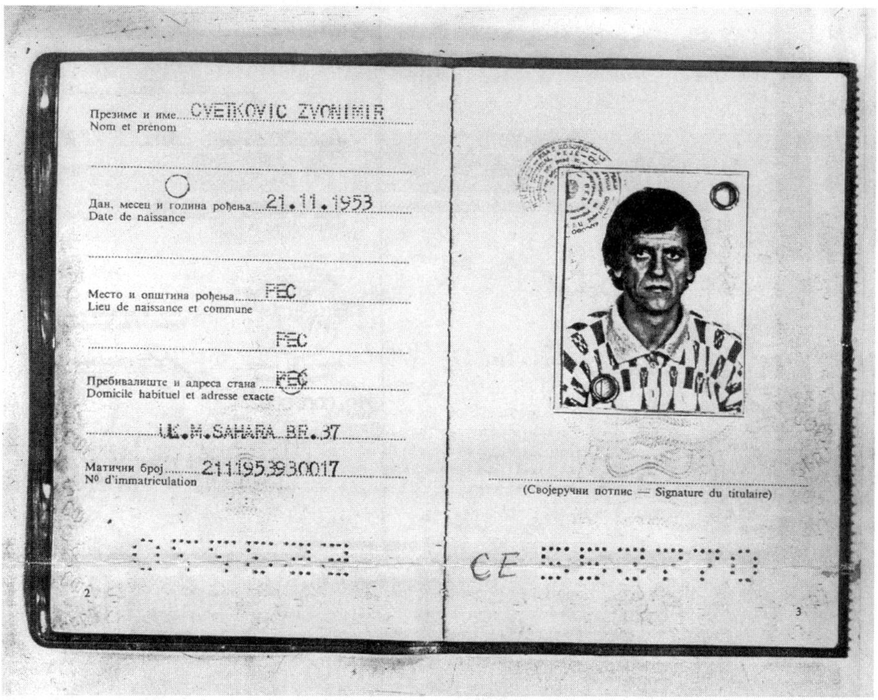

PHOTOGRAPH NO. 5: *This page of Zvonimir Cvetkovic's passport was found by U.S. journalists in mid-July 1999 in Cvetkovic's abaondoned Petrans trucking company office in Pec, Kosovo.* © HUMAN RIGHTS WATCH

"PJP" refers to the special police forces under the Ministry of Internal Affairs (Posebna Jedinica Policije, or Police Special Unit). OPG stands for Operativna Grupa, or Operative Group, although it is not clear how this group fits into the structure of the Serbian Ministry of Internal Affairs. The fact that Salipur, as a Serbian policeman, was apparently in a military unit together with ethnic Serbian civilians, possibly the Munja group, suggests that the Interior Ministry was aware of the activities of local militias, and may have organized and coordinated them On June 7, 1999, President Milosevic posthumously awarded Salipur, along with 911 other Ministry of Interior employees, the Order of Merit in Matters of Defence and Security of the First Degree for their "supression of terrorism" in Kosovo.[65]

Human Rights Watch obtained two photographs of Salipur together with a group of armed, uniformed men (photographs no. 7 and no. 8). In photograph no. 8, Salipur is seen crouching in the front row on the left, holding an Albanian flag. The identities of the other men are unknown.

In photograph no. 7, Salipur is standing in the middle of the back row wearing a cap in front of what appears to be a flag marking the Albanian-Yugoslav border. To his left is a man identified separately by two individu-

Са дубоком тугом обавештавамо родбину
и пријатеље да је наш драги

Шалипур Видомир - "Муња"

(1970 - 1999)

јуначки погинуо бранећи Свету Српску земљу 8. априла 1999.год.
у својој 29 години живота, од руке шиптарских терориста.
Сахрана ће се обавити 11. априла (на Ускрс) на гробљу
у Добриловићима у 13 часова.
Поворка креће испред породичне куће.

Ожалошћени: *отац Ненад, мајка Рајка*
супруга Снежана, син Петар
браћа Милутин, Владан и Станко
снајке Биљана и Душица
братићи Виктор и Лазар
и остала многобројна родбина и пријатељи

ПОСЛЕДЊИ ПОЗДРАВ ОД КОЛЕГА И СТАРЕШИНА ИЗ ЈЕДИНИЦА "ОПГ" и "ПЈП" - СУП-а ПЕЋ

PHOTOGRAPH NO. 6: *Vidomir Salipur's death announcement.*

© HUMAN RIGHTS WATCH

als as Nebojsa Minic, who has been directly implicated as the leader of a gang that extorted and then killed six members of one family, aged five to twenty-eight, in Pec on June 12 (see section above, A Final Killing). Two people who said they had had direct contact with Minic told Human Rights Watch that he is heavily tattooed with images of a knife, an axe, and a grenade on his forearm, and a dead man on his chest. The man in the front row of photograph no. 7, far left, was identified independently by two people, as well as by KLA sources, as "Milan," allegedly a friend of Salipur's, although no specific allegations were leveled against him. The identities of the other men in the photograph are unknown.

There is also some evidence of the involvement of the Yugoslav Army (VJ) in the attacks on Cuska, Pavljan, and Zahac. Local KLA authorities in Pec told Human Rights Watch in July they possessed a notebook that, they claimed, belonged to an officer in the VJ. Notes in the book mentioned a military build-up in the Cuska area prior to the May 14 killing, they said.

Shortly thereafter, Natasa Kandic from the Belgrade-based Humanitar-

PHOTOGRAPH NO. 7: *Vidomir Salipur standing in the center of the back row wearing a cap. Allegedly the head of a local Pec militia called "Munja", or Lightning, Salipur had a reputation for brutality against ethnic Albanians. To his left is Nebojsa Minic. The date and location of the photograph are unknown, as are the identities of the other men.* © HUMAN RIGHTS WATCH ian Law Center published a report in which she mentioned the notebook of a VJ lieutenant shown to her by the KLA authorities in Pec.[66] She wrote that the book:

> [R]egister[ed] the military activites in the municipality of Pec after March 24. The entry for May 11 said that the focus of military activities should be shifted to Cuska and its vicinity. The local KLA headquarters in Pec also had a document marked confidential bearing the signature of the colonel in charge of the 125th Brigade.[67]

A subsequent article in the Western press claimed that the war crimes tribunal had found Yugoslav Army documents that ordered the "cleansing" of Cuska. A journalist for *USA Today* reported that he inspected a black vinyl, three-ringed notebook that contained a direct order typed on army stationery and stamped by the Supreme Defense Council of the Yugoslav Army Headquarters in Belgrade. The order reportedly said, "The aim of the mili-

PHOTOGRAPH NO. 8: *Vidomir Salipur is crouching in the front row, far left. The date and location of the photograph are unknown, as are the identities of the other men.* © HUMAN RIGHTS WATCH tary activity should be to cleanse Cuska and the surrounding villages and terrain."[68] The article said that investigators from the war crimes tribunal had found the notebook on July 2 near an abandoned military headquarters in Kosovo.

LJUBENIC (LUBENIQ)

With its proximity to the Albanian border and a high degree of KLA activity in the area, the village of Ljubenic just south of Pec was a constant focus of police attention and activity during 1998 and 1999. According to the OSCE, it was also the home village of a local KLA commander.[69]

According to villagers in Ljubenic, between March 24 and June 10, 1999, more than eighty villagers were killed by Serbian forces in different incidents. On July 10, Italian KFOR announced a possible mass grave containing 350 bodies, but these allegations turned out to be false. Thus far, tribunal investigators have discovered only nine bodies in three different sites around the village, but Human Rights Watch has received reports of over eighty execution-style killings in the area during this period.[70]

The first known incident in Ljubenic took place on May 25, 1998, when two Serbian policemen were ambushed by the KLA and wounded on the Pec-Djakovica road near the village.[71] Police forces then shelled Ljubenic from a distance before entering the village, separating the men and women, and executing nine of the men.[72] On May 29, the entire village fled, mostly to Albania, due to the government's spring offensive.

According to the OSCE, about 650 Albanians and 120 Serbs were living in the village as of January 1999.[73] During the NATO campaign, the most serious incident took place on April 1. Numbers vary, but at least sixty-three men were killed at this time, according to numerous witnesses. At least twenty-five more people, nine of them from Ljubenic, were killed over the next week in the mountains to the west.

According to one of the village elders who spoke with Human Rights Watch, sixty-three men died on April 1, although witnesses and survivors who spoke with journalists claimed that the number was closer to eighty.[74] Eight different eyewitnesses spoke with a variety of foreign journalists who wrote about the killings in the English-language press. Their reports are highly consistent. Six of them saw the killings taking place, one heard the shooting as she was walking away with the other woman and children, and one saw Serbian forces removing the bodies.

All of the witnesses said that Serbian forces arrived in the village around 7 a.m. on April 1. One claimed that an unidentified man from Pec had warned them the night before that the paramilitary forces were planning to come to the village.[75] Some villagers fled into the nearby mountains when the forces arrived, but those who remained were ordered to gather in one spot. The men were then separated from the women, children, and elderly, who were told to leave the village on foot. The men were then interrogated about having weapons, and two men were shot in front of the group. Shortly thereafter, the security forces—one witness said three men—opened fire on the group. Nine villagers survived.

Numbers vary, but at least sixty-three men were killed

One woman who was sent away on foot told the *London Times*:

> They told the women and children to go to Albania as they said we always wanted to do. . . . We had to leave the men behind but when we reached a main road we heard shooting and I knew something terrible had happened. Later when I reached Albania I learnt that my father had died.[76]

A man who survived the shooting told the *Chicago Sun Times,* "They divided the women and children from the men and told them to go to Albania. After that, they executed two men from the village in front of us, and after a while they started to shoot us, using all different kinds of weapons."[77] One witness claimed to have seen "irregular forces" taking the bodies away on tractors.[78]

According to the testimonies provided to journalists, the nine survivors, some of them injured, crawled to a nearby forest, and then into the mountains. One wounded sixteen-year-old boy died. Most of the others eventually made it to Albania.

Some of those who escaped before the killing were then attacked over the next week in the mountains. According to the village elder who spoke with Human Rights Watch, nine people from Ljubenic were killed in the mountains, as well as fourteen people from Bucane (Buqan), three people from Krusevac (Krusec), and one from Prilep (Prejlep). Many bodies are still missing, he said. The high number of landmines in the area has prevented a final tally by villagers or investigators from the war crimes tribunal.

One survivor who was in the mountains told a journalist from the Associated Press, "We were attacked from all sides. . . . They threw people from the rocks down into the streams."[79] Another survivor told the *Irish Times,* "We ran up the mountain, we ran down the mountain, we lost nine people in all. Four were women, two were children. Everywhere we went were the bullets."[80]

The area around Ljubenic had a lot of KLA activity in the eighteen months preceding the April 1 killings, which may have been a motivation. Furthermore, four different witnesses told journalists that one of the armed Serbs who opened fire said that the KLA had killed his brother.[81] One of these four witnesses claimed that the man said his brother had been taken off a train some months before and killed by the KLA. Another witness said the man appeared to be the youngest of the group.

The OSCE report on Kosovo also mentions a man who said his brother had been killed by the KLA. The report quotes a survivor of the killing who overheard the armed Serb as saying "Your KLA killed my brother! Is what they did to my brother okay?" One old man reportedly tried to negotiate with the Serbian forces, and reminded them of what had happened in May 1998 when the police killed nine men. The armed Serbs allegedly responded: "The 'police?' Well, this is not the police, this is the army!" and then shot the old man.[82] One witness who spoke with the *Providence Journal* gave a similar account, although it is not known if this is the same man who spoke with the OSCE. According to this witness, the armed Serbs interrupted the elderly Albanian who was trying to negotiate and said, "You son of a bitch old man, come here. . . . We are not Serbian police. We are Serbian soldiers."[83]

The OSCE report, which puts the number killed on April 1 at sixty-six, includes the findings of an OSCE visit to Ljubenic on July 1, 1999. Near where the men had been killed, the report says, the OSCE saw scattered clothes and empty bullet casings at the spot from which the Serbian forces were said to have shot. In a nearby house, five sites were seen where bodies appeared to have been burned.[84]

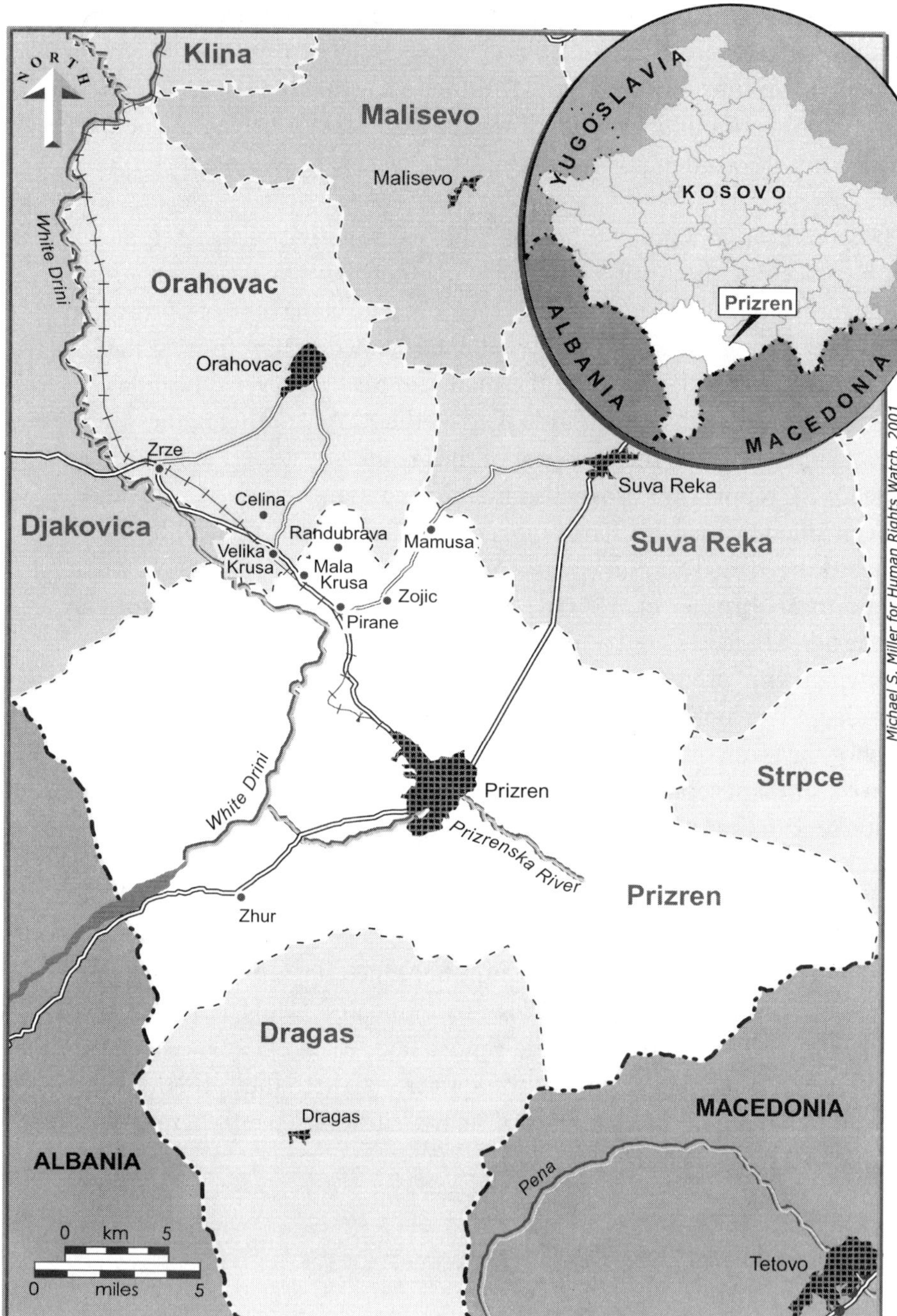
NORTH
Klina
Malisevo
Malisevo
YUGOSLAVIA
KOSOVO
Prizren
ALBANIA
MACEDONIA
White Drini
Orahovac
Orahovac
Zrze
Celina
Djakovica
Randubrava
Mamusa
Velika Krusa
Mala Krusa
Zojic
Pirane
Suva Reka
Suva Reka
Michael S. Miller for Human Rights Watch, 2001
Strpce
White Drini
Prizren
Prizrenska River
Prizren
Zhur
Dragas
Dragas
MACEDONIA
ALBANIA
Pena
0 km 5
0 miles 5
Tetovo

11

PRIZREN MUNICIPALITY

The Prizren municipality, located in Kosovo's southwestern corner, had a relatively mixed ethnic population. According to the OSCE, 78 percent of the population was ethnic Albanian, 5 percent Serbian, and 17 percent other national communities, such as Turks and Roma.[1] Throughout 1998 and early 1999, the municipality was less severely affected by the war than Djakovica and Decani to the northwest. However, villages in the northeastern part of the municipality, in the direction of Suva Reka and Orahovac, were trouble spots due to the ongoing presence of the KLA.

Prizren municipality was the site of many crimes during the period of NATO bombing, including in the city of Prizren itself, especially the neighborhood of Tusus. Villages north of the city on the border with Orahovac municipality, such as Pirane, Mala Krusa, Mamusa (Mamushe), Zojic (Zojiq), and Randubrava (Randobrave), were particularly hard hit due to KLA activity in the area and the use of certain villages as rebel transit routes. The villages of Pirana (Pirane) and Mala Krusa, stretching north along the main road to Celina and Zrze (Xrxe), are covered separately in the chapter on the Prizren- Djakovica Road.

The Yugoslav Army's Third Army, responsible for Kosovo, had a barracks in Prizren, and witnesses claimed that the army was very active in the municipality, coordinating actions with the police. Based in Prizren was the army's 549th Motorized Brigade, commanded by Col. Bozidar Delic (see Forces of the Conflict). Prizren was also one of the seven regional bases in Kosovo of the Serbian police, known as a Sekretarijat Unutrasnjih Poslova (Secretariat for Internal Affairs), or SUP. The Prizren SUP covered the municipalities of Prizren, Orahovac, Suva Reka, and Gora. The commander of Prizren SUP throughout 1998 was Col. Gradimir Zekavica, and Lt. Milan Djuricic was the section head of Prizren SUP's police department.[2] A new SUP head was apparently appointed in January 1999: Col. Milos Vojnovic, who was also assistant chief of the police department in the Serbian Ministry of Internal Affairs.[3] But, based on awards issued to MUP officers after the war, Col. Zekavica was commander during the war (see Forces of the Conflict).

PRIZREN CITY

A historic Ottoman outpost with several fourteenth century Serbian Orthodox churches as well as centuries-old mosques, the city of Prizren, in south-western Kosovo, was largely spared the physical devastation suffered by so many other cities in Kosovo. Ethnically diverse, its pre-war population was roughly two-thirds ethnic Albanian, but with sizeable numbers of ethnic Serbs, Roma, Turks, Vlachs, and Muslim Slavs. It was not known as an important center of KLA activity and, in comparison to other Kosovo cities, both Albanian and Serb, relations among the various ethnic groups were relatively peaceful prior to the conflict.

At the outset of the NATO bombing campaign, the OSCE has reported, Serbian military and police shelled a few areas of the city and destroyed the historic seat of the "League of Prizren," an important historical monument for Kosovo's ethnic Albanians.[4] Yet, with the exception of the Tusus neighborhood, the "ethnic cleansing" of Prizren was carried out with a lesser degree of violence and fewer wanton attacks than in many other parts of Kosovo. Thus, Jamie Shea, NATO spokesman during the air strikes, was either exaggerating or misinformed when he stated on May 17, 1999, that Prizren was the city that "has probably suffered the most over the last months in the whole of Kosovo."[5] Serbian forces cleared some areas of Prizren systematically, but many ethnic Albanians remained in the city throughout the conflict. Because of the obvious dangers outside, men generally stayed within their homes for weeks and months at a stretch.

In April 1999, on at least two occasions, Serb police and military rounded up hundreds of men in Prizren and forced them to serve on trench-digging brigades near the border with Albania. Human Rights Watch interviewed two men who were taken from their homes on April 24 to serve in such brigades.[6] They were initially brought to Prizren's sports center, near the military barracks, and given outdated army uniforms to wear; then they were brought to the Dragash municipality south of Prizren and made to dig trenches for a month. Other Prizren natives who fled the city in mid-April reported that they had left in order to escape a similar round up. One man stated that he had been held at the sports center for five hours with about 200–300 other people, but was released after a doctor certified that he was disabled.[7]

Tusus Neighborhood

The May 26 attack on the Tusus neighborhood of Prizren, in which Serb forces killed some twenty-seven to thirty-four people and burned over one-hundred homes, was the most violent episode in Prizren during the conflict. In the first half of June, Human Rights Watch interviewed three refugee eyewitnesses from Tusus in Albania.[8] A Human Rights Watch researcher then visited the Tusus area on June 14, just after NATO's entry into Kosovo, photographing the devastation and interviewing additional witnesses. In all, Human Rights Watch heard the testimonies of fourteen Tusus residents.

The Tusus violence was apparently sparked by the killing of at least two Serbian police officers on Ramiz Sadik street, a major avenue that cuts through the area. Several witnesses told Human Rights that they had heard about the killings, while one witness, L.V., stated that he saw the bodies on May 26 in the early morning. "One [of the police] was lying on his back," L.V. explained. "The other was face down, with lots of bullet holes in his back; his back was bloody."[9] Kosovapress, a KLA press organ, reported higher numbers of Serb losses, stating that twenty-one Serbian police and paramilitaries were killed in Tusus by a KLA commando unit the night before the attack.[10] The Serbian Ministry of Internal Affairs website, gives the names and photographs of two policemen killed in Tusus on May 26: Milosav Rajkovic (born in 1975), and Zlatomir Stankovic (born in 1957).[11]

The Tusus violence was apparently sparked by the killing of at least two Serbian police officers.

By about 7:30 a.m. on May 26, the Serbian forces had begun a violent rampage though the neighborhood. F.K., a thirty-three-year-old Tusus resident, told Human Rights Watch that he and sixteen members of his family "stayed in the basement and heard lots of shooting." The gunfire, he said, "was non-stop, very close, maybe fifty meters away from our house. After a half hour of shooting, they started burning and demolishing houses in the neighborhood. They smashed everything."[12] He said that the fires continued through the early evening, at which time his family finally escaped by climbing over their garden wall, walking through burning timbers to reach a road out of the neighborhood.

Other families described how Serbian forces entered their homes, sometimes to kill, sometimes to conduct searches. L.V., a sixteen-year-old boy, told Human Rights Watch:

> More than fifteen Serbs came in the house. They asked us, "Are there KLA here?" They searched the house, staying inside for about five minutes. They were special police, wearing a red insignia of the Serbian flag on their arms. They took me outside and said, "We're going to kill you. Take a last look at your family because we're going to kill you."[13]

When L.V. was brought outside, however, a man whom he believed was the Serbian commander told the others to release him. L.V.'s mother was also harassed; she said that she thought the security forces were going to take her away but that her mother-in-law's screaming saved her.[14] More than one

Burnt house in the Tusus neighborhood of Prizren. On May 26, 1999, Serbian police rampaged through the neighborhood, killing between twenty-seven and thirty-four civilians and burning countless homes.

group of Serbian security forces visited their house, which is centrally located on Ramiz Sadik Street.

Just off Ramiz Sadik Street was the home of the Abdulmexhidi family. J.A., a nineteen-year- old woman, described the family's ordeal:

> The police came to our house around noon and ordered all the men to face the wall. There were six Serbs in green camouflage uniforms; the word police was written across their chest. We were inside the house at the time. They came inside and they ordered everyone outside, except my father and uncle.[15]

F.A., her mother, continued:

> They called the women from inside the house and demanded money from us. They said they'd kill our husbands. They put a Kalashnikov to my husband's head. I gave them 2,000 DM and the men gave them 1,500 DM. Everyone came outside. They ordered us to leave and they kept the men . . . . When we left, we saw the men being beaten. They kicked the men in the stomach and back, and hit them with the butt of their guns.[16]

Six men, including F.A.'s husband, her brother-in-law, and her two sons, age seventeen and twenty-one, were forced to stay behind. F.A.'s daughter described what happened next. She explained: "[T]he men were facing the wall with their hands up. When we got to the road, we heard shooting, the sound of Kalashnikovs."

F.A. returned to the house the next day, finding it blackened and burned, its roof caved in. The family's small dog had been shot. She saw blood everywhere around the house but no sign of her relatives. "Someone suggested to me that the men were in jail, not dead, but I knew they were dead," she told Human Rights Watch. Two days later she found their bodies in the morgue.

Residents who stayed in the area throughout the attack said that the security forces left the neighborhood in the mid-afternoon. At about 4 p.m., after the security forces were gone, a truck arrived to pick up the bodies of the dead. The group of people handling the truck were said to include an ethnic Albanian driver, four Serbian civil servants, and four Roma, charged with retrieving the bodies. "Their truck was full of dead bodies," said one witness. "It was open in the back and you could see them. The gypsies were going house to house looking for bodies. They threw them in the back of the truck like sacks."[17] According to another witness, who said that she saw numerous bodies wrapped in white sheets in the back of the truck, one of the civil servants carried a camera and was photographing the dead.[18]

The perpetrators of the attack appear to have been a mix of special police forces and paramilitaries.

Human Rights Watch interviewed two people who picked up bodies at the local morgue in the following days. M.B., age sixty-five, said that he and a few friends picked up about two dozen bodies from the morgue that Friday, including a thirty-four-year-old woman who was completely burned; she had lived on his street. He recalled: "The doctor at the morgue told us that we had to decide: either we bury them or they would put them in a mass grave. I transported some of the bodies in a horse cart."[19] Another sixty-five-year-old man, F.D., went to the morgue for several days in a row, each time picking up a couple of bodies. He attended a funeral for many of the dead that Sunday at a cemetery near the local mosque.

The perpetrators of the attack appear to have been a mix of special police forces and paramilitaries. One woman said that they wore green camouflage uniforms; some wore masks, and some had bandanas on their heads. An eleven-year-old remembered them as carrying "big knives" and "smoking cigars."[20] One witness reported the presence of "Greeks and Russians who didn't even speak Serbian."[21]

Estimates of the total number of neighborhood residents killed range from twenty-seven to thirty-four. Two witnesses said that they had each personally seen more than twenty-five corpses.[22] When Human Rights Watch visited Tusus on June 14, 1999, about three weeks after the killings, residents claimed that thirty-four people had been killed, and they provided the names of twenty-six of them. The area was physically devastated: entire streets were blackened, with nearly every house on them reduced to charred wreckage. Approximately one hundred homes were badly damaged.

Bilbildere Neighborhood

Another Prizren neighborhood in which killings were reported is Bilbildere. On the morning of May 16, 1999, two ethnic Albanian men were said to have been summarily executed there by paramilitaries. Human Rights Watch interviewed three relatives of the men who were killed, all members of a single family.

The witnesses said that almost all of the residents of the neighborhood fled to Albania in late April, leaving only their family and six others. Three weeks passed without incident, but then early on Sunday, May 16, a group of Serbian police arrived and searched the house for weapons. Not long after the police left, a large group of paramilitaries arrived. E.M., a twenty-six-year-old woman, told Human Rights Watch what happened:

> At about 9:00 a.m. Arkan's men came, nearly one hundred of them. They had light blue bandanas around their heads, and special vests that they wore open; you could see their chests. They wore necklaces with crosses and other emblems. Most of them had shaved heads; some had beards. There was a Russian with a beard; he didn't speak Serbian . . . . They had greasepaint on their faces, under their eyes. They wore camouflage green uniforms, like soldiers, but a few had dark blue ones . . . . They didn't come into our house but were all over the neighborhood. We were terrified.[23]

E.M. said that the paramilitaries took away her two brothers-in-law, Elez Muharremi and Enez Muharremi, as well as Fatmir Muharremi, the son of Enez. Not long after the men were taken away the remaining family members heard automatic weapon fire. A.M., the mother of the two older men, explained: "I heard the sound of shooting. 'I'm afraid they've killed them,' I told my other son . . . . it was a burst of fire from an automatic weapon."[24] After the paramilitaries left the neighborhood, the family found the bodies of two of the men in the bathroom of a neighboring home.

Enez's surviving brother told Human Rights Watch:

> I heard the women cry out when they found the bodies so I ran over. A neighbor told me, "don't go in, you won't be able to bear the sight," so I didn't go in. I went to the police station to get the police, but on the way I ran into three police. They came to the house with me and we entered the bathroom together. That's when we saw the bodies: they were lying on the floor. There was blood everywhere. Enez had been shot twice in the chest and arm; Fatmir had been shot in the chest and foot. The police never took the bodies to the morgue.[25]

As of June 1999, the whereabouts of the other brother-in-law, Elez Muharremi, were not known.

Krusha Madhe
Velika Kruša
50

12

THE PRIZREN–DJAKOVICA (GJAKOVE) ROAD

Orahovac (Rrahovec) and Prizren Municipalities

One of the first regions to be hit by Serbian and Yugoslav government attacks after the NATO bombing was a series of villages along a ten kilometer stretch of road between Prizren and Djakovica. From Bela Crkva and Zrze in the north to Pirane in the south, government forces, mostly army units, systematically shelled the area before special ground forces moved in to the villages. Sometimes with the help of local Serbs from the area, men of fighting age were separated from women and children. Between March 24 and 26, police and paramilitary forces, without any reported defense by the KLA, executed hundreds of men. The killings at Bela Crkva and Velika Krusa are among the six incidents listed in the ICTY's initial indictment of Slobodan Milosevic and the four other top government officials.

The intensity of the violence in this area had a number of causes. First, the government clearly wanted to clear the border region with Albania at the start of the campaign. Control of the border was necessary to minimize infiltration from Albania by the KLA, to prepare for a possible NATO ground invasion, and to facilitate the "ethnic cleansing" of Albanians from other parts of Kosovo. The border areas were cleared, which then made it easier to deport Albanians from Pec, Suva Reka, the Drenica region, and other parts of the province. Control of the Prizren-Djakovica road for troop movement and supplies was clearly a strategic priority for the government.

Second, many of the villages under attack, such as Velika Krusa, were well known for their ongoing support for and presence of the KLA throughout 1998 and 1999. Nearby Retimlje (Reti) was a fortified KLA base. Arms were most likely flowing through these villages from Albania since 1998, and the

KLA was seen frequently in and around the area, sometimes attacking police on the main road.

One final motivation may have been the wealth of the region. This southwestern part of Kosovo had the province's most fertile land, and the area was known for its relatively wealthy residents, which may have attracted paramilitaries interested in looting and theft.

One important incident along the road around Djakovica, detailed in the chapter The NATO Air Campaign, was NATO's bombing of a civilian convoy. On April 14, NATO aircraft repeatedly bombed refugees over a twelve-mile stretch of road between Djakovica and Decani, injuring thirty-six and killing seventy-three civilians around the villages of Bistrazin, Gradis, Madanaj, and Meja. NATO and U.S. spokespersons initially claimed the target was an exclusively military convoy and that Serb forces may have been responsible for the attacks on civilians. NATO officials later admitted that about a dozen NATO planes had been involved in numerous attacks on the two convoys, dropping a total of nine bombs.

BELA CRKVA (BELLACERKE)

Serbian police first arrived in Bela Crkva, which had some 3,000 inhabitants, one week before the NATO bombing began. They burned a few houses, shot livestock, and stole some items from private homes, villagers said. According to one villager, a twenty-eight-year-old man named Eqerem Zhuniqi was killed at this time.[1]

What witnesses believed to have been Serbian special police forces and paramilitary units entered the village again around 3 a.m. on March 25. Witnesses reported a mixture of men in blue and green military uniforms, some of them masked, and many wearing a white ribbon on their sleeves. Immediately, they began stealing cars and valuables like televisions.

At least sixty military-age men, fearful for their lives, fled right away into the nearby hills. Other villagers remained to see what would happen. One woman, N.Z., told Human Rights Watch:

> On March 25, the night after NATO started bombing, I was sleeping. At about 3 a.m., my husband woke me up and said, "we have to move, tanks are in the village." I took some clothes I could find and went to the door. As soon as I came to the door, there were tanks maybe ten meters away from us.[2]

N.Z. stayed in her house with her family for approximately twenty minutes, deciding what to do. Eventually, the tanks withdrew from the center. But around 4:30 a.m., N.Z.'s family saw smoke and flames at the edge of the village. Residents from that part of the village began coming to the center, saying that government forces were setting homes on fire. At this point, N.Z.'s family, and between 300 and 400 other villagers including approximately fifty military-age men, decided it was time to flee.

The area around Bela Crkva is relatively flat, so the group sought shelter in the wooded gully of the Ballaj stream less than one mile from the village. At times they hid in the stream itself, which was only knee deep.

The group first intended to head towards the village of Rogovo. But they heard shots from that direction, and decided to go towards Zrze instead. In the distance, they saw Bela Crkva burning. By 6:00 a.m. it was getting light, but the group decided to stay in the stream bed due to the shooting.

Sometime around 8:00 a.m., the group made its way towards the railroad bridge that crosses the stream. Twelve people from the families of Clirim Zhuniqi and Xhemal Spahiu were about fifty meters ahead of the main group. They were the first ones to encounter the police on the bridge.

N.Z. recounted what happened:

> We started walking towards Zrze, not knowing the police were behind the bridge. We walked towards the bridge, which was about twenty meters away. The first family was of a man [Clirim], his wife, and three children. When he saw the police, they surrendered. The people next to us said we should surrender as well. We began to walk, and the police started shooting at us, but no one was wounded. We all lay down.[3]

Another woman in the group, S.Z., told Human Rights Watch:

> There was a stream with bushes that was a hiding place. The village was hiding there. The stream was about up to our knees with water. The Serbs found us—maybe about twenty Serbs—I couldn't count because we couldn't see them all. The said, speaking Serbian, "Everyone, hands up, come out from that hiding place." I didn't understand what they were saying but some of our men understood Serbian and they explained.[4]

Before the police came to the larger group, the Zhuniqi and Spahiu families members were ordered out of the stream bed into a nearby field. One witness claimed that the men were forced to strip. Another witness said that he saw men in "green uniforms with white bandanas" shoot Clirim, his wife, and their three children, as well as the family of Xhemal Spahiu. He said:

> They killed all of them with an automatic gun in a field maybe 500 meters away from their house. I could see it [the killing] very well. It happened only 200–300 meters away from me. I was hiding in the stream near the bridge. I recognized one of the men [shooting], who was from Velika Hoca.[5]

According to the witnesses, an Albanian doctor from Bela Crkva named Nesim Popaj, aged thirty-six, tried to negotiate with the Serbian commander, pleading with him to spare the lives of the villagers. Popaj allegedly explained that they were not members of the KLA but just villagers who wanted to work in peace. The commander responded by saying: "You're terrorists, bring out your guns."

They killed all of them with an automatic gun in a field maybe 500 meters away from their house.

During this discussion, witnesses said, the commander was stepping down on the neck of Shendet Popaj, the doctor's seventeen-year-old nephew, who was lying prone on the ground. Abruptly ending the discussion, the commander—described by one witnesses as a medium-height man, around thirty-five years old, in a green camouflage uniform with three stars on his shoulders—shot Dr. Popaj with three bullets in front of his wife and three children, after which he killed Shendet. The witness noted specifically that the commander, believed by the witness to be a captain, had a distinguishing feature: a recognizably deformed mouth.

One witness, one of four men to survive the subsequent shooting, told Human Rights Watch:

> First they killed the doctor, who was a leader of the village. They killed him with an automatic weapon from about one meter away. The doctor was saying, "please don't kill us, we're villagers who want to work; we're not with the KLA." The Serbs were saying, "you're terrorists; bring out your guns." They said "Where is NATO to save you now?" A captain gave the orders. He killed the doctor himself, while they were debating. The doctor was the most respected man in the village. He had studied in the West: in Sarajevo, Zagreb,

> and Germany. After they killed the doctor, they immediately killed his nephew. The captain had his foot on the nephew's neck. They shot the nephew in the head.
>
> The captain was normal height [approximately one meter eighty centimeters tall]. He was wearing a helmet. Had three gold stars on his shoulder, no mask. He had a strange, scrunched up mouth. No moustache or beard. He was in his thirties, maybe thirty-five or so.
>
> When the police were separating me from my children, my children were trying to come to me. When they killed the doctor, the doctor's wife and three children were watching; they were about twenty meters away and they saw everything. They were all screaming; the police were trying to keep them away. There was a total of about twenty police.[6]

The security forces then separated men over the approximate age of fourteen from the women and children. The men were told to undress, in what the villagers thought was an apparent attempt to humiliate them in front of their wives and children. One explanation, however, may have been a police attempt to look for military uniforms underneath the civilian clothes.[7] The Serb forces, described by one woman as wearing green uniforms with a white arm band or ribbon on their sleeves, then proceeded to search the mens' clothes and strip them of their identity documents, jewelry, and money, including 40,000 DM from one man, Muharem Zhuniqi. At this point, the women and children were told to walk along the railroad track towards Zrze. The men were ordered to dress and sent back towards the river bed.

The female villagers who were walking along the tracks told Human Rights Watch that, just after departing, they heard a burst of gunfire that lasted several minutes without interruption. N.Z. testified: "When we had walked for maybe ten meters, we heard shots of an automatic gun, three or four minutes without interruption. The women all started to cry, 'They killed our husbands!'"

In a separate interview, another woman recalled: "The Serbs directed the group I was in to the village of Zrze. While we were being directed over the bridge, we heard automatic weapons firing for a few minutes. We didn't even dare turn our heads to see what was happening."[8]

Human Rights Watch spoke with two men who were among those ordered to the river bed. In separate interviews, they testified that the Serbian forces had opened fire on them with automatic weapons. Six men initially survived, but two of these men later died from their wounds.

Human Rights Watch interviewed the first survivor on April 16 in Kukes, a few days after he had entered Albania. At the time, he had bandages on his right shoulder, right arm, and head wounds he said he had sustained during the shooting in Bela Crkva, as well as some shrapnel wounds he sustained later in the head and arm from shelling near the village of Nogavac (Nagafc). A visit to a doctor in Tirana, Albania, later revealed that the man had a bullet lodged in his shoulder.

The man said he was among the first men in the group to be shot. He fell back into the water, he said, and was then covered by the other falling bodies, which saved his life. He told Human Rights Watch:

> After killing the doctor and his nephew, they told us to go back down to the stream. Then they immediately started to fire on us. The captain didn't say anything; he just started shooting, and the rest started shooting too. They kept shooting for about five to ten minutes. When they started shooting, I was the first to fall; I was hit by a bullet in my left shoulder. Dead people fell on top of me.

The stream near Bela Crkva where Serbian forces executed sixty-four ethnic Albanians.

© JOANNE MARINER/HUMAN RIGHTS WATCH

> After they stopped firing, they looked around to see who was breathing. I could hear them say, "this one is breathing." They checked to see who was alive and they killed them. I was covered up by bodies.
>
> I stayed like that for about twenty minutes. After ten minutes I heard shooting. They were killing people up the stream. When I got up, I saw dead people all around me. Five others survived, but others later died. Forty-two people were killed.[9]

Some thirty minutes after the second round of firing, when the witness realized that the Serb forces had moved on, he stood up and saw, in addition to the estimated forty men dead in the river, the dead bodies of seven elderly people from Bela Crkva, as well as two persons unknown to him, lying in a field about a hundred meters away from the stream. He then proceeded to walk towards Zrze, where he told the women from the village what had happened.

This was corroborated by N.Z., who had been sent to Zrze with the other

From ICTY's 1999 indictment of Slobodan Milosevic et al.

On or about 25 March 1999, forces of the FRY and Serbia attacked the village of Bela Crkva (Orahovac/Rahovec municipality). Many of the residents of Bela Crkva fled into a streambed outside the village and sought shelter under a railroad bridge. As additional villagers approached the bridge, a Serbian police patrol opened fire on them killing 12 persons, including 10 women and children. The police then ordered the remaining villagers out of the streambed, at which time the men were separated from the women and small children. The police ordered the men to strip and then systematically robbed them of all valuables. The women and children were then ordered to leave. The village doctor attempted to speak with the police commander, but he was shot and killed, as was his nephew. The other men were then ordered back into the streambed. After they complied, the police opened fire on the men, killing approximately 65 Kosovo Albanians. (Those persons killed who are known by name are set forth in Schedule B which is attached as an appendix to the indictment.)

women. She told Human Rights Watch that one man, the survivor quoted above, came to Zrze. He was silent at first, she said, and then he explained what had happened to the other men. She confirmed that he was wounded in the shoulder.

The husband of N.Z.'s sister-in-law then went back to the river bed with some women to see if there were any other survivors. He brought back five other men, N.Z. said, but two of them subsequently died.

The other survivor interviewed by Human Rights Watch told the same story. He said:

> They separated us, and ordered us to walk in the bed of the stream. When we started, they opened fire on us. I fell down, and was covered by five or six dead bodies. I stayed for about one hour in the water, the dead covered me. When I no longer heard any noise, I stood up. I myself was fully covered in blood. I saw five people who were injured. Later, only three of them survived. I was so horrified, that I hid in some bushes. After about one hour, two women, relatives of some of these people, came, and saw the bodies. One of them discovered two of her sons, fifteen and sixteen years old. There were forty-five dead people, who were buried two days later by people from the village.[10]

Human Rights Watch spoke with four different individuals who saw the dead bodies or then helped with their burial in the field near the stream. One man said, aside from the group of men killed in the stream, he found twelve people from two families—seven children, three women, and two men—near the bridge. He told Human Rights Watch:

> After the Serbs left, I went down to the stream with the wife of one of the men to see what had happened to them. I found the bodies, as well as five people who were wounded but still alive . . .
>
> We buried the bodies two days after they were killed. We were too scared to bury them before that. We buried them in a field just near the stream by the bridge. It took two nights to bury them—for safety reasons we worked only at night. The first night, twenty to thirty people worked eight hours to bury them. The second night, about fifteen people spent four hours burying them.[11]

On July 6, the victims were provided a proper Muslim burial, after they were examined by British forensics experts working for the war crimes tribunal. According to the ICTY, seventy-seven bodies were exhumed from the site.[12]

CELINA (CELINE)

On March 25, hours after the NATO bombing began, Serbian and Yugoslav troops moved in on the village of Celina. Some villagers fled into the nearby hills, but hundreds of ethnic Albanians were trapped in the village. Over the next three days, more than sixty-five of them were killed, including twenty-two people from one family who were caught in a small ravine behind their house. ICTY forensic teams exhumed sixty-nine bodies in spring 1999.

Human Rights Watch researchers interviewed three witnesses to the abuses in Celina, each of them in a different place on a different date. Their testimonies are largely consistent with one another, and match press accounts from the village, as well as the human rights report from the OSCE.

All three witnesses, one of them an admitted KLA soldier, claimed they first heard tanks and heavy military vehicles near Celina around 1:00 a.m on March 25. Between 4:00 a.m. and 6:00 a.m., the village was being shelled.

Fearful for their lives, many men, some of them KLA fighters, fled into the surrounding fields and hills at this time. Women and children, including Albanians from the nearby villages of Opterusa (Opterushe), Zociste (Zozishte), Bela Crkva, Retimlje, Mala Hoca (Hoca e Vogel), and Brestovac (Brestoc), hid in basements and nearby caves. Government security forces entered Celina by 6:00 a.m.

All of Human Rights Watch's witnesses fled Celina on the morning of the 25th, and then returned to see the bodies of those who had been killed. One man claimed that he saw some of the killing while he was hiding near the village on a small hill. Interviewed at length at the Morina border post in Albania, where he was waiting for his family to leave Kosovo, the thirty-year-old man said that he had watched from atop the hill as government forces shelled the Celina mosque and burned the school. A former soldier in the Yugoslav Army (1986–1987), the man claimed that the commander of the forces was an

ICTY forensic teams exhumed sixty-nine bodies in spring 1999.

army major because he saw the stars on his shoulder and heard his subordinates calling him "Major." The government troops, however, seemed to be paramilitaries, he said. They were in green camouflage uniforms and had white bandanas on their sleeves.

The women and children of the village, together with the remaining men, were ordered outside their homes, where they were forced to hand over money and jewelry, the witness told Human Rights Watch. Many people were then sent into the basements of their homes, but some women were sent to Zrze.

Later in the day, the security forces left Celina, and the witness entered the village to see what had happened. He went first to his own home, where he saw that his father, two nephews, and two family guests had been killed. He said:

> My father was killed by a bullet through the nose. Another guy was killed by a bullet in the head, and the other by a bullet to the stomach. It was my father, two sons of my uncle, and two visitors from Celina and Bela Crkva. One of them had a bullet to the forehead, the other had a bullet in the back of the neck. I thought one of them might be alive, but we went back to hide on the hill.[13]

The witness stayed in the area over the next four days, walking in the hills around Nogavac and Mala Hoca, and sometimes going back to Celina when it was safe. The Serbian forces set up a local base in the house of Burhan Hasani, he said. During this time, he saw a number of dead bodies in the village, and witnessed some executions from afar.

First, he said, eight people were killed from the Dina family on March 25, although he only saw the bodies from the window of their house after they had been killed. "I just saw their bodies and the blood," he said. Then, on March 26, all of the remaining villagers were gathered in the center of Celina. Approximately fifteen men were separated from the group and forced to take off their shirts. One teenage boy was killed with a knife, he said, and then the rest of the men were killed by automatic gunfire and burned with gasoline. The witness said:

> I saw all the men were naked from the waist up. . . . The men were lined up next to a garage. Fifteen or sixteen men. I know them all, only three of them

> were guests—two from Hoca e Vogel [Mala Hoca] and one from Krusa e Vogel [Mala Krusa.] I saw them take their shirts off on the orders of the police. Then they took their money.
>
> They took one guy from the crowd. First they showed their knife. One of them licked the sharp side of the knife. Then one of them cut his throat. It was a long, black knife about half an arm's length, with a curved blade. The victim was Alban Rexhepi, thirteen years old. Then they killed the rest of the men.
>
> Using a small bucket full of gasoline from a car, they spilled fuel on the bodies. After the police left, I saw two other [ethnic Albanian] guys who witnessed the scene. I knew fourteen of the victims—we were related. All of them were burned. They were killed with automatic guns. One man—tall and bald—gave the order.[14]

This account was corroborated by an elderly couple from Zrze whose family members died in Celina, as well as by another witness statement given to the press. The elderly couple heard about the killings on March 27 and went to Celina to help with the burial. According to them, seventeen men had been shot and burned. "We saw all the bodies," the wife said. "You could see that they had been executed and then the bodies were burned."[15] In a *New York Times* article written from Albania during the war based on refugee accounts, one man says he saw fifteen people, most of them from the Rexhepi family, burned in Celina. "Their shirts were stripped off," said the fifty-year-old witness, and "gasoline was thrown on them, and they were set on fire."[16]

Later on March 25, when the security forces were not present, the witness entered the village to look for survivors. At that time, he saw more dead bodies in a field, although he did not remember exactly how many people had been killed at that spot. All together, between March 25 and 27, the witness claimed to have seen seventy-two dead persons in Celina, primarily from three families (two Albanian and one Roma): the family of Mytar Zeqiri, the family of Elki Zeqiri, and the family of Faik Saliu (Rom).

On March 28, security forces surrounded and captured the witness in the hills, along with a large group of ethnic Albanian men and women with whom he had been hiding. One man, Agim Ramadani (aged twenty-three or twenty-four) was separated out and executed, he said. Another man, Sakip Rexhepi, aged thirty-five, was taken and was missing as of mid-April, when the witness was interviewed. The group was then taken to Velika Krusa, where there was a military checkpoint. A mute man, Vefia Rexhepi (aged thirty-six) was killed near a pond along the way, and Nait Elshani (aged thirty-three) was shot closer to Velika Krusa, he claimed. The rest of the group was taken by bus to the border village of Zur, from where they were ordered to walk into Albania on March 28. The witness said he recognized the faces of three policemen, one of whom was from Velika Hoca.

The testimony above is largely corroborated by two other witnesses from Celina. One of them, a forty-four-year-old man interviewed in a refugee camp in Durres, Albania, told Human Rights Watch that he had fled Celina with his family in the early morning of March 25. Around 6 p.m. that day, the man went back into Celina with some other villagers to collect his three trucks. Although he did not see any of the bodies, women in the village told him that eighteen people had been killed and burned, and that members of the Dina and Myftari families had also been killed.[17] He said:

> When I went back, people told me that the Serbs had gathered eighteen people in one house, stripped them, and then burned them after pouring oil on them. A woman named Nerxhivan Rexhepi told me this, saying the people killed were from her family. Another man came and told me that the same had happened to the Dina family, where five people were killed. Another told of the same thing happening to the Myftari family, where sixteen people were killed. It was said that fifty other people were killed in Celina as well.[18]

On March 27, the man and his family were in the hills with a large group of Albanians, estimated at 10,000 to 15,000 people, from the area. The police and army in green camouflage uniforms with white bandanas surrounded the group, he said, and then separated out many of the fighting age men, who were then forced to strip. One youth of about twenty whose family name was Ramadani, was taken away and executed, he said. Although the witness did not know the victim's first name, the family name matches that provided by the first Celina witness, suggesting that they were in the same group in the hills. The second witness said:

The police and army in green camouflage uniforms with white bandanas surrounded the group.

> When about half of us were naked, they took a young boy away to the side. Two soldiers walked him away about fifty meters to a pit. They were wearing green uniforms and white bandanas. They made him kneel. Then they shot him with a pistol three times from behind. Then they said to us: "Make sure you give us everything you have or we'll shoot you like we did him." They wanted more money. All together, we must have given them 500,000 or 600,000 DM.[19]

The group was then forced to walk toward Velika Krusa. At a body of water between Velika Krusa and Kushaj village, some young men were forced to stand in the cold water up to their necks, he said. In Velika Krusa, the witness heard that two men had been killed, although he did not witness their murders or see the bodies. One of the victims, he heard from others, was a mute man named Vefair Rexhepi who was shot and then "fell into the water"—a statement that matches the testimony of the first witness. The other victim was Nait Kabashi from Obtorush, which is the same first name but a different family name from that given by the first witness. From Velika Krusa, trucks and buses took the group close to the Albanian border.

The third Human Rights Watch witness was a KLA soldier, interviewed in Celina after NATO's entry into Kosovo.[20] He showed Human Rights Watch a list of seventy-three people killed in Celina on March 25, as well as six people missing as of mid-June 1999.

The man claimed to have watched from a nearby hill on March 25 as Serbian police attacked and killed twenty-two members of the Zeqiri family in a small ravine behind their house. Only one thirteen-year-old boy survived, he said. The bodies were buried one month later. Another seven people were burned in a car on March 26, he said. Human Rights Watch was shown a burned car where the killings allegedly took place.

Press accounts largely corroborate the three witness testimonies provided above. In one article, a villager from Celina showed the reporter the spot on a path—"almost a tunnel, with overhanging brush"—where twenty-two people were killed; most likely the location where the Zeqiri family was killed. German peacekeepers in the area claimed that there were seventeen grave sites in the village.[21]

In the article, the man from Celina also claims that he was captured with other villagers in the woods on March 28, and "a few [men] were shot." Later, the man was forced to stand in a creek up to his neck before being taken by truck to near the Albanian border—a statement that matches the testimony of the second witness.

Another article by the same journalist mentions the killing of fourteen men in Celina on March 26. "There were fourteen males in that group," a witness said. "And I am the only one to survive."[22]

The human rights report from the OSCE, "Kosovo/Kosova: As Seen, As Told," also corroborates the general account of events. According to the report, one man hiding in the woods on March 25 watched as thirteen men were taken into a building, and then there was shooting from inside. The witness then claimed to have seen the police pile the bodies up and set them on fire.

Villagers from Celina also told the OSCE that they had been captured in the woods after the initial attack, and forced to walk to Velika Krusa, where trucks took them to Zur. Witnesses claimed that two men were executed during the walk, one of them a mute.[23]

VELIKA KRUSA AND MALA KRUSA (Krushe e Madhe and Krushe e Vogel)

Velika Krusa and Mala Krusa (Greater and Lesser Krusa) lie approximately one mile apart, on the border between the Orahovac and Prizren municipalities. Velika Krusa was a predominantly ethnic Albanian village with approximately 2,000 inhabitants, while Mala Krusa had a larger Serbian population, approximately 18 percent, according to the OSCE. The KLA was active in and around the villages throughout 1998 and 1999.[24] Journalists and members of the OSCE-KVM mission repeatedly saw and met KLA soldiers in the area.

The events in the two villages, the first massacres from Kosovo reported during the NATO air war, should be presented together since the two populations intermingled during the attacks. However, due to limited time and resources, Human Rights Watch only focused on Velika Krusa, where more than ninety men were killed, and interviewed eight witnesses who observed killings and other war crimes in that village. The events in Mala Krusa are only mentioned briefly in this section, even though more than one hundred men are believed to have lost their lives there. Both villages are mentioned in the ICTY indictment of Slobodan Milosevic and his four top officials.

As with most of the villages along the Prizren-Djakovica road, such as Bela Crkva and Celina, police and army units began shelling Velika and Mala Krusa in the early morning of March 25, between 3:00 and 5:00 a.m. By the next day, government forces had entered the villages. Witnesses from Velika Krusa described a combination of special police and army, wearing dark blue uniforms with "police" written on the back and green camouflage, respectively. Most of the forces had white arm bands, they said. Some of the men had painted faces and bandanas; some had long hair, other had shaved heads.

The KLA was not in the area at the time of the attack. In the chaos, most of the civilians attempted to hide in cellars or flee into the nearby hills and woods. Many civilians fled to the nearby village of Nogavac, where others from the region were also gathering.[25] Many people also gathered in the woods between Velika and Mala Krusa. Security forces began looting and burning many of the private homes on March 26, and they eventually captured the civilians who were hiding outside of the villages.

According to press accounts and the OSCE, the women and children in the woods were separated from the men and sent either to Velika Krusa or to the border with Albania. The men were marched into a Serb-owned house in Mala Krusa, where they were shot with automatic weapons. The victims, at least one hundred men, were then covered with hay and set on fire. ICTY forensic teams found only fourteen bodies in Mala Krusa, but reported clear evidence of grave tampering.[26] The building where the killings took place had been demolished with explosives. Human Rights Watch visited Mala Krusa on June 19, 1999, and found a large crater at the site where villagers said the massacre had occurred.

In Velika Krusa, more than ninety villagers were killed in various parts of the village between March 26 and March 28. Based on testimonies from eight witnesses, Human Rights Watch compiled a list with forty-three victim names. ICTY forensics teams exhumed ninety-eight bodies from three different sites in Velika Krusa, although some of those killed may have been KLA soldiers killed in combat.[27]

The victims, at least one hundred men, were then covered with hay and set on fire.

There is also strong evidence that government forces attempted to conceal the killings in both Velika and Mala Krusa by burning and removing some of the bodies. Witnesses in Velika Krusa saw the police removing bodies with trucks and army vehicles and dumping them in the river. NATO later found a truck in the river that had bones in the back. In Mala Krusa, the house where the men were shot, was set on fire and blown up.

Velika Krusa (Krusha e Madhe)

The precise details of the killings in Velika Krusa are not entirely clear since they took place at different times in different parts of the village. One man, for example, R.E., told Human Rights Watch that he helped bury three men killed in Velika Krusa: Selim Taha (aged approximately seventy), Daim Taha (aged approximately sixty-five), and Qamil Taha (aged approximately sixty), all of whom were killed on or around March 27. Qamil was found on the road leading out of the village, while Selim and Daim were killed in the gardens of their respective homes. R.E. also believed Bajram Hoti (aged approximately thirty) and a local teacher, Osman Sejfullahu (aged approximately fifty-seven), were also killed. R.E. did not see the

Funeral in Velika Krusa where more than ninety men were killed.

PHOTO BY ALBAN BUJARI

killings or the bodies, but found their identity documents lying in the road surrounded by lots of blood.[28]

Human Rights Watch first visited Velika Krusa on June 15, 1999, three days after NATO's entry into Kosovo. German KFOR troops were not allowing anyone near a roofless house in the village where bodies had reportedly been found. A German television journalist was able to take a look, however, and told Human Rights Watch that there were approximately twenty burned skeletons inside.[29] In total, ICTY teams found ninety-eight bodies at three different sites around the village, forty bodies, thirty-four bodies, and twenty-four bodies respectively. Although the tribunal has not made its forensic reports public, some individual investigators have spoken to the press. John Bunn, the head of Scotland Yard's forensic team that investigated Velika Krusa, said that the victims in the village had been shot in the back of the head at close range.[30] Pointing to a room in a burned house in Velika Krusa, Sue Black, a Scottish forensic anthropologist working with the same team said, "They herded people into there, shot them and set fire to the premises."[31] [Maybe use this part at the front of the section . . . to the end]

As stated above, there is also strong evidence that Serbian police tried to conceal the killing by burning or removing bodies. Villagers saw police dumping dead bodies into the nearby river. According to the OSCE, KFOR later removed a truck from the river, and bones were found in the back.[32]

The OSCE report is supported by a man from Nogavac, R.E., who helped bury many of the dead in Velika Krusa. He told Human Rights Watch that he saw the Serbian police removing some of the bodies:

> Four days after the killings, the Serbian police arrived with bulldozers, a truck, and some army vehicles. They collected corpses and took them away. We weren't able to film this. We don't know what they did with the bodies.[33]

According to witnesses in Velika Krusa who spoke with Human Rights Watch, on March 26, security forces rounded up all of the men, women, and children left in the village, as well as those they had captured hiding in the vicinity. The women were sent to the mosque and the men were separated into groups. S.G., a nineteen-year-old man from Velika Krusa, told Human Rights Watch what he saw after the security forces entered the village:

> They separated men from women and put the men in the garden of a house. They beat the men, including me. They killed two young men at the begin-

> ning, then they started bringing others away in small groups to kill us. But they let the old men and the very young men go. I survived because, when they asked me how old I was, I said sixteen. The let me leave with the group of old and young men.[34]

One man, R.D., who fled into the hills when the assault began, said the security forces separated the men into three groups. He did not see the separations while in hiding, but he found twenty-five bodies in various parts of the village over the next four days, five of which were burned.[35]

"I survived because, when they asked me how old I was, I said sixteen."

According to R.D., one group was sent to Nogavac, one group to the Velika Krusa mosque, and one group down the hill from the village. Of the group that was sent to Nogavac, he said, fifteen of eighteen people were killed. He did not see them being shot but found their bodies in a field at the edge of the village and then helped with the burial. The dead, he said, included Fahri Hoti (aged approximately thirty), Asaf Hoti (aged approximately twenty-six), Plahe Hoti (aged approximately thirty), Bajram Duraku (aged approximately twenty-eight), and two other unidentified members of the Duraku family.

Two victims were also found dead in the mosque, R.D. said. This was corroborated by another Velika Krusa resident who was held in the mosque and witnessed the shootings. He told Human Rights Watch that he had been put on the second floor of the mosque together with approximately forty other men from the village. The men were robbed of their money, he said, but allowed to go after spending one night in detention. As he was leaving, he saw two men shot. He told Human Rights Watch:

> I was about to leave the mosque. We were at the door when I saw them shoot two men less than ten meters away, and we heard them scream. I heard the shots, one shot for each, and I saw them fall. I didn't see why they shot them. But I think they thought they were KLA. The men who were shot were Besalet Krasniqi (aged between twenty-eight and thirty) and Bedri Sefulahu (aged twenty-six).[36]

Another Velika Krusa resident told Human Rights Watch that he was in a nearby field tending to his cattle when the attack began in the evening of

March 25. Someone told him that the villagers were gathering together for safety, he said, so he ran back to the village. On the way, he was shot at with what he believed was a shoulder-fired weapon, perhaps a rocket-propelled grenade. He was wounded by shrapnel in the leg and right buttock—wounds that were observed by Human Rights Watch in Albania eight days after the attack.

"Their bodies fell on top of me. Their blood was in my face . . ."

The man hid in a private house for the night together with four other villagers. The next day, March 26, the five men were captured by police and taken to the center of the village, where most of the other villagers were gathered. According to the witness, the security forces separated out forty men, and then shot them with automatic guns. "They shot them with machine guns, like this," he told Human Rights Watch, while making a motion of shooting a machine gun. "It happened right in front of me."[37]

One man from Velika Krusa, whose two brothers were killed, told Human Rights Watch that seventeen men had been killed and burned, although he did not witness the killings. It is not clear whether these seventeen men were a part of the forty killed men mentioned above. There was one survivor, the man told Human Rights Watch: S. H.

S. H. was featured on a television documentary on Kosovo produced by the British program Panorama called "The Killing of Kosovo." In the show, the survivor is shown lying in a hospital bed with bandages covering most of his body, including his head. He is severely burned but able to recount what happened to him in Velika Krusa:

> They fired at us with Kalashnikovs. As the shots sounded, I fell to the ground. The others were all killed. Their bodies fell on top of me. Their blood was in my face . . . Another policeman brought the petrol. And they sprinkled it over the dead bodies and set fire to it. After that, I knew I had to act fast or I would be burned alive.[38]

S.H. escaped the fire and eventually made it out of Kosovo to Albania.

Evidence of the killing in Velika Krusa was also provided by a local water engineer, Milaim Bellanica, who filmed some of the dead in the village on April 1, and then managed to smuggle the video out of Kosovo by hiding it underneath a tractor. Broadcast on the BBC on April 4, the footage was heavily edited because of its graphic content. It shows dead men in civilian clothes, who have apparently been shot in the head or under the jaw. In the Panorama documentary, Bellanica said he saw sixty-four corpses in Velika Krusa, of which he was able to identify twenty-six by name.

The Yugoslav government denounced the film and allegations of a massacre in Velika Krusa as "a new propaganda bomb" by the West which was using "the worn-out scenario of monstrous lies and loathsome accusations."[39]

Mala Krusa (Krusha e Vogel)

Press accounts and the OSCE report on Kosovo, as well as indirect testimony provided to Human Rights Watch, provide some details on the killing in Mala Krusa. According to the accounts, approximately one hundred men were captured in the woods outside of the village on March 26 and forced with their hands above their heads into a barn in the village. They were then shot with automatic weapons, covered with hay, and set on fire.

Human Rights Watch interviewed one man, a resident of Nogavac, who said that two survivors of the Mala Krusa massacre stayed at his house in Nogavac for approximately one week, beginning a few days after the killing. The man, R.E., said:

> Two survivors of a massacre near Krushe e Vogel [Mala Krusa] lived with me for seven days in my house. About one hundred young men were killed. It wasn't done by the same Serbs as those who killed people in Krushe e Madhe [Velika Krusa]. I've forgotten the name of one of the survivors; the other is P. R. The first guy had a burned face.
>
> P.R. told me that the men were separated from the women and placed in a one-story house, half of which was filled with hay. First the Serbs killed the men with a burst of automatic weapon fire, then they set fire to the house. These guys were lucky to fall under the dead bodies. P.R. escaped without being hurt but his brother was killed. One of his cousins was killed when he tried to escape. Only ashes are left of that house.
>
> P.R. arrived at my house at 4:00 p.m. on Friday. He was almost unconscious, walking in a complete daze, in shock. Some of his hair was burnt but otherwise he was physically okay. He said that the Serbs and Albanians used to live together in his village. The massacre was committed by masked neigh-

bors; he recognized some of their voices. In Velika Krusa, it was Arkan soldiers.

The other survivor, P.R.'s friend, arrived about two days later. We didn't have time to go back to Krushe e Vogel [Mala Krusa] and bury the bodies. We were again forced by the Serbs to leave our homes.[40]

According to an article in the London *Observer* by John Sweeney, eight men survived the shooting in Mala Krusa and tried to run away. Two were shot during the attempted escape, but six survived.[41] The article, which was further developed into a television documentary, also claimed that the survivors recognized some Serbian neighbors from the village among their killers.

On April 3, 1999, CNN aired an interview with an alleged survivor of the executions, M.K. With bandaged hands and his face covered with burns, he said on camera, "They rounded up all the villagers. Then they separated men from women. To the women they said, 'You may go to the border'... But they put us men in two big rooms and started to shoot us. They said, 'Now NATO can save you.'"[42]

M.K. said that the Serbian forces then covered the bodies with straw and lit them on fire. He escaped when they left to get more gasoline, and eventually made it out to Albania, where he was interviewed by CNN.

An earlier article on Mala Krusa by Sweeney presents another witness who claims to have seen Serbian forces burning between fifteen and twenty bodies in Mala Krusa and dumping them into the Drini River on March 27, although this might be the same incident mentioned above regarding Velika Krusa. While hiding in the woods near the river, the witness told Sweeney, he saw "the Serbs pour some liquid into the back of the lorry. Had they just been setting the lorry on fire, it would not have been necessary to do that. Then the lorry started to burn. It burnt all night. Had the lorry been empty, it would not have burned for so long."[43]

ZRZE (XERXE)

Zrze is a small village at the strategic junction of the Prizren-Djakovica road and the road to Orahovac. Before the war, it had approximately seven Serbian families. The police station was responsible for some of the surrounding villages, including Bela Crkva, Celina, Velika Krusa, Nogovac, Potocane (Potocane) and Sopnic (Sapniq).

With one notable exception, the police and army apparently did not bother the ethnic Albanian residents of the village during the last week of March and all of April, and very little of the village was destroyed. On the contrary, villagers from the area, such as Bela Crkva, were sent to Zrze and allowed to gather there (see section on Bela Crkva). Albanians ran some basic shops during the NATO bombing and were not prohibited from giving food and water to the thousands of internally displaced Albanians who passed through Zrze on their way out towards Albania. Some refugees in Albania told Human Rights Watch that the villagers of Zrze helped them during their expulsions.

On and around May 4, however, the villagers and internally displaced Albanians who were seeking shelter in Zrze, were all forcibly displaced. Some people were robbed or had their identity documents destroyed along the way.

The police and army also had a checkpoint near Zrze, perhaps to screen the tens of thousands of ethnic Albanians who were being deported towards Albania. Witnesses from Mitrovica, Pec, and other locations in Kosovo reported seeing beatings at the checkpoint, and some killings. Upon entry into Kosovo in June 1999, ICTY forensics teams exhumed eighteen bodies from around the village.

The army and police arrived in Zrze on March 25, the day after NATO bombing began. They occupied a grain storage facility, from where they had wide views southward down the valley towards Velika Krusa. Snipers from the top of the grain elevators were considered a threat by villagers, and one man was said to have been killed, although his death remains unconfirmed.

Police stole cows and lambs for meals during their stay, villagers said, as well as many local cars and trucks. And some Albanians were charged fines by the police when they used the local roads. The wheat warehouse was also allegedly used as a collection point for looted goods from the area. Villagers said they saw the police bringing many valuables, such as television sets and satellite dishes, into the warehouse, and then transporting them away in stolen trucks.

For the most part, the abusive police were not from the area. Villagers in Zrze said that the local police, run by a man named Zvonko, were not violent, and at times they even helped protect local Albanians from the police and paramilitaries that had come from other parts of Serbia. One man claimed that, about one month before the NATO bombing, Zvonko helped get him released from a police interrogation.[44] One woman said that, during the bombing, the local police were "helpful." She said:

> The regular policemen actually helped us, but when the other policemen came, the local police said they couldn't help us. . . . The regular police did not levy fines, but the others would fine us every time we would go on the main road. They [the regular police] also helped us to avoid executions of people by other policemen and soldiers.[45]

On May 4, police and soldiers began going house to house at the edge of the village robbing local Albanians. The villagers were given one hour to pack their things and head for Albania, which all of them did. No violence was reported during this time.[46]

The only serious violence reported in Zrze prior to the expulsions was the alleged rape of a local woman on April 5. Human Rights Watch interviewed two people who testified that a twenty-two-year-old woman, whose name is being withheld, was sexually assaulted by unknown Serbian men. One man staying in Zrze during the war, who was originally from Bela Crkva, told Human Rights Watch that he saw the woman, a relative of his, taken by an "army captain," although it is not clear if the perpetrator was in the army, police, or paramilitaries.

"They caught her by the hair and put a gun to her head, and they told her husband that she was theirs."

> She [the alleged victim] is twenty-two and very beautiful. The army captain said: "This woman is not yours anymore." It was on April 5 in the morning. They entered the house and grabbed her. They caught her by the hair and put a gun to her head, and they told her husband that she was theirs. An old man [name withheld] went to the soldiers' house to try to get her back but it took him an hour to get her. She was very traumatized when she returned. She fainted and she was sobbing. She's still ill. She said that the police threatened her. They said that Albanian women are very strong—so strong that they can have sex with the whole Serbian army. She faced all sorts of insults; she was in shock and was very reluctant to talk about it. We were afraid she had been raped, but we asked her and she said no.[47]

In a separate interview, a woman from Bela Crkva who was sheltering in the same house in Zrze talked about the alleged rape of the same person, claiming that, after the attack, the woman wanted to kill herself. She said:

> In Zrze, the Serbs grabbed a woman and put a knife to her throat, and they kept her for one hour. Her name is [same as witness above, but withheld to protect the victim]. She is tall and very good looking. She told the women that she had been raped. She kept saying she wanted to kill herself. She was married and was chosen by the Serbs in front of her husband. They pointed a knife at her and tried to kiss her, while she tried to escape. They said, "if anyone makes a move, we're going to kill you." Nobody dared to move. We had to put our hands up. She was the most beautiful woman in the whole area . . .
>
> When she returned, she was in shock, crying and crying. She wanted to kill herself by sticking her fingers in the light socket. She couldn't talk. We couldn't leave her alone because we were afraid she would kill herself. She cried for hours and pulled her hair out. That evening she told her mother-in-law that she had been raped. It happened on Wednesday, about a week or so ago.[48]

13

SUVA REKA (SUHAREKE) MUNICIPALITY

Suva Reka town, with approximately 10,000 inhabitants (90 percent ethnic Albanian), and its surrounding villages were continuous areas of conflict in 1998 and 1999. A KLA presence in the hills around the town made the region a regular target of police and army actions. Many villages suffered killings and the destruction of civilian property at the hands of the police before the NATO intervention.[1]

During the NATO bombing, most of the abuses in Suva Reka took place in the first week when many residents were expelled and a series of killings took place, as reflected in the chapter Statistical Analysis of Violations. Thousands of people were either deported to Albania, some by bus, or they fled into nearby areas controlled by the KLA, such as Djinovce (Gjinoc) and Budakovo (Budakove).[2] Looting and burning of civilian property was widespread.

Former employees of the OSCE and those who had rented their homes to the OSCE were under particular threat. The most serious incident was the killing in Suva Reka town of at least twenty-four members of the extended Berisha family, including eleven children aged sixteen or younger, which had rented two houses to the OSCE. In Trnje village, six kilometers southwest of Suva Reka, at least twenty-four people were killed, including seven children aged fifteen or younger.

According to the Suva Reka office of the Council for the Defense of Human Rights and Freedoms, 430 people were killed in the Suva Reka municipality during the bombing, and sixty-seven people were missing as of late August 1999.[3] The KLA-appointed mayor after the war, Haki Gashi, said that 427 people had been killed in the municipality, although approxi-

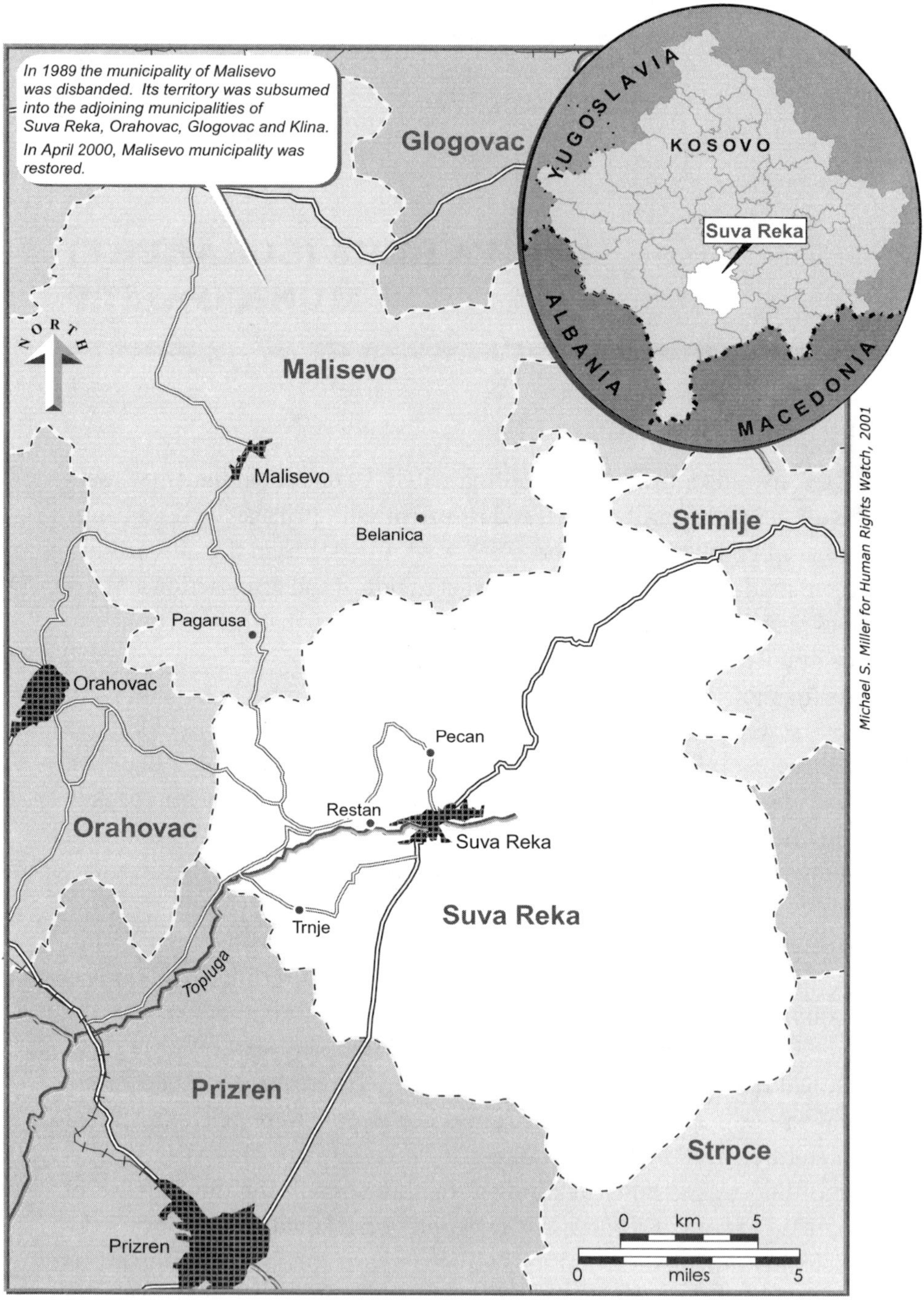
In 1989 the municipality of Malisevo was disbanded. Its territory was subsumed into the adjoining municipalities of Suva Reka, Orahovac, Glogovac and Klina.
In April 2000, Malisevo municipality was restored.
YUGOSLAVIA
KOSOVO
Suva Reka
ALBANIA
MACEDONIA
Glogovac
NORTH
Malisevo
Malisevo
Belanica
Stimlje
Pagarusa
Orahovac
Pecan
Restan
Suva Reka
Orahovac
Trnje
Suva Reka
Topluga
Prizren
Strpce
0 km 5
Prizren
0 miles 5
Michael S. Miller for Human Rights Watch, 2001

mately eighty of these people had been KLA soldiers.[4] Human Rights Watch did not confirm these numbers or clarify whether KLA soldiers killed in combat were distinguished from those summarily executed (the latter, no less a war crime than deliberate killings of civilians.) Aside from the forty killings in Suva Reka town documented in this section (all of them on March 25 or 26), Human Rights Watch confirmed the deliberate killing of eleven male civilians and the rape of at least two women in one village (which will remain nameless to protect the victims and their families), the killing of at least twenty-four people in Trnje village, and at least twelve killings in Belanica, a village where tens of thousands of displaced Albanians had assembled. According to the OSCE, killings of smaller numbers of people also took place in the following villages: Bukos (Bukosh), Budakovo (Budakove), Vranic (Vraniq), Geljance (Gelanc), Sopina (Sopine), Musutiste (Mushtishte), and Lesane (Leshane).[5]

Former employees of the OSCE and those who had rented their homes to the OSCE were under particular threat.

The war crimes tribunal exhumed three grave sites in Suva Reka town containing 103 bodies. One of them contained fifty-five bodies, and the other two contained fifteen and thirty-three respectively.[6]

According to witness testimonies, most of the abuses in the municipality were committed by Serbian police or paramilitaries who were said to have worn a variety of uniforms, either blue, grey, or green. Some wore black masks, while others had long hair. And many of them, witnesses said, wore white bandanas around their arms. A name mentioned as a leader of local forces by at least four witnesses was "Misko" Nisevic, who was well known in Suva Reka town as the owner of the Hotel Boss and, more importantly, the local head of state security.[7]

The police station in Suva Reka was under the Secretariat for Internal Affairs (SUP) of Prizren municipality, which covered Prizren, Orahavac, Gora, and Suva Reka (see Forces of the Conflict). As of February 1998, the chief of the Suva Reka police station was Lt. Dobrivoje Vitosevic, and Sub Lt. Radojko Repanovic was his deputy.[8]

Interestingly, after the first wave of Albanians were expelled from Suva Reka in late March, the police generally allowed Albanians to stay in the town. There was even an attempt to register people at this time, and men were obliged to report to the police station once a day.

SUVA REKA (SUHAREKE) TOWN

The OSCE presence in Suva Reka (November 1998 to March 1999) helped provide a sense of security for ethnic Albanians in and around the town. Predictably, abuses increased around March 20 when the OSCE withdrew from Kosovo. Some skirmishes between the KLA and police took place in the villages around Suva Reka, and Serbian police harassed and beat some ethnic Albanian residents. Tension increased on March 22 when at least seven ethnic Albanians were killed by the police or "disappeared" in unclear circumstances.

More serious violence began after the first NATO bombs fell on March 24. Serbian police and paramilitaries took up positions around the town and systematically forced residents to leave, witnesses said. The police organized buses for some people for deportation to the border with Albania. One resident of Suva Reka, a journalist, told Human Rights Watch:

> After the first bombs, on March 25, in the early morning we heard shots from guns and one armored vehicle from the Berisha neighborhood. We heard the news that they had massacred them [the Berisha family] while some were still sleeping. There was panic among the population, and [there was a rumor] that a part of town should move to the other part, on the other side of the road. We stayed for two days, and I saw fire and smoke. We even saw fire and smoke from the Balkan rubber factory. We think they burnt people there, because of the smell.
>
> Two days later, on March 27, Serb paramilitaries came to the other side of town, looking for some people by name, and they burned some houses where the OSCE had been staying. The population got scared, in every house there were about a hundred people. When they came to twenty or thirty meters away from us, I said: "Let's just go and leave town."

The worst incident involved the families of Nexhat and Faton Berisha, who had rented their adjacent houses to the OSCE. Between twenty-four and forty-two people from the Berisha family were killed, six of them in front of their homes and the others in a shopping center near the town's center. Two women and one male child survived.

According to a family member who lived next door and witnessed the incident, the police first arrived around 5:00 a.m. on March 25 and demanded money from Nexhat and Faton Berisha. The police beat Nexhat and took any equipment the OSCE had left behind. The witness said he recognized one of the policemen as Miki Petrovic, brother of Zoran Petrovic, whom another witness claimed to have seen in the area. The witness described how the police came again the next day and shot members of the family:

Between twenty-four and forty-two people from the Berisha family were killed.

> At 12:00 noon another group of police came back, some twenty to thirty, and surrounded these two houses [of Nexhat and Faton]. We were in touch with them by telephone. Both families were in the house of Faton in the night of the twenty-fifth and twenty-sixth. They came and knocked on the door, and took all the people outside. I was watching from my window. The women and children passed by our house, the others were near the house of Nexhat. At one point, they called the men—Sedat, Bujar, Nexhat, Nexhmedin and Faton, and Fatime, the mother of Faton. Without any sign, they just started to shoot at them, with a burst of gunfire. Some people went into the houses and set them on fire. I again recognized Miki Petrovic, but I didn't recognize any of the others. I got upset when I saw how they killed members of my family. The others started to run down to the shopping center. I didn't know then the destiny of the rest of the family, I just heard a lot of shots.
>
> They were in new police uniforms, with white bandanas around their arms, and shaved heads. I didn't see Zoran Petrovic, but Flaka[9] said that she saw him. The house of Faton and Nexhat was burned, it is only two to three meters away from mine. I was afraid that it would also catch my house. I was thinking to go out, but the snipers were waiting for us. At that moment, I heard a lot of shooting and there was a lot of fire, but I didn't know what was happening. We went with six children in the toilet, put handkerchiefs in the mouth of the kids, we were afraid the Serbs would hear us. The police had taken the six bodies and put them behind Nexhat's house, but when the roof started burning, pieces fell down on them and they burnt. It burnt until the evening. As a doctor[10] I couldn't believe bodies could burn that much.
>
> I stayed in the house until after 6:00 p.m., when the police came in the house and wanted to burn it. They were in groups of three policemen, and went from house to house. They opened the door, they didn't know we were

> inside, so I went and opened the door for them. At first he wanted to shoot me at once, but I talked in Serbian with him. My brother gave 1,000 DM, so they released us. We took our cars, and we all went to Albania: five adults and six children.
>
> When I arrived in Albania, I found out that the rest of the family had been killed as well, Flaka told me. They put them in one cafeteria in the shopping center. There was the family of the sons of my uncle, and three other families. These families went out of the house because they were scared, and they wanted to go to the other side of town through the shopping center. They caught them, and put them in the cafeteria. First, they threw some grenades in that place, and people who survived were killed with guns. Flaka, Mirela and Arben[11] survived, but were wounded. Later, they brought a truck, and put them all on the truck, and went towards Prizren. People who saw the truck saw blood dripping down to the road. Flaka, Mirela and Arben jumped off the truck near Ljutoglav. People who were there took them to the doctor of the KLA. In total, forty-eight people were killed in half an hour.[12]

The OSCE's report on Kosovo includes information provided by one of the survivors, Flaka. She said that on March 21, the police questioned her husband as to why he had allowed the OSCE to stay in his house. On March 25, as the witness above testified, the police visited her home around 5:00 a.m. They beat her husband unconscious in her house (the above witness was not able to see this) and stole any goods of value left by the OSCE.

According to her testimony in the OSCE report, the police came again on March 26. She explained how, after shooting some of her relatives in front of the house, she and a group of other uninjured family members were chased to another part of town, where they were forced into a cafe. Citing her testimony, the report states:

> Around midday on 26 March the police came again. A policeman she knew (and named in the interview) called her brother-in-law's son outside and shot him dead. The police screamed at them and when the families ran outside they found their house "under siege" from police, Serb civilians and "Gypsies" (Maxhupet). Some of the family were shot dead immediately. The interviewee was among a group of other family members who were chased to a different part of the town, apprehended and pushed into a café.
>
> She saw the police shoot every person in the room with machine-guns

> and rifles. She had her four children—two girls aged sixteen and fourteen and two sons aged ten and two years old—gathered around her. They were all killed. She was trying to protect her two-year-old son with her legs but he was shot and died.[13] She was also hit in the abdomen with a bullet that had passed through her elder son's body. She encouraged him to pretend he was dead but as the perpetrators collected the bodies and took them outside they saw that her eldest son was still breathing and shot him again. She heard him cry out once. At least twelve children under age seventeen were killed and ten adults including a pregnant woman. The interviewee pretended to be dead as the police removed all valuables from their bodies. . . . She was placed in a truck on top of other bodies including the children. On the way towards Prizren she jumped from the truck and was found by people who took her to UCK-held territory where her wounds were treated. She then spent some time moving around Kosovo avoiding the shelling. She left Kosovo on 9 May.[14]

The OSCE report also states that two witnesses saw a truck full of dead men, women and children "on or around March 26" drive into the garden of the high school, where the bodies were set on fire, although neither the OSCE nor Human Rights Watch confirmed that these bodies were those of the Berisha family. Serbs, whose names were recorded by the witnesses, were repeatedly seen unloading the bodies.[15]

"They were pointing their guns at our chests, and demanded money and gold."

Other killings took place on March 25 in the neighborhood where the Berisha family lived. One woman, N.E., who lived a few hundred meters from the Berisha house, explained how security forces entered her home and executed her son, Fadil (aged twenty-six) and brother-in-law Medi (aged fifty). She said:

> We woke up at 5:10 a.m. on Thursday, March 25, because of gunshots. We went to the door, and saw they were in the house of our neighbor. Right away, some of them came to us. In total, there were seven of us, but only two men: Fadil and Medi. They came inside and asked the owner: "Where are the children?" They caught my son Fadil and the brother of my husband, Medi, and started to body search them. They were pointing their guns at our chests, and demanded money and gold. We gave them all we had. They took Medi, a lawyer, in another room, and asked him something. They brought him back,

then they took Medi and Fadil in another room. They started shooting in front of our feet, and told us to get out of the house.

We didn't see them being shot, but we heard the shots when we were still in the house. There were eight of them [police], and two of them went into the room with them. With us, there were four inside, and two at the door. They started shooting [at us and at them] at about the same time. They had green camouflage uniforms, white bandanas, and knives. They didn't have masks. I didn't recognize any of them, but I remember the one who gave the orders. He was short, had a black hat, he was dark skinned, a little bit fat, no moustache or beard, about thirty-five to forty years old. They spoke in Serbian, but outside, when they started to insult us, they sometimes used Albanian words. Neither Fadil nor Medi had fought with the KLA. Medi has worked in court, and later worked in the Balkan factory. Fadil was a mathematics teacher.[16]

Another female family member who was in the house at the same time confirmed N.E.'s account and then found Fadil and Medi's bodies when she returned to Kosovo in June. She said:

We left Medi and Fadil, and went to Semetishte, and then on to Albania. When I came back from Albania, I saw signs of the bodies inside the house, there was hair on the floor. We found the body of Medi on August 29, and buried him yesterday. He was in a graveyard on the road to Restan. People of KFOR took Medi's body out, together with some others. Fadil was found two weeks ago in a graveyard on the road to Pecan.[17]

In describing another incident, a woman told of four policemen coming to her home, shooting her uncle and, apparently, her father. She told Human Rights Watch:

On March 25, about 7:00 a.m., we were staying in this room. There were ten of us in the room, only two men, my father Avdyl (aged forty-seven) and my uncle Osman (aged forty-one). At first, they [the Serbs] were staying outside near this window. Then they broke the door, came in, and told us to go outside. But at the door they stopped us and asked if there was someone upstairs. First they had taken money from my uncle.

There were four Serbs: one inside, one at the door, one in the yard, and one at the gate. They had masks, gray uniforms, no camouflage, patches,

> white bandanas on the arm with nothing on it. I didn't recognize any of them. They took us outside, separated my uncle and he was shot in the yard. My sister is an invalid, and my father was carrying her. We went on the road to Pecan. They gathered other people from the neighborhood. They stopped us near the school, a few hundred meters away from our house. The put us all in a [unfinished] building without a roof. We stayed there, and they told my father to put my sister Aferdita (fourteen) on the ground. They told all of us to get out of the building, and kept my father there. Me and my sister carried Aferdita. They told us to go to the KLA, and we don't know anything else anymore. After about ten meters, we heard shots from the building. We had to go on to Pecan. They later found the body of my uncle in the graveyard of the Berisha family. We don't know what they did to my father.[18]

Yet another woman, whose daughter was among those killed with the Berisha family (see above), explained how two other members of her fam-

Serbian police forced Myrete Berisha, aged thirty-five, and her three children to leave Suva Reka at the end of March. After four days on the road in a convoy of tractors, she arrived safely at the Morina border crossing with Albania. She was interviewed by Human Rights Watch in Kukes, Albania on April 26, 1999:

"I had tried to hide what was going on from my son. My son was afraid when the police were shooting. He was saying that they're bad police. I'd say, "no, they're good police; they're just trying to kill some birds, because the birds steal corn from us. It's better to kill the birds." I'd make up anything. When he asked why he had to sleep with all his clothes on—he was hot—I'd say, "It's better to do this because we may leave at night to find a better house, and it will be cold out." He asked, "Why do we need a better house?" I explained that we needed a better bathroom—we didn't have a very nice bathroom—that we'd get a nice house with a nice bathroom like grandfather has. Of course now, at the Italian refugee camp, he complains, "Why did you tell me that we were finding a good house; I want to go back to Suhareke [Suva Reka]; our house was better; we have no bathroom here," on and on."

ily, one of them a mechanic for the OSCE, were killed by armed Serbs that same day:

> At 5:45 a.m. on March 25, we woke up from gun shots. I woke up, my husband Raif (aged fifty-seven) was still sleeping. I went upstairs to see if there were police at the school or not. I didn't see any of them in the streets or the school, but I heard a lot of gunfire. I went down again, and I heard the gun shots coming closer to us. I woke my husband up, and we discussed what to do. I proposed the attic, but he said no, they can burn the house. We discussed whether we should go to the attic or the basement.
>
> My husband was still dressing when they came inside the yard. There were a lot of them in the yard, and a lot of them in the street. About twenty in the yard, maybe more. They had grey uniforms, white bandanas, I didn't see any masks. They were screaming, and asked for the owner of the house. My husband went out to speak with them, but they didn't let him speak. They asked: "Do you have children inside the house?" My husband started to scream to us: "Get out!" When I went out, I saw my husband lying on the ground, I don't know why. They took me to him, and told my husband to get up. They told both of us to put our hands in the air. They didn't allow him to say anything. They pointed a gun at us, and I begged them not to shoot us, we were innocent.
>
> They were talking through a walkie-talkie. They kept us for five minutes, and then one of them said: "Go away, women!" I went to the house of my brother-in-law Kadri, and when I got there, I saw Mina, Kadri, and Bardhyl [family members] in a line with guns pointed at them by twenty Serbs. When they saw me, they told me to get in the line. They didn't know the others had released me. Mina and I started to scream: "Don't shoot at us!" But Bardhyl and Kadri didn't say anything. Mina wanted to save her son Bardhyl, so she gave 1,000 DM and a gold necklace. She said: "Please, just release my son!"
>
> One of them started to scream that we had to go away. One policemen came and took us outside the gate and onto the street. When we went onto the street, we heard shots, but we didn't see it happening. They told us to leave for Semetishte. They only spoke Serbian. Later, they found the bodies in the house of Bardhyl.[19]

Human Rights Watch spoke separately with Bardhyl H., aged twenty-six, who confirmed the above account. He added his personal story, which included hiding in a basement for twenty-eight days, during which time he kept a journal:[20]

> The day after NATO started bombing, before 6:00 a.m., we were surrounded by the police. We were sleeping, my father, mother and me. They [Serbian security forces] came up the steps, and were in the yard. One of them on the steps started to scream: "Come on, open the door, fast!" I was in the bedroom on the first floor, my parents were in the living room. When I went out from the room, I saw my parents in the hallway. I ran down and opened the door. One of them was in front of the door, and he pointed a Kalashnikov at us. We went out with our hands up. For twenty minutes, they abused us in the yard, asking all kinds of questions and pushing us.

"Mina wanted to save her son Bardhyl, so she gave 1,000 DM and a gold necklace."

> We had two cars in the garage, and they told me to open the doors and they took the car keys from me. In the meantime, they had brought my uncle and his wife here, after about fifteen minutes [see above testimony]. They separated us men, and told the women to get out of here. My mother started to beg them: "Please release my son!" Before they had been checking the house, and my mom gave them money, about 1,000 DM.
>
> But they started to push the women to leave. After the women left, they took us up the steps to the house and started to shoot at us. We jumped into the hallway, and fortunately I was not hit. I managed to go up the stairs and went to the attic. Both my father and my uncle were hit and killed. When I went upstairs, the house of my uncle, which is connected to ours, was burning, and they shot with a gun to burn our house as well. I stayed in the attic for ten to fifteen minutes, but the house was burning, so I jumped from the balcony and went into the yard of my uncle. I went inside a little shed, which was not burned, and stayed until the evening. Then I went into the basement of the house and stayed there for twenty-eight days. The first ten days, it was difficult to get food, I just ate sugar and jam from the house. And I found some baby food I ate. It was hard to get water. After ten days, I found a gas can in the house of my neighbor, and I could make pancakes, french fries etc. For water, I went down in the well with a plastic canister of three liters and took water. During the night, I sometimes went out in the yard, but during the day the police were in the streets. After that, I went outside, and went to the area where there were still people from Suva Reka.

> There were twenty to thirty Serbs, probably paramilitaries, in the yard [on the day of the killing]. It was not regular police. My mother says the uniform was black, but I think it was dark blue. They had white bandanas around their arms, and all of them were young, seventeen or eighteen years old. They had no masks, no insignia, and nothing written on the bandanas. There were no signs at all. They had Zastava cars. I didn't see any other weapons, just automatics. They only spoke Serbian to us.
>
> The bodies stayed here for a long time, I don't know how long. None of us were ever in the KLA, my father was a quiet man, he never hurt anybody.[21]

"The first ten days, it was difficult to get food, I just ate sugar and jam from the house."

A male resident of Suva Reka told Human Rights Watch how Serbian forces killed at least ten other men in another incident on March 25. He said:

> The day after NATO bombing, at 6 a.m., Serb paramilitaries, police and Serb civilians entered Albanian homes. The police went from house to house, gathered the men, and brought them to a house maybe thirty meters away from my house. We managed to escape. When they asked for money and gold, Fadil Berisha gave them 200 DM, but it wasn't enough, and they shot him. Ahmet Kryeziu (aged fifty-four) gave them 500 DM, but he was killed anyway by the same guys. Abdullah Elshani (aged approximately forty-two) and Osman Elshani (aged approximately thirty-three) were also gathered and brought to the same place. Again, they gave money, then they were shot. In total, ten or eleven people were killed this way in this house. I was in our yard, maybe twenty or thirty meters away. There were four or five men wearing ordinary police uniforms, carrying machine guns.[22]

Exactly how many people were killed in Suva Reka town on March 25 is unclear. But based on the testimonies in this report, at least forty people were killed, including eleven children aged sixteen or under and seven women.

After March 29, many of Suva Reka's residents were allowed to stay in the town. Ethnic Albanians interviewed by Human Rights Watch reported continued harassment, looting and burning, but no serious physical maltreatment during this time. The authorities distributed registration cards to the

Albanian residents and ordered the men to report to the police station once a day. Food was available at Serbian-run stores. One woman originally from Recan, X.X. (initials altered) said that, around the beginning of May, she was in the village of Shtime:

> We stayed there one night, and they [Serbian police] gave us biscuits and cakes. Then they told us to go to Suva Reka and go to houses that were not burned yet. We stayed in Suva Reka for one week. We didn't have any problems there. All men had to report every day to the police station. They were told not to accommodate any refugees or KLA people. We got a registration card in Suva Reka. The Serbs told us we could walk freely, but that we should be careful of bombing. But only men walked in the streets; the rest didn't go out. There was not sufficient food in Suva Reka, only the food we found in the house. There were no shops anymore, they've burned them all.[23]

"At least forty people were killed, including eleven children."

Some Albanians, however, were expelled from Suva Reka around May 21, some of them on buses organized by the police. The witness above, X.X., told Human Rights Watch:

> Yesterday [May 21] at 9:00 a.m., they told us to leave. My husband went to the police station as usual, and that's where they told him we should leave. All people in Suva Reka had to leave, but they were all people from surrounding villages. We went to the main road, and there were three buses waiting that took us to Zhur. We were treated well in the bus, there were no problems. At the border, they took 50 DM from me.[24]

BELANICA (BELLANICE)

North of Suva Reka town, Belanica is a small farming village with three hundred families and an estimated 3,000 people, all of them ethnic Albanians, set amidst bucolic orchards and vineyards. The houses are spread around a large grassy field, with a school and medical clinic in its center.

The villagers in Belanica had to flee their homes on a number of occasions during the government's summer 1998 offensive. At least one villager is known to have died at this time when he returned during the shelling to care for his livestock. Otherwise, the villagers were generally spared direct violence, even though the KLA was active in the area.

That changed with the onset of NATO bombing. Over the period of a few days, tens of thousands of ethnic Albanians, most of them displaced from nearby villages, gathered in Belanica, where they were harassed, beaten, and robbed by Serbian police and paramilitaries, before being expelled to Albania. There are strong allegations of rape, and more than two dozen men from the Belanica area are believed to have been killed.

Belanica is a unique case in the Suva Reka municipality since both the KLA and the Serbian forces allowed Albanian civilians to congregate there. The KLA told civilians who were fleeing the shelling of their villages that Belanica was safe. Meanwhile, Serbian police and Yugoslav Army soldiers also directed the internally displaced towards the village because, they said, there was no fighting there. Somewhere between 12,000 and tens of thousands of ethnic Albanians, depending on the witness, crammed into the village, most of them huddled together with their tractors in the central field. Shortly thereafter, the police and paramilitaries attacked the village, which suggests that Belanica might have been used by Serbian forces as a gathering point for the internally displaced to expedite their expulsion from Kosovo, as well as the looting and robberies that accompanied the "ethnic cleansing."

Villagers in the Suva Reka municipality began to flee their villages due to police harassment and attacks just after the OSCE departed Kosovo on March 20. By March 24, the commencement of NATO bombing, thousands of refugees had fled to the hills and forests due to government shelling or fear of attacks. Many gathered in Pagarusa village where the KLA was located.

Refugees testified to Human Rights Watch that the KLA directed them to Belanica beginning around March 25. Thousands went to Belanica on March 31 when Pagarusa was shelled. One eighteen-year-old woman from Duhel told Human Rights Watch:

> We stayed four nights in Pagarusa, beginning on the night of March 26. When they [government forces] began to shell the village on March 31, people began to flee. Many shells fell; I couldn't even count them. Two women were killed by the shelling, one from Banja village in the Malisevo district and one from Decani.

> We left Pagarusa for Belanica on March 31. We went to Belanica because the KLA told us to go there; they said there was no shelling there. But it seems this was also the army's goal; they wanted us to concentrate there, and that's why they didn't shell it.[25]

By March 31, at least 12,000 displaced ethnic Albanians were in Belanica, according to one person who was present, most of them women, children, and elderly, since the men of fighting age had fled into the hills. Most other witnesses claimed the number was much higher, even up to 100,000 from the surrounding villages. The most authoritative journalistic research on Belanica was conducted by John Daniszewski from the *Los Angeles Times*, who interviewed more than two dozen villagers from Belanica and the surrounding area, and published a series of articles that focused on one family. In one of his articles, "The Death of Belanica," he estimated that 80,000 people from fifty different villages were in Belanica.[26]

According to the article, on the evening of March 31, a KLA soldier warned those in Belanica that the KLA was retreating, leaving it open to attack. An estimated 1,600 more young men fled into the hills.

The details given in the article closely match the testimony of twenty witnesses interviewed by Human Rights Watch, both in Albania when they were refugees and back in Kosovo in August. According to most of the testimonies, the government's attack began on April 1, although three people said it began on March 31. Around 6:00 a.m. on April 1, most witnesses said, shells fell on the lower end of Belanica. By early afternoon, Serbian troops dressed in blue and black uniforms, some with ski masks and others with face paint, entered the village, shooting wildly into the air. Tanks and armored vehicles roared into the center of the village.

One witness originally from Dobrodeljane (Doberdolan) claimed that the police tried to register some of the internally displaced. According to the witness, the Serbian forces said that no one would be hurt and that people could go home after the registration process, although the police did shoot at a few young men who were trying to escape.[27]

The most common police and paramilitary activity was robbery.

All of the witnesses, however, agree on what came next: terror and banditry at the hands of the Serbian police and paramilitaries. Many men were beaten over the next few days, they said, and an unknown number were killed in the village.

The most common police and paramilitary activity was robbery. Every person interviewed said that the government forces demanded money and jewelry from men, women, and children in return for their lives. Deutsche Marks were demanded to save a person's life. When people could not pay, they were killed. One woman told Human Rights Watch:

> They kept coming up to the tractors. It was mostly women and children on the tractors. They would come up and do things like pull the pin from a grenade and say, "I'm going to drop this in there with you if you don't give me some Deutsche Marks." They would also grab the children by the throat and pull out a knife, saying, "We'll kill the kid if you don't pay up."[28]

Another woman told Human Rights Watch:

> I heard lots of screaming, lots of gun shots. They hit people when the people refused to give them money. The police kept coming up and saying "Give us money or we will kill you." People with no money had no way of saving themselves.
>
> At one point, the police came up to a man on the tractor in front of me. They said, "Give us money!" He didn't have anything for them. He was from Ostrozub (Astrazup) village. So they pulled him off the tractor and killed him. When he didn't give them anything they [four policemen] pulled him off the tractor by his arms and legs. They brought him around to the back of a house, then I couldn't see him anymore. I heard shooting and I could see one of the policemen aiming his gun and firing. The man didn't come back to his tractor.[29]

Yet another woman said:

> The people who were killed had no money. The soldiers wouldn't accept [Yugoslav] dinars; they demanded Deutsche Marks. I saw a woman with her wounded son. A policeman came up to her and said, "Give me 1,000DM or I'll kill him." She pleaded with others to giver her money so that she could pay the policeman, and she got some. Her son was not killed.[30]

One fifty-three-year-old man originally from Duhel said that he saw the police kill five people. He told Human Rights Watch:

> The scariest part was that the Serbs were shooting in the air and my children were scared. I saw them killing five people about fifteen meters away from me. They were asking the victims for money. They didn't have money, so the Serbs shot them dead. I don't know the people who were killed.[31]

One woman, H.S., explained how the police took away her seventeen-year-old son, Ifraim, and demanded money for his return. She said:

> After the registration, they came to the tractors and demanded money. I had met a relative and was in their tractor. They took my son of seventeen, Ifraim Shala, away and took him to a basement. They said: "Your son is in the KLA, you have to give us money or we'll kill him." I had to give them jewelry to get my son back. They kept him for one hour in the basement, and came four times to ask for money and jewelry before the let my son go. They threatened me, and said: "Whore, give me all your money." They beat up my son when he came out of the basement. They beat him with the butt of a gun. In total, they beat him three times.
>
> They also did this to other people. They just roamed around the crowd, asking for money. When you gave money, they left, but then came back again, and asked again for money. This continued several times, until there was no more money, and then people got beaten. I saw several people get beaten. They wore blue uniforms, and some of them black uniforms, with black bulletproof vests with [Cyrillic] letters on the back. Some had masks, you could just see the eyes.[32]

Human Rights Watch interviewed two other men who were taken for brief periods into the basement of a house in Belanica. Both of them were interrogated about the KLA, threatened with death, and beaten, but eventually released.

H.S. also witnessed the security forces shoot three men because they did not have any money. She said:

> In the light of the tractor, I saw two men from Marali [Moralija in Serbian] in a tractor with a trailer maybe two tractors away from mine. The same three masked men who had asked us for money came to them, and asked for money. They grabbed them by their clothes, and demanded money. The men said they didn't have any money. Then they shot them with a small gun,

> you could barely hear the shooting. One of the men was around fifty, the other around thirty-five. I heard that others were killed as well, but I haven't seen that. Those who had money were told to leave, those who didn't were stopped and beaten up. We heard gunshots all the time, and threats, like: "You asked for NATO, so go to NATO, go to Albania."[33]

One woman, aged seventy, gave detailed testimony about how the police broke into her home and killed her seventy-seven-year-old husband. The elderly couple had decided to stay in their home with a young child, she said, because they were too tired to go into the field:

> We put on a fire and tried to warm up some food. As we were sitting there, four or five men suddenly came in. My husband can't see so well; he didn't know they were soldiers. He said to them "Welcome!" and then offered them cigarettes. They knocked the cigarette pack from his hand. Then one of the soldiers shot him in the arm. Then they shot him again, this time in the chest. My husband said, "Oh, mother," and fell on the ground.
>
> There was a small child with us in the house; they kicked him, but didn't kill him. Then they went to the second floor, searched the house, and told me to leave. There was a tank nearby; as I was leaving the house, they fired a shell at the building. The house was destroyed.[34]

Another witness, a journalist from Belanica, said that he saw the police shoot a mentally handicapped and deaf man because he did not give them money. He said:

> Just minutes before we left, in the house of my cousins, they killed Agim Bytyqi, a retarded man from Nishor [Nisor in Serbian], who was between thirty-eight and forty years old. I saw it happen. I was only twenty to thirty meters away. He couldn't talk, he was deaf and dumb. I think they were asking him for money, and when he didn't answer, they shot him with a burst of gunfire from an automatic gun.[35]

Lastly, two different witnesses, interviewed seperately, reported the killing of two men from Moralija village (Marali) in Orahovac municipality, Osman and Bekim Vrenezi. One witness, a cousin of the two men, told Human Rights Watch that the police took Osman and Bekim away, claiming that they were in the KLA. He said:

> At 4:00 or 5:00 p.m., they took two of them, Osman (aged twenty-seven) and Bekim (aged fifteen), and said they were members of the KLA. They asked for money, but we didn't have a bank with us, and we didn't have any money left to give. They had all of our money, 2,500 Deutsche Marks and gold. We were without money. They kept saying that they were KLA. Then they took them away, and we didn't see what happened. We were afraid to leave our family. The KLA later found them [dead] in Belanica.[36]

The other witness, a man from the same village but unrelated to the family, claimed to have seen Osman and Bekim Vrenezi get shot, ostensibly because they did not give enough money to the police. He told Human Rights Watch:

> At 7:30 p.m., two people from my village, Osman Vrenezi, twenty-seven years old, and Bekim Vrenezi, sixteen years old,[37] were killed. They asked them for money. They had 900 Marks, but they wanted 1,000, which they didn't have. I heard the shots, and I saw them fall down.[38]

It is not clear how many people were killed in Belanica since the Albanians came from such a wide range of villages. All together, witnesses cited in the *Los Angeles Times* article claimed to have seen twenty-two people killed, although this is not presented as a total figure for the village. Human Rights Watch confirmed twelve killings based on twenty witness interviews, although at least one of these is also mentioned in the *Los Angeles Times* article.[39] A follow-up article by John Daniszewski cites the mayor of Belanica, Gani Zogaj, as saying that thirteen men from the village were killed.[40] According to the war crimes tribunal, three bodies were found in the village.[41] Again, since the victims came from the surrounding area, relatives may have taken their bodies away for burial.

Human Rights Watch confirmed twelve killings based on twenty witness interviews.

Human Rights Watch also heard serious allegations about rape in Belanica, but was unable to document any specific cases. Ethnic Albanians suggested that rape had taken place, but they were unwilling to speak about it. The *Los Angeles Times* article also mentions how gunmen threatened women with rape. One witness claimed that two women were taken into an abandoned house and raped, but this allegation remains unconfirmed. Other women are in the article as reporting sexual harassment, such as security forces making them take off their shirts to check for money.

Beginning April 1, the Albanians in Belanica were ordered to leave the village, and many of the homes were set on fire. Convoys of tractors and people on foot were sent in two directions: south to Suva Reka town, Prizren, and then Morina on the border with Albania, or northwest to Malisevo, and then to Orahovac, Zrze, Prizren, and Morina. Police and army units were very present along all of the roads, witnesses said. Some Albanians were forced to stay for twenty-four hours in Malisevo until the Malisevo police organized three buses and many trucks to bring the people to Zur village near the border.

Some men were detained by security forces during the journey to Albania. One man from Belanica explained how four men were taken on the road between Malisevo and Ostrozub (Astrazup), three of whom were later found dead. He said:

> We went from Malisevo to Ostrozub, where they stopped Shaban Zogaj, the son of my neighbor, and took him away. They hit him with the butt of an automatic gun, and he was lying down on the asphalt. Then they told us to leave, and we didn't know what happened to him. When we came to Orahovac, they took three young guys: Sami Zogaj (aged twenty), Sali Zogaj (aged thirty-three), and Elmi Zogaj (aged nineteen). [We heard] they were shot on April 5. We later went to take their bodies in Orahovac and reburied them here [in Belanica].[42]

Human Rights Watch interviewed Shaban Zogaj's father about the incident. As of August 19, he had no information about Shaban's whereabouts or condition. He said:

> In Ostrozub, I was with the tractor, and two tractors and a truck were behind me with my family. When we left Ostrozub, near the INA gas station, they stopped my tractor again, and took my son Shaban (thirty-three) from the tractor. I didn't see it happen, I was in front of him. I asked someone if they [the rest of his family] were coming, and someone said no. I stopped my tractor, and waited. When they came, I asked my [other] son: "Are all of you here?" My son said: "Father, they have detained Shaban." I went to the truck, and asked my family if we had any money left. We had 2,000 DM. I took the money, and went back. My son Ismail told me not to go. But I said I wanted to go. He tried to stop me but he couldn't. So my son started to swear and

> said: "Please don't go, we already lost one [family member], I don't want to lose another." But I went, and my son came behind me, and said: "Don't go, it's over. They hit him and he was lying on the asphalt." But I didn't want to stop. I came very close, but then the police told me: "Your son is now our son, and we know what we will do with him." They brought me back. I tried to give them money, but it didn't help. I went back [to my family] and we went on. It is hard to leave family behind, it would have been better if I had seen him being killed. I don't know what happened to him. Since I've come back [to Kosovo], only five days ago, I haven't tried to find him. Tomorrow I'll go to Istok, where they are digging up graves.[43]

Human Rights Watch also interviewed a family member of the three other Zogaj men who corroborated the story. Elmi, Sami, and Sali were taken off their tractor in Orahovac, the witness said, and the family was forced to move on. He told Human Rights Watch:

> We left them in the hands of God. They killed them five days later. We found them on June 19 in the graveyard of Orahovac. We exhumed all three bodies, and we recognized them from their clothes. Sali had been beaten in Belanica and his jawbone was broken. He was executed at close distance. He was shot in the head. Sami was also shot in the head. Elmi was shot in the chest. Their jackets were all covered with bullet holes.[44]

VILLAGE IN THE SUVA REKA MUNICIPALITY[45]

On April 21, Serbian security forces surrounded a small village in the Suva Reka municipality that will remain nameless due to the nature of the crimes that took place there. All of the village's men fled into the hills except for eleven older men who stayed behind with between 200 and 300 women and children. All of the eleven men were killed and thrown into a village well. The women were held for three days in private houses, where some of them were sexually abused and raped.

Human Rights Watch first learned of the abuses in late April while interviewing refugees in northern Albania. At that time, the women of the village reported being held for three days in private houses by Serbian forces. Two of the women interviewed openly acknowledged having been raped, while witnesses gave Human Rights Watch the names of four other women whom they believe were sexually abused.

As refugees in Albania, the women told Human Rights Watch that the police had taken away eleven elderly men. Some women claimed to have seen one of these men lying dead near the road as they were marched out of the town on April 24, but they didn't know who it was. One elderly woman testified that she had overheard the police talking about how they had killed the men and thrown them into a deep well. The other men were missing, they said.

All of the eleven men were killed and thrown into a village well.

When Human Rights Watch visited the village on August 1, different villagers confirmed that the same eleven men mentioned by the women had been killed. The men were thrown into a village well, which was then mined. Forensics experts from the war crimes tribunal discovered twelve bodies (a twelfth man was killed on May 5).

According to villagers in the area, the KLA had been active in the Suva Reka municipality throughout 1998 and 1999 in the Petrovo area, with a base in Budakovo. During the NATO bombing, the KLA was also in the village of Lanishte (Llanishte).

The police first came to the village on April 5, villagers said. They demanded money and jewelry at this time, and burned some of the homes, but they did not directly abuse any of the village inhabitants. According to the OSCE report, the villagers prepared a local guard in anticipation of another government attack.[46]

The police surrounded the village again in the early afternoon of April 21. The men of the village, including some people from nearby villages, fled into the hills to join the KLA. A large number of people from the villages east of Suva Reka gathered near Lanishte, where the KLA was based. There was fighting in the area for three days, one witness said, leaving sixty Albanians injured and two dead, as well as five Serbian policemen killed.[47] According to the Serbian Ministry of the Interior, nineteen policemen were injured in "terrorist attacks" in the Suva Reka municipality between April 22 and 24, although it is not clear whether they were injured in the fighting mentioned by the witness.[48] After three days, the KLA sent the civilian population, as many as 10,000 people according to one witness, to Petrovo. Some civilians went to Racak.

The only people with direct knowledge of what occurred in the village after April 21 are the women and children who remained there, and their

Serbian captors. According to survivors—Human Rights Watch spoke with twelve women—the police captured all of the 200 to 300 women and children (including fifty women from nearby villages and the eleven elderly men) in a field. The men were searched and taken away. The women were divided up randomly for confinement in three private houses.

During this time, the women were repeatedly threatened and harassed. The police demanded the women place their money and jewelry in a bucket that was passed around. When the booty was inadequate, one witness said, a policeman held a knife to a three year-old boy, saying that he would kill him if the mother didn't produce gold or money.[49] Certain women were ordered to cook and clean for the Serbian forces. Some were forced to have sex with their captors.

The two rape victims interviewed by Human Rights Watch were held in the same house, which was crowded with frightened women and children. Women held in other houses described similar conditions. One of the victims described how she was sexually abused on two occasions, during one of which she was raped. At approximately 4 p.m. on her second day of captivity, she said, she was "chosen" from among a large group of women by a man in a green camouflage uniform. The man took her to another house and raped her. She told Human Rights Watch:

"He had sex with me: he did whatever he wanted."

> [The rapist] said "come here." He took me away from all the women and did whatever he wanted with me. He was small, about forty or so, dark-skinnned, a Gypsy. The Serbs have recruited Gypsies. I knew he was a Gypsy because of the way he looked: they're black, dark-skinned. There's lots of them in Suva Reka. He was in a green camouflage uniform, the same as the Serbs, with red stripes on the shoulder. . . .
>
> The Gypsy took me to another house, about five minutes' walk away. He was alone with me for half an hour or an hour. He had sex with me: he did whatever he wanted. It was a cousin's house. We left around 5:00 p.m [50]

The following day, another man demanded she go with him to a different house some ten minutes' walk away. According to the woman's account, the man did not tell her where he was taking her or why, but instead pushed her forward with his gun when she started crying.

The house was full of members of the Serbian security forces, she told

Human Rights Watch. They asked her questions, using a mixture of gestures and very basic words to communicate, as the woman hardly understood Serbian. They asked her age, whether she had any children, and the whereabouts of her husband. They asked her for money. When she told them that she had none, they ordered her to take off her clothes. She started crying and pulling out her hair, which made the men laugh. They put on some music.

After she took off her clothes, the men approached her one by one as she stood before them naked. She told Human Rights Watch that all of them looked at her, then they left her alone in the room with the man she believed to be their commander and another officer, who was naked on a bed. The victim was made to lie on the bed with the officer who, she said, touched her breasts but did not force her to touch him. The commander, whom she recognized as such because he had gold stars on his cap and had issued orders to others, reclined on his back about ten feet away. "I kept crying all the time and pushing his hands away," she said. "Finally he said to me, I'm not going to do anything. The commander just stared at us."

After approximately ten minutes, the other soldiers returned to the room and, still nude, the woman was forced to serve them coffee. She was then ordered to put her clothes back on and clean up. She picked up the dirty cups and dishes and swept the floor, she said. Then she was returned to the house with the other women. When the others asked what had happened to her, she refused to tell them.

The second rape victim told Human Rights Watch that the police took her away from the house where she was being held and brought her to another house. There she was placed in a room and forced to strip naked. One after the other, five members of the Serb forces entered the room to look at her body, but it was only the last man who raped her, she said. While he was assaulting her, the other four entered the room and watched. The woman also stated that someone had placed a walkie-talkie under the bed in the room, and that throughout the ordeal the Serbian forces shouted at her via the walkie talkie to scare her. In all, she was held in the room for about half an hour. She explained:

> Five soldiers came into the room where I was naked, one by one. Only the last one had physical contact with me; the others just looked, and said to me: "If the others ask, say that we had contact." Each one spent a few minutes with me.... The last guy stayed longer than the others. After a while the other

guys burst into the room and found us having sex; they stayed and watched. I was in the room no more than a half hour.[51]

Other women held in the village told Human Rights Watch that they had seen or heard other women being taken by the Serbian forces during their three days in captivity. One elderly woman said that, on the third night, the police entered one house shining a flashlight in the faces of the women, many of whom were trying to cover their heads with their scarves. They found one woman and said, "You come with us." She returned approximately two hours later and, when asked what happened, said, "Don't ask me anything."[52]

Human Rights Watch spoke with a doctor from the United Arab Emirates refugee camp in Kukes, Albania, where the refugees from the village were staying in late April. He said that three other women from the village had come to him on April 27 to report that they had been raped. The doctor said that one of these women showed obvious signs of severe emotional distress.[53]

She returned approximately two hours later and, when asked what happened, said, "—Don't ask me anything."

On Saturday, April 24, all of the women in the village were forced to walk to a nearby village, where they were held in the local school for two days and two nights without food or water, although no one reported further physical abuse. On April 26, the Serbian Red Cross came and provided the women and children with milk, bread, and canned food. The group was then taken in two buses to the village of Zur, where they were forced to walk across the border into Albania.

The residents of the village returned to their homes on June 16. Human Rights Watch visited the village on August 1. Only two of the twenty-eight houses were not damaged in some way, mostly by fire.

Villagers told Human Rights Watch that twelve men in total had been killed in the village. One of them was killed on May 5 in a field. The eleven others were all killed on or around April 21. The names provided were exactly the same as those provided to Human Rights Watch by the female refugees in Albania. Their ages, from forty-nine to ninety-one, also matched. Furthermore, the villagers said, all eleven bodies were found in a local well, which was also mined. Human Rights Watch saw the freshly-dug graves of the eleven men on the edge of the village. According to her

November 10 report to the UN Security Council, ICTY prosecutor Carla Del Ponte said that forensics experts had discovered twelve bodies in the village.[54]

According to the villagers, the first government forces to arrive in the village were in blue or green uniforms. On the second day, however, they were joined by armed men in green uniforms believed to be army personel. Many of the men had brown armbands; some perpetrators had long hair and beards and others wore black ski masks. One of the policemen, a witness said, had black hair with a dyed yellow streak in front. One of the rape victims said that most of the Serbs in the house where she was taken were carrying foot-long knives on their belts.

TRNJE (TERRNJE)

Human Rights Watch spoke with three eyewitnesses to a mass killing on March 25 in the village of Trnje, six kilometers southwest of Suva Reka town. Interviewed separately, the witnesses reported direct knowledge of between twenty-four and thirty-six killings at the hands of security forces in green uniforms, and the total number may be higher.[55] One of the witnesses saw Serbian forces taking away the bodies four days later.

All three witnesses, two from Trnje and one originally from Studecane, testified that government security forces entered the village around 6:00 a.m. on March 25. It appears that two houses on the edge of the village were targeted. One witness, I.G., a survivor of the shooting in his house, told Human Rights Watch:

> Two police came inside the house, and inside the living room, and eight or ten were outside with guns. The police who came inside told us to go outside. They didn't even allow us to put on our shoes. I went out, and saw the other policemen [in our yard], and lots of police outside the gate, and another group of police coming from the direction of the school. The other police were standing at the wall, pointing their automatic guns at us. They told us to sit down, and we all sat down in a line, my father was the last one. My father came to me and said he would go inside the house, but when he went two other policemen inside the house shot him in his neck and killed him.

> Then one of them came to me, and asked me where the men were, because there were only three men, and the rest were all women and children. From their pocket they took out some insignia or emblem of the KLA, put it in my mouth, and told me to ask for NATO. Then they hit me with the butt of a gun in the back of my head. They broke my skull, I was operated on [later]. I fell down, and lost consciousness for a moment. When I opened my eyes again, I saw a line of eight policemen who started to shoot at us with an automatic [gun]. Only two of us survived, me and my cousin N. B. from Studenqan [Studencane]. One third young kid survived for thirty hours, but then he died. I was not hit. After they killed everyone, they burned three houses. Only one room was okay.[56]

The man later left his house to look for other people in the village. In the house of the Voci family, he saw Ali Voci lying dead. At the house of a relative, he saw Shemsi and Votim (a seven-year-old child) also lying dead. In total, the man believes that thirty-six people were killed on March 25 in the village, and another nine were killed thereafter during the war. But he was only able to provide the names of twenty-four victims.

Witnesses reported direct knowledge of between twenty-four and thirty-six killings.

Human Rights Watch spoke with another survivor, N.B., who corroborated I.G's account.[57] He said that he had come to Trnje to be with his family because there had been shooting and shelling in his home village of Studecane since the OSCE left on March 20. He explained how, in Trnje on March 25, one of the men in green uniform was holding a KLA patch in his hand and demanding to know who was the owner of a house. It was this man, N.B. said, who gave the order to shoot:

> The man with the [KLA] emblem in his hand gave the order: "Shoot!" In one second, they started to shoot, and we all fell down. They hit me in my left hand.[58] I saw it was all covered with blood, and I couldn't move it. After I fell down, I heard one shot—they were shooting at me because I was moving. But the bullets didn't hit me. I stayed like that for three to five minutes, and when I didn't hear anything, I stood up. I saw that one child about nine years old was still moving. I went to my car, about five meters away, and at that moment I.G., who was on the right, stood up. He was all bloody on his head and neck. We asked each other where we were hit, and we saw that the others weren't moving anymore.[59]

The third witness was in a different house from N.B. and I.G. This seventy-one-year-old man saw security forces—he did not know if they were police or army—enter the village on the early morning of March 25. They came inside the gate of his home, he said, and burned the stable. Between ten and twelve armed men then came inside his house. They threw a hand grenade, he said, but no one was injured.

"I knew they came to take the bodies."

The forces then went to other houses in the village, including that of I.G. After some time, the witness left his home to look around. He saw the dead bodies of Shemsi Gashi (aged forty), the wife of his son (name unknown), and Votim Gashi (aged seven). Some people were killed in another house, he said, including Barie Gashi, Ajmane Gashi, and Besarta Gashi, all members of his family, as well as Rahime Voci (aged fifty to fifty-five), Ramadan Krasniqi (aged seventy-three), Refie Kransiqi (aged forty-eight or forty-nine), Behjare Krasniqi (pregnant, aged twenty-three or twenty-four). Two hundred meters away were the bodies of the witness' nephews, Shaban Gashi (aged thirty-eight) and Hamzi Gashi (aged thirty-five), as well as those of Muhamet Krasniqi (aged sixty-three), and Refki Reshaj (aged forty-nine). Finally, Haki Gashi (aged seventy-three) was killed in the street and Mehmed Limani (aged fifty-five) was killed in the witness' yard.[60]

On March 29, four days after the killing, N.B. claims to have seen Serbian forces removing the bodies from Trnje in a truck. He said:

> Early in the morning I heard a truck come from Leshane [Lesane in Serbian]. I heard them stop, and they opened the metal doors, and I knew they came to take the bodies. I heard when they put them in the truck, and I heard the Serbs complain about the smell. They put them all in, and went back to Leshane. They also burnt the car, my tractor, and another room where Musli was.
>
> In the evening, I went out into Musli's yard, and saw that they had taken all the bodies, there was just one child's jacket left in the yard. I didn't see anyone in the village, and I didn't know what to do. I decided to go to Mamushe, where the people from Studencan were hiding. I arrived at midnight, but the people were afraid to take in refugees, so I stayed two nights in the mosque. Then people from Pagarushe came, and we took a truck and went to Albania. We put up a white flag to show we had surrendered.[61]

14

VUCITRN (VUSHTRRI) MUNICIPALITY

Located in north central Kosovo, Vucitrn municipality had a prewar population of approximately 90,000 people, 90 percent of whom were ethnic Albanians. Serbs were located primarily in the town of Vucitrn and a few surrounding villages. Since early 1998, the KLA had been present in the Cicavica mountains, which run parallel to the main road and railway line between Mitrovica and Pristina. Numerous KLA attacks along that stretch were recorded throughout 1998 and early 1999.

On February 25, 1999, the Yugoslav Army began what it called "winter exercises" in the Vucitrn area. As the OSCE later reported, the exercises were in fact an army operation to clear the road and rail links north into Serbia by pushing the KLA back into the mountains, which it did.[1]

Vucitrn town was shelled the day NATO bombing began, and thousands of residents were expelled in that first week of the air campaign. On April 3, buses were organized to send residents to Macedonia. Another wave of forced expulsions took place around April 15.

Sporadic incidents took place to the northwest and southwest of Vucitrn during the bombing, although most of the civilians had fled the area due to ongoing fighting. By the end of April, many displaced persons had gathered in Veliki Kicic (Kqiqi i Madhe) to the north of Vucitrn. On May 2, they were forcibly dispersed in different directions.

Tens of thousands of ethnic Albanian displaced persons gathered throughout April in the Shala region of the municipality, where KLA forces were present, to the north and east of Vucitrn town. A government offensive in late April and early May succeeded in breaking through KLA lines in the north of the region near Bajgora (Bajgore) and Meljenica (Melenice) vil-

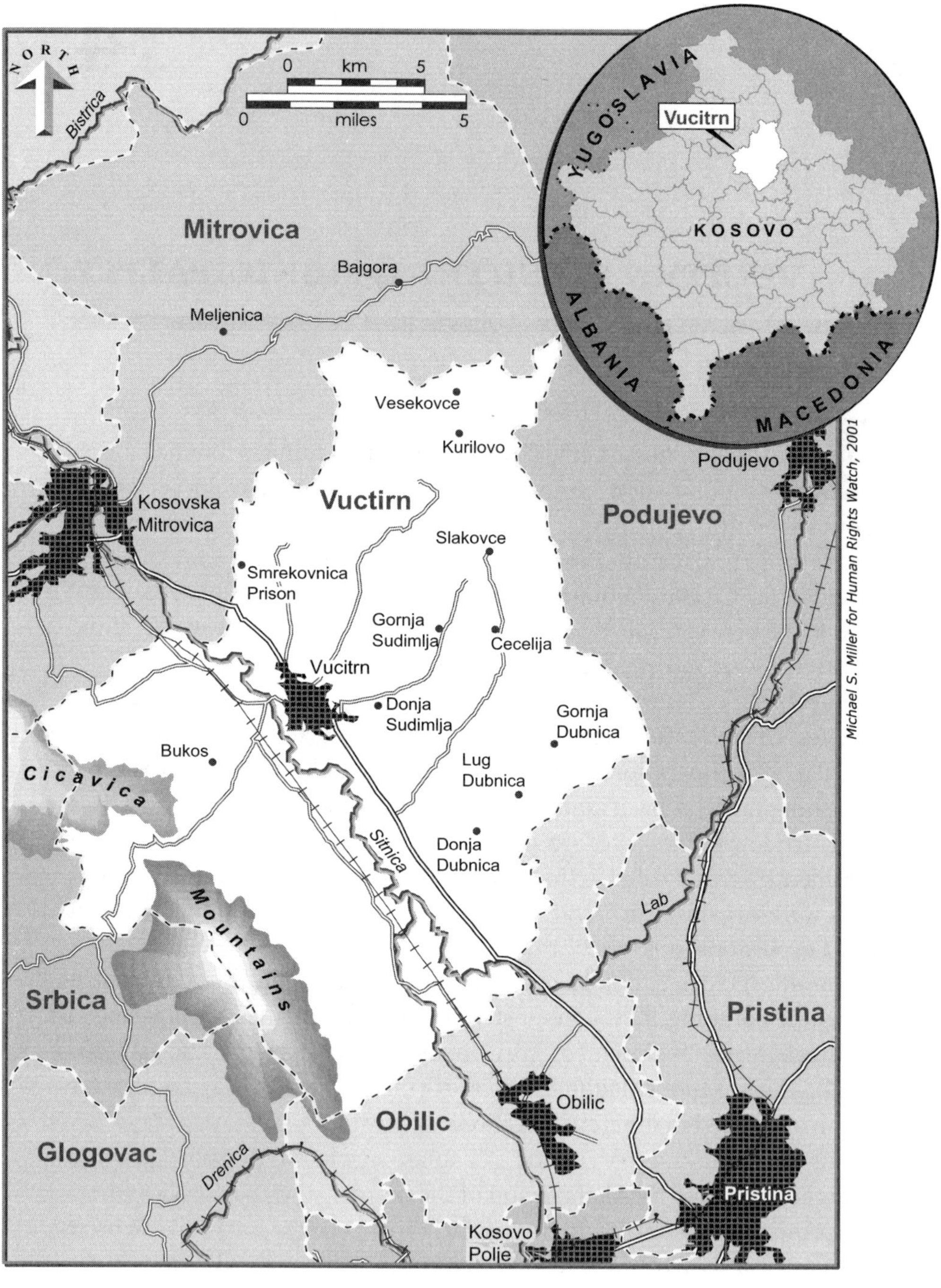

NORTH
0 km 5
0 miles 5
Bistrica
Mitrovica
Bajgora
Meljenica
Vesekovce
Kurilovo
Vuctirn
Kosovska Mitrovica
Slakovce
Smrekovnica Prison
Gornja Sudimlja
Cecelija
Vucitrn
Donja Sudimlja
Gornja Dubnica
Bukos
Lug Dubnica
Cicavica
Sitnica
Donja Dubnica
Mountains
Srbica
Obilic
Glogovac
Drenica
Kosovo Polje
Pristina
Podujevo
Lab
YUGOSLAVIA
Vucitrn
KOSOVO
ALBANIA
MACEDONIA
Michael S. Miller for Human Rights Watch, 2001

lages. Displaced persons fled primarily in two directions: east toward Podejevo or south along the Slakovce River.

Police and paramilitary forces caught up with the convoy that traveled south. On May 2 and 3 between Gornja Sudimlja and Donja Sudimlja (Studime e Eperme and Studime e Poshtme), police and paramilitaries killed an estimated one hundred men, as described below. Random executions, including the shooting of twelve people from one family, took place in and around the villages during May. In total, forensic teams from the war crimes tribunal discovered ninety-eight bodies in Gornja Sudimlja. According to Vucitrn residents and U.N. employees in Kosovo after the war, another mass killing of sixty-nine men took place in Vucitrn town on May 22, although this incident is not documented in this report. The ICRC recorded sixty-nine men missing from Vucitrn on that same day, although it is not clear whether these are the same men reportedly killed.[2]

Also covered in this chapter is the treatment of ethnic Albanian men held in Smrekovnica prison in the north of the municipality. Most of the men, more than 3,000 according to the OSCE,[3] were expelled from Kosovo in late May and early June with reports of physical abuse in detention.

GORNJA SUDIMLJA AND DONJA SUDIMLJA (STUDIME E EPERME AND STUDIME E POSHTME)

The May 2 Convoy Attack

While in Kukes, Albania, during the NATO bombing, Human Rights Watch researchers interviewed six Kosovar Albanians who had witnessed the attack on the convoy near Gornja Sudimlja. Interviewed separately, they provided consistent accounts of how Serbian police and paramilitaries pulled ethnic Albanian men from a convoy of tractors, and then shot some of the men in their custody.[4] Subsequent interviews were conducted with ethnic Albanians from the area who had been taken from the convoy and held in detention (see section on Smrekovnica prison). Finally, in August, Human Rights Watch visited Gornja Sudimlja and Donja Sudimlja and interviewed an additional nine villagers, who corroborated the first witnesses' versions of events and provided further details.

According to the interviewees, Serbian forces ordered a group of ethnic

Albanians from the town of Vucitrn and the surrounding villages to leave their homes at the end of March and the beginning of April. Five buses took ethnic Albanians to the border with Albania at this time. Some ethnic Albanians were allowed to stay in the area around Vucitrn until May 2, while others had to move several times because of ongoing small arms attacks or shelling by Serbian forces.

Ultimately, many displaced persons ended up in villages to the northeast of Vucitrn that were under the marginal control of the KLA, such as Bajgora, Vesekovce (Vesekofc), Kurilovo (Kurillove), and Slakovce (Sllakovc), where the KLA had a field hospital. The area became overcrowded, and several witnesses reported that they stayed in houses with more than one hundred persons, while others were forced to sleep outside.

Government forces broke through the KLA's front line near Bajgora and Meljenica, forcing those sheltering in the area to flee.

In the beginning of May, Serbian and Yugoslav forces launched an offensive and shelled several villages in the region around Bajgora. On May 2, government forces broke through the KLA's front line near Bajgora and Meljenica, forcing those sheltering in the area to flee.[5] A convoy of refugees set out southward towards the villages of Slakovce and Cecelija (Ceceli), where they were joined by other ethnic Albanians who had sought refuge in those places. At that point, the convoy consisted of several hundred vehicles and three to five thousand refugees, witnesses estimated, and stretched all the way to the village of Gornja Sudimlja. The Serbian and Yugoslav forces followed the refugees as they traveled, burning many houses in Slakovce and Cecelija.

Witnesses told Human Rights Watch that they stopped to rest and discuss their plans in Gornja Sudimlja, which had been occupied by the KLA until May 2. Yugoslav Army forces were based in a warehouse in Donja Sudimlja, some said, a village the refugees would have to pass through to get to Vucitrn. A thirty-year-old woman from Novo Selo Begovo (Novoselle e Begut), S.A., who was on the first tractor of the convoy, told Human Rights Watch what happened around 8 p.m. on May 2:

> [We] decided to tie a white cloth to our tractor, to show that we wanted to surrender. But before we got to Studime e Poshtme [Donja Sudimlja], they started shooting and shelling us in an awful way. I used a mattress to cover

> my children, and we drove on to Donja Sudimlja. When we got to the warehouse, we saw a line of soldiers on the left hand side of the road.
>
> They stopped us, and told us to get out of our tractors, and put our hands behind out heads, and then to sit down on the road. The soldiers started cursing us, and walked among us, kicking and beating some of us. One woman was beaten just because her child was crying.[6]

"The soldiers started cursing us, and walked among us, kicking and beating some of us."

The soldiers, who were joined by policemen and paramilitaries between 8:30 and 9 p.m., went from tractor to tractor in the convoy, cursing and threatening the refugees. At the same time, the soldiers coming from Slakovce and Cecelija had also reached the convoy. The men had either blue or green uniforms. Some of them had beards, while others were masked.

K.B., a thirty-four-year-old Albanian man from Vucitrn who had been hiding in the villages, told Human Rights Watch what happened next:

> When they [the police and paramilitaries] arrived at my part of the convoy, they asked my brother where his KLA uniform was, and his gun. But he said he didn't have any because he wasn't a member of the KLA. Then they hit him with the butt of a gun, after which they came to me, and told me to get off the trailer. When I got off, he hit me with his gun on my cheekbone, forehead and mouth, breaking one of my teeth. Then they stabbed me with a bayonet, and almost cut off part of my ear. They took me by my elbow, pointed a gun at my back, and dragged me some twenty meters away. They pushed me towards a little stream, and I jumped over it, and fell down. When I got up, they hit me four times in the back of my head with a gun, and once in my ribs. Later, a doctor told me that they had broken one of my ribs. I fell again, and lay there for about two minutes, after which I got up, and went back to the tractor.
>
> After I was beaten, I saw three soldiers or policemen drag away two girls between seventeen and twenty years old. They took them away some twenty or thirty meters, so I couldn't see what happened to them. But when they came back after fifteen or twenty minutes, I saw that their shirts had been ripped apart in the middle.[7]

Human Rights Watch inspected and photographed K.B.'s wounds during the interview in Kukes, Albania. The top of his left ear was torn, but had been repaired by a doctor in one of the refugee camps, and his right front tooth was broken. Others fared worse. Z. A., a forty-four-year old man from Novosella, related what happened to his family:

> At about 9:00 p.m., the paramilitaries and army stopped us. I couldn't see them very well, it was already dark. They took away our money and jewelry. Then two paramilitaries with masks and bandanas took my uncle, Remzi Aliu (aged fifty-four), and my nephew, Ramadan Aliu (aged thirty-eight). They asked them for money. Then they took them away some thirty meters, and shot them with a burst of gunfire from their automatic weapons. Then they took Hajrula Aliu and his wife, but they gave them [the police and paramilitaries] 500 German marks, so they didn't kill them.[8]

B.A., a nineteen-year-old man from Donja Sudimlja, told a similar story:

> When they [the soldiers coming from Cecelija] came to us, a Serbian soldier grabbed my brother, who was twenty-seven years old, by his elbow and took him some three meters away from the tractor. There, he asked for money, and soon after that he shot my brother with a pistol in the back.
>
> At the same time, they took my uncle, shot at him and kicked him, and he fell on the ground. We saw two bodies lying on the ground, and we thought they were both dead. After that, they took my father as well, and while they pointed a pistol at his throat, they demanded money. My father gave them one hundred German marks, but they asked for one thousand. I told my father to give it to him, so my father came back to the tractor and gave him another nine hundred marks. They then released my father, but right away they caught my cousin, and asked him for money as well. So my father again gave them five hundred marks, after which they released my cousin. After the army left, we heard my uncle asking for me to come and help him. A few minutes later, my father and grandfather went to him and carried him to the tractor, because he had been hit in his lower leg, so he couldn't walk. When they turned my brother over, they saw he was dead.[9]

Another man from Gornja Sudimlja explained how he witnessed three men being pulled from his tractor and shot:

> There were about fifteen paramilitaries near my tractor. They shone a flash-

light on the father of a four year old. One of them pushed the son aside with a gun and shot the father, Agim Gerguli [aged thirty-seven or thirty-eight], who was a father of four children. Then they asked something from Enver Gerguli [aged forty], my relative, but he was deaf and dumb, so he didn't answer. They took him by his collar off the tractor, and I got off the tractor and begged them to save his life. They said I should give money or they would make him speak. I gave him 800 German Marks and they said it was okay. Then another guy came. He took my brother two meters away and shot him.

"He pointed the Kalashnikov at my jaw. He said: 'You have two minutes to give me 1,000 marks.'"

He came back again with a flashlight and found another relative, Naman [aged thirty-nine]. He took him to the other side of the tractor and asked for money. I gave them 1,400 marks, but they killed him two meters away with a Kalashnikov. I thought he was maybe still alive, and I told him to tumble and go through the water. But there was a guy who understood [what I said], and they shot him again with the Kalashnikov. After that, he pointed the Kalashnikov at my jaw. He said: "You have two minutes to give me 1,000 marks." But I didn't have any money. My wife and kids were in the tractor, and they told me to get money from my wife. But she didn't have any money either, so I gave them my brother's money. They were counting down: "Two minutes, one minute . . . two seconds, one second," and then I pushed the gun down, and the gun fell, and I ran and jumped into the stream. I stayed there for one minute, thinking he would come and find me. I couldn't walk, I just crawled in the woods, twenty or thirty meters away from the tractor. Then I heard them say: "Gotovo, gotovo!" ["Enough, enough"] They got in a car and started to drive down.[10]

Human Rights Watch also interviewed Z.G.'s brother, M.G., a man who witnessed a killing and then lost an arm due to a gunshot wound. He told Human Rights Watch that his tractor was stopped somewhere between Gornja and Donja Sudimlja. One unidentified man tried to escape the convoy at this time and was shot, he said. The police then demanded money from M.G., who provided some, but was shot anyway in the arm. He said:

They came to my tractor with a flashlight, and told me to climb down. They asked me for money, and I gave 300 DM to a policeman from Serbia in a

> police uniform with good looks who was bald. After I gave 300 DM, he took out his automatic weapon and told me to turn around. I thought he would shoot me, and he did shoot me with two bullets in my right arm, and one in my back. I fell down on my left arm, and I tried to move my right arm, but I couldn't, so took my arm with my other hand. I felt my arm was getting colder. After they [the Serbian forces] left, I asked my neighbor for water, which I got. He asked me if I was alive, and they took me in the tractor. When I heard they [the Serbian forces] were coming back, they took me into the forest. I stayed there all night with my mother.[11]

The next morning, M.G.'s brothers came into the forest with their father and the bodies of Agim, Enver, and Naman. They left the bodies in the graveyard and took M.G. into the garden of his house. That evening, a doctor came from Vucitrn and treated his wounds. Then, on May 4, M.G. was taken to Slakovce, which was back under the control of the KLA, and a doctor amputated the arm with a sharp knife—a fact that was confirmed independently for Human Rights Watch by the doctor who performed the procedure.

Yet another man from Gornja Sudimlja, S.B., witnessed the security forces execute his son, who had been married that morning, and two other men from the village. He told Human Rights Watch:

> When they came to my tractor, there were three men: my son, Adnan, Eshref Rashica [aged approximately thirty], and Ismet Statovci [aged between twenty-seven and thirty]. First, they caught Ismet, took him off the tractor, and started to beat him. They asked him where he was from. He said he was from Firaja. Then another one said: "Just take him and kill him." They killed him with an automatic gun, I heard two booms, he was only three or four meters away.
>
> Then they came back and took my son. They grabbed his right arm, took him to the other side of the road. I went with him, but they hit me with the butt of a gun on my left cheekbone, and I fell. I heard them shoot my son, I heard two booms. I saw him lying, he was shot in his upper back. After that, they caught Eshref, and killed him as well. I heard them talk over the radio, asking how many people were killed. One of the guys said seventy-five, and then they said: "just go until you have one hundred."[12]

A fifty-nine-year-old farmer from Gornja Sudimlja, H.A., told Human

Rights Watch how men in police uniforms shot his brother and son, killing the latter. He said:

> They came to the tractor and took my brother Haki, and my son Rahman (aged twenty-seven) from the tractor. They took 1,100 DM from my brother and son, and then shot at my son and brother. My brother was wounded in his right ankle[13] and they killed my son. I wasn't even three meters away, and they shot him in front of us, in front of his mother. The men who did it were in police uniforms, and were wearing masks. When my brother fell down, they shot him again with one bullet in his back.[14] The bullet went through.[15]

Other witnesses interviewed by Human Rights Watch reported how men unknown to them were executed in front of their eyes. The soldiers and paramilitaries walked up and down the tractor convoy, they said, harassing, robbing and sometimes executing the refugees. The witnesses all reported hearing repeated shooting during the period between approximately 9 and 10:30 p.m. Around 11:30 p.m., policemen from Vucitrn came and ordered the convoy to move on towards Vucitrn. Around 12 a.m., May 3, they arrived in town.

"I heard them shoot my son, I heard two booms."

Several witnesses reported that they saw many dead bodies along the road to the city, but the exact number of executed persons from the convoy is unknown. Four separate witnesses claimed to have seen twenty-five, thirty, seventy, and "over a hundred" dead bodies, respectively. The varying numbers may result from the fact that the witnesses were located in different parts of the convoy, so that those towards the front of the line saw fewer than those at the back. Investigators from the war crimes tribunal discovered ninety-eight bodies in Gornja Sudimlja.[16]

Precise numbers were also provided by those who helped bury the victims. Z.G., for example, said that he returned to Gornja Sudimlja around 5 a.m. on May 3, and saw seventy-two bodies between the graveyard and the location where his relatives had been killed. He said:

> In the graveyard there were ninety-two bodies. All dead bodies were destroyed—without arms, legs, or a head. Only two bodies had not been mutilated. We put covers over them. We just opened several graves, and put five or six bodies in one place. We buried them with a few men, and had some

> help from the KLA, but we couldn't bury all of them on May 3, we could only bury thirty-four bodies.[17]

The commander of the KLA unit responsible for Donja and Gornja Sudimlja said that his soldiers buried ninety-two victims from the convoy attack. He said:

> There were ninety-two dead bodies, all from the column. The victims were mostly drivers of tractors and trailers. There were a lot of deserted tractors, and some people were shot dead on tractors. The majority of them were shot at a close distance, maybe two or three weren't. I think most people were shot in their heads or upper bodies. We buried them on May third, fourth, and fifth. We found many bullet casings there, of automatic weapons produced in Yugoslavia, and also some casings from pistol bullets. There is also a video of the bodies made by an amateur.[18]

Human Rights Watch obtained and viewed a copy of the video tape. It shows the village of Gornja Sudimlja the day before the attack, and on the day of the attack. The tape also shows footage of between twenty and twenty-five dead bodies, many of them apparently shot in the head, although it cannot be concluded with certainty from the video how they died. The bodies are filmed individually close up and are never seen against a recognizable landmark in the village. Moreover, there is a pause between the footage of the village and the footage of each of the bodies, either because recording was paused or because of subsequent editing. Nevertheless, the position of the bodies is consistent with witness statements and the tape appears credible.

The account of the attack on the convoy collected from witnesses interviewed by Human Rights Watch matches the information provided by foreign journalists who covered the incident, either from Albania during the war, or from inside Kosovo after June 1999. All together, five media accounts in the English-language press include nine eyewitness statements, all of which mention the police and paramilitary killings that took place on May 2 and 3. One man claimed that eleven members of his family were killed.[19] One woman told a journalist from the *Independent* (London), "They killed my husband before my eyes. . . . At first they beat the men with rifle butts, then they killed them. All through the journey I closed my eyes because I did not want to remember the scene."[20]

Detentions and Expulsions

Since the convoy of displaced persons reached Vucitrn, the Albanians were directed towards an agricultural cooperative near Motel Vicianum, where they spent the night sitting in a fenced off area, guarded by the police and some soldiers. Witnesses told Human Rights Watch that several thousand refugees were there, and that the area was so crowded it was impossible to stretch their legs, let alone sleep. The guards roamed among the refugees all night, checking their papers, and in several cases beating people.

In the morning, somewhere between 8:00 and 10:00 a.m., May 3, approximately thirty policemen entered the compound. Three different witnesses separately identified a policeman named Petrovic, who they claimed was a police commander in Vucitrn, as the officer in charge. One of these three witnesses did not know his first name, but the other two claimed his name was Dragan Petrovic.[21]

The witnesses concurred that the police ordered the men between the ages of eighteen and sixty to separate themselves from the women, children and elderly men. The police checked the identity papers of the 500 to 600 men who had been separated. From this group, all of the tractor drivers were allowed to rejoin their families, all together about 200 men.

A large truck then came, witnesses said, loaded fifty to sixty of the remaining men, and took them away in the direction of Mitrovica. Approximately ten to twenty minutes later, the truck returned empty and transported another group of men in the same direction. Witnesses reported that the truck returned to reload with men at least eight times.

While the men were being transported, the tractor drivers were told to load their families onto their vehicles and drive towards Mitrovica. Those who were among the first to leave the compound told Human Rights Watch that, as they drove by, they saw the truck used to transport the men parked outside the Smrekovnica prison. The witnesses claimed that they saw several of the men who had been taken away from the agricultural cooperative in Vucitrn, including some of the witnesses' own family members.

Another witness, who was not part of the convoy in Gornja Sudimlje, claimed to have seen ethnic Albanian men in and around the Smrekovnica prison on May 3. This thirty-eight-year-old man from Bajgora, S.B., interviewed in Kukes, said he had arrived in Smrekovnica on the morning of May 2 on foot with another group of approximately 3,000 villagers from the Bajgora area. Around 5 p.m. that day, the police had come to his uncle's house, where he was hiding, and ordered him to join the rest of the group in the Smrekovnica school yard, which is next to the prison. S.B. told Human Rights Watch that he saw several thousand men being held in the prison, although it is not clear how he arrived at this number or whether he saw these people in the prison or around it. He also claimed that approximately 300 men staying with him in the school yard were taken to the prison. A few men were released from the prison every hour, he said, and all of them appeared to have been beaten.[22]

Back in Vucitrn, the convoy of mostly women, children, and elderly traveled under police escort through Smrekovnica to Kosovska Mitrovica and then alone through Srbica, Pec and Klina, where the displaced persons spent one night. From Klina, a smaller road was taken south to Prizren, and then to the Morina border crossing with Albania, which they crossed on May 4.

Other Killings

After the initially displaced in the convoy were deported, between 15,000 and 40,000 ethnic Albanians remained in the area between Cecelija (Ceceli) and Dubnica (Dumnice), a few kilometers to the south, where the KLA had regained control. In addition, the police told some families in Vucitrn that it would be safe for them to return to Gornja and Donja Sudimlja. The KLA also assumed positions in the villages. Shortly thereafter, however, government forces assumed positions on the high ground around the villages, which cut off access to Vucitrn. The only entry point into the town, where food was available, was along a stream which runs from Gornja Sudimlja through Donja Sudimlja to Vucitrn. At various times during May, ethnic Albanian villagers were shot and killed while trying to get to or from Vucitrn.[23]

According to the local KLA commander, on May 17, around 8:00 p.m., his soldiers found six men who had been shot near the stream. All of them had been killed from a range of approximately fifteen to twenty meters, he said. Two of the men survived.

Human Rights Watch interviewed one of the two survivors, V.Z.. He said that he was traveling on foot with seven other men from Gornja Sudimlja back to Vucitrn, where he had spent most of the war with relatives. His home is near the stream that leads to town, so when the group approached it, he went off for a minute to check his house. He explained what happened next:

> We went down through the stream together at 7:00 p.m. We came close to my house and I told them to keep going, I just wanted to see my house. We were about 200 meters away from my house. When I took my first steps, I was maybe four meters away from the others, I heard a burst of gunfire. I ran and hid in a stone house. I didn't know where to go. I stayed a little while, and I heard shots all the time.
>
> I heard gun shots, and I was afraid they were in front of me. I just ran and hid in some bushes, 300 or 400 meters away from the stream. I saw another group of Serbs coming with a tractor from Sfracaku [Svracak], but they didn't see me. I was only 150 meters away, but they didn't see me. I saw they had uniforms, but I don't know which ones, [because] I was lying down. During that time, I heard a lot of shots, it took one hour.
>
> I thought they would see me, so I waited for them to come when they finished with the others. I could only see one of the persons that was shooting, he was close to me. He was lying in the apple orchard, and when he saw me, he started shooting and screaming at me. He was wearing a green camouflage uniform. Even in my house, there was one person on the second floor.[24]

Another killing took place on May 23, but there were no direct witnesses. Another KLA commander, who claimed to have been responsible for a battalion in the Sudimlja and Samodraza (Samadrexhe) area, said he found the bodies of eight women, aged approximately fourteen to thirty-one on May 24 near the stream. Two of them had been cut with a knife near the mouth, he said, and some of them had their clothes torn off, leading him to believe that some of them had been raped.[25]

The KLA commander for Sudimlja, interviewed separately, also claimed that KLA soldiers found the bodies of eight women and girls, aged between twelve and thirty, near the stream around 12 a.m. on May 23. Six of the bodies were in the river and two girls were a few meters away, he said. The commander also believed that two of the girls had been raped because their shirts had been torn off, but a medical examination was not performed, he said.[26]

Government forces killed twelve members of the Gerxhaliu family.

The last reported killing took place on May 31, when government forces killed twelve members of the Gerxhaliu family who lived in Donja Sudimlja close to the main road near the stream. After clashing with Serbian forces, KLA soldiers found three men from the family, Xhemail, Selatin, and Shaban (Selatin's son), shot near their house. Nine other members of the family, including six children under the age of fourteen, were killed inside the house.[27]

One sixty-eight-year-old man from the family, Sali Gerxhaliu, said that he woke up on May 31 to the news that his three relatives had been killed near their house. He hitched up his horse and cart and went to collect the bodies. He said:

> When I came to the stream, I saw that one of Selatin's arms had been cut off by gunfire, and he was hit in his neck. Shaban was shot in his eye, and you could see a fracture in his skull. Xhemail was shot in his chest and in his lower belly. All of them were shot with bullets. There were seven or eight bullets in Xhemail, all of them had been shot more than once. I started to cry for my relatives.[28]

After collecting the bodies, Sali Gerxhaliu, his friend Ismet, and Xhemail's daughter decided to look in the family home, since they realized that none of their relatives had come looking for them. Xhemail's daughter held the horse as Sali Gerxhaliu looked inside:

> So I went inside the house, and I saw nine of them in a room. From the door, I saw Sale lying with her arms in front of her head. Two boys were close to Sale and two women. It looked like they were sleeping. The boys were sitting with their legs down. I said: "Allah, Allah, they are all dead, all nine of them." I went outside again, and took the three bodies to the graveyard. At the graveyard, I met some other people, and I told them there were twelve people dead. They asked whether they should bury them, but I said it would be better to wait, and call some police.[29]

Sali Gerxhaliu did call the police in Vucitrn, who came to investigate the crime scene. He explained:

> The police and an investigation judge came and took pictures. They said they would give us copies, but they never did. When they came, the investigative judge, a woman from Montenegro, started crying. One policeman asked her

> why she was crying. The woman said: "What did these kids do?" But one of the policemen, Dragan Petrovic, said: "This is a war, comrade." I said to him: "A war is of men against men, so go in the forest, and fight with the KLA. These are kids that were sleeping." But Petrovic just looked at me. After they took pictures, they said we shouldn't bury them, because they would bring people from Kosovska Mitrovica. They went to Vushtrri [Vucitrn] with a car, but then they came back, and told us to bury them after all.[30]

"The police and an investigation judge came and took pictures."

Dragan Petrovic was mentioned by three other villagers from the area, who claimed they saw him in Vucitrn dealing with the convoy after the attack in Gornja Donja Sudimlja on May 3.

Human Rights Watch also spoke with Shukri Gerxhaliu's son, a forty-four-year-old man from the village. He said that he heard two loud explosions from NATO bombs around 4:00 a.m. on May 31. Then, around 7:00 a.m., Serbian forces entered the village. Most of the men managed to slip away but they later learned that three men from the Gerxhaliu family, Selatin, Shaban and Xhemail, had been killed. Later in the day, the man went into the Gerxhaliu house and saw the nine bodies. He said:

> When I went inside the house, from the door of the room, I saw a son of Selatin sitting, and to the right of him, there was an old woman and two children, who she was trying to protect. Next to her, there were the wife of Nexhmedin and her son. The others had been trying to hide in the room.[31]

The KLA battalion leader also told Human Rights Watch about the Gerxhaliu killing, claiming that the men were not members of the KLA. He said:

> I went to see the dead people [of the Gerxhaliu family]. Three of them were outside up the hill, and they were shot from a close distance. Selatin, Xhemail and Shaban were not members of the KLA, I had never heard of them before. Nine of them were in one room. When I saw the children, I couldn't stay there. Some were hit in the face, others in the chest. They were executed by Yugoslav Kalashnikovs, we found the shells. The children were aged from around five to eighteen, and there were also some women. This case was also investigated by the Serbs. Even for them it was strange. There were two police positions, left and right of the village. They blamed each other: the police

said the military had done it, and the other way around. It was the military police who did the investigation.[32]

SMREKOVNICA (SMREKONICE) PRISON

On May 22 in Kukes, Albania, Human Rights Watch interviewed six Kosovar Albanian men who had been released that day from Smrekovnica prison near Mitrovica, a minimum security prison built in the 1970s. All of the men described abusive treatment by Serbian authorities, including beatings in detention.

Over the next two weeks, dozens of other ethnic Albanian men from the Vucitrn and Mitrovica area entered Albania and told of their detentions in Smrekovnica. All of them told of regular beatings by police during their imprisonment, especially during interrogations about their activity in or knowledge of the KLA.[33] On many of the interviewees, Human Rights Watch saw obvious signs of physical abuse, including black eyes, severe bruises on inmates' backs, legs and buttocks, and skin abrasions. Most of the men were forced to sign confessions that they were engaged in terrorist activities before being released.

Human Rights Watch saw obvious signs of physical abuse.

Human Rights Watch interviewed more than thirty former detainees, and their testimonies were remarkably similar. All of the men were arrested in Vucitrn or Mitrovica or other villages in those areas, where the KLA was active. Some were arrested on May 2, taken from a refugee convoy near Sudimlja (see section on Donja Sudimlja).

The prisoners were held in conditions that fell far short of minimal acceptable standards. All of the former detainees said that their cells were extremely overcrowded, and in some cells it was impossible to sit down due to the overcrowding. A fifty-two-year-old man from Resnik said that seventy-six persons were crowded into his cell, which measured four by eight meters,[34] while a forty-three-year-old man from the Podujevo area said that his four-by-five-meter room held thirty-six men.[35] The detainees were not provided with mattresses or blankets and were forced to sleep on the concrete floor.

Without exception, the detainees were interrogated, some as many as five times, about their possible connections to the KLA. During these interrogations, the men reported being beaten, some severely. A.K., age twenty-seven, was first held for two weeks in a school in Srbica and then transferred to Smrekovnica prison, where he was held for another two weeks. He told Human Rights Watch:

> I was interrogated five times: two times in the school in Skenderaj [Srbica], and three times in the prison [in Smrekovnica]. They asked me if I was a member of the KLA, who I knew in the KLA, whether I had given money to the KLA if I had connections in the KLA, etc. Whenever I said I didn't know any KLA, they'd beat me up with [wooden] sticks, rubber police batons or the butt of a gun. They'd hit me in my back and on my hands.[36]

"Whenever I said I didn't know any KLA, they'd beat me up with [wooden] sticks, rubber police batons or the butt of a gun."

Other interviewees also stated that they were severely beaten on their backs, heads, hands and knees during interrogations, some of which took place in technical and medical schools in Mitrovica, which allegedly served as police headquarters during the war.

One former detainee from Dolak village, who was released from the prison and arrived in Albania on June 7, told Human Rights Watch:

> Forty-two of us went to the technical school [in Mitrovica] and the rest went to the medical school We were placed in a basement and then they started beating us up. There were five or six police and soldiers. We were facing the wall so it was hard to see. They hit us with rubber batons, iron rods, and the butts of the automatic weapons. They kicked us. Not much punching with fists, except one guy who was punched in the eye. [Human Rights Watch saw the man with bruising around his eye.][37]

Former detainees said Serbian youths in Mitrovica had thrown stones at them as they were being transported to or from the technical school, and some of them even participated in the beatings. One man said:

> Serbian kids also came into the basement and hit us with metal rods and threw stones at us. The kids said, "Let us beat them." They were different ages, eleven, twelve, or so. They had been in the street playing. When we were taken off the truck, they were there; they threw stones at us. The kids insulted our mothers and called us terrorists.[38]

Another man, said: "I was hit in the back by a kid. It was lighter than a beating by an adult. Compared to being hit by the police, it was like being tickled."[39]

Another former detainee claimed that, on May 28, the prisoners were threatened with sexual abuse. Men described as "paramilitaries" forced some of the prisoners, mostly younger boys around fourteen years old, to stand naked, after which they were verbally threatened with rape. According to the witness, six young prisoners were then taken away, but Human Rights Watch found no other evidence to prove that further sexual abuse took place.[40]

Besides physical mistreatment, the men reported that prisoners were provided insufficient food, about 200 grams of bread per person per day. The men from the Vucitrn region all reported that they had not received any food at all for forty-eight hours, from the moment they were detained in Vucitrn on the evening of May 2, until about 8:00 p.m. on Tuesday, May 4. Some former detainees reported that the food improved about ten days into their detention, when the authorities began to serve warm meals.

It is unknown how many detainees were still in Smrekovnica when the war ended on June 12. Many prisoners being held in other detention facilities in Kosovo, such as in Lipljan or Prizren, were transferred to prisons inside Serbia proper, where many of them remain as of September 2000. (See Abuses After June 12, 1999.)

15

STATISTICAL ANALYSIS OF VIOLATIONS

Between March and December 1999, Human Rights Watch conducted more than 600 interviews with victims and witnesses to international humanitarian law violations in Kosovo. The information from these interviews is presented in other chapters of this book in testimony cited from interviews and case studies. This chapter uses statistics derived from the interviews to examine the trends and patterns of the crimes committed that may not be evident from narrative information. The numbers and graphs will deal in a systematic and substantive way with the reports of who was killed, when, where, and by whom.

The chapter, prepared in conjunction with the Science and Human Rights Program of the American Association for the Advancement of Science (AAAS), is the first large-scale data project conducted by Human Rights Watch.[1] It hopefully contributes to the growing field of human rights and statistical analysis.[2]

The interviews were conducted by Human Rights Watch researchers, usually with a interpreter, in Albania and Macedonia between March 28 and June 12, 1999, and in Kosovo between June 12 and December 31, 1999. Interviewees were selected for their knowledge of specific abuses inside the province. All interviews were conducted with a view to eliciting open narratives of what the interviewee had seen or experienced inside Kosovo between March 20 and June 12, 1999, rather than through standardized questionnaires. On return to New York, the interview documents were coded by trained volunteers for violation types, time and place of violations, victims, and perpetrators. A database was created, which is available for public use at http://hrdata.aaas.org.

Executions by Municipality Reported to Human Rights Watch

Credit: All maps, graphs, and charts designed by Matt Zimmerman. © Human Rights Watch

LIMITATIONS OF THE DATA

The statistics presented in this chapter shed light on the nature of war crimes in Kosovo, but they do have limitations. Most importantly, Human Rights Watch did *not* randomly sample the interviewees. On the contrary, researchers purposefully sought out not only the victims and witnesses of violations, but specifically those with knowledge of the most serious violations, such as torture, sexual violence, and executions. Therefore, these data cannot be extrapolated to general findings for Kosovo as a whole. Nor can these data provide information about the total number of persons killed, or give a complete picture of violations throughout the province.

Human Rights Watch activities were largely in the municipalities in Kosovo that were known to have been hardest hit by the war, such as Glogovac, Orahovac, Djakovica, Prizren, and Srbica. However, additional focus was directed to municipalities in the southwest, such as Djakovica and Orahovac, because researchers in North Albania during the war documented a heavy flow of refugees from those areas. Some northeastern and central municipalities, specifically Podujevo and Kosovo Polje, where many killings took place, are under-reported in this chapter and in the report as a whole.

Lastly, the process of coding and database creation is imperfect, particularly when dealing with complex narratives, as is the case with many war crimes in Kosovo. In complicated scenarios, it is not always easy to prepare statistical data that records accurately what occurred, where, and when. Kosovo is further complicated by confusion and ambiguity concerning place names in Serbian and Albanian, as well the fact that some of the same village names appear in up to four different municipalities.

Because of concerns like these, the Human Rights Watch Kosovo database was repeatedly checked and adjusted to eliminate errors, a process that is ongoing. To reduce errors, all instances for which the number of execution victims was over ten but considered imprecise were dropped from the total number of reported executions. In addition, the top five municipalities for executions, as well as some of the other municipalities, were carefully reviewed an additional time to eliminate faulty entries or records that counted the same execution violation more than once.

Like the report in general, these data only deal with violations committed between March 20 (when the OSCE withdrew from Kosovo) and June 12, 1999 (when NATO entered Kosovo). Note that for clarity, all percentages have been rounded to the nearest integer.

GENERAL FINDINGS

From the large body of Human Rights Watch interviews, 577 interviews were coded because the interviewee had direct knowledge of a human rights or humanitarian law violation. From these 577 interviews, Human Rights Watch recorded more than 35,000 unduplicated violations, although many were suffered in succession by the same individuals.[3] It must be noted that a violation may involve one or more victims. In many cases, for instance, the populations of whole villages or cities were expelled, such as the village of Ade or Pec city, or entire households were killed, like the Berisha household in Suva Reka. Again, the number of violations reported to Human Rights Watch cannot be extrapolated to suggest how many violations were committed in Kosovo as a whole.

The main violations reported to Human Rights Watch are depicted in Graph 1 below. Only those violations reported more than one hundred times are shown.

Graph 1: number of violations reported to Human Rights Watch, by type, for number in excess of 100.

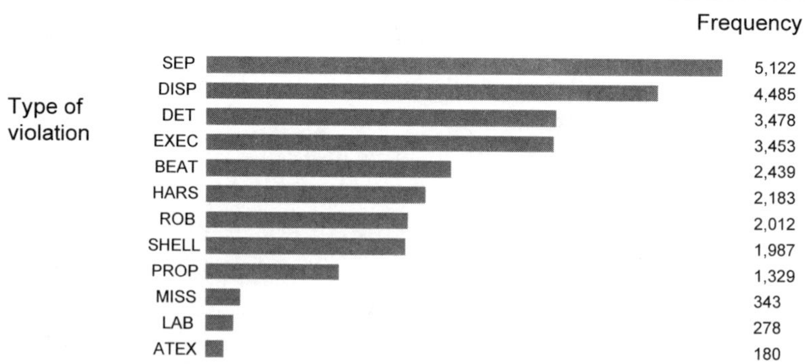

Note: This graph should not be construed to suggest the frequency or relative frequency of violations in Kosovo, since Human Rights Watch tried to document the worst of the abuses. Executions, for example, are likely to be overrepresented in comparison to indiscriminate shelling since researchers purposefully sought out evidence of individual cases of such killings. The figures for the violations, and their full names are: separations of men, women and children (5,122), forced displacement (4,485), detentions (3,478), executions (3,453), beatings (2,439), harassment (2,183), robbery (2,012), indiscriminate shelling (1,987), private property destruction (1,329), missing persons (343), forced labor (278), and attempted execution (180).

With 5,122 reported violations, the forced separation of men, women and children[4] was the most commonly reported violation. Displacement,[5] with 4,485 reported violations, was the second most common, which is understandable given that it was a dominant violation of the conflict—more than 850,000 Kosovar Albanians were expelled from Kosovo, according to UNHCR, and thousands more were internally displaced. The third most frequent violation was detention[6] with 3,478 reported violations, followed by extrajudicial executions with 3,453 violations.

Future reports by Human Rights Watch and others may focus on the patterns of these violations: when and where they occurred over time, and in what circumstances. Also of interest is whether certain violations tended to take place in isolation or together with other violations. For the sake of simplicity, however, this report focuses on only one of the violation types, albeit the most serious of the crimes: executions.

An Analysis of Extrajudicial Executions

It should be noted that extrajudicial executions by state actors—deliberate killings with no judicial process—may be over-reported in relation to other violations in this chapter since Human Rights Watch researchers actively sought to document such deliberate killings as a priority. At the same time, many extrajudicial executions committed in Kosovo are clearly not included in the 3,453 cases; just as an example, information on large-scale killings in Beleg, Goden, Kacanik, and Podujevo were not included in these data or the geographic chapters. In addition, the bodies of some people reported missing to Human Rights Watch during the data collection period have since been discovered. Despite these concerns, the body of information on executions collected by Human Rights Watch is large enough to draw some significant conclusions about the pattern of killings by Serbian and Yugoslav forces.

In the 3,453 documented executions, Human Rights Watch obtained the names of 916 people, or 27 percent of the victims. The rest of the victims were unidentified by witnesses.

The Gender of Execution Victims

As is clear from the cases documented in other chapters of this report, Serbian and Yugoslav forces summarily executed males at a much higher rate than females.

Of the 3,453 execution victims reported to Human Rights Watch, the gender of the victim was known for 2,232 people (65 percent). Of these 2,232 victims, 2,055 of the people were male (92 percent) and 177 were female (8 percent). This breakdown is depicted in Graph 2 at right.

Graph 2: Gender of Execution Victims

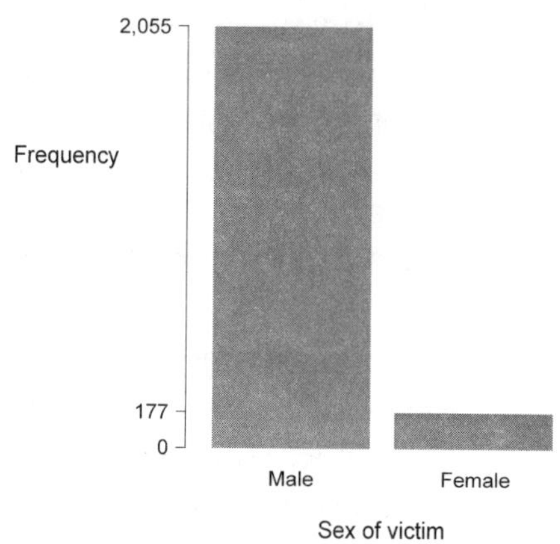

These findings would be expected if the data dealt with deaths in combat or even summary executions of combatants, since the KLA's forces were predominantly male. But, as the case studies in other chapters make clear, the vast majority of summary execution victims were civilians who did not participate in combat. Take, for example, the killings of approximately ninety prisoners in the Dubrava prison or the roughly 300 men taken from refugee convoys and killed in Meja.

Clearly this represents a targeting of Kosovar Albanian males. This finding is reinforced by the fact that, during the NATO bombing, many males were either in hiding within Kosovo, fighting with the KLA, or living abroad, while women were more likely to have stayed at home during the war, where they were susceptible to abuse.

The Ages of Execution Victims

Of the 3,453 known victims of summary execution, Human Rights Watch obtained the age of 630 people (18 percent). Of the victims for whom age was known, 530 were males (84 percent) and one hundred were females (16 percent). The fact that the age of victims was known in only 18 percent of the cases should be considered when conducting an analysis, since bias may have been introduced. Witnesses might have only provided ages for the youngest or oldest of the victims, for example, in order to emphasize the

Graph 3: Ages of male execution victims

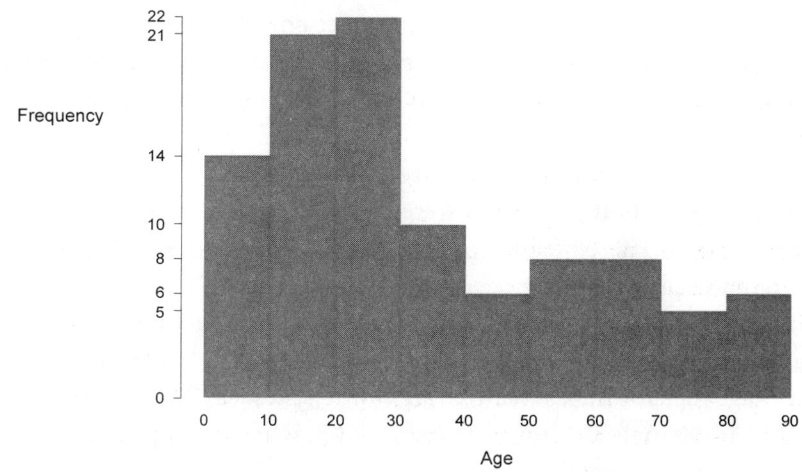

Graph 4: Ages of female execution victims

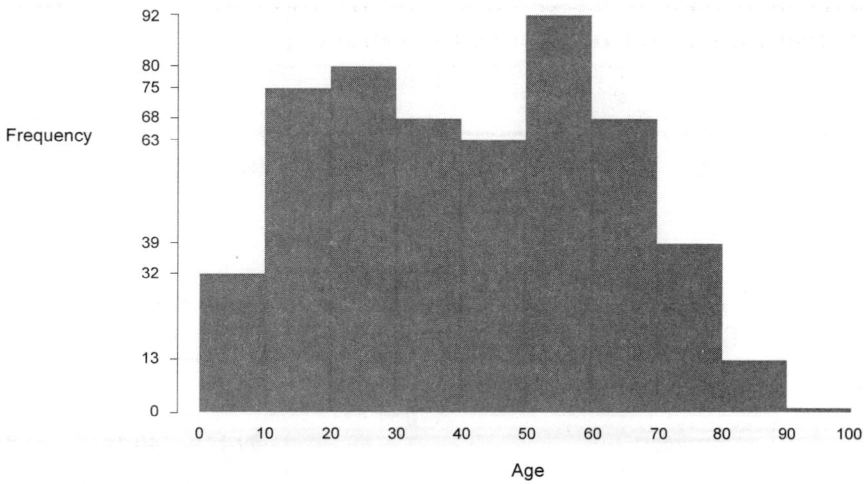

seriousness of the crimes. Even given this possibility, however, these data reflect some interesting results that deserve mention.

Notably, the ages of summary execution victims differ for men and women. For male execution victims, the average age was 40.3 years. For female victims, the average age was 32.7 years. Graphs 3 and 4 depict the age distributions for male and female summary execution victims.

It is clear that the pattern of violation is different for male and female. The killings of men and boys tended to target equally males between the ages of 10 and 70, with a falloff at higher ages. The summary executions of females were high for ages 10–30, then fell off to a uniform level for those over 30.

In both cases, the murder of children below ten were lower. However, female children in that age group were proportionately more likely to be killed than males. These qualitative comments based on Graphs 3 and 4 are reflected in the summary comparison statistics in Figure 1 below.

As Figure 1 shows, 75 percent of the male execution victims were below 56 years of age, while 75 percent of female execution victims were under 50. The "average" age for males was 40.3 and for females was 32.7. Similarly, 25 percent of the female victims were below 14.5, whereas 25 percent of the male victims were below 22.

At first glance, the results are counter-intuitive. Most notably, based on the case studies, one would expect to see a rise in executions of military age

Figure 1: Comparison of summary statistics for age

NAME	MEANING	ALL	MALE	FEMALE
Maximum	Largest Value	90	90	87
Third Quartile	75% of the values are less than this value	56	56	50
Median	50% of the values are less than this value	38	40	24
First Quartile	25% of the values are less than this value	20	22	14.5
Minimum	Smallest value	0	0	3
Mean	"average"	39.1	40.3	32.7
n	how many values	630	530	100

men, who were targeted for killing during village sweeps, such as in the villages of Cuska, Bela Crkva, and Meja. In numerous cases, men between the ages of 18 and 50 were separated from women and children and killed. However, there are a number of plausible explanations for the discrepancies in the victims' ages.

First, as mentioned above, there were relatively fewer fighting age males in the villages during the NATO bombing. Many men between the ages of 20 and 50 were either hiding in the hills (fearful of being targeted), fighting with the insurgency, or living abroad. In many villages, women and children were left behind with a smaller number of older men. So, while the case studies provide testimonial evidence that military age males were targeted for execution, this is not reflected in these data since military age men were relatively less present in the areas susceptible to attack.

Second, the case studies show how men were frequently killed by government security forces after having been separated from women and children, such as in Bela Crkva or Izbica. Executions of females, however, more often took place in group killings (such as the execution of an entire family) and not from the deliberate targeting of women. The killing of twelve members of the Gerxhaliu family on May 31 in Gornja Sudimlja[7] or the Berisha family in Suva Reka[8] on March 25 are examples where a family—men, women and children—was killed together. In other words, women were more likely to be killed in groups for which the killers did not distinguish between gender or ages, thereby including some younger female victims.

A third possibility is that executions of women were related to sexual violence which involved younger female victims. Unfortunately, it is impossible to prove this theory with the data collected. Although Human Rights Watch coded for rape and sexual violence in the database, which would theoretically allow an analysis of whether female executions and sexual violence tended to occur at the same time, the sensitive nature of sexual violence in Kosovar Albanian society rendered the data on those crimes unreliable, in the opinion of Human Rights Watch. In other words, sexual violence was under-reported both in testimony and in the database.

One point to consider with these data on ages is the *rate* of killing. For example, it looks as though government forces were not summarily executing older men and women at a high rate. However, given the fact that there are fewer older people in the population than middle-aged or younger adults, then the elderly were being killed at a relatively higher rate. The opposite is true for children under age ten. Since it is likely that there are more children of that age in the population than adults or elderly, then the rate of children being killed is less than that of adults.[9]

Executions Over Time

Plotting the total extrajudicial executions reported to Human Rights Watch over time reveals a great deal about the systematic and coordinated nature of the violations in Kosovo. As Graph 5 demonstrates, total summary executions took place in three very distinct waves.

From the beginning of the offensive on March 20, there was a clear and rapid spike in extrajudicial executions, culminating around March 25–27, just after the commencement of NATO bombing. This was followed by a significant drop off, with a low point around April 5–6. A second wave of extrajudical executions peaked around April 27–28. A third but significantly smaller wave of executions reached its zenith around May 10–11, followed by a precipitous drop-off that peters out by June 12, with the exception of a minor bump around May 30–31.

The three distinct surges in executions suggest that the killings were not the result of random violence by government forces. Rather, that data supports other evidence that they were carefully planned and implemented strikes that fit into the government's larger strategic aims.

Graph 5: Reported Executions Over Time

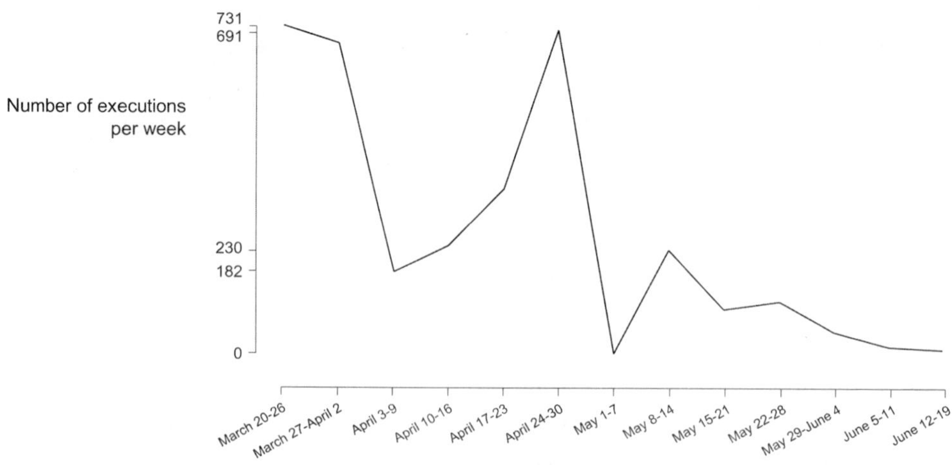

Of course, Graph 5 summarizes only those executions reported to Human Rights Watch and not the total number of executions committed in Kosovo. However, the pronounced nature of the three waves, based on 3,453 executions, strongly suggests the purposeful and coordinated nature of the violations. Although not all executions are represented, the findings based on partial data are strong and clear.

Executions by Municipality

Of the 3,453 extrajudicial executions reported to Human Rights Watch, 66 percent of the executions for which we have municipality identification occurred in the following five municipalities: Djakovica, Orahovac, Srbica, Glogovac, and Suva Reka. With the exception of Podujevo, where Human Rights Watch conducted little research, this clearly reflects the municipalities that were most impacted by the war and associated security operations from 1998 to 1999. Thirty-five percent of the reported executions took place in Djakovica and Orahovac municipalities alone, as shown in Figure 2 below.

Again, Figure 2 should not be interpreted as a representation of total extrajudical executions in the municipalities or in Kosovo as a whole since it reflects only those executions reported to Human Rights Watch. Two municipalities in particular stand out as having been undercounted due to only partial research in those areas: Podujevo and Kosovo Polje. With these

Figure 2: Top municipalities of reported extrajudicial executions

MUNICIPALITY	REPORTED EXECUTIONS	PERCENT	CUMULATIVE PERCENT
1. Djakovica	645	18%	18%
2. Orahovac	583	17%	35%
3. Srbica	431	12%	47%
4. Glogovac	368	11%	58%
5. Suva Reka	248	7%	65%

Note: The other municipalities where Human Rights Watch gathered reports of executions, in descending order, are: Pec, Kacanik, Prizren, Vucitrn, Istok, Lipljan, Pristina, Kosovoska Mitrovica, Decan, Gnjilane, Obilic, Urosevac, Podujevo, Leposavic, Stimlje, Strpce, Kosovo Polje, Klina, Kosovoska Kamenica, Zvecan, Novo Brdo, Gora, Vitina and Zubin Potok.

notable exceptions, the data can be taken as a relatively fair reflection since Human Rights Watch documented a high percentage of the major killing sites across Kosovo. These data were collected in Albania and Macedonia during the war, as well as inside Kosovo after the war, so that all geographic areas were covered.[10]

Intense killing "sprees" tended to occur in municipalities over short periods of times.

The coordinated nature of extrajudicial executions in Kosovo is further revealed when the killings are examined by municipality. As the graphs below reveal, intense killing "sprees" tended to occur in municipalities over short periods of times, suggesting a strategic order to commit executions in certain areas or, in the least, the deployment of forces known for brutality and disregard with orders to terrorize the civilian population without legal constraints. More sporadic executions in the municipalities may not be reflected in the graphs since Human Rights Watch tended to focus on the larger-scale incidents.

The intensity of executions in any given municipality over a short period suggests that, as in Graph 5, the killings were not random events. Rather,

Graph 6: Extrajudicial Executions in Djakovica over time

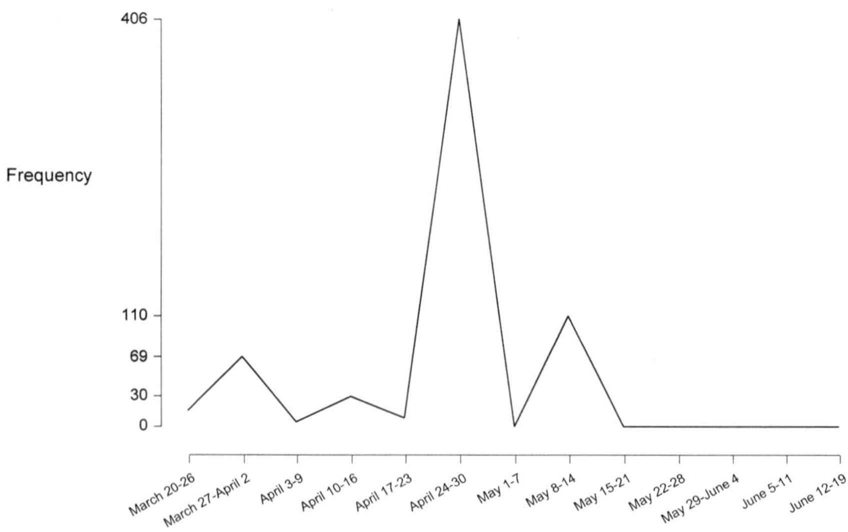

Graph 7: Extrajudicial Executions in Orahovac over time

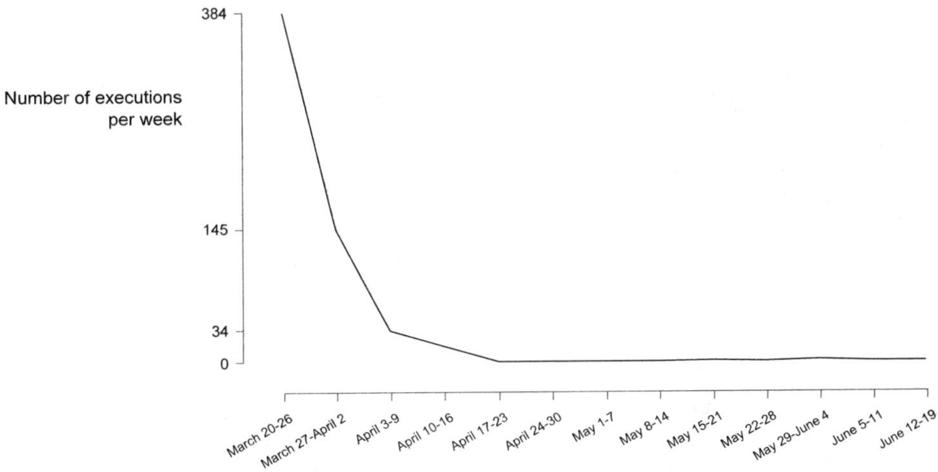

Graph 8: Extrajudicial Executions in Srbica over time

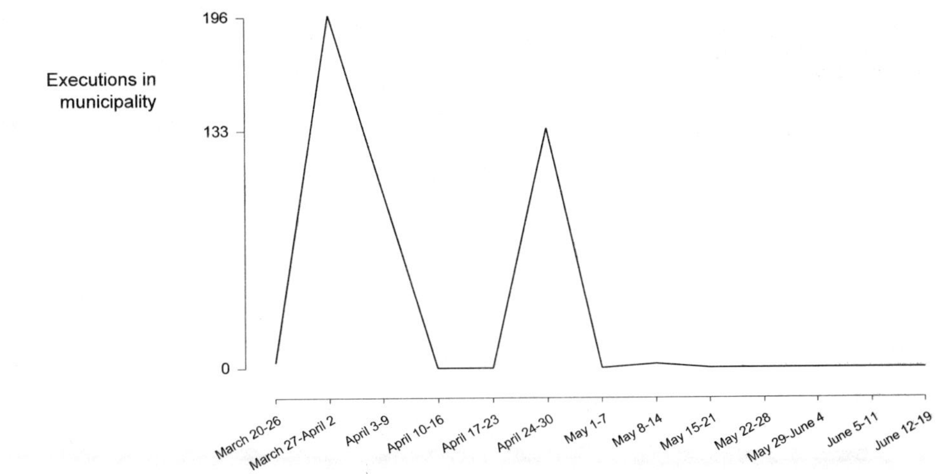

Graph 9: Extrajudicial Executions in Glogovac over time

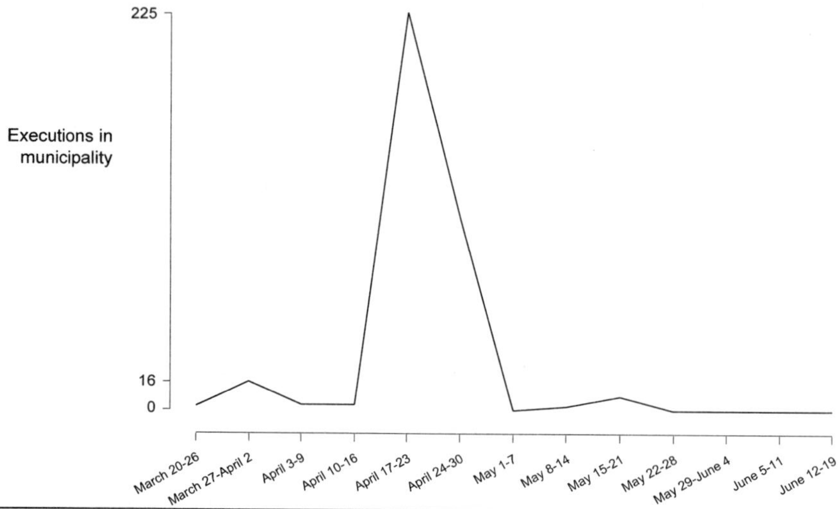

Graph 10: Extrajudicial Executions in Suva Reka over time

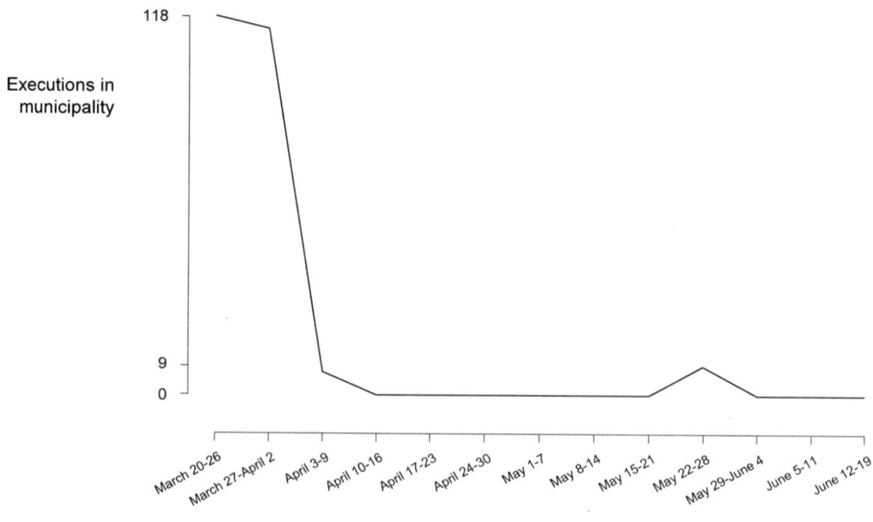

there were distinct periods when killings were intense, suggesting they were the result of a premeditated and coordinated policy of violence. Our anecdotal research also supports the conclusion that executions in each municipality were specific and purposeful.

Executions and Expulsions: a Correlation

Evidence of a centrally coordinated attack on Kosovar Albanians is strengthened by another statistical study on the outflow of refugees from Kosovo to Albania. The April 2000 study conducted by the AAAS found that the refugee flows into Albania occurred in three separate waves.[11] From late March to late May 1999, the report said, 95 percent of the Kosovar Albanian refugees who entered Albania did so during one of three "distinct phases," as shown in Graph 11.

To explain the graph, the report concluded:

Graph 11: Number of Kosovar Albanians entering Albania at Morina border crossing, by two-day period, from the AAAS report "Policy or Panic"

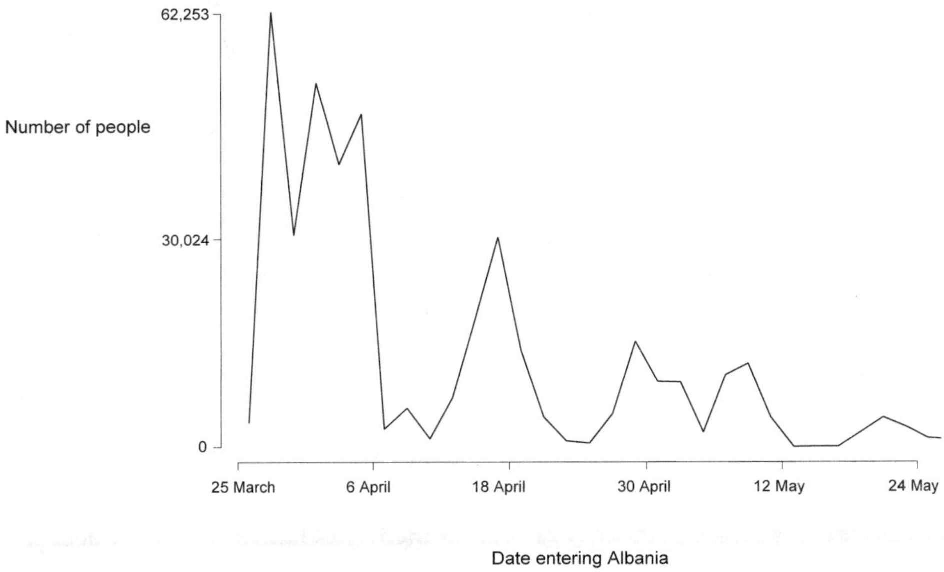

> It is our conclusion that the evictions were not spontaneous: mass migration on this scale and in this pattern could only have been driven by a centralized policy, not by individual decisions or emotions of either Kosovar Albanians or local Yugoslav military or police officials . . .
>
> The coherence of the phases, and their apparent coordination across broad regions of Kosovo suggests that Yugoslav authorities devised and implemented a policy to attempt to clear at least certain regions of ethnic Albanians.[12]

As may be evident from Graph 11, the timing of the three refugee waves to Albania documented by AAAS coincides closely with the three waves of executions documented by Human Rights Watch (Graph 5).[13] This is made even more clear when the AAAS data on expulsions and the Human Rights Watch data on executions are compared more directly in Graph 12.

As Graph 12 shows, the peaks and valleys of the three phases, and even the final bump, closely match for both executions reported to Human Rights Watch and refugee outflows to Albania. In other words, the executions in Kosovo over time appear to parallel expulsions.[14] The difference in magnitude for the second wave could be attributable to the fact that most of the executions documented by Human Rights Watch in that time frame occurred in the north and central municipalities, particularly Srbica and Glogovac. A large percentage of those expelled from these municipalities went to Macedonia, where they would not have been picked up by the AAAS data.

This strong relationship further suggests that there was a centrally devised and implemented strategy to target Kosovar Albanians. The three phases of killings and expulsions seem tied to the strategic objectives of the military and political leadership in Belgrade.

One explanation is that government forces committed executions in order to expedite the expulsions—a theory that is supported by some case studies. In many villages documented in this report, such as Celina and Korenica, police, army, or paramilitary forces committed executions before, or in the process of, expelling the civilian population from a village or city. It is also understandable that killings would rise along with executions since government forces were unleashed on an area to be "cleansed." Often these were areas of KLA activity where policemen and soldiers had been killed, giving the government forces a justification, in their own mind, for violence.

The three waves of expulsions and executions can be further analyzed by municipality. AAAS found that the three phases of expulsions (Graph 11) related to different regions of Kosovo. Specifically, in the first phase of expulsions, most of the refugees came from western and southwestern Kosovo. In the second phase, most of the refugees came from the northern and central municipalities. In the final phase, refugees came largely from the western and southern municipalities. This geographic distribution is represented in Graph 13, taken from the AAAS report, which shows the propor-

Graph 12: AAAS data on expulsions (top) and Human Rights watch data on executions (bottom) over time

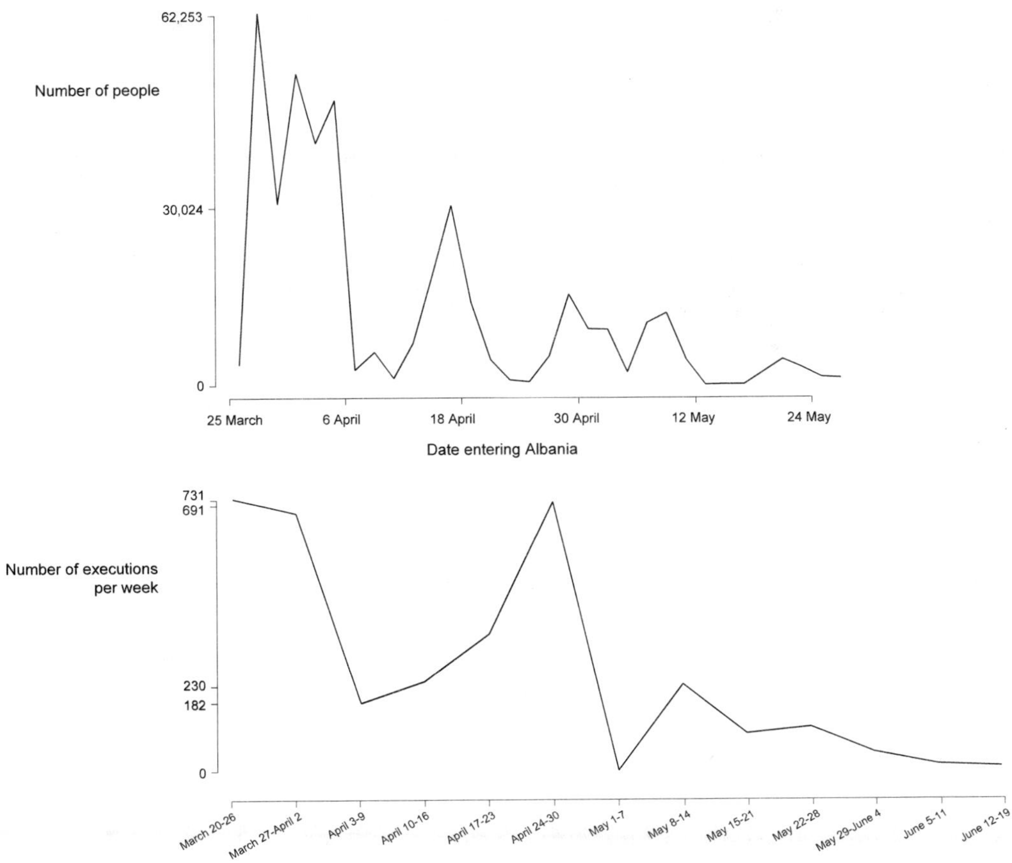

tion of refugees to Albania that came from the southwestern Kosovo municipalities (Suva Reka, Orahovac, Prizren, and Djakovica).

The Human Rights Watch data shown in Graph 6 through 10 are consistent with these findings. Namely, the municipalities in Kosovo's southwest, like Djakovica, Orahovac, Suva Reka and Prizren (see Graph 14), have large numbers of killings in the first time period. The northern municipalities like Glogovac were more likely to see executions in the second phase. In the third phase, the executions reported to Human Rights Watch were again mostly in the southwestern municipalities of Djakovica and Prizren.

Naturally, there are some exceptions. The killings in the north-central municipality of Srbica, for example (Graph 8), fall more neatly into the first and third phases rather than the second. The first phase is explained by the March 28 killing of between 146 and 166 men in Izbica, a former stronghold of the KLA that was attacked early on by government forces. The third phase surge is due to the killings in Rezala and Cirez as part of the government's offensive in Drenica.

Graph 13: Proportion of Kosovar Albanians entering Albania who originated from municipalities in the south and west, by two-day period. From AAAS' "Policy or Panic."

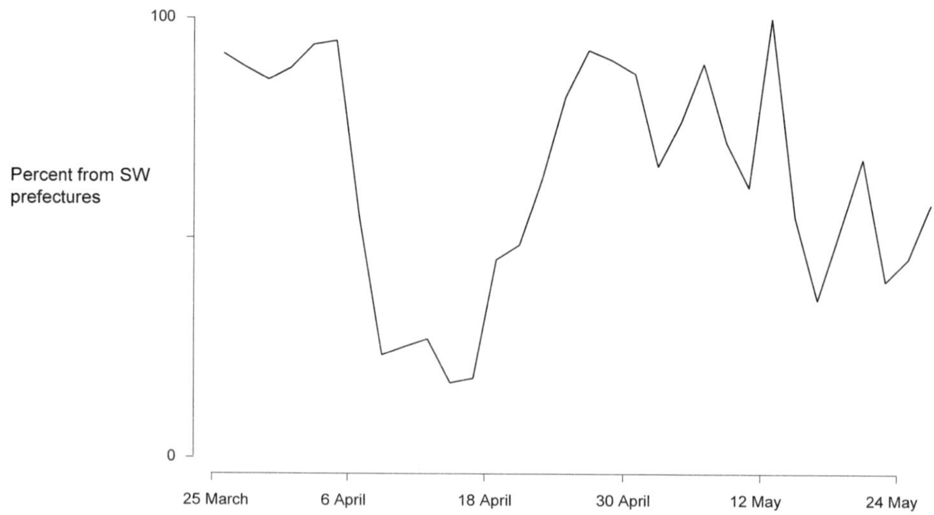

Graph 14: Extrajudicial Executions in Prizren over time

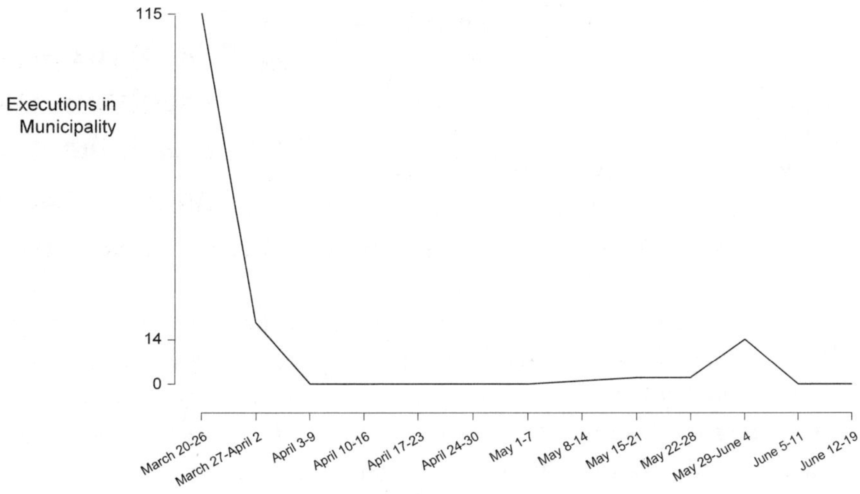

Graph 15: Extrajudicial Executions in Pec over time

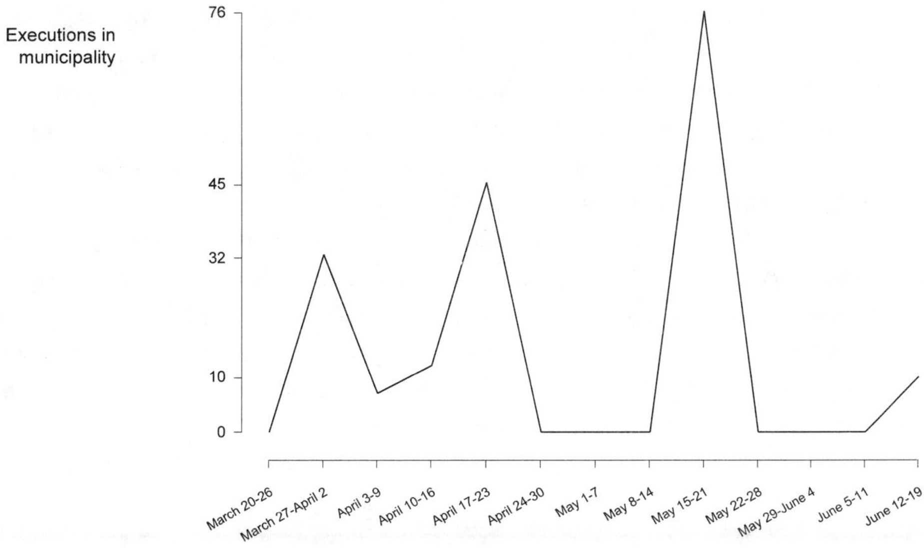

Likewise, the killings in Pec (see Graph 15) tend to mirror the first and second phase. The surge around May 14 represents the killing of seventy people in the villages of Cuska, Zahac and Pavlan. As mentioned in the detailed section on these villages in the chapter on Pec, it remains unclear why these three villages were attacked at this time, since they had remained intact throughout the war and were apparently devoid of any KLA presence. Possibilities range from revenge (KLA General Agim Ceku's family is from Cuska) to local paramilitaries plundering the three untouched villages in the area.

The three phases of expulsions closely match the three phases of executions.

This correlation between executions and expulsions was also studied by the AAAS, which conducted a second study on killings in Kosovo, *Political Killings in Kosova/Kosovo,* published in September 2000, in conjunction with the American Bar Associations's Central and East European Law Initiative (ABA/CEELI). The report's analysis of killings across Kosovo was based on 3,353 interviews collected by Human Rights Watch, ABA/CEELI, the Center for Peace Through Justice, and Physicians for Human Rights. The study concluded that approximately 10,500 Kosovar Albanians were killed between March 20 and June 12, 1999, with a 95 percent confidence interval from 7,449 to 13,627.[15]

The study compared the executions documented by these four organizations with the original AAAS report on expulsions and found very similar results to those presented by Human Rights Watch in Graph 12; namely, the three phases of expulsions closely match the three phases of executions. Similarly, as the AAAS-ABA/CEELI report states, "the pattern of killings by municipality closely follows that of refugee flows."

The strikingly similar conclusions reached by Human Rights Watch and the AAAS-ABA/CEELI report is in part due to the fact that Human Rights Watch provided its interview data for the AAAS-ABA/CEELI report. However, Human Rights Watch interviews accounted for only 577 of the 3,353 total interviews (17 percent). The similar findings should, therefore, be taken as independent confirmation of the results.

Perpetrators of Executions

Human Rights Watch asked all witnesses and victims of violations whether they could identify the type of perpetrator involved in the abuse: Serbian police, Yugoslav Army, paramilitary, or "other," for example, local Serbs, NATO, or the KLA. The results for the perpetrators of executions are presented below, but they must be taken only as an indication of perpetrator trends rather than definitive statements.

The main reason for this was Kosovar Albanians' difficulty in identifying Serbian and Yugoslav forces. While some witnesses and victims were confident in their identifications, many others, due to lack of knowledge about the forces and the generally stressful environment, were unable to distinguish between the police, army, and paramilitaries.

This was made more difficult by the large array of government forces used in the campaign, such as military police in the army, special antiterrorist forces in the police, paramilitaries, and local armed groups (see Forces of the Conflict). There were few standard uniforms and badges and insignia were not always displayed.

In addition, the scenarios in which these abuses took place were complex: one type of force might have shelled a village, another invaded it, and a third committed executions. Human Rights Watch asked witnesses which type of government force was "present" at the scene of a violation. This does not necessarily mean that it was that government force which actually committed the particular killings, but it can corroborate the testimonial evidence that most large-scale operations involved combined military and police or paramilitary forces.

Of the 3,453 extrajudicial executions reported to Human Rights Watch, witnesses claimed to have identified the Serbian police in 1,768 executions (51 percent), the Yugoslav Army in 1,173 cases (34 percent), and paramilitaries in 1,154 cases (33 percent). More than one perpetrator type may have been present at any execution.

The results are counterintuitive since the narrative chapters in this report suggest that paramilitaries were responsible for much of the worst killing, although the police and army were hardly exempt. Again, the fact that witnesses had difficulty identifying the different forces and that larger operations often involved a mix of forces probably account for the contradictory results.

When identifying perpetrators, it is easier to identify those with command responsibility for a notorious unit or a region where largescale killings took place. Given the intensity of the deliberate and unlawful killings in certain areas of Kosovo over short periods of time, as depicted in Graphs 6 through 10, as well as Graphs 14 and 15, it is highly likely that the various commanders in charge of the given municipalities were aware of the killings that took place in their respective areas of responsibility. Despite this, there is no evidence that military or political leaders took any steps to punish those responsible for the killings, or to minimize further such killings taking place as the conflict continued.

16

THE NATO AIR CAMPAIGN

From the beginning of Operation Allied Force—NATO's bombing campaign against the Federal Republic of Yugoslavia—NATO and allied government and military officials stressed their intent to limit civilian casualties and other harm to the civilian population. The practical fulfillment of this legal obligation and political imperative turned upon a range of decisions relating to targeting, weapons selection, and the means of attack. Despite precautions, including the use of a higher percentage of precision-guided munitions than in any other major conflict in history, civilian casualties occurred.

Human Rights Watch conducted a thorough investigation of civilian deaths as a result of NATO's bombing campaign in the Federal Republic of Yugoslavia. On the basis of this investigation (detailed in a February 2000 report, "Civilian Deaths in the NATO Air Campaign"), Human Rights Watch found that there were ninety separate incidents involving civilian deaths throughout the Federal Republic of Yugoslavia during the seventy-eight day bombing campaign. Some 500 Yugoslav civilians are known to have died in these incidents. Between 278 and 317 of the dead—between 56 and 60 percent of the total number of deaths—were in Kosovo.[1]

Thirty-two of these incidents with civilian deaths occurred in Kosovo, the majority involving attacks on mobile targets or military forces in the field.[2] Attacks in Kosovo overall were more deadly for civilians than those elsewhere in the Federal Republic of Yugoslavia—a third of the incidents (thirty-two out of ninety) account for more than half of the civilian deaths in the country. Seven incidents of civilian deaths that were particularly deadly were a result of attacks on convoys or transportation links. Because

Damage from a NATO bomb along the Pristina-Pec highway.

pilots' ability to identify these mobile targets properly was so important in avoiding civilian casualties, these incidents raise the question whether flying at high altitudes precluded proper target identification and caused unnecessary loss of life. Insufficient evidence exists to answer that question conclusively at this point.

There were ninety separate incidents involving civilian deaths throughout the Federal Republic of Yugoslavia during the seventy-eight day bombing campaign. Some 500 Yugoslav civilians are known to have died.

Another factor in assessing the higher level of civilian deaths in Kosovo is the possible government use of ethnic Albanian civilians as "human shields." There is some evidence that Serbian and Yugoslav forces used internally displaced civilians as human shields in the village of Korisa on May 13, and may thus share the blame for the eighty-seven deaths there. (For further discussion on the use of "human shields" by government forces, see March-June 1999: An Overview.)

INTERNATIONAL HUMANITARIAN LAW AND ACCOUNTABILITY

Rules of international humanitarian law arise from international agreements such as the Geneva Conventions, or develop as international customary law. States have an obligation to ensure compliance with all provisions of international humanitarian law, and to suppress all violations. War crimes constitute some of the most serious violations of international humanitarian law, known as grave breaches, and are generally intentional or deliberate acts. These violations give rise to the specific obligation to search for and punish those responsible, regardless of the nationality of the perpetrator or the place where the crime was committed. Examples of war crimes are wilful killing, torture or inhuman treatment of noncombatants, wilfully causing great suffering or serious injury to body or health of noncombatants, or launching an indiscriminate attack in the knowledge that the attack will cause excessive loss of life or injury to civilians.

Human Rights Watch found no evidence of war crimes in its investigation of NATO bombing in Kosovo. The investigation did conclude, however, that NATO violated international humanitarian law. Human Rights Watch has called on NATO governments to establish an independent and impartial commission, competent to receive confidential information, that would investigate violations of international humanitarian law and the extent of these violations, and would consider the need to alter targeting and bombing doctrine to ensure compliance with international humanitarian law. Such a commission should issue its findings publicly. Human Rights Watch also called for NATO to alter its targeting and bombing doctrine in order to bring it into compliance with international humanitarian law.

With respect to NATO violations of international humanitarian law in Kosovo, Human Rights Watch was concerned about a number of cases in which NATO forces:

- took insufficient precautions identifying the presence of civilians when attacking convoys and other mobile targets; and

- caused excessive civilian casualties by not taking sufficient measures to verify that military targets did not have concentrations of civilians (such as at Korisa).

THE STANDARDS APPLIED

The conduct of warfare is restricted by international humanitarian law—the laws of war. International humanitarian law applies expressly and uniquely to armed conflict situations, with distinct provisions to regulate international and non-international (internal) armed conflicts. In evaluating NATO's use of military force in the Federal Republic of Yugoslavia, the laws of war provide the most relevant standards.

As explained in the chapter on Legal Standards in the Kosovo Conflict, beginning February 28, 1998, the conflict in Kosovo could be characterized as an internal armed conflict, which obliged both government forces and the KLA to respect basic protections of international humanitarian law—the rules of war—in particular, Article 3 common to the four Geneva Conventions of 1949, Protocol II to those conventions, and the customary rules of war. With the initiation of the NATO bombing on March 24, 1999, the conflict in Kosovo and all of the Federal Republic of Yugoslavia, to the extent that it involved NATO and Serbian and Yugoslav forces, became an international armed conflict to which the full body of international humanitarian law applied.

Protocol I additional to the Geneva Conventions of 1949 provides the basis for the evaluation here of NATO's bombing. This protocol has been ratified by most NATO members, and the U.S. government, while not a party, has declared that it accepts all of the relevant standards. The basic principle of Protocol I, and of the laws of war generally, is that the civilian population and individual civilians shall enjoy general protection against dangers arising from military operations. This turns in large part on the requirement that attackers must distinguish between civilians and combatants and between military objectives and civilian objects. They must take all feasible precautions to avoid or minimize harm to civilians, and to this end may not attack civilians directly, or combatants and civilians indiscriminately.

Damage to civilian objects and civilian casualties that are incidental to lawful attacks on military objectives are known in military terminology as "collateral damage." The legality of an attack turns upon various factors. First, the attackers must do everything feasible to verify that they are aiming at something specific—they cannot lash out blindly. Second, the attackers must establish that the objective to be attacked is a legitimate military objective. And third, the attackers must establish whether an attack would endanger civilians and civilian objects, and must weigh this risk against the military advantage to be gained. Attacks which may be expected to cause incidental loss of life or injuries to civilians, or to cause damage to civilian objectives *are indiscriminate* if this harm to civilians is "excessive in relation to the concrete and direct military advantage anticipated" (Protocol I, article 57 (2)). The International Committee of the Red Cross (ICRC), the principal authority on the interpretation of international humanitarian law, has cautioned that the argument of proportionality can never justify very high civilian casualties and damage, whatever the military advantage envisioned.

In researching each of the incidents involving civilian deaths in Kosovo, Human Rights Watch sought to gather the facts that can enable analysts to assess the legitimacy of the real or perceived military objectives targeted; the care taken and procedures and criteria employed to confirm the military nature of the targets; the proportionality of the civilian deaths and the means employed in the attack in relation to the military objectives, where these were known; the correlation of civilian deaths to the location and nature of the targets selected; the timing of target selection as a factor in its appropriateness and the minimization of civilian harm; the methods and conditions under which distinct weapons systems were employed; and, the potentially indiscriminate nature of some weapons systems in general and under certain conditions.

In assessing specific attacks, with a view to general observations on the conduct of the air war, the primary issue is whether due care was taken for the protection of civilians. Was the prospect of civilian deaths sufficiently taken into account in the targeting, the weaponry employed, and the means and conditions under which weapons were employed? This involves a review of the selection of targets, and the procedures through which these were determined, matters beyond the scope of the present report. So too is the larger question of whether the military objectives identified and targeted by NATO forces were wholly within what is permissible under humanitarian law. The following analysis addresses those aspects of the air war conducted in Kosovo only through the cost in civilian lives, as a factor in assessing the larger picture of compliance with international humanitarian law.

CASE STUDIES OF CIVILIAN DEATHS IN KOSOVO

The incidents in Kosovo involving civilian deaths provide a part of the picture from which to consider NATO's conduct of the war.[3] At issue is whether NATO effectively adhered to the humanitarian law imperative that the civilian population be protected against dangers arising from military operations. At the core is the principle of civilian immunity from attack and its complementary principle requiring the parties to a conflict to do everything feasible to distinguish civilians from combatants at all times. Several incidents, which accounted for a large proportion of civilian deaths, clearly illustrate troubling aspects of NATO actions, and are presented below.

The most dramatic losses of civilian life from the NATO offensive in Kosovo came from attacks on fleeing or traveling refugees mistaken for military forces. Repeated attacks on refugees over a twelve-mile stretch of the Djakovica-Decan road in Kosovo took the lives of seventy-three civilians; attacks near Korisa in Kosovo killed as many as eighty-seven displaced persons and refugees; and two incidents involving attacks on civilian buses, at Luzane and Savine Vode, caused additional civilian losses. An estimated nineteen civilians died in the two attacks on Dubrava prison.

The most dramatic losses of civilian life from the NATO offensive in Kosovo came from attacks on fleeing or traveling refugees mistaken for military forces.

In all of these incidents, the principal concern is whether every feasible precaution was taken to accurately distinguish civilians from combatants. At the same time, there are questions as to whether the decisions to attack might have been made on the basis of incomplete and/or seriously flawed information. The public statements by NATO concerning particular attacks, and the changes in the way attacks were characterized, also bear some analysis, in particular insofar as such statements may show an intent to justify clearly unlawful attacks in which civilian casualties were clearly excessive.

Moreover, there is a question as to whether NATO's determined effort to avoid pilot casualties precluded low-flying operations that might have helped to identify targets more accurately. This was and continues to be a major issue in the public debate about Operation Allied Force. For many weeks in the initial stages of the war, NATO airplanes were not flying below 15,000 feet. If the height at which the NATO pilots flew had little effect on with identification of and attacks upon targets, then the issue is irrelevant. But if precision would have been greater (and civilian casualties lessened) had NATO pilots flown lower, it could be argued that there may have been a point at which NATO was "obligated" to have its pilots fly lower.[4] In the case of attacks such as those at Djakovica-Decan, described below, in which flying at a higher altitude seems to have been a factor in a pilot's failure to properly identify a target, the conclusion again is that inadequate precautions were taken to avoid civilian casualties.

The incident at Korisa, described below, also raises important questions of Yugoslav responsibility for some of the civilian deaths attributed to NATO bombing. In this case, NATO did not apply adequate precautions in executing its airstrikes. But Yugoslav military forces may share the blame for the eighty-seven civilian deaths at Korisa: there is some evidence that displaced Kosovar civilians were forcibly concentrated within a military camp there as human shields.

Direct Yugoslav responsibility has been shown for killings at the Dubrava prison that Yugoslav authorities attributed to NATO bombing. Human Rights Watch researchers in Kosovo found that some eighty-six prisoners there were victims of extrajudicial executions—cold-blooded murder—by Yugoslav forces in the days after NATO bombed the prison. The NATO attack on May 21 was, however, responsible for nineteen deaths at the facility prior to the massacre of prisoners; an earlier NATO attack killed four civilians at the prison.[5]

Seven of the thirty-two incidents in Kosovo in which civilians died occurred as a result of attacks on targets in densely populated urban areas. Three incidents occurred in Djakovica, two in Pristina, and two in Prizren.The targets in almost all of these attacks were military/police barracks, headquarters, and other facilities, or factories. In these cases there was little doubt as to the apparent objective of the attack, or that these locations constituted lawful military objectives.

A discussion of the major legal and policy issues raised in selected incidents in Kosovo follows:

Refugees on the Djakovica-Decan Road

On April 14, during daylight hours, NATO aircraft repeatedly bombed refugees over a twelve-mile stretch of road between Djakovica and Decan in western Kosovo, injuring thirty-six and killing seventy-three civilians—deaths Human Rights Watch was able to document. The attacks began around 1:30 p.m. and persisted for about two hours, causing civilian deaths in numerous locations on the convoy route near the villages of Bistrazin, Gradis, Madanaj, and Meja. NATO and U.S. spokespersons initially claimed the target was an exclusively military convoy and that Serb forces may have been responsible for the attacks on civilians. Pentagon spokesman Ken Bacon said that NATO commander Gen. Wesley Clark had received reports that "after the convoy was hit, military people got out and attacked civilians." "The pilots state they attacked only military vehicles," NATO said, adding that the "reported incident will be fully investigated once all mission details have been reviewed." There are also various NATO reports of Serbian deception in placing dead civilians at the site of the bombing. German Defense Minister Rudolf Scharping, in particular, put the blame for civilian casualties on Yugoslav forces.[6]

On April 15, NATO began to backtrack. It said one plane had "apparently" dropped a bomb on a civilian vehicle traveling with a military convoy. The reference to a strictly military convoy was modified: "Serbian police or army vehicles might have been in or near the convoy." NATO acknowledged that it had bombed civilian vehicles by mistake: "Following a preliminary investigation, NATO confirmed that apparently one of its planes dropped a bomb on a civilian vehicle traveling with a convoy yesterday."

Reporters from U.S. media went to the scene on April 15. They interviewed refugee survivors and observed shattered farm tractors, burned bodies identified as refugees, bomb craters, shrapnel, and bomb remnants with U.S. markings. The refugee column had apparently been divided in two main groups. Over the next few days, NATO wavered from insisting its forces attacked only military vehicles to an explanation that two convoys had been targeted, that the refugees had been at the rear of military columns, and that the civilian death toll was limited. On April 16, NATO spokesman Jamie Shea and Gen. Giuseppe Marini declared that "in one case and one only, we have proof of civilian loss of life. Otherwise, we are sure that we targeted military vehicles."

NATO finally admitted that the pilot of a U.S. F-16 mistakenly fired on what he believed to be military trucks, and

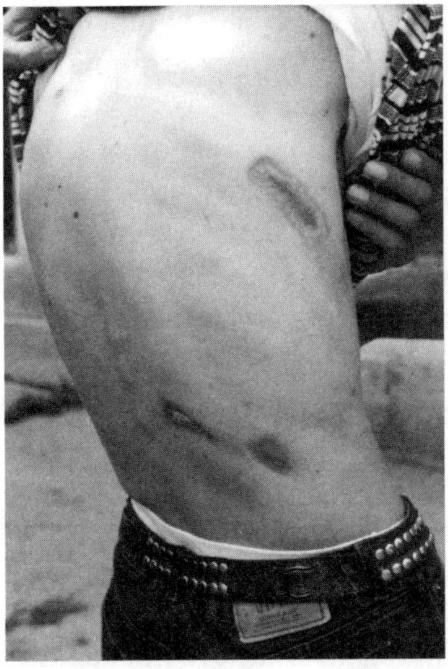

Seventy-three civilians died and thirty-six were injured, including this ethnic Albanian man, when NATO bombed a convoy of internally displaced persons on the road between Djakovica and Decan on April 14. "In my tractor fourteen people died," he said. © FRED ABRAHAMS/HUMAN RIGHTS WATCH

expressed "deep regret." Later, on April 19, NATO modified its account of a single pilot's error, declaring that about a dozen planes had been involved in numerous attacks on the two convoys, dropping a total of nine bombs. Convoluted explanations continued for a number of days after the incident; NATO and the United States seemed incapable of reconstructing what had occurred. There were widespread press reports of the use of cluster bombs, which the United States denied.[7]

The reported change in NATO rules of engagement would indicate that the alliance recognized it had taken insufficient precautions in mounting this attack.

In addition to the press reporting of this incident and the endless damage control by NATO and U.S. spokespersons, Human Rights Watch obtained extensive forensic details of the incident from the Yugoslav government.[8] No evidence whatsoever was ever produced to indicate Serb responsibility for any of the deaths, though Tanjug reported the deaths of three Serbian "policemen" in the bombings who it said "were securing the safe passage for the convoy."[9] This tends to suggest that military or police were present among the refugee vehicles, but Human Rights Watch found no basis to support the claim that the convoys themselves were primarily composed of military vehicles.[10]

General Clark stated in September that NATO consistently observed Yugoslav military vehicles moving on roads "intermixed with civilian convoys." After the Djakovica-Decan incident, General Clark said, "we got to be very, very cautious about striking objects moving on the roads.[11] Another NATO officer, Col. Ed Boyle, said: "Because we were so concerned with collateral damage, the CFAC [Combined Forces Air Component Commander] at the time, General [Michael] Short, put out the guidance that if military vehicles were intermingled with civilian vehicles, they were not to be attacked, due to the collateral damage."[12] When this directive was actually issued, and why it may not have served to avoid the subsequent three incidents, remains an important question. Nevertheless, the reported change in NATO rules of engagement would indicate that the alliance recognized it had taken insufficient precautions in mounting this attack, in not identifying civilians present, and in assuming that the intended targets were legitimate military objectives.

Displaced Civilians in the Korisa Woods

On May 13, almost a month after the Djakovica-Decan incidents, as many as eighty-seven displaced Kosovar civilians were killed and sixty wounded when bombs were dropped during the night on a refugee camp in a wooded area on the Prizren-Suva Reka road, near the village of Korisa. There have been various conflicting reports of the number of dead, from 48 to 87.[13] The Yugoslav government claimed the attackers used cluster bombs, and the *White Book* published by the Ministry of Foreign Affairs includes photographs of the remains of tactical munitions dispensers (TMDs) it says are from the site. NATO spokespersons vociferously denied the use of cluster bombs,[14] and Human Rights Watch has been unable independently to confirm that cluster bombs were indeed used in this attack.

In an official statement on May 15, NATO spokesman Maj. Gen. Walter Jertz acknowledged the attack, deeply regretting any "accidental civilian casualties." He insisted, nonetheless, that the attack was against Yugoslav army forces in the field:

> This was a legitimate military target. The Serb claims of an attack involving cluster bombs against a non-military target are both false. NATO identified Korisa as a military camp and command post. Military equipment including an armored personnel carrier and more than ten pieces of artillery were observed at this location. The aircraft observed dug-in military positions at the target before executing the attack. NATO cannot confirm the casualty figures given by the Serbian authorities, nor the reasons why civilians were at this location at the time of the attack.[15]

The NATO statement further stressed that military positions had been positively identified and that the bombs employed included laser-guided precision guided missles and non-guided gravity bombs:

> Immediately prior to the attack at 23:30—11:30 p.m.—local time Thursday night an airborne forward air controller confirmed the target, so the identification and attack system of his aircraft, having positively identified the target as what looked like dug in military reveted positions, he dropped two laser guided bombs. Following his attack, he cleared his wingman to also attack the same target using two more laser guided bombs. Approximately

> 10 minutes later, the third aircraft engaged the target with . . . six gravity bombs. A total of 10 bombs were dropped on the target.[16]

The same day, Pentagon spokesman Kenneth Bacon said at a news briefing that the incident would be reviewed, but that major changes in operations should not be expected:

> This accident at Korisa did not shake NATO's resolve in any way. . . . NATO deeply regrets civilian casualties. . . . We try very hard to avoid these casualties, but combat is inherently dangerous and accidents cannot be avoided . . . this mission, like every other, will be reviewed, and the airmen and their commanders will learn what they can from it and continue. But I don't anticipate that there will be a sweeping change. We can't cross legitimate military targets off the list, and we won't.[17]

On May 16, a Kosovar refugee who witnessed the NATO strike on Korisa reported to Deutsche Welle that FRY police forced some 600 displaced Kosovars to serve as human shields there before the attack. "We were told something bad would happen to us if we left the place," said the eyewitness, interviewed by the station's Albanian service. He said Serbian police hinted at what was about to happen. "Now you'll see what a NATO attack looks like," the refugee quoted one policeman as saying. The refugee said he finally went to sleep underneath a tractor only to be woken up by explosions and the cries of children and adults. He said he and others managed to scale a two-meter wall surrounding the plot and fled in the direction of the village as Serbian paramilitaries fired bullets around them.[18] On the basis of available evidence it is not possible to determine positively that Serbian police or Yugoslav army troops deliberately forced civilians to group near them, nor to establish the motive for such action.

The laws of war expressly forbid shielding. Article 28 of the Geneva Convention IV stipulates that "The presence of a protected person may not be used to render certain points or areas immune from military operations." Protocol I, article 51(7), elaborates:

> The presence or movements of the civilian population or individual civilians shall not be used to render certain points or areas immune from military operations, in particular in attempts to shield military objectives from

> attacks or to shield, favour or impede military operations. The Parties to the conflict shall not direct the movement of the civilian population or individual civilians in order to attempt to shield military objectives from attacks or to shield military operations.

The protocol stresses, however, in art. 51(8), that such violations of the laws of war do not in any way release an adversary from obligations to respect civilian immunity. An authoritative new commentary on humanitarian law states: "If one party to a conflict breaks this rule, this does not exempt the other side from the regulations applicable in military attacks. . . . The military commander must therefore take into account the column of refugees used by the adversary as a shield."[19]

For NATO, then, the question is whether its target designation was made with the knowledge that hundreds of displaced civilians were present in this wooded area—there is no evidence to this effect—and secondly, whether sufficient measures were taken to verify that the target had no such concentrations of civilians. On this score, the excessive civilian death toll in what NATO has itself described as a lamentable accident suggests that verification was inadequate.

Bombing of Dubrava Prison

Another case of Yugoslav deception involves civilian deaths and NATO bombing that damaged the large Dubrava prison complex near Istok. According to NATO and former Dubrava prisoners interviewed by Human Rights Watch, Yugoslav Army and Serbian police forces were based adjacent to the penitentiary, which was fully operational well into the NATO air campaign, housing common criminal offenders and political detainees serving out their terms.

The Penitentiary Institute Istok, as it was officially called, was hit twice by NATO, causing civilian deaths among both prisoners and guards. In the first attack, at 1:15 p.m. on May 19, three prisoners and a guard were reported killed. The second attack occurred on May 21, in which at least nineteen prisoners were killed. An investigation undertaken by Human Rights Watch, based on eyewitness testimony, found that prisoners were lined up and fired upon by Serb police and prison guards inside the penitentiary walls after the May 21 attack, and some eighty or so prisoners were killed. (For detailed documentation of the killings, see the section on Dubrava prison in Istok Municipality).

The Yugoslav government initially reported that nineteen people were killed in the Dubrava Penitentiary as a result of the May 21 attack.[20] However, four days later, the Yugoslav press reported from the official Tanjug agency that "in days-long bombardment of the Penitentiary Institute Istok, some 100 prisoners died, and some 200 were wounded." On May 27, Tanjug quoted Vladan Bojic, a judge in Pec's District Court, saying that ninety-six corpses had been pulled from the ruins. On May 29, the Yugoslav government stated that "The number of casualties in the Correctional Institution in Istok is increasing."[21] On May 30, Tanjug reported a total of ninety-three killed.[22] In July, the Yugoslav government claimed that NATO bombs killed ninety-five inmates and injured 196.[23]

While NATO readily acknowledged the air strikes at Istok and justified the attacks on the grounds that it had targeted military objectives "in the vicinity of a prison,"[24] Human Rights Watch has determined that Yugoslav forces were likely responsible for the majority of the deaths which occurred after the bombing. On May 22, according to eyewitnesses, prison officials ordered approximately 1,000 prisoners to line up in the prison yard. After a few minutes, they were fired upon, and grenades were thrown at them from the prison walls and guard towers, killing at least seventy people. Over the next twenty-four hours, prison guards, special police, and possibly paramilitaries attacked prisoners who were hiding in the prison's buildings, basements, and sewers, killing at least another twelve people.

Journalists who visited the Dubrava prison on May 21, just after the morning bombing, reported seeing between ten and twenty bodies.[25] Serb authorities again opened the prison for journalists on May 24. Reporting for the BBC, Jacky Rowland said it was unclear how the victims in the prison had died, but that three days after the first journalists' tour, the dead numbered forty-four. The condition of the prisoners' bodies viewed there did not conform with the government's claim that they had died in the bombing. Post-war visits to the prison by journalists confirmed that prisoners had been killed execution-style after the bombing.[26]

Given the degree of civilian casualties in the two attacks on the Dubrava prison, it appears that NATO did not apply adequate precautions in executing its airstrikes on nearby military objectives, and therefore must be held accountable for the civilian deaths that occurred as a direct result of those attacks. But Yugoslav forces must be held fully responsible for approximately eighty-six of the ninety-five deaths Yugoslav authorities acknowledged at Dubrava, as these were prisoners who were executed extrajudicially well after the NATO strikes.

NATO's Use of Cluster Bombs

One of the issues of most intense public interest that has emerged from Operation Allied Force is NATO's use of cluster bombs. There are seven confirmed and five likely incidents involving civilian deaths from cluster bomb use by the United States and Britain. Altogether, some ninety to 150 civilians throughout Yugoslavia died from NATO cluster bombs.

The most serious incident involving civilian deaths and the use of cluster bombs occurred on May 7 in Nis, Serbia. The mid-day attack on Nis airfield, which is located inside the urban zone, killed fourteen civilians and injured twenty-eight. NATO confirmed the attack on Nis airfield,[27] and on May 8, NATO Secretary General Solana confirmed NATO responsibility for the attack, stating that "NATO has confirmed that the damage to the market and clinic was caused by a NATO weapon which missed its target."[28] According to U.S. Air Force sources, the CBU-87 cluster bomb container failed to open over the airfield but opened right after release from the attacking airplane, projecting submunitions at a great distance into the city.[29]

After the incident in Nis, the White House quietly issued a directive to the Pentagon to restrict cluster bomb use (at least by U.S. forces).[30] Human Rights Watch considers this to have been the right move, but is concerned, given these risks, that cluster bombs were being used in attacks on urban targets in the first place. The mid-May prohibition against the further use of cluster bombs clearly had an impact on the level of civilian deaths as the war continued, particularly as bombing with unguided weapons (which would otherwise include cluster bombs) significantly intensified towards the end of the month. Nevertheless, the British air force continued to drop cluster bombs (official chronologies show use at least on May 17, May 31, June 3, and June 4),[31] indicating the need for universal, not national, norms regarding cluster bomb use.

Elderly Serb woman waiting to depart Prizren in a convoy of fleeing Serb civilians on June 14, 1999.

17

ABUSES AFTER JUNE 12, 1999

INTRODUCTION

The adoption of Security Council Resolution 1244 on June 10, 1999, and the conclusion of the Military Technical Agreement between NATO and the Governments of Serbia and the Federal Republic of Yugoslavia brought an end both to the NATO bombing and mass expulsions and killings by Serbian and Yugoslav security forces. In accordance with the terms of the agreement, the NATO-led Kosovo Force (KFOR) entered the province on June 12, and the Yugoslav Army and Serbian police (and paramilitaries) began a phased withdrawal from Kosovo, followed by a suspension of NATO air strikes. By June 20, all Serbian and Yugoslav security forces had withdrawn, leaving Kosovo under the control of KFOR.

The departure of Yugoslav and Serbian security forces brought an end to more than a decade of increasingly bloody and systematic persecution of Kosovar Albanians. But it did not bring an end to violence or gross violations of human rights in Kosovo. The province's Serb and Roma minorities—who many ethnic Albanians collectively regarded as active or complicit in atrocities by government forces—were immediately targeted for revenge. Thousands had already departed with the government's forces. Those who remained were forced to leave the province or concentrated in enclaves after widespread and systematic arson of Serb and Roma homes, beatings, detentions, and murders. As of July 2001, an estimated 1,000 Kosovo Serbs and Roma were missing and unaccounted for.[1]

Violence soon spread to include attacks on other minorities, particularly Muslims who spoke Slavic languages rather than Albanian, Croats, and ethnic Turks. Kosovar Albanians regarded as collaborators with the Serbian or

Yugoslav state and their families were also attacked. At the same time, political violence between Kosovar Albanian political parties and factions and rivalries among former Kosovo Liberation Army officers (both sometimes linked to economic issues and corruption) led to some high-profile killings, even after the October 28, 2000, municipal elections.

ATTACKS ON MINORITIES

The KLA and ethnic Albanian civilians carried out widespread burning and looting of homes belonging to Serbs, Roma and other minorities, and destroyed many Orthodox churches and monasteries in the immediate aftermath of KFOR's arrival in Kosovo. Attackers combined this destruction with killings, harassment and intimidation designed to force people from their homes and communities, a pattern which continues today. Members of minority groups in Kosovo have been detained, beaten, and sometimes tortured, with as many as 1,000 Serbs and Roma reported unaccounted for after abductions since the end of the conflict. The elderly and infirm who remained in their homes have frequently borne the brunt of this violence and intimidation, and many now live as virtual prisoners in their homes. The demographic consequences have been profound: At least 150,000 members of Kosovo's minorities fled the province for Serbia and Montenegro, most within the first six weeks of KFOR's initial deployment.[2] In addition to those non-Albanians who fled the province, there has been substantial internal displacement inside Kosovo, with the majority of Serbs and other minorities concentrated into enclaves like Northern Mitrovica or Kosovo Polje.

Members of minority groups in Kosovo have been detained, beaten, and sometimes tortured, with as many as 1,000 Serbs and Roma reported unaccounted for.

Although a desire for revenge and retaliation provides some of the explanation for the violence, especially in the cases of arson and looting of property, Human Rights Watch's research suggests that a great deal of the violence is politically motivated; namely, the removal from Kosovo of non-ethnic Albanians in order to better justify an independent state. There is also clear evidence that some KLA units were responsible for violence against minorities beginning in the summer of 1999, and continuing throughout 2000 and early 2001. Human Rights Watch has no evidence, however, of a coordinated policy to this end of the political or military leadership of the former KLA, which has made public statements condemning attacks against minorities.[3]

The willingness of almost all Kosovar Albanians to remain silent about such attacks, either from fear of speaking out or because of a belief in the collective guilt of Serbs and Roma, has created a permissive environment for violence against minorities. Human Rights Watch interviews with Kosovar Albanians from all walks of life suggest a widespread acceptance of the view that wartime atrocities now mean that Serbs have forfeited the right to remain in Kosovo and to retain their property and goods, irrespective of their involvement in abuses. On the other hand, many of the same respondents privately expressed their revulsion at the violence perpetrated against minorities.

A great deal of the violence is politically motivated; namely, the removal from Kosovo of non-ethnic Albanians.

No estimates exist for the number of minority homes destroyed in the postwar period, but Human Rights Watch researchers visiting formerly mixed communities throughout Kosovo during the summer of 1999 observed wide-spread arson and looting of homes. Seventy-six Orthodox churches, monasteries, or religious sites have been damaged or destroyed since June 1999 according to the Serbian Orthodox Church in Kosovo.[4] Human Rights Watch researchers visited a number of the sites.

The intent behind many of the killings and abductions that have occurred in the province since June 1999 appears to be the expulsion of Kosovo's Serb and Roma population rather than a desire for revenge alone. In numerous cases, direct and systematic efforts were made to force Serbs and Roma to leave their homes.[5] Human Rights Watch documented the harassment of elderly Serb women in formerly mixed communities in Prizren and Gnjilane municipalities, for example, and received reports of widespread efforts to remove Serbs from their homes in Pristina and Lipljan. Roma have been driven from their homes in Pristina and elsewhere by intimidation and other harassment.

Grenade and rocket attacks on minority homes are another method of "persuading" residents to leave. Such attacks against Serbs have been reported in the municipalities of Lipljan, Vitina, Gnjilane, Obilic, Orahovac, Kosovo Polje, Pec, Prizren, and Vucitrn. Attacks against Roma have been reported in Stimlje, Pristina, and Pec municipalities. The homes of the Gorani, another ethnic group of Slavic Muslims, have been subjected to grenade attacks in Gora municipaliy and other Muslim Slavs (Bosniaks) have suffered grenade attacks in Prizren, Pec, and Istok. In Pristina, Serbs and Roma have received threatening telephone calls and visits by armed men in civilian clothing and KLA uniforms in which they are flatly told to leave. The double grenade attack on a marketplace full of Serb civilians in the town of Kosovo Polje in September 1999, which killed two and left forty-seven wounded, can be understood in the same context. Even those who do choose to leave are not immune from violence: in October 1999 a KFOR-escorted convoy of 150 Serbs leaving Kosovo was attacked in Pec. Vehicles were stoned and their occupants pulled out and beaten before the vehicles were set on fire. At least fifteen Serbs were wounded during the attack.

According to a survey carried out by UNHCR, more than 150,000 of the 210,000 displaced persons from Kosovo in Serbia and Montenegro fled after June 12.[6] Approximately 143,000 of the 210,000 displaced persons from Kosovo in Serbia and Montenegro are Serbs and more than 25,000 are Roma. Several thousand Roma and Serbs also entered Macedonia during the same period, and an unknown number fled to other third countries. In addition, as noted, there has been substantial displacement of the remaining minority populations within Kosovo into mono-ethnic enclaves (sometimes consisting of a single apartment building), generally under KFOR protection. Significant numbers of minority populations not associated with abuses against Albanians, including Gorani, Muslim Slavs, and Croats have also been displaced from their homes by harassment and intimidation, including violent attacks. The explanation as to why those not implicated in attacks against Albanians should be targeted is complex: part of the explanation appears to be that, as speakers of Slavic languages, these minorities are associated with Yugoslavia in general and with Serbia in particular. In addition, such minorities may also be perceived to have had a privileged status in Kosovo, notably during the crackdown against Albanians in the 1990s.

Most of the Serb populations in the municipalities of Pristina, Pec, Prizren, Urosevac, and Istok have fled their homes, as have large numbers from the town of Gnjilane. According to a February 2000 report of the inter-agency Ad-Hoc Task Force on Minorities, only 700 to 800 Serbs remain in

Pristina, compared to an estimated 20,000 in 1998.[7] The Task Force also reported that only 120 Serbs remain in the town of Prizren and twenty-three in the town of Urosevac. Those Serbs displaced inside Kosovo are mostly concentrated in towns and villages which had an historic Serb majority and which were fairly quickly assigned KFOR protection, including Kosovo Polje, Babin Most (Babimoc), Plemetina (Plementine), Strpce, Gracanica (Pristina municipality),Velika Hoca (Orahovac municipality), Dobrotin and elsewhere in Lipljan municipality (where the Serbs population is estimated at 9,500), Gnjilane municipality (estimated at 12,500), the northern part of Kosovska Mitrovica, and the northern municipalities of Leposavic and Zubin Potok.[8] In addition, only a few hundred of the 6,000 Serb refugees from Croatia resettled in Kosovo remain, according to UNHCR, after two collective centers for such refugees were burned.

As noted above, there are at least 25,000 Roma displaced from Kosovo in Serbia and Montenegro, as well as several thousand in camps in Macedonia.

Serb children leaving Prizren with their families on June 14, 1999. Most of the Serbian population in the municipalities of Prizren, Pristina, Pec, Urosevac, and Istok fled their homes after the war due to revenge attacks.

© JOANNE MARINER/HUMAN RIGHTS WATCH

There has also been substantial internal displacement, but the size of the remaining population is unknown.[9] The European Roma Rights Center (ERRC), a Budapest-based Roma rights organization, reported in July 1999 that none of the Roma communities it had visited held more than half of their pre-conflict Roma population. February 2000 estimates from the Ad Hoc Task Force on Minorities indicated that between 115 and 140 Roma remained in Pristina town. The November 1999 report from the Task Force estimated that there were a further 300–600 Roma elsewhere in Pristina municipality at that time.[10] Other areas with significant Roma populations as of early 2000 included Kosovo Polje (between 1,700 and 2,800), Obilic (around 1,200), Lipljan (around 1,500), Urosevac (4,200), and Prizren (4-5000).[11]

Violence against the Albanian-speaking Ashkali Roma continued after the October 28, 2000, municipal elections. On November 8, four Ahkali men were murdered execution-style by unknown assailants outside the village of Dosevac (Dashevc) near Srbica. The men, living in tents, had just returned to their homes with the assistance of UNHCR.[12] In response to the killings, Head of UNMIK Bernard Kouchner said "Somewhere in Kosovo, extremists want to undermine the return of decent people to their homes."[13]

Members of other minorities have also been displaced inside Kosovo or have left the province altogether. In November 1999, 293 ethnic Croats were evacuated from Kosovo to Zagreb, after they complained of harassment, arson, and not being permitted to speak Croatian.[14] The ethnic Croat population in Janjevo was placed under heavy KFOR protection and appeared stable. Attacks against the Croat and Roma communities in the village intensified in March 2000 however, following the removal of the permanent KFOR guard, and decreased only after the permanent protection was renewed.

The Muslim Slav population of Kosovo (sometimes referred to as Bosniaks) have also fled Pristina in significant numbers, mainly for Bosnia, leaving around 1,600 to 1,800 out of a pre-war population between 3,500 and 4,000.[15] The estimated 23,000 to 25,000 Muslim Slavs in Prizren municipality (who sometimes refer to themselves as Torbesh) have come under significant pressure to leave, including grenade attacks and the murder of a Torbesh family of four in January and of a Muslim Slav man in February, which led to some departures.[16] The Muslim Slav population in Pec appears relatively secure but members of the community have nevertheless come under attack: in April, a group of fifteen Albanian men attacked and beat a seventy-year-old Bosniak woman. (The woman had reportedly been mistaken for a Serb.) There have also been attacks on the homes of Gorani, who are distinct from the Muslim Slav/Bosniak community.

Generally unidentified groups of armed ethnic Albanians have carried out abductions of Serbs and Roma throughout Kosovo since early June 1999. In some cases, these forces have detained, questioned, beaten, and then released those abducted. However, according to the International Committee of the Red Cross (ICRC), as of April 2001, approximately more than 500 of those abducted remain unaccounted for.[17]

According to Ranko Djinovic, president of the Association of the Families of the Missing and Kidnapped in Kosovo and Metohija, 1,230 non-Albanians went missing in Kosovo between January 1998 and November 2000. Twenty percent of these people went missing before the NATO intervention, Djinovic said, 5 percent during the air war, and 75 percent after NATO's entry into Kosovo.[18] This number may be too high, however, as some names on the association's list are reported twice and others who were reported missing were in detention and have been subsequently released.

In May 2000, the ICRC published a book listing missing persons from Kosovo registered up to that point. According to the ICRC, 450 persons went missing between June 10, 1999, and March 31, 2000. Human Rights Watch reviewed the ICRC list and, according to the names, at least 309 of these people were clearly members of minorities (non-Albanian.)[19] This matches closely with figures from the Humanitarian Law Center which, between March 24 and August 10, 1999, registered 318 missing non-Albanians.[20] The ICRC figure of total missing as of April 2001 was 3,525, but no ethnic breakdown was available.[21]

The rape of women from minorities has also been reported since June 1999. Roma women have suffered in particular. The European Roma Rights Center has documented three incidents of rape of Roma women by persons in KLA uniform. The center interviewed an eyewitness who reported that his sister and wife had been raped by four uniformed men in Djakovica on June 29, 1999. They also interviewed the relative of a woman from Kosovska Mitrovica who had been raped on June 20, 1999 by six men in KLA uniforms.[22]

On July 26, 1999, KFOR received a report from a middle-aged Serb woman in Gnjilane that she had been raped by two Kosovar Albanian men.[23] Two Kosovar Albanian woman witnessed the two men entering the woman's apartment. The OSCE recorded the rape of a Roma woman in Prizren in October 1999 by several Albanian men.[24] One of the perpetrators, who was subsequently arrested by KFOR, had allegedly raped another Roma woman in the area. The February Task Force on Minorities report also documented the rape of a pregnant Ashkali woman in Urosevac in November 1999, and the rape and attempted rape of several Roma women that same month in the Djakovica area.[25]

According to KFOR statistics, in the approximately five months between KFOR's arrival on June 12 and early November 1999 there were 379 murders in Kosovo, with 135 victims of the Serbs. No separate figures were kept for persons from other minorities, but the figures underscore both the scale of the lawlessness in post-war Kosovo and the violence between Albanians and Serb paramilitaries and civilians that continued in Kosovska Kamenica, Kosovska Mitrovica, and several other areas over the summer. Between January 30 and May 27, 2000, KFOR reported ninety-five murders in Kosovo.[26] Twenty-six of the victims were Serbs, seven were Roma, two were Muslim Slavs, fifty-two were Albanians, and eight were of unknown ethnicity. Although, the statistics show a steep decline in the murder rate, it is important to emphasize that murder (together with other serious crimes such as aggravated assault, arson and kidnapping) still disproportionately affect minorities, who now comprise far less than 10 percent of Kosovo's resident population.[27]

Some of the worst violence against minorities has occurred in and around the divided city of Kosovska Mitrovica, which has also been the scene of extensive internal displacement. Following the wartime displacement of around 8,000 Albanians from the (now predominantly Serb) northern side of the Ibar river, more than 2,000 Serbs have been displaced from the (now predominantly Albanian) southern side of the river. Between 8,000 and 10,000 Roma have also been forced from the southern side of the river. Despite the somewhat belated efforts of KFOR and U.N. police to secure the city, incidents of harassment and intimidation have reduced the minority populations on both sides of the Ibar.

The city has been effectively partitioned, with a heavy deployment of KFOR peacekeepers designed to keep communities apart and to protect isolated pockets of Serbs and Roma in the southern part of the city and Albanians, Muslim Slavs, and Turks in the northern part (most of them concentrated in the so-called "Bosniak" quarter). Some of the worst violence in Mitrovica followed a February 2, 2000, rocket attack on a UNHCR bus under KFOR escort traveling from a Serb enclave, the village of Banja, to Kosovska Mitrovica. The attack left an elderly Serb man and woman dead and three others wounded, and sparked a wave of tit-for-tat violence in northern Mitrovica that left eight non-Serbs dead and forced more than 1,700 Albanians, Muslim Slavs, and Turks to flee to the southern part of the city. UNHCR bus lines connecting minority enclaves were suspended for two months after the attack.

After the events of the spring of 2000 minorities remained a target, with much of the violence designed to force them to leave Kosovo. The Ad Hoc Task Force on Minorities report from May stated that "the last remaining Serb in Klobukar [a village in Novo Brdo municipality] was stabbed in the chest on 14 February, and her body was discovered the next day in her burning house."[28] On February 26, Josip Vasic, a prominent doctor and member of the Serb National Council was shot dead on the street in Gnjilane.[29] A twenty-nine-year-old Serb man was shot dead on March 11 while working in his fields in the village of Donja Brnjica (Bernica e Poshteme), near Pristina. On March 27, a Roma man was found strangled in Istok. On March 28, an elderly Serb women was beaten in her home in Prizren. The woman subsequently died of her wounds. On April 3, 2000, Metodije Halauska, an eighty-six-year-old ethnic Czech was kidnapped from his home in Pristina, beaten and shot in the back of the head. On April 8, the body of an unidentified elderly woman was found in the burned remains of a Serb house in Pec.[30] Two Roma teenage boys aged seventeen and eighteen and a forty-eight-year-old Roma woman were also found shot dead in Pec on the same day. On April 9, a Serb man was shot dead in a restaurant in Gnjilane. Three other Serbs were also killed during that same week.

The weeks surrounding the first anniversary of NATO's entry into Kosovo were particularly bloody with a series of grenade and landmine attacks and "drive-by" shootings targeting Serbs that left eleven dead and more than a dozen wounded. On May 22, a seventy-year-old Serb farmer was shot dead in Gojbulja (Gojbuja) village (Vucitrn municipality).[31] Two days later a fifty-one-year-old Serb man was shot dead in the town of Vitina. On May 28, two men and a four-year-old boy were killed and two men were wounded in a "drive-by" shooting in Cernica (Gnjilane municipality).[32] A May 31 "drive-by" shooting in Babin Most village left one Serb man dead and another wounded. On June 1, a group of Serbs returning from a funeral were fired upon by ethnic Albanians in the village of Klokot (Gnjilane municipality), killing one woman and wounding three men.[33] On June 2, two Serb men driving on a road connecting two Serb villages were killed after their car hit a landmine. A woman and two children in the car were wounded. The road had previously been cleared of mines, the mine.[34] A grenade attack in the Serb enclave of Gracanica on June 6 left a further five wounded.[35] On June 15, two Serb men were killed and another man was wounded after their vehicle drove over a landmine near the village of Lepina (Lipljan municipality) in what a KFOR spokesperson described as a "deliberate, carefully planned, attack."[36]

Service with an international organization has not been sufficient to provide minorities with immunity from violence. In October 1999, a U.N. official from Bulgaria was shot dead on Pristina's main street, after reportedly being mistaken for a Serb. The same month, a grenade was thrown into the Pristina apartment of a Serb interpreter working for the U.N., slightly wounding her. She had earlier been forced to move apartments because of harassment. On May 15, the body of twenty-five-year-old Petar Topoljski, a Serb UNMIK translator, was found in the village of Rimaniste, near Pristina.[37] Topoljski had not appeared for work for the previous week, after his name, photograph, and address were published in the Kosovo daily newspaper *Dita,* together with allegations that he was a Serb paramilitary who had participated in the mass expulsions of Albanians from the province. (The newspaper was temporarily shut down by UNMIK for eight days after the paper's editor refused to apologize for publishing the story, print a retraction, or agree to refrain from making similar accusations in the future. The paper also reprinted the article when the ban was lifted.)

VIOLENCE AGAINST ETHNIC ALBANIANS

As the events in Mitrovica and the murder statistics make clear, violence has not been confined to non-Albanians. On June 12, 2000, two ethnic Albanians were killed and a third injured in an attack by Serb assailants in the village of Cubrelj (Qubrel). As noted above, the violence in northern Mitrovica that followed the February rocket attack on a UNHCR bus left eight non-Serbs dead and forced almost two thousand others to flee their homes. In addition to Serbian attacks on Albanians in Mitrovica, there has also been considerable Albanian-on-Albanian violence. Albanians accused of "collaboration" with Serbian authorities have been beaten and forced from their homes, notably in the municipalities of Prizren, Djakovica, and Klina. Albanian Catholics and the families of Albanians who worked for the Serbian state have encountered particular difficulties.[38]

Albanian political moderates have also been threatened. In October 1999, Veton Surroi and Baton Haxhiu, the publisher and editor of a leading Albanian language daily, *Koha Ditore,* were accused of being "pro-Serb vampires" who "should not have a place in free Kosovo" by KosovaPress, the official news agency of the KLA. The article stated that "it would not be surprising if they become victims of possible and understandable revenge acts"—a clear incitement to violence against the two journalists. The attack followed the publication of editorials in *Koha Ditore* and a strong commentary by Surroi condemning attacks against minorities, which concluded that the climate created by such attacks was likely to have profound and negative consequences for democracy in Kosovo, and would affect all of its inhabitants, minority and Albanian.

Albanians accused of "collaboration" with Serbian authorities have been beaten and forced from their homes.

The struggle for primacy among the factions of the former Kosovo Liberation Army and Ibrahim Rugova's Democratic League of Kosovo (LDK) have also led to violence. The murder of an LDK politician and the kidnapping and interrogation of another in the Drenica region in November 1999 was followed by a spate of execution-syle murders of prominent KLA fighters.[39] According to the *New York Times,* twenty-three KLA members were killed between June 1999 and May 2000.[40] Although the killings are frequently attributed to rivalries within organized crime, some of the murders, including the killing in May of political moderate and prominent former-KLA leader Ekrem Rexha (known as Commander "Drini"), have a clear political dimension.[41] On June 15, 2000, gunmen wearing the KLA insignia killed Alil Dresaj, a senior LDK politician.[42]

Violence against members of political parties continued after the October 28, 2000, municipal elections, although it was not always clear whether the killings were politically motivated. A member of the LDK in Klina, Hazir

Raci, was killed three days after the elections.[43] On November 16, an LDK member of Pec's new Municipal Council, Shkelzen Hyseni, was attacked and wounded in his home.[44] On November 23, a founding member of the LDK and advisor to Ibrahim Rugova, Xhemail Mustafa, was killed by two unknown gunmen at 3:00 p.m. outside his apartment in the Dardania neighborhood of Pristina.[45]

RESPONSE OF THE INTERNATIONAL COMMUNITY

Statements by the leaders of NATO countries and the U.N. in the crucial first months after NATO entered Kosovo asserted that what was happening there was different than the violence in the spring; that the world was witnessing individual acts of revenge; that there was no equivalence between Serbia's persecution of its Albanian minority and the post-war per-

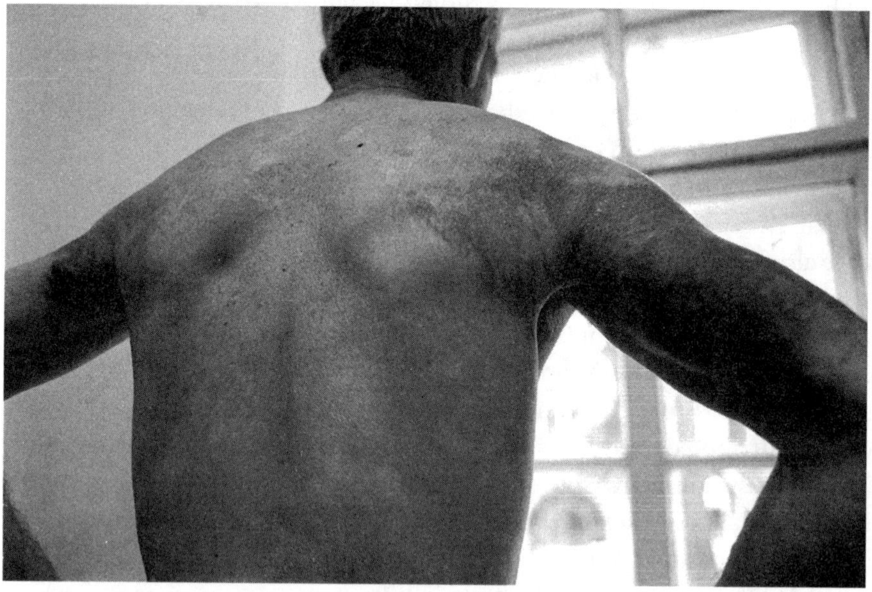

This Kosovar Albanian man was held for two days in Prizren by the KLA and severely beaten. German KFOR troops freed him and numerous other captives on June 18, 1999.

© JOANNE MARINER/HUMAN RIGHTS WATCH

secution of minorities in Kosovo. In his introduction to a 400-page OSCE report detailing postwar abuses against minorities in Kosovo, Bernard Kouchner, the head of UNMIK wrote, "It is not fair to make comparisons with the situation before or during the war.... it is no longer a matter of a policy... the crimes we see are the acts of individuals."[46] Condemnation of attacks on minorities was frequently equivocal. During a July 29, 1999, visit to Kosovo, U.S. Secretary of State Madeline Albright was asked about the killing of fourteen Serb farmers in the village of Gracko. Her response was that it "was obviously a dreadful incident. We can't forget that there were some pretty disgusting things that took place before, but the system is set up in order to protect them. They should stay."[47] The ambiguity of her response typified the ambivalent reaction of Western leaders to violence against minorities in Kosovo.

NATO failed to take decisive action to curb the forced displacement and killings of Kosovo's minorities in the first months.

NATO failed to take decisive action to curb the forced displacement and killings of Kosovo's minorities in the first months. Initially, KFOR was solely responsible for security, but it balked at civilian policing tasks and detained few suspects. Most were released quickly, their freeing justified by the absence of a legal framework to warrant their continued detention. Thus, from the earliest days of the U.N. and NATO presence in Kosovo, violence and criminality (including attacks on minorities) were effectively undeterred. More recent efforts by U.N. police have been hampered by a flawed local judiciary that is reluctant to detain or convict Albanian defendants, particularly in cases involving violence against minorities. The inevitable result has been a climate of impunity in the province.

The issue of violence against minorities has commanded considerable attention among international actors in Kosovo. The creation of the UNHCR and OSCE-led Ad Hoc Task Force on July 14, 1999, has undoubtedly played a crucial role in the development of these humanitarian initiatives and in advocating better protection of minorities. A report of the task force from November 1999 listed a variety of measures designed to improve the security for at-risk populations in Kosovo, including: "reinforcement of doors, installation of emergency calling devices in homes, and the establishment of a hotline between lead agencies and KFOR."[48] The report also notes that "UNHCR has designed a special humanitarian distribution network for needy minority groups, and interim systems for providing medical care to minority groups who are otherwise denied access."[49] There is also little doubt that without KFOR protection, minority enclaves in Orahovac, Gracanica, and Prizren would no longer exist.

Nevertheless, the overall response of the international community to abuses against minorities has been belated and inadequate, particularly in the area of security. The withdrawal of Serbian police and Yugoslav military units, while bringing a welcome end to widespread abuses against Kosovar Albanians, left a security vacuum for Serb and other minority civilians that has only been partially filled by KFOR peacekeepers and U.N. police. In the crucial first two months of the international intervention, there were no more than a handful of U.N. police, leaving KFOR troops to perform civilian policing functions. In order to bridge the gap, France and Italy deployed paramilitary police units and other contingents utilized military police to perform civilian policing functions, including investigations of complaints.

KFOR's response to attacks and threats against minorities during the first months of the operation was uneven, with minorities receiving round-the-clock protection in some areas, while those in others were forced from their homes. KFOR's overall record on preventing the abduction, detention, and murder of Serbs and Roma during that crucial period was poor. A KFOR officer in eastern Kosovo told Human Rights Watch at the end of June 1999 that his unit did not even try to keep track of the abductions because of their frequency. In many cases, KFOR officers from all contingents expressed the view that the commission of such crimes was inevitable. Efforts by a Human Rights Watch researcher to report an incident of harassment in Ljubizda village on June 30, 1999, to the German KFOR contingent required multiple visits to local posts, and then to the contingent headquarters in Prizren, where a civilian-military implementation cell (CMIC) officer appeared uninterested in the details of the case.

KFOR's lack of consistency and frequently inadequate response can be explained in part by concern about protecting its own forces, differing interpretations of the mandate by each national contingent, and lack of experience in civilian policing. It is also important to recall that prior to its entry into Kosovo on June 12, 1999, KFOR was prepared to encounter resistance from armed Serb military and civilians. This is evidenced by the preponderance of heavy weapons, including tanks and artillery, that NATO amassed on the Macedonian and Albanian borders, and that were later deployed throughout Kosovo. It is reasonable to assume that such a fighting force was not psychologically prepared immediately to protect the population they had expected to have to subdue, and which they regarded as responsible for creating the refugee crisis. In addition, with much of the initial force consisting of heavy armor, KFOR was not initially equipped to perform small patrols in villages with a mixed population, nor to respond quickly to violent protests or other civil unrest.

Civilian policing resources were not provided by U.N. member governments during the crucial first months of the operation. At the end of July 1999, there were only around 200 international police in Kosovo, most of them engaged in establishing a headquarters and training procedures. While the failure to deploy police quickly may have been partly the result of logistical constraints on the part of contributing governments, the failure to arrest and prosecute criminal acts against minorities and others during the first few months of the international civilian mission created a culture of impunity for such violence. As of October 19, 2000, UNMIK had deployed 4,162 civilian police officers, including border police, just below the authorized strength of 4,718.[50] On December 16, 2000, the OSCE-administered police academy (an eight-week basic training course) graduated its eleventh class of trainees for the Kosovo Police Service (KPS), raising the total number of graduates to 2,851. Forty-five percent of the new class' 312 cadets are non-Albanian. Fifty-nine members of the graduating class are women.[51]

As the United Nations police and Kosovo Police Service have belatedly begun to carry out their duties, their efforts have been frustrated by delays in establishing an effective judiciary. Part of the delays was due to UNMIK's wrangling with Albanian judges over which legal system should apply.

Ethnic Albanian children scramble atop the ruins of a Serbian Orthodox Church in Djakovica that was blown up in July 1999.

© FRED ABRAHAMS/HUMAN RIGHTS WATCH

Although several hundred local judges have now been appointed, the inability of the United Nations to persuade minority judges to take up their positions, and pressures on ethnic-Albanian judges have resulted in a nascent court system that is reluctant to detain or pass guilty verdicts on Albanian defendants, no matter how serious the charges or strong the evidence. On the other hand, Serb and other minority defendants frequently find themselves in pre-trial detention and eventually convicted even where cases are very weak.[52] Some U.N. officials in Kosovo now admit that just as the Kosovo Police Service requires a high-degree of international control and supervision, the courts system also demands international judges and prosecutors to ensure equal access to justice for all plaintiffs and due process for all defendants. At present, the flawed functioning of the judiciary is doing little to check Kosovo's cycle of impunity and insecurity.[53]

NATO and U.N. officials are well aware that persons linked to the former KLA and the KLA's successor, the Kosovo Protection Corps are implicated in violence against minorities.

The familiar refrain from the United Nations is that the poor security situation is the result of a lack of resources. It is true that there is still a shortfall of civilian police and insufficient funds to pay judges and prosecutors adequately. But the United Nations and OSCE have hundreds of personnel in their Pristina headquarters, and KFOR maintaisn the presence of more than 42,000 troops, including 32,000 from NATO countries. The more fundamental shortcoming is the lack of political will. Senior NATO and U.N. officials are well aware that persons linked to the former KLA and the KLA's successor, the Kosovo Protection Corps[54] are implicated in violence against minorities and in criminal activities, but have chosen to do little about it.[55] NATO officials have been at pains to avoid accusing former members of the KLA of such violence. Indeed, General Wesley Clark, the Supreme Allied Commander of NATO forces in Europe, went so far as to state in August 1999 that there was no evidence of KLA involvement in attacks, saying "I'm not going to point fingers at the KLA."[56]

Notwithstanding General Clark's exhoneration of the KLA, NATO officers on the ground told Human Rights Watch that their intelligence revealed precisely the opposite. United Nations police have also gathered ample evidence of abuses by persons linked to the KLA and KPC, which were compiled in an internal UNMIK report in February 2000.[57] Despite this evidence, few people have been arrested or charged for their role in such activities, nor has significant pressure been brought to bear on the political leadership of the former KLA or the KPC to curb such abuses in their ranks.

With the exception of concerns about ongoing attacks by Albanian armed groups in southern Serbia and Macedonia,[58] NATO governments are generally unwilling to confront the ambiguous role played by elements of the former KLA in Kosovo since June 1999. It took almost a year before international officials, including U.N. Secretary-General Kofi Annan, NATO Secretary-General Lord Robertson and U.S. State Department special envoy James O'Brien were finally willing to concede that attacks against minorities in Kosovo were systematic in nature.[59] The unwillingness of the world's most powerful military alliance even to suggest that local KLA units might be involved, and its failure to take action against those units, strongly suggests that its political leaders in Washington, London, Paris, Berlin, and elsewhere, as well as those in the United Nations, wish to avoid any confrontation with the political and military leadership of the former KLA. Their failure to do so is especially striking given that the Security Council authorized the U.N. and NATO to administer and secure Kosovo. Unless NATO governments are prepared to hold all persons accountable for acts of violence and crime in Kosovo, irrespective of their political connections, the cycle of impunity and insecurity looks set to continue.

KOSOVAR ALBANIAN PRISONERS IN SERBIA SINCE WAR'S END

On June 10, 1999, just after NATO and the Yugoslav Army signed the Military Technical Agreement that ended the war, an estimated 2,000 Kosovar Albanians were transferred from prisons in Kosovo to prisons in Serbia proper, notably in Sremska Mitrovica, Nis, Prokuplje, and Pozarevac.[60] The majority of the prisoners were civilians unlawfully arrested by Serbian security forces during the war. According to the Serbian press, the Serbian Ministry of Justice ordered the prisoners' transfer "for their own safety."[61]

As of March, 2001, approximately 1,400 of these Kosovar Albanian prisoners had been released, an estimated 150 of them under a Yugoslav

Amnesty Law passed in February 2001.[62] The remaining detainees registered and visited by the International Committee of the Red Cross— approximately 480 people— were in different stages of their legal proceedings.

Some of the Kosovar Albanians in Serbian prisons on political charges may have been involved with the Kosovo Liberation Army. But the vast majority were picked up in sweep actions by the Serbian police who were clearly on orders to arrest large numbers of Albanian men. As emerged in the Spring 2000 trial of the 143 men from Djakovica, the police arrested people who were hiding in their houses.[63] Beatings at the time of arrest were common, including during the April 27, 1999, arrest of former student activist and KLA spokesman Albin Kurti, although later treatment in the Serbian prisons was better.[64]

Prisoners transferred to Serbia from Lipljan prison on June 10 told Human Rights Watch how prison guards tied their hands and loaded them onto buses, beating those who moved. One prisoner said:

> They tied us with ropes and put us in groups of fifty. We could not sit. They started withdrawing and shooting in the air. We were afraid they would kill us there. At 6:00 a.m., June 10, they held us until 12:00 p.m. without food or water. Then they put us onto buses with our heads down. Half of us were on the floor. It was cold. They beat those who moved.[65]

The Serbian government sporadically released some of the prisoners throughout 1999 and 2000, usually after they had been found innocent at trial. On June 25, 1999, 166 men were released and brought back to Kosovo by the ICRC.[66] Another fifty-four men were released from Sremska Mitrovica prison on October 4.[67] Between January 27 and 29, forty-nine men were released, after seventeen or more months in custody, among them the author and journalist Halil Matoshi.[68]

On the other hand, convictions in Serbian courts continued throughout 1999 and 2000. On May 22, 2000, the 143 men from Djakovica were convicted and sentenced to a combined 1,632 years in prison for conspiracy against the state and terrorism in a trial that failed to meet international standards, according to human rights groups based in Serbia.[69] (On April 23, 2001, the Serbian Supreme Court released the defendants pending a review of the case by the district court.) On July 10, 2000, five Kosovar

Albanian students from Belgrade University were sentenced to prison terms ranging from six to twelve years for terrorist acts, despite court testimony that they had been tortured to extract confessions.[70] Human Rights Watch monitored three days of the trial and observed numerous procedural violations, such as collusion between the prosecution and the chief judge, the admission of dubious evidence, and the broadcast on state television of taped confessions.[71] On the third day of the trial, November 25, 1999, after one of the defendants gave a detailed and graphic account of the torture inflicted upon him in detention, president of the chamber, Judge Dragisa Slijepcevic responded: "Since the public is at this trial, I would like to say: Do you think that the police in European countries deal with detainees any differently?"

"Since the public is at this trial, I would like to say: Do you think that the police in European countries deal with detainees any differently?"

–Judge Dragisa Slijepcevic

The political prisoners were routinely denied the right to a fair trial. Courts sentenced Kosovar Albanians on the basis of forced confessions, and judges frequently refused to allow the introduction of evidence that could have disproved the charges. The prosecution's primary evidence against those convicted was often the highly unreliable and discredited "paraffin test," which checks for traces of gunpowder on defendants' hands.

Two Belgrade-based organizations, the Humanitarian Law Center (HLC) and Group 484, conducted extensive monitoring of the trials that continued throughout the spring and summer of 2000. In a press statement demanding the release of Kosovar Albanians unlawfully detained during the Kosovo conflict, the HLC highlighted:

> [G]rave violations of due process by Serbian judicial bodies and correctional institutions against ethnic Albanians who were arrested in the 24 March–10 June period this year on charges of terrorism and other criminal acts against the constitutional order of FR Yugoslavia . . .[72]

The HLC reported that, in many cases it monitored, detention periods were excessive, lawyers were denied access to their clients, and trials were scheduled before the defense had even seen the indictment. The HLC also appealed for the release of twenty-five minors, eleven women, approximately 200 wounded, and fifty ailing prisoners among the Kosovar Albanians who were in Serbian prisons at the end of 1999.[73]

Some prominent cases were also tried in Serbian courts. On December 9, 1999, a well-known Albanian pediatrician and poet, Dr. Flora Brovina, was sentenced to twelve years in prison by a Nis court for anti-state activities.[74] She was accused of providing food, clothing, and medical supplies to the KLA, as well as planning terrorist acts. In June, the Serbian Supreme Court ruled that her case should be retried by the Nis municipal court, and a retrial began on September 14, 2000. On November 2, 2000, newly elected Yugoslav President Vojislav Kostunica granted her an amnesty, and she returned to Kosovo.

Dr. Brovina, founder and head of the League of Albanian Women, was arrested by Serbian police in civilian clothes in front of her Pristina apartment on April 20, 1999. Originally held in Kosovo's Lipljan prison, Brovina was transferred to Pozarevac prison on June 10. She was allowed visits by the ICRC, her lawyers, and her husband, but meetings had to be held in the Serbian language.[75] Her trial was also reported to have numerous procedural irregularities.[76]

Reports have also emerged of Kosovar Albanian families paying bribes for the release of family members in Serbian prisons. An article in the *Washington Post* claimed that families had paid more than $10,000 per prisoner.[77] A report on prisoners by the International Crisis Group (ICG) claims that Serbian lawyers have promised to secure the release of Kosovar Albanians for fees ranging between 10,000 and 50,000 DM.[78]

Some lawyers in Serbia who represent Kosovar Albanian defendants encountered threats and physical violence. On December 3, 1999, an ethnic Albanian lawyer working with the Humanitarian Law Center, Teki Bokshi, was abducted from the highway near Belgrade as he drove back from visiting Kosovar Albanian clients in Sremska Mitrovica prison. According to the Humanitarian Law Center, Bokshi was stopped along with two colleagues by police in civilian clothes in a gray Mercedes car with official plates.[79] He was released after one week.

On March 16, another Humanitarian Law Center lawyer, Husnije Bytyqi, and his wife were seriously beaten by unknown assailants in their Belgrade apartment. Bytyqi, who was scheduled to defend six Kosovar Albanians facing terrorism charges the following day, required surgery due to his head injuries. Bytyqi had reportedly received threats from Serbian lawyers in

Kosovo, whom he had accused of taking bribes to secure the release of Albanian prisoners.[80]

In February 2001 the newly elected Yugoslav parliament passed an Amnesty Law to allow for political prisoners to be released, although the law did not apply to those acussed of having committed terrorist acts. By mid-March 2001, 157 Kosovar Albanians had been released under the law.[81]

Despite these releases, the issue of Kosovar Albanian prisoners in Serbia remains a highly sensitive issue in Kosovo, especially among the families of detainees. According to the International Crisis Group report, their continued imprisonment has "a corrosive effect on both international and local peace-building efforts in Kosovo."

Clearly, Milosevic tried to use the prisoners as a bargaining chip and as a means to undermine the international administration in Kosovo. Throughout 1999 and 2000, Albanians became increasingly frustrated with the international community's inability to secure the prisoners' release.

After his election in October 2000, Yugoslav President Vojislav Kostunica pledged to respect human rights and reestablish the rule of law in Yugoslavia. Correcting miscarriages of justice such as those perpetrated against Kosovo Albanian political prisoners is an essential part of upholding that pledge. According to the Yugoslav constitution and federal law, the Yugoslav president is empowered to pardon those indicted or convicted of federal crimes, such as hostile activity against the state and terrorism.

ICTY investigators marked bullet holes in the village of Cuska.

© FRED ABRAHAMS/HUMAN RIGHTS WATCH

18

WORK OF THE WAR CRIMES TRIBUNAL

The International Criminal Tribunal for the former Yugoslavia was founded in May 1993 to prosecute war crimes committed on the territory of the former Yugoslavia since 1991.[1] As of March 15, 2001, sixty-two individuals were under public indictment, thirty-six of whom were in custody. Twenty people had been convicted and two had been acquitted.[2]

The tribunal's first public reference to Kosovo was on March 10, 1998, just after the Serbian government's first large-scale attack in the Drenica region, when the tribunal's prosecutor stated that its jurisdiction "is ongoing and covers the recent violence in Kosovo."[3] Three days later, the U.S. government announced that it was providing $1,075,000 to support the Tribunal's investigations in Kosovo.

On June 12, 1998, the Contact Group meeting in London urged the tribunal to undertake a "rapid and thorough investigation" of possible humanitarian law violations in Kosovo.[4] On July 7, then-chief prosecutor of the tribunal Justice Louise Arbour, wrote a letter to the Contact Group in which she reaffirmed the tribunal's mandate and intentions in Kosovo:

> The prosecutor believes that the nature and scale of the fighting indicate that an "armed conflict," within the meaning of international law, exists in Kosovo. As a consequence, she intends to bring charges for crimes against humanity or war crimes, if evidence of such crimes is established.[5]

Throughout 1998, a number of top western politicians and political bodies publicly supported the tribunal's work on Kosovo. On August 31, the U.S.

ambassador-at-large for war crimes issues, David Scheffer, announced that he was not able to visit Belgrade and Kosovo because he had been denied a Yugoslav visa. He told a press conference in Zagreb, Croatia:

> The United States is cooperating fully with the Tribunal as it investigates the conflict in Kosovo. We are ensuring that relevant information is provided to the Tribunal in a timely manner so that its investigations can proceed efficiently. We urge other governments to cooperate with and provide information to the War Crimes Tribunal regarding the conflict in Kosovo.[6]

In early July, the tribunal sent its first team of investigators to the Federal Republic of Yugoslavia and into Kosovo itself to investigate the conflict. Small teams followed up for brief periods in September.

The Yugoslav authorities refused to accept the jurisdiction of the tribunal, and frustrated the work of investigators by denying them visas or forbidding them from carrying out investigations in Kosovo. Only a few tribunal investigators were able to gain access to the province in 1998 and early 1999, and they were officially prohibited by the Yugoslav authorities from interviewing persons or gathering evidence. The Yugoslav authorities based their refusal to cooperate with the tribunal on their view that the conflict in Kosovo was an internal dispute with "terrorists," a view repeatedly rejected by the tribunal, the U.N. Security Council, and other international actors, including Human Rights Watch.[7]

In October 1998, a Finnish forensic team sponsored by the European Union was granted permission by Yugoslav authorities and the local Kosovo courts to exhume bodies from six sites in Kosovo: Gornje Obrinje, Orahovac, Golubovac (Golubofc), Glodjane, Klecka, and Volujak. The first three burial sites contained the bodies of victims of alleged crimes by Serbian and Yugoslav forces; the later three burial sites were expected to hold the bodies of victims of crimes by the KLA.[8]

The Finnish team was allowed to conduct investigations into the sites at Klecka and Volujak—both sites of alleged KLA crimes. However, while attempting to reach Gornje Obrinje on December 10, where Human Rights Watch concluded that Serbian forces killed twenty-one members of one ethnic Albanian family in September 1998,[9] the Finnish team was blocked by a convoy of Serbian police. About ten armored personnel carriers manned by heavily armed police forces insisted on accompanying the forensic team to Gornje Obrinje, which was located deep within territory under the partial control of the KLA.[10]

The Serbian police insisted that the team be accompanied by a Serbian court official and members of a Belgrade-based forensic team, and refused to allow the team to proceed without police escort, which the leaders of the forensic team opposed, out of fear of provoking a confrontation with the KLA. During a two-hour negotiation session between the forensic team and the Serbian police, a plainclothes policeman violated the diplomatic immunity of Finnish ambassador Timothy Lahelma by opening the doors of his diplomatic vehicle, grabbing his camera, and removing the film from the camera. According to members of the forensic team interviewed by Human Rights Watch, police repeatedly attempted to shelter their armored vehicles from KLA attack by moving them behind diplomatic vehicles belonging to the E.U. contingent of the Kosovo Diplomatic Observer Mission (KDOM). Anticipating a confrontation between the KLA and the Serbian police, the forensic team decided to abandon its attempt to reach Gornje Obrinje.

On January 18, 1999, three days after the killing of forty-five ethnic Albanians in Racak (see Background), Chief Prosecutor Arbour attempted to enter Kosovo through Macedonia in order to investigate the reported atrocities in Racak. She did not have a Yugoslav visa, having been denied one by the authorities, and was refused entry into the country. Back in The Hague, Arbour stated unequivocally that she would investigate the Racak massacre "with or without access to the territory." Regarding the fears of evidence tampering, she said:

> Evidence of tampering—should such evidence become available, is, in fact, excellent circumstantial evidence of guilt. If one can trace where the order to tamper came from, it permits a pretty strong inference that it was done for the purpose of hiding the truth, which demonstrates consciences of guilt.[11]

Ten days after the killings, the Finnish forensic team was allowed to conduct autopsies on forty of the Racak victims along with teams from Yugoslavia and Belarus. Their report, released March 17, 1999, provided no details on post-mortem findings. The report did conclude that "there were no indications of the people being other than unarmed civilians."[12]

During the NATO bombing of Yugoslavia, the tribunal set up an office in Tirana, Albania, to interview refugees, and it worked closely with governmental and nongovernmental organizations collecting information on international humanitarian law violations from Albania and Macedonia.

On April 7, the U.S. State Department issued a statement that named nine commanders in the Yugoslav Army, placing them on notice that "VJ and MUP forces are committing war crimes and crimes against humanity in Kosovo"—crimes for which commanders can be indicted by the Tribunal.[13] The statement added:

> No commander of the VJ or MUP is immune from prosecution, now or in the future. Any commander of the VJ or MUP who plans, instigates, orders, or even aids or abets in a war crime, crimes against humanity, or genocide, is individually responsible for crimes committed in Kosovo. There is no statute of limitations for war crimes, crimes against humanity, or genocide within the jurisdiction of the International Tribunal.[14]

The statement identified the following individuals as commanders in Kosovo:

- Colonel Milos Mandic, Commander, 252nd Armored Brigade, deployed central Kosovo (Home Garrison: Kraljevo, Serbia);
- Major General Vladimir Lazarevic, Commander, Pristina Corps;
- Colonel Mladen Cirkovic, Commander, 15th Armored Brigade, HQ Pristina;
- Colonel Dragan Zivanovic, Commander, 125th Motorized Brigade, HQ Kosovska Mitrovica and Pec;
- Colonel Krsman Jelic, Commander, 243rd Mechanized Brigade, HQ Urosevac;
- Colonel Bozidar Delic, Commander, 549th Motorized Brigade, HQ Prizren and Djakovica;
- Colonel Radojko Stefanovic, Commander, 52nd Mixed Artillery Brigade, HQ Gnjilane;
- Colonel Milos Djosan, Commander, 52nd Light Air Defense Artillery-Rocket Regiment, HQ Djakovica;
- Major Zeljko Pekovic, Commander, 52nd Military Police Battalion, HQ, Pristina.

On May 27, 1999, the tribunal announced its highest level indictments to date: that of Yugoslav President Slobodan Milosevic and four other top officials for "murder, persecution, and deportation in Kosovo" between January 1 and late May 1999. The indictees are:

- Slobodan Milosevic, President of the FRY, Supreme Commander of the Yugoslav Army, and President of the Supreme Defense Council;
- Milan Milutinovic, President of Serbia and member of the Supreme Defense Council;
- Dragoljub Ojdanic, Chief of Staff of the Yugoslav Army;
- Nikola Sainovic, Deputy Prime Minister of the FRY;
- Vlajko Stojiljkovic, Minister of Internal Affairs of Serbia.

TOP ROW, LEFT TO RIGHT: *Former Yugoslav President Slobodan Milosevic, Former Serbian Minister of Internal Affairs Vlajko Stojiljkovic, Former Yugoslav Deputy Prime Minister Nikola Sainovic.* BOTTOM ROW, LEFT TO RIGHT: *Former Chief of the Yugoslav Army General Staff Dragoljub Ojdanic, Serbian President Milan Milutinovic (as of July 2001).* AFP PHOTOS

Slobodan Milosevic, Milan Milutinovic, Dragoljub Ojdanic, and Vlajko Stojiljkovic were charged with violating the laws or customs of war (murder and persecutions on political, racial, or religious grounds) and crimes against humanity (deportation and murder). Nikola Sainovic was charged on the basis of individual criminal responsibility for these same crimes.[15] The initial indictment did not relate to crimes committed in Bosnia or Croatia, only to crimes committed in Kosovo during the first five months of 1999.

The tribunal established an office in Pristina shortly after NATO's entry into Kosovo in June 1999 to better deal with the formidable task of investigations. The first exhumation season lasted from June to October 1, 1999. Six weeks later, the newly appointed Chief Prosecutor, Carla Del Ponte, presented her preliminary findings to the U.N. Security Council in New York. As of November 10, 1999, she reported, the tribunal had completed work at 195 of 529 reported grave sites in Kosovo, exhuming 2,108 bodies. Del Ponte pointed out, however, that this did not represent the total number of bodies. Exhumations were ongoing, and the tribunal had also "discovered evidence of tampering."[16] The next exhumation round lasted from April to October 2000. According to Del Ponte's November 2000 address to the Security Council, tribunal teams examined an additional 325 sites, exhuming 1,577 bodies and the partial remains of 258 others. Del Ponte stated that the provisional total of exhumed bodies over two years is "almost 4,000 bodies or parts of bodies." She added that an accurate figure will never be possible "because of deliberate attempts to burn the bodies or to conceal them in other ways."[17]

On September 29, 1999, Del Ponte made the tribunal's work in Kosovo a top priority.[18] The main focus, she announced, was the investigation and prosecution of Milosevic and the other leaders indicted in May. Thereafter, indictments of other individuals in positions of political and military authority may follow. In addition, the tribunal is investigating perpetrators of particularly egregious crimes—so-called "notorious offenders." This would include those who committed rape or sexual violence during the conflict.

The tribunal also recognized that it "has neither the mandate nor the resources" to be the main investigatory and prosecutorial agency in Kosovo.[19] The vast majority of crimes committed during the armed conflict will have to be dealt with by the local Kosovo police and judiciary, currently under the mandate of the United Nations Mission in Kosovo (UNMIK).

In her November 2000 address to the Security Council, Del Ponte also stressed the need to arrest Slobodon Milosevic, who lost his reelection bid in September and was then forcibly removed from office on October 5, 2000. Del Ponte urged the U.N. to pressure the new Yugoslav authorities to cooperate in Milosevic's arrest and extradition to The Hague, stating that "it would be inconceivable to allow Milosevic to walk away from the consequences of his actions."[20] She also called on the Security Council to modify the tribunal's statute so that it might deal with post-war abuses against Serbs and other minorities in Kosovo. According to the current statute, with the exception of genocide, the tribunal only has jurisdiction over crimes committed in armed conflict.

The vast majority of crimes committed during the armed conflict will have to be dealt with by the local Kosovo police and judiciary.

After coming to power in October 2000, new Yugoslav President Vojislav Kostunica stated that cooperating with the tribunal was "not a priority." In November, however, he agreed that the tribunal could reopen its office in Belgrade. Newly-appointed Foreign Minister Goran Svilanovic said, "We cannot and should not avoid facing the consequences of war and responsibility of crimes."[21] Although several Serbian government representatives have spoken out in favor of cooperation with the tribunal, Kostunica himself repeatedly denigrated the international body as an anti-Serb institution. His negative position on the tribunal changed somewhat after strong pressure from the U. S. government.

In October 2000, the U.S. Congress laid down strict guidelines in the 2001 Foreign Operations Assistance Act, prohibiting the U.S. government from continuing aid to Belgrade unless Yugoslavia cooperates with the tribunal, including "the surrender and transfer of indictees or assistance in their apprehension." According to the legislation, the Bush administration had to decide by March 31, 2001, whether to halt U.S. aid, effectively blocking approximately $50 million allocated for Yugoslavia.

In late January 2001, del Ponte visited Belgrade to meet with the new Yugoslav government. In a press conference after her return to The Hague, the prosecutor said she was disappointed with the level of cooperation she had received, although she remained "cautiously hopeful." Her meeting with President Kostunica, she said, "did not lead to any meaningful dialogue."[22]

The Yugoslav government's cooperation with the tribunal improved slightly before the March 31 deadline imposed by the U.S. government. The Yugoslav government began debate on a new law to allow for full cooperation with the tribunal and the surrender of indictees, and the tribunal was granted permission to conduct investigations inside Yugoslavia, including the hearing of witnesses and access to documents and archives.[23] In addition, two Bosnian Serb indictees ended up in the custody of the tribunal. The first such person, Blagoje Simic, former mayor of Samac, turned himself over to the tribunal on March 12, 2001. Ten days later, Milomir Stakic, former mayor of Prijedor, was arrested by the Serbian police and handed over to the tribunal.[24]

On April 1, Serbian police and special police arrested former President Milosevic on charges of corruption. The government made no commitment to transfer him to the tribunal. At least publicly, as of late April, none of the investigations involved his role in war crimes or crimes against humanity committed during the wars of Yugoslav succession.

On April 2, the U.S. government certified that conditions had been met for continued economic assistance to Yugoslavia. Full U.S. support for a future international donors' conference, however, was withheld, pending continued cooperation with the tribunal. State Department spokesman Richard Boucher said that the U.S. government "would expect" Yugoslavia to deliver Milosevic to the tribunal but that support for continued aid would not be "based on a single step alone."[25] As of April 2001, at least eight persons indicted by the tribunal were believed to be living in Serbia, including the four former Serbian and Yugoslav officials indicted along with Milosevic and three Yugoslav Army officials indicted on charges relating to the capture of Vukovar, Croatia, in November 1991.

On June 28, under strong international pressure, the Serbian government transferred Milosevic to the tribunal in The Hague. He appeared before the court for his arraignment on July 2, refused defense counsel, and denounced the proceedings as a political trial.

DOMESTIC WAR CRIMES TRIALS

Although the vast majority of those accused of having committed war crimes left Kosovo after the war, a few suspects remained in the province. These individuals have been investigated and prosecuted locally before domestic Kosovar courts. Approximately forty individuals accused of war crimes were in custody in Kosovo as of August 2000. The precise number of detainees was unknown since some individuals had been released and others had escaped hospitals or detention facilities, including thirteen people who escaped from the detention facility in Northern Mitrovica in September 2000 and one person who escaped from the U.S. military's Camp Bondsteel.[26] At least three of the accused were Roma, and the rest were Serbs. According to police statistics reported in the press, as of December 2000, the local judiciary had indicted twenty-two people for war crimes and nine for genocide.[27]

In June 2000, UNMIK announced the establishment of the Kosovo War and Ethnic Crimes Court (KWECC) to deal with the prosecution of war crimes committed during the conflict. The court's mandate was to cover events from January 1999 on and to include ethnically motivated crimes committed after the NATO bombing, but the idea was scrapped.

Throughout 2000 and 2001, some war crimes trials were proceeding through the local court sometimes with the participation of international judges. One war crimes trial was completed on September 20, 2000, resulting in a twenty-year sentence for Milos Jokic for killing one man and ordering another to be killed. In June 2001, courts with international judges sentenced three Serbian men to prison terms for their roles in crimes against ethnic Albanians. Zoran Stanojevic, a former policeman, received fifteen years imprisonment for taking part in the Racak massacre, Cedomir Jovanovic, an alleged member of a paramilitary group, received twenty years imprisonment for crimes committed in Orahovac municipality, and Andjelko Kolasinac, former mayor of Orahovac town, received a five-year sentence for the same. All three verdicts were heavily criticized by human rights monitors for the lack of due process during the proceedings.

The local courts are plagued by underfunding, poor organization, and political manipulation.

UNMIK is at odds on how to deal with the local war crimes prosecutions. On the one hand, the international administration wants the justice system to begin functioning, and there is pressure from the Albanian community to hold criminals accountable. On the other hand, the local courts are plagued by underfunding, poor organization, and political manipulation, and there is little chance of Serbian war crimes defendants receiving a fair trial in the Albanian-dominated system.[28] A January 2000 OSCE report on the Kosovo judiciary concluded that, regarding war crimes trials against Serbs, there are "real concerns as to the actual bias of the courts."[29]

After the war, some trials for crimes committed during the armed conflict had also begun in Serbian courts. Two Kosovar Albanians, Bekim and Luan Mazreku, were charged with joining the KLA, raping Serbian women, and then executing Serbian civilians in the Kosovo village of Klecka in 1998 (see Background, Abuses by the KLA).[30] On April 18, 2001, after a year-long trial, both men were found guilty of terrorism and sentenced to the maximum twenty years in prison. Citing a biased court, a limited right to defense, and the use of force to extract a confession, the Humanitarian Law Center, which monitored the trial, concluded that the court "presented no evidence to prove that the Mazrekus had committed these crimes."[31]

On July 19, 2000, a court in Pozarevac, Serbia, convicted two Serbian policemen of the murder of three ethnic Albanians in Kosovo in 1999.[32] Boban Petkovic from Velika Hoca was sentenced to four years and nine months in prison for the May 9, 1999, murder of Ismail Durguti, Sezair Miftari, and Miftari's wife Sefkija. Djordje Simic was sentenced to one year in prison for being an accessory to the murders.

On December 20, 2000, a military court in Nis sentenced two Yugoslav Army reservists, Nenad Stamenkovic and Tomica Jovic, to four and a half years in prison for murdering two Kosovar Albanian civilians in Susica village. Army Captain Dragisa Petrovic was found guilty of incitement to murder and sentenced to four years and ten months. In a review of the case, the Humanitarian Law Center welcomed the verdict but criticized the sentence as "too mild." The defendants were found guilty of murder rather than a war crime, the organization said, as is allowed under Article 142 of the Yugoslav Criminal Code.[33] The presiding judge, Col. Radenko Miladinovic, said that the sentence was lenient because the soldiers were suffering from "war psychosis" at the time of the crime.[34]

On April 19, 2001, the Yugoslav Army announced that military courts had begun twenty-four proceedings against soldiers suspected of having committed war crimes in Kosovo.[35] On April 24, the army stated that the military prosecutor had ordered investigations against, "soldiers, noncommissioned officers and officers . . . for crimes resulting in deaths and injuries of civilians as well as deprivation of their basic human rights during combat activities in the province of Kosovo in 1998 and 1999."[36]

According to Radio B92, on May 24, 2001, Serbia's new head of police Sreten Lukic, who was head of the Kosovo police in 1998 and 1999, announced that sixty-six police officers were under investigation for crimes allegedly committed against ethnic Albanians during the NATO bombing. On July 14, 2001, Serbian Justice Minister Vladan Batic said war crimes trials of Serbian citizens would begin in the coming weeks.

INVESTIGATIONS OF NATO AND THE KLA

Consistent with its mandate to investigate all sides, on May 14, 2000, the tribunal formed an internal committee to assess the allegations that NATO committed humanitarian law violations during the bombing campaign against Yugoslavia, and to determine whether the tribunal should commence investigations. In a report made public on June 8, the committee recommended against a further investigation into the bombing campaign as a whole or into specific bombing incidents. "[E]ither the law is not sufficiently clear," the report concluded, "or investigations are unlikely to result in the acquisition of sufficient evidence to substantiate charges against high level accused or against lower accused for particularly heinous offences."[37]

As of July 2001, tribunal investigations against the KLA continued. In her September 29, 1999, statement, Carla Del Ponte specified that her office would investigate the civilian and military leaders "of whichever party to the conflict" who may have committed crimes during the armed conflict.[38] In a press conference in Pristina on June 21, 2000, Del Ponte stressed that, while her focus was upon the Serbian and Yugoslav leadership, the upper hierarchy of the KLA was also a target of investigation. Breaking from the practice of providing no details about ongoing investigations, she announced that "five episodes" of alleged KLA crimes were under investigation, although she refused to specify the incidents.

Del Ponte stressed that the upper hierarchy of the KLA was also a target of investigation.

Del Ponte has also criticized the post-conflict abuses against Serbs and Roma in Kosovo, calling them "the seeds of future revenge and lasting instability in the region."[39] In her November 2000 address to the U.N. Security Council, she asked that the tribunal's statute be amended so that her office could prosecute the ongoing crimes taking place after the armed conflict.

Four months later, with the outbreak of armed conflict in the Presevo valley of southern Serbia and the northern regions of Macedonia, Del Ponte announced that the tribunal's mandate did indeed cover on-going events in the former Yugoslavia, specifically Kosovo, southern Serbia and Macedonia. In a press conference in The Hague on March 21, 2001, the chief prosecutor said that "the continuing violence in each area [Kosovo, southern Serbia and Macedonia] does indeed satisfy the legal criteria for the definition of "armed conflict" for the purposes of crimes set out in the statute of the tribunal." She also announced that her office had opened two investigations: the first into activities against Serbs and other minorities in Kosovo by unidentified Albanian armed groups from June 1999 until the present; and a second investigation into the activities of the Liberation Army of Presevo, Medvedja and Bujanovac (UCPMB) in southern Serbia from November 1999 until the present.[40]

19

LEGAL STANDARDS IN THE KOSOVO CONFLICT

INTRODUCTION

Human Rights Watch reported extensively on human rights abuses in Kosovo from 1990, the year Kosovo's autonomy was revoked, through 1997.[1] The police abuses, arbitrary arrests, and violations of due process that characterized the state's treatment of ethnic Albanians during that period were violations of the International Covenant on Civil and Political Rights, to which the Federal Republic of Yugoslavia is a party, and were additionally prohibited under Yugoslav domestic law. The growth of armed opposition to abusive direct rule from Belgrade, in the form of the Kosovo Liberation Army, and the intensification of fighting between government forces and this armed insurgency from the spring of 1998, altered the nature of the conflict, the types of abuses committed, and the applicable law.

From February 28, 1998, fighting between the various Serbian and Yugoslav security forces and the KLA could be characterized as a non-international (internal) armed conflict under international humanitarian law (the laws of war). The law applicable during this period includes Article 3 common to the four Geneva Conventions of 1949, Protocol II to those conventions, and the customary laws of war—all of which apply to both government forces and armed insurgents. Documented violations of international humanitarian law during this period included the execution of non-combatants, the use of disproportionate military force, indiscriminate attacks against civilians, and the systematic destruction of civilian property by the Serbian special police and the Yugoslav army, as well as serious violations by the KLA, such as forced expulsions, hostage-taking, and summary executions.

With the initiation of NATO bombing on March 24, 1999, the conflict in

Kosovar Albanian refugees entering Albania.

Kosovo and in all of the Federal Republic of Yugoslavia, to the extent it involved NATO and Serbian or Yugoslav forces, bcame an international armed conflict to which the full body of international humanitarian law applied. During this period, NATO committed violations of humanitarian law in its bombing campaign in the Federal Republic of Yugoslavia (see The NATO Air Campaign). Serbian and Yugoslav security forces were responsible during this period for the mass deportations and widespread killing of ethnic Albanian civilians between March and June 1999. The withdrawal of Serbian and Yugoslav forces from Kosovo and the cessation of the NATO bombing campaign on June 12, 1999, ended the state of armed conflict in Kosovo. Protocol I provides that application of the Geneva Conventions shall cease on the close of military operations.

KOSOVO AS AN INTERNAL ARMED CONFLICT

International humanitarian law makes an important distinction between international and non-international (internal) armed conflicts, which determines the applicable law. Article 2, common to the four Geneva Conventions of 1949, states that an international armed conflict must involve a declared war or any other armed conflict which may arise "between two or more of the High Contracting Parties" to the convention. The official commentary to the 1949 Geneva Conventions broadly defines "armed conflict" as any difference between two states leading to the intervention of armed forces.[3]

An internal armed conflict is more difficult to define, since it is sometimes debatable whether hostilities within a state have reached the level of an armed conflict, in contrast to internal tensions, disturbances, riots, or isolated acts of violence. The official commentary to Common Article 3 of the Geneva Conventions, which regulates internal armed conflicts, lists a series of conditions that, although not obligatory, provide some pertinent guidelines. First and foremost among these is whether the party in revolt against the de jure government, in this case the KLA, "possesses an organized military force, an authority responsible for its acts, acting within a determinate territory and having the means of respecting and ensuring respect for the Convention."[4]

Other conditions outlined in the convention's commentary deal with the government's response to the insurgency. Another indication that there is an internal armed conflict is the government's recognition that it is obliged to use its regular military forces against an insurgency.[5]

Internal armed conflicts that reach a higher level of hostilities are governed by the 1977 Protocol II to the Geneva Conventions, which is more elaborate than Common Article 3 in its protection of civilians (see below). Protocol II is invoked when armed conflicts:

> [T]ake place in the territory of a High Contracting Party between its armed forces and dissident armed forces or other organized armed groups which, under responsible command, exercise such control over a part of its territory as to enable them to carry out sustained and concerted military operations and to implement this Protocol.[6]

Finally, internal armed conflicts are also governed by customary international law, such as the customary international norms enunciated in United Nations General Assembly Resolution 2444.[7] Adopted by unanimous vote on December 19, 1969, this resolution expressly recognizes the customary law principle of civilian immunity and its complementary principle requiring the warring parties to distinguish civilians from combatants at all times. The preamble to this resolution states that these fundamental humanitarian law principles apply "in all armed conflicts," meaning both international and internal armed conflicts.[8]

Interpreting its jurisdiction over violations of customs of war committed in the territory of the former Yugoslavia, the ICTY has held that this jurisdiction includes "violations of Common Article 3 and other customary rules on internal conflict" and "violations of agreements binding upon the parties to the conflict, considered *qua* treaty law, i.e. agreements which have not turned into customary international law," such as Protocol II to the Geneva Convention.[9]

THE APPLICABILITY OF COMMON ARTICLE 3 AND PROTOCOL II

As of February 28, 1998, the hostilities between the KLA and government forces had reached a level of conflict to which the obligations of Common Article 3 apply. Given the subsequent intensity of the conflict until June 1999, Human Rights Watch is also evaluating the conduct of the KLA and government forces based on the standards enshrined in Protocol II to the Geneva Convention.[10]

On February 28, Serbian special police forces launched their first large-scale, military attack on the Drenica villages Likosane and Cirez which were suspected of harboring KLA members (see "Background"). Between that date and the withdrawal of Serbian and Yugoslav forces from Kosovo in June 1999, the KLA and the government were engaged in ongoing hostilities involving military offensives, front lines, and the use of attack helicopters and heavy artillery (the latter two exclusively by the government). The KLA possessed small arms and light artillery.

Although the KLA was primarily a guerrilla army without a strong centralized hierarchy and with strong regional divisions, the insurgency was an organized military force for the purposes of international humanitarian law. The KLA had seven "operational zones," each with a commander, chief of staff, brigades, and battalions. The General Staff ("Shtabi i Pergjishme"), albeit without total control over the regional commanders, coordinated military actions and political activities, a structure which allowed decisions to be transmitted down to the fighters.

During 1998, seasoned war correspondents, as well as Human Rights Watch researchers who encountered the KLA, at times observed discipline among KLA fighters manning checkpoints and their tendency to apply similar policies and procedures (for example, with regard to granting journalists access to areas under KLA control). Such discipline was an indication that the fighters were receiving orders regarding policy and that the fighters were answerable at least to regional commanders. There were also cases, however, when a clear lack of discipline and training was observed, which points to some structural weaknesses within the KLA. Despite this, it was clear by mid-1998 that the KLA leadership was able to organize systematic attacks throughout large parts of Kosovo. It also coordinated logistical and financial support from the Albanian diaspora in Western Europe and the United States. Arms flowed regularly from Albania's north. This coordination only increased as the war progressed, although the KLA always maintained a distinctly regional character.

As of February 28, 1998, the hostilities between the KLA and government forces had reached a level of conflict to which the obligations of Common Article 3 apply.

From April until mid-July, 1998, the KLA tenuously held as much as 40 percent of the territory of Kosovo, although most of that territory was retaken by government forces by August 1998. Until then, however, the KLA had held a number of strategic towns and villages, and manned checkpoints along some of Kosovo's important roads; by September 1998 their area of control had been reduced to some parts of Drenica and a few scattered pockets in the west, especially at night.[11]

Although the KLA's command structure was damaged as a result of the government's summer offensive, the nucleus of the organization continued to exist. A separate armed Albanian organization known as FARK (Forcat Armatosur e Republikes se Kosoves—Armed Forces of the Republic of Kosova), which had a separate base in Northern Albania and was mostly present in the Metohija (Dukagjin) region of Kosovo, was an added complication. By September 1998, it was clear that this alternative group, comprised mostly of ethnic Albanians with past experience in the Yugoslav Army and Serbian police, did not agree with the KLA's military strategy, criticizing its lack of professionalism. However, FARK and the KLA never engaged in hostilities against one another.

As mentioned in the chapter Forces of the Conflict, KLA spokesmen repeatedly expressed the organization's willingness to respect the rules of war, which is one of the factors to be considered in determining whether an internal armed conflict exists that would invoke Protocol II standards.[12] In an interview given to the Albanian-language newspaper *Koha Ditore* in July 1998, KLA spokesman Jakup Krasniqi said:

> From the start, we had our own internal rules for our operations. These clearly lay down that the KLA recognizes the Geneva Conventions and the conventions governing the conduct of war.[13]

KLA Communique number 51, issued by the KLA General Staff on August 26, stated that, "The KLA as an institutionalized and organized Army, is getting increasingly professional and ready to fight to victory."[14]

In November 1998, Human Rights Watch researchers had a meeting with two KLA representatives, Hashim Thaci and Fatmir Limaj, to discuss the KLA's commitment to the laws of war. The KLA representatives admitted that, in a war situation, "problems" did occur. But they stressed that the KLA was committed to the Geneva Conventions and respected international humanitarian law. Despite repeated requests, however, the representatives refused to provide any evidence of the KLA's stated commitment. The KLA has a soldiers' code of conduct, they said, but it could not be viewed. Disciplinary measures for abusive soldiers were in place, they claimed, but no details were provided. Detainees were treated humanely, they emphasized, but they could not be visited due to "security reasons."

"The KLA recognizes the Geneva Conventions and the conventions governing the conduct of war."

–KLA spokesman Jakup Krasniqi

There were reported but unconfirmed cases of KLA soldiers being disciplined by their own commanders for having harassed or shot at foreign journalists, but there are no reported cases of KLA combatants being punished for targeting ethnic Serb or Albanian civilians for murder, abusing those in detention, or any other violation of Common Article 3 or Protocol II.

Finally, through its words and actions, the Yugoslav government clearly recognized the KLA as an organized armed force. In addition to the Serbian regular and special police, which operate similar to a military organization, the government was obliged to use its regular military forces, the Yugoslav Army, against the insurgents. During the period between February 28, 1998, and June 12, 1999, the conditions of article 3 and Protocol II were satisfied. Human Rights Watch is, therefore, evaluating the conduct of both the government and the KLA based on the principles outlined in Common Article 3 and Protocol II.

Common Article 3 and the Protection of Noncombatants

Article 3 common to the four Geneva Conventions has been called a convention within a convention. It is the only provision of the Geneva Conventions that directly applies to internal (as opposed to international) armed conflicts.

Common Article 3, Section 1, states:

> In the case of armed conflict not of an international character occurring in the territory of one of the High Contracting Parties, each Party to the conflict shall be bound to apply, as a minimum, the following provisions:
>
> (1) Persons taking no active part in the hostilities, including members of

> armed forces who had laid down their arms and those placed *hors de combat* by sickness, wounds, detention, or any other cause, shall in all circumstances be treated humanely, without any adverse distinction founded on race, colour, religion or faith, sex, birth or wealth, or any other similar criteria.
>
> To this end the following acts are and shall remain prohibited at any time and in any place whatsoever with respect to the above-mentioned persons:
>
> (a) violence to life and person, in particular murder of all kinds, mutilation, cruel treatment and torture;
> (b) taking of hostages;
> (c) outrages upon personal dignity, in particular humiliating and degrading treatment;
> (d) the passing of sentences and the carrying out of executions without previous judgment pronounced by a regularly constituted court, affording all the judicial guarantees which are recognized as indispensable by civilized peoples.

Common Article 3 thus imposes fixed legal obligations on the parties to an internal armed conflict to ensure humane treatment of persons not, or no longer taking an active role in the hostilities.

Common Article 3 applies when a situation of internal armed conflict objectively exists in the territory of a State Party; it expressly binds all parties to the internal conflict, including insurgents, although they do not have the legal capacity to sign the Geneva Conventions. In Yugoslavia, the government and the KLA forces were parties to the conflict and therefore bound by Common Article 3's provisions.

The obligation to apply article 3 is absolute for all parties to the conflict and independent of the opposing party's obligation. That means that the Yugoslav government cannot excuse itself from complying with article 3 on the grounds that the KLA is violating article 3, and vice versa.

The application of article 3 does not confer any status upon the insurgent party, from which recognition of additional legal obligations beyond common article 3 would flow. Nor is it necessary for any government to recognize the KLA's belligerent status for article 3 to apply.

In contrast to international conflicts, the law governing internal armed conflicts does not recognize the combatant's privilege[15] and therefore does not provide any special status for combatants, even when captured. Thus, the Yugoslav government was not obliged to grant captured members of the KLA prisoner of war status. Similarly, government combatants who were captured by the KLA need not be accorded this status. Any party can agree to treat its captives as prisoners of war, however, and all parties were required to treat captured combatants—and civilians—humanely. Summary executions, whether of combatants or civilians, violated the prohibition on "murder of all kind."

Because the KLA forces were not "privileged combatants," they could be tried and punished by the Yugoslav courts for treason, sedition, and the commission of other crimes under domestic laws.

Common Article 3 thus imposes fixed legal obligations on the parties to an internal armed conflict to ensure humane treatment of persons not, or no longer taking an active role in the hostilities.

Protocol II and the Protection of Noncombatants

Protocol II elaborates upon Common Article 3's injunction of humane treatment and provides a more comprehensive list of protections for civilians in internal armed conflicts. While not an all-inclusive list, the following practices, orders, and actions are prohibited:

- Orders that there shall be no survivors, such threats to combatants, or direction to conduct hostilities on this basis.
- Acts of violence against all persons, including combatants who are captured, surrender, or are placed *hors de combat.*
- Torture, any form of corporal punishment, or other cruel treatment of persons under any circumstances.
- Pillage and destruction of civilian property. This prohibition is designed to spare civilians the suffering resulting from the destruction of their real and personal property: houses, furniture, clothing,

provisions, tools, and so forth. Pillage includes organized acts as well as individual acts without the consent of the military authorities.[16]

- Hostage taking.[17]

- Desecration of corpses.[18] Mutilation of the dead is never permissible and violates the rules of war.

Protocol II also states that children should be provided with care and aid as required. Article 4, paragraph 3 states that no children under the age of fifteen shall be "recruited by the armed forces or groups."

Protection of the Civilian Population

The distinction between civilians and combatants is fundamental to the laws governing both internal and inaternational armed conflicts. In situations of internal armed conflict, generally speaking, a civilian is anyone who is not a member of the armed forces or of an organized armed group of a party to the conflict. Accordingly, "the civilian population comprises all persons who do not actively participate in the hostilities."[19]

Full-time members of the Serbian or Yugoslav governments' armed forces and KLA combatants are legitimate military targets and subject to attack, individually or collectively, until such time as they become hors de combat, that is, surrender or are wounded or captured.[20]

Policemen without combat duties are not legitimate military targets, nor are certain other government personnel authorized to bear arms such as customs agents.[21] Policemen with combat duties, however, would be proper military targets, subject to direct attack.

Civilians may not be subject to deliberate individualized attack since they pose no immediate threat to the adversary.[22] The term "civilian" also includes some employees of the military establishment who are not members of the armed forces but assist them.[23] While as civilians they may not be targeted, these civilian employees of military establishments or those who indirectly assist combatants assume the risk of death or injury incidental to attacks against legitimate military targets while they are at or in the immediate vicinity of military targets.

In addition, both sides may utilize as combatants persons who are otherwise engaged in civilian occupations. These civilians lose their immunity from attack for as long as they directly participate in hostilities.[24] "[D]irect participation [in hostilities] means acts of war which by their nature and purpose are likely to cause actual harm to the personnel and equipment of enemy armed forces," and includes acts of defense.[25]

The distinction between civilians and combatants is fundamental to the laws governing both internal and inaternational armed conflicts.

"Hostilities" not only covers the time when the civilian actually makes use of a weapon but also the time that he is carrying it, as well as situations in which he undertakes hostile acts without using a weapon.[26] Examples are provided in an United States Army Field Manual cited by the ICRC, which lists some hostile acts as including:

> sabotage, destruction of communication facilities, intentional misleading of troops by guides, and liberation of prisoners of war. . . . This is also the case of a person acting as a member of a weapons crew, or one providing target information for weapons systems intended for immediate use against the enemy such as artillery spotters or members of ground observer teams. [It] would include direct logistic support for units engaged directly in battle such as the delivery of ammunition to a firing position. On the other hand civilians providing only indirect support to the armed forces, such as workers in defense plants or those engaged in distribution or storage of military supplies in rear areas, do not pose an immediate threat to the adversary and therefore would not be subject to deliberate individual attack.[27]

Persons protected by Common Article 3 include members of both government and KLA forces who surrender, are wounded, sick or unarmed, or are captured. They are *hors de combat,* literally, out of combat.

Designation of Military Objectives

The fundamental distinction between civilians and the military also applies to the nature of facilities that may be legitimate objects of attack. To constitute a legitimate military objective, the object or target, selected by its nature, location, purpose, or use, must contribute effectively to the enemy's military capability or activity, and its total or partial destruction or neutralization must offer a definite military advantage in the circumstances.[28]

Legitimate military objectives are combatants' weapons, convoys, installations, and supplies. In addition:

> an object generally used for civilian purposes, such as a dwelling, a bus, a fleet of taxicabs, or a civilian airfield or railroad siding, can become a military objective if its location or use meets [the criteria in Protocol I, art. 52(2)].[29]

To constitute a legitimate military object, the target must 1) contribute effectively to the enemy's military capability or activity, and 2) its total or partial destruction or neutralization must offer a definite military advantage in the circumstances.

The laws of war characterize all objects as civilian unless they satisfy this two-fold test. Objects normally dedicated to civilian use, such as churches, houses and schools, are presumed not to be military objectives. If they in fact do assist the enemy's military action, they can lose their immunity from direct attack. The presumption that an object is civilian in nature would not include objects such as transportation and communications systems that can have a military purpose. In such circumstances, it is necessary to analyze whether the facility or utility meets the two-part test, above.

The attacker also must do everything "feasible" to verify that the objectives to be attacked are not civilian. "Feasible" means "that which is practical or practically possible taking into account all the circumstances at the time, including those relevant to the success of military operations."[30]

Prohibition of Indiscriminate Attacks and the Principle of Proportionality

Even attacks on legitimate military targets, however, are limited by the principle of proportionality. This principle places a duty on combatants to choose means of attack that avoid or minimize damage to civilians. In particular, the attacker should refrain from launching an attack if the expected civilian casualties would outweigh the importance of the military target to the attacker. The principle of proportionality is codified in Protocol I, article 51 (5):

Among others, the following types of attacks are to be considered as indiscriminate: . . .

(b) an attack which may be expected to cause incidental loss of civilian life, injury to civilians, damage to civilian objects, or a combination thereof, which would be excessive in relation to the concrete and direct military advantage anticipated.

If an attack can be expected to cause incidental civilian casualties or damage, two requirements must be met before that attack is launched. First, there must be an anticipated "concrete and direct" military advantage. "Direct" means "without intervening condition of agency . . . A remote advantage to be gained at some unknown time in the future would not be a proper consideration to weigh against civilian losses."[31]

Creating conditions "conducive to surrender by means of attacks which incidentally harm the civilian population"[32] is too remote and insufficiently military to qualify as a "concrete and direct" military advantage. "A military advantage can only consist in ground gained and in annihilating or weakening the enemy armed forces."[33]

The second requirement of the principle of proportionality is that the foreseeable injury to civilians and damage to civilian objects not be disproportionate, that is, "excessive" in comparison to the expected "concrete and definite military advantage."

The attacker should refrain from launching an attack if the expected civilian casualties would outweigh the importance of the military target to the attacker.

Excessive damage is a relative concept. For instance, the presence of a soldier on leave cannot serve as a justification to destroy the entire village. If the destruction of a bridge is of paramount importance for the occupation of a strategic zone, "it is understood that some houses may be hit, but not that a whole urban area be leveled."[34] There is never a justification for excessive civilian casualties, no matter how valuable the military target.[35]

Indiscriminate attacks are defined in Protocol I, article 51 (4), as:

a) those which are not directed at a specific military objective;
b) those which employ a method or means of combat which cannot be directed at a specific military objective; or

c) those which employ a method or means of combat the effects of which cannot be limited as required by this Protocol; and consequently, in each such case, are of a nature to strike military objectives and civilians or civilian objects without distinction.

The Protection of Civilians from Displacement

There are only two exceptions to the prohibition on displacement, for war-related reasons, of civilians: their security or imperative military reasons. Article 17 of Protocol II states:

> The displacement of the civilian population shall not be ordered for reasons related to the conflict unless the security of the civilians involved or imperative military reasons so demand. Should such displacements have to be carried out, all possible measures shall be taken in order that the civilian population may be received under satisfactory conditions of shelter, hygiene, health, safety and nutrition.

The term "imperative military reasons" usually refers to evacuation because of imminent military operations. The provisional measure of evacuation is appropriate if an area is in danger as a result of military operations or is liable to be subjected to intense bombing. It may also be permitted when the presence of protected persons in an area hampers military operations. The prompt return of the evacuees to their homes is required as soon as hostilities in the area have ceased. The evacuating authority bears the burden of proving that its forcible relocation conforms to these conditions.

Displacement or capture of civilians solely to deny a social base to the enemy has nothing to do with the security of the civilians. Nor is it justified by "imperative military reasons," which require "the most meticulous assessment of the circumstances"[36] because such reasons are so capable of abuse. As the ICRC commentary to Protocol II states:

> Clearly, imperative military reasons cannot be justified by political motives. For example, it would be prohibited to move a population in order to exercise more effective control over a dissident ethnic group.[37]

Mass relocation or displacement of civilians for the purpose of denying a willing social base to the opposing force is prohibited as it responds to such a wholly political motive.

Even if the government were to show that the displacement were necessary, it still has the independent obligation to take "all possible measures" to receive the civilian population "under satisfactory conditions of shelter, hygiene, health, safety, and nutrition."

Displacement or capture of civilians solely to deny a social base to the enemy has nothing to do with the security of the civilians.

YUGOSLAV DOMESTIC LAW

The federal constitution of Yugoslavia, promulgated in 1992, established Yugoslavia as a democratic state "founded on the rule of law."[38] The forty-nine articles of the section on rights and freedoms guarantee all Yugoslav citizens basic civil and political rights, such as free speech, free association, and the right to a fair trial.

Yugoslav laws guarantee all defendants the right to due process. Article 23 of the federal constitution forbids arbitrary detention and obliges the authorities to inform a detainee immediately of the reason for his or her detention and grant that person access to a lawyer. Article 24 obliges the authorities to inform the detainee in writing of the reason for his or her arrest within twenty-four hours. Pre-trial detention ordered by a lower court may not exceed three months, unless extended by a higher court to a maximum of six months. Article 25 outlaws torture, as well as any coercion of confessions or statements. The use of force against a detainee is also a criminal offence.

Section 1, Article 11 of the constitution guarantees the rights of minorities to "preserve, foster and express their ethnic, cultural, linguistic and other attributes, as well as to use their national symbols, in accordance with international law." Section 1, Article 20 states that: "Citizens shall be equal irrespective of their nationality, race, sex, language, faith, political or other beliefs, education, social origin, property, or other personal status."

Articles 46 and 47 guarantee minorities the right to education and media in their mother tongue, as well as the right to establish educational and cultural associations. Article 48, however, places restrictions on free association for minorities that are susceptible to a broad and arbitrary interpretation.

> Members of national minorities have the right to establish and foster unhindered relations with co-nationals within the Republic of Yugoslavia and outside its borders with co-nationals in other states, and to take part in international nongovernmental organizations, *provided these relations are not detrimental to the Federal Republic of Yugoslavia or to a member republic.* [Emphasis added.]

The federal constitution of Yugoslavia, promulgated in 1992, established Yugoslavia as a democratic state "founded on the rule of law."

The Yugoslav constitution also guarantees that the government will respect international law. Article 10 states: "The Federal Republic of Yugoslavia shall recognize and guarantee the rights and freedoms of man and the citizen recognized under international law." Article 16 adds:

> The Federal Republic of Yugoslavia shall fulfill in good faith the obligations contained in international treaties to which it is a contracting party. International treaties which have been ratified and promulgated in conformity with the present Constitution and generally accepted rules of international law shall be a constituent part of the internal legal order.

Regarding combatants' respect for international humanitarian law, Yugoslav law is also very clear. The Yugoslav Law on Defense, article 19, obliges soldiers to respect international law dealing with the wounded, prisoners, and civilians. The article says:

> Members of the Yugoslav Army participating in an armed conflict are obliged under all circumstances to abide by the rules of international humanitarian law and other rules on humane treatment of wounded and prisoners, and on the protection of civilians.[39]

Serbia's Law on Internal Affairs also addressed the behavior of the police. Article 33 states that employees of the Ministry of Internal Affairs are obliged to carry out all orders by the minister or their superior, "with the exception of the ones ordering performance of a deed that constitutes a criminal act."[40]

SELECT KOSOVO HUMAN RIGHTS BIBLIOGRAPHY

Human Rights Watch Reports on Kosovo

Kosovo: Rape as a Weapon of "Ethnic Cleansing," 3/00
Civilian Deaths in the NATO Air Campaign, 2/00
A Village Destroyed: War Crimes in Kosovo, 10/99
Abuses Against Serbs & Roma in the New Kosovo, 8/99
"Ethnic Cleansing" in the Glogovac Municipality, 7/99
NATO's Use of Cluster Munitions, 5/99
Kosovo Flashes #1-50, 3–6/99
A Week of Terror in Drenica, 2/99
Detentions and Abuse in Kosovo, 12/98
Humanitarian Law Violations in Kosovo, 10/98
Persecution Persists: Human Rights Violations in Kosovo, 12/96
Human Rights Abuses of Non-Serbs in Kosovo, Sandzak & Vojvodina, 10/94
Open Wounds: Human Rights Abuses in Kosovo, 3/94
Abuses Continue in the Former Yugoslavia: Serbia, Montenegro & Bosnia-Hercegovina, 7/93
Human Rights Abuses in Kosovo, 10/92
Human Rights in a Dissolving Yugoslavia, 1/91
Yugoslavia: Crisis in Kosovo, 3/90

Other Reports on Kosovo

American Association for the Advancement of Science (AAAS) and the Institute for Legal and Policy Studies, *Policy or Panic? The Flight of Ethnic Albanians from Kosovo, March-May 1999,* April 2000.

American Bar Association (CEELI program) and AAAS, *Political Killings in Kosova/Kosovo,* September 2000.

American RadioWorks documentary, *Massacre at Cuska,* www.americanradioworks.org.

Amenesty International reports available at www.amnesty.org.

Balkan Human Rights Web Page, www.greekhelsinki.gr/.

Bar Human Rights Committee of England and Wales, *Kosova 2000: Justice, Not Revenge,* February 2000.

Council for the Defense of Human Rights and Freedoms, various reports available at: www.albanian.com/kmdlnj/.

European Roma Rights Center, *Roma in the Kosovo Conflict,* February 2000.

Helsinki Committee for Human Rights in Serbia, *Status of National Minorities in Kosovo,* May 1998.

Humanitarian Law Center reports available at www.hlc.org.yu.

Independent International Commission on Kosovo, *The Kosovo Report,* October 2000.

International Crisis Group, *Reality Demands: Documenting Violations of International Humanitarian Law in Kosovo 1999,* June 2000.

International Crisis Group, *Kosovo Albanians in Serbian Prisons: Kosovo's Unfinished Business,* January 2000.

International Helsinki Federation, various reports and statements available at www.ihf.hr.org.

International Press Institute, *The Kosovo News and Propaganda War,* September 1999.

Lawyers Committee for Human Rights, *Protection of Kosovar Refugees and Returnees: The Legal Principles,* June 1999

Lawyers Committee for Human Rights, *Kosovo: Protection and Peace-Building—Protection of Refugees, Returnees, Internally Displaced Persons, and Minorities,* August 1999.

Lawyers Committee for Human Rights, *A Fragile Peace: Laying the Foundations for Justice in Kosovo,* October 1999.

Medecins Sans Frontieres, *Kosovo: Accounts of a Deportation,* April 1999.

Organization for Security and Cooperation in Europe (OSCE), *Kosovo/Kosova: As Seen/As Told,* Parts I and II, December 1999.

Physicians for Human Rights, *War Crimes in Kosovo: A Population-Based Assessment of Human Rights Violations Against Kosovar Albanians,* August 1999.

Society for Threatened Peoples, *Kosovo: War, Expulsion, Massacres,* August 1998

United Nations High Commissioner for Refugees and OSCE, *Assessments of the Situation of Ethnic Minorities in Kosovo* (July 1999, November 1999, February 2000, June 2000).

United Nations Special Rapporteur on the Situation of Human Rights in Bosnia and Herzegovina, the Republic of Croatia and the Federal Republic of Yugoslavia, *Periodic Report on the Situation of Human Rights in Bosnia and Herzegovina, the Republic of Croatia and the Federal Republic of Yugoslavia* (September 24, 1999) and *Addendum* (November 1, 1999).

United States Department of State, *Ethnic Cleansing - An Accounting,* December 1999, *Erasing History: Ethnic Cleansing in Kosovo,* May 1999

United States Department of State, *Kosovo Judicial Assessment Mission Report,* April 2000.

NOTES

Chapter 2. Background

1 For a good description of the evolution of the KLA, *see* Tim Judah, *Kosovo, War and Revenge* (New Haven and London: Yale University Press, 2000).
2 Ruza Petrovic and Marina Blagojevic, Migration of Serbs and Montenegrins from Kosovo and Metohija, Serbian Academy of Science and Arts, June 7, 1988.
3 For details, *see* Helsinki Watch (now Human Rights Watch), *Yugoslavia: Crisis in Kosovo,* March 1990.
4 Petrovic and Blagojevic, Migration of Serbs and Montenegrins from Kosovo and Metohija.
5 Judah, *Kosovo, War and Revenge,* p. 49.
6 Laura Silber and Allan Little, *Yugoslavia: The Death of a Nation,* (New York: Penguin USA, 1995).
7 On August 25, 2000, Ivan Stambolic was abducted by unknown persons from the Kosutnjak Park in Belgrade. As of August 2001, his whereabouts remained unknown. Stambolic's family accused Milosevic and his wife, Mirjana Markovic, former Serbian Interior Minister Vlajko Stojiljkovic, and former State Security Chief Rade Markovic of organizing the abduction because they feared Stambolic would reenter politics.
8 Tim Judah, "Kosovo's Road to War," *Survival,* July 1, 1999.
9 After six months in prison, Vllasi was charged with "counter-revolutionary acts" on August 28, as well as culpability in the deaths of twenty-four ethnic Albanians who had been shot by Serbian police on March 28, 1989 (see below), even though he was in prison at the time. He was convicted, but released after approximately one year in prison. (*See* Helsinki Watch (now Human Rights Watch) and the International Helsinki Federation for Human Rights, *Yugoslavia: Crisis in Kosovo,* March 1990.)
10 Ibid., by Helsinki Watch and the International Helsinki Federation for Human Rights, *Yugoslavia: Crisis in Kosovo,* March 1990.
11 The Program for the Realization of Peace, Freedom, Equality, Democracy, and Prosperity of the Socialist Autonomous Province of Kosovo, item 6, Republic of Serbia, March 30, 1990
12 Under pressure from the West, Albania's support for Kosovo's independence ceased with the change of government in 1992.

13 For documentation on human rights abuses following the revocation of Kosovo's autonomy, *see* Human Rights Watch, "Human Rights Abuses of Non-Serbs in Kosovo, Sandzak and Vojvodina," *A Human Rights Watch Report,* vol. 6, no.6, October 1994, Human Rights Watch; *Open Wounds: Human Rights Abuses in Kosovo,* (New York: Human Rights Watch, 1994); Human Rights Watch, "Abuses Continue in the Former Yugoslavia: Serbia, Montenegro & Bosnia-Hercegovina," *A Human Rights Watch Report,* vol. 5, no. 11, July 1993; Helsinki Watch (now Human Rights Watch), "Human Rights Abuses in Kosovo," A Human Rights Watch Report, vol. 8, no. 63, October 1992; *Human Rights in a Dissolving Yugoslavia,* 1/91, *Yugoslavia: Crisis in Kosovo,* 3/90.

14 The Serbian government constructed settlements for relocated Serbs throughout Kosovo. Ethnic Albanians referred to the newcomers as "colonizers."

15 Kosovar Albanians were requested to pay the LDK three percent of their annual income.

16 Ivo H. Daalder, "Kosovo: Bosnia Deja Vu," *Washington Post,* April 17, 1998.

17 Judah, *Kosovo: War and Revenge,* p. 113.

18 In response to a Freedom of Information Act request, Human Rights Watch received an unclassified cable sent from the U.S. embassy in Belgrade on December 2, 1996, highlighting the "lack of awareness [among Albanians] that U.S. policy toward Kosovo does not, repeat not, support its independence." The public affairs officer who sent the cable was concerned that "98 percent of Albanians do not know that the U.S. does not support Kosovo's independence" and he called for more clarity on this position from Washington, especially in the programming of the Voice of America.

19 The LDK spurned offers to support Milosevic's opponents in elections, like Milan Panic in 1992, because they thought their goal of independence was more achievable with the internationally despised Milosevic in power. A similar trend was discernible in October 2000 when the Albanians feared the victory of Vojislav Kostunica would undercut their drive for independence.

20 For documentation of the abuses in Albania between 1992 and 1996, *see* Human Rights Watch, *Human Rights in Post-communist Albania,* May 1996. The destabilization of Albania culminated in the 1997 collapse of the so-called pyramid schemes, multimillion dollar financial scams, and resulting months of anarchy. Arms depots were looted throughout the country and tens of thousands of small arms made their way across the border into Kosovo.

21 The Dayton Agreement divided the former Yugoslav republic of Bosnia Hercegovina into two entities: Republika Srpska and the Federation of Bosnia and Herzegovina. After large-scale ethnic cleansing during the war, Republika Srpska had an almost exclusively Serbian population.

22 Among those killed were Stana Radusinovic, a Serbian emigrant from Albania, and Blagoje Okulic, a Serbian refugee from Knin, who were killed while sitting in a Serb-owned cafe in the city of Decan. Two Serbian policemen, Zoran Dasic and Safet Kocan, were wounded.

23 Interview with former KLA commander of the Llap region Rrustem Mustafa (a.k.a . Remi), published in the Kosovo daily *Zeri* between April 21 and May 4, 2000.

24 On June 16, a Serbian policeman, Goran Mitrovic, was wounded by gunfire at the bus station in Podujevo. The next day, policeman Predrag Georgovic was shot dead in the village Sipolje (Shipol), while his colleague, Zoran Vujkovic, was wounded. The police station in the village of Luzane (Lluzhane) was also attacked. Then, on August 2, four police stations in Podujevo (Podujeve) and Pristina were attacked, but no one was hurt. Six days later, there were several explosions at a Serbian settlement being built near Decan (Decane).

On August 28, three grenades were thrown at the police station in Lolopak (Lollopak) near Pec, causing no casualties but substantial material damage. That same day, an inspector with the Serbian police, Ejup Bajgora, was killed by automatic gunfire near his home in Donje Ljupce (Lupqi i Poshtem) near Podujevo. Finally, on October 26, a Serbian police officer, inspector Milos Nikic, and an employment office employee, Dragan Rakic, were ambushed and killed by unknown attackers in the village of Surkis (Surkish) near Podujevo. *See* Human Rights Watch, "Persecution Persists: Human Rights Violations in Kosovo," A Human Rights Watch Report, vol. 8, no. 18, December 1996.

25 For a description of police violence in 1996, *see* Human Rights Watch, *Persecution Persists.*

26 The vaguely worded agreement called for "the normalization of the educational system of Kosovo for Albanian youth," and "the return of the Albanian students and teachers back to schools."

27 According to the U.S. government, the outer wall of sanctions was to stay in place until Yugoslavia met the following demands: compliance with the terms of the Dayton Accords, cooperation with the International Criminal Tribunal for the Former Yugoslavia, regulated relations between the successor states of the former Yugoslavia and a restoration of civil and political rights in Kosovo. This position was emphasized on numerous occasions by European and U.S. diplomats.

28 See Human Rights Watch, *Persecution Persists.*

29 Human Rights Watch interview with Deputy Minister Rade Drobac, Belgrade, Yugoslavia, July 19, 1996.

30 U.N. peacekeepers had been stationed in Macedonia since 1991 to preserve the unity of the state, which is still seen as a vital buffer between competing countries in the southern Balkans. For information on human rights conditions in Macedonia, *see* Human Rights Watch, *A Threat to Stability: Human Rights in Macedonia,* (New York, Human Rights Watch, April 1996), and Human Rights Watch, *Police Violence in Macedonia,* (New York, Human Rights Watch, April 1998).

31 *See* Human Rights Watch, "Discouraging Democracy: Elections and Human Rights in Serbia," *A Human Rights Watch Report,* vol. 9, no. 11, September 1997.

32 The three fighters were Rexhep Selimi, Muje Krasniqi, and Daut Haradinaj.

33 Statement by the Contact Group on Kosovo, Moscow, February 25, 1998.

34 Press conference by U.S. Special Representative Robert S. Gelbard, Belgrade, Pristina, Serbia and Montenegro, February 22, 1998.

35 Press conference by U.S. Special Representative Robert S. Gelbard, Belgrade, Serbia and

Montenegro, February 23, 1998. Gelbard repeated his condemnation of Albanian terrorist actions again on February 25 during an address at the U.S. Institute of Peace in Washington.

36 For a list of organizations considered terrorist groups by the U.S. government, see: www.state.gov/www/global/terrorism/, March 2001.

37 Adem Jashari, a known KLA fighter who became a local hero and martyr after his death, had already been convicted in absentia by a Pristina court on July 11, 1997, for terrorist acts along with fourteen other ethnic Albanians, in a trial that clearly failed to conform to international standards. See press release, "Human Rights Watch/Helsinki Condemns Political Trial in Kosovo," July 15, 1997.

38 *See* Human Rights Watch, *Humanitarian Law Violations in Kosovo,* (New York: Human Rights Watch, 1998).

39 "Interior Ministry Spokesman Gives Press Conference," Tanjug, March 7, 1998.

40 The International Criminal Tribunal for the former Yugoslavia, "Prosecutor's Statement Regarding the Tribunal's Jurisdiction Over Kosovo," The Hague, March 10, 1998.

41 Press Statement by James P. Rubin, U.S. Department of State Spokesman, March 2, 1998.

42 London Contact Group Meeting, March 9, 1998, Statement on Kosovo. Available at: www.secretary.state.gov/www/travels/980309_kosovo.html, March 2001.

43 The Contact Group adopted four measures, although it did not specify how they were to be implemented: a) U.N. Security Council consideration of a comprehensive arms embargo against the FRY, including Kosovo; b) Refusal to supply equipment to the FRY which might be used for internal repression, or for terrorism; c) Denial of visas for senior FRY and Serbian representatives responsible for repressive action by FRY security forces in Kosovo; d) A moratorium on government-financed export credit support for trade and investment, including government financing for privatization, in Serbia.

44 On March 10, 1998, the prosecutor's office at the war crimes tribunal stated that the violence in Kosovo fell within its mandate.

45 Contact Group Statement on Kosovo, Bonn, March 25, 1998.

46 Contact Group Statement on Kosovo, Rome, April 29, 1998.

47 Members of the Kosovar Albanian group, known as the G5, were: Ibrahim Rugova, Pajazit Nushi (head of the Council for the Defense of Human Rights and Freedoms), Machmut Bakalli (former head of the Kosovo Communist Party), Fehmi Agani (leading member of the LDK, who was murdered by Serbian police during the NATO bombing), and Veton Surroi (publisher of the independent newspaper *Koha Ditore*).

48 Media Center Pristina, *Dialogue not Separatism and Terrorism,* Third Amended Edition, (Pristina: Media Centar Pristina, 1998), pp 96–97.

49 Conclusions of the European Union General Affairs Counsel, May 25, 1998.

50 In his book, *Kosovo, War and Revenge,* Tim Judah claims that Rugova was promised a meeting with Clinton in return for agreeing to meet Milosevic. Judah, *Kosovo, War and Revenge,* p. 154.

51 Negotiations foundered, largely because the Albanians, who had formed a larger group called the G15, refused to negotiate during an offensive that so severely affected civilians.

52 See Human Rights Watch, *Humanitarian Law Violations in Kosovo.*

53 For information on the university law, *see* Human Rights Watch, "Deepening Authoritarianism in Serbia: The Purge of the Universities," *A Human Rights Watch Report,* vol. 11, no. 2, January 1999. For information on the Serbian media, especially Serbia's broadcast media laws, see "Restrictions on the Broadcast Media in FR Yugoslavia," a September 1998 report by Free2000, the international committee to protect free press in Serbia that is affiliated with the Serbia-based Association of Independent Electronic Media (ANEM). See http://www.free2000.opennet.org/, March 2001.

54 Declaration by the European Union on Kosovo, Brussels, June 9, 1998.

55 Statement on Kosovo issued at the meeting of the North Atlantic Council in Defense Minister Session, Brussels, June 11, 1998.

56 Statement by NATO Secretary General Dr. Javier Solana on Exercise "Determined Falcon," Brussels, June 13, 1998.

57 Contact Group Statement on Kosovo, London, June 12, 1998.

58 See ANEM's website at: www.anem.opennet.org/index.phtml

59 *See* Humanitarian Law Center, *Spotlight Report No. 28,* January, 1999, and Human Rights Watch, *Detentions and Abuse in Kosovo.*

60 See Human Rights Watch, *A Week of Terror in Drenica.*

61 Ibid.

62 "Persons missing in relation to the events in Kosovo from January 1998," International Committee of the Red Cross, First Edition, May 2000.

63 Humanitarian Law Center, "Kosovo—Disappearances in Times of Armed Conflict," *Spotlight Report No. 27,* August 5, 1998.

64 See Human Rights Watch, "Humanitarian Law Violations in Kosovo."

65 For details of the Klecka case, *see* Human Rights Watch, "Humanitarian Law Violations in Kosovo."

In April 2000, two Kosovar Albanians, Luan and Bekim Mazreku, went on trial in Nis, Serbia, for allegedly executing Serbian civilians in Klecka. On May 30, their trials were indefinitely postponed and, as of September, there had been no verdict. See trial monitoring reports by the Serbia-based organization, Group 484, April 21 and September 20, 2000.

66 *Koha Ditore,* July 11, 1998.

67 Reuters, July 29, 1998.

68 U.N. Security Council Resolution 1199, September 23, 1998.

69 Statement NATO Secretary General Javier Solana, Vilamoura, Portugal, September 24, 1998.

70 Dejan Anastasijevic, "Slamming the Door," *Vreme,* no. 415, October 3, 1998.

71 The creation of a large-scale human rights department was an innovation for OSCE missions. The human rights findings during the KVM's mission, as well as during and after the NATO bombing, were later presented in two useful reports: OSCE/ODIHR, *Kosovo: As Seen as Told,* Parts I and II.

72 On the occasion of his dismissal, Stanisic issued a brief statement that included these lines: "The service under my leadership functioned in line with its constitutional and legal framework, and it was under the constant legal control of the Serbian Supreme Court. The service linked its activities and the responsibilities primarily to the institu-

tion of the Serbian president." BBC Worldwide Monitoring, "Text of statement issued by Serbian security chief on his dismissal," Source: Beta news agency, Belgrade, October 28, 1998.

73 Perisic, Chief of the Yugoslav Army General Staff from August 1993 to November 1998, was generally considered more inclined toward compromise with the West. For an interesting account of Perisic's negotiations with western military leaders, see "Serbs' Offensive Was Meticulously Planned," by R. Jeffrey Smith and William Drozdiak, April 11, 1999, *The Washington Post.* See also, "Vengeful After First Setbacks, Army Chose Unrepentant Force," by Michael R. Gordon and Thom Shanker, *New York Times,* May 29, 1999.

74 See the interview with former KLA commander of the Llap region Rrustem Mustafa (alias Remi), published in the Kosovo daily *Zeri* between April 21 and May 4, 2000. Commander Remi states, "The UCK [?] welcomed the [KVM] agreement, and in general it was profitable for us, for further mobilization, for the training of our soldiers, and for pulling our strength together so that we could continue the way that we had already started."

75 OSCE/ODIHR, *Kosovo/Kosova: As Seen, As Told—Part I,* pp 26–29.

76 OSCE/ODIHR, *Kosovo/Kosova: As Seen, As Told—Part I,* pp. 384.

77 Smith and Drozdiak, "Serbs' Offensive Was Meticulously Planned."

78 *See* Human Rights Watch, "Yugoslav Government War Crimes in Racak," A Human Rights Watch report, January 1999.

79 Statement by Serbian President Milan Milutinovic, *Borba,* January 18, 1999.

80 The Rambouillet Accords, Interim Agreement for Peace and Self-Government in Kosovo, February 23, 1999, Appendix B, paragraphs 8 and 21.

81 OSCE/ODIHR, *Kosovo/Kosova: As Seen, As Told—Part I,* p 27.

82 Press conference of German Foreign Minister Fischer, April 6, 1999, World Hall of the Foreign Office, and Tony Paterson, "Germany Gives Details of Covert Plan," *Times* (London), April 9, 1999.

83 John Goetz and Tom Walker, "Serbian Ethnic Cleansing Scare Was A Fake, Says General," *Sunday Times,* April 2, 2000.

Chapter 3. Forces of the Conflict

1 For an indication of the diversity of Serbian and Yugoslav forces, see the Military Technical Agreement signed between the International Security Force (KFOR) and the Governments of the Federal Republic of Yugoslavia and the Republic of Serbia on June 9, 1999. The agreement says that "FRY forces" refers to: "regular army and naval forces, armed civilian groups, associated paramilitary groups, air forces, national guards, border police, army reserves, military police, intelligence services, federal and Serbian Ministry of Internal Affairs local, special, riot and anti-terrorist police, and any other groups or individuals so designated by the international security force ("KFOR") commander."

2 Photographs of members of security forces obtained by Human Rights Watch show that government troops often wore colored ribbons on their arms. Countless witness statements also describe this. The ribbons may have served to identify units engaged in particular operations or to reduce the possibility of KLA infiltration.

3 Human Rights Watch interview, name and place witheld, July 19, 1999.

4 Human Rights Watch interview with R.N., Cegrane, Macedonia, May 18, 1999.

5 After the change in Serbian and Yugoslav governments in late 2000, Serbian courts began to try some VJ soldiers for crimes committed in Kosovo during the war. See "The Work of the War Crimes Tribunal."

6 In mid-December, 2000, Kertes gave an interview to *Nedeljni Telegraf*, in which he admitted providing funds to the ruling parties, as well as to the army and the police (*see* Danijela Bogunovic, "They Always Asked! More for More!," *Nedeljni Telegraf*, December 13, 2000). He was arrested two days later and charged with embezzling $2 million and $700,000 in separate cases (*see* "Serbia Police Seize Milosevic Ally," Associated Press, December 15, 2000).

7 *Beta*, April 9, 1998. Commander of the Yugoslav Third Army Gen. Nebojsa Pavkovic, with responsibility for Kosovo, later defended the killings in Drenica by calling them "the liquidation of a few members, a consequence." See General Pavkovic's interview with Frontline, available at: www.pbs.org/wgbh/pages/frontline/shows/kosovo/interviews/pavkovic.html, (March 20, 2001).

8 Momicilo Perisic was Chief of the VJ General Staff from August 1993 to November 1998, during which time he commanded the VJ and is believed to have remained in close contact with his Serbian counterparts in the Republika Srpska Krajina and the Republika Srpska.

From 1990 to 1991, Perisic was commander of the Yugoslav National Army's (JNA) artillery school in Zadar, Croatia. Thereafter, he became chief of staff of the JNA's newly formed Bileca Corps and commanded that Corps until 1992. In 1992, he became chief of staff and deputy commander of the 3rd Army. In August 1993, he was promoted to Colonel General and appointed VJ Chief of Staff, replacing Zivota Panic.

In 1997, Perisic was tried in absentia by a Zadar court and sentenced to twenty years in prison for war crimes and atrocities allegedly committed during the VJ attack on Zadar. In January 2001, Perisic was appointed a Deputy Prime Minister of the new Serbian government, prompting a protest from the Croatian Foreign Minsitry.

9 In addition to extensive witness testimony collected by Human Rights Watch, the extent of the cooperation between MUP and VJ was reflected in a Serbian Ministry of Internal Affairs statement released after the war regarding a meeting of the MUP and VJ leadership:

> The extremely successful and efficient cooperation during the previous period was emphasized, particularly regarding the fight against Albanians separatists and terrorists in Kosovo and Metohija, as well as special unity between the Yugoslav Army and the police forces in the defense from NATO aggression. (Announcement, MUP website, April 10, 2000.)

10 OSCE/ODIHR, *Kosovo/Kosova: As Seen, As Told, Part I*, p. 21.

11 Constitution of the Federal Republic of Yugoslavia, articles 135 and 136.

12 FreeB92 News, November 1, 2000.

13 Although there is no express provision in the Yugoslav constitution or any federal law that SDC decisions must be unanimous, this interpretation has been generally accepted and follows from the provisions of the Yugoslav constitution, in particular Article 1, which defines the Federal Republic of Yugoslavia as a sovereign state founded on the equality of citizens and the *equality of the constituent republics* (emphasis added). The SDC rules of procedure are not public.

14 "Djukanovic: Milosevic not Supreme Commander," Radio B92, March 16, 1999.

15 Ojdanic replaced Col. Gen Momcilo Perisic on November 3, 1998. He retired from military service on December 30, 2000.

16 "Three Thousand Officers, Non-Commissioned Officers, Soldiers and Civilians Employed in the Services of the VJ," *Politika,* June 16, 1999.

17 According to the United Kingdom Ministry of Defence, the chief of the VJ's counter intelligence service was Col. Gen. Geza Farkas. See www.mod.uk/news/kosovo/yugoforces.htm, April 20, 2001.

18 The First Army was commanded by General Srboljub Trajkovic. At the outset of the NATO bombing, the Second Army was commanded by General Radosav Martinovic. He was replaced by Colonel General Milorad N. Obradovic just after the start of the air strikes and subsequently placed on pension.

19 See the following for more information: the website of the Federation of American Scientists (www.fas.org/man/dod-101/ops/kosovo.htm, March 20, 2001), the United Kingdom's Ministry of Defense website (www.kosovo.mod.uk/, March 20, 2001), and the Jane's Defense Weekly website (www.janes.com/regional_news/europe/news/kosovo/jwa990401_01_n.shtml, March 20, 2001), as well as a report by the International Crisis Group, *Reality Demands,* June 2000.

20 Ibid.

21 See Jane's World Armies at www.janes.com/regional_news/europe/news/kosovo/jwa990401_01_n.shtml, March 2001.

22 Zoran Miladinovic, "Always Among the Prominent," *Vojska,* October 29, 1998. Cirkovic was also the commander of the Kosovski Junaci barracks in Pristina. B.K., "Dedication to the Call," *Vojska,* November 5, 1998. Cirkovic was also publicly named as commander of the 15th Armored Brigade by the U.S. State Department on April 7, 1999.

23 A June 25, 1998, article in *Vojska* (Vladica Krstic, "Write a Letter, Soldier,") said that Zivanovic was scheduled to replace Col. Srba Zdravkovic. Zivanovic was also publicly named as commander of the 125th Motorized Brigade by the U.S. State Department on April 7, 1999. An armored mechanized unit based in the Vojvoda Petar Bojovic barracks in Pec belonged to the brigade under the command of Major Milicko Jankovic. Ljiljana Bascarevic, "The Harmony Between Knowledge and Experience," *Vojska,* October 22, 1998.

24 Zoran Miladinovic, "Care for the Soldiers is the Priority," *Vojska,* November 12, 1998, refers on page nineteen to the "motorized unit of Pristina Corps, from Prizren, under the command of Bozidar Delic." According to the article, the unit "conducts complex

tasks of securing the frontier, control of communications in the border area. . . . Since the beginning of the conflict in Kosovo and Metohija, the unit has had many clashes with terrorist bands which have tried to penetrate our country from the territory of the Republic of Albania." Delic was also publicly named as commander of the 549th Mechanized Brigade by the U.S. State Department on April 7, 1999.

25 Jelic was publicly named as commander of the 243rd Mechanized Brigade by the U.S. State Department on April 7, 1999.

26 "Human Factor Makes No Mistakes," *Vojska,* September 10, 1998. This is one of three artillery brigades in the Third Army, with others in Aleksinac and Vranje. It was based in Gnjilane in the Knez Lazar barracks. Stefanovic was also publicly named as commander of the 52nd Mixed Artillery Brigade by the U.S. State Department on April 7, 1999. The State Department also identified Col. Milos Djosan as commander of the 52nd Light Air Defense Artillery-Rocket Regiment, based in Djakovica.

27 Zoran Miladinovic, "Right Fighters at the Right Place," *Vojska,* May 7/14, 1998. Pekovic was also publicly named as commander of the 52nd Military Police Battalion by the U.S. State Department on April 7, 1999. According to *Vojska,* the Military Police of the Pristina Corps have a special antiterrorist unit, commanded by Second Lieutenant Milija Vukanic. Zoran Miladinovic, "Terrorists Have No Chance," *Vojska,* May 7/14, 1998, and Branko Kopunovic, "People Who Pass Their Shadow," *Vojska,* May 7/14, 1998.

28 According to a researcher on the VJ at Belgrade's Institute of Contemporary History, one of the VJ's two fighter regiments (Lovacki Puk) at Pristina's Slatina airport consisted of two squadrons of MIG-21 planes. "Units Filled to the Maximum," *Nasa Borba,* May 4, 1998.

29 "Decrees on Promotions and Appointments," *Vojska,* December 31, 1998, and January 7, 1999.

30 Zoran Miladinovic, "In Challenge You See a Hero," *Vojska,* October 8, 1998. Mirko Starcevic's position in the Third Army was also evident by his appearance at a press conference in Pristina on April 24, 1998, when he informed journalists about recent attacks on the army near the border with Albania. He was presented as "a representative of the Yugoslav Army Corps in Pristina."

31 "Decrees on Promotions and Appointments," *Vojska,* December 31, 1998 and January 7, 1999.

32 "General Stojimirovic Vows to Defend FRY," Tanjug, March 26, 1999.

33 "General: Kosovars Have 'Nothing But Praise' for Serb Army," Beta, July 17, 1999.

34 In a letter published on August 24, 1999, in *Blic,* these "generals of the Yugoslav Army's Third Army," together with Vladimir Lazarevic, countered claims that they had threatened some members of Serbia's political opposition. Reported by Radio B2-92, August 24, 1999.

35 United Kingdom Ministry of Defense website, www.kosovo.mod.uk/, accessed March 2001.

36 R. Jeffrey Smith and Dana Priest, "Yugoslav Eviction Operation 'Basically Done'; Government Forces in Kosovo Digging In For an Extended Stay," *Washington Post,* May 11, 1999.

37 Branko Kopunovic, "With Sword and Shield," *Vojska,* April 23, 1998, and "Who are the New Generals," *Vojska,* January 22, 1998, which describes Stojimirovic as having been the commander of the Corps' motorized brigade and then its chief of staff before becoming overall commander.

38 "Decrees on Promotions and Appointments, *Vojska,* December 31, 1998 and January 7, 1999. Stojimirovic replaced Major General Miodrag Simic. Zoran Miladinovic, "Well Based Confidence of the People," *Vojska,* January 15, 1998, and Zoran Miladinovic, "Practical Modes of Training," *Vojska,* January 15, 1998. *See also,* "General Stojimirovic Vows to Defend FRY," Tanjug, March 26, 1999.

39 Branko Kopunovic, "With Sword and Shield," *Vojska,* April 23, 1998.

40 "The War That We Were Involved in Was the Most Unequal War Ever Known," *Politika,* November 27–30, 1999. Evidence that the 63rd Parachutist Brigade was active in Kosovo comes from various sources. On October 15, 1999, President Milosevic awarded the 63rd Parachutist Brigade with the Order of the National Hero, which was accepted by Lieutenant Colonel Todorov. In his acceptance speech, Todorov said that his forces has lost many men "in the defense of Yugoslavia from European and domestic forces, and in the fight against Shiptar (a pejorative term for Albanians) terrorists in the year 1998 and in the defense of the last defensive war." *Politika,* October 15, 1999. In addition, a colonel from the 63rd Parachutist Brigade, Goran Ostojic, was reported to have died in August 1998 after being sent "to the front." Srboljub Bogdanovic and Daniel Bukumirovic, "Special Upbringing," *Evropljanin,* August 27, 1998. Lastly, in a October 1998 speech, former Chief of the VJ General Staff Momcilo Perisic said: "I congratulate the soldiers, sub-officers, officers, and civilians in the service of the 63rd Parachute Brigade of the Special Forces Corps. . . . In complex circumstances, remaining faithful to the traditions of parachuting and keeping the pride of the profession, you have shown how the motherland is to be protected and preserved. With professional responsibility and readiness to withstand all efforts, in the best possible manner you have confirmed the status of an elite unit of the Yugoslav Army." "They Confirm the Sattus of an Elite VJ Unit," *Vojska,* October 15, 1998.

41 B. Kopunovic, "When 'Otters' Fly with Falcons," *Vojska,* May 7/14, 1998. The article also says that, among the members of the 72nd Brigade are "the popular and well known Falcons [Sokolovi]."

42 Federation of American Scientists website, www.fas.org/man/dod-101/ops/kosovo.htm, (March 2001).

43 Branko Kopunovic, "People Who Pass Shadows," *Vojska,* May 7/14, 1998.

44 *Vecernje Novosti,* June 30, 1999.

45 Republic of Serbia, Autonomous Province of Vojvodina, Kovacica District, Department of General Management and Public Service, Local Office of Debeljaca, Number III-111/99-05, March 26, 1999, 2621 Debeljaca.

46 Maggie O'Kane, "Kosovo 'Cleaner' Tells How Villages Were Emptied," *Guardian* (London), April 27, 1999.

47 Ibid.

48 *Frontline,* Public Broadcasting System, available at: http://www.pbs.org/wgbh/pages/frontline/shows/kosovo/interviews/pavkovic.html, (March 20, 2001).

49 Ibid.

50 U.S. Department of State, Press Statement by James P. Rubin, Spokesman, April 7, 1999, "Responsibility of Individual Yugoslav Army and Ministry Of Internal Affairs Commanders for Crimes Committed By Forces Under Their Command in Kosovo." The other named commanders were: Major General Vladimir Lazarevic, Commander, Pristina Corps; Colonel Mladen Cirkovic, Commander, 15th Armored Brigade, HQ Pristina; Colonel Dragan Zivanovic, Commander, 125th Motorized Brigade, HQ Kosovska Mitrovica and Pec; Colonel Krsman Jelic, Commander, 243rd Mechanized Brigade, HQ Urosevac; Colonel Bozidar Delic, Commander, 549th Motorized Brigade, HQ Prizren and Djakovica; Colonel Radojko Stefanovic, Commander, 52nd Mixed Artillery Brigade, HQ Gnjilane; Colonel Milos Djosan, Commander, 52nd Light Air Defense Artillery-Rocket Regiment, HQ Djakovica; and Major Zeljko Pekovic, Commander, 52nd Military Police Battalion, HQ, Pristina.

51 Jane's World Armies (www.janes.com/defense/news/kosovo/jwa990401_01_n.shtml/, March 2001.)

52 "The Yugoslav Army's Third Army Commander Lieutenant General Nebojsa Pavkovic: Kosmet is not Lost," *Vojska,* June 16, 1999.

53 For details on the MUP, see its website, also in English, at www.mup.sr.gov.yu/domino/mup.nsf/pages/index-e, (March 20, 2001).

54 On February 7, 2001, Sokolovic was found dead in his car in Zajecar, Serbia, with a bullet wound to his head. Initial autopsy reports concluded the death was a suicide. "Solokovic Postmortem Indicates Suicide," Radio B92, February 8, 2001.

55 The Indictment of Milosevic et al., Case IT-99-37-I, International Criminal Tribunal for the Former Yugoslavia, May 24, 1999.

56 For details on the Draskovic incident, see Human Rights Watch report, "Curtailing Political Dissent: Serbia's Campaign of Violence and Harassment Against Government Critics," April 2000.

57 Milanka Ivezic, "Successfully, Professionally, Responsibly, and with Discipline," *Policajac,* No. 4/97, April 1997, "Appointments and Assignments in the Ministry," Policajac, No. 4/97, April 1997, and Filip Svarm, "Go to Kosovo," *Vreme,* March 28, 1998.

58 Svarm, "Go to Kosovo," and the Federation of American Scientists website: www.fas.org/man/dod-101/ops/kosovo.htm, accessed March 2001.

59 United Kingdom, Ministry of Defense, www.kosovo.mod.uk/mupstruct.htm, accessed March 2001.

60 Dejan Anastasijevic, "How the Police Renounced Slobodan Milosevic," *Vreme,* October 19, 2000.

61 "SAJ Belgrade Won First," *Policajac,* No. 6/97, June 1997.

62 Gradisa Katic, "They Train for Years for an Operation That Takes Several Seconds," *Blic,* March 15, 1998, which reports that the SAJ took part in the March 1998 attack on Donji Prekaz, along with the PJP and regular police.

63 Prior to this, Lukic was assistant chief of police in Belgrade. On August 2, 1997, he accompanied Serbian Minister of Internal Affairs Vlajko Stojiljkovic on a visit to the SAJ in Belgrade. "Adroitness, Skillfulness and Professionalism," *Policajac,* No. 9/97, August 1997.

64 "Sreten Lukic Promoted to the Rank of Two-Star General of the Police," *Politika,* May 13, 1999.

65 Milan and Sredoje Lukic have been charged, together with Mitar Vasiljevic, for the mass murder of approximately 135 Bosnian Muslims around the eastern Bosnian town of Visegrad between May 1992 and October 1994.

66 *See* Chuck Sudetic, "The Reluctant Gendarme," *Atlantic Monthly,* April 2000.

67 What's New: Foreign Diplomats Visit Kosovo and Metohija, MUP website (March 20, 2001).

68 Tom Walker, "Belgrade Pledges to Wipe Out 'Terrorists' in Kosovo," *Times (London),* June 11, 1998.

69 What's New: Foreign Diplomats Visit Kosovo and Metohija, MUP website (March 20, 2001).

70 *See* Human Rights Watch, *Humanitarian Law Violations in Kosovo,* October 1998.

71 KDOM, Daily Report for August 21, 1998.

72 R. Jeffrey Smith, "Taps Reveal Coverup of Kosovo Massacre," *Washington Post,* January 28, 1999.

73 Dejan Anastasijevic, "How the Police Renounced Slobodan Milosevic," *Vreme,* October 19, 2000.

74 *See* "Serbian Government Promotes Rights Abuser: New Interior Ministry Appointee Commanded Police in Kosovo," Human Rights Watch press release, February 2, 2001.

75 Z. Miladinovic, "Gift From the People," *Vojska,* No. 331, December 10, 1998.

76 M. Manic and S. Kovacevic, "Will and Readiness to Carry Out All Security Tasks," *Policajac,* No. 18/98, October 1998.

77 "Everything Binds Us to This Land," *Policajac,* No. 18/98, October 1998.

78 "We Are Doing the Best We Can," *Policajac,* No. 4/97, April 1997.

79 "In Complex Security Circumstances, They Fulfill Their Obligations With Success," *Policajac,* No. 3/98, February 1998. Col. Zekavica was awarded the Order of Merit in Matters of Defense and Security of the First Degree on July 7, 1999 (see "Examples of Heroism and Patriotism," *Politika,* July 11, 1999).

80 "At New Duties," *Policajac,* No. 1/99, January 1999.

81 "Confidence Arrived Through Work and Good Results," *Policajac,* No. 3/98, February 1998.

82 "Good and Alert," *Policajac,* No. 8/98, April 1998.

83 "Ability to Persevere in the Fight Between Good and Evil," *Policajac,* No. 8/98, April 1998.

84 "At New Duties," *Policajac.*

85 *See* Human Rights Watch, *A Week of Terror in Drenica,* February 1999.

86 "Policeman Milan Tenic Killed," *Policajac,* No. 8/98, April 1998.

87 Milanki Mijatov, "We Are Capable of More and Better," *Policajac,* No. 4/99, February 1999, and Dejan Anastasijevic, "Bloody Weekend in Drenica," *Vreme,* March 7, 1998.

88 See "Justice for Kosovo" on the American RadioWorks website: www.americanradioworks.org, (March 20, 2001).

89 Gajic was with Sreten Lukic for the meeting with foreign diplomats in Pec on June 7, 1999. According to one press account, after the public affairs debacle in March 1998,

when Albanian families were massacred in Drenica, Gajic was appointed to oversee security in the western region of Kosovo during the spring offensive. Tom Walker, "Belgrade Pledges to Wipe Out 'Terrorists' in Kosovo," *The Times* (London), June 11, 1998.

90 United Kingdom, Ministry of Defense, www.kosovo.mod.uk/mupstruct.htm, (March 20, 2001).

91 Dejan Anastasijevic, "The Boys From Brazil," *Vreme,* October 19, 2000, and "How the Police Renounced Slobodan Milosevic," *Vreme,* October 19, 2000; Robert Block and Matthew Kaminski, "Was Serbian Revolt the People's Alone?" *Wall Street Journal,* October 23, 2000.

92 *See* VIP Report 1975, February 28, 2001, which cites the newspaper *Vecernje Novosti,* as well as the VIP Report from May 7, 2001. Milorad Ulemek's (or Lukovic's) nickname "Legija" has also caused confusion because there are at least two other men known as "Legija" in Serbia's paramilitary structures.

93 Human Rights Watch interview with J.J., Belgrade, Yugoslavia, November 2, 1998.

94 Human Rights Watch interview with VJ soldier, Decan, Kosovo, September 24, 1998.

95 United Kingdom, Ministry of Defense, www.kosovo.mod.uk/mupstruct.htm, March 20, 2001.

96 Srboljub Bogdanovic and Daniel Bukumirovic, "Special Upbringing," *Evropljanin,* August 27, 1998, and Filip Svarm, "Go To Kosovo," *Vreme,* March 28, 1998.

97 Anastasijevic, "The Boys from Brazil."

98 See, for example, Zoran B. Mijatovic, "How the SPS and JUL Destroyed the State Security Service," *Nedeljni Telegraf,* November 8, 2000.

99 Andrew Purvis and Dejan Anastasijevic, "The Bloody Red Berets," Time.com, March 12, 2001.

100 VIP Report, May 7, 2001.

101 Ibid.

102 United Kingom, Ministry of Defense, www.kosovo.mod.uk/mupstruct.htm, March 20, 2001.

103 See "Justice for Kosovo," American RadioWorks website.

104 *Vecernje Novosti,* June 30, 1999.

105 Arkan's Tigers were also known as the Serb Volunteer Guard. They were founded by Zeljko Raznatovic ("Arkan"), who was indicted by the ICTY on September 30, 1997, for crimes in Bosnia. He was killed by gunmen in a Belgrade hotel in January 2000.

106 The White Eagles were a paramilitary formation under the command of Vojislav Seselj, a deputy prime minister in the Serbian government and head of the Serbian Radical Party.

107 According to the OSCE, the Republika Srpska Delta Force came from the Ministry of Internal Affairs of the Republika Srpska. See OSCE/ODIHR, *Kosovo/Kosova: As Seen, As Told, Part I.* p. 24.

108 Ibid.

109 Ibid.

110 Human Rights Watch interview with M.J., Dobratin, Kosovo, July 13, 1999.

111 Philip Sherwell, "Focus the Ethnic Cleansing Business: "We Didn't Rape or Kill Enough. . . ," *Sunday Telegraph* (London), June 27, 1999.

112 James M. Dorsey "Death Factory: For These Serbs, Ethnic Cleansing Was a Business Proposition," *Wall Street Journal Europe,* August 31, 1999.
113 Jack Kelley, "Remorseless Troops Tell About Pillaging Kosovo," *USA Today,* July 22, 1999.
114 See "Justice for Kosovo," American RadioWorks website.
115 Ibid.
116 Humanitarian Law Center, *Kosovo Roma: Targets of Abuse and Violence, March 24-September 1, 1999,* 1999.
117 See the following: Roy Gutman, "Russian 'Volunteers' Allegedly Helped Serbs," *Newsday,* June 22, 1999; Maggie O'Kane, "Russian Soldiers' Peace Role Gives Refugees Chills," *Guardian* (London), June 24, 1999; "Retour des Russes sous l'habit de la KFOR: Tusus n'y croit pas," France 3 Infos, June 21, 1999.
118 Ron Ben-Yishay, "The Israeli Soldiers of the Serb Army," *Tel Aviv Yedi'ot Aharonot,* June 11, 1999.
119 "Danish Mercenary Set Free With Charges," *Agence France Presse,* August 31, 1999.
120 Sainovic chaired the commission for cooperation with the OSCE's KVM mission and was a member of the Serbian delegation at the Rambouillet talks in February 1999. On May 11, 2001, the Yugoslav parliament voted to lift the immunity of Sainovic and Jovan Zebic, both former Yugoslav Deputy Prime Ministers. Sainovic and Zebic are wanted by the Belgrade District Court to answer charges that they abused their official position to help President Milosevic siphon off state funds.
121 Statute of the International Criminal Tribunal for the Former Yugoslavia, Adopted May 25, 1993, amended May 13, 1998. Articles two through five of the statute list the punishable crimes: Grave breaches of the Geneva Conventions of 1949, violations of the laws or customs of war, genocide, and crimes against humanity (such as murder, deportation, torture, and rape).
122 In a January 16, 2001, interview with Belgrade's Radio B92, General Pavkovic was asked directly about civilian casualties and mass graves in Kosovo. He answered: "The thing I do know is that the Army firmly observed all the terms of the Geneva Convention and the international agreements." When asked "How about war crimes?" Pavkovic responded, "I am not aware of any such thing." See http://www.b92.net/intervju/eng/2001/0116.phtml, April 28, 2001.
123 March 26, 1999, Announcement, MUP website, March 20, 2001.
124 May 4, 1999, Announcement, MUP website, March 20, 2001.
125 See www.pbs.org/wgbh/pages/frontline/shows/kosovo/interviews/pavkovic.html (March 20, 2001).
126 Radio B92 interview with Gen. Nebojsa Pavkovic, available at http://www.b92.net/intervju/eng/2001/0116.phtml, April 22, 2001.
127 The police records were left behind in Pec district offices and were viewed by Human Rights Watch in July 1999.
128 See "Justice for Kosovo," American RadioWorks website.
129 In 2001, the new Serbian government and the VJ began prosecuting some cases. See Work of the International Criminal Tribunal for the former Yugoslavia.

130 Dusan Stojanovic, "Milosevic Makes Public Appearance," Associated Press, November 25, 2000.

131 Members of the Security Organs and Services on the Security Day May 13, MUP website, (March 20, 2001).

132 "Humanitarian Law Center Director's letter to the Yugoslav Army's General Staff," *Danas,* August 21, 2000.

133 In 1998, a splinter group tried to form a parallel fighting force: FARK—Forcave Armatosure e Republikes e Kosovos (Armed Forces of the Republic of Kosova), under the command of Bujar Bukoshi, prime minister of the self-proclaimed Kosovo government. FARK was disbanded and, by March 1999, its members were fighting alongside the KLA.

134 The British press published unconfirmed reports in October 1999 that Ceku was under investigation by the war crimes tribunal for crimes committed by Croatian Army forces against ethnic Serbs in 1993. The tribunal neither confirmed nor denied the speculation, in accordance with its policy of not commenting on investigations. See, "Kosovo Commander Denies War Crimes in Croatia," Agence France Presse, October 12, 1999.

135 Other members of the KLA's General Staff included Jakup Krasniqi, Azem Syla, Xhavit Haliti, Rame Buja, and Sokol Bashota, all in the political directorate, as well as Fatmir Limaj and Rexhep Selimi.

136 Rexha was gunned down by unknown assailants in front of his home in Prizren on May 8, 2000.

137 For details on some of the KLA personalities, see reports by the International Crisis Group, *Critical Implementation Issues and a "Who's Who" of Key Players,* March 1999, *Who's Who in Kosovo,* August 1999, and *What Happened to the KLA?,* March 2000. See also Zoran Kusovac, "The KLA: Braced to Defend and Control," *Jane's Intelligence Review,* April 7, 1999.

138 *Koha Ditore,* July 12, 1998.

139 KLA Communique Nr. 51, as published in *Koha Ditore,* August 26, 1998.

140 "Kosovo Reintegration Efforts are Bearing Fruits," IOM release, March 16, 2000.

141 The demilitarization agreement signed by the KLA on June 20, 1999, tended to confirm that non-Kosovo Albanians had participated in the KLA. Point 23(e) stipulated the withdrawal from Kosovo of "all UCK personnel, who are not of local origin, whether or not they are legally within Kosovo, including individual advisors, freedom fighters, trainers, volunteers, and personnel from neighboring and other States." (The "Undertaking of Demilitarization and Transformation by the UCK" is available at www.kforonline.com/resources/documents/uck.htm, March 20, 2001.)

142 For details, see, Roger Boyes and Eske Wright, "Drugs Money Linked to the Kosovo Rebels," *The Times* (London), March 24, 1999; Frank Viviano, "Separatists Supporting Themselves with Traffic in Narcotics," *San Francisco Chronicle,* June 10, 1994; "Speculation Plentiful, Facts Few About Kosovo Separatist Group," *Baltimore Sun,* March 6, 1998; Zoran Kusovac, "Another Balkans Bloodbath?—Part One, *Jane's Intelligence Review,* February 1, 1998; "TV report says Kosovo Albanians involved in Illegal Business in Germany," BBC Worldwide Monitoring, AND news agency, Berlin, June 28, 1999.

143 "Sreten Lukic Promoted to the Rank of Two-Star General of the Police," *Politika,* May 13, 1999. See also the MUP website.
144 "Awards for the Defense of the Homeland," *Policajac,* July 1999.
145 "Three Thousand Officers, Non-commissioned Officers, Soldiers and Civilians Employed in the Services of the VJ," *Politika,* June 16, 1999.
146 Ibid.
147 "Examples of Heroism and Patriotism," *Politika,* July 11, 1999. See also the MUP website. There Djordjevic is called a Lieutenant General, Stavanovic is a Major General, and Lukic is a Major General.
148 "Radojko Stefanovic New Commander of the Pristina Corps," *Hronika,* December 30, 1999.
149 "The War That We Were Involved in Was the Most Unequal War Ever Known," *Politika,* November 27–30, 1999.
150 May 13, 2000 Announcement, MUP website (March 20, 2001).
151 July 5, 2000, Announcement, MUP website (March 20, 2001).

Chapter 4. March–June 1999: An Overview

1 According to UNHCR statistics, the total number of refugees from Kosovo on June 9 was 862,979. This figure excludes those who had sought asylum in Europe prior to March 1999. No precise figures exist for the total population of internally displaced in Kosovo between March and June 1999 but most estimates range between 500,000 and 600,000, which includes the more than 200,000 persons internally displaced prior to March.
2 The expulsion of virtually all foreign journalists from Pristina on March 25 completed the removal of all foreign witnesses from Kosovo.
3 OSCE/ODIHR, *Kosovo/Kosova: As Seen, As Told,* Part I, p. 37.
4 See the following press accounts: "[T]he death toll from Kosovo's war was about 2,000 at the end of last year [1999], but that figure is substantially higher now," Anne Thompson, "A worsening terror: Disappearances Grow in Kosovo," Associated Press, March 18,1999; "... more than 1500 people have been killed," Charles Trueheart, "Kosovo Delegation Vows Anew to Sign Peace Agreement; West to Reapply Pressure on Belgrade," *Washington Post,* March 16, 1999; "... more than 2,000 deaths," Kurt Schork (Reuters), "A Year Ago, Serb Attack Kicked Off Kosovo War," *Seattle Times,* March 5, 1999. See also, *The Kosovo Report,* The Independent International Commission on Kosovo, October 2000.
5 UNHCR Press Briefing Note: Kosovo, Tuesday, February 2, 1999.
6 According to a November 1998 survey of 285 villages in Kosovo carried out jointly by UNHCR and a group of humanitarian NGOs, 210 villages had been affected by the fighting in 1998. Twenty-eight percent of the homes in those villages (9,809) had been completely destroyed, and 15 percent (5,112) of the homes had severe damage. [UNHCR Pristina,"IDP/Shelter Survey Kosovo: Joint Assessment in 20 Municipalities," November 12, 1998.]

7 Out of an estimated Kosovo population of 1.8 million, 850,000 Kosovars were refugees, and as many as 600,000 were internally displaced. Given that approximately 200,000 of the total population were Serbs, Roma, and other minorities, the percentage of displaced Albanians from Kosovo may have been as high as 90 percent.

8 UNHCR contingency plans prepared by the UNHCR Special Envoy for the Former Yugoslavia prior to March 24 put the maximum number of refugees from Kosovo that could be expected as a result of intensified hostilities in the province at 100,000. "The Kosovo refugee crisis: an independent evaluation of UNHCR's emergency preparedness and response," UNHCR Evaluation and Policy Analysis Unit, February 2000.

9 OSCE/ODIHR, *Kosovo/Kosova: As Seen, As Told, Part I*, pp. 21–30.

10 Ibid.

11 For a Seselj statement on forced expulsions published in The Greater Serbia Journal on October 14, 1995, see: www.alb-net.com/cleansing.htm, (accessed March 2001).

12 Human Rights Watch found few cases of "identity cleansing" among refugees arriving in Macedonia. This may be due to the weaker base of support for the KLA in eastern Kosovo (the point of origin for most refugees arriving in Macedonia). Another possibility is that Macedonia, unlike Albania, would not permit such a large influx of Kosovo Albanians to remain indefinitely.

13 Bolstered by four years of a United Nations preventive deployment of peacekeepers, Macedonia had avoided the civil conflict that engulfed the other republics of the Socialist Federal Republic of Yugoslavia. The election of a multi-ethnic government coalition had mitigated tensions between the large ethnic Albanian community, whose experience of persistent discrimination had strengthened calls among many of its members for greater autonomy, and the larger ethnic Macedonian population, whose fears of a greater Albania were inflamed by such calls.

For more on human rights in Macedonia, see Human Rights Watch, "Police Violence in Macedonia," April 1998, and Human Rights Watch, *A Threat to Stability: Human Rights in Macedonia* (New York: Human Rights Watch, 1996).

14 The Macedonian government periodically closed its borders to Kosovo refugees until the international community agreed to transfer out of the country some of those already present in Macedonia. For more on the Macedonian government's treatment of refugees during the war, see a Human Rights Watch statement, "Macedonia Must Keep Border Open To Refugees," April 1, 1999.

15 After the end of the war, some western politicians even claimed that the return of refugees was the original objective of the NATO action—a temporal impossibility, further contradicted by NATO's own predictions about possible refugee flows that might follow the start of the bombing.

16 Human Rights Watch interviews, Bogovine, Macedonia, April 5, 1999; Neprosteno, Macedonia, April 10–11, 1999; Kukes, Albania, April 17 and April 26, 1999; Kukes, Albania, May 12–13 and May 22, 1999; Kukes, Albania, June 6, 1999.

17 Prior to March 1999, more than 90 percent of the population of Leposavic and approximately 75 percent of the populations of Zubin Potok and Zvecan were Serbs.

18 Human Rights Watch interviews, Bogovine, Macedonia, April 4, 1999.

19 Human Rights Watch interviews, Kukes, Albania: April 16–19, 1999; April 23, 1999;

April 26, 1999; May 10, 1999; May 11, 1999; May 13, 1999; May 22, 1999; June 2, 1999 and June 7, 1999.

20 Many of them were displaced again during the forcible expulsion of large sections of Pristina in March and April 1999. (Human Rights Watch interviews, Dzepciste, Macedonia, April 3, 1999).

21 Human Rights Watch interviews, Podujevo town, Dobratin village (Podujevo municipality), July 13, 1999; Kukes, Albania, May 22, 1999.

22 For more information on events in Kosovo Polje and Obilic municipalities during 1998, see: OSCE/ODIHR, *Kosovo/Kosova: As Seen, As Told,* pp. 235–239 and pp. 268–273. Some details on the KLA's brief capture of the Belacevac mine, and the nine Serbs who went missing, can be found in a Human Rights Watch report, *Humanitarian Law Violations in Kosovo,* October 1998.

23 Human Rights Watch interviews, Bogovine, Macedonia, April 4, 1999; Kukes, Albania, April 4 and April 14, 1999; Kukes, Albania, June 8, 1999.

24 Human Rights Watch interviews, Bogovine, Macedonia, March 31, 1999 and April 5, 1999; Kukes, Albania, April 29, 1999 and May 10, 1999.

25 For more information on Ade see: Human Rights Watch, *Kosovo Human Rights Flash #32,* April 29, 1999.

26 Human Rights Watch interviews, Morina, Albania, April 28, 1999; Kukes, Albania, April 29, 1999; Tetovo, Macedonia, April 30, 1999.

27 Human Rights Watch interviews, Krume, Albania, April 2, 1999; Kukes, Albania, April 8 and 9, 1999.

28 Human Rights Watch interviews, Morina, Albania, April 4, 1999; Kukes, Albania, April 8, 1999; Morina, Albania, April 28, 1999.

29 OSCE/ODIHR, *Kosovo/Kosova: As Seen, As Told,* pp. 216–226.

30 Human Rights Watch interviews, Neprosteno, Macedonia, April 8 and 11, 1999; Zelino, Macedonia, April 12, 1999; Orasje, Macedonia, April 14, 1999; Senekos, Macedonia, April 16 and 17, 1999; Gostivar, Macedonia, April 18, 1999.

31 Human Rights Watch interviews, Orasje, Macedonia, April 12 and 14, 1999; Kotlina, Kosovo, August 8, 1999. See also, Amnesty International, "FRY: Killings in the Kacanik Area," April 9, 1999.

32 Human Rights Watch interviews, Senekos, Macedonia, April 16, 1999; Gostivar, Macedonia, April 18, 1999; Kukes, Albania, April 18, 1999; Kukes, Albania, May 14, 1999.

33 Human Rights Watch interviews, Neprosteno, Macedonia, April 8, 1999; April 10–11, 1999.

34 "Yugoslavs are Crying 'Crocodile Tears': Cohen — 100,000 Kosovars May be Dead, Says Defense Secretary," *Toronto Star,* May 17, 1999; David E. Rosenbaum, "Crisis in the Balkans: the Dead: U.S. Official Calls Tallies of Kosovo Slain Too Low," *New York Times,* April 19, 1999.

35 U.S. Department of State, "Erasing History: Ethnic Cleansing in Kosovo," May 1999; Transcript of Press Conference by Jamie Shea and Brigadier General Giuseppe Marani, NATO Headquarters, April 17, 1999.

36 "UN Sets Kosovo Dead at 11,000," Reuters, August 3, 1999, and "Kouchner's Spokeswoman Comments on Kosovo Death Figures," Agence France Press, August 3, 1999.

37 See, for example: Charles A. Radin and Louise D. Palmer, "Number of missing Kosovars is challenged," *The Boston Globe,* April 21, 1999.
38 For transcripts of the program, plus two other reports on war crimes in Kosovo, see: www.americanradioworks.org, (accessed March 2001).
39 "Milosevic Tried to Cover up Kosovo Crimes: Official," Agence France Presse, May 26, 2001, and "A Dark Secret Comes to Light in Serbia," by Carlotta Gall, *New York Times,* June 1, 2001.
40 Beta News, July 17, 2001, and Madame Carla Del Ponte, Prosecutor, ICTY, "Remarks to the Security Council," November 10, 1999.
41 ICRC Statement, "Persons Unaccounted for in Connection with the Kosovo Crisis," April 10, 2001. Prior to this statement, ICRC had said that 3,368 persons from Kosovo remained missing as of June 27, 2000. The majority of the missing are Kosovo Albanians, but also include 400 Serbs, one hundred Roma and persons from other minorities. Seventy-four percent disappeared between March and June 1999. ICRC, "Update 00/01 on ICRC activities in the Federal Republic of Yugoslavia," June 27, 2000.
42 Madame Carla Del Ponte, Prosecutor, ICTY, "Remarks to the Security Council," November 10, 1999.
43 Address to the Security Council by Madame Carla Del Ponte, prosecutor, International Criminal Tribunals for the former Yugoslavia and Rwanda, November 21, 2000, New York.
44 Human Rights Watch interview with N.B., Studencane, Kosovo, August 29, 1999.
45 Paul B Spiegel and Peter Salama, "War and mortality in Kosovo, 1998–99: an epidemiological testimony," *The Lancet,* Vol. 355, No. 9222, June 24, 2000.
46 Political Killings in Kosova/Kosovo, Central and East European Law Initiative of the American Bar Association and the American Association for the Advancement of Science, Washington D.C., October 2000.
47 Other known lawyers killed during the war were Urim Rexha from Djakovica, Mehdi Elshani from Suva Reka, and Ismet Gashi from Prizren.
48 Human Rights Watch interview with Nekibe Kelmendi, Pristina, Kosovo, July 25, 1999.
49 OSCE/ODIHR, *Kosovo/Kosova: As Seen, As Told, Part I,* p. 236.
50 May 7, 1999, Announcement, MUP website, www.mup.sr.gov.yu/domino\mup.nsf/pages/index, (accessed March 2001).
51 OSCE/ODIHR, *Kosovo/Kosova: As Seen, As Told, Part I,* pp. 151–152.
52 For a tribute to Mehmeti and Dervishi, see Robert Elsie, "Gone but not Forgotten," *Guardian,* April 3, 1999.
53 The findings of this research are set out in full in a separate Human Rights Watch report: "Kosovo: Rape as a Weapon of Ethnic Cleansing," *A Human Rights Watch Report,* vol. 12, no. 3, March 2000.
54 Human Rights Watch received credible reports of rape from the Center for the Protection of Women and Children, based in Pristina (Prishtina) (twenty-nine cases); the Albanian Counseling Center for Women and Girls, an NGO in Albania (twenty-eight cases); the Yugoslavia-based Humanitarian Law Center (four cases) and; the Kosovo-based Council for the Defense of Human Rights and Freedoms (four cases). Médécins Sans Frontières (MSF), with offices in Kosovo before and after the war, reported four

cases, and other medical personnel working in Kosovo and Albania confirmed an additional eight cases. Physicians for Human Rights interviewed four victims of sexual violence, and Amnesty International documented another three cases of rape, although two were also counted by Human Rights Watch.

55 Human Rights Watch interview, R.G., Kukes Refugee Camp, Albania, June 5, 1999.
56 Human Rights Watch interview, P.J., Kukes Refugee Camp, Albania, June 5, 1999.
57 UNHCR Press Briefing Note: Kosovo, Tuesday, February 2, 1999.
58 UNHCR Press Briefing Note: Kosovo, April 13, 1999.
59 UNHCR Press Briefing Note: Kosovo, May 13, 1999.
60 Statistic from: "The Kosovo refugee crisis: an independent evaluation of UNHCR's emergency preparedness and response," UNHCR Evaluation and Policy Analysis Unit, February 2000. This figure excludes those who had sought asylum in Europe prior to March 1999.
61 No precise figures exist for the total population of internally displaced in Kosovo between March and June 1999 but most estimates range between 500,000 and 600,000.
62 OSCE/ODIHR, *Kosovo/Kosova: As Seen, As Told.* pp. 98–99.
63 The American Association for the Advancement of Science, East-West Management Institute and the Institute for Legal and Policy Studies, *Policy or Panic: The Flight of Ethnic Albanians from Kosovo, March–May 1999,* May 2000. The report is available at: http://hrdata.aaas.org/kosovo/policyorpanic/, (accessed March 2001).
64 Human Rights Watch interview with M.B., Skopje, Macedonia, April 2, 1999.
65 Human Rights Watch interview with X.P., Skopje, Macedonia, April 2, 1999.
66 Human Rights Watch interview with N.J., Tetovo, Macedonia, March 31, 1999.
67 Human Rights Watch interview with S.K., Skopje, Macedonia, April 2, 1999.
68 See Human Rights Watch, Kosovo Human Rights Flash # 16, "Violent Ethnic Cleansing in Djakovica," April 3, 1999.
69 Human Rights Watch interview, name unknown, Krume, Albania, April 2, 1999.
70 International Criminal Tribunal for the former Yugoslavia, "Prosecutor of the Tribunal against Slobodan Milosevic and others: Indictment," June 1999.
71 See Human Rights Watch, "Detentions and Abuse in Kosovo," *A Human Rights Watch Report,* vol. 10, no. 10, December 1998.
72 Human Rights Watch interview with A.S. Prizren, Kosovo, June 13, 1999.
73 See Human Rights Watch, "Kosovo: Rape as a Weapon of 'Ethnic Cleansing.'"
74 Human Rights Watch interview with R.N., Glogovac, Kosovo, November 5, 1999.
75 For more information on destruction during 1998, see Human Rights Watch, *A Week of Terror in Drenica,* February 1999. pp. 57–62.
76 UNHCR Pristina, "IDP/Shelter Survey Kosovo: Joint Assessment in 20 Municipalities," November 12, 1998.
77 UNHCR GIS Unit, Pristina, Kosovo, "UNHCR Shelter Verification: Agency Coverage," November 9, 1999.
78 Status Report, United Nations Interim Administration Mission in Kosovo, July 14, 2000.
79 Physicians for Human Rights, *War Crimes in Kosovo: A Population-Based Assessment of Human Rights Violations Against Kosovar Albanians,* August 1999.

80 Protocol II, Article 14, of the Geneva Conventions states: "It is therefore prohibited to attack, destroy, remove or render useless, for that purpose, objects indispensable to the survival of the civilian population, such as foodstuffs, agricultural areas for the production of foodstuffs, crops, livestock, drinking water installations and supplies and irrigation works."

81 "Balkan Crisis: Cleaning Wells in Kosovo," ICRC News 99/37, September 8, 1999.

82 For more information on the case, see: Human Rights Watch, "Kosovo: Rape as a Weapon of 'Ethnic Cleansing'."

83 R. Jeffrey Smith, "Carcasses Dumped in Wells as Serb Crackdown Ended," *Washington Post,* December 10, 1998.

84 Valerie Reitman, "Kosovo Wells Emerging as Mass Graves," *Los Angeles Times,* August 10, 1999.

85 Human Rights Watch interview with Dr. Asllani, Pec, Kosovo, July 23, 1999.

86 *Corriere Della Sera,* July 6, 1999.

87 Human Rights Watch interview, Kukes, Albania, April 4, 1999.

88 Human Rights Watch interview with A.H., Cegrane, Macedonia, May 15, 1999.

89 Human Rights Watch interview with H.M., Stenkovac II refugee camp, Macedonia, May 10, 1999.

90 Human Rights Watch interview with I.X., Cegrane, Macedonia, May 15, 1999.

91 The four C's insignia is a Serbian nationalist symbol, comprising a cross and four Cyrillic S's. It is derived from the slogan "Only Unity Saves the Serbs" (Samo Sloga Srbina Spasava).

92 Human Rights Watch interview with H.S., Neprosteno, Macedonia, April 22, 1999.

93 International Crisis Group, *Reality Demands: Documenting Violations of International Humanitarian Law in Kosovo 1999* (Brussels: International Crisis Group, 2000).

94 OSCE/ODIHR, *Kosovo/Kosova: As Seen, As Told,* pp. 94–96.

95 See also, Ian Fisher, "Refugees 'Human Shield' Witnesses Say They Were Held in Targeted Village," *New York Times,* May 31, 1999.

96 Human Rights Watch interview, Stenkovac II refugee camp, Macedonia, May 9, 1999.

97 OSCE/ODIHR, *Kosovo/Kosova: As Seen, As Told, Part I,* pp. 94–96.

98 Physicians for Human Rights, *War Crimes in Kosovo: A Population-Based Assessment of Human Rights Violations Against Kosovar Albanians,* August 1999.

99 International Campaign to Ban Landmines, *Landmine Monitor Report 2000,* August 2000.

100 "103 Killed and 394 Disabled by Mines," KosovaLive, November 20, 2000.

101 Report of the Secretary General on the United Nations Interim Administration Mission in Kosovo, June 6, 2000 (S/2000/538).

102 Status Report, United Nations Interim Administration Mission in Kosovo, July 14, 2000.

103 Lord Robertson of Port Ellen, secretary general of NATO, "Kosovo One Year One—Achievement and Challenge," March 21, 2000.

104 Basic Points of the Statement by the Representative of the Federal Republic of Yugoslavia at the International Seminar on Anti-Personnel Mines, Budapest, March 26-28, 1998. For details of statement and the FRY government's position, see Human Rights Watch, *Humanitarian Law Violations in Kosovo.*

105 International Campaign to Ban Landmines, *Landmine Monitor Report 2000,* August 2000.

106 Consolidated Minefield Survey Results: Kosovo, the HALO Trust, Pristina, August 14, 1999.

107 Kosovo Crisis Fact Sheet #133, U.S. Agency for International Development, December 10, 1999.

108 Military Technical Agreement Between the International Security Force ("KFOR") and the Governments of the Federal Republic of Yugoslavia and the Republic of Serbia, Article II, Paragraph 2.

109 Press Briefing by the Secretary-General's Special Representative for Humanitarian Affairs in Kosovo, September 29, 1999.

110 See Human Rights Watch, "Ticking Time Bombs: NATO's Use of Cluster Munitions in Yugoslavia," *A Human Rights Watch Report,* vol. 11, no. 6 (D), June 1999.

111 See Human Rights Watch, "Civilian Deaths in the NATO Air Campaign," *A Human Rights Watch Report,* vol. 12, no. 1 (D), February 2000.

112 International Campaign to Ban Landmines, *Landmine Monitor Report 2000,* August 2000. See also Human Rights Watch, "Civilian Deaths in the NATO Air Campaign," *Cluster Bombs: Memorandum for CCW Delegates,* December 16, 1999, and "Ticking Time Bombs: NATO's Use of Cluster Munitions in Yugoslavia."

113 Estimates of overall dud rates vary from the conservative 2 to 5 percent claimed by manufacturers, to up to 23 percent observed in acceptance and operational testing, to some 10 to 30 percent observed on the ground in areas of Iraq after the Gulf War. Human Rights Watch has used a conservative estimate of 5 percent mechanical and fuse failures to estimate the humanitarian effect. For details, see Human Rights Watch, "Ticking Time Bombs: NATO's Use of Cluster Munitions in Yugoslavia."

114 NATO, "Teaching Kids to Stay Away—Cluster Bomb Fact-Sheet," http://kforonline.com, July 6, 2000.

115 BBC News, "Kosovo Mine Expert Criticizes NATO," May 23, 2000.

Chapter 5. Drenica Region

1 The intertwined history of Drenica's two municipalities and the geographic pattern of the abuses make it logical to treat the region as a whole rather than as separate municipalities as we have done elsewhere in the report.

2 For more information on the attacks *see*: Human Rights Watch, *Federal Republic of Yugoslavia: Humanitarian Law Violations in Kosovo* (New York: Human Rights Watch, 1998), pp. 18–37.

3 Ibid., pp. 33–37.

4 For more information on the attacks *see*: Human Rights Watch, *A Week of Terror in Drenica: Humanitarian Law Violations in Kosovo* (New York: Human Rights Watch, 1999).

5 As of May 15, 2000, more than 200 persons from the Drenica region remained missing,

presumed dead. ICRC, "Persons Missing in Relation to the Events in Kosovo from January 1998," May 15, 2000.

6 International Criminal Tribunal for the Former Yugoslavia, "The Prosecutor of the Tribunal against Slobodan Milosevic, Milan Milutinovic, Nikola Sainovic, Dragoljub Ojdanic, Vlajko Stojiljkovic," section 98.f, May 24, 1999.

7 Human Rights Watch interview with S.E., Kukes, Albania, March 25, 1999.

8 Human Rights Watch interview with H.D., Stenkovac I refugee camp, Macedonia, June 9, 1999.

9 Human Rights Watch interview with S.E., Kukes, Albania, March 25, 1999. For the full account of her story, see Human Rights Watch, *Kosovo Human Rights Flash no. 39,* May 19, 1999.

10 Human Rights Watch interviews with Z.D. and S.E., Stenkovac I refugee camp, Macedonia, June 9, 1999, and Kukes, Albania, March 25, 1999.

11 Human Rights Watch interview with H.D., Stenkovac I refugee camp, Macedonia, June 9, 1999.

12 Human Rights Watch interview with F.A., Kukes, Albania, June 2, 1999.

13 Human Rights Watch interview with S.E., Kukes, Albania, March 25, 1999.

14 Ibid.

15 Human Rights Watch interview with Z.D, Stenkovac I refugee camp, Macedonia, June 9, 1999.

16 Human Rights Watch interview with H.D., Stenkovac I refugee camp, Macedonia, June 9, 1999.

17 Human Rights Watch interview with I.H., Kukes, Albania, June 3, 1999.

18 Amnesty International, "Federal Republic of Yugoslavia: Killings in the Izbica Area," *Kosovo Update,* May 25, 1999.

19 Human Rights Watch interview with A. H., Vaise, Albania, June 3, 1999.

20 Human Rights Watch interview with F. A., Kukes, Albania, June 2, 1999.

21 Ibid., and Human Rights Watch interview with A.H., Vaise, Albania, June 3, 1999.

22 NATO Press Conference by Jamie Shea and Brigadier General Giuseppe Marani, April 17, 1999. (To read a transcript of the briefing and see the aerial images, *see* http://www.nato.int/kosovo/all-frce.htm, March 2001).

23 Human Rights Watch interview with H.D., Stenkovac I refugee camp, Macedonia, June 9, 1999.

24 Remarks to the Security Council by Madame Carla Del Ponte, Prosecutor, International Criminal Tribunal for the former Yugoslavia, November 10, 1999, New York.

25 "Serbs move Albanian bodies to area bombed by NATO—Albanian TV," BBC World Wide Monitoring Service, report by Albanian TV (Tirana), April 22, 1999.

26 Human Rights Watch interview with X.X., Kosovo, October 11, 1999, location omitted and initials altered.

27 Human Rights Watch interview with M.D., Srbica, Kosovo, October 11, 1999.

28 Ibid.

29 Human Rights Watch interview with X.X., Kosovo, October 11, 1999.

30 Human Rights Watch interview with M.D., Srbica, Kosovo, October 11, 1999.

31 Ibid.

32 Julian Borger and Owen Bowcott, "War crimes: Serbs accused of obliterating evidence of mass graves," *The Guardian,* June 17, 1999.

33 Human Rights Watch interview with M.D., Srbica, Kosovo, October 11, 1999.

34 International Management Group, "Assessment of Damaged Buildings and Local Infrastructure in Kosovo," January 1999.

35 Human Rights Watch, *Humanitarian Law Violations in Kosovo,* pp. 33–37.

36 A list given to Human Rights Watch by Muqolli family members in a Macedonian refugee camp on May 8, 1999, had forty-four names and seven unknown victims, while a list given to Human Rights Watch in Poklek on June 25, 1999, had forty-eight names. Media accounts have cited other figures, such as fifty-two (*Irish Times,* June 18, 1999) and sixty-two (Associated Press, June 17, 1999).

37 Human Rights Watch interview with F.M., Cegrane refugee camp, Macedonia, May 8, 1999.

38 Human Rights Watch interview with R.M., Stari Poklek, Kosovo, June 25, 1999.

39 U.N. Assessment, GIS Unit Pristina, January 28, 1999.

40 A number of villagers from Staro Cikatovo requested anonymity in return for their testimony. The letters A.A., B.B., C.C., etc. are therefore used in this section to protect their identities.

41 Human Rights Watch interview with A.A., Stenkovac II refugee camp, Macedonia, May 9, 1999.

42 Human Rights Watch interview with B.B., Cegrane refugee camp, Macedonia, May 8, 1999.

43 Ibid.

44 Human Rights Watch interview with A.A., Stenkovac II refugee camp, Macedonia, May 9, 1999.

45 Human Rights Watch interview with D.D., Stenkovac II refugee camp, Macedonia, May 9, 1999.

46 Human Rights Watch interview with C.C., Cegrane refugee camp, Macedonia, May 12, 1999.

47 Human Rights Watch interview with E.E., Stenkovac II refugee camp, Macedonia, May 9, 1999.

48 Human Rights Watch interview with A.A., Stenkovac II refugee camp, Macedonia, May 9, 1999.

49 Human Rights Watch interview with C.C., Cegrane refugee camp, Macedonia, May 12, 1999.

50 OSCE, *Kosovo/Kosova: As Seen, As Told, Part I,* pp 190–191.

51 As of the close of the 1999 exhumation season, the ICTY had confirmed twnety-five bodies in Vrbovac, but had yet to confirm finding any bodies in Stutica. As of May 15, the ICRC had received reports of more than one-hundred missing persons from the area, including seventy-five from Vrbovac and twenty-seven from Stutica. (ICRC, "Persons Mising in Relation to the Events in Kosovo from January 1998," May 15, 2000.)

52 Human Rights Watch interview with R.K., Vrbovac, Kosovo, October 1, 1999.

53 Human Rights Watch interview with F.P., Vrbovac, Kosovo, September 29, 1999.
54 Human Rights Watch interview with R.N., Cegrane refugee camp, Macedonia, May 18, 1999.
55 Human Rights Watch interview with M.H., Poklek, Kosovo, October 2, 1999.
56 Human Rights Watch interview with S.G., Vrbovac, Kosovo, October 1, 1999.
57 Human Rights Watch interview with B.R., Vrbovac, Kosovo, October 1, 1999.
58 Human Rights Watch interview with Z.Z., Poljance, Kosovo, October 4, 1999. (Initials altered).
59 Human Rights Watch interview with A.D., Trstenik, Kosovo, October 2, 1999.
60 Human Rights Watch interview with Y.Y., Globare, Kosovo, October 8, 1999. (Initials altered).
61 Human Rights Watch interview with A.S., Cirez, Kosovo, October 13, 1999.
62 Human Rights Watch interview with Z.K., Gladno Selo, Kosovo, October 10, 1999.
63 Human Rights Watch interview with R.B., Stutica, Kosovo, June 25, 1999.
64 Human Rights Watch interview with A.A., Stutica, Kosovo, October 9, 1999.
65 Human Rights Watch interview with A.S., Stutica, Kosovo, October 5, 1999.
66 Human Rights Watch interview with Z.K., Gladno Selo, Kosovo, October 10, 1999.
67 Human Rights Watch interview with F.R., Cirez, Kosovo, July 11, 1999.
68 Human Rights Watch interview with M.F., Cirez, Kosovo, July 11, 1999. According to M.F. the victims were Rahim F. (18); Nazif F. (16); Dritan B. (16); Fidaim Z. (28); Mehmet M. (40); Halit H. (41) and; Ferti S. (28).
69 Human Rights Watch interview with Q.Q. (initials altered), Dosevac, Kosovo, October 5, 1999.
70 Human Rights Watch interview with A.S., Stutica, Kosovo, October 5, 1999.
71 Human Rights Watch interview with F.R., Cirez, Kosovo, July 11, 1999.
72 Human Rights Watch interview with A.A., Stutica, Kosovo, October 9, 1999.
73 Human Rights Watch interview with A.D., Trstenik, Kosovo, October 2, 1999.
74 Human Rights Watch interview with Z.K., Gladno Selo, Kosovo, October 10, 1999.
75 Human Rights Watch interview with F.R., Cirez, Kosovo, July 11, 1999.
76 Human Rights Watch interview with A.S., Cirez, Kosovo, October 13, 1999.
77 Human Rights Watch interview with Z.Z., Poljance, Kosovo, October 4, 1999. (Initials altered).
78 Human Rights Watch interview with Q.Q., Dosevac, Kosovo, October 5, 1999. (Initials altered.)
79 Human Rights Watch interview with representatives from the Council for the Defense of Human Rights, Glogovac, Kosovo, October 12, 1999.
80 Human Rights Watch interview with A.S., Cirez, Kosovo, October 13, 1999.
81 Human Rights Watch interview with R.B., Stutica, Kosovo, June 25, 1999.
82 Human Rights Watch interview with S.G., Vrbovac, Kosovo, October 1, 1999.
83 Human Rights Watch interview with Y.Y., Globare, Kosovo, October 8, 1999. (Initials altered.)

84 Human Rights Watch interview with A.D., Trstenik, Kosovo, October 2, 1999.
85 Human Rights Watch interview with R.B., Stutica, Kosovo, June 25, 1999.
86 Human Rights Watch interview with Z.K., Gladno Selo, Kosovo, October 10, 1999.
87 Human Rights Watch interview with A.A., Stutica, Kosovo, October 9, 1999. (Initials altered?)
88 Human Rights Watch, *A Week of Terror in Drenica,* pp. 42–47.
89 Villagers came to Glogovac from Staro Cikatovo, Trstenik, Poklek, Banjica, Domanek, and Gladno Selo, among other towns?.
90 For more information on abuses in Glogovac town, *see*: Human Rights Watch, "'Ethnic Cleansing' in the Glogovac Municipality," *A Human Rights Watch Report,* vol.11, no. 8, July 1999.
91 Human Rights Watch researchers in Drenica in September 1998 also encountered some soldiers of the Yugoslav Army with KLA pins on their uniforms, clearly as a sarcastic trophy statement.
92 Human Rights Watch interview with N.B., Stenkovac refugee camp, Macedonia, May 8, 1999.
93 Human Rights Watch interview with B.K., Senekos refugee camp, Macedonia, May 23, 1999.
94 Human Rights Watch interview with A.H., Cegrane refugee camp, Macedonia, May 15, 1999.
95 Human Rights Watch interview with A.G., Stenkovac refugee camp, Macedonia, May 8, 1999.
96 Human Rights Watch interview with thirty-five-year-old man, Neprosteno refugee camp, Macedonia, April 30, 1999.
97 Human Rights Watch interview with I.X., Cegrane refugee camp, Macedonia, May 15, 1999.
98 Human Rights Watch interview with B.B., Cegrane refugee camp, Macedonia, May 13, 1999.
99 Human Rights Watch interview with X.D., Cegrane refugee camp, Macedonia, May 14, 1999.
100 Human Rights Watch interview with R.M., Cegran refugee camp, Macedonia, May 8, 1999.
101 Human Rights Watch interview with N.B., Stenkovac refugee camp, Macedonia, May 8, 1999. N.B. claimed that he spent three days in a field hospital in the refugee camp due to head wounds. Human Right Watch saw a scar on the back of his head where he claimed to have been injured by the police.
102 Human Rights Watch interview with twenty-three-year-old man from Glogovac, Neprosteno refugee camp, Macedonia, April 29, 1999.
103 Human Rights Watch interview with M.S., Neprosteno refugee camp, Macedonia, May 23, 1999.
104 Human Rights Watch interview with A.H., Cegrane refugee camp, Macedonia, May 15, 1999.
105 Human Rights Watch interview with C.C., Cegrane refugee camp, Macedonia, May 12, 1999.

106 Human Rights Watch interview with H.M., Stenkovac II refugee camp, Macedonia, May 10, 1999.
107 Human Rights Watch interview with B.B., Cegrane refugee camp, Macedonia, May 13, 1999.
108 Human Rights Watch interview with A.H., Cegrane refugee camp, Macedonia, May 15, 1999.
109 Human Rights Watch interview with X.D., Cegrane refugee camp, Macedonia, May 14, 1999.

Chapter 6. Djakovica (Gjakove) Municipality

1 OSCE/ODIHR, *Kosovo/Kosova: As Seen, As Told, Part I.*
2 For a good overall description of abuses in the municipality see International Crisis Group, *Reality Demands: Documenting Violations of International Humanitarian Law in Kosovo 1999,* (Brussels: International Crisis Group, June 2000).
3 See Human Rights Watch, "Civilian Deaths in the NATO Air Campaign," February 2000.
4 Since NATO's entry into Kosovo, Roma have been subjected to repeated harassment and violence by ethnic Albanians, many of whom view Roma as a group as having participated in crimes or collaborated with FRY state repression. In Djakovica, sections of the Roma neighborhood Brekoc were burned down and throughout mid-1999 approximately 600 Roma were living in a refugee camp on the outskirts of the city. Fifteen Djakovica Roma were reported killed or missing in political violence as of August 1999. (See chapter on Abuses After June 12, 1999.)
5 Human Rights Watch interview with Faton Polloshka, Djakovica, Kosovo, July 24, 1999.
6 Copies of the lists are on file in the Human Rights Watch office, New York.
7 Peter Finn, "On Polloshka's List, A Record of Horror," *Washington Post,* June 20, 1999.
8 John Kifner, "Mass Grave, Now Empty, Called Massacre Evidence," *New York Times,* June 23, 1999.
9 Human Rights Watch interview, name withheld, Djakovica, Kosovo, July 24, 1999.
10 Human Rights Watch interview with Faton Polloshka, Djakovica, Kosovo, July 24, 1999.
11 Although the *Washington Post* named Zdravkovic as the commander of the 125 Motorized Brigade, an article in the Yugoslav Army's *Vojska* magazine named Col. Dragan Zivanovic as the "future commander" of the brigade, without specifying when he would take command. (Vladica Krstic, "Write a Letter, Soldier," *Vojska,* June 25, 1998.) Zivanovic was also publicly named as commander of the 125th Motorized Brigade by the U.S. State Department on April 7, 1999. See the chapter on Forces of the Conflict.
12 Peter Finn and R. Jeffrey Smith, "Sudden Death in Kosovo's 'Heart of Darkness,'" *Washington Post,* April 30, 1999.
13 In an April 7, 1999, statement, U.S. State Department spokesman James Rubin announced that Colonels Mandic and Stefanovic, as well as seven other police and

army commanders, were "on notice" that their "forces are committing war crimes and crimes against humanity in Kosovo." See statement by James P. Rubin, State Department Spokesman, April 7, 1999.

14 OSCE/ODIHR, *Kosovo/Kosova: As Seen, As Told, Part I.*

15 Between March 24 and June 12, three doctors from the city were killed, two in Djakovica (Dr. Izet Hima and Dr. Masar Radoniqi) and one in nearby Raca (Dr. Bedri Beqa). The deputy manager of the hospital, Esat Bicuri, was also killed. According to doctors at the Djakovica hospital, which remained open throughout the war, the police and army set up field hospitals in the Disco Tiffany and in a Catholic Church.

Human Rights Watch interviews with Dr. Juniku, Djakovica, Kosovo, July 26, 1999, and Dr. Burim Sahatqija, Djakovica, Kosovo, August 4, 1999.

16 Finn, "On Polloshka's List, A Record of Horror."

17 Between March 24 and June 12, six workers of the Mother Theresa Society in the Djakovica municipality were killed. Two others were wounded, and nine are missing. Another eight were temporarily detained and beaten, and the office was burned on March 25.

Human Rights Watch interview with Sadik Polloshka and Peter Quni, Djakovica, Kosovo, July 23, 1999.

18 According to the indictment, the other three men killed were Sylejman Begolli, Arif Bytyqi, and Urim Bytyqi. The OSCE's report on Kosovo, "As Seen, As Told," page 174, also mentions this incident, although the description is different from that provided in the indictment.

19 Finn, "On Polloshka's List, A Record of Horror".

20 List of Persons Killed in the Period March to May, 1999, Council for the Defense of Human Rights, July 1999.

21 *See* Human Rights Watch, "Violent Ethnic Cleansing in Djakovica," *Kosovo Flash no.16,* April 3, 1999.

22 Human Rights Watch interview with X.K, Krume, Albania, April 2, 1999.

23 Human Rights Watch interview, name unknown, Krume, Albania, April 2, 1999.

24 Human Rights Watch interview with N.C., Djakovica, Kosovo, July 24, 1999.

25 Human Rights Watch interview with A.N., Djakovica, Kosovo, July 24, 1999.

26 Human Rights Watch interview with G.J., Djakovica, Kosovo, July 25, 1999.

27 Human Rights Watch inspected the hole in the bricks of the attic, from which one could indeed see down the street.

28 Human Rights Watch interview with A.N., Djakovica, Kosovo, July 24, 1999.

29 *See* Finn, "Sudden Death in Kosovo's 'Heart of Darkness'." According to the article, the killings took place in this order:

1. One unknown man not from Djakovica
2. Rexh Guci, 43, and his brother
3. Fehmi Lleshi, 46, butcher, and his wife
4. Hysen Deda, 77, his wife, Saja, 65, daughter Drita, 33, and her son, 6
5. Twenty people from five families, including twelve children (see below)
6. Jonuz Cana, 65, wife, daughter and son
7. Hasan Hasani, his wife, daughter and brother-in-law

8. Hasani's brother, son and daughter
9. Melahim Carkaxhiu, 36
10. Gezim Berdeniqi, 40.
11. Osam Dika, 70, and three sons
12. Skender Dylatahu, 34, and his brother
13. Myrteza Dinaj, 55, his son and four refugees

30 ICTY indictment of Milosevic, Milutinovic, Sainovic, Ojdanic and Stojiljkovic, para. 98(G).

31 Human Rights Watch interview with N.C., Djakovica, Kosovo, July 24, 1999.

32 Human Rights Watch interview with A.N., Djakovica, Kosovo, July 24, 1999.

33 Human Rights Watch interview with G.J., Djakovica, Kosovo, July 25, 1999.

34 Human Rights Watch interview with Faton Polloshka, Djakovica, Kosovo, July 24, 1999.

35 Human Rights Watch interview with V.V, Krume, Albania. April 10, 1999.

36 Human Rights Watch interview with R.R., Djakovica, Kosovo, June 15, 1999.

37 Human Rights Watch interview with Hekuran Hoda, Djakovica, Kosovo, July 24, 1999.

38 Human Rights Watch interview with L.V. Djakovica, Kosovo, July 23, 1999.

39 Human Rights Watch interview with B.E., Djakovica, Kosovo, July 24, 1999.

40 Human Rights Watch interview with Faton Polloshka, Djakovica, Kosovo, July 24, 1999.

41 Human Rights Watch interview with S.G., Djakovica, Kosovo, June 15, 1999.

42 Human Rigts Watch interview with Fuat Haxhibeqiri, Djakovica, Kosovo, June 20, 1999.

43 Among those men released, according to the council, are Nezhdet Mejzini, Tomor Dyla, Afrim Gala, Nevruz Bakida, Ahmet Bakida (brother of Nevruz), Gezim Qela, Afrim Qela (brother of Gezim), Mirsad Qela (brother of Gezim and Afrim), and Hazmi Morina.

44 Fredrik Dahl, "Serb Court Orders Release of 143 Kosovo Albanians," Reuters, April 23, 2001.

45 Human Rights Watch interview with A.H., Djakovica, Kosovo, July 20, 1999.

46 Human Rights Watch interview with Dr. Sejoullah Hoxha, Pristina, Kosovo, July 21, 1999.

47 Human Rights Watch interview with Silvana Mirija, Tirana, Albania, July 24, 1999.

48 NATO press conference by Jamie Shea and Brigadier General Giuseppe Marani, Brussels, April 20, 1999.

49 Meja was also the site of a NATO attack on a convoy of internally displaced Albanians on April 14.

50 International Committee of the Red Cross, "Persons Missing in Relation to the Events in Kosovo from January 1998," First Edition, May 2000.

51 Human Rights Watch interviews, Kukes, Albania, April 28, 1999.

52 Human Rights Watch interview with V.A., Kukes, Albania, April 30, 1999.

53 Human Rights Watch interview with R.R., Kukes, Albania, June 4, 1999.

54 Human Rights Watch interview with A.S., Kukes, Albania, April 30, 1999.

55 Human Rights Watch interview with M.B., Kukes, Albania, June 4, 1999.

56 International Committee of the Red Cross, "Persons Missing in Relation to the Events in Kosovo from January 1998."
57 Human Rights Watch interview with M.Z., Kukes, Albania, April 30, 1999.
58 Human Rights Watch interview, name not provided, Kukes, Albania, April 29, 1999.
59 Human Rights Watch interview, Kukes, name not provided, Albania, April 29, 1999.
60 Human Rights Watch interview with Ray Wilkenson, Kukes, Albania, April 29, 1999.
61 Human Rights Watch interview with M.J., Kukes, Albania, April 29, 1999.
62 Human Rights Watch interview with L.J., Kukes, Albania, April 29, 1999.
63 Human Rights Watch interview with F.S., Kukes, Albania, April 29, 1999.
64 Human Rights Watch interview with V.A., Kukes, Albania, April 30, 1999.
65 Human Rights Watch interview with M.B., Kukes, Albania, April 30, 1999.
66 Human Rights Watch interview with K.S., Kukes, Albania, April 30, 1999.
67 Rame Mehmeti (aged forty-three) and Mehmet Mehmeti (aged nineteen) are both on the ICRC's list of missing people from Meja. According to the list, which was last updated on May 15, 2000, the two men, who were originally from Brovina, were last seen in Meja on April 27, 1999.
68 Human Rights Watch interview with A.S. Kukes, Albania, April 30, 1999.
69 The man in charge of the Roma street cleaning crews was Faton Polloshka, director of the Djakovica Public Works Department (see section on Djakovica). According to Polloshka, interviewed by Human Rights Watch on June 19, the municipal workers took approximately thirty bodies from Meja, although many more are believed to have been killed, whose whereabouts are unknown.
70 Milutin Prasevic's name also came up in interviews in Koronica (see section on Koronica). One man claimed that Prasevic was among the policemen harassing the villagers in early April. Human Rights Watch interview with M.M., Koronica, Kosovo, July 26, 1999. On June 7, 1999, officer Prasevic from the Djakovica police was posthumously awarded the Order of Merit in Matters of Defence and Security of the First Degree. *Politika,* October 15, 1999.
71 Human Rights Watch interview with K.H., Meja, Kosovo, July 25, 1999.
72 Human Rights Watch interview with Marie Colvin, Kukes, Albania, April 30, 1999. Human Rights Watch interview with Ian Fisher, Korenica, Kosovo, June 16, 1999.
73 Jonathan S. Landay, "Evidence Mounts of War Crimes," *Christian Science Monitor,* June 21, 1999.
74 See http://www.mup.sr.gov.yu/domino\mup.nsf/pages/index-e, January 21, 2000.
75 Human Rights Watch interview with K.H., Meja, Kosovo, July 25, 1999.
76 Human Rights Watch interview with M.M., Koronica, Kosovo, July 26, 1999.
77 Human Rights Watch interview with K.H., Meja, Kosovo, July 25, 1999.
78 Human Rights Watch interview with A.S., Kukes, Albania, April 30, 1999.
79 Human Rights Watch interview with F.B., Kukes, Albania, April 29, 1999.
80 Among the missing from Guska are: Gjon Dedaj, aged approximately fifty-five, Pjeter Dedaj, aged approximately fifty-two, and Martin Dedaj (Pjeter's son), aged approximately twenty-nine.
81 Human Rights Watch interview with M.M., Korenica, Kosovo, July 26, 1999.

82 Ibid.
83 Human Rights Watch interview with Anton Dedaj, Korenica, Kosovo, June 16, 1999.
84 Human Rights Watch interview with Tom Dedaj, Korenica, Kosovo, June 16, 1999. The fact that some paramilitaries were wearing red arm bands suggests a possible central command.
85 Ibid.
86 Human Rights Watch interview with K.M., Korenica, June 16, 1999.
87 Human Rights Watch interview with R.R. and S.R., Kukes, Albania, June 4, 1999.

Chapter 7. Istok (Istog) Municipality

1 UNHCR GIS Unit, Pristina, Kosovo, "UNHCR Shelter Verification: Agency Coverage," November 9, 1999.
2 OSCE/ODIHR, *Kosovo/Kosova: As Seen, As Told, Part I,* pp 208–210.
3 M.Manic and S. Kovacevic, "Will and Readiness to Carry Out All Security Tasks," *Policajac,* No. 18/98, October 1998.
4 By mid-2000, many more Dubrava survivors had been released. In September, seventy-nine of them held a hunger strike in front of Dubrava prison to highlight the plight of the Albanian prisoners still in Serbian custody.
5 See interviews with Ahmet Ahmeti (Izabela Kisic, "Tukli su nas, mucili elektrosokovima i pucli," *Danas,* November 5, 1999); Bajrush Xhemaili ("Former Kosovar Prisoner Says Serbs 'Massacred' Over 100 Inmates," BBC Worldwide Monitoring of *Beta News Agency,* August 26, 1999); and Remzi Tetrica ("We Were Attacked With Automatic Weapons, Snipers and Bombs in Dubrava Prison," *Kosova Sot,* September 30, 1999); and information from Naser Husaj (Carlotta Gall, "Stench of Horror Lingers in a Prison in Kosovo," *New York Times,* November 8, 1999.)
6 "NATO Crimes in Yugoslavia: Documentary Evidence, 25 April–10 June 1999," Yugoslav Ministry of Foreign Affairs, Belgrade, July 1999, p. 319.
7 OSCE/ODIHR, *Kosovo/Kosova: As Seen, As Told, Part I,* pp. 213–214.
8 "We Were Attacked With Automatic Weapons, Snipers and Bombs in Dubrava Prison," *Kosova Sot,* September 30, 1999.
9 "Report on the Trial of the So-called 'Djakovica Group'," Group 484, Volunteer Center for Direct Human Rights, April 2000.
10 "Former Kosovar Prisoner Says Serbs 'Massacred' Over 100 Inmates," BBC Worldwide Monitoring.
11 Hoti (age fifty-six), head of the Party of National Unity (Unikomb), was arrested on May 14, 1993, and subsequently sentenced to five years in prison.
12 Paul Watson, "NATO Bombs Ignite Prison Chaos—KLA Officers Reported to be Among Inmates," *Toronto Star,* May 22, 1999.
13 A.K. was arrested in Pec in August 1998, and sentenced in November 1998 to one year in prison for "terrorist acts." Human Rights Watch inspected A.K.'s verdict from the Pec district court, signed by Judge Goran Petronijevic, but the document number and pre-

cise court dates are not provided here to protect the identity of the witness. A.K. told Human Rights Watch that he had joined the KLA in June 1998, and had fought in Glodjane under Ramush Haradinaj, the KLA's regional commander in the area.

14 Human Rights Watch interview with A.K., Pec, Kosovo, November 17, 1999.

15 B.K. was arrested in September 1998 and sentenced to one year in prison that March 1999 for terrorist activities. He admitted to Human Rights Watch to having been a KLA battalion commander. The precise dates of his arrest and sentencing are not provided to protect the identity of the witness.

16 Human Rights Watch interview with B.K., near Pec, Kosovo, November 17, 1999.

17 NATO press conference, NATO Headquarters, Brussels, May 20, 1999.

18 Yugoslav Ministry of Foreign Affairs, NATO Raids on Manufacturing and Civilian Facilities on May 19 and in the Night Between May 19 and 20, 1999.

19 Ibid.

20 Jacky Rowland, "Bombs, Blood and Dark Despair," *Scotland on Sunday,* May 23, 1999.

21 Paul Watson, "Dispatch from Kosovo: 20 Killed, 10 Wounded as NATO Targets Prison," *Los Angeles Times,* May 22, 1999.

22 Ibid.

23 "NATO Hits Kosovo Jail Again Friday Night," *Associated Press,* May 21, 1999.

24 NATO Morning Briefing, NATO Headquarters, Brussels, May 22, 1999.

25 Watson, "NATO Bombs Ignite Prison Chaos."

26 "Former Kosovar Prisoner Says Serbs 'Massacred' Over 100 Inmates," BBC Worldwide Monitoring.

27 Izabela Kisic, "Tukli su nas, mucili elektrosokovima I pucli," *Danas,* November 5, 1999.

28 "At Least 19 Killed in NATO Bombardment of Prison In Istok," Tanjug, May 21, 1999.

29 "NATO Aircraft Attack Prison In Istok Six Times in One Day," Tanjug, May 22, 1999.

30 "Dozens of Inmates Killed in NATO Air Strikes on Istok Prison," Tanjug, May 22, 1999.

31 Human Rights Watch interview with B.K., near Pec, Kosovo, November 17, 1999.

32 Human Rights Watch interview with A.K., Pec, November 17, 1999.

33 Bajrush Xhemaili was head of the Council for the Defense of Human Rights and Freedom's sub-council in Urosevac/Ferizaj, as well as a member of the council's presidency in Pristina. He was arrested in 1993 and sentenced on August 5, 1993, to eight years in prison. He was released on June 8, 1999, and is currently active in the Party for Democratic Prosperity, the new political party headed by Hashim Thaci, former political director of the KLA and current prime minister of Kosovo's self-appointed Provisional Government.

34 "Former Kosovar Prisoner Says Serbs 'Massacred' Over 100 Inmates," BBC Worldwide Monitoring of *Beta News Agency,* August 26, 1999.

35 Human Rights Watch interview with B.K., near Pec, Kosovo, November 17, 1999.

36 Human Rights Watch interview with A.K., Pec, November 17, 1999.

37 A *New York Times* reporter, Carlotta Gall, who visited Dubrava prison on November 7, 1999, saw weapons in the basement of the cultural center, including a spade, metal spikes, wooden bars and metal piping. ["Stench of Horror Lingers in a Prison in Kosovo," by Carlotta Gall, *The New York Times,* November 8, 1999.]

38 Gall, "Stench of Horror Lingers in a Prison in Kosovo."

39 Ibid.
40 "We Were Attacked with Automatic Weapons, Snipers and Bombs in Dubrava Prison," *Kosova Sot,* September 30, 1999.
41 Human Rights Watch interviewed another former prisoner who was in Lipljan prison from May 24 to June 9 but was not in Dubrava who also reported having to walk through a cordon of policemen. Human Rights Watch interview with R.M., Glogovac, Kosovo, November 5, 1999.
42 Humanitarian Law Center Communique, October 10, 1999.
43 Human Rights Watch interview with A.K., near Pec, Kosovo, November 17, 1999.
44 Human Rigths Watch interview with B. Z., Glogovac, Kosovo, November 5, 1999.
45 "Number of Persons Killed in NATO raids on Istok prison Still Uncertain," Tanjug, May 25, 1999.
46 On May 24, Vladan Bojic was quoted on the state-run Belgrade Radio as saying that NATO had "committed the biggest mass murder of inmates in the history of modern civiliazation," and that the court would begin to investigate the crime.
47 FRY MFA, NATO Raids on Manufacturing and Civilian Facilities on May 29th and in the Night Between May 29th and 30th 1999.
48 Yugoslav press reports; "Identifikovano 86 mrtvih," *DAN,* 27 May 1999, p. 2; "Jos sedam leseva," *DAN,* 30 May 1999.
49 "NATO Crimes in Yugoslavia: Documentary Evidence, 25 April–10 June 1999," p. 319, Yugoslav Ministry of Foreign Affairs, Belgrade, July 1999.
50 "Istok Prison's Unanswered Questions," BBC World News, May 25, 1999.
51 Daniel Williams, "Kosovo Revisited; At War's End, Old Places Seen in New Light," *Washington Post,* June 26, 1999.
52 Ibid.
53 Gall, "Stench of Horror Lingers in a Prison in Kosovo."
54 "Spanish Teams Excavating Mass Burial Site," Associated Press, August 13, 1999.
55 Remarks to the Security Council by Madame Carla Del Ponte, Prosecutor, International Criminal Tribunal for the former Yugoslavia, New York, November 10, 1999.
56 William Booth, "Doctor Tells of Life Among Serbia's Captives," *Washington Post,* July 19, 1999.
57 Paul Watson, "NATO Bombs Ignite Prison Chaos—KLA Officers Reported to be Among Inmates," *Toronto Star,* May 22, 1999.
58 Human Rights Watch interview with Faton Mexhmeti Ramusij, Babaloc (Baballoq), July 17, 1999.

Chapter 8. Lipljan (Lipjan) Municipality

1 Human Rights Watch interview with A.I., Cegrane refugee camp, Macedonia, May 4, 1999.
2 Human Rights Watch interview with B.S., Neprosteno refugee camp, Macedonia, April 29, 1999.
3 OSCE/ODIHR, *Kosovo/Kosova: As Seen, As Told, Part I,* pp. 254–265.

4 Large numbers of people from surrounding villages took shelter in Lugadzija as a result. The village of Smolusa, which was also not directly attacked, served as a similar refuge.
5 Human Rights Watch interview with S.S., Zelino, Macedonia, May 7, 1999.
6 Ibid.
7 Human Rights Watch interview with B.D., Kukes, Albania, April 18, 1999. The chapter on Lipljan in OSCE/ODIHR, *Kosovo/Kosovs: As Seen, As Told* contains a similar account of events in the village.
8 Human Rights Watch interview with K.G., Neprosteno refugee camp, Macedonia, April 29, 1999; Human Rights Watch interview with B.D., Kukes, Albania, April 18, 1999.
9 The chapter on Lipljan in OSCE/ODIHR, *Kosovo/Kosova: As Seen, As Told* includes witness accounts of an attack on Gornje Gadimlje on March 26, forcible expulsions on March 29 and the subsequent influx of large numbers of displaced persons in mid-April.
10 Human Rights Watch interview with B.H., Kukes, Albania, April 18, 1999.; Human Rights Watch interview with B.D., Kukes, Albania, April 18, 1999.; Human Rights Watch interview with B.E., Kukes, Albania, April 19, 1999. Witnesses cited in *As Seen, As Told* indicate that the population was expelled on April 17 but are otherwise consistent.
11 Human Rights Watch interview with M.L., Negotino refugee camp, Macedonia, May 6, 1999.
12 Human Rights Watch interview with S.S., Zelino, Macedonia, May 7, 1999.
13 Human Rights Watch interview with Q.F., Neprosteno refugee camp, Macedonia, April 27, 1999.
14 Ibid.
15 Human Rights Watch interview with F.P., Neprosteno refugee camp, Macedonia, April 29, 1999.
16 Human Rights Watch interview with M.L., Neprosteno refugee camp, Macedonia, April 27, 1999.
17 Human Rights Watch interview with A.A., Cegrane refugee camp, Macedonia, May 1, 1999.
18 Ibid.
19 "As Seen, As Told," Lipljan chapter.
20 Human Rights Watch interview with B.B., Cegrane refugee camp, Macedonia, May 1, 1999.
21 Human Rights Watch interview with F.P., Neprosteno refugee camp, Macedonia, April 29, 1999.
22 Human Rights Watch interview with B.B., Cegrane refugee camp, Macedonia, May 1, 1999. "As Seen, As Told," Lipljan chapter.
23 Human Rights Watch interview, Bogovine, Macedonia, May 6, 1999.
24 Witness statements in the Lipljan chapter of "As Seen, As Told" confirm the deaths and most of the details of the attack provided by the woman.
25 Human Rights Watch interview with Y.S., Cegrane refugee camp, Macedonia, May 20, 1999.
26 "As Seen As Told," includes a detailed account of the killings and describes twenty-six

or twenty-seven dead. See also, Julian Borger, "A Joyous Welcome from the Living, a Grisly Reminder from the Dead," *Guardian*, June 14, 1999. Borger's account, written after a visit to the village, reports twenty-six graves. The ICTY has exhumed 26 bodies from the site.

27 Human Rights Watch interview with J.K., Cegrane refugee camp, Macedonia, May 3, 1999.

28 Ibid.

29 Gregor Mayer, "Mass graves come to light after KFOR enters," Deutsche Presse-Agentur, June 14, 1999. See also, David Rohde, "In Kosovo, Signs of Massacres and a Cover-Up," *New York Times*, June 14, 1999.

30 OSCE/ODIHR, *Kosovo/Kosova: As Seen, As Told*, Lipljan chapter.

31 The ICTY exhumed twenty bodies from graves in the village.

32 Susan Milligan and Mary Leonard, "Serb atrocity evidence mounting," *Boston Globe*, June 18, 1999.

33 Human Rights Watch interview with F.B., Cegrane refugee camp, Macedonia, May 1, 1999.

34 Human Rights Watch interview with F.G., Slovinje, Kosovo, July 24, 1999.

35 Human Rights Watch interviews with F.B., Cegrane refugee camp, Macedonia, May 1, 1999; F.G., Slovinje, Kosovo, July 24, 1999.

36 On June 25, 1999, British military police with KFOR arrested a Serb man from Slovinje, after investigating allegations that he had participated in the killings as a paramilitary.

37 Human Rights Watch interview with Z.G., Slovinje, Kosovo, July 23, 1999.

38 Human Rights Watch interview with F.B., Cegrane refugee camp, Macedonia, May 1, 1999; interview with M.B., Cegrane, Macedonia, May 4, 1999; interview with F.G., Slovinje, Kosovo, July 24, 1999.

39 Human Rights Watch interview with I.N., Slovinje, Kosovo, July 23, 1999.

40 Human Rights Watch interview with M.B., Cegrane refugee camp, Macedonia, May 4, 1999.

41 Human Rights Watch interview with K.G., Neprosteno refugee camp, Macedonia, April 29, 1999.

42 Human Rights Watch interview with H.K., Slovinje, Kosovo, June 22, 1999.

43 Human Rights Watch interview with F.G., Slovinje, Kosovo, July 24, 1999.

44 Human Rights Watch interview with S.B., Slovinje, Kosovo, July 24, 1999.

45 Human Rights Watch interview with F.B., Cegrane refugee camp, Macedonia, May 3, 1999. (Follow-up interview in Lugu i Demas (near Slovinje village), Kosovo, July 23, 1999.)

46 Yonuz's wife Havushe Pacolli (b. 1946) died of a heart attack on April 18.

47 Human Rights Watch interview with F.G., Slovinje, Kosovo, July 24, 1999.

48 Ibid.

49 Human Rights Watch interview with F.B., Cegrane refugee camp, Macedonia, May 3, 1999. (Follow-up interview in Lugu I Demas (near Slovinje village), Kosovo, July 23, 1999.)

50 Human Rights Watch interview with S.B., Slovinje, Kosovo, July 24, 1999.

51 Ibid.
52 Human Rights Watch interview with H.K., Slovinje, Kosovo, June 22, 1999.
53 Human Rights Watch interview with Z.G., Slovinje, Kosovo, July 23, 1999.
54 Human Rights Watch interview with S.B., Slovinje, Kosovo, July 24, 1999.
55 In addition to the sixteen killed on April 16, the body of heart-attack victim Havushe Paccolli had also been buried at the site.
56 Human Rights Watch interview with S.S., Slovinje, Kosovo, June 24, 1999.
57 Ibid.
58 Ibid.
59 Ibid.
60 Human Rights Watch interview with P.F., Slovinje, Kosovo, June 24, 1999.
61 Ibid.
62 Ibid.
63 The Berisha family were less fortunate. On June 12, the day that NATO forces entered Kosovo, the family were on their way to Smolusa from Slovinje to collect food when they triggered an explosive device believed to be an unexploded NATO bomb. Sixty-one-year old Shaban, twenty-seven-year-old Mehaz and twenty-five-year Ibrahim were killed instantly and several other family members were badly wounded. Human Rights Watch interview with the Berisha family, Slovinje, Kosovo, June 24, 1999.
64 "Paramilitary" is an imprecise term in Kosovo that can variously describe any irregular forces including armed civilians and persons in uniforms from the regular security services wearing masks to hide their faces.
65 Human Rights Watch interview with D.N., Slovinje, Kosovo, July 23, 1999.

Chapter 9. Orahovac (Rrahovec) Municipality

1 For details, see Human Rights Watch, *Humanitarian Law Violations in Kosovo,* October 1998.
2 In February 1999, for instance, the KLA admitted to the abduction of two Serb civilians from Velika Hoca. One of the men was killed and the other was severly beaten. See OSCE/ODIHR, Kosovo/Kosova: *As Seen, As Told, Part I,* p. 37.
3 "In Complex Security Circumstances, They Fulfill Their Obligations With Success," *Policajac,* No. 3/98, February 1998.
4 "At New Duties," *Policajac,* No. 1/99, January 1999.
5 A survivor of the massacre told Human Rights Watch that the KLA had a base in Drenoc, but not in Pusto Selo. Human Rights Watch interview, Pusto Selo, Kosovo, June 26, 1999. See also "Report of the High Commissioner for Human Rights on the Situation of Human Rights in Kosovo," U.N. Doc. E/CN.4/2000/10, 27 September 1999, para. 35 (stating that previous fighting between the KLA and Serbs in the area led to reprisal killings in Pusto Selo); and OSCE/ODIHR, *Kosovo/Kosova: As Seen, As Told, Part I.* (chapter on Orahovac, which notes that fighting between KLA and Serbs had taken place in the region around Pusto Selo prior to the massacre).
6 Human Rights Watch interview with B.K., Pusto Selo, Kosovo, June 26, 1999.

7 Human Rights Watch interview with T.K., Pusto Selo, Kosovo, June 26, 1999.

8 Human Rights Watch interview with B.K., Pusto Selo, Kosovo, June 26, 1999.

9 Human Rights Watch interview with B.K., Pusto Selo, Kosovo, June 26, 1999.

10 Human Rights Watch interview with R.K., Pusto Selo, Kosovo, June 26, 1999.

11 At approximately this time the first reports of the Pusto Selo killings appeared in Kosovapress, the KLA's news agency. It released a short bulletin on the massacre on April 3, publishing a list of ninety-nine of the dead the following day. "Rahovec: Bodies of 136 massacred people found in a village near Rahovec," Kosovapress, April 3, 1999, and; "The list of the executed and massacred people in the village of Pastasel, Commune of Rahovec," Kosovapress, April 4, 1999.

12 The photographs were posted on the web site of the U.S. Department of State: http://www.state.gov/www/regions/eur/rpt_9905_ethnic_ksvo_7b.html, (March 22, 2001).

13 See, for example, "NATO: Aerial photo may show mass graves in Kosovo," CNN, April 11, 1999; "Mountain Refugees and Mass Graves," ABC.NEWS.com, April 11, 1999.

14 Human Rights Watch interview with T.K., Pusto Selo, Kosovo, June 26, 1999. The U.S. Department of State, in its May 7, 1999 update on the Kosovo crisis, stated that KLA sources mentioned exhumations in Pusto Selo beginning on April 23, and that the bodies were sent to Orahovac by truck. U.S. Department of State, "Fact Sheet: The Ethnic Cleansing of Kosovo," May 7, 1999.

15 Panorama, "The Valley of the Dead," broadcast July 5, 1999 (available on the Internet at http://news.bbc.co.uk/hi/english/static/inside_kosovo/, (March 22, 2001)).

16 "NATO Photos of Kosovo Mass Graves are Fake: Report," Agence France Presse, April 24, 1999.

17 In late 1999, as a body count of the ethnic Albanians killed during the conflict was beginning to be established, numerous analyses were published arguing that NATO had greatly exaggerated the extent of Serb atrocities (see "March-June 1999: An Overview"). Because the aerial photograph of the grave site at Pusto Selo was among the most compelling pieces of evidence produced by NATO during the war in support of its claims of mass killings, the absence of physical proof of the killings—that is, the 106 missing corpses—was widely reported in critical accounts of NATO's wartime conduct. An article by Alexander Cockburn is notable in this respect. In it, Cockburn notes the claim that 106 ethnic Albanians were killed by Serb forces in Pusto Selo, stating that NATO "rushed out" photographs of the graves. Asserting that "[n]othing to buttress that charge has yet been found," he neglects to mention, however, that survivors of the events had come forward and described the massacre in detail, as well as telling of the subsequent exhumation of the bodies. See Alexander Cockburn, "Where's the Evidence of Genocide of Kosovar Albanians?" *Los Angeles Times,* October 29, 1999. Cockburn perhaps obtained most of the information in his article from a report by Stratfor.com, a Texas think tank. Yet the Stratfor.com report, unlike Cockburn's article, points out that the villagers of Pusto Selo explained that the Serbs had removed the bodies of their dead. See Stratfor.com, "Where Are Kosovo's Killing Fields?" October 17, 1999 (available at http://www.stratfor.com/crisis/kosovo/genocide.htm (March 21, 2001)).

18 Human Rights Watch interview with T.K., Pusto Selo, Kosovo, June 26, 1999.

Chapter 10. Pec (Peja) Municipality

1 Lodja is a village of 2,800 people just outside of Pec where intense fighting took place between the KLA and government forces in the summer of 1998. In mid-August the police pushed the KLA from the village with ground and air power, looted the valuables, and then systematically destroyed all of the village's 284 houses, including the mosque, with bulldozers. Photographs of the destroyed village, taken in February 1999, can be viewed on the Human Rights Watch website: www.hrw.org/hrw/campaigns/kosovo98/photo/pics299/299a.htm, (March 23, 2001).
2 Those killed were Zoran Stanojevic (17), Svetislav Ristic (17), Ivan Obradovic (15), Dragan Trifovic (17), Vukosav Gvozdenovic (18), and Ivan Radevic (25).
3 The local branch of the Council for the Defense of Human Rights and Freedoms claimed that more than 500 people in the Pec municipality had been killed during the war, although it is not clear how many of these people were civilians. Human Rights Watch interview with Dr. Neshat Asllani, Pec, Kosovo, July 15, 1999.
4 "Special Report, Retribution in Kosovo," VIP Daily News Report, Issue 1559, July 28, 1999.
5 M. Manic and S. Kovacevic, "Will and Readiness to Carry Out All Security Tasks," *Policajac,* No. 18/98, October 1998.
6 Matthew McAllester, "Written in blue. . . ," *Newsday,* August 15, 1999.
7 OSCE/ODIHR, *Kosovo/Kosova: As Seen, As Told, Part I,* pp 284–290.
8 Human Rights Watch interview Dr. Neshat Asllani, Pec, Kosovo, July 23, 1999.
9 Human Rights Watch interview with X.H., Tirana, Albania, March 29, 1999.
10 Human Rights Watch interview, Durres, Albania, March 31, 1999.
11 Human Rights Watch interview with Mehe Muzlukaj, Tirana, Albania, March 29, 1999.
12 Human Rights Watch interview with Bujar Tabaku, Tirana, Albania, March 29, 1999.
13 Human Rights Watch interview with Father Jovan, Pec, Kosovo, July 17, 1999.
14 "Bloody Traces, Interview with Father Sava," *Nin Magazine,* July 8, 1999.
15 Human Rights Watch interview with Pec Imam, Pec, Kosovo, July 19, 1999.
16 Human Rights Watch interview with Agim, Pec, Kosovo, July 18, 1999.
17 Human Rights Watch interview with Ibrahim, Pec, Kosovo, July 18, 1999.
18 On June 26, 1999, a woman believed to have been "Kaplan's" sister was raped and killed by men in KLA uniforms.
19 Human Rights Watch interview with Dr. Ibrahim Rexhaj, Pec, Kosovo, July 15, 1999.
20 NATO press conference by Jamie Shea and Brigadier General Giuseppe Marani, Brussels, April 20, 1999.
21 The U.S. State Department report, "Ethnic Cleansing in Kosovo: An Accounting," is available at www.state.gov/www/global/human_rights/kosovoii/op.html, (March 23, 2001).
22 Elisabeth Bumiller, "Deny Rape or Be Hated: Kosovo Victims' Choice," *New York Times,* June 22, 1999; this states: "For now, State Department officials in Washington say they have received refugee reports that Serbs were using the Hotel Karagac in the town of Pec and an army camp near Djakovica as rape camps."

23 See Peter Finn, "Signs of Rape Scar Kosovo; Families' Shame Could Hinder Investigation," *Washington Post*, June 27, 1999.
24 OSCE/ODIHR, *Kosovo/Kosova: As Seen, As Told, Part I*, p. 290.
25 In September, Agim Ceku became the head of the newly-formed Kosovo Protection Corps, the successor to the Kosovo Liberation Army.
26 Human Rights Watch interview with A.A., Ulcin, Montenegro, Yugoslavia, June 15, 1999.
27 Testimony of Ceku family members, Lawyers Committee for Human Rights, Witness Project, Massacre in Qyshk te Pejes, Kosovo. See the Witness Project website: www.witness.org, (March 23, 2001).
28 Website of the Serbian Secretary of Information, www.serbia-info.com, (March 23, 2001), "Albanian terrorism after Milosevic-Holbrooke Accord," February 25, 1999, and BBC Worldwide Monitoring, Serbian Radio, Belgrade, "Serbia: Shoot-out Reported in Pec as Police Arrest Six Albanians," December 22, 1998.
29 The Centre for the Protection of Women and Children, War Chronicle of the Week, December 22, 1998.
30 Human Rights Watch interview with A.A., Ulcin, Montenegro, Yugoslavia, June 15, 1999.
31 Testimony of Ceku family members, Lawyers Committee for Human Rights, Witness Project, Massacre in Qyshk te Pejes, Kosovo. See the Witness Project website: www.witness.org, (March 23, 2001).
32 Ibid.
33 Human Rights Watch interview with B.B., Cuska, July 15, 1999.
34 Human Rights Watch interview with A.S., Ulcin, Montenegro, Yugoslavia, June 15, 1999.
35 Human Rights Watch interview with B.B., Cuska, Kosovo, July 15, 1999.
36 Ibid.
37 Human Rights Watch interview with C.C., Cuska, Kosovo, July 16, 1999.
38 Human Rights Watch interview with D.D., Rozaje, Montenegro, Yugoslavia, June 8, 1999.
39 Human Rights Watch interview with A.A., Ulcin, Montenegro, Yugoslavia, June 15, 1999.
40 Human Rights Watch interview with C.C., Cuska, Kosovo, July 16, 1999.
41 Human Rights Watch saw what appeared to be bullet scars below the witness' left knee and above his right knee. At the time of interview, in July 1999, the witness was still wearing a cast from his right knee down to his ankle. When visited one year later, in July 2000, the man had left the area for further medical treatment.
42 Human Rights Watch interview with B.B., Cuska, Kosovo, July 15, 1999.
43 "Kosovo Crisis - The Awful Truth," *Time*, June 28, 1999.
44 Human Rights Watch interview with A.A., Ulcin, Montenegro, Yugoslavia, June 15, 1999.
45 Ibid.
46 Human Rights Watch interview with D.D., Rozaje, Montenegro, Yugoslavia, June 8, 1999.

47 Human Rights Watch interview with F.F., Pec, Kosovo, July 15, 1999.
48 Human Rights Watch interview, Cuska, July 15, 1999.
49 "Kosovo Crisis—The Awful Truth," *Time*, June 28, 1999.
50 Human Rights Watch interview with B.B., Cuska, Kosovo, July 15, 1999.
51 Human Rights Watch interview with F.F., Pec, Kosovo, July 15, 1999.
52 Human Rights Watch interviews with villagers in Zahac, Kosovo, July 17, 1999.
53 The others were killed on May 12 (one person), June 10 (seven people), and June 14 (one person).
54 Human Rights Watch interviews with villagers in Pavljan, Kosovo, July 17, 1999.
55 Human Rights Watch interview with G.G., Pavljan, Kosovo, July 17, 1999.
56 Human Rights Watch interview with H.H., Cuska, Kosovo, July 16, 1999.
57 Human Rights Watch interview with B.B., Cuska, Kosovo, July 15, 1999.
58 One of the people who identified the man as a commander also claimed that he had taken her away into a home, apparently with the aim to rape her. According to the woman, the man told her she knew what she had to do to save her family. For an unknown reason, she was then let go.
59 Human Rights Watch later interviewed the same ethnic Albanian who, without suggestion, identified the man in photograph no. 3 as Srecko Popovic.
60 For more information from the American RadioWorks report, including photographs, see their website: www.americanradioworks.org, (March 23, 2001).
61 Smith and Montgomery later confronted Cvetkovic directly in Montenegro, where he was living after the war. He denied being in Cuska or ever being in uniform.
62 Human Rights Watch interview with I.I., Zahac, Kosovo, July 22, 1999
63 Human Rights Watch interview with H.H., Cuska, Kosovo, July 16, 1999.
64 For an article on Salipur, see Paul Salopek, "The Merciless Life and Death of a Paramilitary Killer; Sadistic Cop Tortured Town," *Chicago Tribune*, June 27, 1999.
65 *Policajac*, July 1999.
66 Kandic later confirmed her report directly to Human Rights Watch. Commander of the 125th Motorized Brigade was Col. Dragan Zivanovic (see chapter on Forces of the Conflict). It is possible, however, that the document viewed by Kandic was signed by Col. Djordje Nikolic, a representative of Col Zivanovic. Human Rights Watch obtained a document from the 125th Motorized Brigade, dated June 2, 1999, and marked "Military Secret", that was signed by Col. Djordje Nikolic, Representing Commander. The document [No. 2824-1, June 2, 1999] was unimportant, ordering all battalion and division commanders to prepare reports and attend a meeting the following day.
67 "Special Report, Retribution in Kosovo," VIP Daily News Report, Issue 1559, July 28, 1999.
68 Jack Kelley, "U.N. Records Link Serbs to War Crimes," *USA Today*, July 14, 1999.
69 OSCE/ODIHR, *Kosovo/Kosova: As Seen, As Told, Part I*, pp.?.
70 Remarks to the U.N. Security Council by Madame Carla Del Ponte, November 10, 1999.
71 Tanjug, May 25, 1998. [Is there a news title?]
72 See Human Rights Watch, *Humanitarian Law Violations in Kosovo*, (New York: Human Rights Watch, 1998).

73 OSCE/ODIHR, *Kosovo/Kosova: As Seen, As Told, Part I*, p. 290.
74 Human Rights Watch interview with K.B., Ljubenic, Kosovo, July 19, 1999.
75 Chris Stephen, "Kosovo's Heights of Mass Murder," *Scotsman*, July 10, 1999.
76 James Pringle, "Serbs Killed 350 in Orgy of Violence," *Times* (London), July 10, 1999.
77 Michael Smith, " Large Grave Found: Massacre Detailed," *Chicago Sun Times*, July 10, 1999.
78 Paul Salopek, "A Village Ripe with Sorrow, Loss," *Chicago Tribune*, June 22, 1999.
79 Jim Heintz, "U.N. Reports New Possible Mass Killing Site in Western Kosovo," Associated Press, July 9, 1999.
80 Chris Stephen, "Kosovo's Heights of Mass Murder," *Scotsman*, July 10, 1999.
81 Ibid., and "Her Family's War—'Where is the World'," *Providence Journal*, August 8, 1999; James Pringle, "Serbs Killed 350 in Orgy of Violence," *Times* (London), July 10, 1999.; and Sylvie Groult, "Kosovo Massacre Survivor Tells of Miraculous Escape," Agence France Presse, July 11, 1999.
82 OSCE/ODIHR, *Kosovo/Kosova: As Seen, As Told, Part I*, p. 290.
83 "Her Family's War—'Where is the World'," *Providence Journal*..
84 OSCE/ODIHR, *Kosovo/Kosova: As Seen, As Told, Part I*, p. 290.

Chapter 11. Prizren Municipality

1 OSCE/ODIHR, *Kosovo/Kosova: As Seen, As Told, Part I*, p. 331.
2 "In Complex Security Circumstances, They Fulfill Their Obligations With Success," *Policajac*, no. 3/98, February 1998.
3 "At New Duties," *Policajac*, no. 1/99, January 1999.
4 OSCE/ODIHR, *Kosovo/Kosova: As Seen, As Told, Part I*, pp. 332–335.

Serbian sources, in contrast, claim that the building was destroyed by aerial cluster bombs dropped by NATO. See Committee for National Solidarity, "Aide Memoire on the Use of Inhumane Weapons in the Aggression of the North Atlantic Treaty Organization Against the Federal Republic of Yugoslavia," May 15, 1999.

The League of Prizren was founded in 1878, bringing together representatives of all Albanian inhabited regions to demand autonomy from the Ottomans. The establishment of the League was a landmark in the movement for Albanian self-determination. The building that was destroyed—where the League was organized—archived historic documents relating to the League's creation and activities.

5 Press conference given by NATO Spokesman Jamie Shea and SHAPE Spokesman Major General Walter Jertz, Brussels, Belgium, May 17, 1999. (Available at www.nato.int/kosovo/press/p990517b.htm, April 19, 2001.)
6 Human Rights Watch interview with R.G., Kukes, Albania, June 6, 1999; Human Rights Watch interview with F.K., Kukes, Albania, June 9, 1999. Human Rights Watch also interviewed the relatives of six other men who were said to have been taken at the same time. The six were killed in the attack on the Tusus neighborhood of Prizren only days after they were released from digging trenches. Human Rights Watch interviews with F.A., H.A., and J.A., Prizen, Kosovo, June 14, 1999.

7 Human Rights Watch interview with L.G., Morina border crossing, Albania, April 14, 1999.

8 The *Washington Post* interviewed several refugee eyewitnesses within days of the incident. See John Ward Anderson, "Massacre Reported in Kosovo," *Washington Post,* May 30, 1999. The UNHCR also reported on the incident based on refugee testimonies. See UNHCR, Kosovo Crisis Update, June 2, 1999 (stating that twenty-five people were allegedly killed on May 26 in Tusus), available at www.ess.uwe.ac.uk/Kosovo/Kosovo-Current_News209.htm, (March 23, 2001).

9 Human Rights Watch interview with L.V., Prizren, Kosovo, June 14, 1999. Another witness told Human Rights Watch that his wife saw the bodies of two Serbian police in the street at about 7:30 that morning. He said that he woke up "to a burst of automatic weapon fire," and that his wife had gone to peer out into the street to see what was happening; she then noticed the bodies. Human Rights Watch interview with F.K., Kukes, Albania, June 9, 1999.

10 "As the Historic City of Prizren Burns, Dozens of Kosovars Murdered," Kosovapress, May 28, 1999. Available on the internet at: http://www.alb-net.com/kcc/052899.htm#7, (March 23, 2001).

11 See the MUP website, www.mup.sr.gov.yu/domino/mup.nsf/pages/index-e, (March 23, 2001).

12 Human Rights Watch interview with F.K., Kukes, Albania, June 9, 1999.

13 Human Rights Watch interview with L.V., Prizren, Kosovo, June 14, 1999.

14 Human Rights Watch interview with A.V., Prizren, Kosovo, June 14, 1999.

15 Human Rights Watch interview with J.A., Prizren, Kosovo, June 14, 1999.

16 Human Rights Watch interview with F.A., Prizren, Kosovo, June 14, 1999.

17 Human Rights Watch interview with L.V., Prizren, Kosovo, June 14, 1999.

18 Human Rights Watch interview with A.V., Prizren, Kosovo, June 14, 1999.

19 Human Rights Watch interview with M.B., Kukes, Albania, June 11, 1999.

20 Human Rights Watch interview with K.V., Prizren, Kosovo, June 14, 1999.

21 Human Rights Watch interview with M.B., Kukes, Albania, June 11, 1999. Press accounts cite other witnesses who claim that Russian "mercenaries" were involved in the Tusus killings. Roy Gutman, "Russian 'volunteers' allegedly helped Serbs," *Newsday,* June 22, 1999; Maggie O'Kane, "Russian soldiers' peace role gives refugees chills," *Guardian* (London), June 24, 1999; "Retour des Russes sous l'habit de la KFOR: Tusus n'y croit pas," France 3 Infos, June 21, 1999.

22 The *Washington Post* reported that one woman claimed to have seen thirty-one bodies at the morgue. Anderson, "Massacre Reported in Kosovo."

23 Human Rights Watch interview with E.M., Kukes, Albania, June 11, 1999.

24 Human Rights Watch interview with A.M., Kukes, Albania, June 11, 1999.

25 Human Rights Watch interview with S.M., Kukes, Albania, June 11, 1999.

Chapter 12. The Prizren—Djakovica (Gjakove) Road

1 Human Rights Watch interview with B.Z., Kukes, Albania, April 15, 1999.
2 Human Rights Watch interview with N.Z., Domaj, Albania, April 15, 1999.
3 Ibid.
4 Human Rights Watch interview with S.Z., Domaj, Albania, April 15, 1999.
5 Human Rights Watch interview with I. Z., Kukes, Albania, April 12, 1999.
6 Human Rights Watch interview with I.Z., Kukes, Albania, April 16, 1999.
7 A documentary on Kosovo produced by Frontline includes an interview with a soldier from the Yugoslav Army who talks about stripping Albanians in order to look for military clothes. The soldier, identified as "K" said: "Yes, they [ethnic Albanians] would forget to change their clothes completely, and they'd be wearing their army underwear. In principle, they had a good system. They were wearing civilian clothes over their uniforms... then they would have their uniforms over their civilian clothing. And another layer of civilian clothing over that . . . and they took it off when appropriate . . ." See http://www.pbs.org/wgbh/pages/frontline/shows/kosovo/interviews/, (March 23, 2001).
8 Human Rights Watch interview with S.Z., Domaj, Albania, April 15, 1999.
9 Human Rights Watch interview with I.Z., Kukes, Albania, April 16, 1999.
10 Human Rights Watch interview with M.P., Kukes, Albania, May 11, 1999.
11 Human Rights Watch interview with S.G., Kukes, Albania, April 15, 1999.
12 Remarks of Carla Del Ponte to the UN Security Council, November 10, 1999, New York.
13 Human Rights Watch interview, Morina border crossing, Albania, April 28, 1999.
14 Ibid.
15 Human Rights Watch interview with R.T. and H.T., Zrze, Kosovo, June 22, 1999. The couple provided the names of sixteen victims: Nasim Rexhepi (aged sixty-six), Muharrem Rexhepi (aged approximately sixty), Nejazi Rexhepi (aged approximately fifty-eight), Shani Rexhepi (aged approximately fifty-five), Teki Rexhepi (son of Muharrem, aged approximately forty-two), Hysni Ibrahimi (aged approximately forty-three), Dërqut Rexhepi (aged approximately forty-three), Naim Rexhepi (Dergut's brother, aged approximately forty), Isa Rexhepi (uncle of Naim, aged approximately fifty), Haki Rexhepi (Isa's brother, aged approximately sixty), Alban Rexhepi (Haki's nephew, aged approximately fifteen), Betullah Rexhepi (aged approximately sixty-five), Muhamet Hajdari, aged approximately seventy, Hajdar Hajdari (age unknown), Refahi Hajdari (son of Muhamet, age unknown), Nebi Krasniqi (guest from Velika Krusha, age unknown).
16 John Kifner, "Refugees Tell of Atrocities," *New York Times*, April 6, 1999.
17 This appears to be different from the incident observed by the first witness in which fifteen or sixteen men were killed and their bodies burned.
18 Human Rights Watch interview, Durres, Albania, March 31, 1999.
19 Ibid.
20 Human Rights Watch interview with Q.R., Celina, Kosovo, June 21, 1999.
21 John Daniszewski, "Beneath Bits of Fresh Earth, Tales of Horror," *Los Angeles Times*, July 3, 1999.

22 John Daniszewski, "Evidence Details Systematic Plan of Killing in Kosovo," *Los Angeles Times*, August 8, 1999.

23 OSCE/ODIHR, Kosovo/Kosova: *As Seen, As Told, Part I*, p. 279.

24 The KLA had checkpoints in the area beginning in spring 1998 and periodically attacked police checkpoints or convoys. On April 27, for example, two policemen, Bojan Nikolic and Srdjan Ilic, were wounded near the Mala Krusa railway station, according to SRNA, the Bosnian Serb press agency, as well as the Serbian Ministry of Interior. According to the Serbian Ministry of Interior, policemen Neven Gloginja (nineteen) and Boban Radenovic (twenty-six) were wounded in a KLA attack on November 14, 1998, near Pirane.

25 Thousands of villagers gathered in and around Nogavac, and there is some indication that they were being directed there by the security forces. Some police were helpful, a few witnesses said, even warning the Albanians that "there are Arkan soldiers in Velika Krusa so we are taking you to Nogavac." But many Albanians reported beatings and robberies, as well as some killings. Nogavac was also shelled at least twice in late March and April, resulting in an undetermined number of deaths. One fifty-four-year-old man who was injured in one of the attacks, said that Nogavac was bombed by Serbian airplanes in the night of April 29.

26 Remarks of Carla Del Ponte to the U.N. Security Council, November 10, 1999, New York.

27 According to Kosovapress, the news agency of the KLA, four KLA soldiers died in Velika Krusa: Fitim Islam Duraku, Enver Eqrem Duraku, Bekim Ismet Gashi, and Dalip Isuf Behra, Kosovapress, May 16, 1999.

28 Human Rights Watch interview with R.E., Kukes, Albania, June 8, 1999.

29 Other press accounts also mentioned twenty charred bodies. See, for example, "NATO Troops Find More Than 20 Charred Corpses in Kosovo House," Agence France Press, June 15, 1999.

30 Tom Cohen, "Victims of Serb Crackdown Reburied," *Associated Press*, August 12, 1999.

31 John Daniszewski, "Victims of Village Massacre Laid to Rest," *Los Angeles Times*, June 28, 1999.

32 OSCE/ODIHR, *Kosovo/Kosova: As Seen, As Told, Part I.*

33 Human Rights Watch interview with R.E., Kukes, Albania, June 8, 1999.

34 Human Rights Watch interview with S.G. Velika Krusa, Kosovo, June 19, 1999.

35 Human Rights Watch interview with R.D., Kukes, Albania, April 26, 1999.

36 Human Rights Watch interview with R.H., Velika Krusa, May 19, 1999.

37 Human Rights Watch interview, Morina border crossing, Albania, April 2, 1999.

38 "The Killing of Kosovo," Panorama, April 1999.

39 Tanjug, April 5, 1999.

40 Human Rights Watch interview with R.E., Kukes, Albania, June 8, 1999.

41 John Sweeney, "What Kind of Men Could Slaughter 100 of Their Own Neighbors? This Kind," *Observer*, October 31, 1999.

42 See http://www.cnn.com/WORLD/europe/9904/03/kosovo.atrocities/, (March 26, 2001).

43 "The Cleansing of Krushe," by John Sweeney, *The Observer,* April 4, 1999.
44 Human Rights Watch interview with E.B., Kukes, Albania, May 22, 1999.
45 Human Rights Watch interview with R.T., Kukes, Albania, May 22, 1999.
46 One family reported that they had been forced to leave the village on April 4, but they had returned two days later because Serbian authorities had closed the Albanian border. They were then expelled again on May 4.
47 Human Rights Watch interview with S.G., Kukes, Albania, April 15, 1999.
48 Human Rights Watch interview with S.Z., Domaj, Albania, April 15, 1999.

Chapter 13. Suva Reka (Suhareke) Municipality

1 Villages around Suva Reka like Restan, Pecan, Slapuzane, Bukos, Semetishte, and Vranic were areas of KLA activity in 1998 and 1999 and, therefore, the targets of government attacks, many of them indiscriminate. Human Rights Watch visited Pecan in February 1999, for example, and observed that only seven of the villages approximately 300 houses were not damaged in some manner from the government's summer offensive. In Slapuzane, where the OSCE-KVM had a small presence, 131 of 142 houses were damaged. For details on the September 1998 destruction and killings in Vranic, see Human Rights Watch, *Humanitarian Law Violations in Kosovo,* Appendix B.
2 According to the OSCE report, the KLA had informed Albanians in the Suva Reka municipality of safe areas where they could go, including: Budakovo (Budakove), Djinovce (Gjinofc), Dubrava (Dubrave), Grejkovce (Grejkoc), Musutiste (Mushtishte), Papaz (Papaz), Savrovo (Savrove), Selograzde (Sellograzde) and Sopina (Sopine).
3 Human Rights Watch interview with Shkender Bytyqi, Suva Reka, Kosovo, August 24, 1999.
4 Human Rights Watch interview with Haki Gashi, Suva Reka, Kosovo, August 24, 1999.
5 OSCE/ODIHR, *Kosovo/Kosova: As Seen, As Told, Part I,* pp 361–370.
6 Remarks of Carla Del Ponte to the U.N. Security Council, November 10, 1999, New York.
7 When first deployed in November 1998, the OSCE-KVM stayed in Miskovic's Hotel Boss. Later, the OSCE—KVM stayed in private houses.
8 *Policajac,* February 1998. Lt. Vitosevic was named by one witness who said he saw him in the village of Vranic the day after a government offensive on September 27, 1998. During this offensive in 1998, two witnesses identified the Suva Reka policeman Milan Sipka by name. See Human Rights Watch, *Humanitarian Law Violations in Kosovo,* Appendix B.
9 Not the survivor's real name.
10 The witness is a gynecologist.
11 None of the survivors' real names.
12 Human Rights Watch interview with A.B., Prizren, Kosovo, August 25, 1998.
13 The OSCE report is slightly inaccurate here since the boy was not the woman's son, and he was hit by grenade shrapnel rather than by a bullet.

14 OSCE/ODIHR, *Kosovo/Kosova: As Seen, As Told, Part I,* p. 363.
15 Ibid.
16 Human Rights Watch interview with N.E., Suva Reka, Kosovo, August 31, 1999.
17 Human Rights Watch interview with Z.E. Suva Reka, Kosovo, August 31, 1999.
18 Human Rights Watch interview with K.E. Suva Reka, Kosovo, August 31, 1999.
19 Human Rights Watch interview with R.H., Suva Reka, August 31, 1999.
20 For more details on Bardhyl's story, including excerpts from his journal, see an article in the *Berliner Zeitung,* Frank Nordhausen, "The Prisoner from Suva Reka" ("Der Gefangene von Suva Reka"), June 29, 1999.
21 Human Rights Watch interview with Bardhyl H., Suva Reka, Kosovo, August 31, 1999.
22 Human Rights Watch interview with H.B., Kukes, Albania, April 12, 1999.
23 Human Rights Watch interview with X.X., Kukes, Albania, May 22, 1999.
24 Ibid.
25 Human Rights Watch interview with S. B., Kukes, Albania, April 4, 1999.
26 John Daniszewski, "The Death of Belanica," *Los Angeles Times,* April 25, 1999.
27 Human Rights Watch interview with H.S. Kukes, Albania, May 18, 1999.
28 Human Rights Watch interview, Kukes, Albania, April 4, 1999.
29 Human Rights Watch interview, Kukes, Albania, April 4, 1999.
30 Human Rights Watch interview with S. B., Kukes, Albania, April 4, 1999.
31 Human Rights Watch interview with H.B., Kukes, Albania, April 4, 1999.
32 Human Rights Watch interview with H.S., Kukes, Albania, May 18, 1999.
33 Ibid.
34 Human Rights Watch interview, name withheld, Kukes, Albania, April 4, 1999.
35 Human Rights Watch interview with S.Z., Belanica, Kosovo, August 15, 1999.
36 Human Rights Watch interview with F.V., Moralija, Kosovo, August 20, 1999.
37 The two witnesses gave different ages for Bekim Vrenezi, fifteen and sixteen respectively.
38 Human Rights Watch interview with R.B., Moralija, Kosovo, August 20, 1999.
39 The only known names of the victims are, according to witnesses: Osman Vrenezi (27), Bekim Vrenezi (15 or 16), Agim Bytyqi (38–40), and Izet Hoxha (77).
40 John Daniszewski, "A Family, A Village Begin Anew in Kosovo War," *Los Angeles Times,* December 30, 1999.
41 Statement of Carla del Ponte to the U.N. Security Council, November 10, 1999, New York.
42 Human Rights Watch interview with I.Z., Belanica, Kosovo, August 19, 1999.
43 Ibid.
44 Human Rights Watch interview with S.Z., Belanica, Kosovo, August 19, 1999.
45 The name of the village has been withheld in order to protect the victims of sexual assault and rape who live there.
46 OSCE/ODIHR, *Kosovo/Kosova: As Seen, As Told, Part I.*
47 Human Rights Watch interview with A.T., Suva Reka village, Kosovo, August 1, 1999.
48 According to the Serbian Ministry of Internal Affairs website (www.mup.sr.gov.yu, (March 21, 2001)), the wounded policemen were: Vlastimir Selenic (1971), Dejan Bajic

(1976), Miodrag Djikic (1971), Srdjan Ilic (1965), Miodrag Djukic (1971), Dejan Tosic (1972), Sinisa Pejev (1960), Branislav Bozic (1969), Slavko Milic (1953), Danijel Spasenov (age unknown), Miodrag Stevanovic (age unknown), Bratislav Stojkovic (1961), Slavoljub Zivkovic (1970), Sasa Krstic (1969), Ljubisa Miljkovic (1968), Dragan Pesic (1969), Slavisa Ivkovic (1964), Vukasin Jovanovic (1963), and Dragan Medic (1970).

49 Human Rights Watch interview, name withheld. Kukes, Albania, April 27, 1999.
50 Human Rights Watch interview, name withheld. Kukes, Albania, April 27, 1999.
51 Human Rights Watch interview, name withheld. Kukes, Albania, April 27, 1999.
52 Human Rights Watch interview, name withheld. Kukes, Albania, April 27, 1999.
53 Human Rights Watch with Dr. Saeed Albloushi, Kukes, Albania, April 27, 1999.
54 Statement of Carla Del Ponte to the U.N. Security Council, November 10, 1999, New York.
55 The OSCE/ODHIR report, *Kosovo/Kosova: As Seen, As Told, Part I,* p. 367, puts the death toll, based on witness and hearsay statements at "around 40."
56 Human Rights Watch interview with I.G., Trnje, Kosovo, August 29, 1999.
57 N.B. lost his wife, daughter-in-law, and grandson in the March 25 attack.
58 Human Rights Watch inspected what appeared to be a bullet wound in his hand.
59 Human Rights Watch interview with N.B., Studencane, Kosovo, August 29, 1999.
60 Human Rights Watch interview with B.G., Trnje, Kosovo, August 29, 1999.
61 Human Rights Watch interview with N.B., Studencane, Kosovo, August 29, 1999.

Chapter 14. Vucitrn (Vushtrri) Municipality

1 OSCE/ODIHR, *Kosovo/Kosova: As Seen As Told,* p. 384.
2 "Persons Missing in Relation to the Events in Kosovo from January 1998," International Committee of the Red Cross, First Edition, May 2000.
3 OSCE/ODIHR, *Kosovo/Kosova: As Seen, As Told, Part I,* pp. 388–390.
4 See Human Rights Watch Kosovo Flash #40, May 20, 1999.
5 A former KLA commander told Human Rights Watch that he was in charge of a fifty-six person unit that was responsible for Gornja and Donja Sudimlja. They retreated from the area, he said, because they did not want to place the 10,000–15,000 internally displaced civilians at risk. The unit returned to the villages after the May 2 offensive. Human Rights Watch interview with M.T., Vucitrn, Kosovo, August 18, 1999.
6 Human Rights Watch interview with S.A., Kukes, Albania, May 13, 1999.
7 Human Rights Watch interview with K.B., Kukes, Albania, May 12, 1999.
8 Human Rights Watch interview with Z.A., Kukes, Albania, May 12, 1999.
9 Human Rights Watch interview with B.A., Kukes, Albania, May XX, 1999.
10 Human Rights Watch interview with Z.G., Gornja Sudimlja, Kosovo, August 14, 1999.
11 Human Rights Watch interview with M.G., Gornja Sudimlja, Kosovo, August 14, 1999.
12 Human Rights Watch interview with S.B., Gornja Sudimlja, Kosovo, August 14, 1999.
13 Human Rights Watch observed the wound.

14 Human Rights Watch observed what appeared to be a bullet wound that had entered the back and exited the middle of the man's torso.

15 Human Rights Watch interview with H.A., Gornja Sudimlja, Kosovo, August 16, 1999.

16 Remarks to the Security Council of Carla del Ponte, November 10, 1999, New York.

17 Human Rights Watch interview with Z. G., Gornja Sudimlja, Kosovo, August 14, 1999.

18 Human Rights Watch interview with M.T., Vucitrn, Kosovo, August 18, 1999.

19 Ray Moseley, "Living and Dead Bear Witness to Atrocities," *Chicago Tribune,* June 16, 1999.

20 Emma Daly, "War in the Balkans: Villagers Saw More Than 100 Men Shot," *Independent,* May 5, 1999.

21 Two other men from the Vucitrn area also identified Dragan Petrovic by name, but in two different events. See below. Human Rights Watch interviews with K.B. and Z.A., Kukes, Albania, May 12, 1999, and with S.A., Kukes, Albania, May 13, 1999.

22 Human Rights Watch interview with S.B., Kukes, Albania, May 13, 1999.

23 In addition to the killings during this period documented below, Human Rights Watch was told about the shooting death of Afrim Bekteshi, aged twenty-seven or twenty-eight, although the precise date and circumstances of his death remain unclear. Human Rights Watch interview with G.I., Vucitrn, Kosovo, August 16, 1999.

24 Human Rights Watch interview with V.Z., Donja Sudimlja, Kosovo, August 19, 1999.

25 Human Rights Watch interview with G.I., Vucitrn, Kosovo, August 16, 1999.

26 Human Rights Watch interview with M.T.,Vucitrn, Kosovo, August 18, 1999.

27 Killed near the family house were: Selatin Gerxhaliu (born 1951 or 1952, husband of Fexhrie), Shaban Gerxhaliu (born 1983, son of Selatin and Fexhrie), and Xhemail Gerxhaliu (born 1937, cousin of family). Killed in the house were: Sala (short for Salihe) Gerxhaliu (born 1918, mother of Selatin), Fexhrie Gerxhaliu (born 1954, wife of Selatin), Muharem Gerxhaliu (born 1985, son of Selatin and Fexhrie), Mexhit Gerxhaliu (born 1987, son of Selatin and Fexhrie), Abdurahim Gerxhaliu (1989, son of Selatin and Fexhrie), Mybera Gerxhaliu (born 1991, daughter of Selatin and Fexhrie), Sabahudin Gerxhaliu (born 1993, son of Selatin and Fexhrie), Sofie Gerxhaliu (born 1963, wife of Nexhmedin), and Safer Gerxhaliu (born 1992, son of Sofie and Nexhmedin).

28 Human Rights Watch interview with Sali Gerxhaliu, Donja Sudimlja, Kosovo, August 16, 1999.

29 Ibid.

30 Ibid.

31 Human Rights Watch interview with Shukri Gerxhaliu, Gornja Sudimlja, Kosovo, August 14, 1999.

32 Human Rights Watch interview with G.I., Vucitrn, Kosovo, August 16, 1999.

33 Corroborative testimony is available in an Amnesty International report, "Smrekovnica Prison — a Regime of Torture and Ill-treatment Leaves Hundreds Unaccounted For," October 1999.

34 Human Rights Watch interview with X.X. (initials altered), Kukes, Albania, May 22, 1999.

35 Human Rights Watch interview with Y.Y. (initials altered), Kukes, Albania, May 22, 1999.
36 Human Rights Watch interview with A.K., Kukes, Albania, May 22, 1999.
37 Human Rights Watch interview, name not provided, Kukes, Albania, June 7, 1999.
38 Human Rights Watch interview, Kukes, Albania, June 7, 1999.
39 Human Rights Watch interview with N.K., Kukes, Albania, June 7, 1999.
40 Human Rights Watch interview with E.H., Kukes, Albania, June 2, 1999.

Chapter 15. Statistical Analysis of Violations

1 Dr. Patrick Ball, Deputy Director of AAAS's Science and Human Rights Program, designed the statistical analysis. Rebecca Morgan, a Human Rights Watch consultant, coordinated the coding process. Dr. Herbert F. Spirer, Professor Emeritus at the University of Connecticut, Adjunct Professor of International Affairs at Columbia University and consultant to AAAS, conducted the statistical analysis and generated the graphs. Fred Abrahams from Human Rights Watch wrote the accompanying text. Outside reviews were conducted by Dr. Fritz Scheuren and Tom Jabine.

Human Rights Watch is grateful to Drs. Ball, Spirer, Jabine and Scheuren for their time and expertise, as well as to the many volunteers, mentioned in the acknowledgement section, who helped to code the data.

This chapter is a joint product of Human Rights Watch and the Science and Human Rights Program of American Association for the Advancement of Science, which operates under the oversight of the AAAS Committee on Scientific Freedom and Responsibility (CSFR). The CSFR, in accordance with its mandate and association policy, supports publication of this chapter as a scientific contribution to human rights. The interpretations and conclusions are those of the authors and do not purport to represent the views of the Board, the Council, the CSFR, or the members of the AAAS.

2 Five other statistical studies of war crimes in Kosovo have been conducted by other organizations: See Central and East European Law Initiative of the American Bar Association and the American Association for the Advancement of Science, *Political Killings in Kosova/Kosovo,* September 2000; American Association for the Advancement of Science, *Policy or Panic? The Flight of Ethnic Albanians from Kosovo, March-May 1999,* April 2000; Physicians for Human Rights, *War Crimes in Kosovo—A Population-Based Assessment of Human Rights Violations Against Kosovar Albanians,* August 1999; Doctors Without Borders/Médécins Sans Frontières, *Kosovo: Accounts of a Deportation,*, April 30, 1999; Paul B Spiegel and Peter Salama, *War and Mortality in Kosovo, 1998–99: An Epidemiological Testimony,* The Lancet, vol. 355, no. 9222, June 24, 2000.

Books on human rights and data analysis that addressed related methods include: Spirer and Spirer, *Data Analysis for Monitoring Human Rights,* Washington: AAAS (1993); Patrick Ball, *Who Did What to Whom?,* Washington, AAAS (1996); Patrick Ball, Herbert F. Spirer and Louise Spirer (eds.), *Making the Case: Investigating Large Scale Human Rights Violations Using Information Systems and Data Analysis,* Washington,

AAAS (2000); Jabine and Claude (eds.), *Human Rights and Statistics: Getting the Record Straight,* Philadelphia, University of Pennsylvania Press (1992); and Patrick Ball, Paul Kobrak and Herbert F. Spirer, *State Violence in Guatemala, 1960–1996: A Quantitative Reflection,* AAAS, Washington, 1999.

3 Human Rights Watch coded for the following violations: robbery, execution, looting, destruction of non-military objects, harassment, displacement, detention, abduction, beating, rape, sexual assault, indiscriminate shelling, separation, "disappearance," forced labor, torture, and human shields.

4 Separation was defined as a case where men and women and children were separated and the fate of one group or another, at the time of the interview, was not known.

5 Displacement was defined as forced expulsion or displacement from an area.

6 Detention was defined as an arrest or imprisonment in which detainees were held in the custody of the state. This includes cases in which detainees were subsequently tortured, "disappeared," or summarily executed.

7 Four of the Gerxhaliu victims were female, aged eight, thirty-six, forty-five, and eighty-one. Three other male victims were under the age of fourteen.

8 At least seven boys and five girls seventeen years of age or younger were killed.

9 This is especially true given that Kosovar Albanians have the highest birthrate in Europe.

10 For a description of the areas covered by Human Rights Watch, see the section on Methodology in the Introduction.

11 American Association for the Advancement of Science, *Policy or Panic? The Flight of Ethnic Albanians from Kosovo, March-May 1999,* April 2000.

12 Ibid.

13 The impact of this comparison is muted slightly by the fact that the AAAS data was predominantly from refugees who entered Albania, while the Human Rights Watch data was not limited in this way. However, Appendix A of the AAAS report explains why their data may be generalized, within limits, to the entire population of Kosovar Albanian refugees during this period, i.e. those who exited to Macedonia, Montenegro or Bosnia-Herzegovina. One important exception mentioned in the report is those who were internally displaced within Kosovo throughout the NATO bombing, for whom there is no information.

14 It is important to note that the time intervals for the two graphs are different: the Human Rights Watch graph is plotted by week, while the AAAS data is plotted by two-day periods. This does not, however, minimize the impact of the comparison. On the contrary, the correlation between the three phases is strengthened by the fact that, using different time intervals, the three phases still match. This helps show that the data are, in statisticians' terms, "robust."

15 The confidence interval indicates that if this study were repeated 100 times using different but independent lists of data, one would expect that in 95 of 100 studies, the estimate would fall within the range of 7,449 and 13,627.

Chapter 16. The Nato Air Campaign

1 Discussion of bombing outside Kosovo is beyond the scope of this report. For further information on bombing elsewhere in the Federal Republic of Yugoslavia, see: Human Rights Watch, "Civilian Deaths in the NATO Air Campaign," February 2000.

2 Each of the thirty-two incidents in Kosovo is set out, together with supporting references, in Annex A of "Civilian Deaths in the NATO Air Campaign," pp. 29–64.

3 For an early account of the use of cluster bombs by NATO in the Federal Republic of Yugoslavia and Human Rights Watch's position, see "Ticking Time Bombs: NATO's Use of Cluster Munitions in Yugoslavia," *A Human Rights Watch Short Report,* vol. 11, no. 6(D), May 1999; and Human Rights Watch, "Cluster Bombs: Memorandum for CCW Delegates," December 16, 1999.

4 The question as to what extent the military is obligated to expose its own forces to danger in order to limit civilian casualties or damage to civilian objects is examined in William J. Fenrick, "Attacking The Enemy Civilian As A Punishable Offense," *Duke Journal of Comparative and International Law,* 1997, p. 546, located at http://www.law.duke.edu/journals/djcil/articles/djcil7p539.htm (March 27, 2001).

5 The eighty-seven deaths in Korisa are counted in the Human Rights Watch total of 500 [cited in the report, "Civilian Deaths in the NATO Air Campaign"]; the seventy-six at Dubrava prison are not.

6 NATO, SHAPE News Morning Update, April 15, 1999; Reuters, 150059 GMT, April 15, 1999.

7 Joie Chen and Jamie McIntyre, "As Serb Force Grows, Limits of Air Attacks Become Apparent," CNN, *The World Today,* April 19, 1999; Sarah Chayes, "General Daniel Leaf Explains the Refugee Bombings," National Public Radio, *All Things Considered,* April 19, 1999.

8 FRY Ministry of Foreign Affairs, *NATO Crimes in Yugoslavia,* vol. 1, pp. 1, 21–26, 32–37; FRY Ministry of Housing, "Photo Documentation of Civilians Who Were Killed By NATO Attacks, from 24.03 until 20.05.1999."

9 Tanjug, Pristina, April 15, 1999.

10 Two eyewitnesses told Human Rights Watch that within the convoy were military vehicles interspersed. Interviews with Kole Hasanaj, Meja, July 25, 1999, and with Safet Shalaj, Djakovica, July 25, 1999.

11 Special U.S. Department of Defense Press Briefing with Gen. Wesley Clark, Supreme Allied Commander, Europe, Topic: Kosovo Strike Assessment; Also Participating: Airmen and Analysts from Operation Allied Force and Post-Strike Assessment Work, Brussels, Belgium, September 16, 1999.

12 Ibid.

13 FRY Ministry of Foreign Affairs, *NATO Crimes in Yugoslavia,* vol. II, pp. 1–17. Though the *White Book* states that there were "only" forty-eight victims in Korisa, Yugoslav and Western press, as well as the U.S. State Department and the U.N. report figures of eighty to eighty-seven victims. Based upon Human Rights Watch investigations and discus-

sions with Western journalists who attempted to reconstruct the incident, it appears certain that more that forty-eight people died in the Korisa attack. The range of deaths reported is thus used.

14 Transcript of Backgrounder given by Peter Daniel and Major General Walter Jertz, in Brussels, May 15, 1999.

15 NATO, Subject: Press Release (99) 079, Statement by the NATO Spokesman on the Korisa Incident, May 15, 1999.

16 Transcript of Backgrounder, May 15, 1999.

17 Transcript, U.S. Department of Defense News Briefing, May 15, 1999.

18 Reuters 152249 GMT, May 15, 1999; Kosovo Chronology, Timeline of events 1989–1999 relating to the crisis in Kosovo, released by the Department of State, Washington, D.C., June 18, 1999.

19 Hans-Peter Gasser, "Protection of the Civilian Population," in Dieter Fleck (ed.), *The Handbook of Humanitarian Law in Armed Conflicts* (Oxford: Oxford University Press, 1995), p. 505, para. 506. Hans-Peter Gasser is a senior legal adviser of the ICRC.

20 Information provided by Yugoslav civil defense authorities; FRY MFA, NATO raids on manufacturing and civilian facilities on May 21st and on the night between May 21st and 22nd 1999.

21 FRY Ministry of Foreign Affairs, NATO Raids on Manufacturing and Civilian Facilities on May 29th and in the Night Between May 29th and 30th 1999.

22 Yugoslav press reports; "Identifikovano 86 mrtvih," *DAN,* May 27, 1999, p. 2; "Jos sedam leseva," *DAN,* May 30, 1999.

23 FRY Ministry of Foreign Affairs, *NATO Crimes in Yugoslavia,* vol. II, p. 319.

24 NATO, Operation Allied Force Update, May 22, 1999, 0930 CET. See also Transcript of Press Conference given by Mr. Jamie Shea and Col. Konrad Freytag in Brussels on Saturday, May 22, 1999.

25 Jacky Rowland, "Bombs, Blood and Dark Despair," *Scotland on Sunday,* May 23, 1999; Paul Watson, "NATO Bombs Ignite Prison Chaos—KLA Officers Reported to be Among Inmates," *Toronto Star,* May 22, 1999; Associated Press, "NATO Hits Kosovo Jail Again Friday Night," May 21, 1999.

26 Carlotta Gall, "Stench of Horror Lingers in a Prison in Kosovo," *New York Times,* November 9, 1999.

27 NATO (SHAPE), ACE News Release—Press Release 99-05-02, May 8, 1999.

28 Transcript of Press Conference given by the NATO Secretary General, Mr. Javier Solana, in Brussels, on Saturday, May 8, 1999 (including Maj. Gen. Jertz).

29 Human Rights Watch correspondence with a U.S. Air Force officer, Novermber 1999.

30 Human Rights Watch discussions with U.S. Air Force and Joiint Chiefs of Staff officers, October 1999.

31 U.K. Ministry of Defense, Royal Air Force, Operation Allied Force News and Downloadable Images (http://www.mod.raf.uk/news/kosovonews.html).

Chapter 17. Abuses After June 12, 1999

1 The Kosovo Liberation Army also abducted, killed, and drove Kosovar Serbs and Roma from Kosovo, as well as ethnic Albanians accused of being "collaborators," in 1998 and early 1999. See section on "Abuses by the KLA" in the Background chapter, as well as Human Rights Watch, "Humanitarian Law Violations in Kosovo," October 1998, pp. 75–87.

2 Between February and April 2000, UNHCR registered 180,000 displaced persons from Kosovo in Serbia and 30,000 in Montenegro respectively. More than 150,000 of the 180,000 displaced persons in Serbia reported that they had fled after June 12, 1999. (See UNHCR *Refugees Daily,* May 23, 2000.)

3 The Kosovo Liberation Army was officially demilitarized in September 1999, and many of its members subsumed into the Kosovo Protection Corps, a civil defense organization headed by former KLA Commander Agim Ceku.

4 "Crucified Kosovo—Destroyed and Desecrated Serbian Orthodox Churches in Kosovo and Metohija (1999–2000)," expanded electronic edition. See: www.kosovo.com/crucified/default.htm (March 21, 2001).

5 By June 2000, international officials were finally willing to concede that attacks against minorities in Kosovo were systematic in nature. In his June 6 report to the Security Council on UNMIK (S/2000/538), U.N. Secretary-General Kofi Annan wrote that attacks on minorities, "appear to be orchestrated." U.S. State Department special envoy James O'Brien stated on June 8 that the violence "seems to be systematic." "Anti-Serb Violence Condemned," AP, June 8, 2000. On May 31, NATO Secretary-General Lord Robertson termed the violence as "ethnic cleansing," noting that "We did not stop ethnic cleansing one year to see ethnic cleansing of another kind take place today." "Kosovo: NATO's Patience Wearing Thin," NATO press release, May 31, 2000.

6 UNHCR Refugees Daily, May 23, 2000.

7 UNHCR-OSCE Ad Hoc Task Force on Minorities "Overview of the Situation of Minorities" (February 11, 2000). UNHCR is the source of the 1998 Pristina population estimate.

8 Information compiled from "Overview of the Situation of Minorities" (February 11, 2000) and from Human Rights Watch field research (June-November 1999).

9 The 1991 Yugoslav census indicated a Roma population of between 30,000 and 40,000 in Kosovo but the real figure is likely to be higher due to non-participation in censuses and continued migration.

10 UNHCR-OSCE Ad Hoc Task Force on Minorities, "Overview of the Situation of Minorities," November 3, 1999.

11 UNHCR-OSCE Ad Hoc Task Force on Minorities "Assessment of the Situation of Ethnic Minorities in Kosovo," February 11, 2000.

12 The victims were Hajzer Ahmeti, Ibush Ahmeti, Isret Bajrami, and Agron Mehmeti.

13 "Ashkali Murder to Have a 'Chilling' Effect on Return of Refugees, Says UNHCR," KosovaLive, November 10, 2000.

14 "Ethnic Croats from Kosovo evacuated to Croatia," Associated Press, November 1, 1999. Quoted in UNHCR Refugee Daily, 11/1/99.
15 UNHCR-OSCE Ad Hoc Task Force on Minorities "Assessment of the Situation of Ethnic Minorities in Kosovo," February 11, 2000.
16 Ibid.
17 ICRC statement, "Person Unaccouted for in Connection with the Kosovo Crisis," April 10, 2001.
18 Press conference of the Association of the Families of the Missing and Kidnapped in Kosovo and Metohija, Belgrade, Yugoslavia, November 10, 2000.
19 "Persons Missing in Relation to the Events in Kosovo From January 1998," ICRC, May 2000. The book of the missing can be searched by name on the ICRC website at: www.familylinks.icrc.org/kosovo.
20 Humanitarian Law Center report, *Kosovo—Disappearances of Non-Albanians 24th March-10th August 1999*. Available at www.greekhelsinki.gr/english/reports/hlc-24-3-10-8-99.html, (March 22, 2001).
21 ICRC Statement, April 10, 2001.
22 European Roma Rights Center, "Press Statement: The Current Situation of Roma in Kosovo," July 9, 1999.
23 OSCE/ODIHR, *Kosovo/Kosova: As Seen, As Told—Part II*, pp.?.
24 Ibid.
25 UNHCR-OSCE Ad Hoc Task Force on Minorities "Assessment of the Situation of Ethnic Minorities in Kosovo," February 11, 2000.
26 UNHCR-OSCE Ad Hoc Task Force on Minorities, "Update on the Situation of Ethnic Minorities in Kosovo (Period Covering February through May 2000)," May 31, 2000.
27 Statistics for aggravated assault over the same period include forty-nine cases of charges against Serbs, two against Roma, two against Muslim Slavs, ninety against Albanians and nine against persons of unknown ethnicity. "Update on the Situation of Ethnic Minorities in Kosovo (Period Covering February through May 2000)."
28 UNHCR-OSCE Ad Hoc Task Force on Minorities, "Update on the Situation of Ethnic Minorities in Kosovo (Period Covering February through May 2000)," May 31, 2000.
29 "U.N. Kosovo Head Condemns Killing of Serb Doctor as 'Sabotage,'" Reuters, March 2, 2000.
30 "Upsurge in Violence in Kosovo in past week: UN," Agence France Presse, April 10, 2000.
31 "Kosovo Farmer Gunned Down in Northern Kosovo," Associated Press, May 22, 2000.
32 KFOR Press Update, May 29, 2000.
33 "Albanians Attack Serbs in Kosovo," Reuters, June 1, 2000.
34 "Landmine Kills Two Serbs in Latest Kosovo Attack," Reuters, June 2, 2000.
35 "Five Serbs Injured in Kosovo Grenade Attack—KFOR," Reuters, June 6, 2000.
36 KFOR Press Update, June 16, 2000; For additional information see: "Two Serbs killed, one injured as car hits landmine in Kosovo," Agence France Presse, June 15, 2000.
37 "Serb Working for UN Killed in Kosovo," Reuters, May 17, 2000.
38 For examples of attacks against Albanian "collaborators" in the months following June 1999, see: OSCE/ODIHR, *Kosovo/Kosova: As Seen, As Told—Part II.*

39 Paul Watson, "Extremist Albanians Target Moderates in Kosovo Strife," *Los Angeles Times,* November 20, 1999.
40 Carlotta Gall, "Kosovo Towns Mourn a Slain Guerrilla Army Commander," *New York Times,* May 12, 2000.
41 For background on Rexha's murder, see Granit Guri, "Elimination of Former KLA Commanders," AIM Pristina, May 18, 2000.
42 "Senior Politician Killed in Kosovo," Agence France Presse, June 19, 2000.
43 "Police Arrest Suspects in Raci Killing," KosovaLive, November 3, 2000.
44 "Peja Municipal Council Member Attacked," KosovaLive, November 16, 2000.
45 R. Jeffrey Smith, "Advocate of Nonviolence Gunned Down in Kosovo," *Washington Post,* November 24, 2000.
46 OSCE/ODIHR, *Kosovo/Kosova: As Seen, As Told—Part II.*
47 Secretary Albright, KFOR Commander General Jackson, and UN Special Representative Kouchner, press remarks, July 29, 1999.
48 UNHCR-OSCE Ad Hoc Task Force on Minorities, "Overview of the Situation of Minorities," November 3, 1999.
49 Ibid.
50 UN Mission in Kosovo, Status Report, October 19, 2000. See:www.un.org/peace/kosovo/pages/kosovo_status.htm, (March 22, 2001).
51 "Class 11 graduates from OSCE Kosovo Police Service School," OSCE press release, December 15, 2000.
52 See, for example, Roy Gutman, "Bias Seen in Judicial System in Kosovo: UN Refuses to Appoint Judges Above the Fray," *Newsday,* April 2, 2000.
53 For more information on Kosovo's post-war judicial system see the following reports: Lawyers Committee for Human Rights, *A Fragile Peace: Laying the Foundations for Justice in Kosovo,* October 1999; United States Department of State, *Kosovo Judicial Assessment Mission Report,* April 2000.
54 The KPC, publically intended for civic defence and emergency relief, is headed by former KLA General Agim Ceku, composed mostly of former KLA combatants, structured along military lines (including special forces units), and supervised by KFOR rather than international civilian authorities. The KPC is widely regarded in Kosovo as the successor force to the KLA.
55 The *New York Times* quoted an unnamed "senior UN official" in February of this year saying that "the unwillingness of the West and KFOR to read the riot act to the KLA remains a central problem here." Steven Erlanger, "Torn Mitrovica Reflects West's Trials in Kosovo," *New York Times,* February 27, 2000.
56 "Clark Sees No Evidence KLA Behind Attacks On Serbs," *Reuters,* 13 August 1999.
57 The existence of the report was first reported in *the Observer* newspaper in March 2000. See John Sweeney and Jens Holsoe, "Revealed: UN-backed Unit's Reign of Terror—Kosovo 'Disaster Response Service' Stands Accused of Murder and Torture," *Observer* (London), March 12, 2000.
58 In late 2000 and early 2001 a group of armed ethnic Albanians calling itself the Liberation Army of Preshevo, Medvedja and Bujanovc (UCPMB) had occupied the buffer zone between Kosovo and southern Serbia in which, based on the Military Technical

Agreement, neither KFOR nor Yugoslav forces were allowed to enter. In March 2001, another group called the National Liberation Army (Ushtria Clirimtare e Kombit, or UCK in Albanian) began occupying villages in north western Macedonia, where ethnic Albanians form a majority.

59 See Report of the Secretary-General on the United Nations Interim Administration in Kosovo (S/2000/538), June 6, 2000; "Anti-Serb Violence Condemned," AP, June 8, 2000; "Kosovo: NATO's Patience Wearing Thin," NATO, May 31, 2000.

60 Neither the Military Technical Agreement nor UN Security Council Resolution 1244, which established the U.N.'s post-war presence in Kosovo, mentioned the prisoners' issue. According to a report by the International Crisis Group, early drafts of the Agreement did contain provisions regarding the prisoners. See International Crisis Group, *Kosovar Albanians in Serbian Prisons: Kosovo's Unfinished Business,* January 26, 2000.

61 "Zatvorenici sa Kosova Izmesteni u Srbiju," *Glas Javnosti,* June 18, 1999.

62 ICRC News 01/10, "Federal Republic of Yugoslavia: Detainees released under amnesty act return home," March 15, 2001.

63 See detailed trial monitoring reports by two Serbian-based organizations: Group 484's Volunteer Group on Human Rights and the Humanitarian Law Center (Communique from July 13, 2000).

64 Kurti was sentenced to fifteen years in prison on March 13, 2000, after ten months in detention. He was still in prison as of April 2001.

65 Human Rights Watch interview with M. K., Barane, Kosovo, November 17, 1999.

66 "Fifty-four Kosova Albanians Released from Serbian Prison," Reuters, October 4, 1999.

67 Ibid.

68 Humanitarian Law Center Communiques, January 29, 2000, and the Associated Press, January 29, 2000.

69 See the trial monitoring reports by Group 484's Volunteer Group on Human Rights (April 2000) and the Humanitarian Law Center (Communique from July 13, 2000.).

70 See Human Rights Watch release, "Belgrade Tries Ethnic Albanian Students For 'Terrorism'—Defendants Allege Torture," December 16, 1999, and "Ethnic Albanian Tells Court He Was Tortured," Reuters, November 23, 1999.

71 See trial monitoring reports by Group 484's Volunteer Group for Human Rights report (April 26, 1999) and two Humanitarian Law Center releases (December 21, 1999, and June 23, 2000.)

72 Humanitarian Law Center Communique, November 8, 1999.

73 Humanitarian Law Center Communique, October 10, 1999. Many of the minors in detention were subsequently released.

74 Brovina was sentenced for seditious conspiracy, according to Article 136 of the Yugoslav Criminal Code, in conjunction with terrorism during a state of war, according to Article 125. On April 10, 2000, Flora Brovina was awarded the PEN/Barbara Goldsmith Freedom-to-Write Award.

75 Human Rights Watch interview with Ajri Begu, Pristina, Kosovo, November 2, 1999.

76 See trial monitoring reports from Group 484.

77 Peter Finn, "Jailed Albanians Walk for a Fee for Freedom," *Washington Post,* October 9, 1999.

78 International Crisis Group, *Kosovar Albanians in Serbian Prisons: Kosovo's Unfinished Business,* January 26, 2000.

79 "HLC Attorney Arrested on Highway After Visiting Detained Clients," Humanitarian Law Center release, December 4, 1999.

80 "Ethnic Albanian Lawyer Beaten by Unknown Assailants," Agence France Presse, March 17, 1999.

81 ICRC News 01/10, "Federal Republic of Yugoslavia: Detainees released under amnesty act return home," March 15, 2001.

Chapter 18. Work of the War Crimes Tribunal

1 U.N. Security Council Resolution 827, May 25, 1993.

2 Fact Sheet on ICTY Proceedings, March 15, 2001. An unknown number of other individuals have been the object of sealed indictments.

3 The International Criminal Tribunal for the former Yugoslavia, "Prosecutor's Statement Regarding the Tribunal's Jurisdiction Over Kosovo," The Hague, March 10, 1998.

4 Contact Group Statement on Kosovo, London, June 12, 1998.

5 Communication from the Prosecutor to the Contact Group Members, The Hague, July 7, 1998.

6 Press conference of Ambassador David Scheffer, Zagreb, Croatia, August 31, 1998.

7 Human Rights Watch first called on the tribunal to undertake an investigation into alleged war crimes in Kosovo on March 7. In a letter to Chief Prosecutor Arbour, Human Rights Watch argued that "The violations of humanitarian law apparently being committed in Kosovo fall under the purview of the International Criminal Tribunal for the former Yugoslavia. . . . By opening an immediate investigation into the apparent war crimes being committed in Kosovo, and signaling that the Tribunal's jurisdiction extends to these atrocities, your office can help to curtail them." See Human Rights Watch press release, "Human Rights Watch Calls on Yugoslav War Crimes Tribunal to Investigate Possible War Crimes in Kosovo," March 7, 1998.

8 For details of these incidents, except Volujak, see Human Rights Watch, *Humanitarian Law Violations in Kosovo,* and Human Rights Watch, *A Week of Terror in Drenica.*

9 See Human Rights Watch, "A Week of Terror in Drenica."

10 See Human Rights Watch press release, "Interference with Kosovo Forensic Team 'Unacceptable,'" December 11, 1998.

11 "Thwarted Kosovo Mission of Louise Arbour," Tribunal Update 109, Institute for War and Peace Reporting, January 18–23, 1999. See also "Don't Tamper with Evidence, UN Prosecutor Tells Belgrade," Agence France Press, January 21, 1999.

12 Report of the EU Forensic Expert Team on the Racak Incident, March 17, 1999.

13 Press Statement by James P. Rubin, Spokesman, April 7, 1999, "Responsibility of Individual Yugoslav Army and Ministry Of Internal Affairs Commanders for Crimes Committed By Forces Under Their Command in Kosovo."

14 Ibid.

15 The Indictment of Milosevic et al., Case IT-99-37-I, International Criminal Tribunal for the Former Yugoslavia, May 24, 1999.

16 Remarks to the Security Council by Madame Carla Del Ponte, Prosecutor, International Criminal Tribunal for the former Yugoslavia, November 10, 1999, New York.

17 Address to the Security Council by Madame Carla Del Ponte, Prosecutor, International Criminal Tribunals for the former Yugoslavia and Rwanda, November 21, 2000, New York.

18 Press Release, "Statement by Carla Del Ponte, Prosecutor of the International Criminal Tribunal for the Former Yugoslavia, on the Investigation and Prosecution of Crimes Committed in Kosovo," September 29, 1999.

19 Ibid.

20 Address to the Security Council by Madame Carla Del Ponte, Prosecutor, International Criminal Tribunals for the former Yugoslavia and Rwanda, November 21, 2000, New York.

21 "Belgrade Pledges War Crimes Purge," BBC News, November 6, 2000.

22 Statement by the Prosecutor, Carla Del Ponte, On the Occasion of Her Visit to Belgrade, The Hague, January 30, 2001.

23 Statement by the Prosecutor Carla Del Ponte, The Hague, March 21, 2001.

24 See Human Rights Watch press releases, "Simic Surrender Not "Cooperation", March 12, 2001, and "Stakic Arrest Welcomed But Milosevic Still Must Be Surrendered to The Hague," March 23, 2001. For details about Stakic's role in Prijedor, see Human Rights Watch, "The Unindicted: Reaping the Rewards of 'Ethnic Cleansing,'" January 1997.

25 "Powell Certified Aid for Yugoslavia," Associated Press, April 2, 2001.

26 As of September 2000, at least twenty detainees had escaped hospitals or detention facilities, including one person who escaped from the U.S. Camp Bondsteel. According to the Belgrade-based Radio B2-92 (August 4, 2000), three Serbian detainees accused of war crimes escaped in early August from a hospital in Northern Mitrovica: Dragan Jovanovic, Vlastimir Aleksic, and Dragisa Peica. In early September 2000, thirteen detainees escaped from the detention facility in Northern Mitrovica, prompting the U.N. authorities to tighten security measures on September 18.

27 "Few War Crimes in Kosova Will Ever Be Prosecuted, Police Say," KosovaLive, December 8, 2000.

28 For informative reports on the post-war justice system in Kosovo see, Lawyers' Committee for Human Rights, "A Fragile Peace: Laying the Foundations for Justice in Kosovo," October 1999, and a U.S. government interagency report, "Kosovo Judicial Assessment Mission Report," April 2000 (available at www.state.gov/www/global/human_rights/kosovoii/042000_kosovo_rpt.pdf, as of March 2001).

29 OSCE Report, "The Development of the Kosovo Judicial System," January 2000.

30 "Group 484 Report on the Trial of Luan Mazreku and Bekim Mazreku," April 21, 2000.

31 Humanitarian Law Center release, "Luan and Bekim Mazreku Denied Fair Trial," September 24, 2000, and "Legal Analysis of the Mazreku Trial."

32 "Policemen Jailed for Murder of Albanians," B2-92, July 19, 2000. See also Carlotta Gall, "Seeing Enemies Everywhere, Serbia Begins a Legal Offensive," *New York Times,* November 29, 1999.

33 Humanitarian Law Center Legal Opinion, "Trial and Sentencing of Yugoslav Army Personnel for the Murder of Two Kosovo Albanian Civilians," December 25, 2000. For details on the case, see R. Jeffrey Smith, "A Yugoslav Officer's Crusade," *Washington Post,* December 20, 2000.

34 R. Jeffrey Smith, "Three Soldiers Convicted in Kosovo Atrocity," *Washington Post,* December 21, 2000.

35 "Yugoslav Army Begin Crime Cases," Associated Press, April 19, 2001.

36 "Officers Charged for Kosovo Killings," Associated Press, April 24, 2001.

37 Final Report to the Prosecutor by the Committee Established to Review the NATO Bombing Campaign Against the Federal Republic of Yugoslavia, June 8, 2000.

38 Press Release, "Statement by Carla Del Ponte, Prosecutor of the International Criminal Tribunal for the Former Yugoslavia, on the Investigation and Prosecution of Crimes Committed in Kosovo," September 29, 1999.

39 Address to the Security Council by Madame Carla Del Ponte, Prosecutor, International Criminal Tribunals for the former Yugoslavia and Rwanda, November 21, 2000, New York.

40 Statement by the Prosecutor Carla Del Ponte, The Hague, March 21, 2001.

Chapter 19. Legal Standards in the Kosovo Conflict

1 Human Rights Watch reports from this period are: "Increasing Turbulence: Human Rights in Yugoslavia," October 1989; "Yugoslavia: Crisis in Kosovo," with the International Helsinki Federation, March 1990; "Yugoslavia: Human Rights Abuses in Kosovo 1990–1992," October 1992; *Open Wounds: Human Rights Abuses in Kosovo,* March 1993; "Persecution Persists: Human Rights Violations in Kosovo," December 1996.

2 Yugoslavia acceded to the four Geneva Conventions on April 21, 1950, and to Protocols I and II on June 11, 1979.

3 International Committee of the Red Cross, *Commentary,* III Geneva Convention (International Committee of the Red Cross: Geneva 1960), p. 23.

4 International Committee of the Red Cross, *Commentary,* IV Geneva Convention (International Committee of the Red Cross: Geneva 1958), p. 35.

5 Ibid.

6 International Committee of the Red Cross Commentary to Protocol II, p. 90.

7 U.N. General Assembly, *Respect for Human Rights in Armed Conflicts,* United Nations Resolution 2444, G.A. Res. 2444, 23 U.N. GAOR Supp. (No. 18) U.N. Doc. A/7433 (New York: U.N., 1968), p. 164.

8 U.N. General Assembly Resolution 2444 affirms:

> . . . the following principles for observance by all government and other authorities responsible for action in armed conflicts:
>
> (a) That the right of the parties to a conflict to adopt means of injuring the enemy is not unlimited;
>
> (b) That it is prohibited to launch attacks against the civilian populations as such;
>
> (c) That distinction must be made at all times between persons taking part in the hos-

tilities and members of the civilian population to the effect that the latter be spared as much as possible.

9 The Prosecution v. Dusko Tadic, Appeals Chamber Decision on the Defense Motion for Interlocutory Appeal on Jurisdiction, para. 89 (October 2, 1995).

10 Human Rights Watch also takes some concepts from Protocol I, since it provides useful interpretive guidance on the rules of war.

11 The ICRC *Commentary* to article 1 of Protocol II addresses the requirements for control over territory. Paragraph 3.3. says: "In many conflicts there is considerable movement in the theater of hostilities; it often happens that territorial control changes hands rapidly. Sometimes domination of a territory will be relative, for example, when urban centres remain in government hands while rural areas escape their authority. In practical terms, if the insurgent armed groups are organized in accordance with the requirements of the Protocol, the extent of territory they can claim to control will be that which escapes the control of the government armed forces. However, there must be some degree of stability in the control of even a modest area of land for them to be capable of effectively applying the rules of the Protocol."

12 The ICRC *Commentary* on Common Article 3, paragraph 1, states that, among other criteria, an internal armed conflict exists when, "the insurgent civil authority agrees to be bound by the provisions of the Convention."

13 *Koha Ditore,* July 12, 1998.

14 KLA Communique Nr. 51, as published in *Koha Ditore,* August 26, 1998.

15 The "combatant's privilege" is a license to kill or capture enemy troops and destroy military objectives. This privilege immunizes combatants from criminal prosecution by their captors for their violent acts that do not violate the laws of war but would otherwise be crimes under domestic law. Prisoner of war status depends on and flows from this privilege. *See* W. Solf, "The Status of Combatants in Non-International Armed Conflicts Under Domestic Law and Transnational Practice," *American University Law Review,* no. 33 (1953), p. 59.

16 International Committee of the Red Cross (ICRC), *Commentary, IV Geneva Convention* (Geneva: ICRC, 1958), p. 226.

17 The ICRC *Commentary on the Additional Protocols,* p. 874, defines hostages as persons who find themselves, willingly or unwillingly, in the power of the enemy and who answer with their freedom or their life for compliance with the orders of the latter and for upholding the security of its armed forces.

18 Protocol II, article 8, states:

> Whenever circumstances permit, and particularly after an engagement, all possible measures shall be taken, without delay, . . . to search for the dead, prevent their being despoiled, and decently dispose of them.

19 R. Goldman, "International Humanitarian Law and the Armed Conflicts in El Salvador and Nicaragua," *American University Journal of International Law and Policy,* vol. 2 (1987), p. 553.

20 A wounded or captured combatant is "out of the fighting," and so must be protected.

21 Report of Working Group B, Committee I, 18 March 1975 (CDDH/I/238/Rev.1; X, 93),

in Howard S. Levie, ed., *The Law of Non International Armed Conflict,* (Dordrecht, Netherlands: Martinus Nijhoff, 1987), p. 67. *See* Rosario Conde, "Policemen without Combat Duties: Illegitimate Targets of Direct Attack under Humanitarian Law," student paper (New York: Columbia Law School, May 12, 1989).

22 M. Bothe, K. Partsch, and W. Solf, *New Rules for Victims of Armed Conflicts: Commentary on the Two 1977 Protocols Additional to the Geneva Conventions of 1949* (The Hague: Martinus Nijhoff, 1982), p. 303.

23 Civilians include those persons who are "directly linked to the armed forces, including those who accompany the armed forces without being members thereof, such as civilian members of military aircraft crews, supply contractors, members of labour units, or of services responsible for the welfare of the armed forces, members of the crew of the merchant marine and the crews of civil aircraft employed in the transportation of military personnel, material or supplies. . . . Civilians employed in the production, distribution and storage of munitions of war. . . ." Ibid., pp. 293–94.

24 Ibid., p. 303.

25 ICRC, *Commentary on the Additional Protocols,* p. 619.

26 ICRC, *Commentary on the Additional Protocols,* p. 618–19. This is a broader definition than "attacks" and includes at a minimum preparation for combat and return from combat. Bothe, *New Rules for Victims of Armed Conflicts,* p. 303.

27 Ibid., p. 303.

28 Protocol I, art. 52 (2).

29 Bothe, et.al., *New Rules for Victims of Armed Conflicts,* pp. 306-07.

30 Ibid., p. 362.

31 Ibid., p. 365.

32 ICRC, *Commentary on the Additional Protocols,* p. 685.

33 Ibid., p. 685. As set out above, to constitute a legitimate military objective, the object, selected by its nature, location, purpose or use must contribute effectively to the enemy's military capability or activity, and its total or partial destruction or neutralization must offer a "definite" military advantage in the circumstances. See Protocol I, art. 52 (2) where this definition is codified.

34 ICRC, *Commentary on the Additional Protocols,* p. 684.

35 Ibid., p. 626.

36 Ibid., p. 1472.

37 Ibid.

38 Constitution of the Federal Republic of Yugoslavia, Section 1, Article 9.

39 Official Gazette of the Federal Republic of Yugoslavia 43/94. Amendments to the law were published in the Official Gazette 28/96.

40 Official Gazette of the Republic of Serbia 44/91. Amendments to the law were published in the Official Gazette 79/91 and 54/96.

INDEX